Scale 1:190,000
or 3 miles to 1 inch
(1.9km to 1cm)

5th edition November 2009

© AA Media Limited 2009
Original edition printed 2005

Copyright: © IGN-Paris 2009
The IGN data or maps in this atlas are from the latest IGN
editions, the years of which may be different. www.ign.fr.
Licence number 9917.

Published by AA Publishing (a trading name of AA Media
Limited, whose registered office is Fanum House, Basing View,
Basingstoke, Hampshire
RG21 4EA, UK. Registered number 06112600).

ISBN: 978 0 7495 6338 7 (paperback)

ISBN: 978 0 7495 6339 4 (spiral bound)

A CIP catalogue record for this book is available from
The British Library.

Printed in Italy by Canale & C. S.P.A., Torino on paper
produced at EMAS (Eco Management and Audit Scheme)
registered paper mills.
Paper: Fenice 80gsm Matt.

The contents of this atlas are believed to be correct at the time
of printing. However, the publishers cannot be held responsible
for loss occasioned to any person acting or refraining from
action as a result of any material in this atlas, nor for any errors,
omissions or changes in such material. This does not affect
your statutory rights.

Photographs on pages II and III are held in the Association's
own library (AA World Travel Library) with contributions from the
following photographers (from left to right):
R Victor, S Day, S Abraham, R Moore, C Sawyer, W Voysey,
C Sawyer, T Oliver, M Busselle.

AA

BIG EASY READ
FRANCE

Atlas contents

Key to map pages	inside front cover
Channel hopping guide	II – III
Route planner	IV – V
Map Legend	VI
France road maps	1 – 201
Corsica road maps	202 – 207
Central Paris	208 – 211
Town plans	212 – 217

Aix-en-Provence	212	Chartres	213	Montpellier	215
Amiens	212	Cherbourg	214	Nancy	216
Angers	212	Clermont-Ferrand	214	Nantes	216
Annecy	212	Coquelles Terminal	I	Nice	216
Avignon	212	Dieppe	214	Orléans	216
Bayeux	212	Dijon	214	Pau	216
Bordeaux	212	Dunkerque	214	Perpignan	216
Boulogne-sur-Mer	III	Folkestone Terminal	I	Poitiers	216
Brest	213	Grenoble	214	Reims	217
Caen	213	La Rochelle	214	Rouen	217
Calais	III	Le Havre	214	St-Malo	217
Cannes	213	Lille	215	Strasbourg	217
Châlons-en-		Limoges	215	Toulon	217
Champagne	213	Lyon-Villeurbanne	215	Toulouse	217
Channel Tunnel	I	Marseille	215	Tours	217

Département map	218
Index to place names	218 – 250
Distances and journey times	inside back cover

Channel Tunnel Terminals

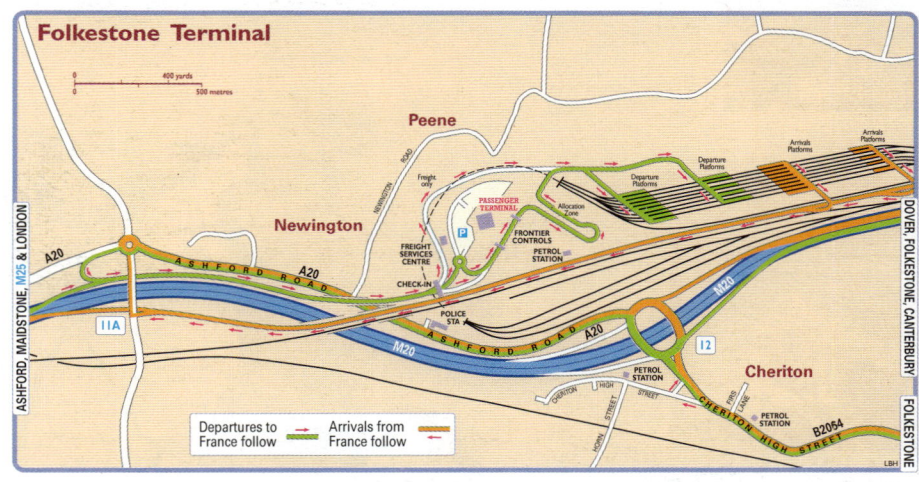

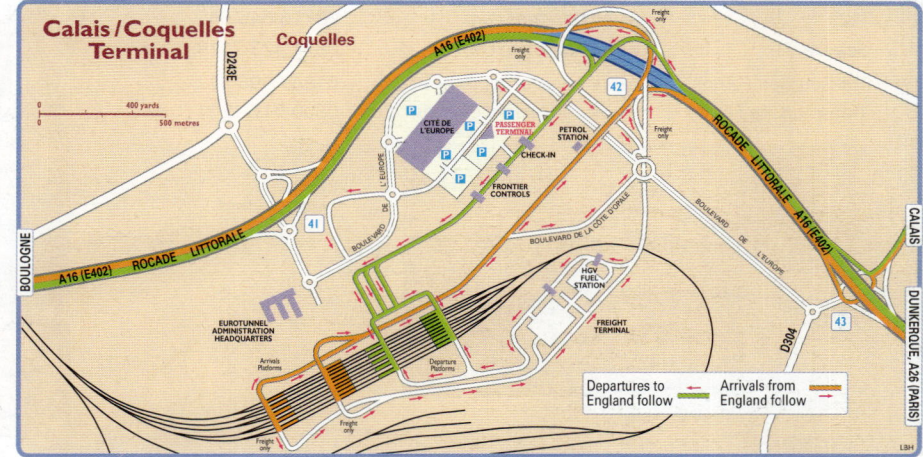

AA European Breakdown Cover

Driving to Europe? Save £10 on AA European Breakdown Cover

AA European Breakdown Cover provides you with a 24-hour English speaking helpline and arranges and helps towards the cost of:
- Emergency roadside repairs
- Towing to the nearest garage
- Alternative transport and accommodation
- Sourcing and delivery of spare parts
- Vehicle recovery to the UK or to your original destination

£10 OFF*
on trips of
six days
or more

Buy now. Call free on
0800 294 0298
and quote Euro Atlas '10

AA For the road ahead

Channel hopping

Whether for 'duty free' shopping, eating and drinking, sightseeing or a combination of all four, it's fun to hop across the Channel. High-speed ferries and the Channel Tunnel have made it easier than ever, Cherbourg is less than three hours sailing, while Calais is only an hour away.

Drive out of the terminal and large shopping complexes and hypermarkets are waiting close by, with large car parks, a fantastic choice of things to buy, and often with eating places all under the same roof. Cité Europe in Calais is the best example.

If you prefer town-centre shopping, colourful markets and tempting patisseries, specialist cheese shops and bakeries, follow the signs for the town centre or Centre-Ville. Boulogne, and Dieppe, for example, are ideal.

France time is normally one hour ahead of British time and remember to drive on the right and go round roundabouts in an anti-clockwise direction!

Vehicle ferries

Destination	Departure port	Operator	Journey time (approx.)
FRANCE AND BELGIUM			
Boulogne	Dover (fast)	LD Lines	1 hour
Caen (Ouistreham)	Portsmouth (March to November)	Brittany Ferries	6 – 7 hours
Caen (Ouistreham)	Portsmouth (March to November) (fast)	Brittany Ferries	3¾ hours
Calais	Dover	Sea France	1½ hours
Calais	Dover	P&O	1½ hours
Calais (Coquelles)	Channel Tunnel - Folkestone Terminal	Eurotunnel	35 minutes
Cherbourg	Portsmouth (March to November)	Brittany Ferries	3 hours
Cherbourg	Portsmouth (summer)	Condor	5 hours
Cherbourg	Poole	Brittany Ferries	4½ – 6½ hours
Cherbourg	Poole (summer) (fast)	Brittany Ferries	2¼ hours
Dieppe	Newhaven	Transmanche Ferries	4 hours
Dunkerque	Dover	Norfolk Line	2 hours
Le Havre	Portsmouth	LD Lines	5½ – 8 hours
Oostende	Ramsgate	Transeuropa	4 hours
Roscoff	Plymouth	Brittany Ferries	6 – 8 hours
St-Malo	Portsmouth	Brittany Ferries	9 – 10¾ hours
St-Malo	Poole (summer) (fast)	Condor	4 hours 35 minutes
St-Malo	Weymouth (fast)	Condor	5¼ hours
CHANNEL ISLANDS			
Guernsey	Weymouth (fast)	Condor	2 hours 10 minutes
Guernsey	Poole (March to October) (fast)	Condor	2¾ hours
Guernsey	Portsmouth	Condor	7 hours
Jersey	Weymouth (fast)	Condor	3 hours 25 minutes
Jersey	Poole (March to October) (fast)	Condor	3 hours
Jersey	Portsmouth	Condor	10½ hours

Ferry services are liable to change at short notice, so please check sailings before planning your journey.

Ferry operators

Operator	Website	Telephone
Brittany Ferries	www.brittany-ferries.co.uk	0871 244 0744
Condor	www.condorferries.com	0845 609 1024
Eurotunnel	www.eurotunnel.com	08705 35 35 35
LD Lines	www.ldlines.co.uk	0844 576 8836
Norfolk Line	www.norfolkline.com	0870 870 1020
P&O	www.poferries.com	08716 645 645
Sea France	www.seafrance.com	0871 423 7119
Transeuropa Ferries	www.transeuropaferries.com	01843 595 522
Transmanche Ferries	www.transmancheferries.co.uk	0800 917 1201

Cherbourg

St Peter Port

Roscoff

15th century castle of St-Malo

Port plans: Cherbourg p.214, Le Havre p.214 and St-Malo p.217.

Boulogne-sur-Mer

Calais

Dover

ENGLISH CHANNEL

Portsmouth Harbour

Boulogne-sur-Mer

Dieppe

Abbey aux Hommes, Caen

Road distances are shown in miles in Britain and kilometres in France and Belgium.

GREAT BRITAIN

ENGLISH CHANNEL

NORTH ATLANTIC OCEAN

Bay of Biscay

SPAIN

IV

GB
E
AND

Grid page references: 1, 2, 6, 8, 12, 14, 16, 18, 20, 30, 32, 34, 36, 38, 40, 42, 44, 52, 54, 56, 58, 60, 62, 64, 72, 74, 76, 78, 80, 82, 90, 92, 94, 96, 98, 106, 108, 110, 112, 120, 122, 124, 126, 134, 136, 138, 140, 148, 150, 152, 154, 164, 166, 168, 170, 180, 182, 184, 186, 188, 196, 198, 200

Places (selected): Folkestone, Dover, Dunkerque, Calais, St-Omer, LILLE, Béthune, Lens, Douai, Arras, Boulogne-sur-Mer, Montreuil, Abbeville, AMIENS, Montdidier, Beauvais, Compiègne, Soissons, St-Quentin, Clermont, Senlis, Pontoise, Meaux, Bobigny, Créteil, Évry, PARIS, Versailles, Provins, Dieppe, Le Havre, ROUEN, Évreux, Dreux, Melun, Fontainebleau, Cherbourg, Bayeux, Ouistreham, CAEN, Lisieux, Bernay, les Andelys, Chartres, Étampes, Pithiviers, Montargis, St-Lô, Coutances, Vire, Argentan, Alençon, Mamers, Nogent-le-Rotrou, Châteaudun, ORLÉANS, Aux, St-Malo, Dinan, Avranches, Fougères, Mayenne, Laval, LE MANS, Vendôme, Blois, Romorantin-Lanthenay, Vierzon, Roscoff, Lannion, Guingamp, St-Brieuc, Morlaix, Brest, Île d'Ouessant, Châteaulin, Quimper, Pontivy, RENNES, Redon, Château-Gontier, Segré, Châteaubriant, la Flèche, TOURS, D357, Loches, Cosne-Cours-sur-Loire, Lorient, Île de Groix, Vannes, Ancenis, ANGERS, Saumur, Chinon, BOURGES, Issoudun, Châteauroux, St-Amand-Montrond, Belle-Île, St-Nazaire, NANTES, Cholet, Bressuire, Châtellerault, le Blanc, la Châtre, Moulins, Montluçon, Île de Noirmoutier, Île d'Yeu, la Roche-sur-Yon, Parthenay, POITIERS, Montmorillon, Guéret, les Sables-d'Olonne, Fontenay-le-Comte, Niort, Montluçon, Bellac, Île de Ré, LA ROCHELLE, Rochefort, Île d'Oléron, St-Jean-d'Angély, Confolens, Rochechouart, LIMOGES, Aubusson, CLERMONT-FERRAND, Saintes, Cognac, Angoulême, Nontron, Ussel, Issoire, Royan, Jonzac, Lesparre-Médoc, Blaye, Périgueux, Bergerac, Sarlat-la-Canéda, Tulle, Brive-la-Gaillarde, Gourdon, Mauriac, St-Flo, BORDEAUX, Libourne, Aurillac, Arcachon, Langon, Marmande, Villeneuve-sur-Lot, Cahors, Figeac, Villefranche-de-Rouergue, Rodez, Biscarrosse, Agen, Nérac, Condom, Castelsarrasin, Montauban, Albi, Milla, Mont-de-Marsan, Dax, Auch, Mirande, TOULOUSE, Castres, Bayonne, Muret, Oloron-Ste-Marie, PAU, Tarbes, St-Gaudens, Carcassonne, Argelès-Gazost, Pamiers, Limoux, Narbo, St-Girons, Foix, PERPIGNAN, Prades, Céret, ANDORRA LA VELLA, Jaca

Spain / ferries: Plymouth, Penzance, Poole, Portsmouth, Weymouth, Newhaven, Santander, Bilbao, SANTANDER, DONOSTIA / SAN SEBASTIÁN, GASTEIZ VITORIA, PAMPLONA / IRUÑEA, BURGOS, LOGROÑO, Channel Islands, Channel Tunnel

km 0 — 150
miles 0 — 100

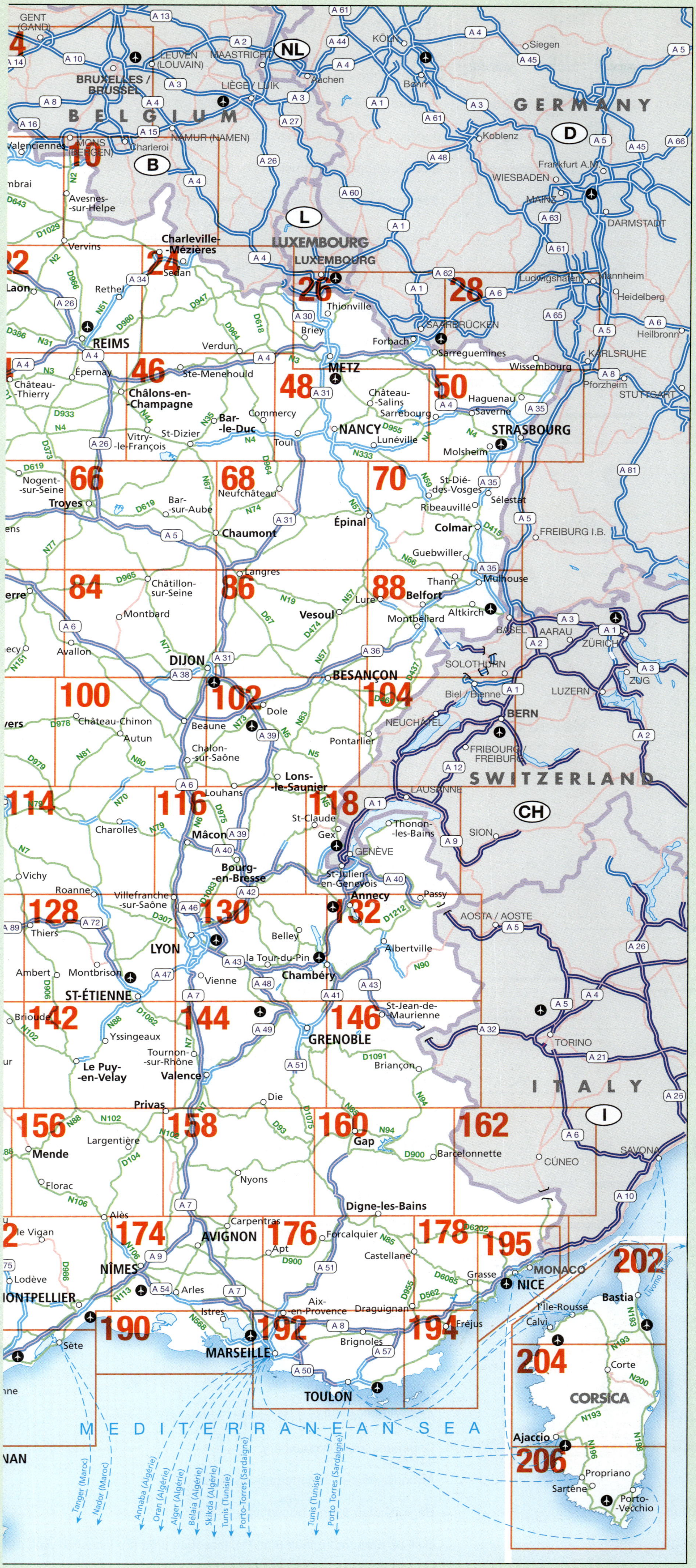

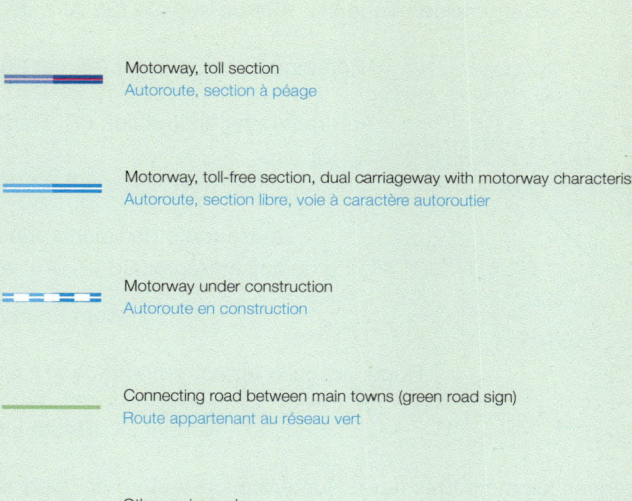

	Motorway, toll section
	Autoroute, section à péage
	Motorway, toll-free section, dual carriageway with motorway characteristics
	Autoroute, section libre, voie à caractère autoroutier
	Motorway under construction
	Autoroute en construction
	Connecting road between main towns (green road sign)
	Route appartenant au réseau vert
	Other main road
	Autre route de liaison principale
	International boundary
	Limite d'État
140	Index to maps in road map section
	Numéros des pages
	Vehicle ferry
	Ferry-boat
	Vehicle ferry-fast catamaran
	Ferry Seacat

Motorway driving in France

Joining a motorway

There are more than 5,000 miles of motorway or *'autoroute'* in France. To join a motorway follow signs with the international motorway symbol or with the word *'par Autoroute'* included. Signs with the words *'péage'* or *'par péage'* lead to toll motorways.

Toll-free motorways

Toll-free motorways are mostly in the vicinity of large cities such as Paris, Bordeaux, Lille, Lyon, Marseille and Metz. There are a few longer-distance toll-free sections such as the A20 from north of Bourges south towards Toulouse and the A75 from Clermont-Ferrand south towards Montpellier. The map shows toll-free motorway sections in blue.

Toll *'péage'* motorways

On most toll motorways a travel ticket is issued when joining and the toll is paid when leaving. Occasionally a toll is paid at intermediate points along the route as well. The travel ticket indicates the toll category for each vehicle. When leaving the motorway the ticket is handed in and the fee paid. Toll booths accept payment in cash Euros or by credit card (note: toll booths will not accept travellers' cheques). On some motorways toll collections are automatic and you should have the correct change ready to throw into the collecting basket. If change is required you must queue in a separate lane.

Service areas

Rest stops or picnic areas, most of which have toilets, are located at regular intervals, normally every 9 miles (15 kilometres). All 24-hour service areas have filling stations and a restaurant or café and are on average every 25 miles (40 kilometres).

Breakdowns

Use of hazard warning lights or a warning triangle are compulsory. Free emergency telephones are located every 1¼ miles (2 kilometres) on most motorways. There are public telephones at rest stops, service areas and toll booths.

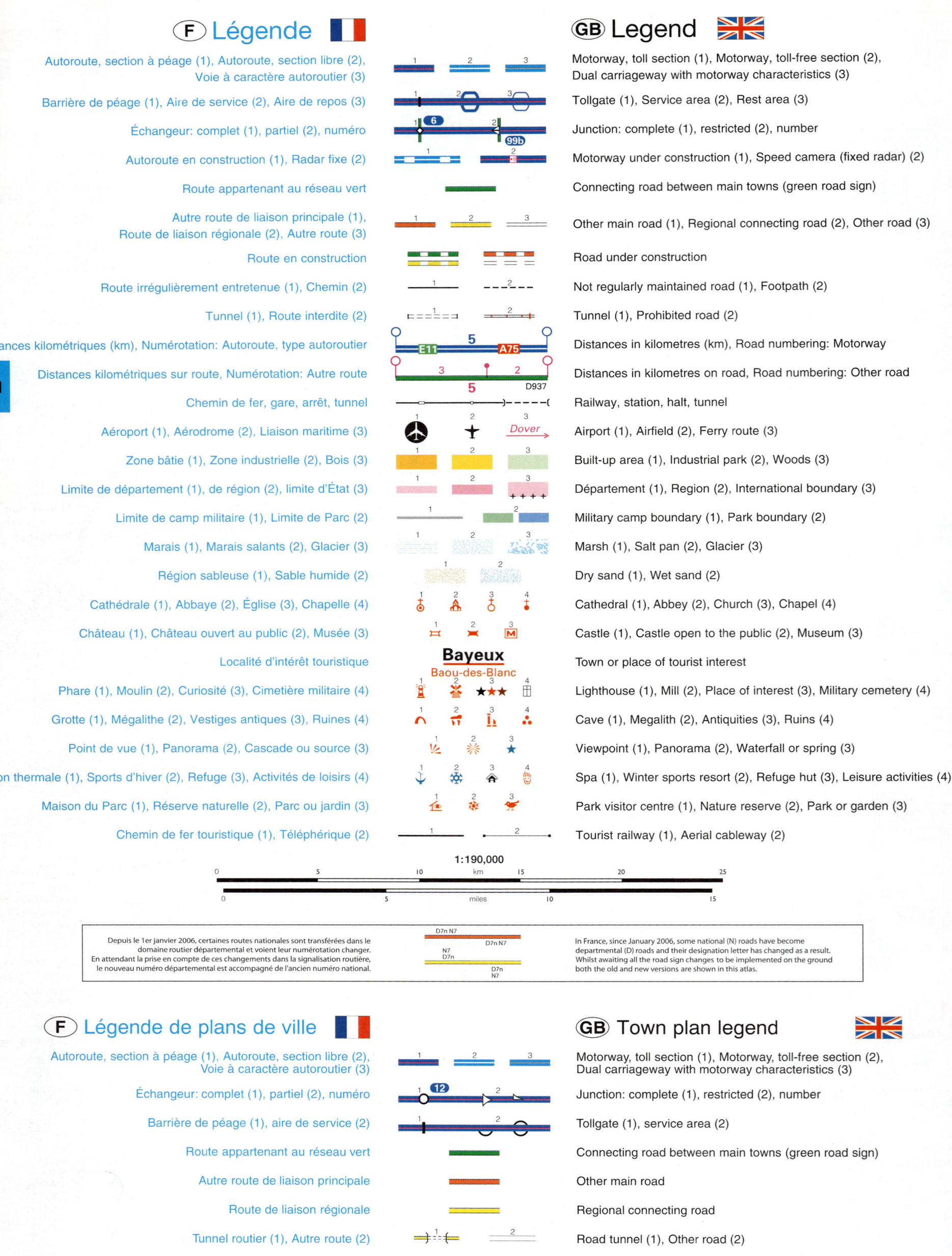

F Légende 🇫🇷 — GB Legend 🇬🇧

Autoroute, section à péage (1), Autoroute, section libre (2), Voie à caractère autoroutier (3) — Motorway, toll section (1), Motorway, toll-free section (2), Dual carriageway with motorway characteristics (3)

Barrière de péage (1), Aire de service (2), Aire de repos (3) — Tollgate (1), Service area (2), Rest area (3)

Échangeur: complet (1), partiel (2), numéro — Junction: complete (1), restricted (2), number

Autoroute en construction (1), Radar fixe (2) — Motorway under construction (1), Speed camera (fixed radar) (2)

Route appartenant au réseau vert — Connecting road between main towns (green road sign)

Autre route de liaison principale (1), Route de liaison régionale (2), Autre route (3) — Other main road (1), Regional connecting road (2), Other road (3)

Route en construction — Road under construction

Route irrégulièrement entretenue (1), Chemin (2) — Not regularly maintained road (1), Footpath (2)

Tunnel (1), Route interdite (2) — Tunnel (1), Prohibited road (2)

Distances kilométriques (km), Numérotation: Autoroute, type autoroutier — Distances in kilometres (km), Road numbering: Motorway

Distances kilométriques sur route, Numérotation: Autre route — Distances in kilometres on road, Road numbering: Other road

Chemin de fer, gare, arrêt, tunnel — Railway, station, halt, tunnel

Aéroport (1), Aérodrome (2), Liaison maritime (3) — Airport (1), Airfield (2), Ferry route (3)

Zone bâtie (1), Zone industrielle (2), Bois (3) — Built-up area (1), Industrial park (2), Woods (3)

Limite de département (1), de région (2), limite d'État (3) — Département (1), Region (2), International boundary (3)

Limite de camp militaire (1), Limite de Parc (2) — Military camp boundary (1), Park boundary (2)

Marais (1), Marais salants (2), Glacier (3) — Marsh (1), Salt pan (2), Glacier (3)

Région sableuse (1), Sable humide (2) — Dry sand (1), Wet sand (2)

Cathédrale (1), Abbaye (2), Église (3), Chapelle (4) — Cathedral (1), Abbey (2), Church (3), Chapel (4)

Château (1), Château ouvert au public (2), Musée (3) — Castle (1), Castle open to the public (2), Museum (3)

Localité d'intérêt touristique — Town or place of tourist interest

Bayeux
Baou-des-Blanc

Phare (1), Moulin (2), Curiosité (3), Cimetière militaire (4) — Lighthouse (1), Mill (2), Place of interest (3), Military cemetery (4)

Grotte (1), Mégalithe (2), Vestiges antiques (3), Ruines (4) — Cave (1), Megalith (2), Antiquities (3), Ruins (4)

Point de vue (1), Panorama (2), Cascade ou source (3) — Viewpoint (1), Panorama (2), Waterfall or spring (3)

Station thermale (1), Sports d'hiver (2), Refuge (3), Activités de loisirs (4) — Spa (1), Winter sports resort (2), Refuge hut (3), Leisure activities (4)

Maison du Parc (1), Réserve naturelle (2), Parc ou jardin (3) — Park visitor centre (1), Nature reserve (2), Park or garden (3)

Chemin de fer touristique (1), Téléphérique (2) — Tourist railway (1), Aerial cableway (2)

1:190,000

| 0 | 5 | 10 | km | 15 | 20 | 25 |

| 0 | 5 | miles | 10 | 15 |

Depuis le 1er janvier 2006, certaines routes nationales sont transférées dans le domaine routier départemental et voient leur numérotation changer. En attendant la prise en compte de ces changements dans la signalisation routière, le nouveau numéro départemental est accompagné de l'ancien numéro national.

D7n N7 / D7n N7
N7 / D7n / D7n N7

In France, since January 2006, some national (N) roads have become departmental (D) roads and their designation letter has changed as a result. Whilst awaiting all the road sign changes to be implemented on the ground both the old and new versions are shown in this atlas.

F Légende de plans de ville 🇫🇷 — GB Town plan legend 🇬🇧

Autoroute, section à péage (1), Autoroute, section libre (2), Voie à caractère autoroutier (3) — Motorway, toll section (1), Motorway, toll-free section (2), Dual carriageway with motorway characteristics (3)

Échangeur: complet (1), partiel (2), numéro — Junction: complete (1), restricted (2), number

Barrière de péage (1), aire de service (2) — Tollgate (1), service area (2)

Route appartenant au réseau vert — Connecting road between main towns (green road sign)

Autre route de liaison principale — Other main road

Route de liaison régionale — Regional connecting road

Tunnel routier (1), Autre route (2) — Road tunnel (1), Other road (2)

Bâtiment administratif (1), église, chapelle (2), hôpital (3) — Administrative building (1), church, chapel (2), hospital (3)

Limite de commune, de canton — Commune, canton boundary

Limite d'arrondissement, de département — Arrondissement, département boundary

Limite de région, d'État — Region, international boundary

Zone bâtie, superficie > 8 ha (1), < 8 ha (2), zone industrielle (3) — Built-up area, more than 8 ha (1), less than 8 ha (2), industrial park (3)

VI

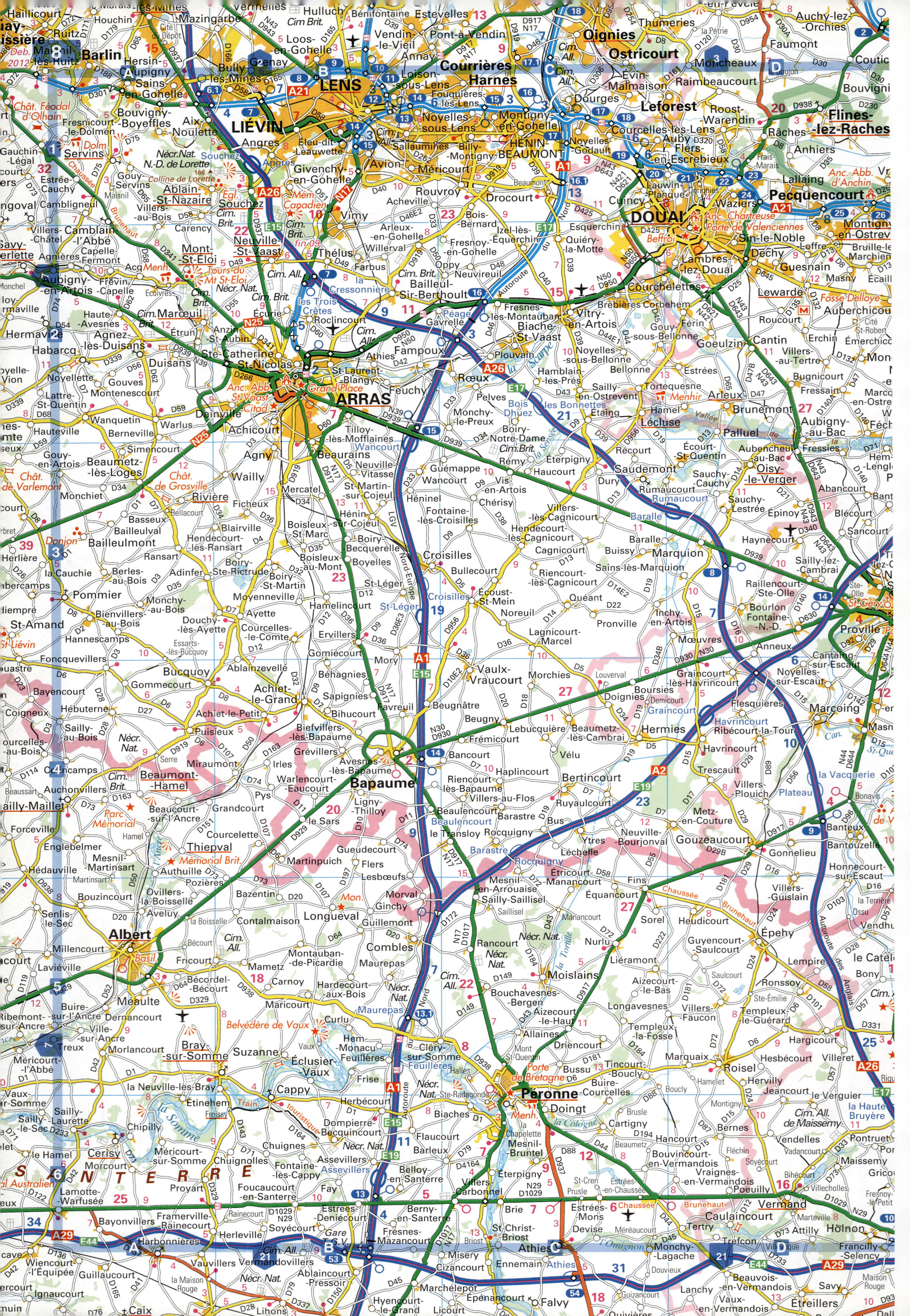

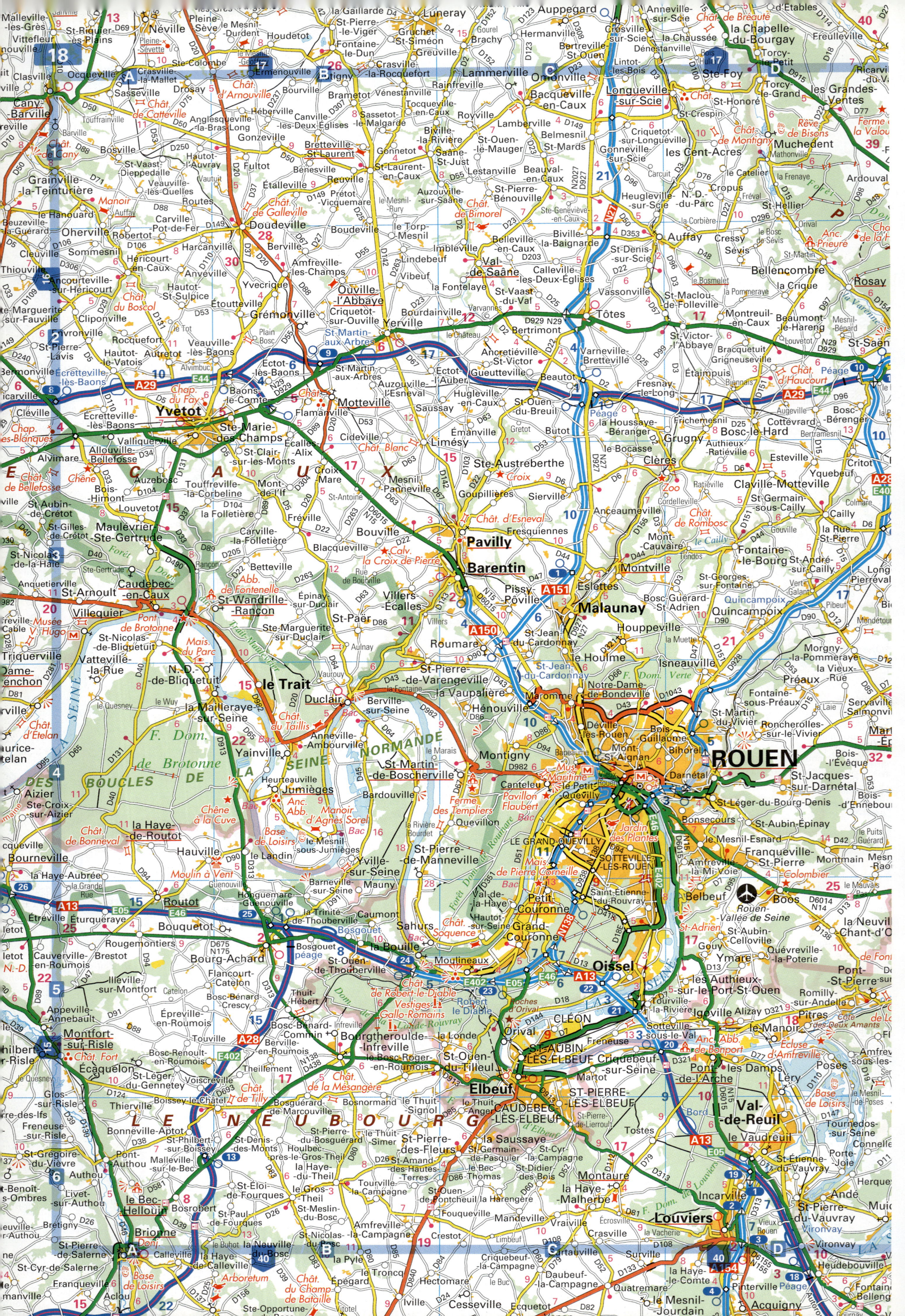

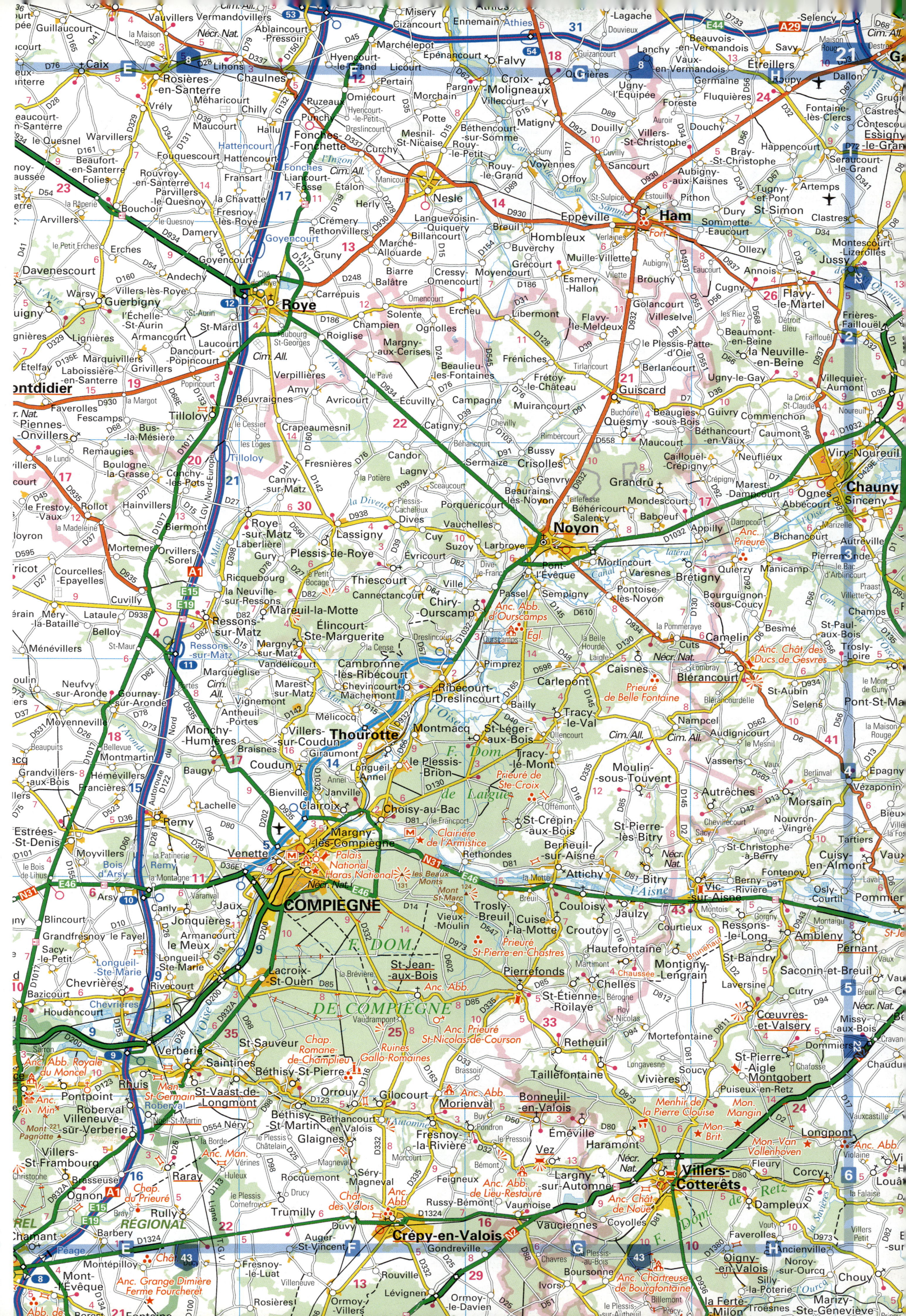

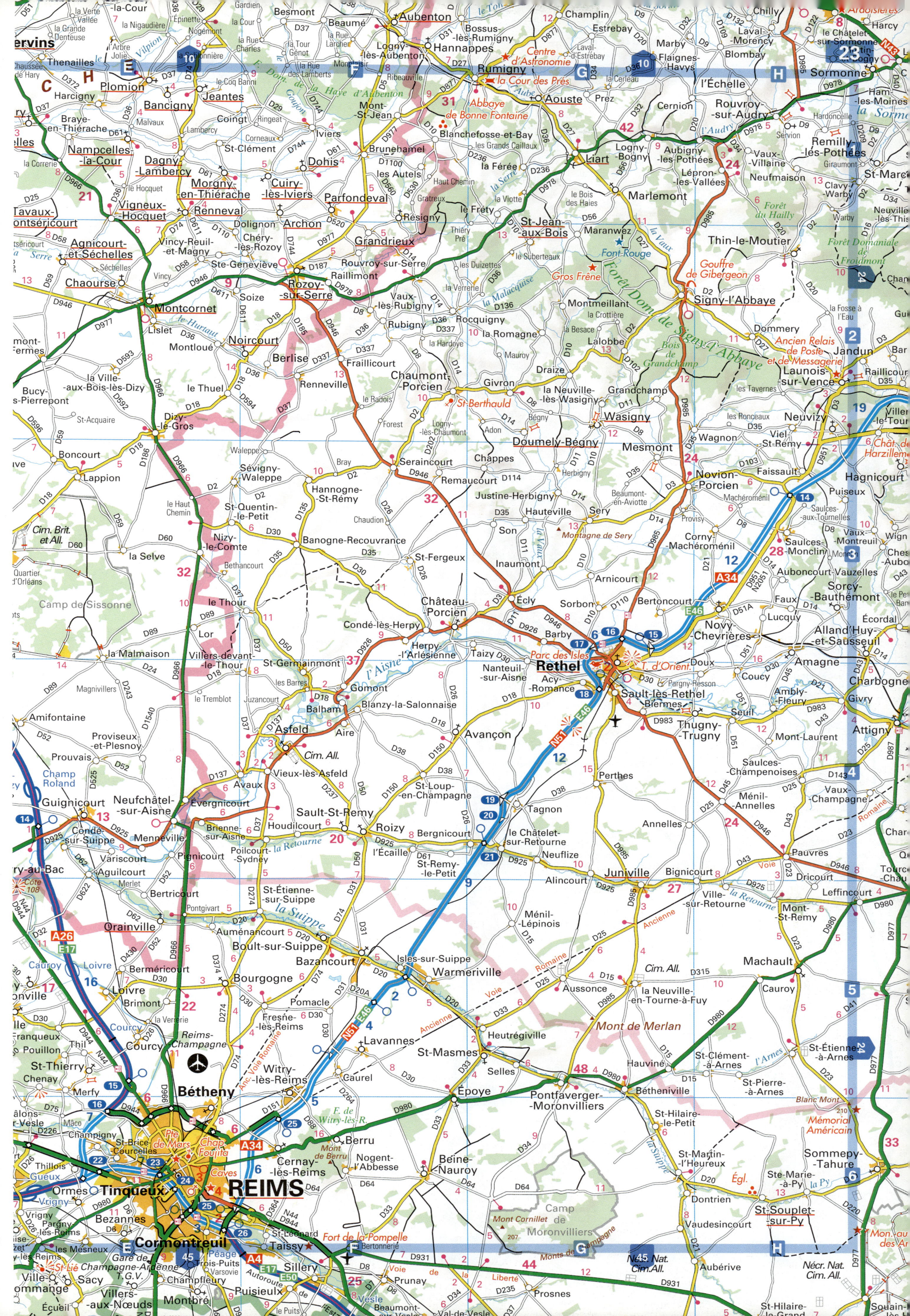

A   B   C   D

1

2

3

C Ô T E   D E S

Î l e s   A b e r s

Phare de l'Île Vierge
Île Vierge
Kélerdut
St-Cava
Plouguerneau
Presqu'Île
Ste-Marguerite
Aber-Wrac'h   Aber Wrac'h
Landéda
D128   D13
Morgan   Coum
Aber Benoît
7
Lampaul-   Lannilis
-Ploudalmézeau   St-Pabu   14
Trémazan   Portsall   3   D26   6   D28   4
Chât.   D168   3   Ploudalmézeau   Tréglonou
Pointe de Landunvez   11   Kersaint   D26   Menhir   3
de Kervignen   Coat-Méal
Radénoc   Argenton   6   D27   Landunvez   15   D26   Bourg-
Plourin   Guipronvel   Blanc
Porspoder   Kerazant   D68   5   D168   18   Tréouergat   4
Menhirs   Milizac   16
Manoir   Brélès   Lanrivoaré   Lanner
de   Kergroadès   Lanvénec   Les Trois
Bel-air   D28   Curés
Phare de Aber Ildut   Lanildut   l'Aber Ildut   D27   Gou
Perros   Erragounan   6   D38   Kerviniou
Lampaul-   D5   15   5   D67   Guilers
-Plouarzel   Menhir   St-Renan   D105   Bohars
Kerescar   de Kerloas   Lamber   12   D5
Phare   Plouarzel   D105   Penfeld
de Trézien   Trégorff   le Bouguen
Ruscumunoc   Kerhornou   19   D67   Kerlazou   Arsenal
Pointe de Corsen   Ploumoguer   D38
Île-Molène   Trébabu   Locmaria-   Plouzané   St-Pierre-
Île   -Plouzané   Kerarmazé   Quilbignon
Molène   a-Trinité   D789   B
Réserve Naturelle   le Conquet   Porsmilin   27   RA
d'Iroise   Lochrist   Ste-Anne-   D38   Pointe
Île de Béniguet   Porsmilin   du-Portzic   des Espagnols   BR
St-Mathieu   Trégana   Goulet de Brest   BRE
POINTE DE ST-MATHIEU   Plougonvelin   Pointe du
Abbaye   D85   Petit Minou
D355
Roscanvel
Lanvarnazal   Quélern
Fort   N.-D. de Roch   St-Fiacre   Taladerc'h   Lanvé
Camaret-   Amadour   D55
sur-Mer   Tour Vauban   D355   D55
Alignements de Lagatjar   D8   P R E S Q U' Î L E
POINTE DE PEN-HIR   Crozon
les Tas de Pois   D887
Pointe de Dinan   Morgat   Cro
D308   Pointe
la Palue   des Gro
Grottes
St-Hernot   Maison
des Minéraux

Î l e   d ' O u e s s a n t

Phare de Créac'h
Niou Uhella   Frugullou   Phare du Stiff
Notre-Dame   3
de Bon Voyage   Ouessant
(Lampaul)
Feunteun Vélen
Phare
de la Jument

Passage du Fromveur

P A R C   **N A T U R E L**

4

5

PARC NATUREL MARIN D'IROISE

6

A   B   C   52   D

Cap
de la Chèvre   Rostudel

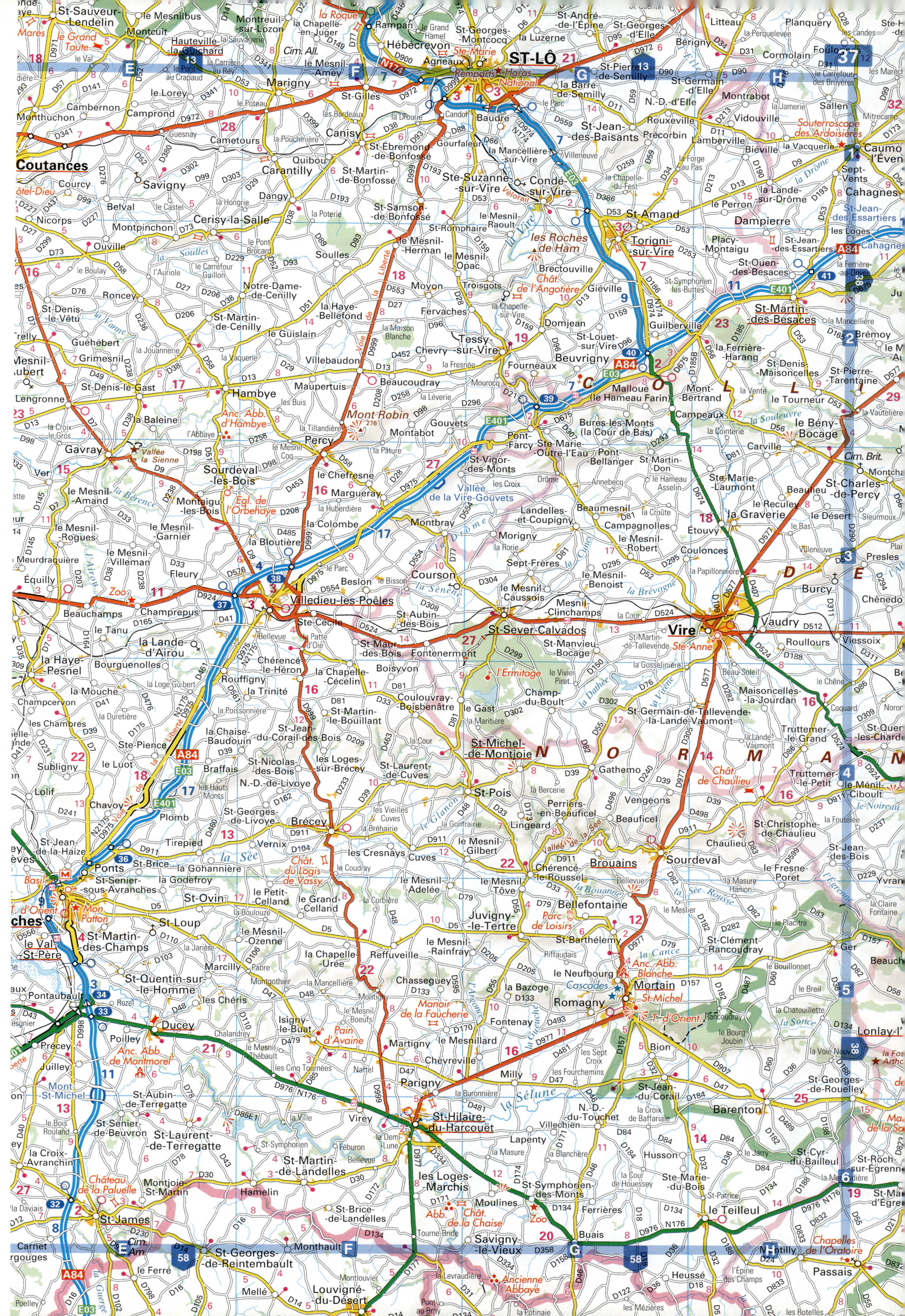

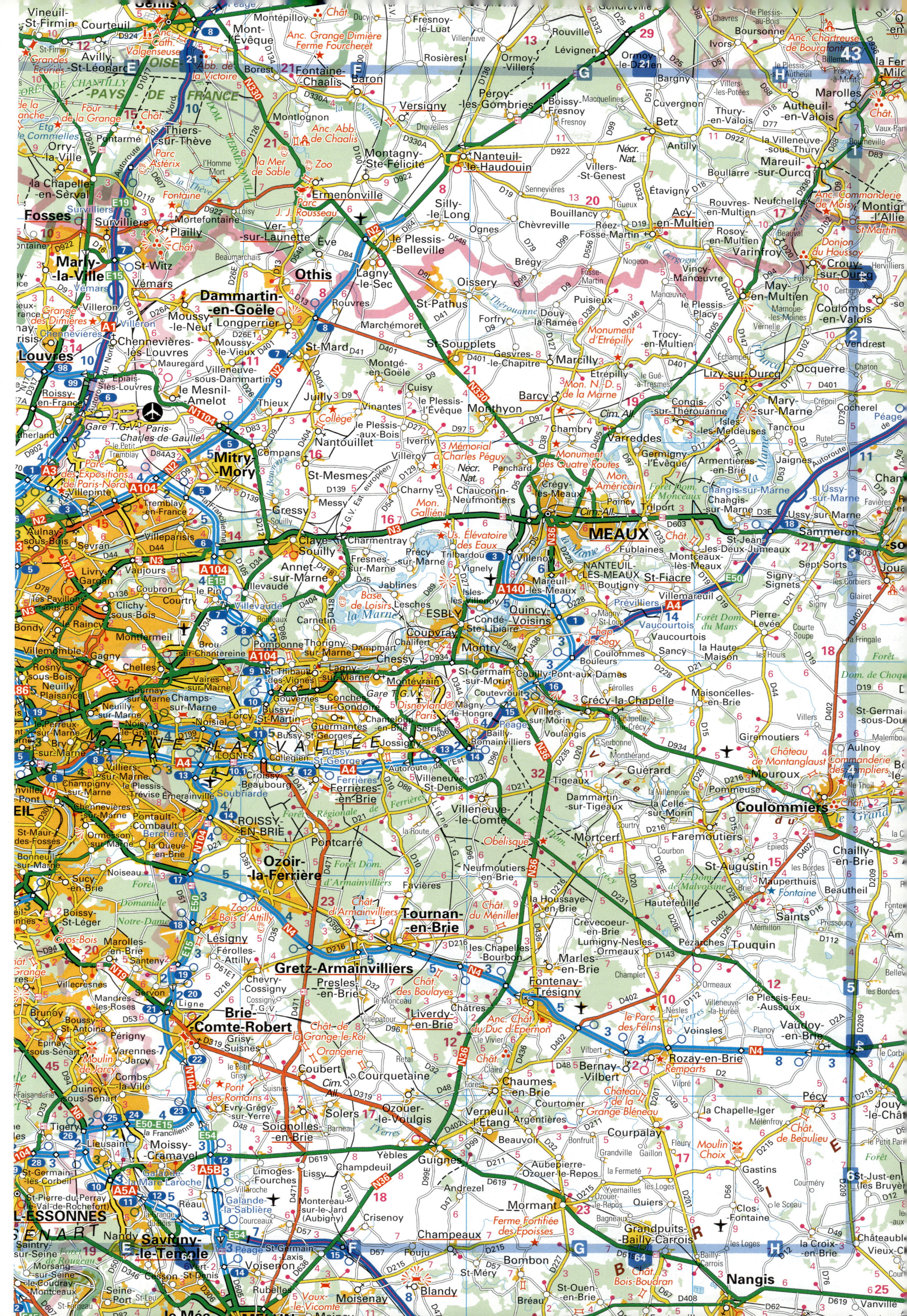

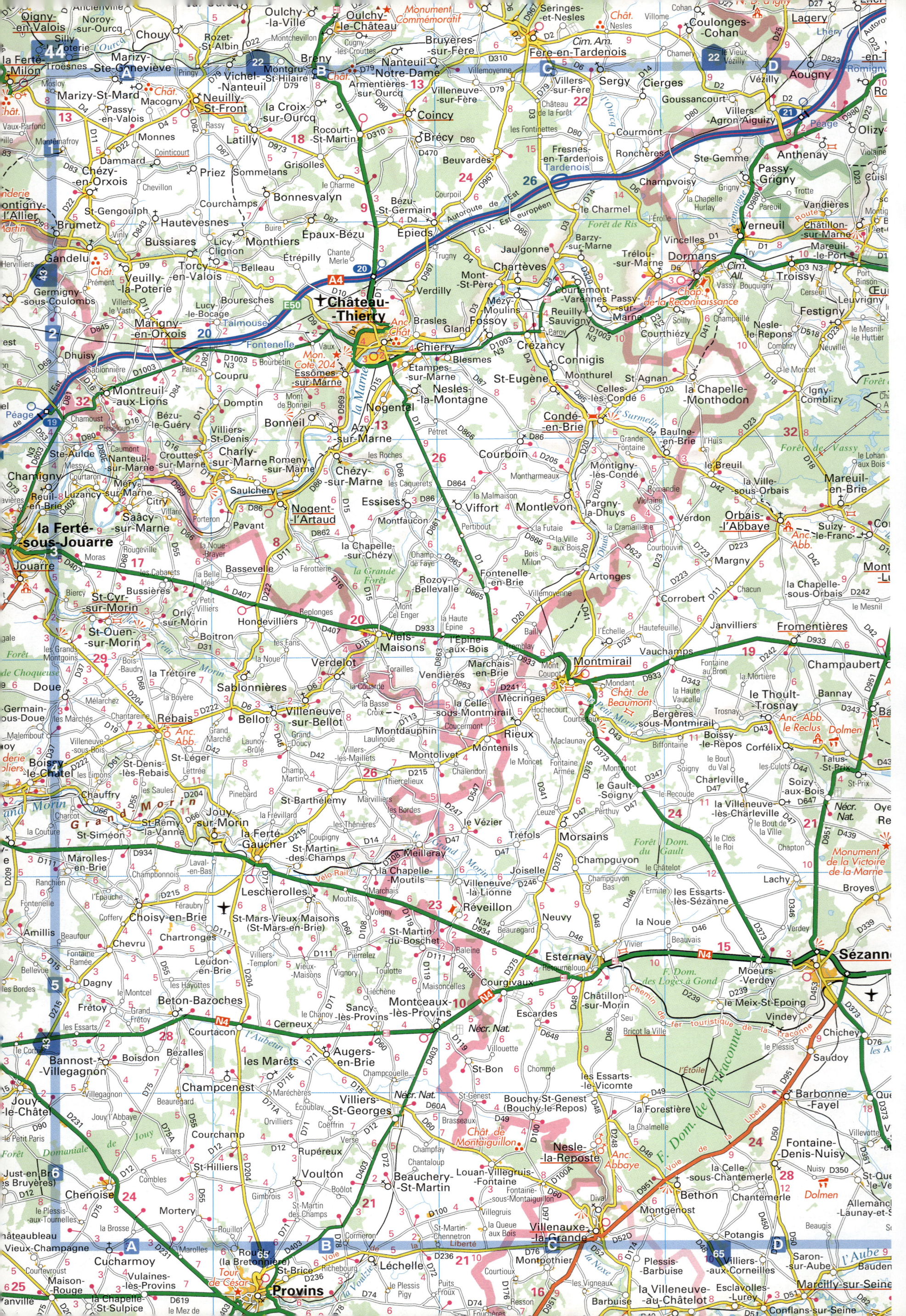

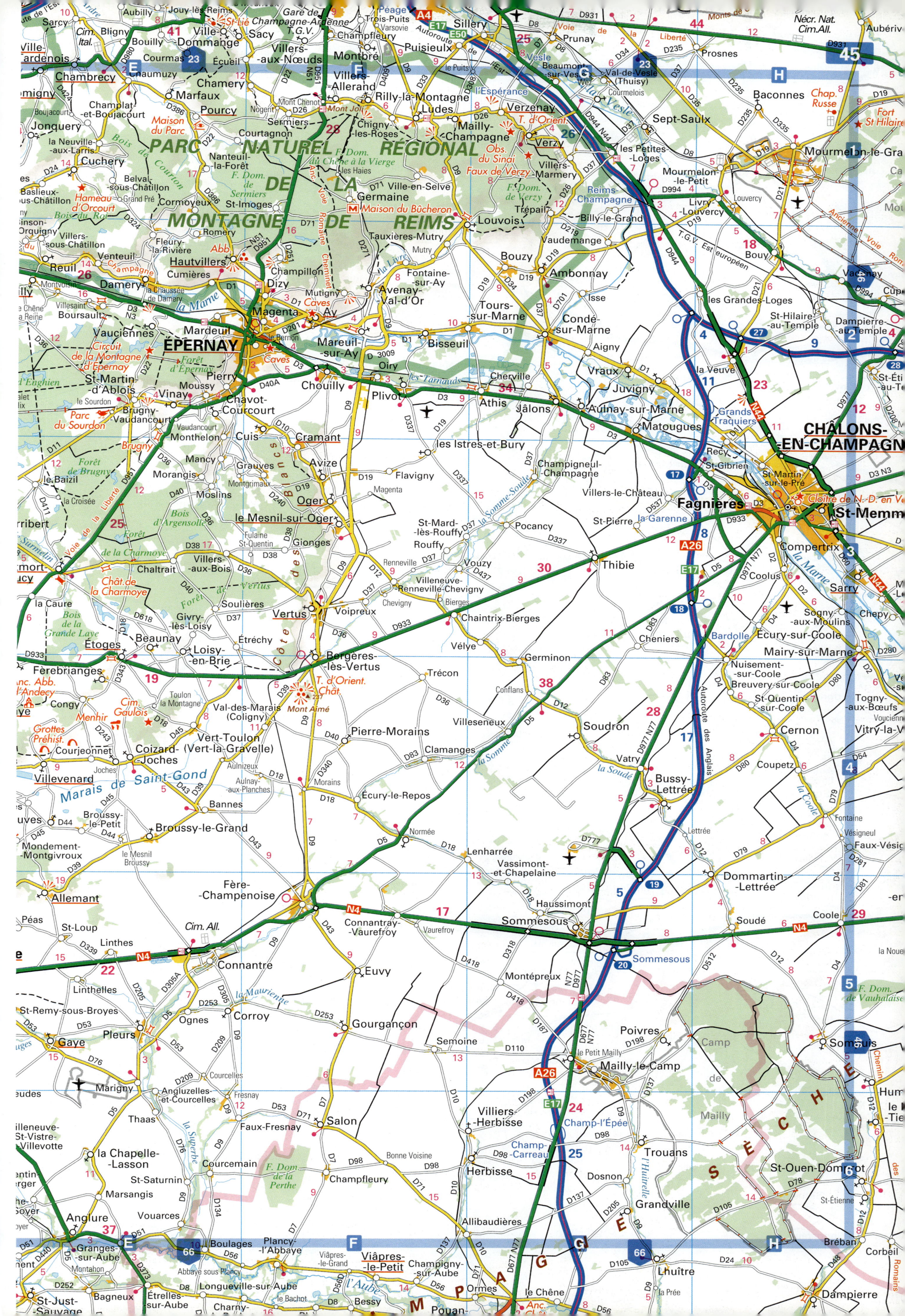

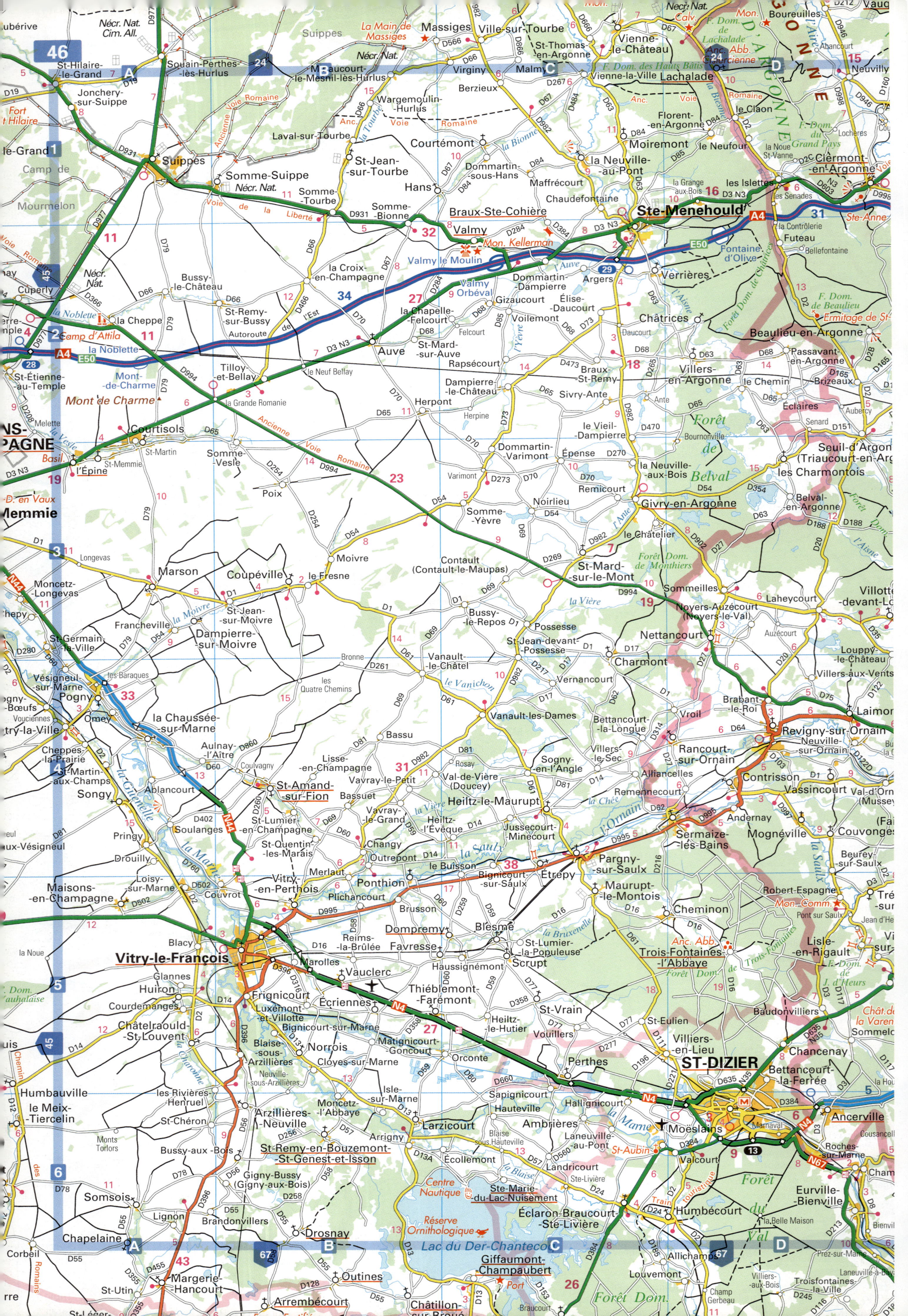

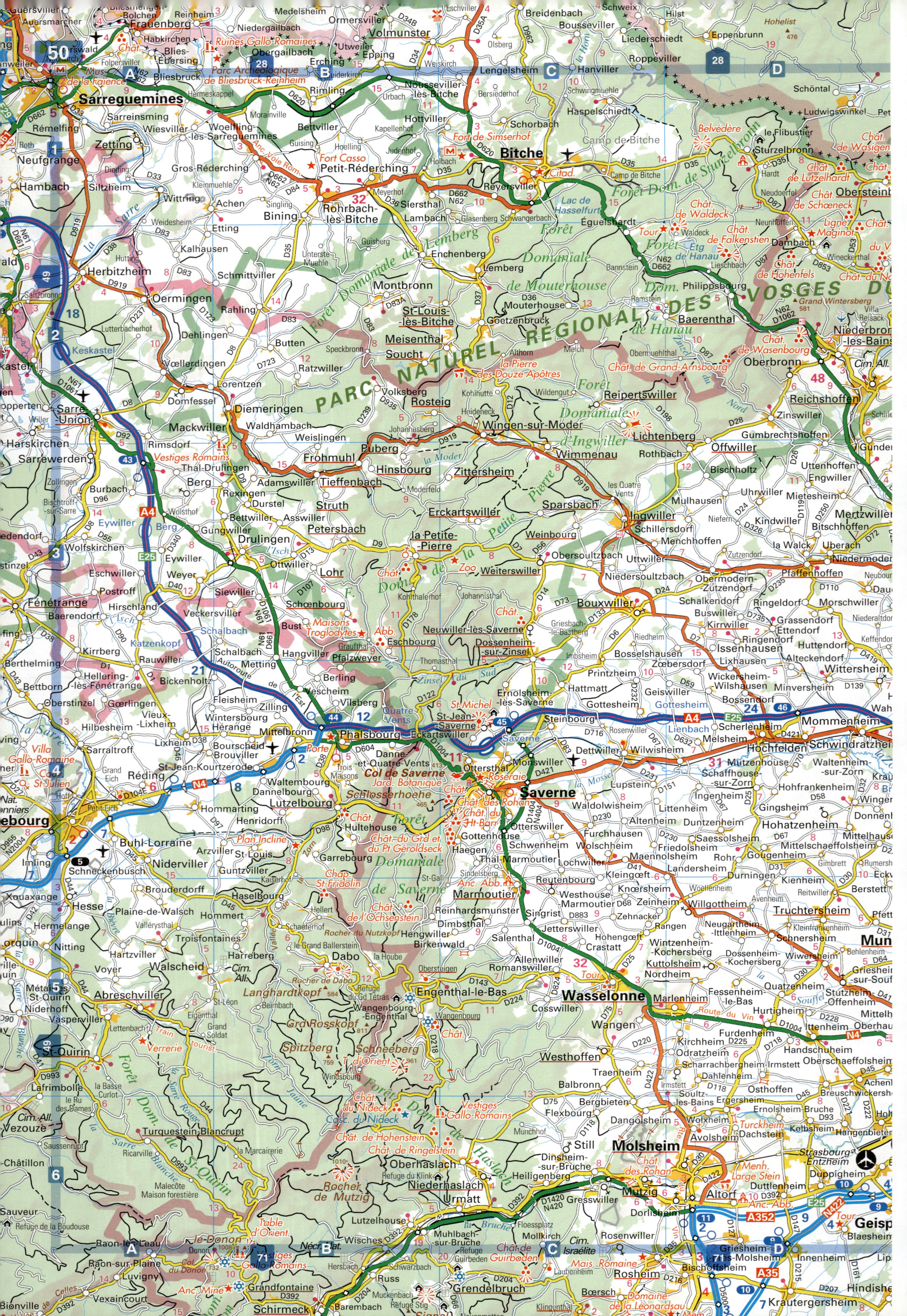

A · B · C · D

D

1

Ar Men

Île de Sein

Île-de-Sein

Chaussée de Sein

Phare de la Vieille

POINTE DU RAZ

2

Cap de la Chèvre 30

Rostudel

des Minéraux

D255 5

D

Pointe de Brézellec

Réserve du Cap Sizun

Pointe du Van

St-They

Baie des Trépassés

Lescoff

Plogoff

Pennéac'h

Kermeur

Cléden-Cap-Sizun

D7

D7

D43

9

Goulien

Quatre-Vents

Toulemonde

Moulin-Castel

3

Beuzec-Cap-Sizun

D7

4

D43

6

5

Pors-Péron

Pont-Croix

D43A

7

D43

6

D784

15

11

Primelin

St-Tugen

Esquibien

Le Pouldu

Confort-Meilar

Audierne

7

Plouhinec

Trébeuzec

5

11

D784

4

23

Plozévet

Menhir

BAIE

D'AUDIERNE

3

4

St-

Notre-D de la J

Phare d'Eckr

POINTE DE PENMARC'H

5

6

A · B · C · D

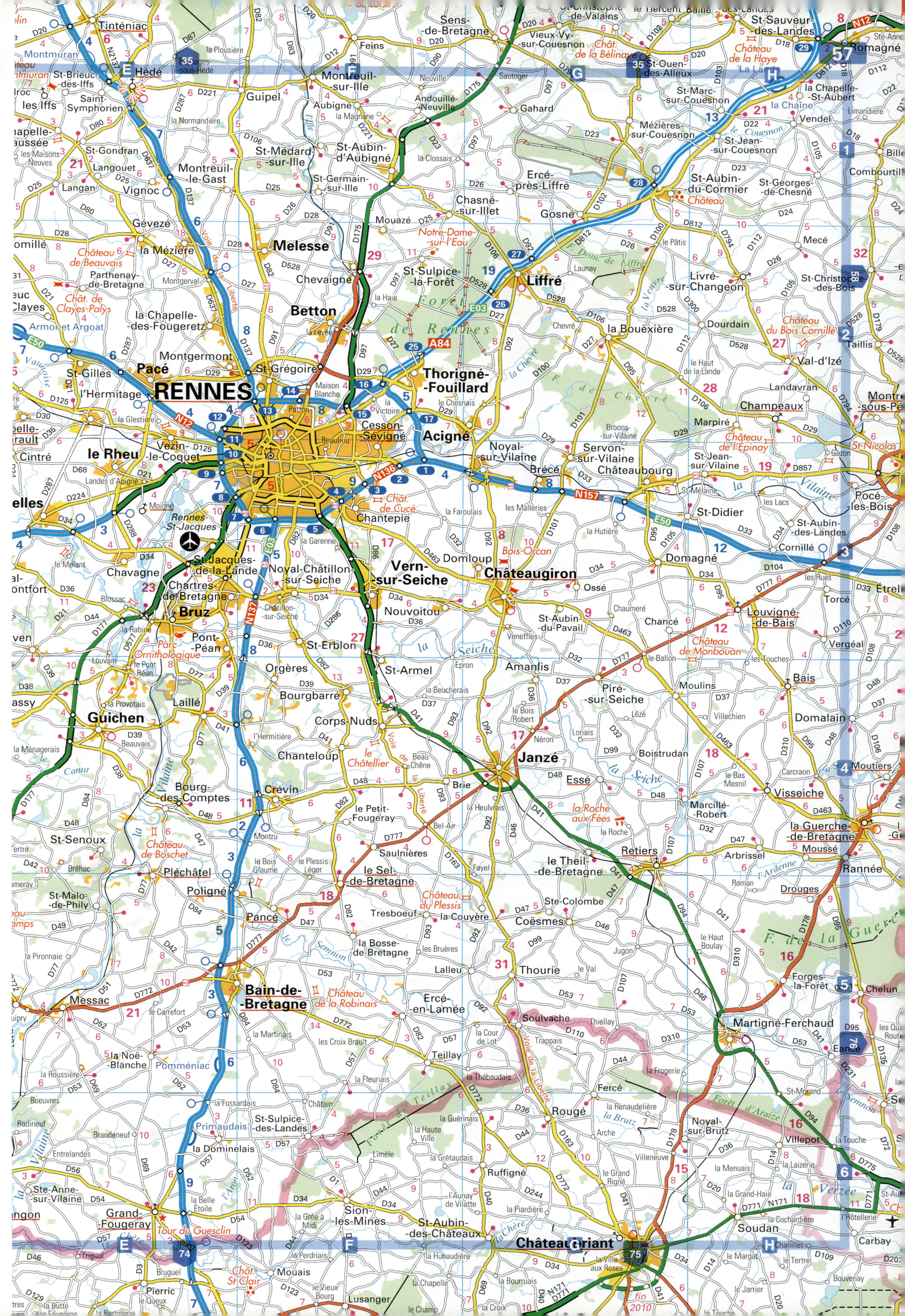

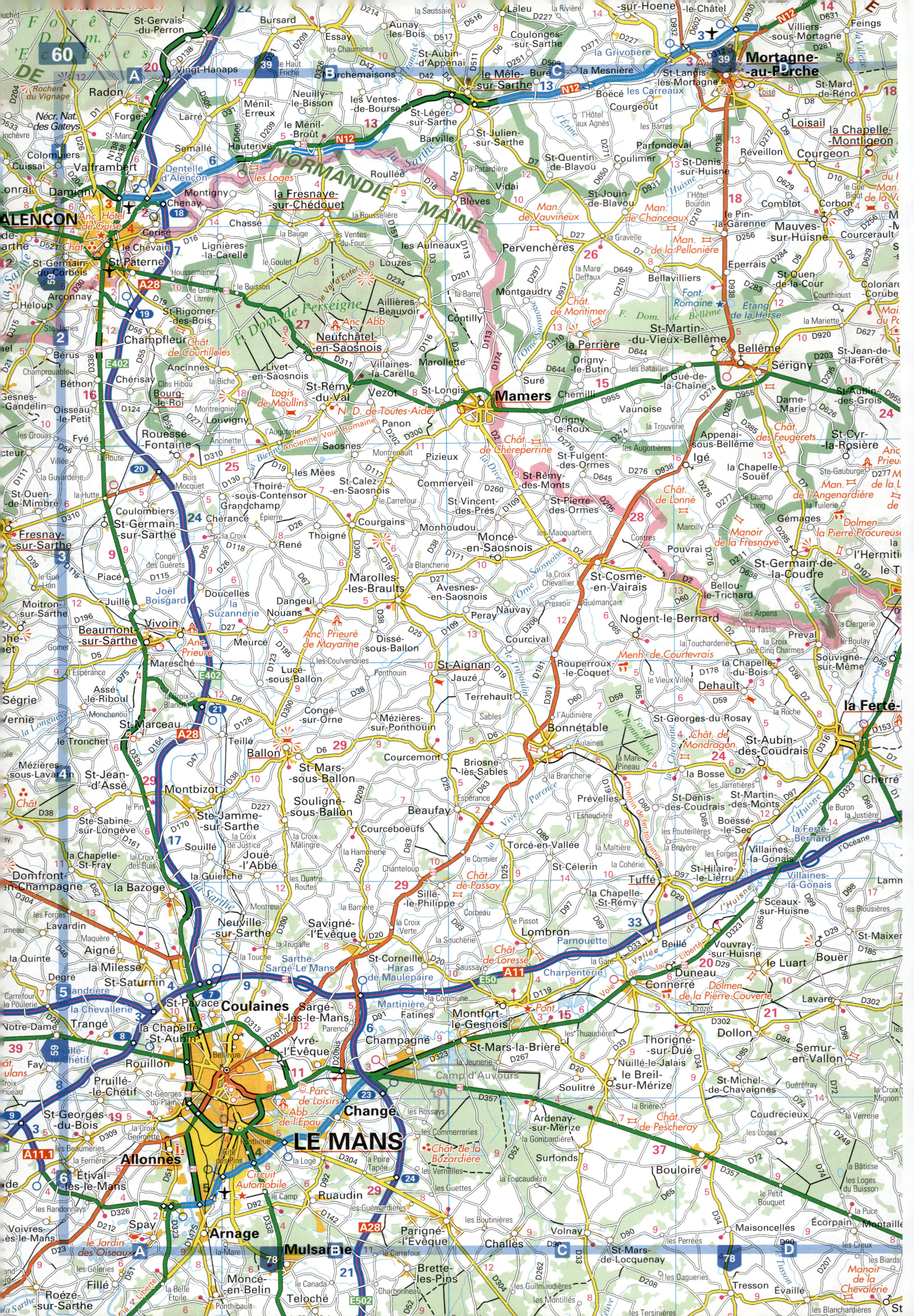

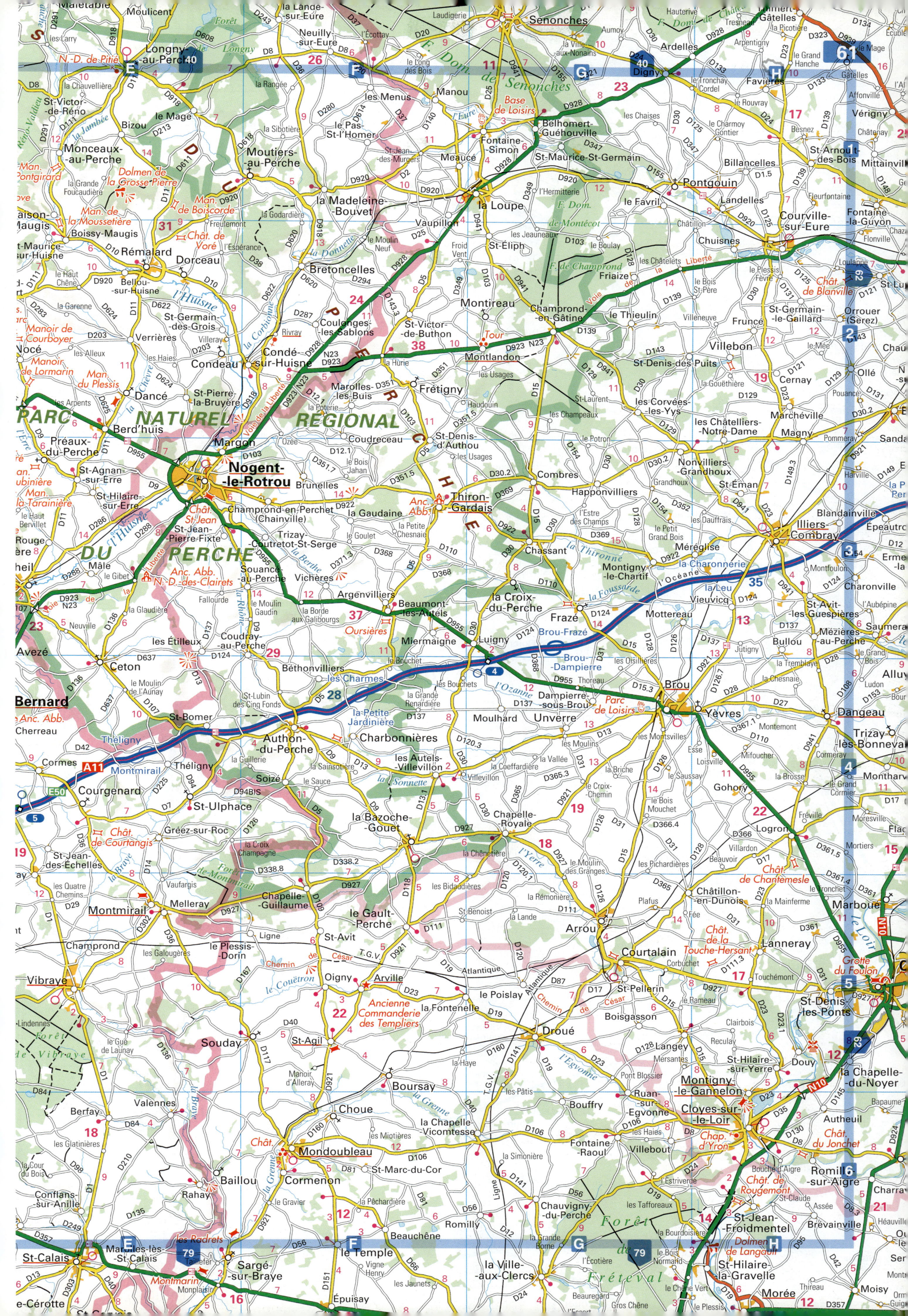

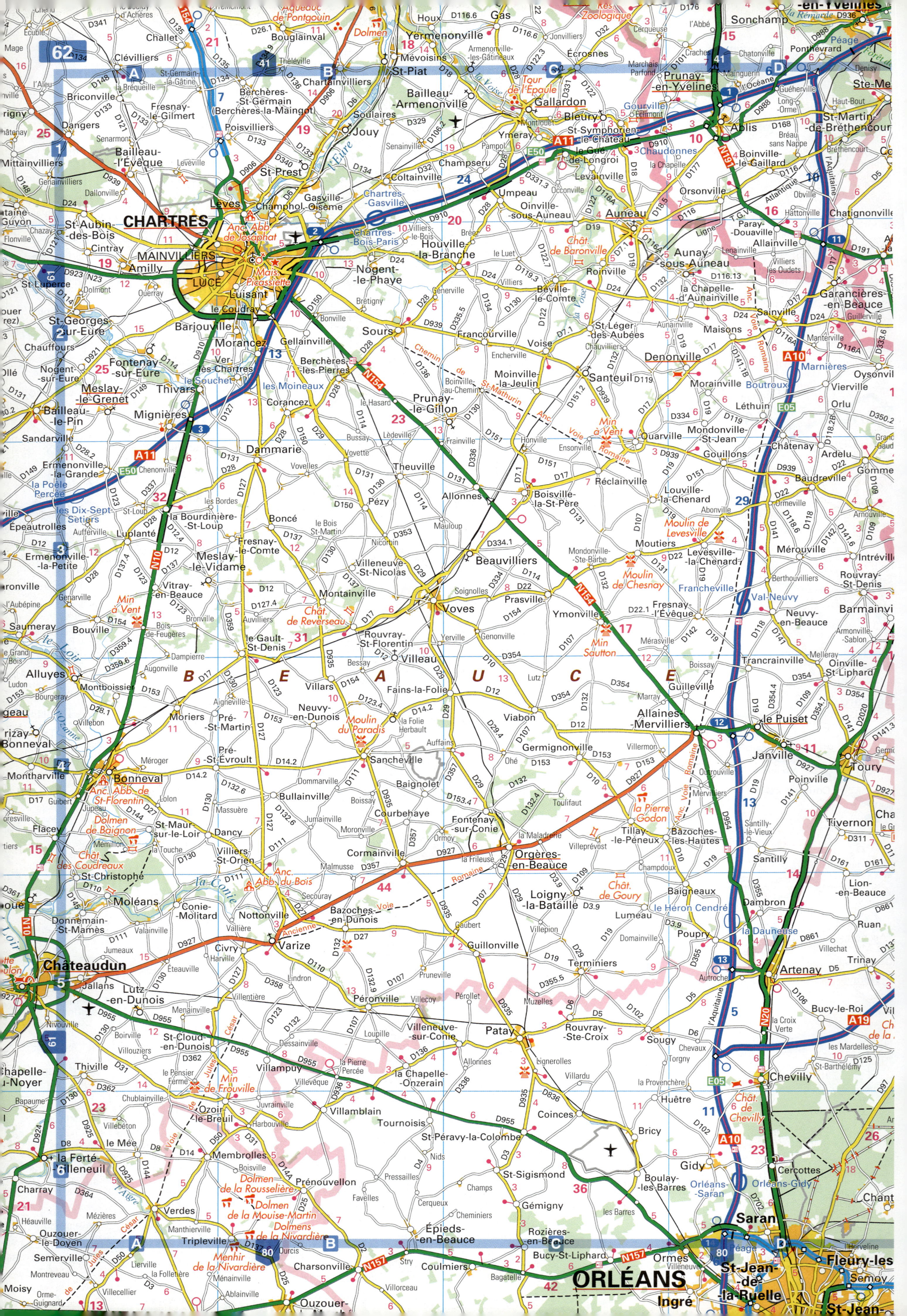

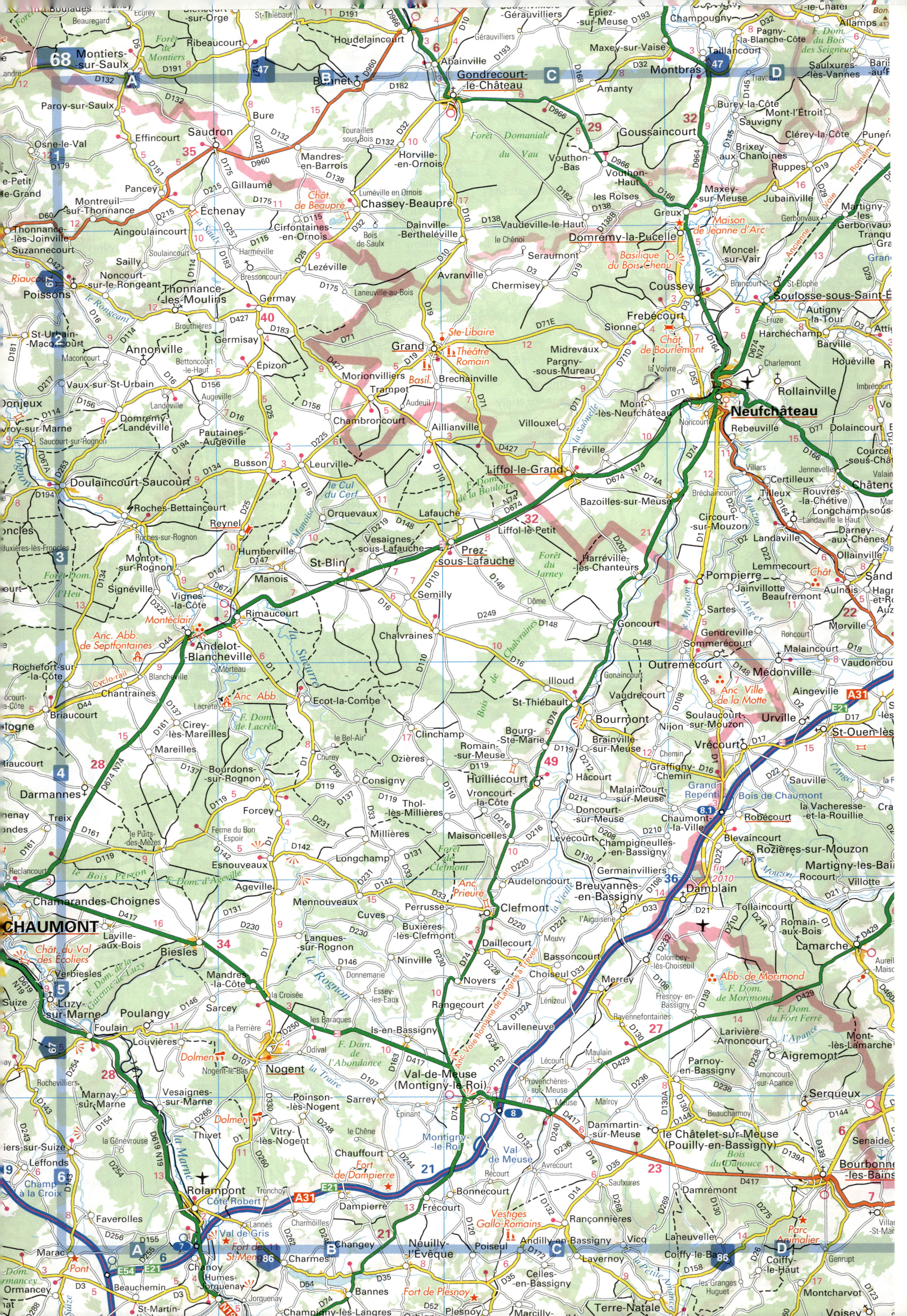

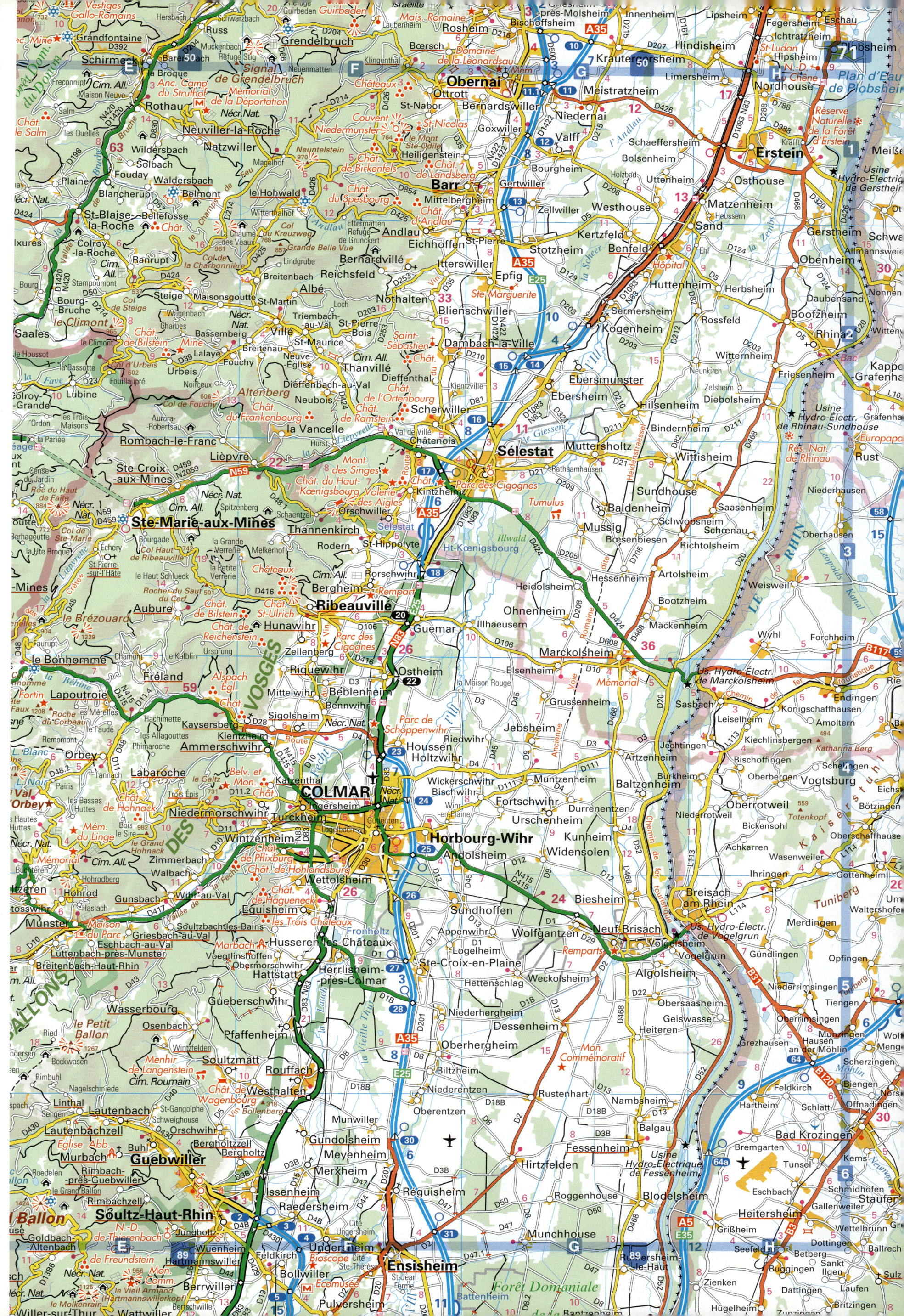

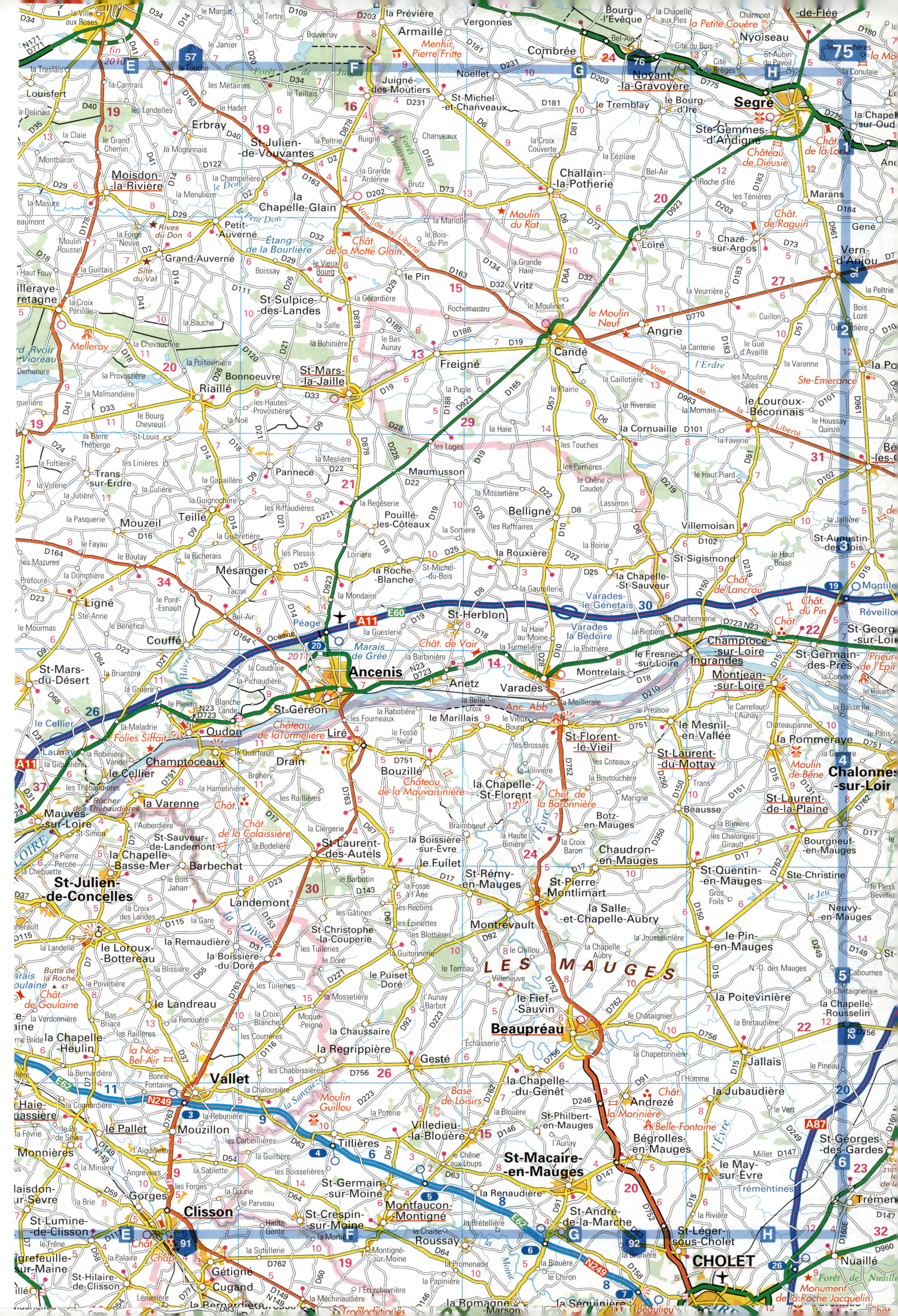

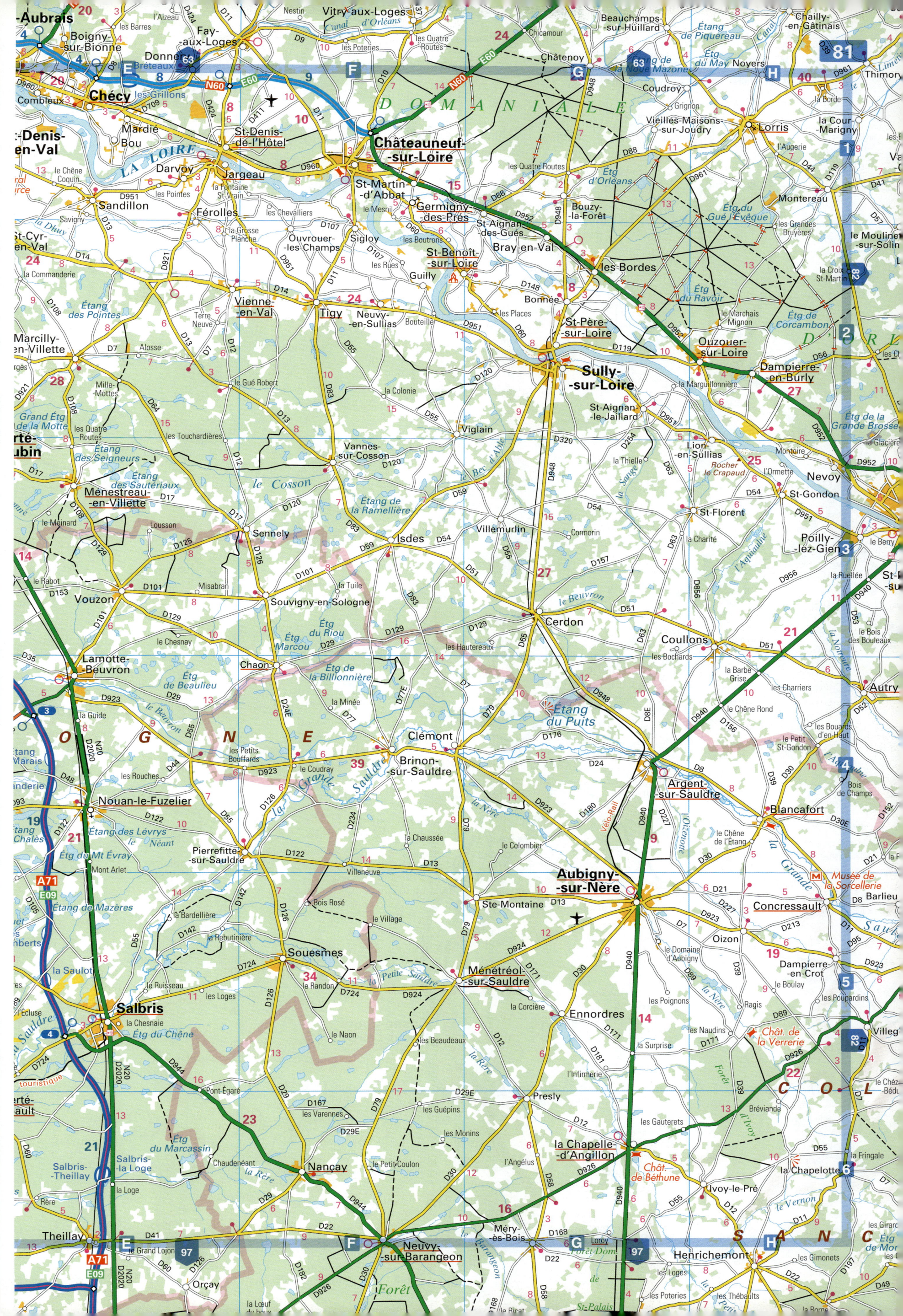

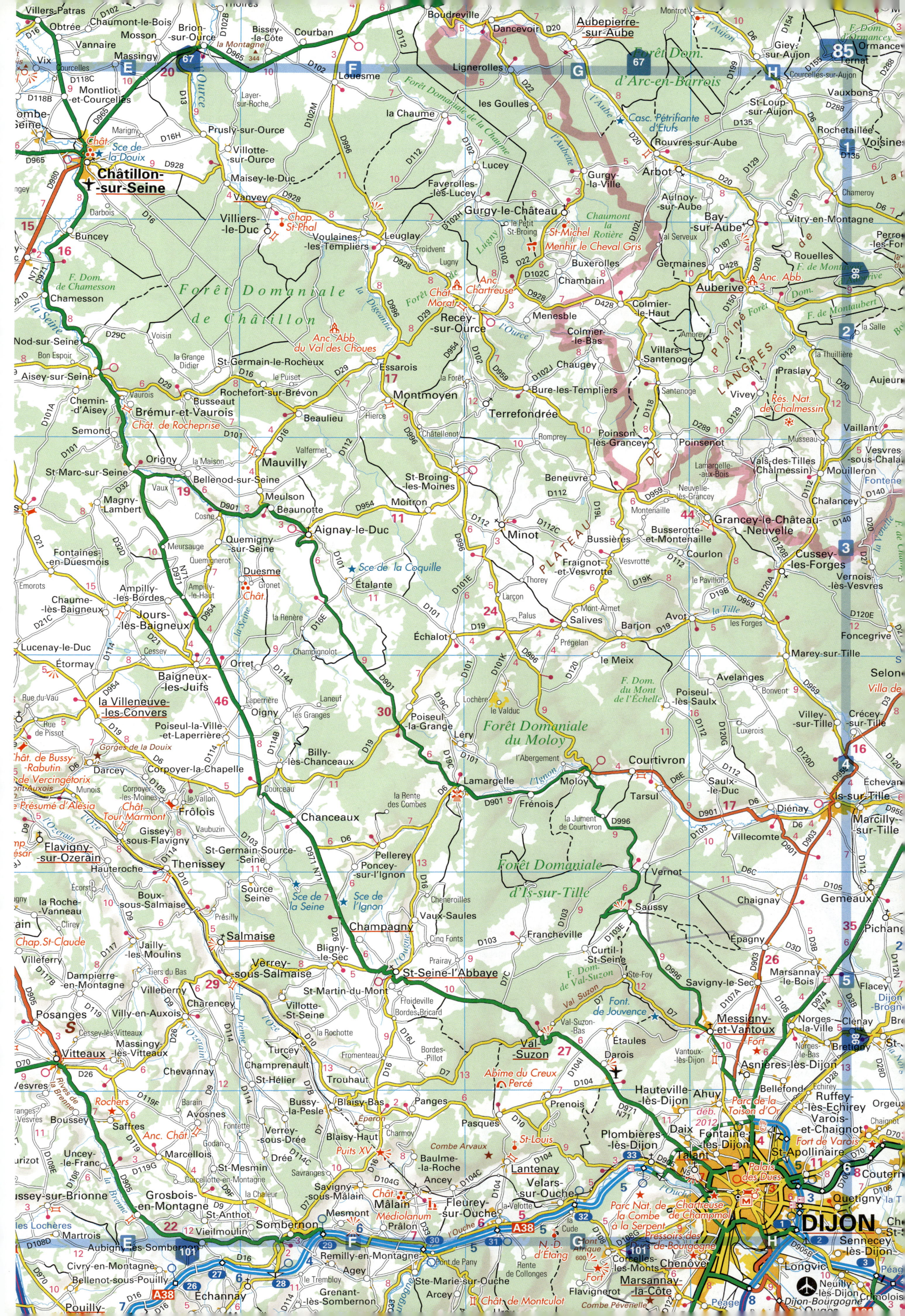

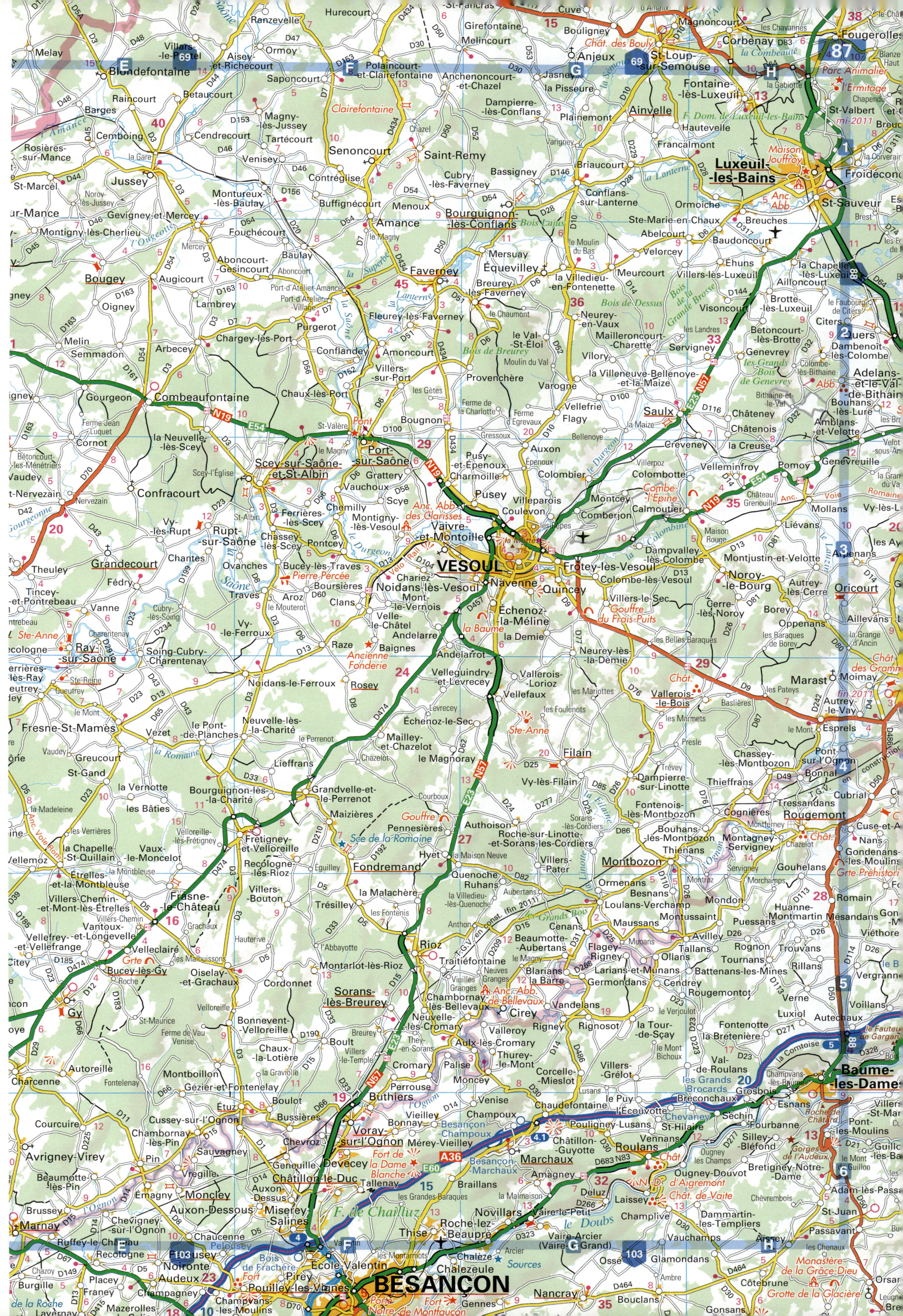

Pointe
de l'Herbaudière

Anc. Abb.
de la Blanche

Pointe
des Charniers

Bourgneuf

Lanterne
des Morts

Pointe de l'Herbaudière

la Madeleine
le Grand Vieil

Phare
des Dames

Bourgneuf-
en-Retz

la Glémerie

la Joussamère

St-Cyr-
en-Retz

l'Herbaudière   **73**

Plage
de Luzéronde

Noirmoutier-en-l'Île

Port
du Collet

les Rivi
aux Guérins

14

Fresnay-
en-Retz

D87

Crypte

Réserve Naturelle
des Marais de Mullembourg

la Haute
Folie

Loyau

le Sud

D64

la Bosse

l'Épine

la Guérinière

Port
des Champs

la Neuve

le Port-
la-Roche

17

Bouin

la Frette

18

Chélevé

le Falleron

de Gille

la Vacheresse

Île
de Noirmoutier

le Fier

8

Barbâtre

les Onchères

la Frândière

la Fosse

25

Passage du Gois
(Praticable à marée basse)

la Croix
Rouge

le Marais
Salé

l'Epoids

MARAIS

la Chauvinerie

les Brochets

les Rochettes

Bois-
de-Céné

D58

la Grande
Croix

Beauvoir-
sur-Mer

11

Abb.

l'Île
Chauvet

Châteauneuf

le Petit Moulin

D71

Base
de Loisirs

Phare
de la Fromentine

le Grand
Pont

le Pré
Cheminée

St-Gervais

18

la Chapelle

la Pierre
Blanche

Belle-
Fontaine

le Mollin

Île d'Yeu, 45 mn

Fromentine

10

D22

la Barre-
de-Monts

la Graffinière

D103

St-Urbain

les Morandières

les Quatre
Moulins

la Croix
Joslain

D75

D948

**Notre-Dame-
de-Monts**

la Grande
Croix

B R E T O N

Min à Vent
de Rairé

Sallertaine

Pont-
Habert

Challa

le Vieux
Cerne

la Vairée

la Botte

D753

le Bloire

14

les Vignes

la Lande

le Perrier

16

fin 2009

Chât.
de la Vérie

**St-Jean-
-de-Monts**

le Bois
Notaire

Soullans

Garanger

Côte

Pointe
du But

Dolmens

l'Île-d'Yeu
(Port Joinville)

Orouet

Villevert

18

Notre-Dame-
de-Riez

Villeneuve

Dolmen
de la Pierre Folle

Chât.
Fort

le Grand Phare

Chât.

Île d'Yeu

St-Sauveur

Atlantis

la Pège

Beaulieu

le Vigneau

Pointe du Châtelet

Menhir

la Croix

Port
de la Meule

St-Hilaire-de-Riez

le Pissot

le Pont

le Plessis

le Fenouiller

D107

Sion sur l'Océan

Corniche Vendéenne

Ganacherie

Pointe de
la Tranche

Sauvage

D6A

**St-Gilles-
-Croix-de-Vie**

Givrand

l'Aigu

D42

Chât.
de Beaumarchais

D38

la Sauzaie

D12

la Chaize-
Giraud

Bretignolles-
-sur-Mer

le Marais Girard

Parc
de Loisirs

St-Nicolas
de Brem

Brem-sur-Mer

les Granges

31

la Salaire

Menhir
la Conche Verte

l'Île
d'Olo

**Olon
-sur-M**

la Girvière

la Chaume

Fort St-Nicolas

Phare de l'Armandèche

**les Sabl
-d'Olon**

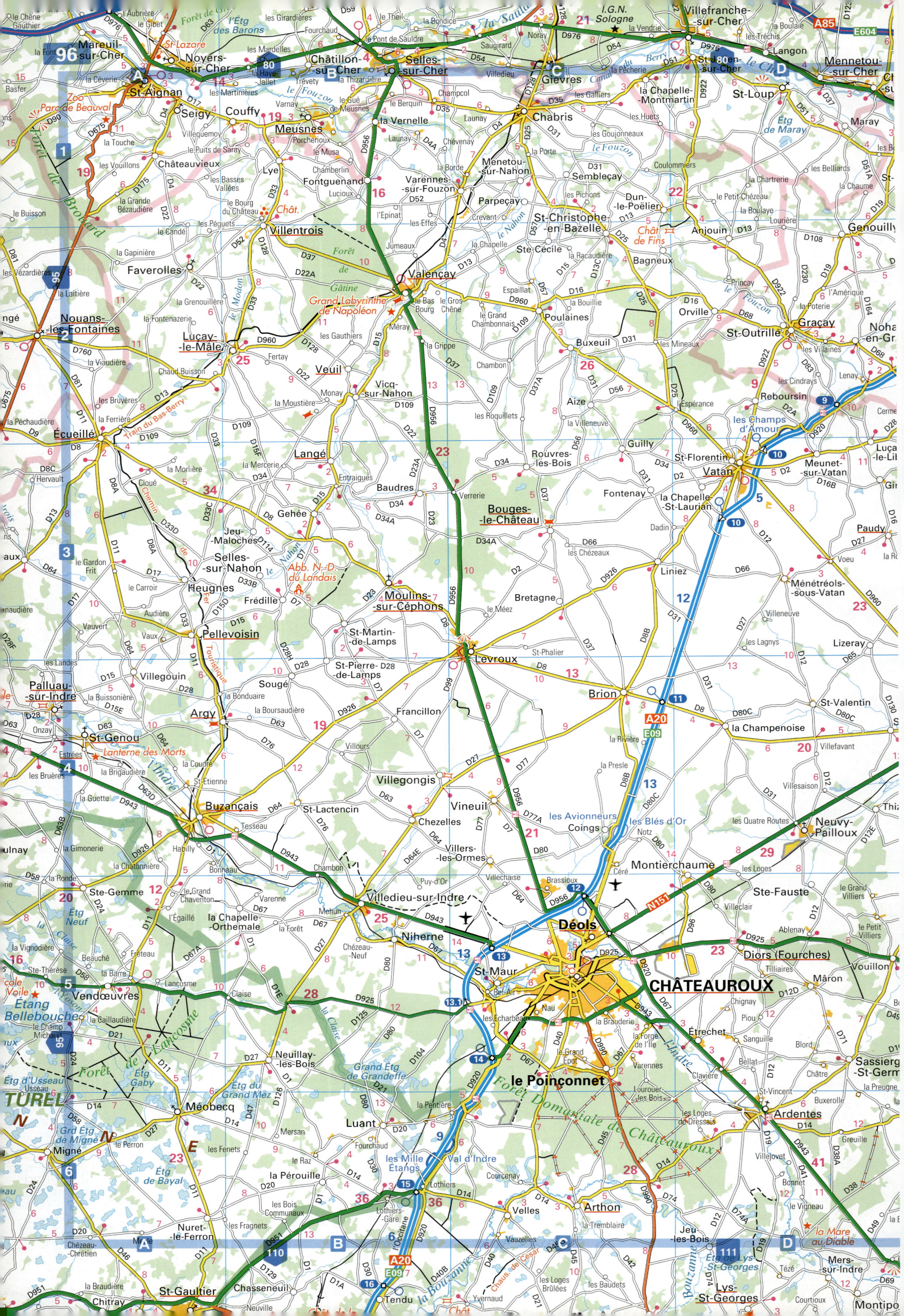

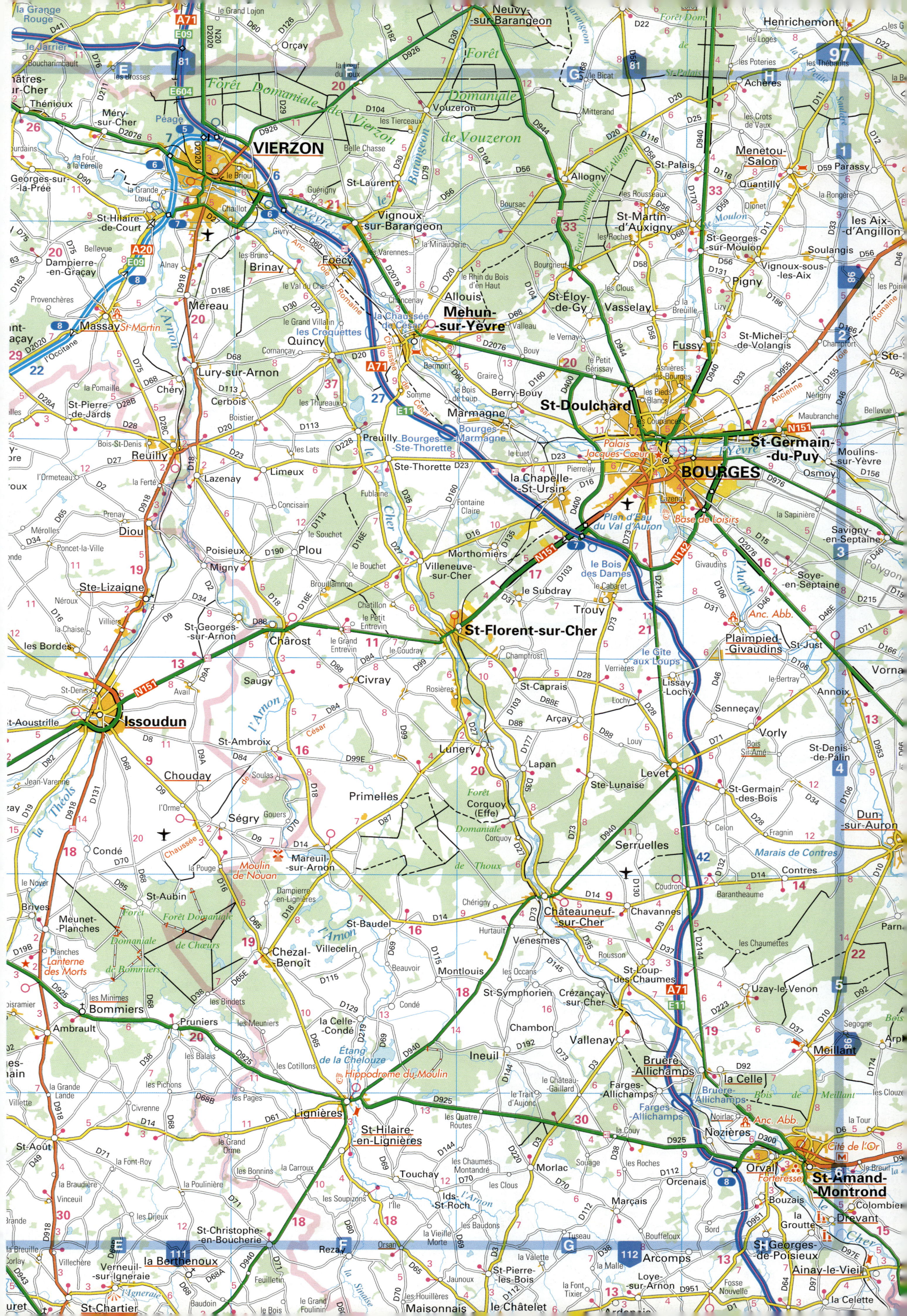

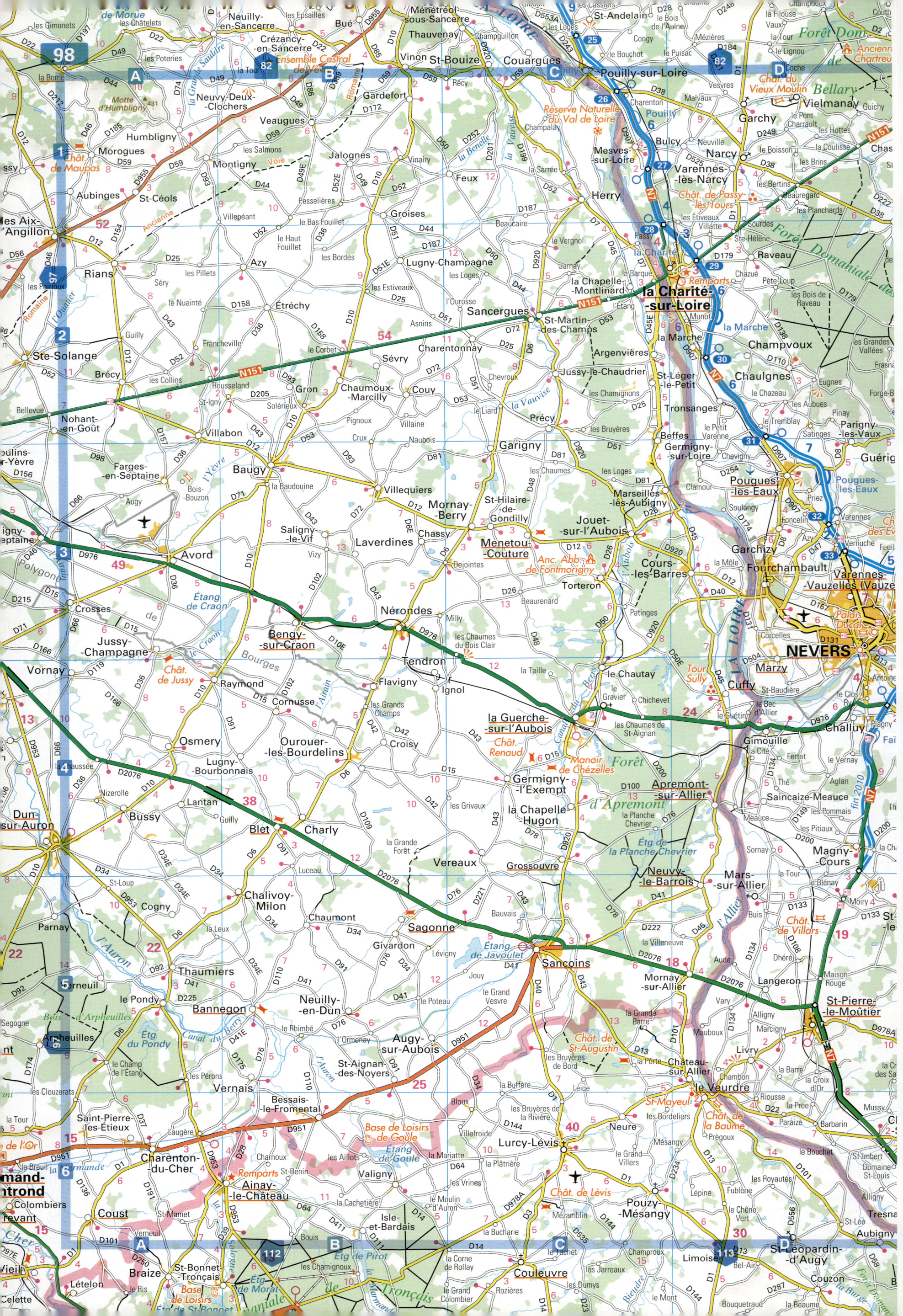

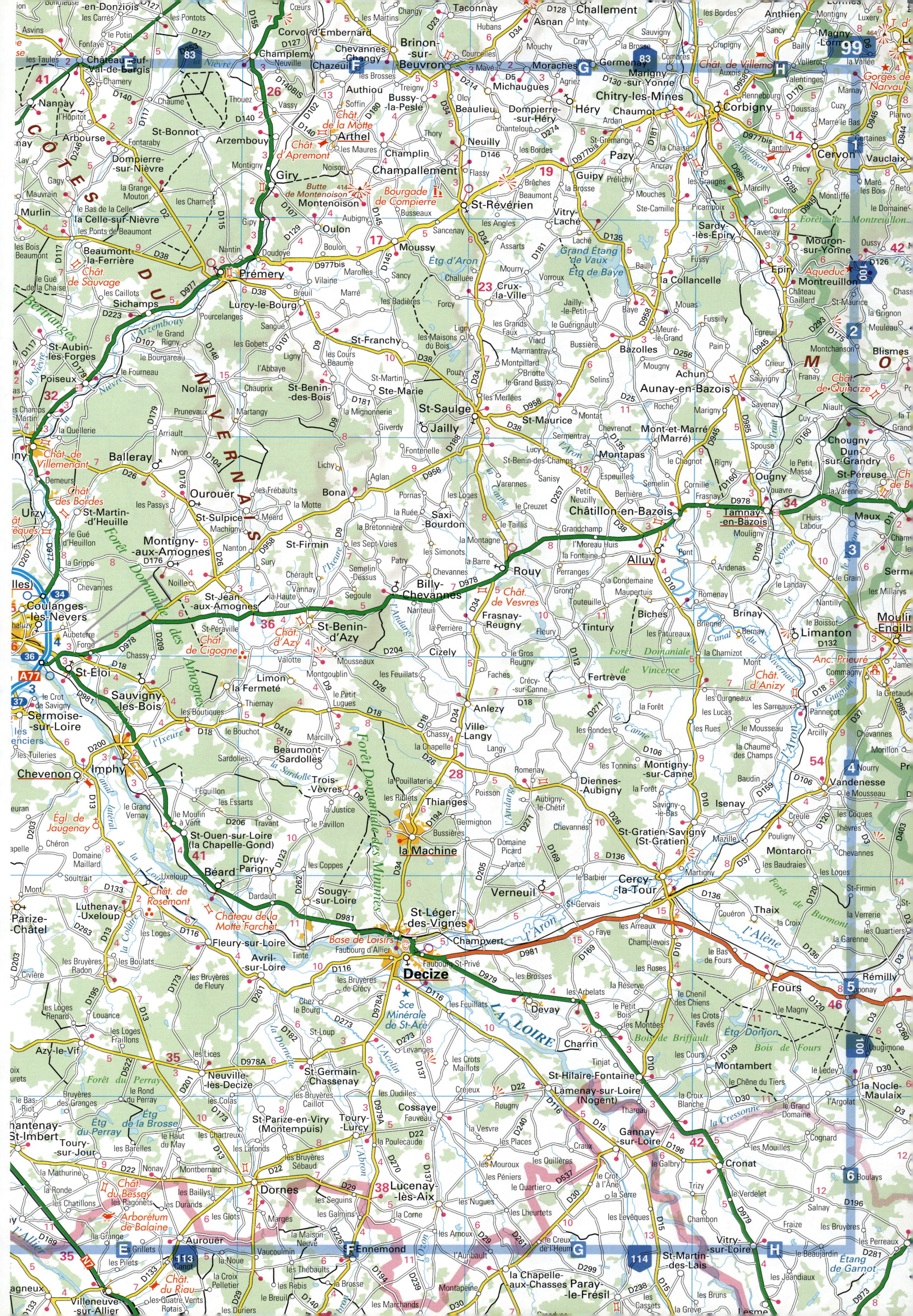

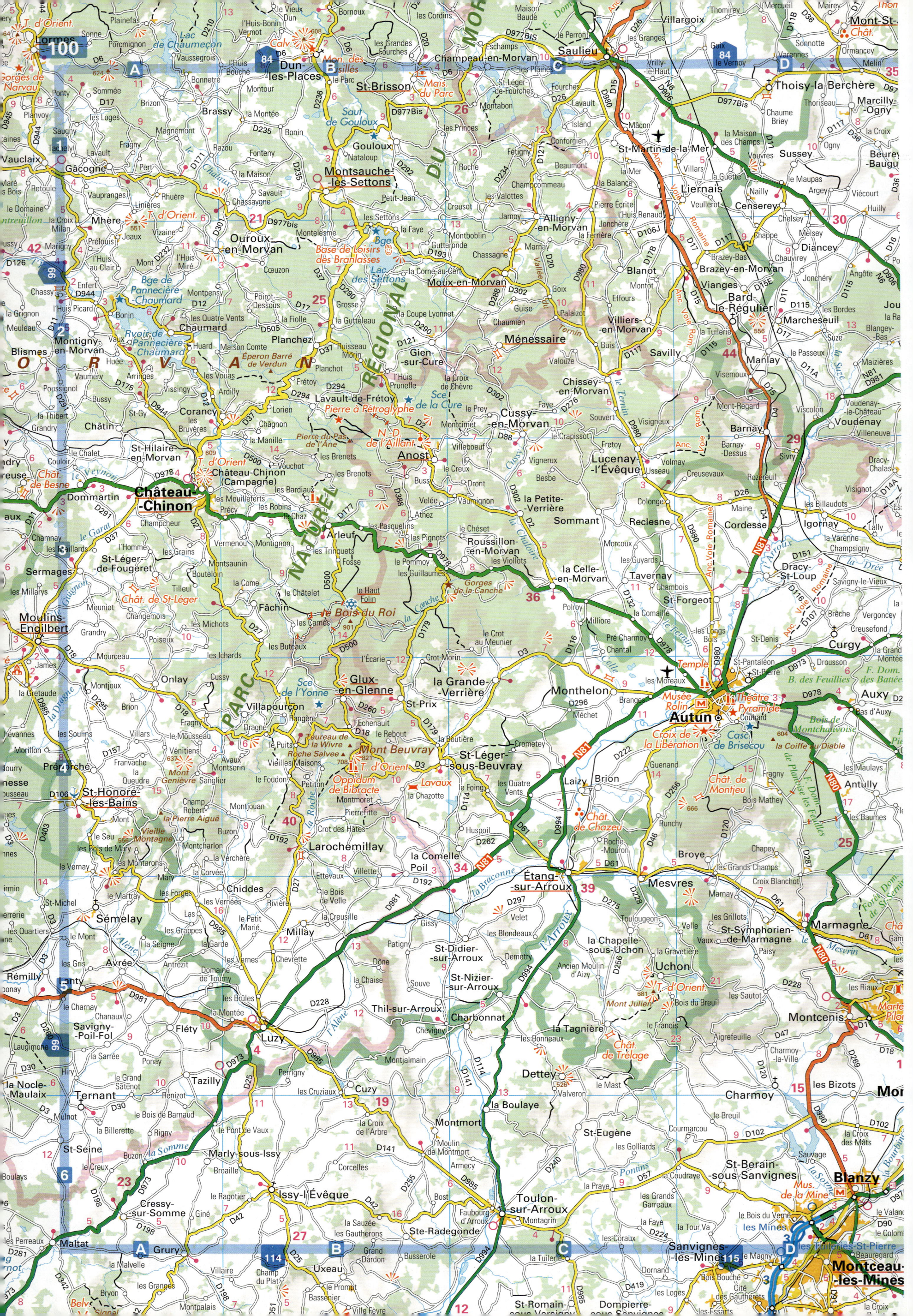

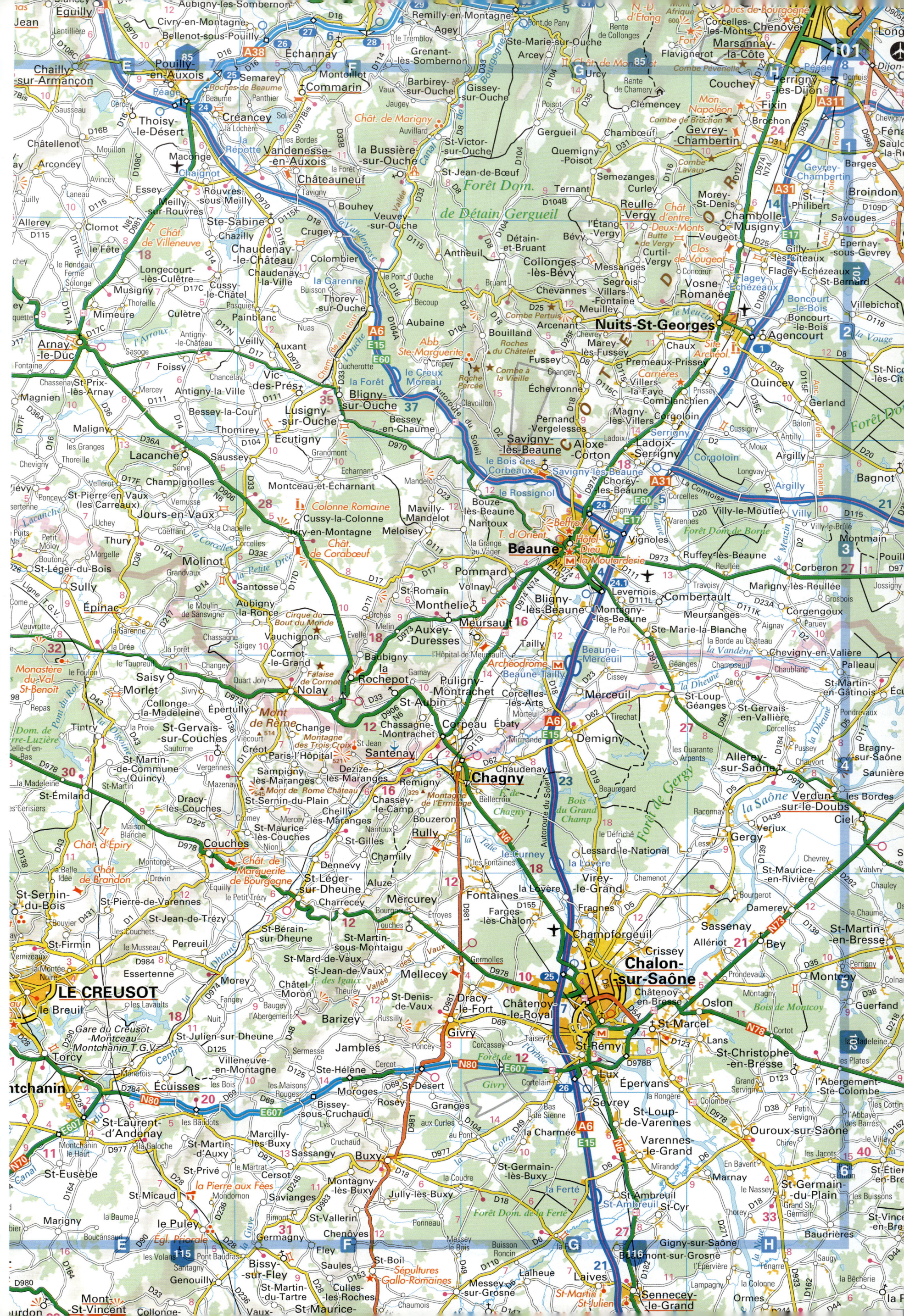

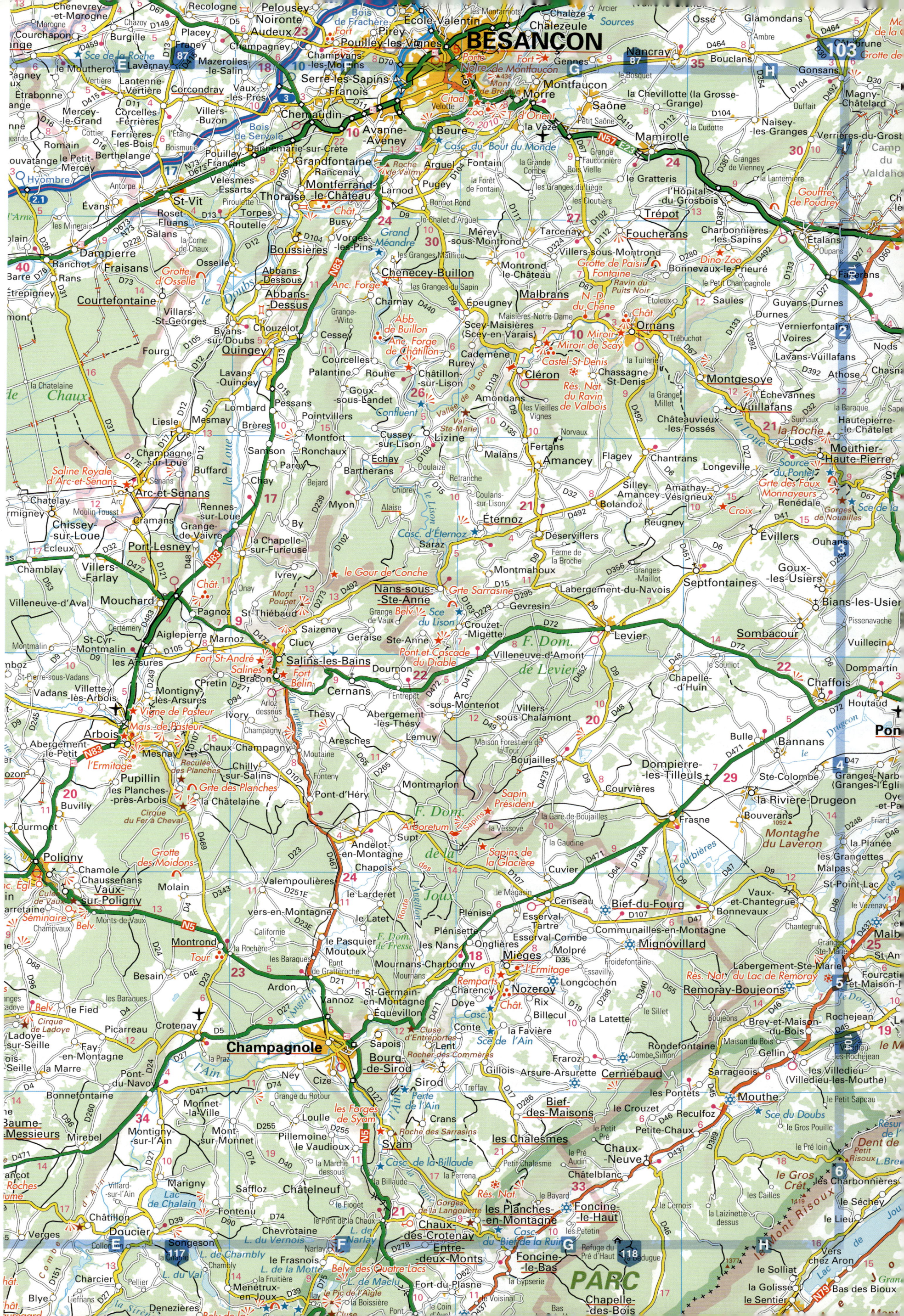

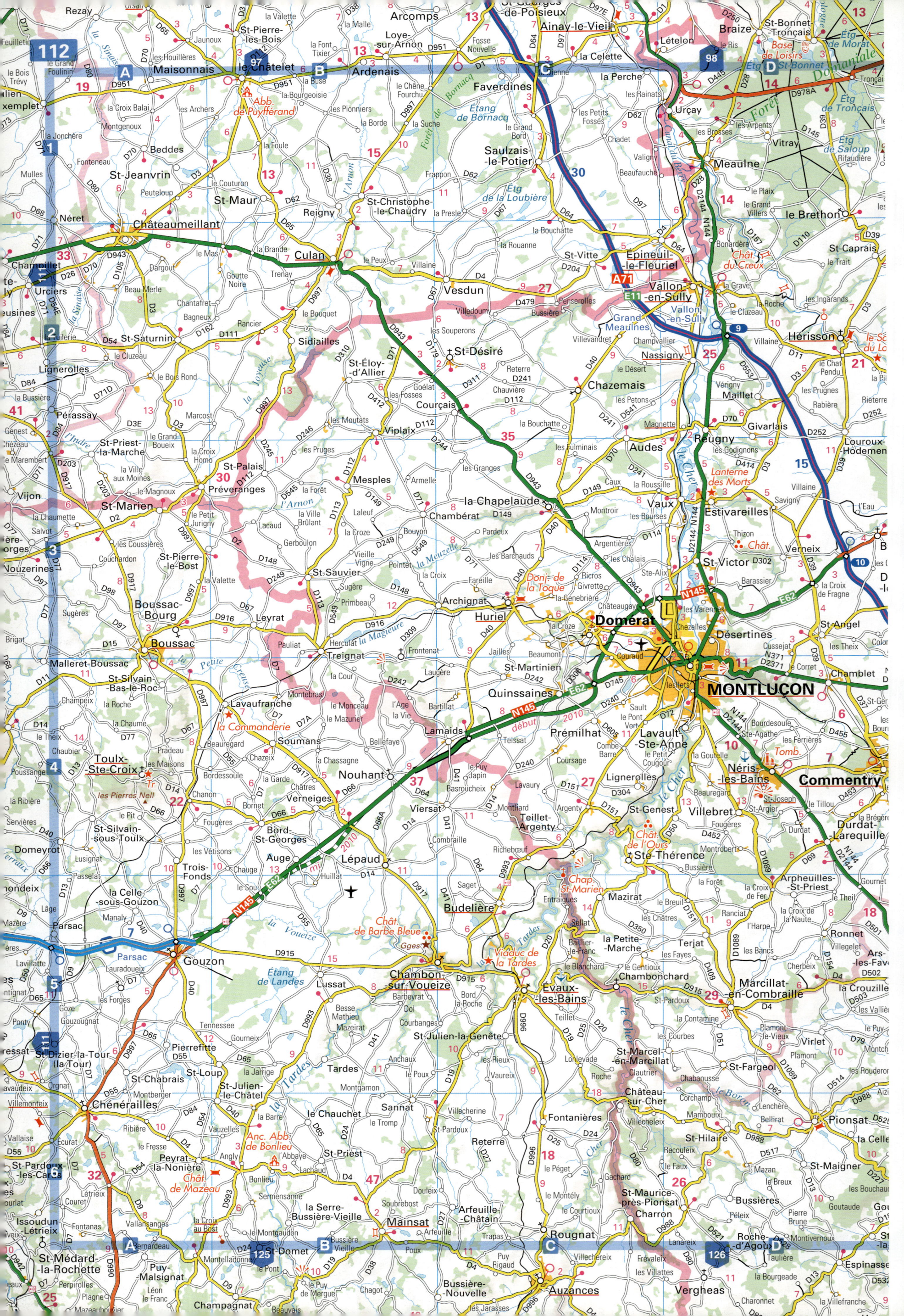

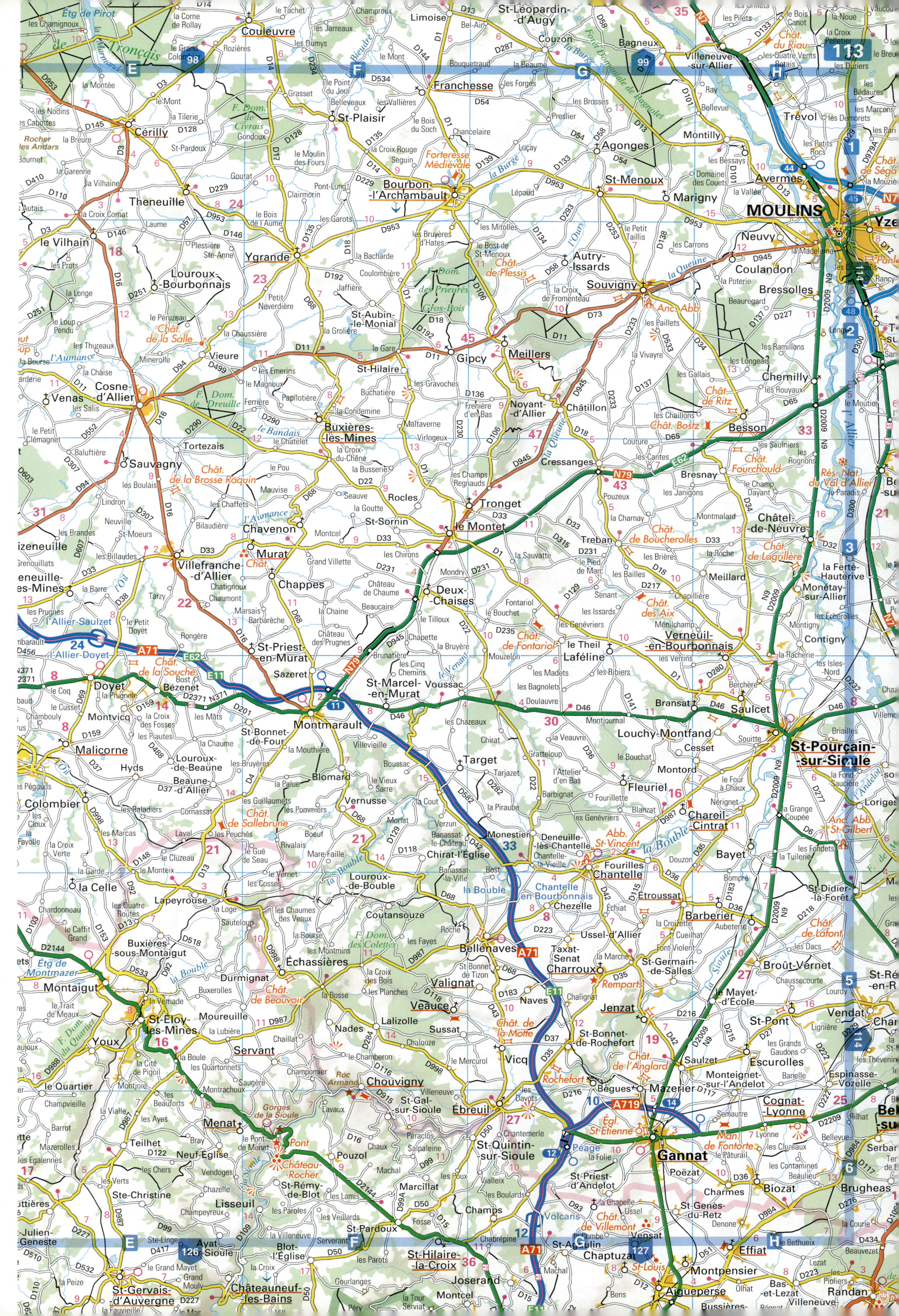

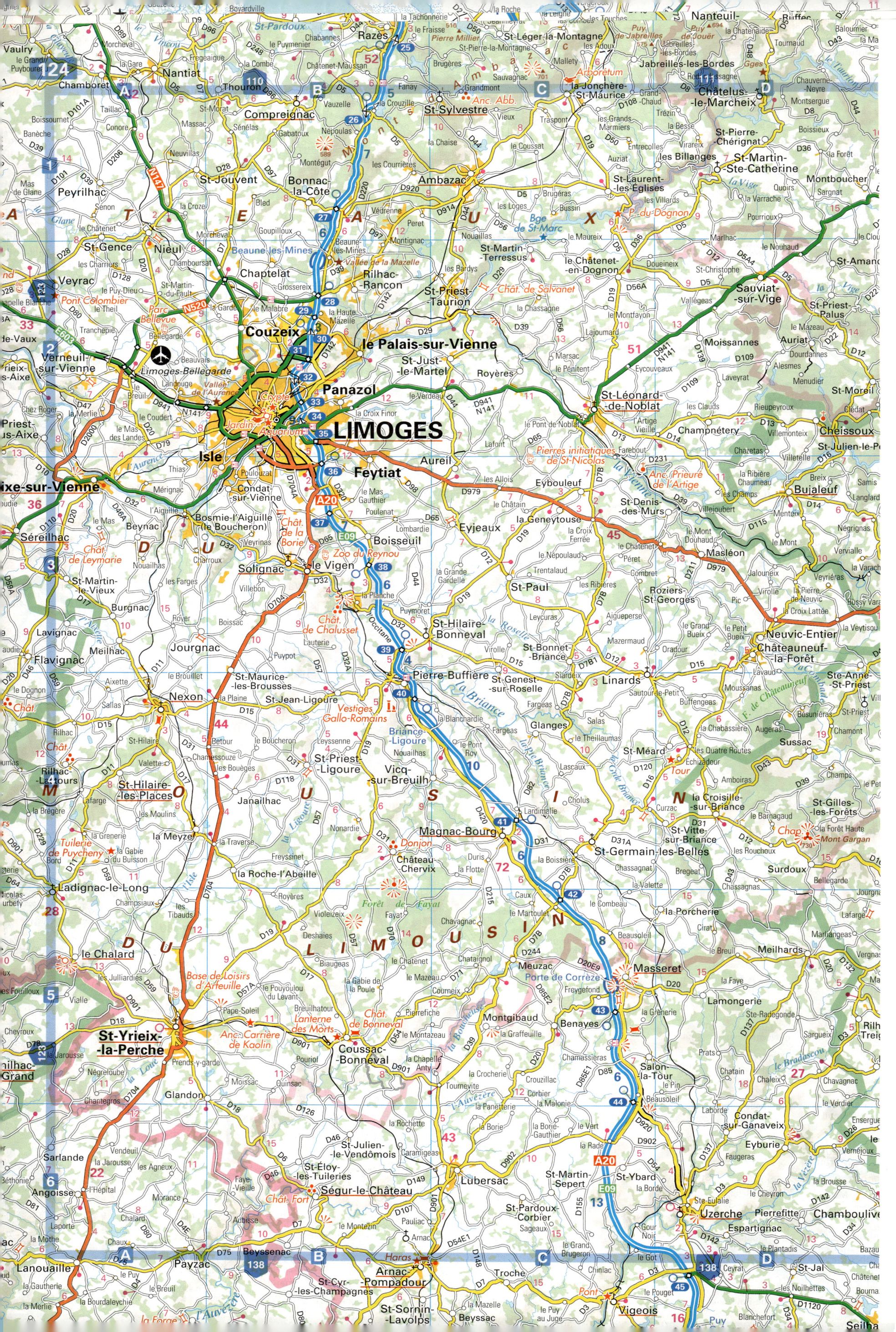

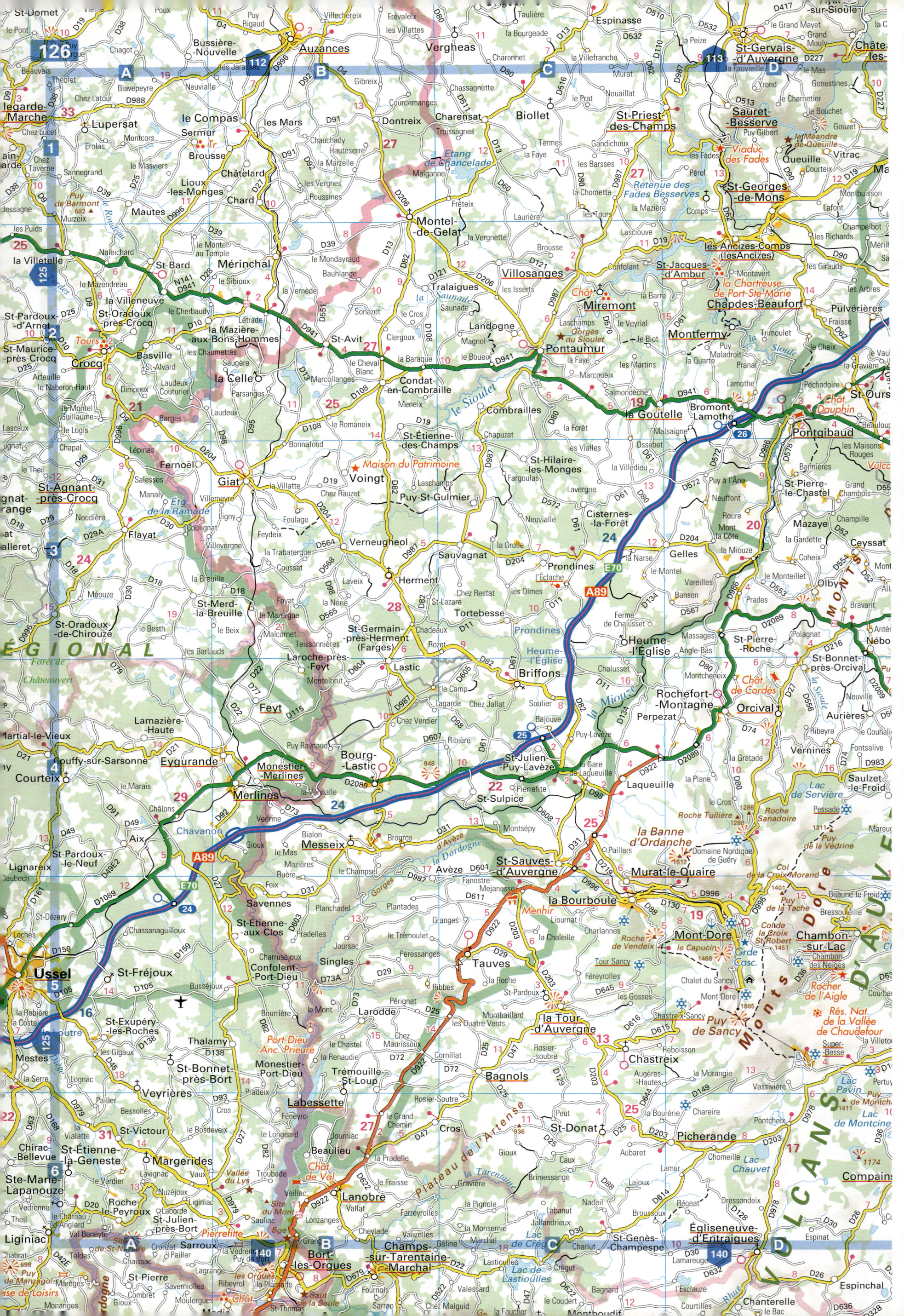

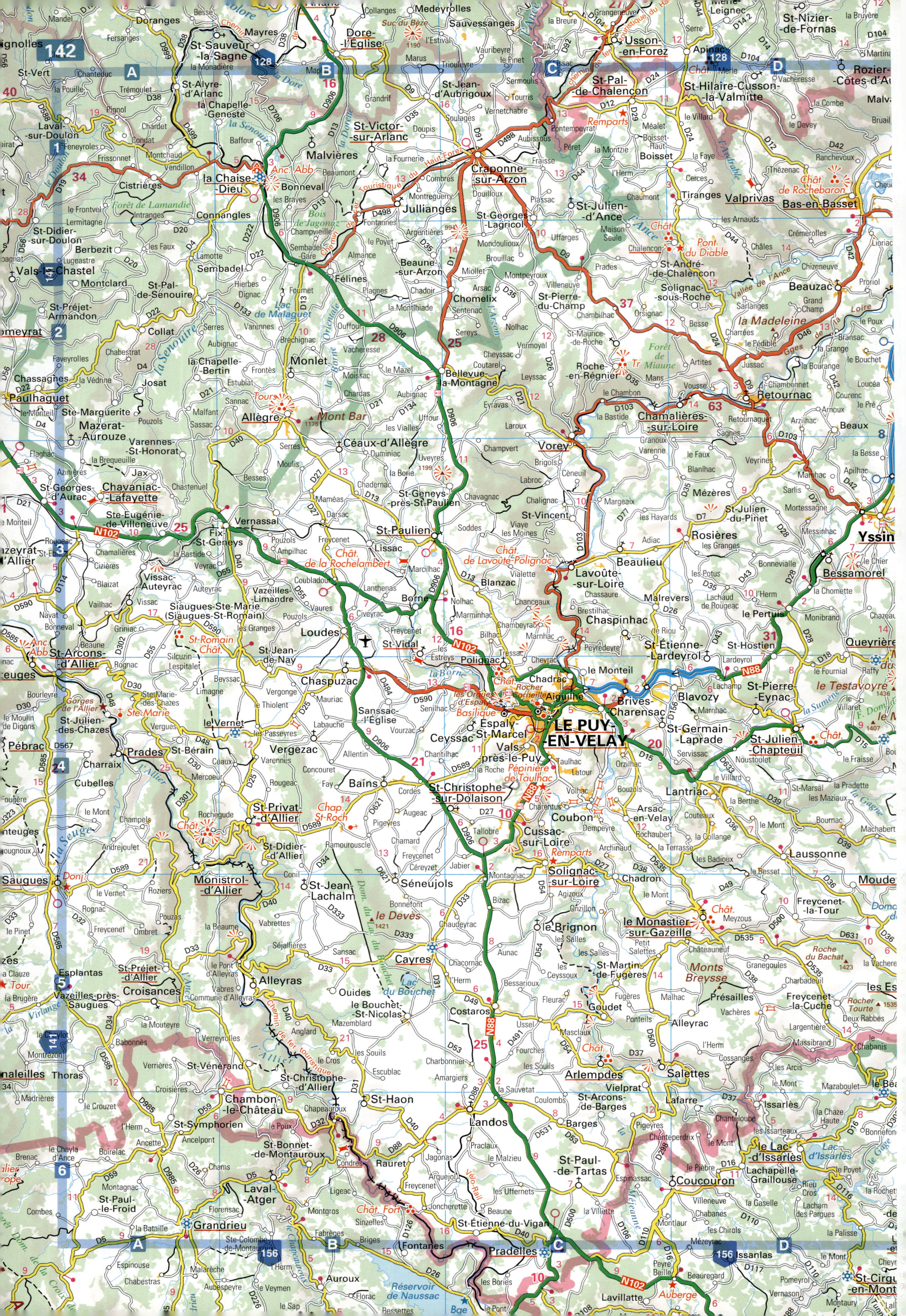

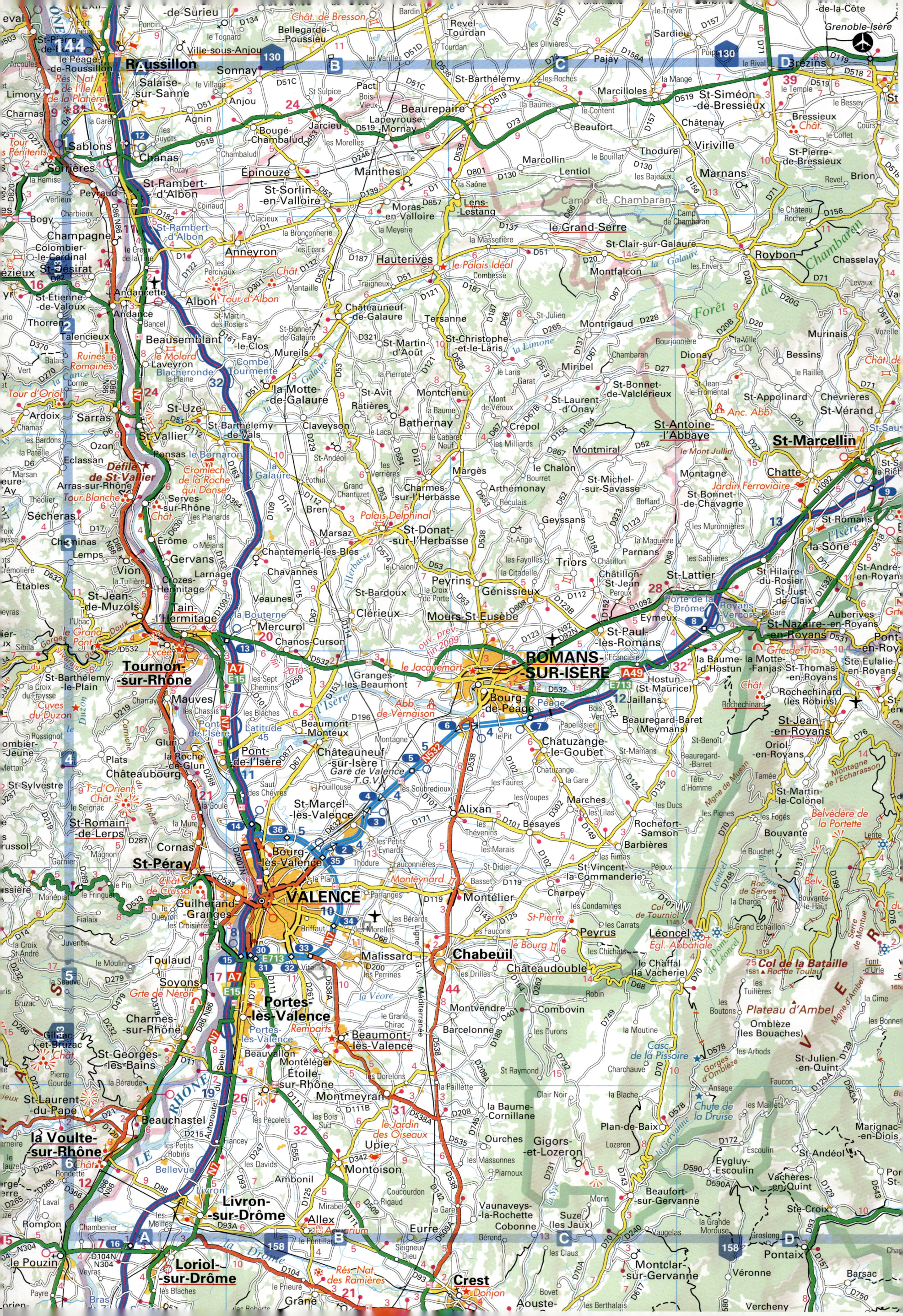

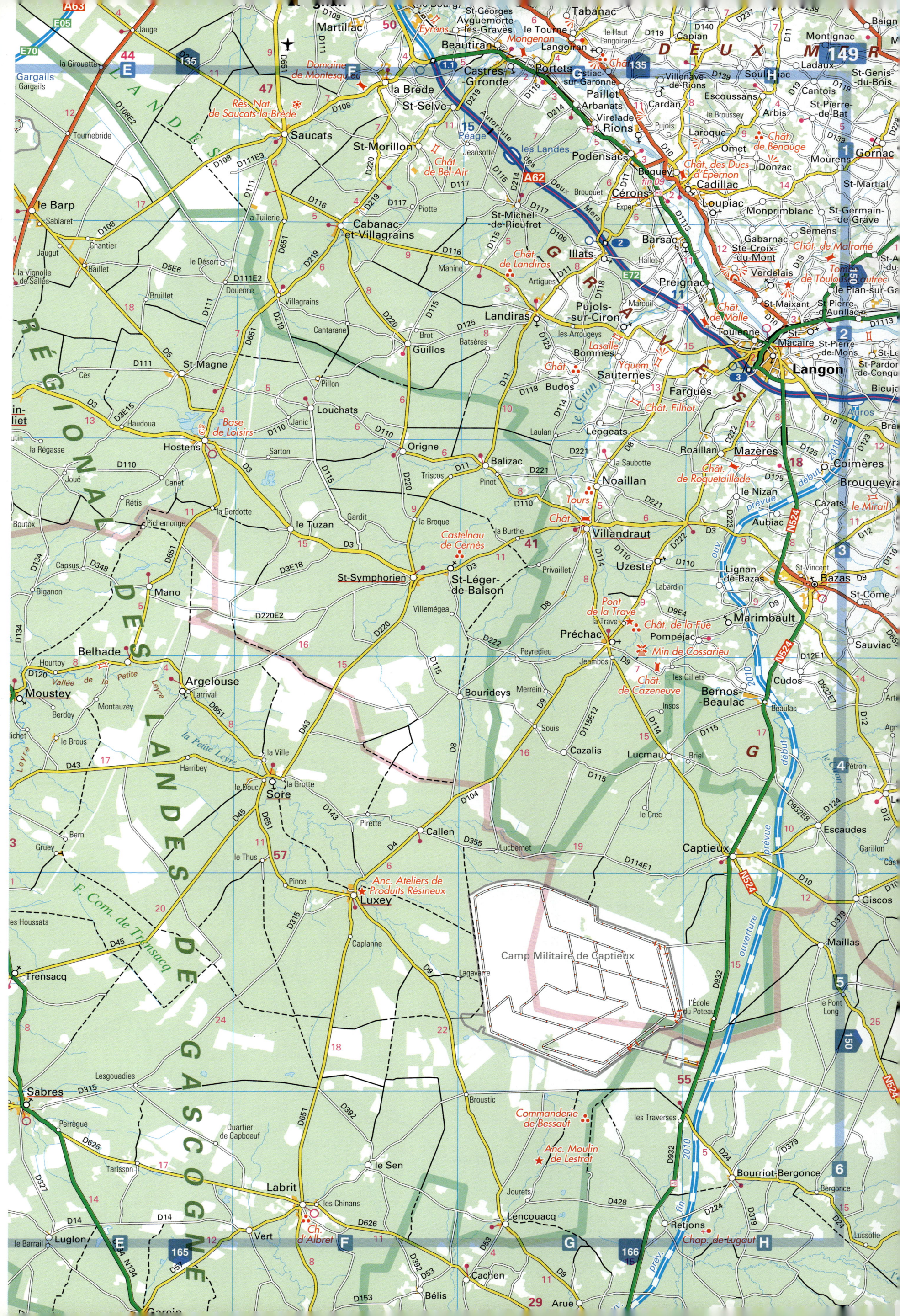

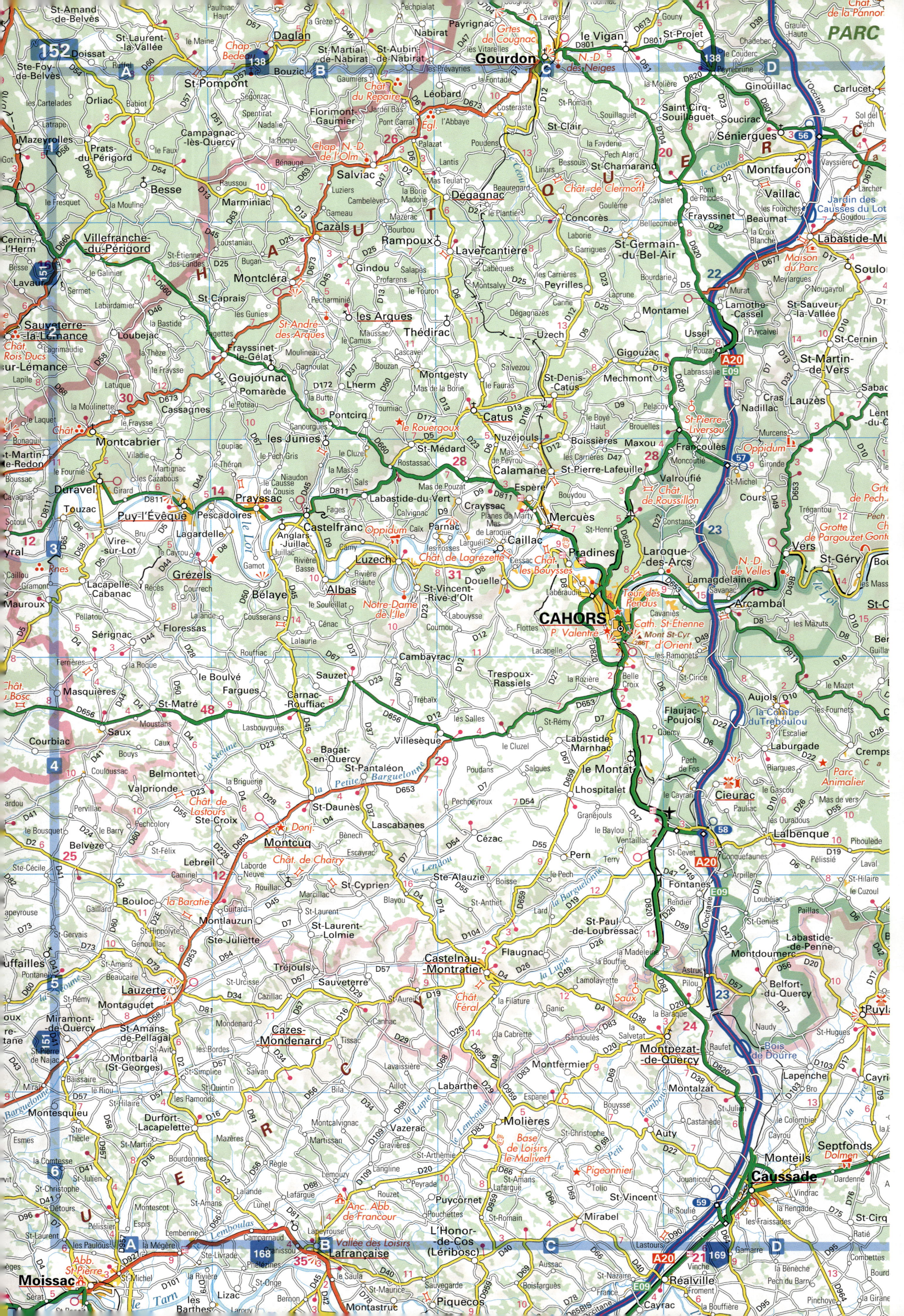

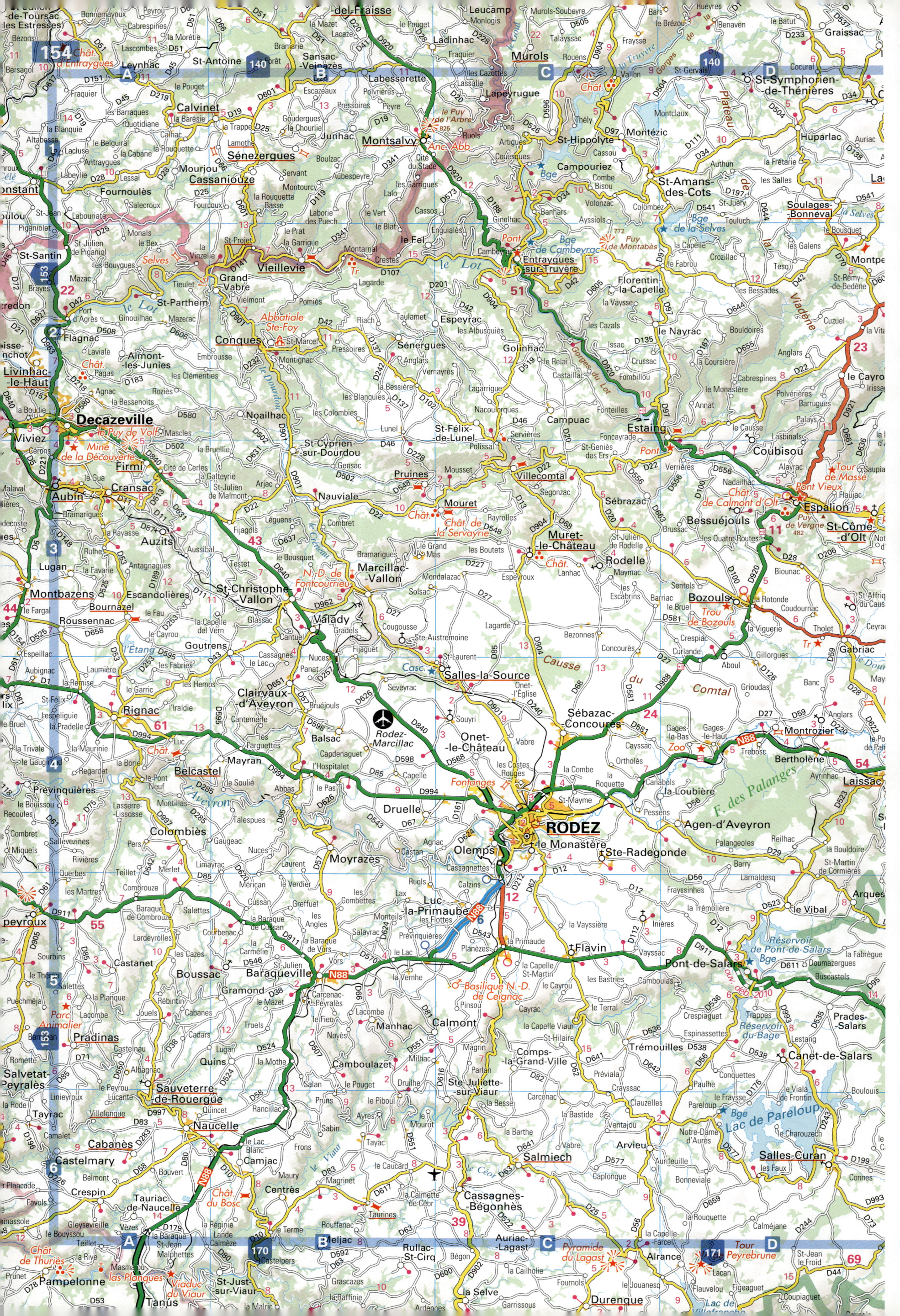

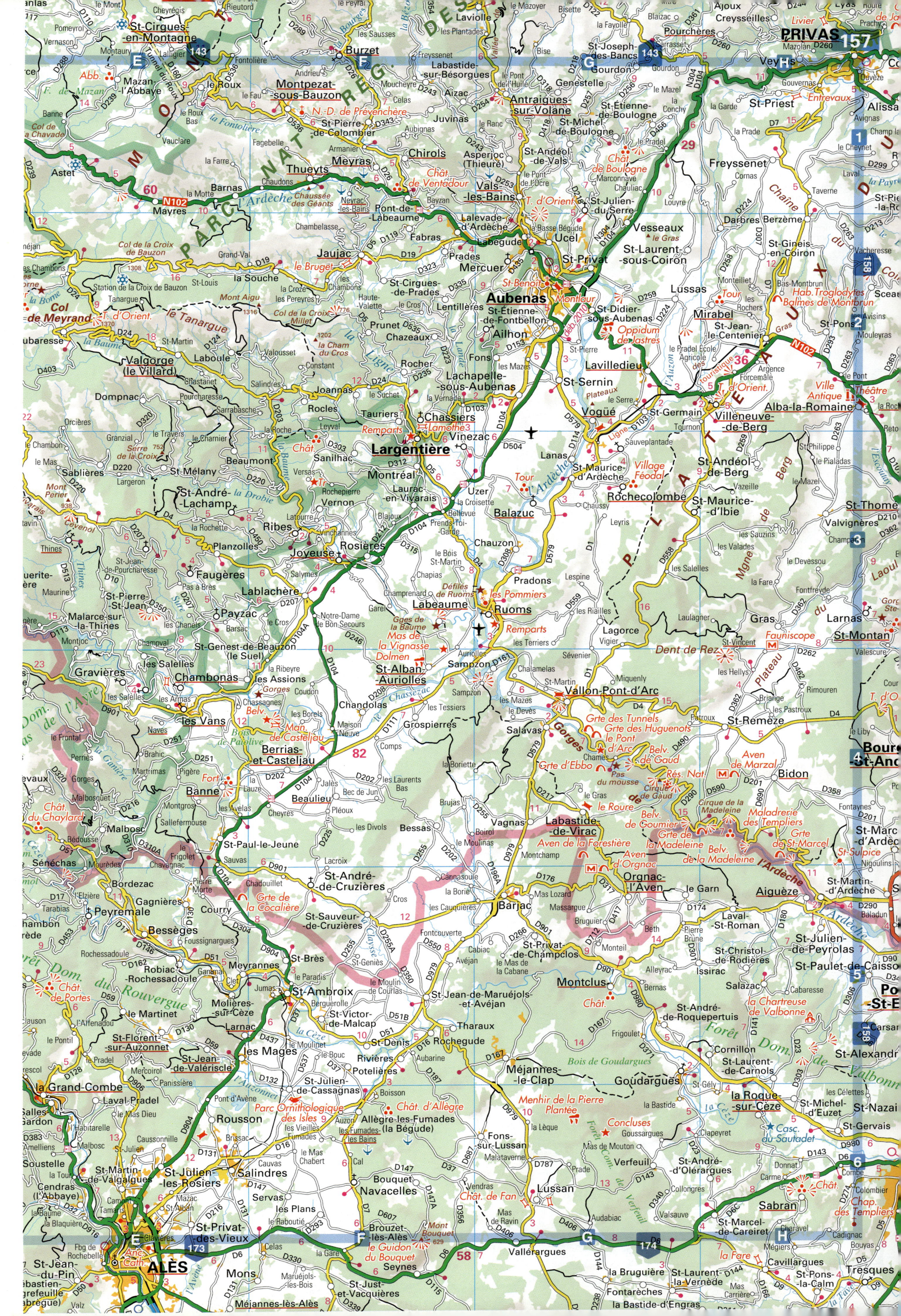

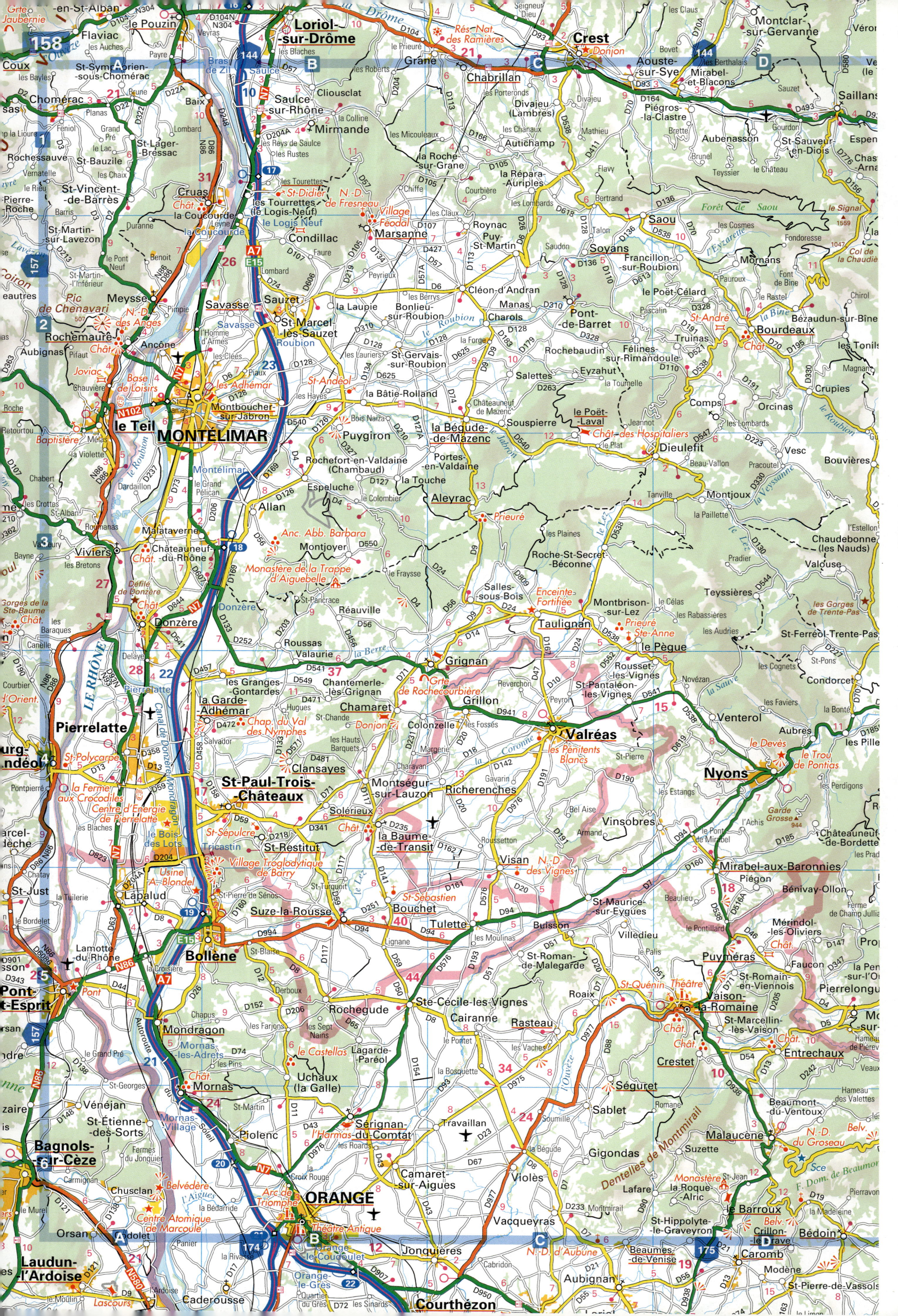

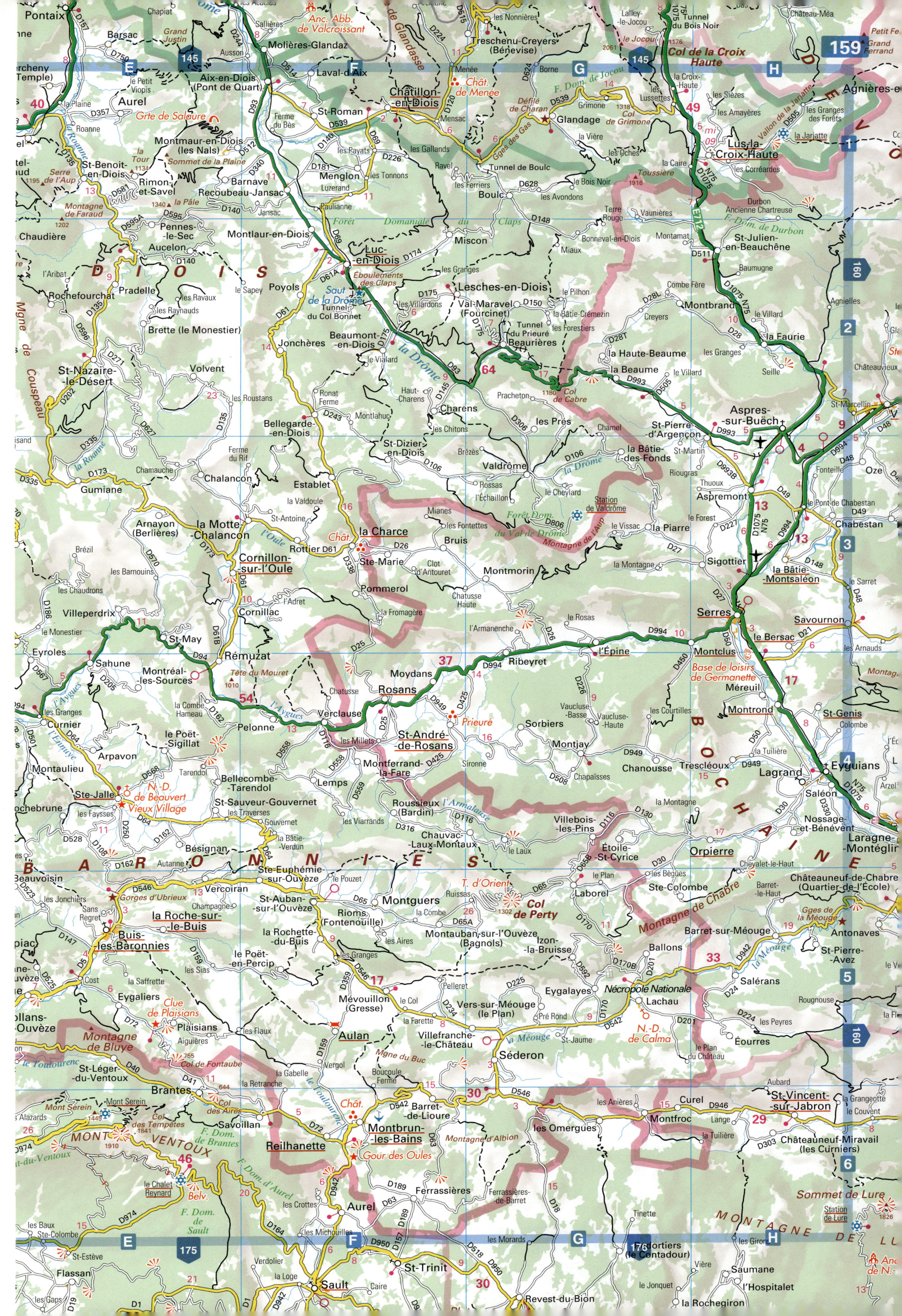

St-Disdier
Petit Ferrand
Grand Ferrand
le Collet
la Motte-en-Champsaur
les Fermonds
Champoléon
du Grand Lac des Estaris
les Infournas
la Motte-en-Champsaur
Charbillac
Route Napoléon
Bénévent-et-Charbillac (les Gentillons)
Chaillol 1600
Orcières
les Marches
Orcières-Merlette 146
D474
Prapic
Noir
Maubourg
Col des Rioupes
D117
D537
les Everras 146
le Noyer
Poligny
St-Bonnet-en-Champsaur
St-Michel-de-Chaillol
la Coche
Serre-Eyrauds
D944
Val du
Drac
Lachaup
Col du Noyer
Réf. Napoléon
St-Étienne-en-Dévoluy
les Étroits
la Joue du Loup
Superdévoluy
l'Enclus
la Fare-en-Champsaur (les Baraques)
St-Julien-en-Champsaur
Chantaussel
St-Laurent-du-Cros
les Farelles
Buissard
Chabottes
St-Michel
St-Jean-St-Nicolas (Pont-du-Fossé)
D944
Archinard
le Mourre Froid 2993
Coutières
Col du Festre
les Garcins
la Cluse
Montagne d'Aurouze 2587
Observatoire du Plateau de Bure
Forêt Domaniale des Sauvas
Station de Laye
Laye
Forest-St-Julien
St-Léger-les-Mélezes
D945
St-Hilaire
Ancelle
Moissière
les Gourniers
Réallon
les Rousses
la Blache
St-Apollinaire
les Chérines
le Petit Vau
Glaise
Montmaur
Chât. du Terrail
la Roche-des-Arnauds
Rabou
Château de Charance
Station Gap-Bayard
Laiterie de Col Bayard
Col Bayard 1248
Chauvet
Réf. Napoléon
les Jaussauds
Romette
la Rochette
D314
les Borels
CHAMPSAUR
les Bernards
Chorges
St-Michel
Serre-Ponçon
Prunières
D241
Ste-Philomène
Furmeyer
Manteyer
St-André
D92
GAP
St-Roch
Man de Rapados
Rambaud
Grand Larra
D94A
les Casses
la Bâtie-Neuve
Montgardin
les Gourres
les Andrieux
D9
la Rama
Lac de Serre-Ponçon
Veynes
Châteauneuf-d'Oze
le Villard
D994
Céüse 2000
Mgne de Céüse 1827
F. Dom. de Céüse
les Durandons
Neffes
Pelleautier
la Freissinouse
St-Auban-d'Oze
les Colombis
Chabrières
la Bâtie-Vieille
les Santons
les Guérins
Avançon
les Olliviers
Chanteloube
le Fein
St-Étienne-le-Laus
Salle du Bal des Demoiselles Coiffées
Rousset
Belv.
St-Michel
Pontis
les Demoiselles Coiffées
le Sauze-du-Lac
l'Adroit de Pontis
Espréaux
Villaret
Col des Guérins 1312
Sigoyer
les Bénéchons
Lettret
Châteauvieux
la Roche
Jarjayes
Valserres
Théus
Bge de Serre-Ponçon
St-Vincent-les-Forts
le Lautaret
Plateau de Dormillouse
le Saix
Esparron
Tournoux
Fouilouse
Tallard
Chât.
Piégut
Venterol
Remollon
les Tourniaires
Rochebrune
les Forests
la Bréole
le Goirands
St-Jean Montclar
Station St-Jean Montclar
Montclar (Serre-Nauze
Barcillonnette
Vitrolles
Lardier-et-Valença
la Saulce
Curbans
Urtis
Gigors
Bréziers
Bellaffaire
Chaumenc
Villaudemard
Plan de Vitrolles
les Roches
Rousset
la Curnerie
Faucon-du-Caire
Turriers
le Forest-loin
St-Martin-lès-Seyne
le Col
Selonnet
Pompiery
la Gineste Haute
Montagne de St-Genis
Pibert
le Caire
Astoin
Bois Noir
Citad.
Seyne
St-Pons
Ventavon
Monêtier-Allemont
Claret
Melve
Gautière
les Hautes-Graves
Bayons
la Rouchaye
la Haute Combe
Chabanon-Selonnet
Bas Chardavon
Auzet
le Grand Puy
l'Écluse
Laze
le Grand Pré
Sigoyer
Villarnaud
la Motte-du-Caire
Clamensane
Esparron-la-Bâtie
Reynier
Ferme Béridon
l'Infernet Bas
le Grand Puy
Upaix
Thèze
la Bréjonnière
Escuyer
le Poët
les Fourniers
Vaumeilh
Nibles
Valavoire
la Sapie
Verdaches
Clues de Verdaches
Barles
St-Clément
le Villard
les Travers
Chabre (École)
Valernes
Châteaufort
Mison
D304
St-Geniez
la Bastide
St-Jérôme
le Verger
l'Adrech
la Silve
Défilé de la Pierre Écrite
Pierre Écrite
Chabert
Rocher de Dromont
N.-D. de Dromont
Authon
le Forest
le Château
Esclangon
la Flogère
Ribiers
Plan de la Baume
Entrepierres
Vilhosc
le Castellard-Melan
Hautes-Duyes
Toge
Pré Forant
le Guéni
la Javie
le Brusquet
Franchironnette
les Chabanons
Citad.
Sisteron
St-Symphorien
la Robine-sur-Galabre
les Ubachons
Draix
le Vieux Noyers
D948
Vilhosc
St-Martin
Champ Roubin
le Villard
N.-D. du Bourg
Bevons
Salignac
Sourribes
les Romans
Thoard
Marcoux
Archail
Noyers-sur-Jabron
Valbelle (les Richaud)
Peipin
Aubignosc
la Tuilière
Beaucouse
Centre Géologique de St-Benoit
Champtercier
DIGNE-LES-BAINS
Forêt Domaniale du Jabron
le Forest
Volonne
Égl. St-Martin
Barras
St-Jérôme
les Épinettes
le Villard
LURE
Anc. Abb. de N.-D. de Lure
Château-Arnoux-St-Auban (les Chabannes)
Parc botanique l'Escale
Châteauneuf-Val-St-Donat
le Belvédère
Mallefougasse-Augès
Terres Rouges
Base de Loisirs Lac des Ferréols
les Dourbes

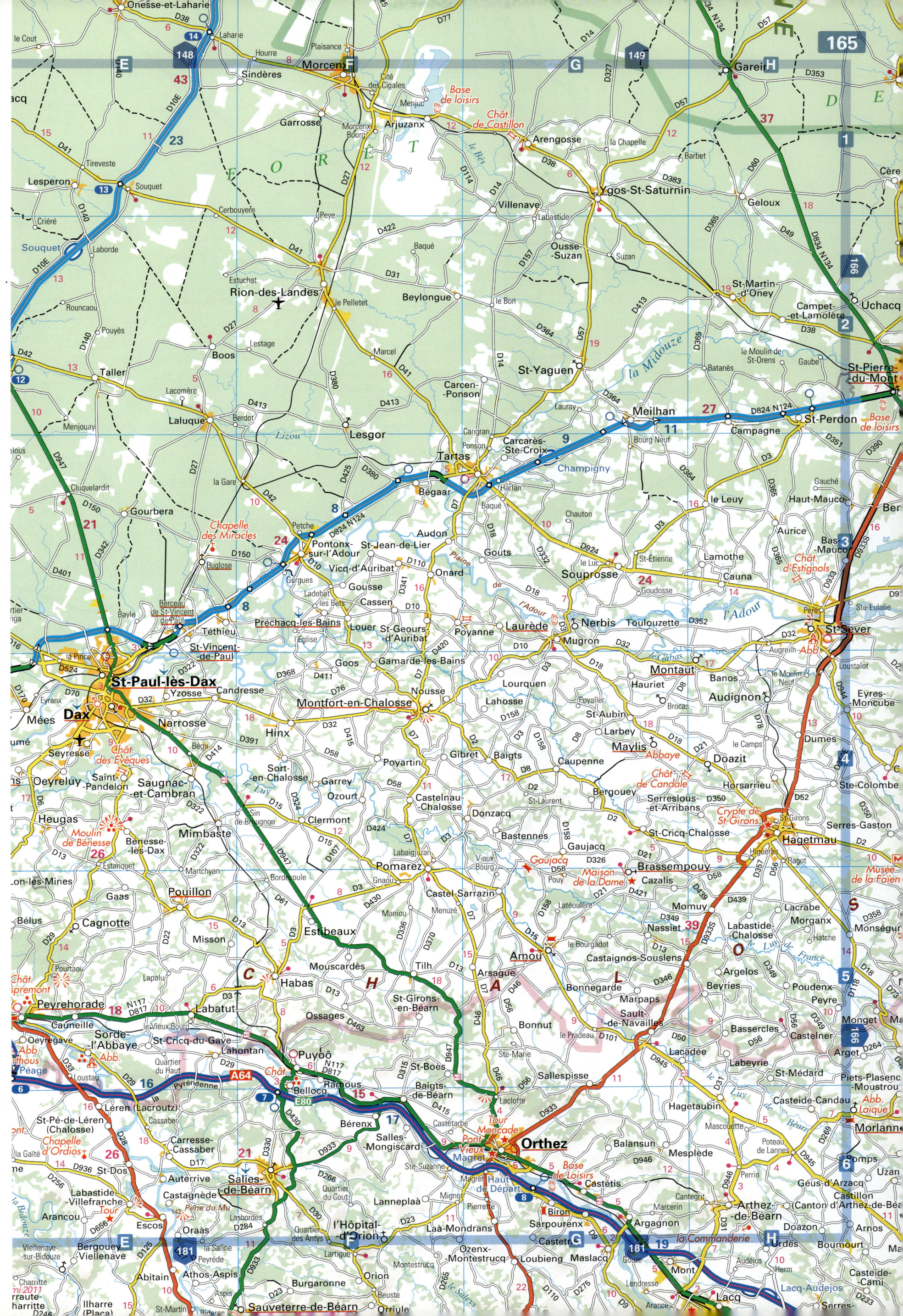

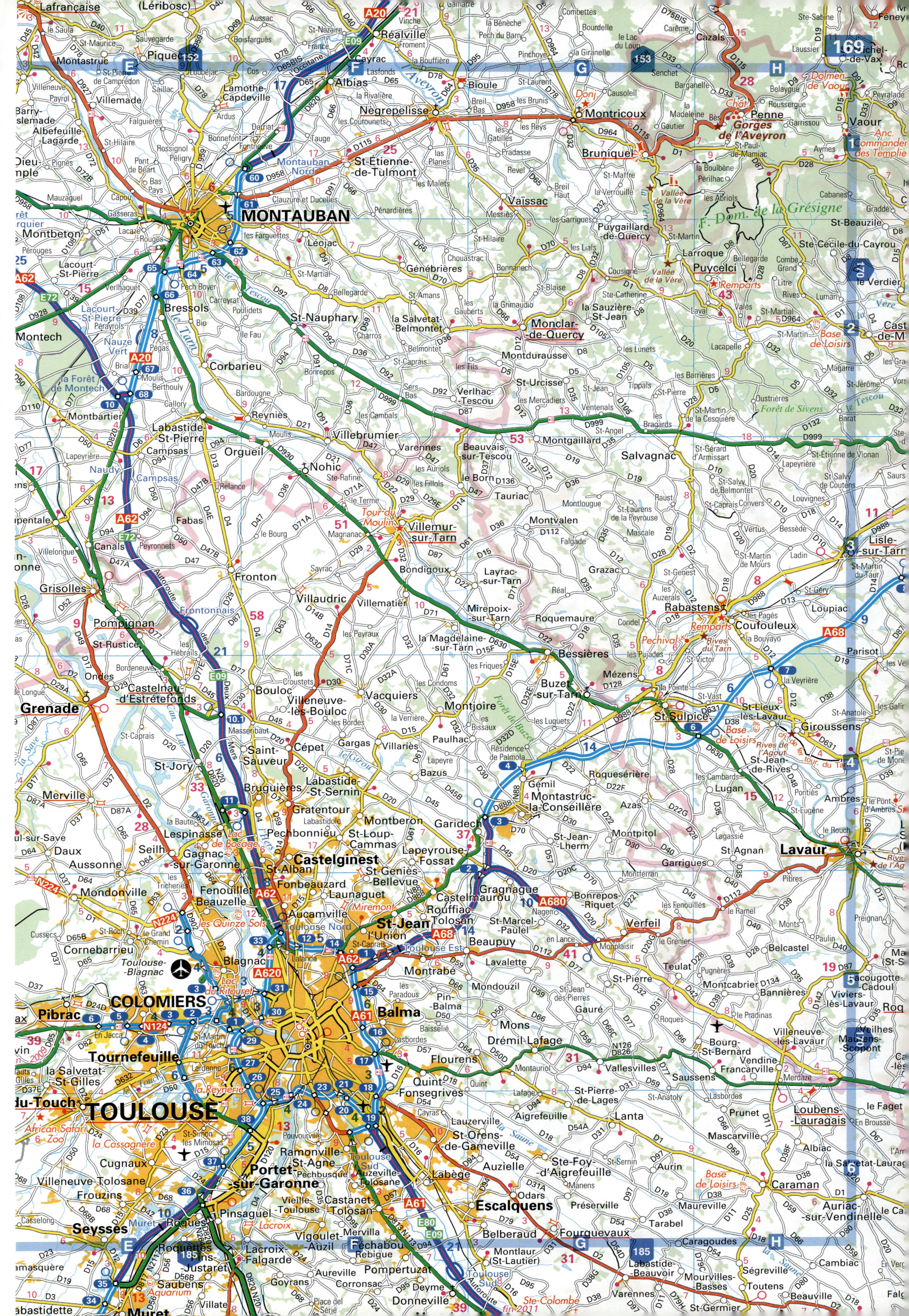

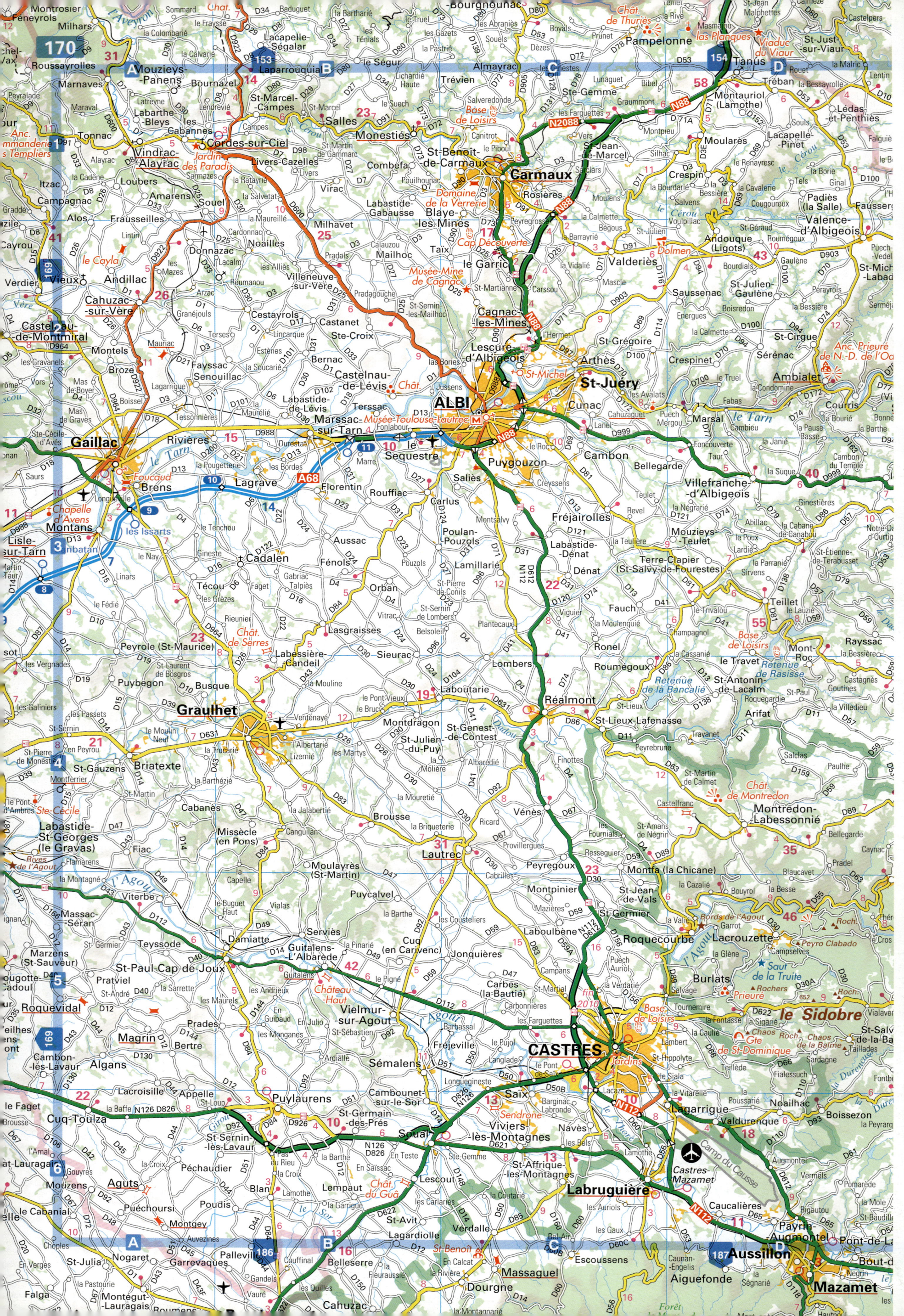

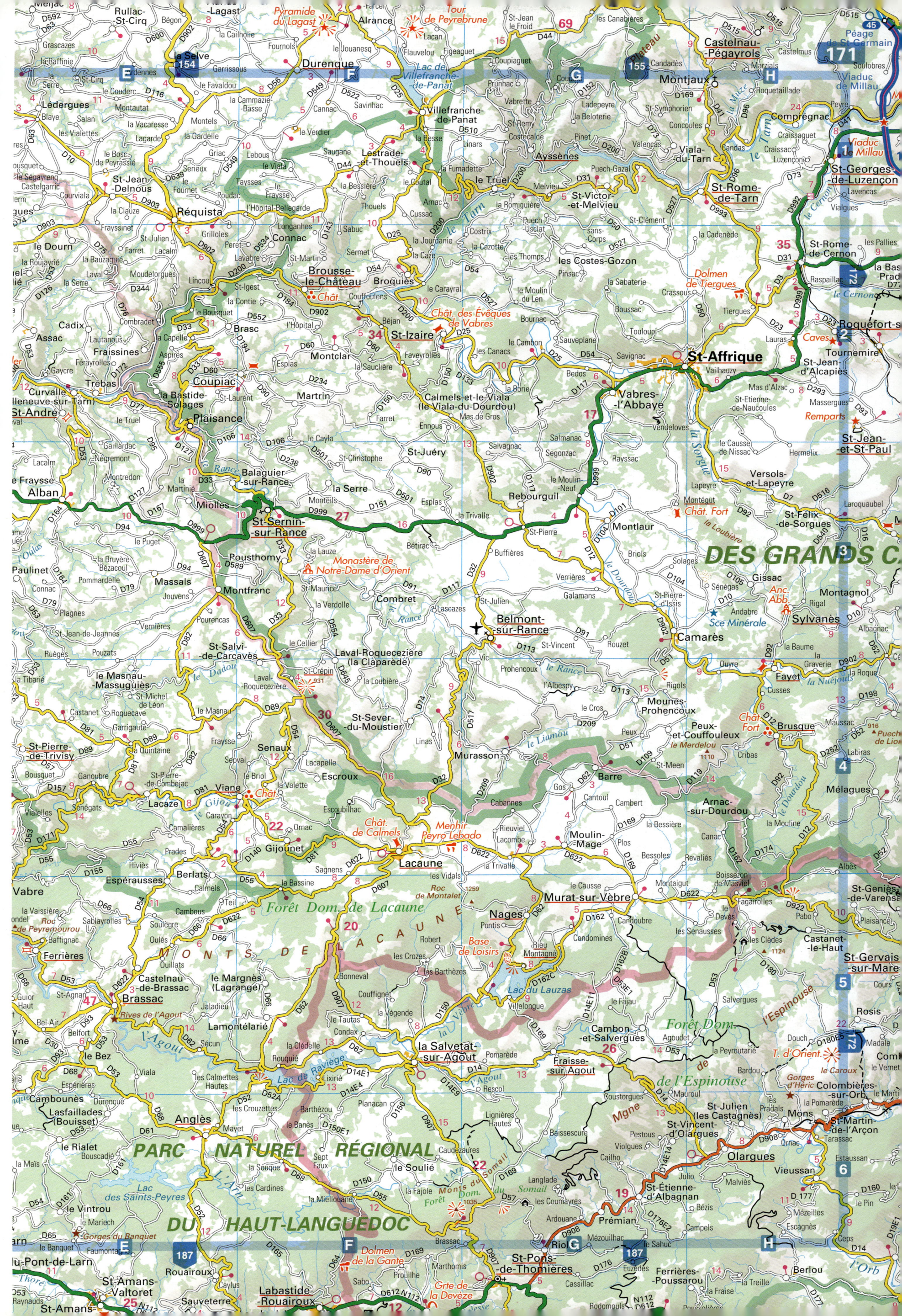

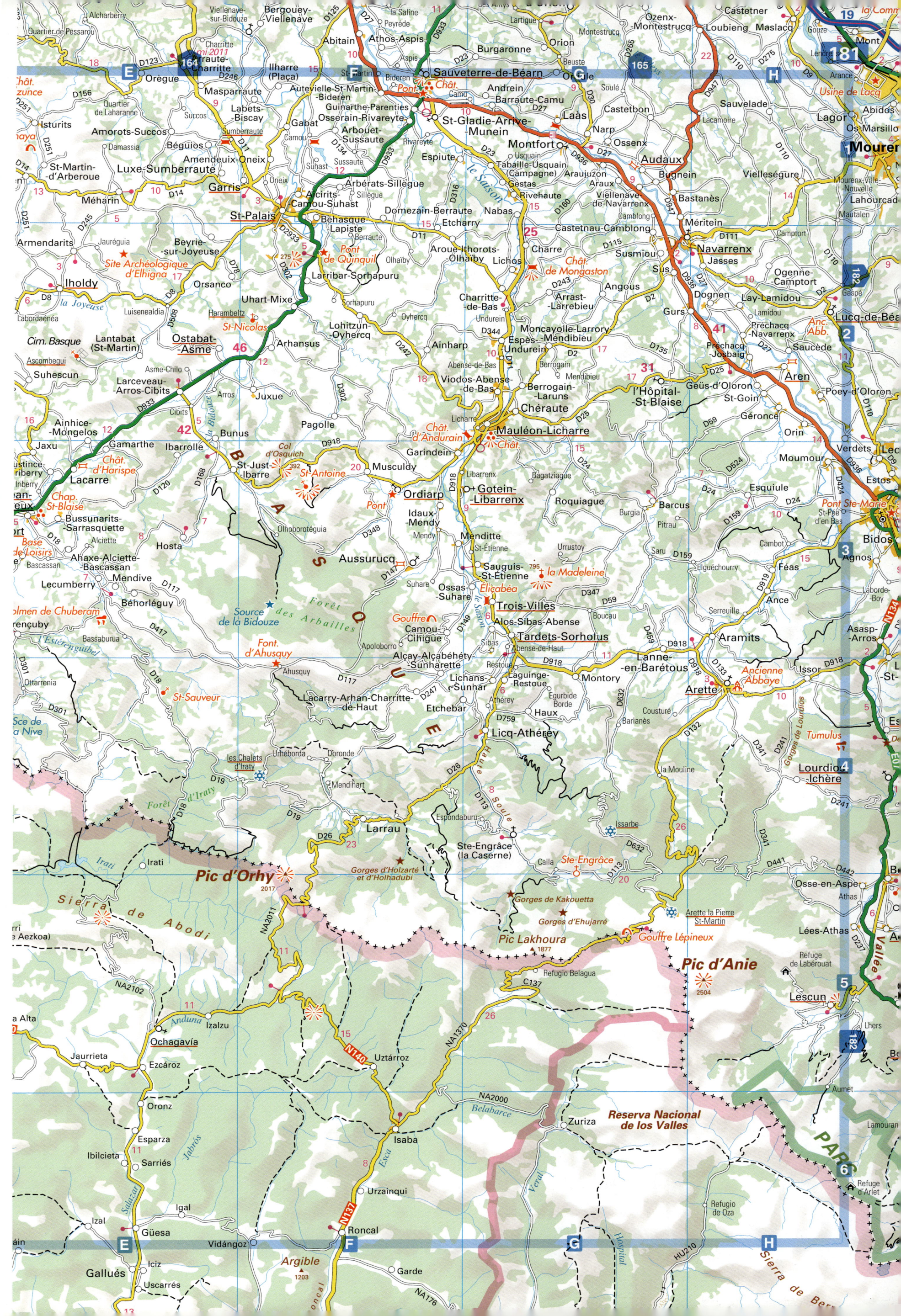

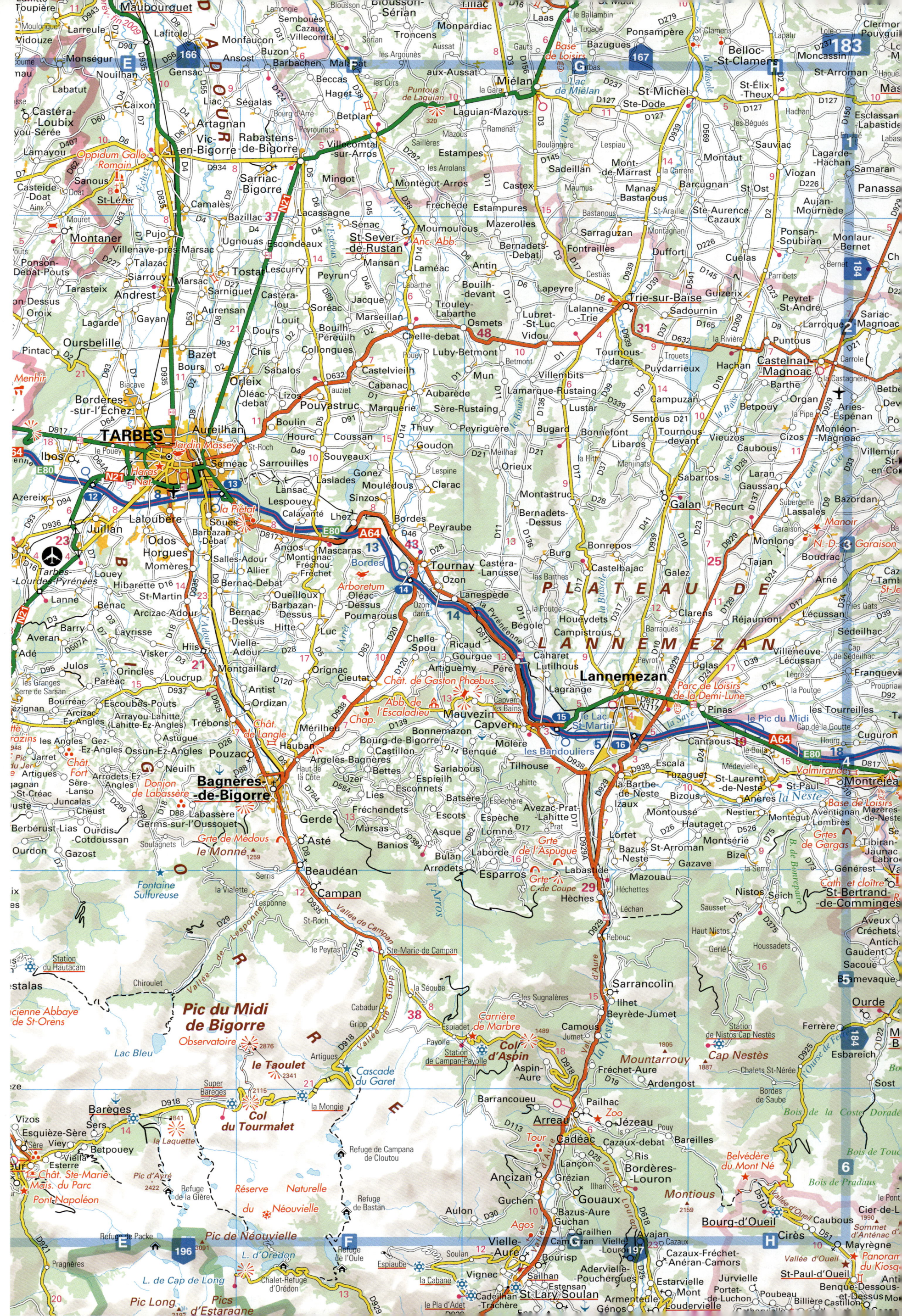

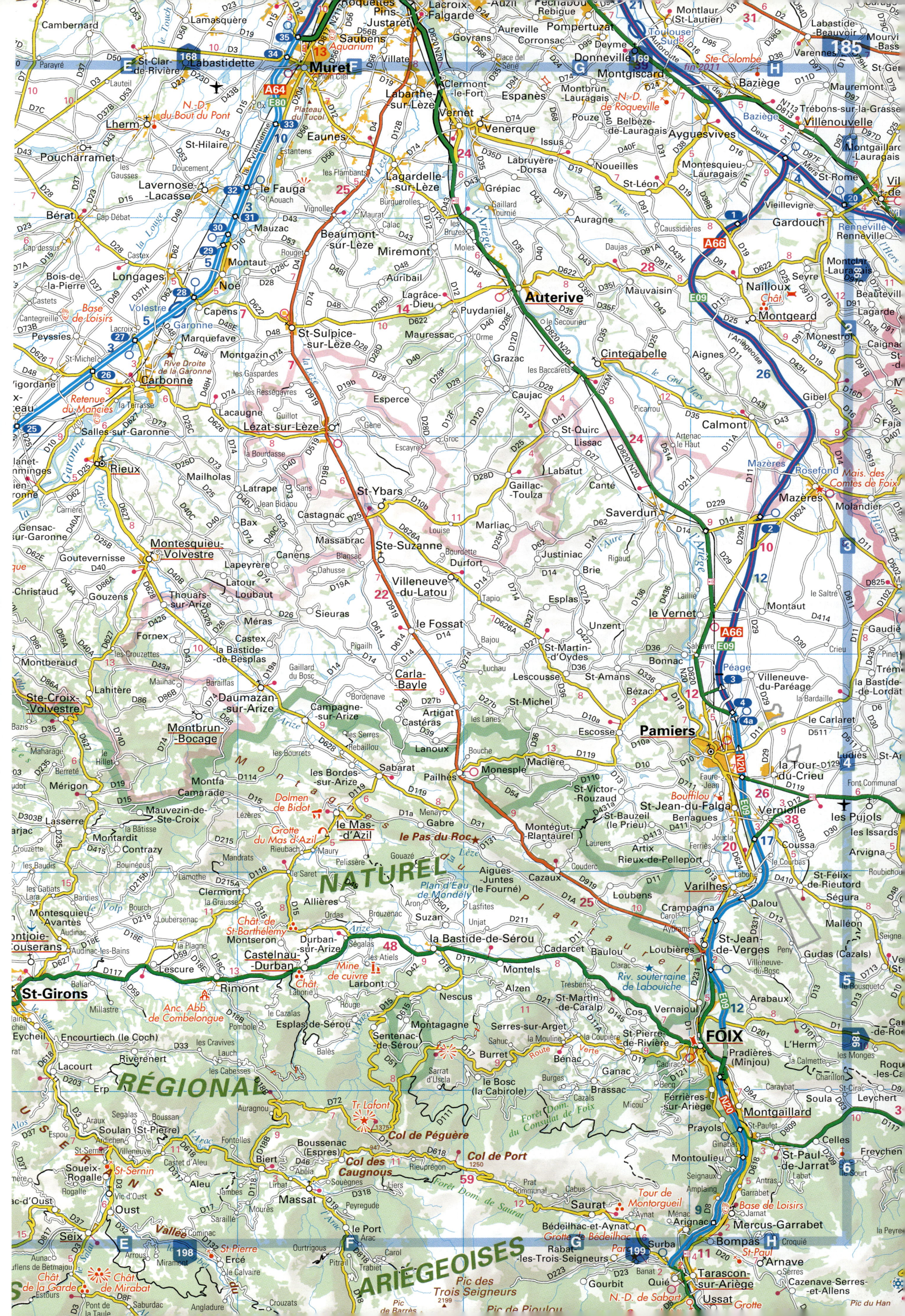

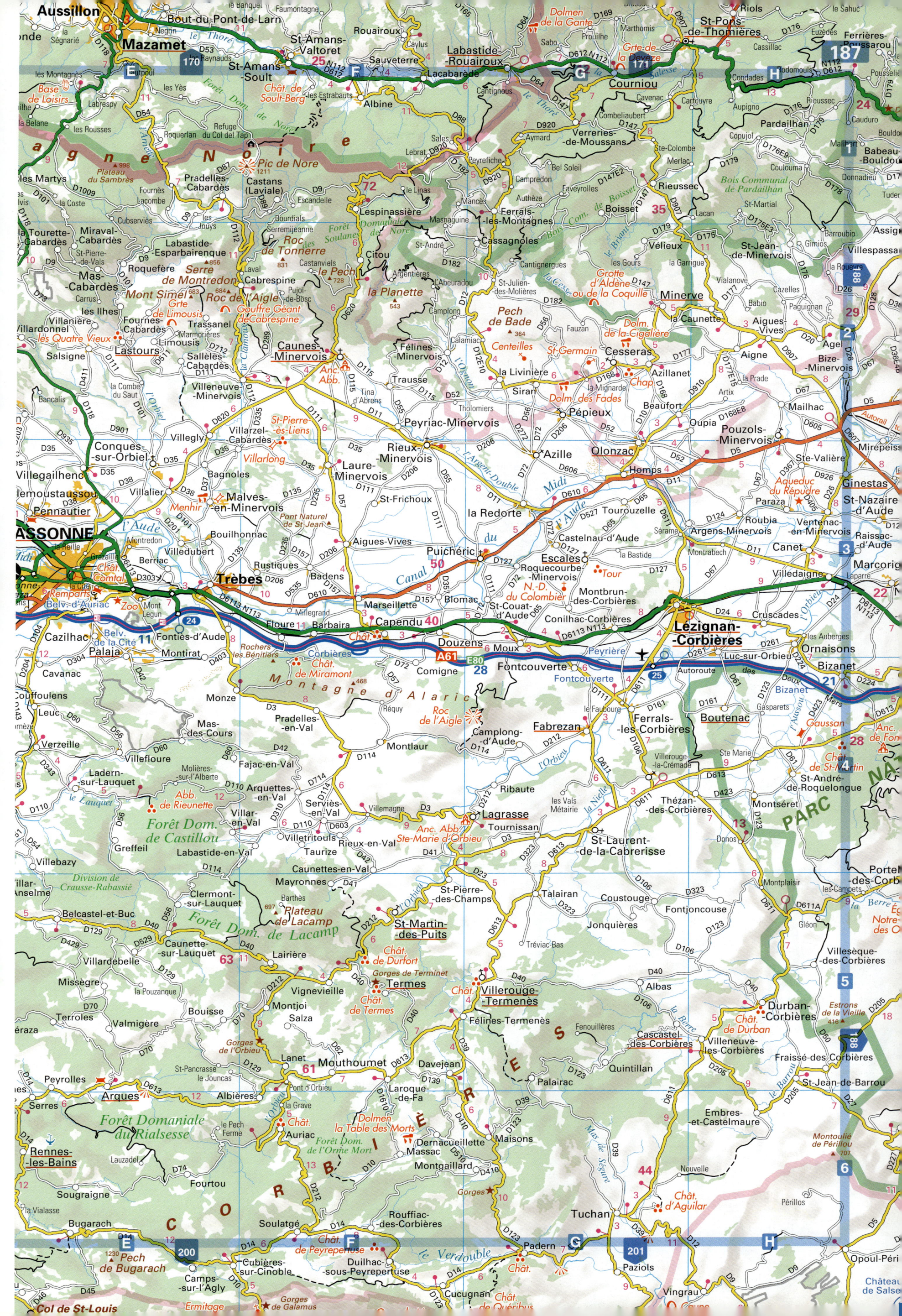

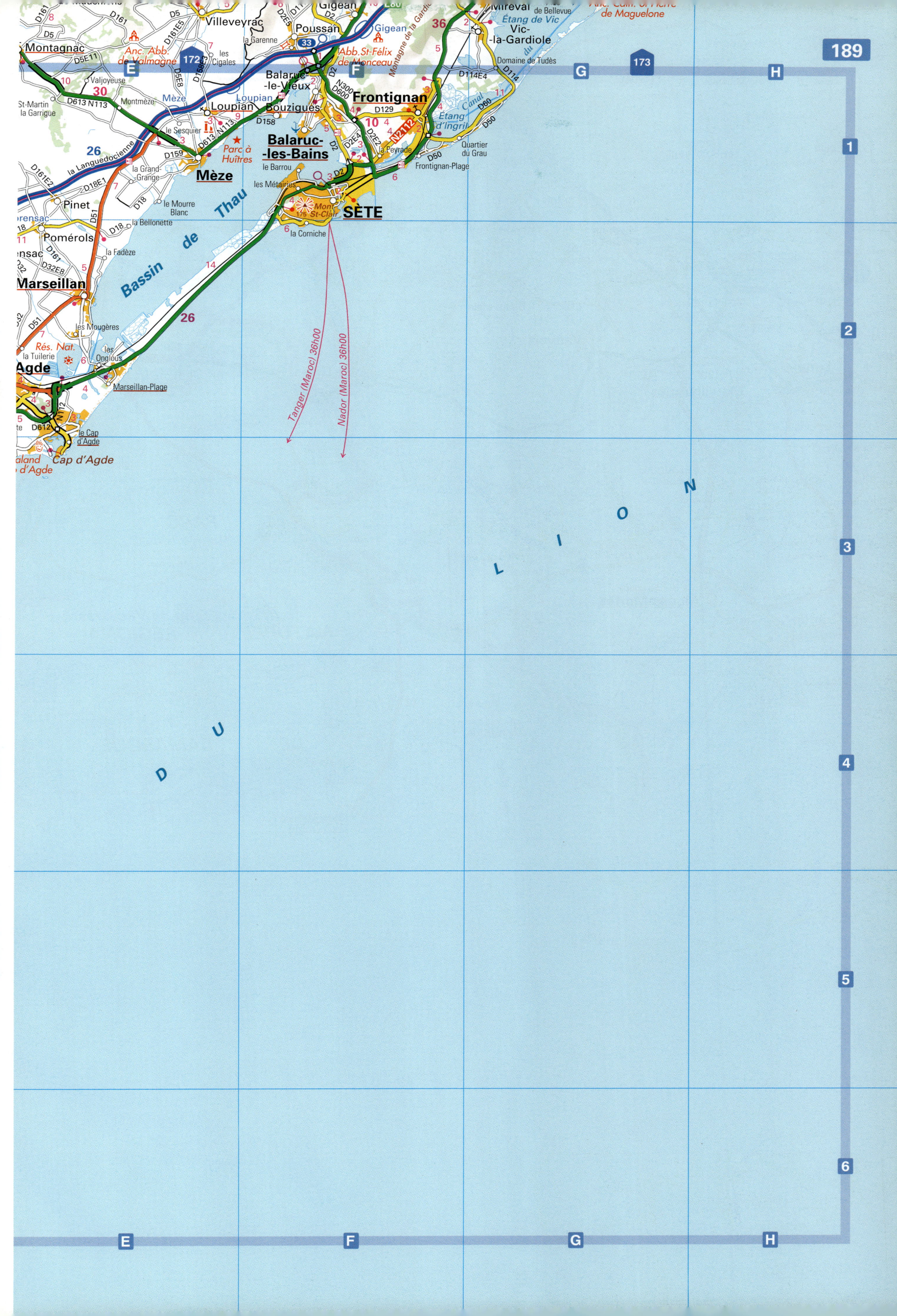

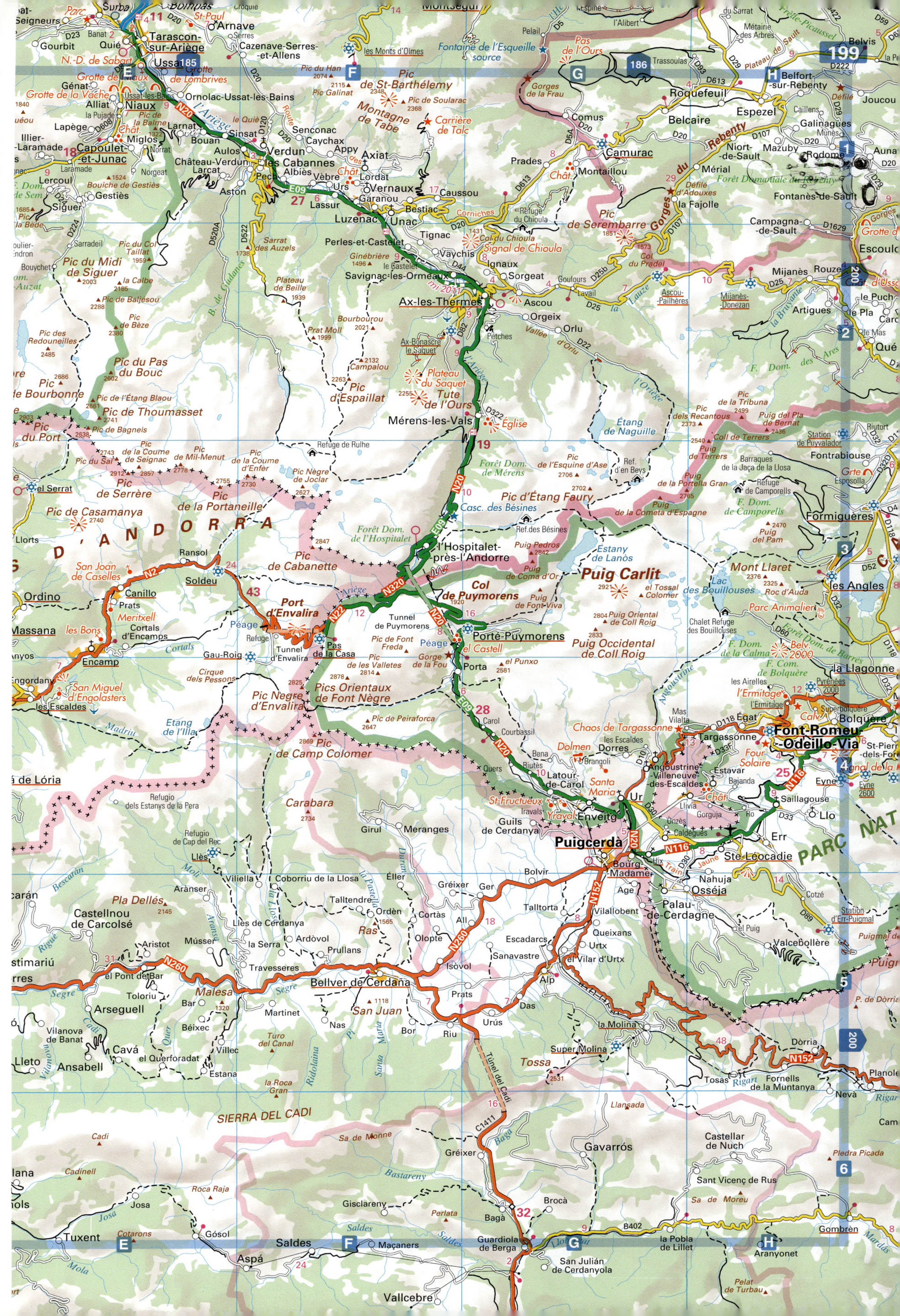

A   B   C   D

1

2

3

4

5

6

A   B   C   D

Marseille 11h30
Nice 5h30
Savona (Italie) 6h00
Marseille 11h30
Toulon (en saison) 5h45
Nice 5h30
Savona (Italie, en saison) 6h00

Punta di l'Acciolu

Tour

Ogliast

9

Phare de la Pietra
l'Île-Rousse
N197
Tour de Saleccia
Tour
Lozari
Parc Botanique
Monticello
304
Monte Négru
8

Punta di Vallitone
D513
D63
Marine de Davia
Corbara
Occiglioni
Punta di Varcale
Citadelle
Algajola
Santa-Reparata-di-Balagna
Marine de Sant'Ambrogio
33
12
Pigna
Couvent de Corbara
Punta Spano
Tour
D71
D557
10
D151
D113
Sant'Antonino
Belgodère
Palasca
Tocconi
D963
D71
Costa
D71
8
Occhiatana
la Revellata
Punta Caldanu
Tour
Lumio
Aregno
D413
D13
Ville-di-Paraso
Speloncato
Grotte des Veaux Marins
Citadelle
D81B
Lavatoggio
6
Bocca di Salvi
Cateri
Avapessa
D663
9
Nessa
17
Pioggiola
D963
Olmi-Cappella
Calvi
N197
San Petru
San Raineru
Montegrosso (Lunghignano)
Muro
Feliceto
Mausoléo
Vallic
N.-D. de la Serra
Petra Maio
Cassano
Zilia
San Parteo
1680
Monte Grosso
D963
Punta di Cantaleli
725
Montemaggiore
D151
Capu di a Conca
Priugiu
Ancn. Couvent d'Alzi Pratu
1937
Capu a u Dente
Monte Padru
15
Calvi-Sainte-Catherine
D51
Santa Restituta
2029
2393
Forêt Territoriale de Tartagine-Melaja
Capo Cavallo
Sémaphore
801
Monte Cintu
Moncale
Calenzana
Cima di a Statoja
Ascu
295
Torre Truccia
Suare
Tarazone
2143
2304
Gorge
Truccia
D81B
la Figarella
Chaos de Bocca Rezza
Monte Corona
Pont Génois
34
Torre Mozza
D251
Forêt Communale d'Ascu
Capu di a Mursetta
Amacu
Capu Ladroncellu
13
l'Argentella
Pieve
Frassigna
Cirque de Bonifatu
Giunte
Capu di l'Argentella
16
16
Refuge de Carrozzu
Punta di Ciuttone
Bocca Bassa
Tour Maraghiu

204   204

CENTRAL PARIS

0   100   200   300   400   500 m

208

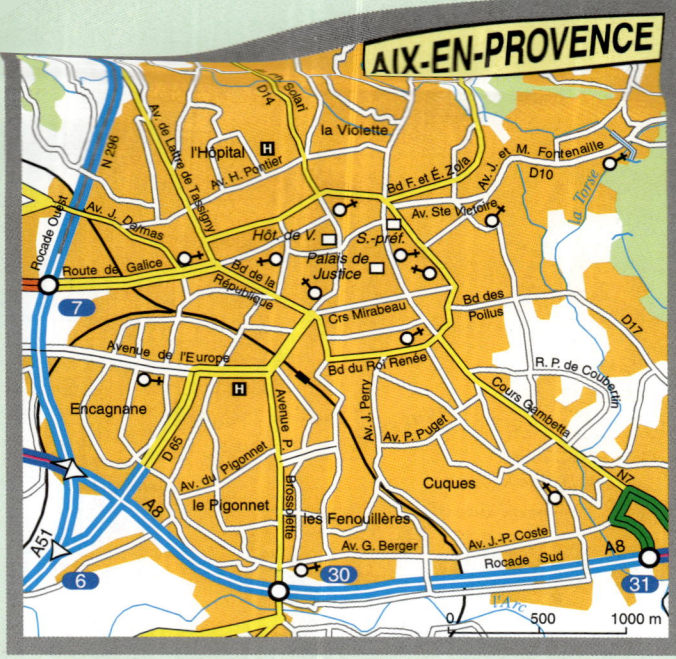

AIX-EN-PROVENCE

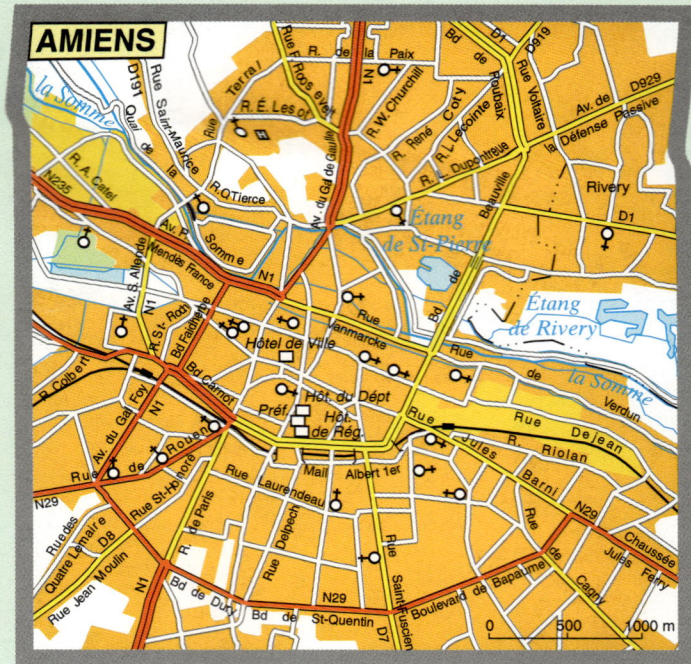

AMIENS

ANGERS

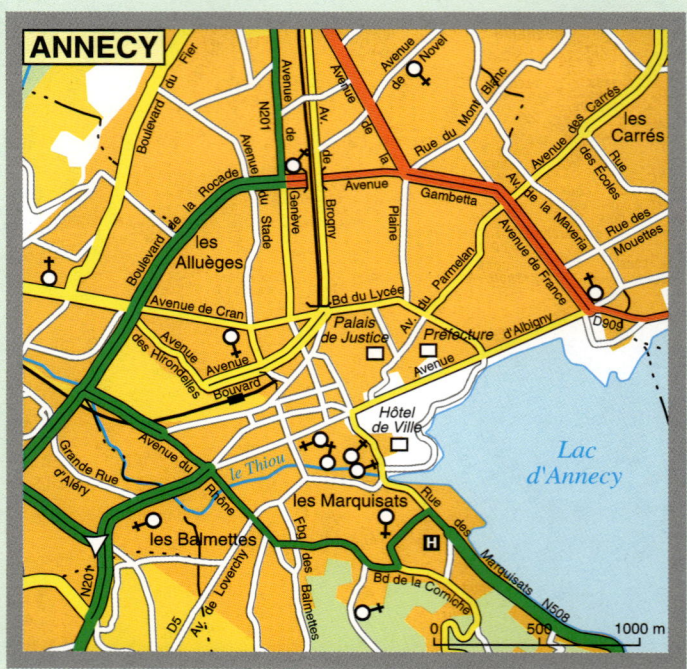

ANNECY

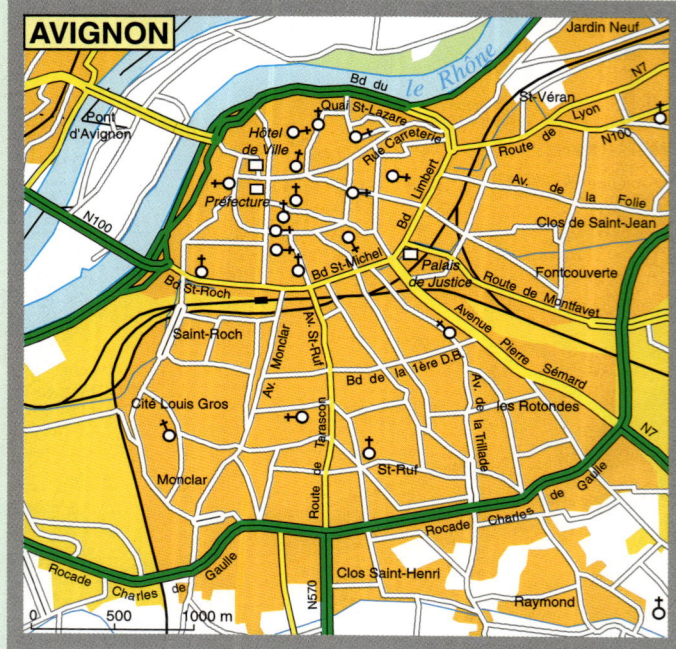

AVIGNON

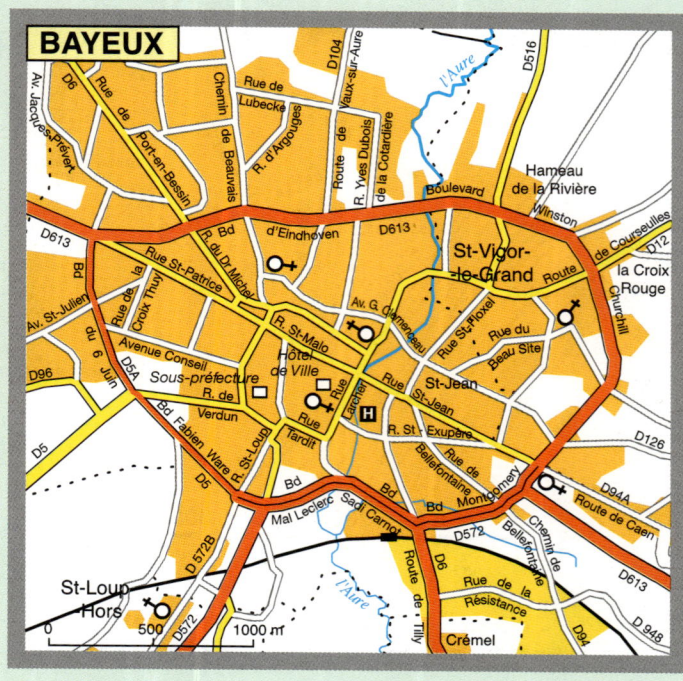

BAYEUX

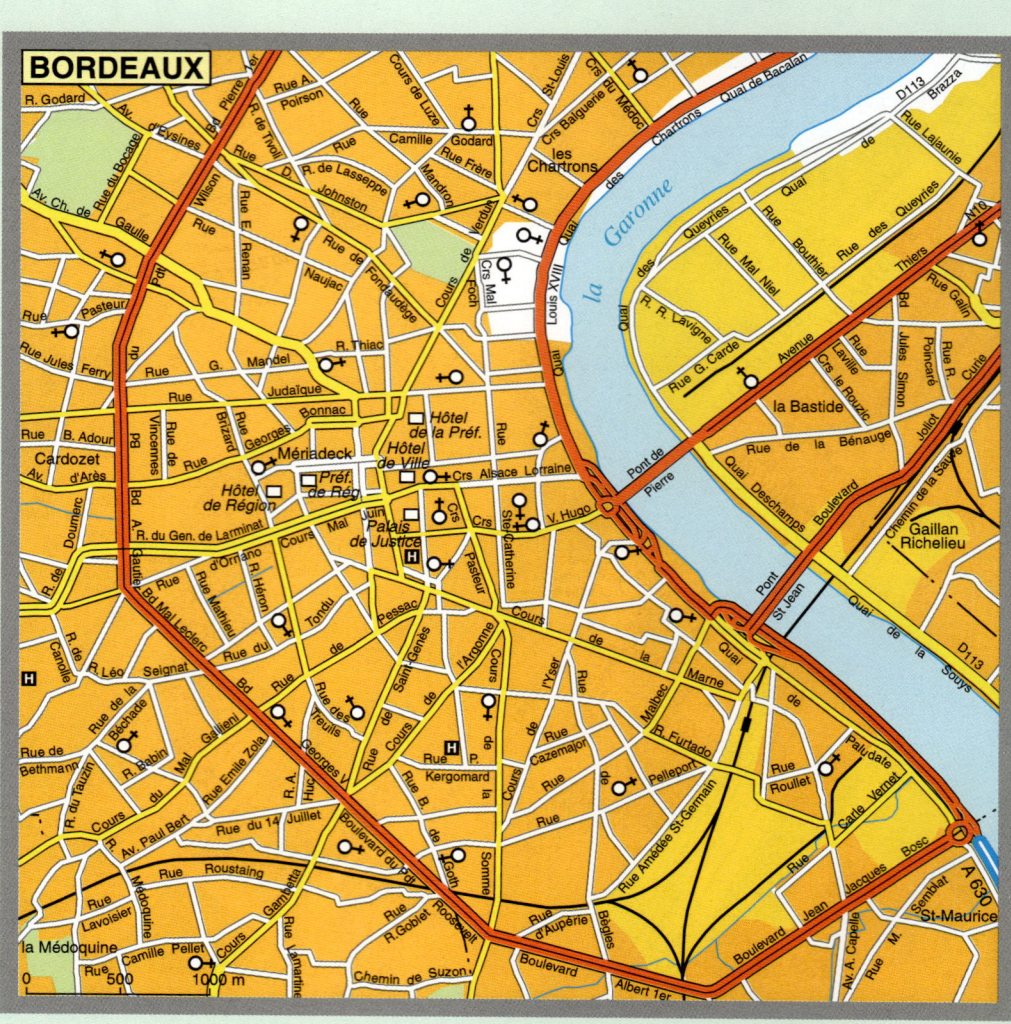

BORDEAUX

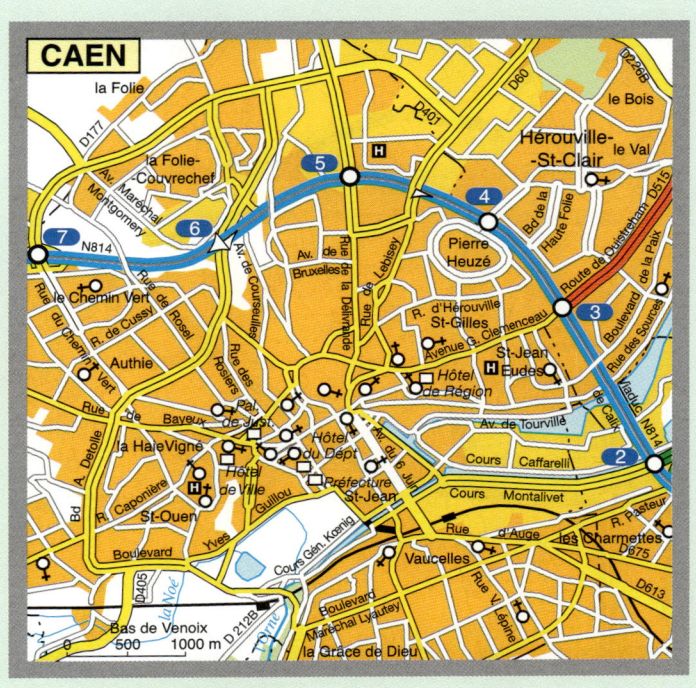

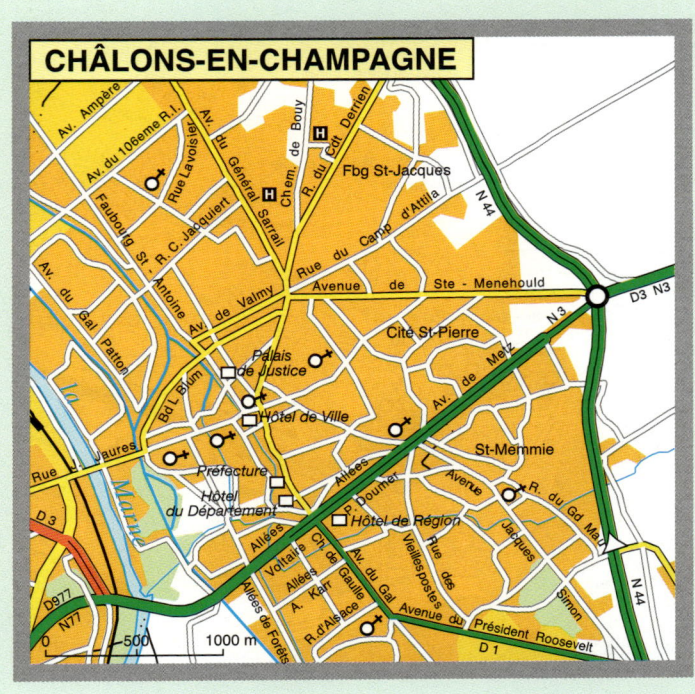

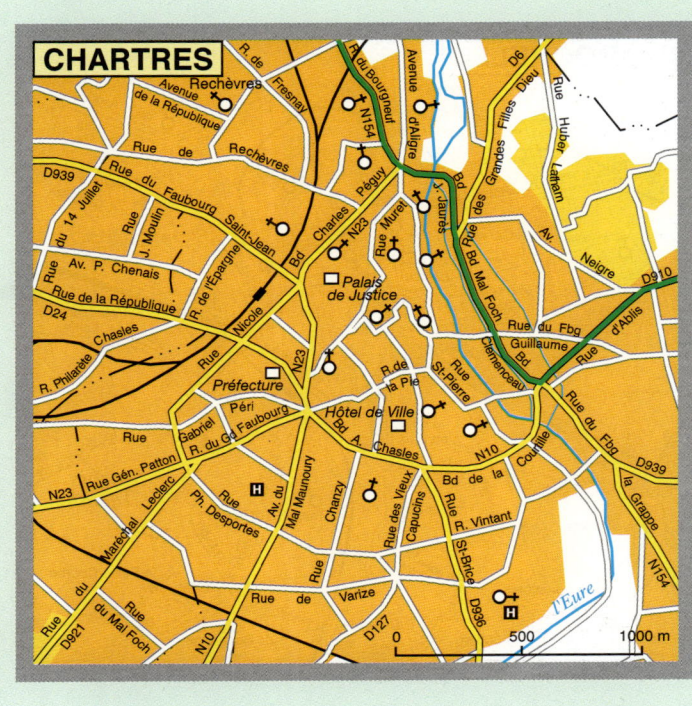

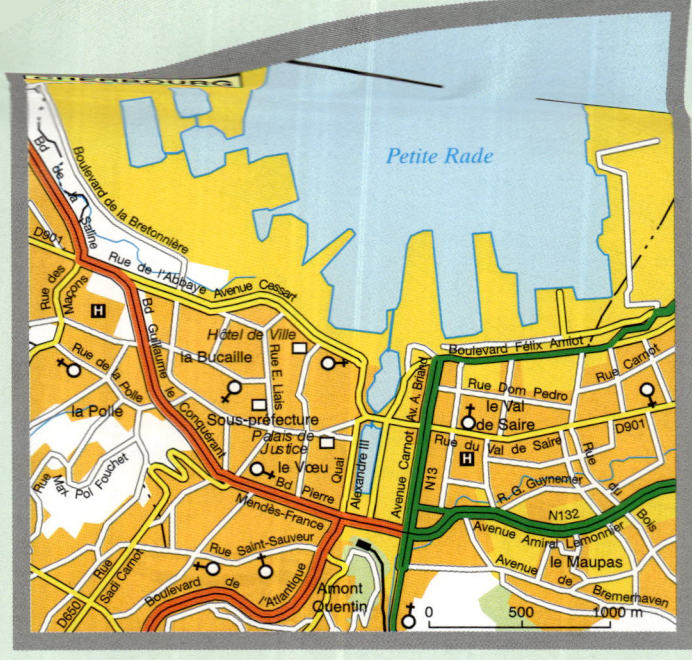

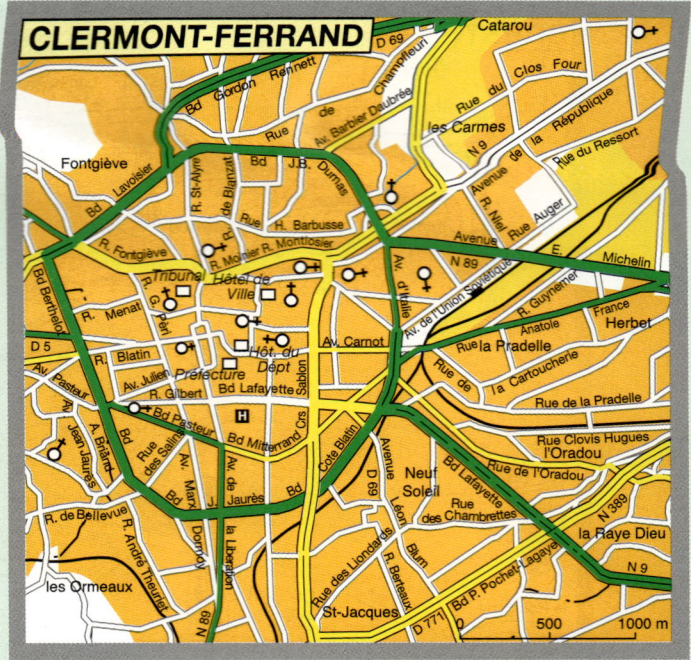

CLERMONT-FERRAND

DIEPPE

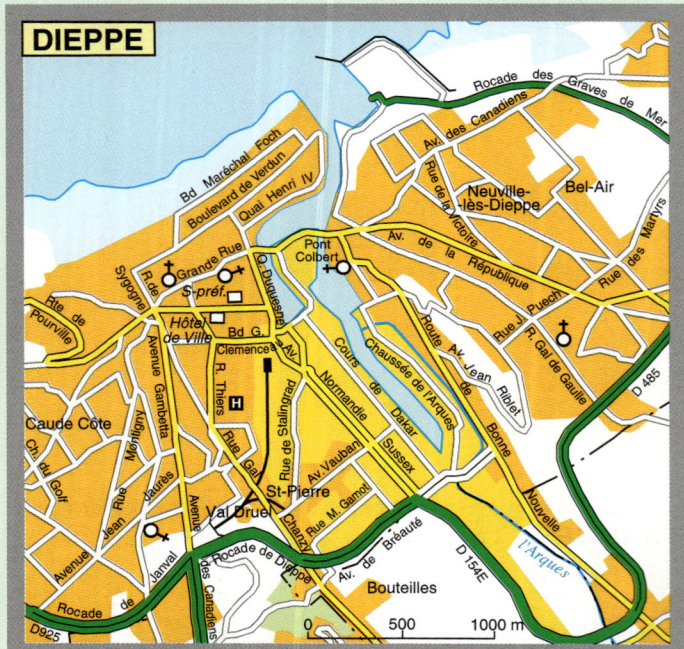

DIJON

DUNKERQUE

GRENOBLE

LA ROCHELLE

LE HAVRE

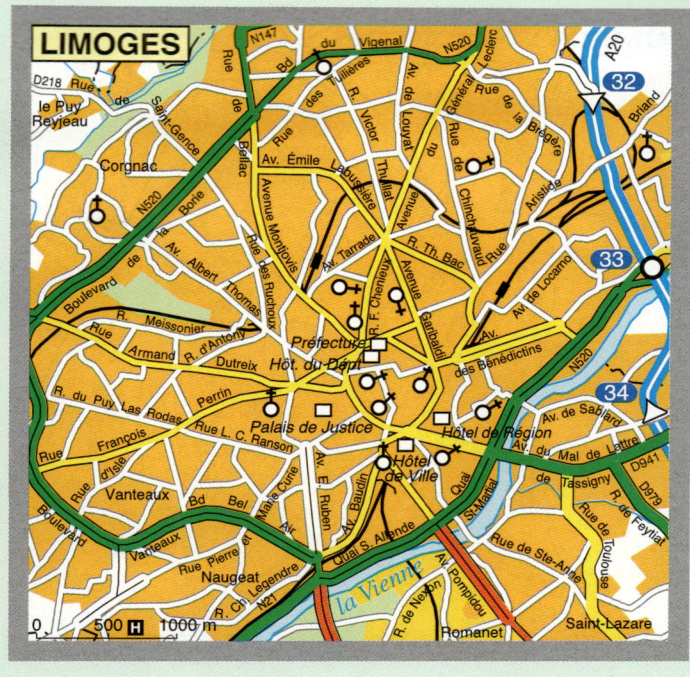

215

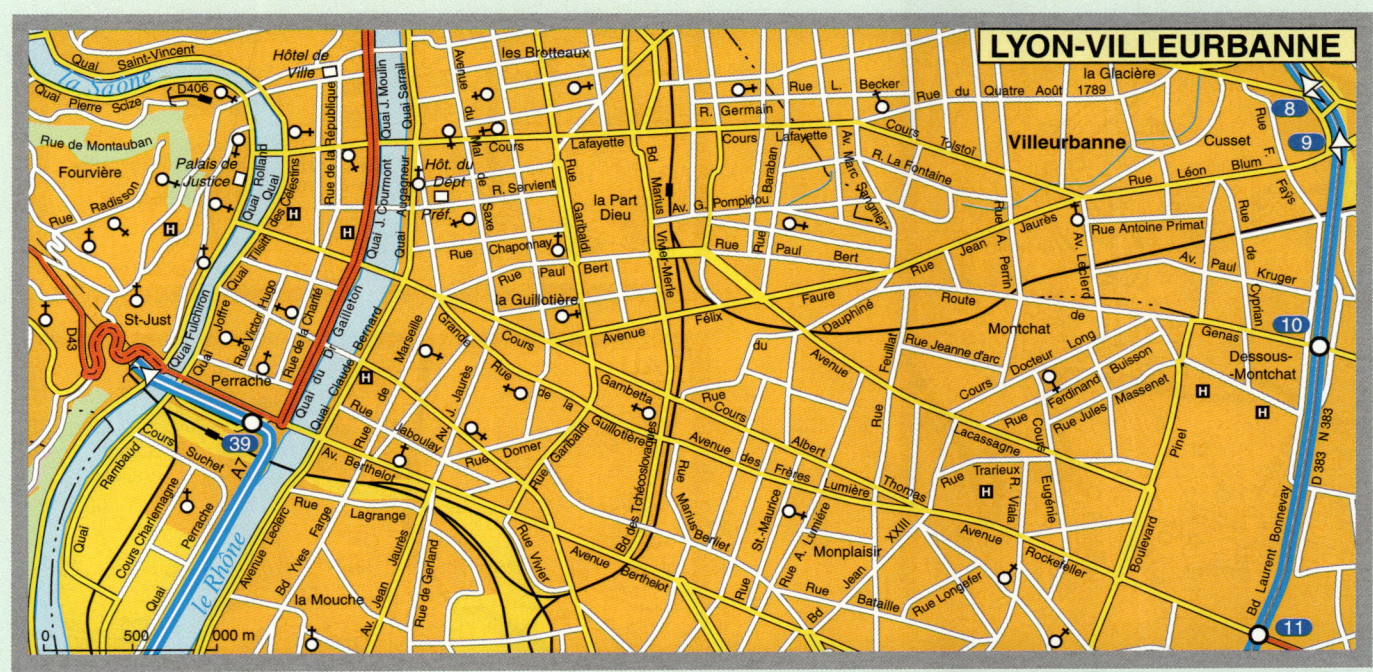

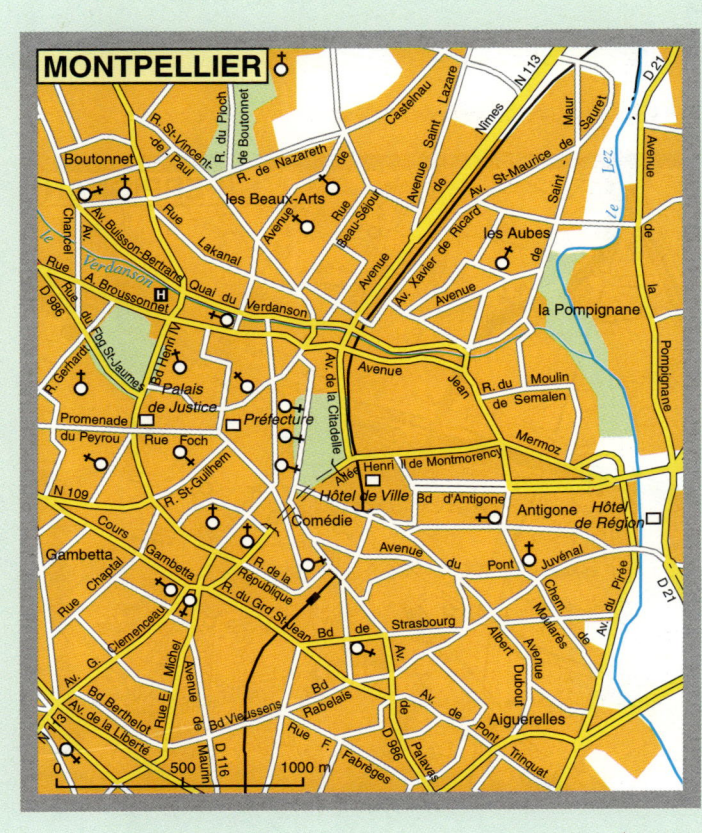

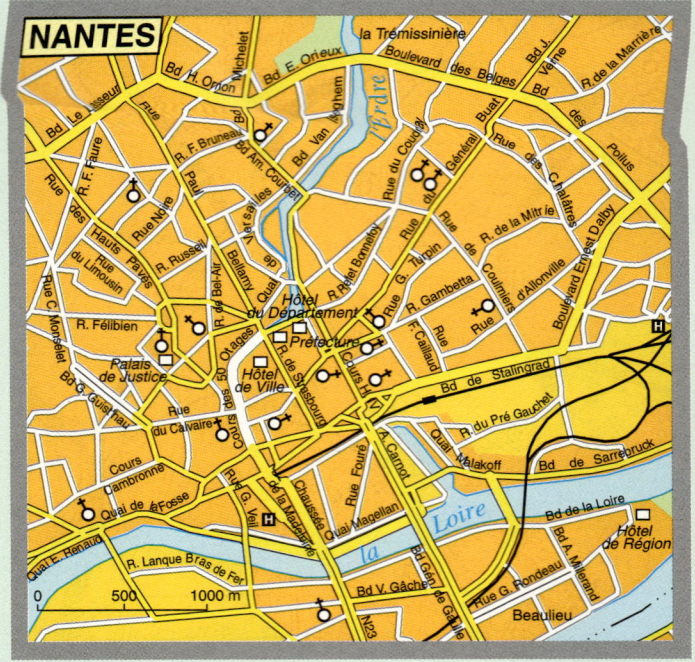

NANTES

ORLÉANS

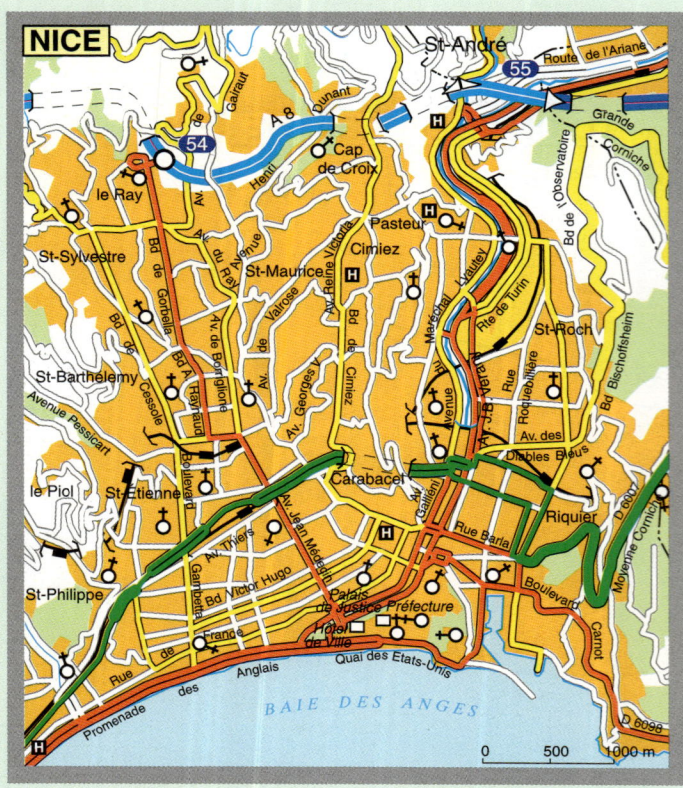

NICE

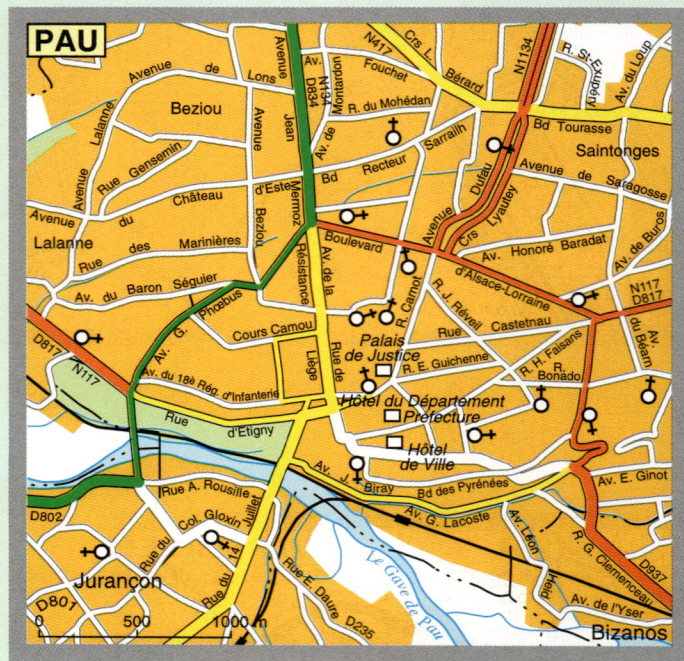

PAU

PERPIGNAN

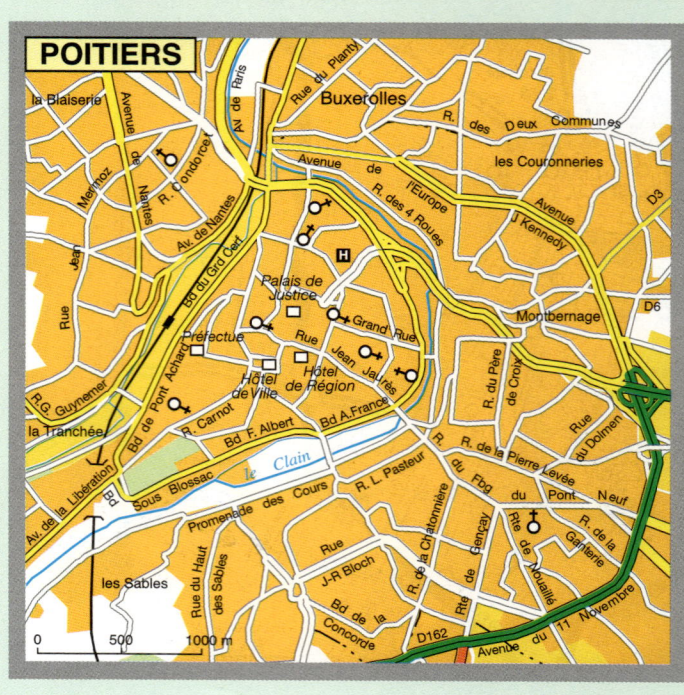

POITIERS

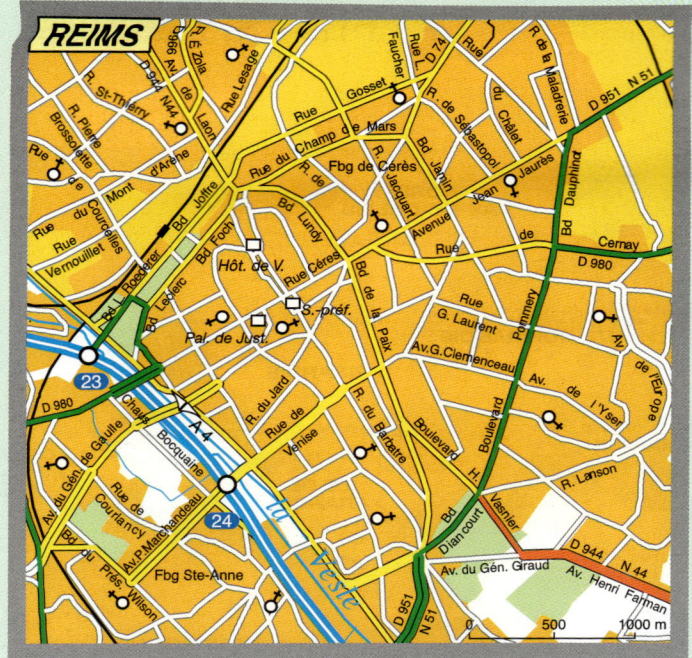

REIMS

ROUEN

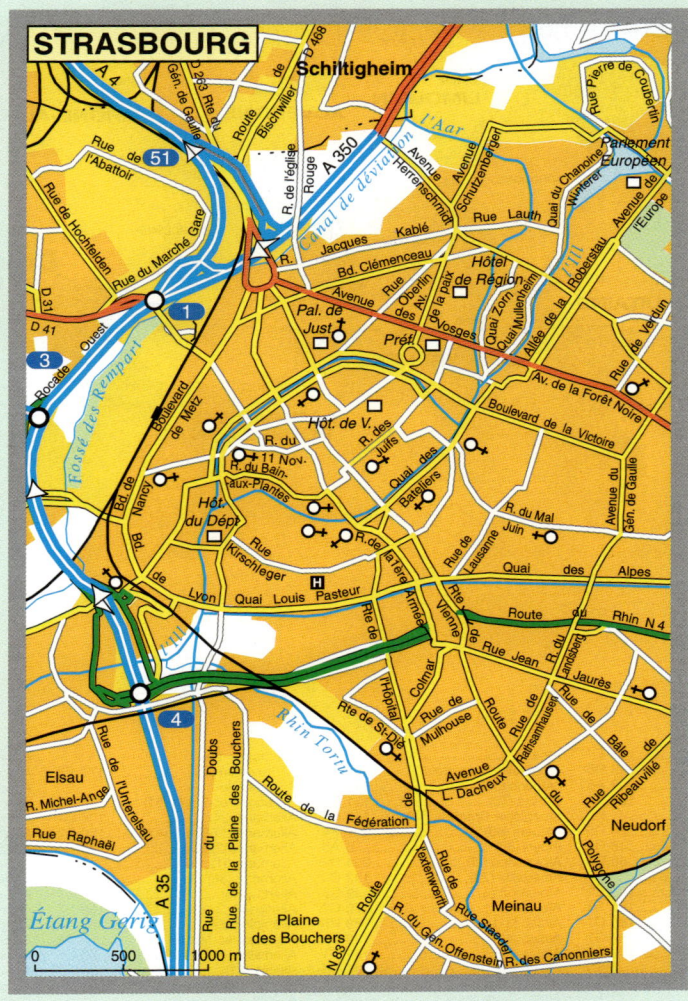

STRASBOURG

ST-MALO

TOULON

TOULOUSE

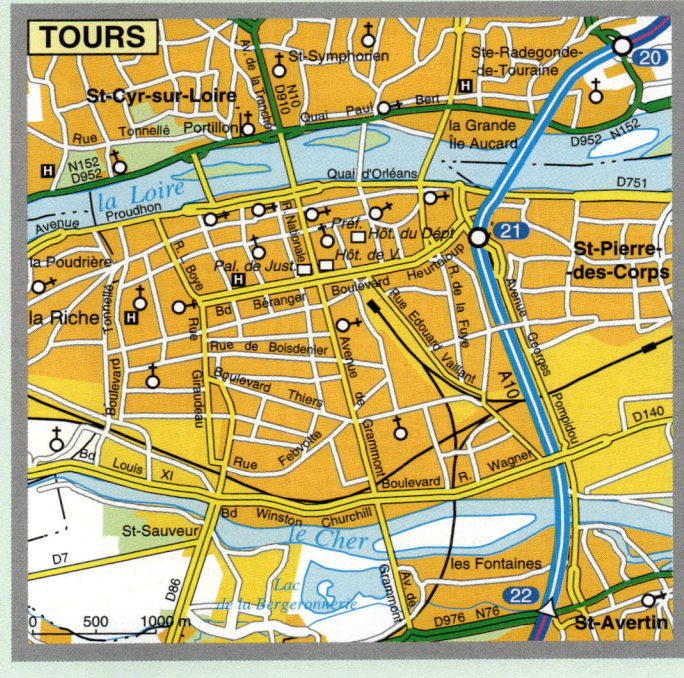

TOURS

Département map
France administrative

218

01 Ain
02 Aisne
03 Allier
04 Alpes-de-Haute-Provence
05 Hautes-Alpes
06 Alpes-Maritimes
07 Ardèche
08 Ardennes
09 Ariège
10 Aube
11 Aude
12 Aveyron
13 Bouches-du-Rhône
14 Calvados
15 Cantal
16 Charente
17 Charente-Maritime
18 Cher
19 Corrèze
2A Corse-du-Sud
2B Haute-Corse
21 Côte-d'Or
22 Côtes d'Armor
23 Creuse
24 Dordogne
25 Doubs
26 Drôme
27 Eure
28 Eure-et-Loir
29 Finistère
30 Gard
31 Haute-Garonne
32 Gers
33 Gironde
34 Hérault
35 Ille-et-Vilaine
36 Indre
37 Indre-et-Loire
38 Isère
39 Jura
40 Landes
41 Loir-et-Cher
42 Loire
43 Haute-Loire
44 Loire-Atlantique
45 Loiret
46 Lot
47 Lot-et-Garonne
48 Lozère
49 Maine-et-Loire
50 Manche
51 Marne
52 Haute-Marne
53 Mayenne
54 Meurthe-et-Moselle
55 Meuse
56 Morbihan
57 Moselle
58 Nièvre
59 Nord
60 Oise
61 Orne
62 Pas-de-Calais
63 Puy-de-Dôme
64 Pyrénées-Atlantiques
65 Hautes-Pyrénées
66 Pyrénées-Orientales
67 Bas-Rhin
68 Haut-Rhin
69 Rhône
70 Haute-Saône
71 Saône-et-Loire
72 Sarthe
73 Savoie
74 Haute-Savoie
75 Paris
76 Seine-Maritime
77 Seine-et-Marne
78 Yvelines
79 Deux-Sèvres
80 Somme
81 Tarn
82 Tarn-et-Garonne
83 Var
84 Vaucluse
85 Vendée
86 Vienne
87 Haute-Vienne
88 Vosges
89 Yonne
90 Territoire de Belfort
91 Essonne
92 Hauts-de-Seine
93 Seine-Saint-Denis
94 Val-de-Marne
95 Val-d'Oise

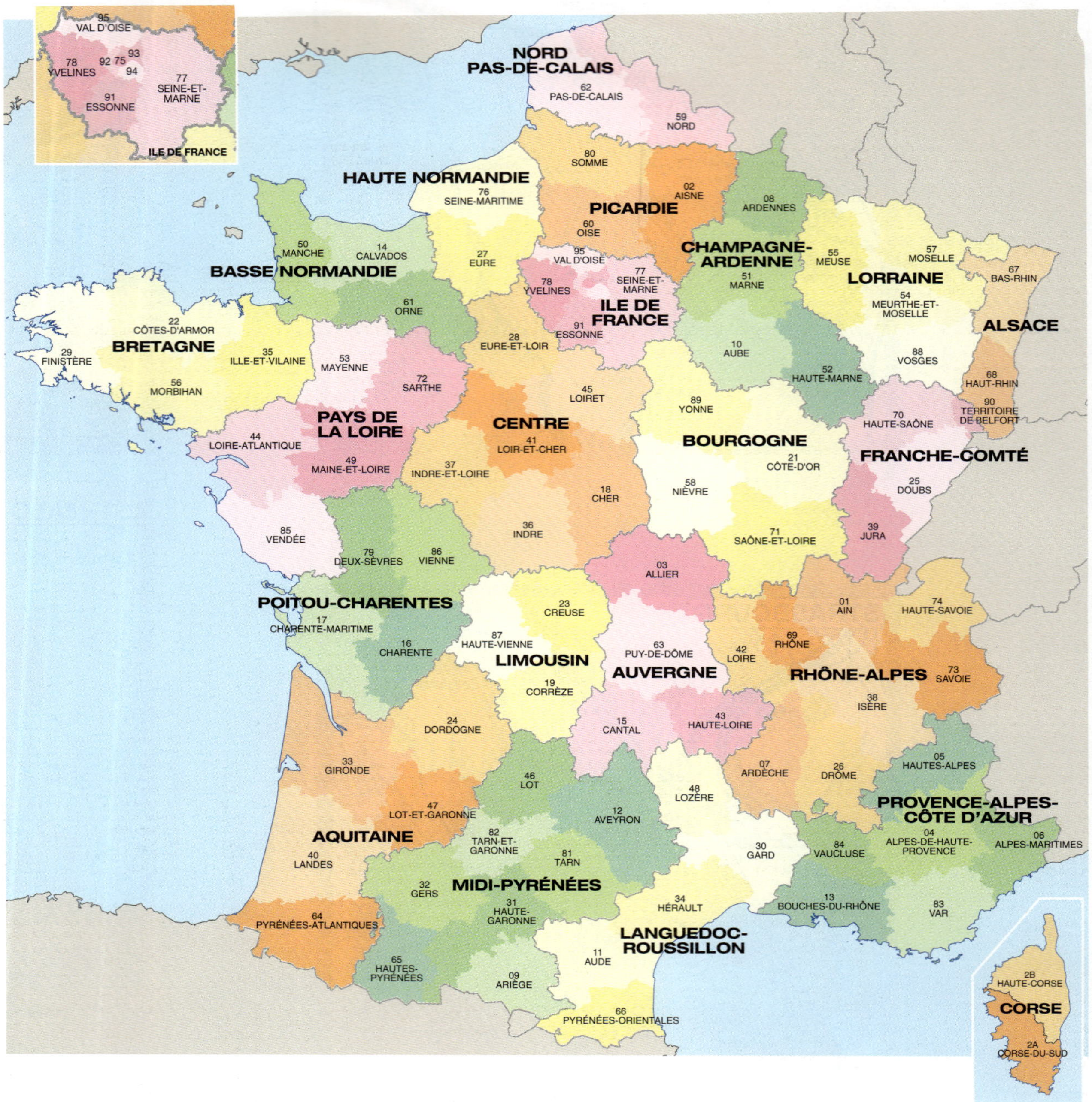
ILE DE FRANCE
95 VAL D'OISE
78 YVELINES
92 75 93 94
91 ESSONNE
77 SEINE-ET-MARNE
NORD PAS-DE-CALAIS
62 PAS-DE-CALAIS
59 NORD
80 SOMME
02 AISNE
60 OISE
PICARDIE
HAUTE NORMANDIE
76 SEINE-MARITIME
27 EURE
BASSE NORMANDIE
50 MANCHE
14 CALVADOS
61 ORNE
CHAMPAGNE-ARDENNE
08 ARDENNES
51 MARNE
10 AUBE
52 HAUTE-MARNE
LORRAINE
55 MEUSE
57 MOSELLE
54 MEURTHE-ET-MOSELLE
88 VOSGES
ALSACE
67 BAS-RHIN
68 HAUT-RHIN
90 TERRITOIRE DE BELFORT
ILE DE FRANCE
28 EURE-ET-LOIR
BRETAGNE
29 FINISTÈRE
22 CÔTES-D'ARMOR
35 ILLE-ET-VILAINE
56 MORBIHAN
PAYS DE LA LOIRE
53 MAYENNE
72 SARTHE
44 LOIRE-ATLANTIQUE
49 MAINE-ET-LOIRE
85 VENDÉE
CENTRE
45 LOIRET
41 LOIR-ET-CHER
37 INDRE-ET-LOIRE
18 CHER
36 INDRE
BOURGOGNE
89 YONNE
21 CÔTE-D'OR
58 NIÈVRE
71 SAÔNE-ET-LOIRE
FRANCHE-COMTÉ
70 HAUTE-SAÔNE
25 DOUBS
39 JURA
POITOU-CHARENTES
79 DEUX-SÈVRES
86 VIENNE
17 CHARENTE-MARITIME
16 CHARENTE
LIMOUSIN
87 HAUTE-VIENNE
23 CREUSE
19 CORRÈZE
AUVERGNE
03 ALLIER
63 PUY-DE-DÔME
15 CANTAL
43 HAUTE-LOIRE
RHÔNE-ALPES
01 AIN
74 HAUTE-SAVOIE
69 RHÔNE
42 LOIRE
73 SAVOIE
38 ISÈRE
07 ARDÈCHE
26 DRÔME
AQUITAINE
24 DORDOGNE
33 GIRONDE
47 LOT-ET-GARONNE
40 LANDES
64 PYRÉNÉES-ATLANTIQUES
MIDI-PYRÉNÉES
46 LOT
12 AVEYRON
82 TARN-ET-GARONNE
81 TARN
32 GERS
31 HAUTE-GARONNE
65 HAUTES-PYRÉNÉES
09 ARIÈGE
48 LOZÈRE
LANGUEDOC-ROUSSILLON
30 GARD
34 HÉRAULT
11 AUDE
66 PYRÉNÉES-ORIENTALES
PROVENCE-ALPES-CÔTE D'AZUR
05 HAUTES-ALPES
04 ALPES-DE-HAUTE-PROVENCE
06 ALPES-MARITIMES
84 VAUCLUSE
13 BOUCHES-DU-RHÔNE
83 VAR
CORSE
2B HAUTE-CORSE
2A CORSE-DU-SUD

A

Aast (64) 182 D2
Abainville (55) 68 B1
Abancourt (59) 8 D3
Abancourt (60) 19 G2
Abaucourt (54) 48 D3
Abaucourt-Hautecourt (55) 25 F6
Abbans-Dessous (25) 103 F2
Abbans-Dessus (25) 103 F2
Abbaretz (44) 74 D2
Abbécourt (02) 21 H3
Abbecourt (60) 20 B5
Abbenans (25) 88 A4
Abbeville (80) 6 D4
Abbéville-la-Rivière (91) 63 F3
Abbéville-lès-Conflans (54) 25 H6
Abbeville-Saint-Lucien (60) 20 B3
Abbévillers (25) 88 D5
Abeilhan (34) 188 C1
Abelcourt (70) 87 H2
Abère (64) 182 D1
l'Abergement-Clémenciat (01) 116 C5
l'Abergement-de-Cuisery (71) 116 C1
l'Abergement-de-Varey (01) 117 F6
Abergement-la-Ronce (39) 102 C2
Abergement-le-Grand (39) 102 D4
Abergement-le-Petit (39) 103 E4
Abergement-lès-Thésy (39) 103 F4
l'Abergement-Sainte-Colombe (71) 101 H5
Abidos (64) 182 A1
Abilly (37) 95 E4
Abitain (64) 165 E6
Abjat-sur-Bandiat (24) 123 F4
Ablain-Saint-Nazaire (62) 8 B1
Ablaincourt-Pressoir (80) 8 B6
Ablainzevelle (62) 8 B3
Ablancourt (51) 46 A4
Ableiges (95) 42 B2
les Ableuvenettes (88) 69 G4
Ablis (78) 62 D1
Ablon (14) 16 B6
Ablon-sur-Seine (94) 42 D5
Aboën (42) 128 D6
Aboncourt (54) 69 E2
Aboncourt (57) 26 C4
Aboncourt-Gesincourt (70) 87 F2
Aboncourt-sur-Seille (57) 48 D4
Abondance (74) 119 F4
Abondant (28) 41 F4
Abos (64) 182 A1
Abreschviller (57) 50 A5
Abrest (03) 114 A6
les Abrets (38) 131 F5
Abriès (05) 147 G5
Abscon (59) 9 E2
l'Absie (79) 92 D6
Abzac (16) 109 G5
Abzac (33) 135 H4
Accolans (25) 88 A4
Accolay (89) 83 G3
Accons (07) 143 F5
Accous (64) 182 A5
Achain (57) 49 F3
Achen (57) 50 A1
Achenheim (67) 50 D5
Achères (18) 97 H1
Achères (78) 42 B3
Achères-la-Forêt (77) 63 H3
Achery (02) 22 A2
Acheux-en-Amiénois (80) 7 H4
Acheux-en-Vimeu (80) 6 C4
Acheville (62) 8 B1
Achey (70) 86 C4
Achicourt (62) 8 B2
Achiet-le-Grand (62) 8 B4
Achiet-le-Petit (62) 8 B4
Achun (58) 99 H2
Achy (60) 20 A3
Acigné (35) 57 G2
Aclou (27) 40 B1
Acon (27) 40 D4
Acq (62) 8 A2
Acqueville (14) 14 B6
Acqueville (50) 12 B2
Acquigny (27) 41 E1
Acquin-Westbécourt (62) 2 A4
Acy (02) 22 B5
Acy-en-Multien (60) 43 G2
Acy-Romance (08) 23 G4
Adaincourt (57) 49 E2
Adainville (78) 41 G5
Adam-lès-Passavant (25) 87 H6
Adam-lès-Vercel (25) 104 A1
Adamswiller (67) 50 B3
Adast (65) 182 D5
Adé (65) 183 E3
Adelange (57) 49 F2
Adelans-et-le-Val-de-Bithaine (70) 87 H2
Adervielle-Pouchergues (65) 197 E1
Adilly (79) 93 F6
Adinfer (62) 8 A3
Adissan (34) 172 C6
les Adjots (16) 108 D6
Adon (45) 82 B2
les Adrets (38) 146 A1
les Adrets-de-l'Estérel (83) 178 B5
Adriers (86) 109 H4
Afa (2A) 204 C5
Affieux (19) 125 E5
Affléville (54) 25 H5
Affoux (69) 129 F2
Affracourt (54) 69 G1
Affringues (62) 1 H4
Agassac (31) 184 C2
Agde (34) 188 D2
Agel (34) 187 H2
Agen (47) 151 F5
Agen-d'Aveyron (12) 154 D4
Agencourt (21) 101 H2
Agenville (80) 7 F3
Agenvillers (80) 7 E3
les Ageux (60) 20 D5
Ageville (52) 68 B5
Agey (21) 101 F1
Aghione (2B) 205 G4
Agincourt (54) 48 D4
Agmé (47) 150 D3
Agnac (47) 150 D1
Agnat (43) 141 H1
Agneaux (50) 37 F1
Agnetz (60) 20 C5
Agnez-lès-Duisans (62) 8 A2
Agnicourt-et-Séchelles (02) 23 E2
Agnières (62) 8 A2
Agnières-en-Dévoluy (05) 160 A1
Agnin (38) 144 A1
Agnos (64) 181 H3
Agny (62) 8 B3
Agon-Coutainville (50) 36 D1
Agonac (24) 137 F1
Agonès (34) 173 E3
Agonges (03) 113 G1
Agos-Vidalos (65) 182 D4
Agris (16) 122 D3
Agudelle (17) 121 F6
Aguessac (12) 155 F6
Aguilcourt (02) 23 E4
Aguts (81) 170 A6
Agy (14) 13 H5
Ahaxe-Alciette-Bascassan (64) 181 E3
Ahetze (64) 164 A6
Ahéville (88) 69 G3
Ahuillé (53) 58 C5
Ahun (23) 111 H6
Ahuy (21) 85 H6
Aibes (59) 10 B3
Aibre (25) 88 B4
Aïcirits-Camou-Suhast (64) 181 F1
Aiffres (79) 107 H4
Aigaliers (30) 174 A1
l'Aigle (61) 40 A4
Aiglemont (08) 24 B1
Aiglepierre (39) 103 E3
Aigleville (27) 41 F2
Aiglun (04) 177 E1
Aiglun (06) 178 C2
Aignan (32) 167 E4
Aignay-le-Duc (21) 85 F3
Aigne (34) 187 H2
Aigné (72) 60 A5
Aignerville (14) 13 G5
Aignes (31) 185 G2
Aignes-et-Puypéroux (16) 122 B6
Aigneville (80) 6 C4
Aigny (51) 45 G2
Aigonnay (79) 108 A3
Aigre (16) 122 B2
Aigrefeuille (31) 169 G6
Aigrefeuille-d'Aunis (17) 107 E5
Aigrefeuille-sur-Maine (44) 74 D6
Aigremont (30) 173 H2
Aigremont (52) 68 D5
Aigremont (78) 42 B3
Aigremont (89) 84 A3
Aiguebelette-le-Lac (73) 131 G5
Aiguebelle (73) 132 C5
Aigueblanche (73) 132 D5
Aiguefonde (81) 170 D6
Aigueperse (63) 127 F1
Aigueperse (69) 115 G4
Aigues-Juntes (09) 185 G4
Aigues-Mortes (30) 173 H6
Aigues-Vives (09) 186 B5
Aigues-Vives (11) 187 F3
Aigues-Vives (30) 173 H4
Aigues-Vives (34) 187 H2
Aiguèze (30) 157 H5
Aiguilhe (43) 142 C4
Aiguilles (05) 147 G6
l'Aiguillon (09) 186 B6
Aiguillon (47) 150 D5
l'Aiguillon-sur-Mer (85) 106 B3
l'Aiguillon-sur-Vie (85) 90 D4
Aiguines (83) 177 F3
Aigurande (36) 111 G3
Ailhon (07) 157 G2
Aillant-sur-Milleron (45) 82 C2
Aillant-sur-Tholon (89) 83 E1
Aillas (33) 150 A3
Ailleux (42) 128 C3
Aillevans (70) 87 H3
Ailleville (10) 67 E3
Aillevillers-et-Lyaumont (70) 69 H6
Aillianville (52) 68 B2
Aillières-Beauvoir (72) 60 B2
Aillon-le-Jeune (73) 132 A4
Aillon-le-Vieux (73) 132 A4
Ailloncourt (70) 87 H2
Ailly (27) 41 E1
Ailly-le-Haut-Clocher (80) 7 E4
Ailly-sur-Noye (80) 20 C1
Ailly-sur-Somme (80) 7 F6
Aimargues (30) 174 A5
Aime (73) 133 E4
Ainay-le-Château (03) 98 B6
Ainay-le-Vieil (18) 98 A6
Aincille (64) 181 E3
Aincourt (95) 41 H2
Aincreville (55) 24 D5
Aingeray (54) 48 B4
Aingeville (88) 68 D4
Aingoulaincourt (52) 68 A1
Ainharp (64) 181 F2
Ainhice-Mongelos (64) 181 E3
Ainhoa (64) 180 C1
Ainvelle (70) 87 G1
Ainvelle (88) 69 E5
Airaines (80) 7 E5
Airan (14) 14 D5
Aire (08) 23 F4
Aire-sur-la-Lys (62) 2 B5
Aire-sur-l'Adour (40) 166 B4
Airel (50) 13 F6
les Aires (34) 172 A6
Airion (60) 20 C4
Airon-Notre-Dame (62) 6 C1
Airon-Saint-Vaast (62) 6 C1
Airoux (11) 186 B2
Airvault (79) 93 G5
Aiserey (21) 102 A2
Aisey-et-Richecourt (70) 87 E1
Aisey-sur-Seine (21) 85 E2
Aisonville-et-Bernoville (02) 9 F5
Aïssey (25) 87 H6
Aisy-sous-Thil (21) 84 C5
Aisy-sur-Armançon (89) 84 C3
Aiti (2B) 205 F1
Aiton (73) 132 B4
Aix (19) 126 A4
Aix (59) 3 H6
les Aix-d'Angillon (18) 98 A2
Aix-en-Diois (26) 159 F1
Aix-en-Ergny (62) 1 H5
Aix-en-Issart (62) 1 G6
Aix-en-Othe (10) 65 G4
Aix-en-Provence (13) 176 A6
Aix-la-Fayette (63) 127 H5
Aix-les-Bains (73) 131 H3
Aix-Noulette (62) 8 A1
Aixe-sur-Vienne (87) 124 A3
Aizac (07) 157 F1
Aizanville (52) 67 G5
Aize (36) 96 C2
Aizecourt-le-Bas (80) 8 C5
Aizecourt-le-Haut (80) 8 C5
Aizelles (02) 22 D4
Aizenay (85) 91 F4
Aizier (27) 15 H2
Aizy-Jouy (02) 22 B4
Ajac (11) 186 C5
Ajaccio (2A) 204 C6
Ajain (23) 111 H5
Ajat (24) 137 H3
Ajoncourt (57) 48 D3
Ajou (27) 40 B2
Ajoux (07) 143 G6
Alaigne (11) 186 C4
Alaincourt (02) 22 A1
Alaincourt (70) 69 F6
Alaincourt-la-Côte (57) 48 D3
Alairac (11) 186 D3
Alan (31) 184 C3
Alando (2B) 205 F2
Alata (2A) 204 C5
Alba-la-Romaine (07) 157 H2
Alban (81) 171 E3
Albaret-le-Comtal (48) 141 F5
Albaret-Sainte-Marie (48) 141 G5
Albas (11) 187 G5
Albas (46) 152 B3
Albé (67) 71 F2
Albefeuille-Lagarde (82) 169 E1
l'Albenc (38) 145 E2
Albens (73) 131 H2
Albepierre-Bredons (15) 140 D3
l'Albère (66) 201 F4
Albert (80) 8 A5
Albertacce (2B) 204 D2
Albertville (73) 132 C3
Albestroff (57) 49 G3
Albi (81) 170 C2
Albiac (31) 169 H6
Albiac (46) 139 E6
Albias (82) 169 F1
Albières (11) 187 F6
Albiès (09) 199 F1
Albiez-le-Jeune (73) 146 C2
Albiez-Montrond (73) 146 C2
Albignac (19) 138 D3
Albigny-sur-Saône (69) 130 A2
Albine (81) 187 F1
Albitreccia (2A) 204 D6
Albon (26) 144 A2
Albon-d'Ardèche (07) 143 F6
Alboussière (07) 143 H5
les Albres (12) 153 H3
Albussac (19) 139 E3
Alby-sur-Chéran (74) 132 A2
Alçay-Alçabéhéty-Sunharette (64) 181 F4
Aldudes (64) 180 C3
Alembon (62) 1 G3
Alençon (61) 60 A2
Alénya (66) 201 F3
Aléria (2B) 205 H4
Alès (30) 157 E6
Alet-les-Bains (11) 186 D5
Alette (62) 1 G6
Aleu (09) 185 E6
Alex (74) 132 B1
Alexain (53) 58 C3
Aleyrac (26) 158 C3
Alfortville (94) 42 D4
Algajola (2B) 202 C5
Algans (81) 170 A5
Algolsheim (68) 71 G5
Algrange (57) 26 B3
Alièze (39) 117 G1
Alignan-du-Vent (34) 188 D1
Alincourt (08) 23 G4
Alincthun (62) 1 G4
Alise-Sainte-Reine (21) 84 D4
Alissas (07) 158 A1
Alix (69) 129 H2
Alixan (26) 144 C4
Alizay (27) 18 D5
Allain (54) 48 B6
Allaines (80) 8 C5
Allaines-Mervilliers (28) 62 D4
Allainville (28) 41 E5
Allainville (78) 62 D2
Allaire (56) 73 H1
Allamont (54) 48 A1
Allamps (54) 48 A6
Allan (26) 158 B3
Allanche (15) 141 E2
Alland'Huy-et-Sausseuil (08) 23 H3
Allarmont (88) 70 D1
Allas-Bocage (17) 121 F6
Allas-Champagne (17) 121 G5
Allas-les-Mines (24) 137 H6
Allassac (19) 138 C2
Allauch (13) 192 B3
Allègre (43) 142 B2
Allègre-les-Fumades (30) 157 F6
Alleins (13) 191 H2
Allemagne-en-Provence (04) 177 E3
Allemanche-Launay-et-Soyer (51) 45 E6
Allemans (24) 136 C1
Allemans-du-Dropt (47) 150 D2
Allemant (02) 22 B4
Allemant (51) 45 E5
Allemond (38) 146 A3
Allenay (80) 6 B4
Allenc (48) 156 B3
Allenjoie (25) 88 D4
Allennes-les-Marais (59) 3 F6
Allenwiller (67) 50 C5
Allerey (21) 101 E2
Allerey-sur-Saône (71) 101 H4
Allériot (71) 101 H5
Allery (80) 6 D5
Alles-sur-Dordogne (24) 137 G5
les Alleuds (49) 77 E6
les Alleuds (79) 108 C5
les Alleux (08) 24 B4
Alleuze (15) 141 F5
Allevard (38) 132 A6
Allèves (74) 132 A3
Allex (26) 144 B6
Alleyrac (43) 142 D5
Alleyras (43) 142 B5
Alleyrat (19) 125 H5
Alleyrat (23) 125 G1
Allez-et-Cazeneuve (47) 151 F4
Alliancelles (51) 46 C4
Alliat (09) 199 E1
Allibaudières (10) 45 F6
Allichamps (52) 46 C6
Allier (65) 183 F3
Allières (09) 185 F5
les Alliés (25) 104 A3
Alligny-Cosne (58) 82 C5
Alligny-en-Morvan (58) 100 C1
Allineuc (22) 33 F6
Allinges (74) 119 E3
Allogny (18) 97 G1
Allondans (25) 88 C4
Allondaz (73) 132 C3
Allondrelle-la-Malmaison (54) 25 F3
Allonne (60) 20 B5
Allonne (79) 107 H1
Allonnes (28) 62 C3
Allonnes (49) 77 H6
Allonnes (72) 60 A6
Allons (04) 178 A1
Allons (47) 150 A5
Allonville (80) 7 G5
Allonzier-la-Caille (74) 118 B6
Allos (04) 161 F5
Allouagne (62) 2 C6
Alloue (16) 109 F6
Allouis (18) 97 F2
Allouville-Bellefosse (76) 17 E5
les Allues (73) 132 D6
les Alluets-le-Roi (78) 42 A3
Alluy (58) 99 G3
Alluyes (28) 62 A4
Ally (15) 139 H3
Ally (43) 141 G3
Almayrac (81) 170 C1
Almenêches (61) 39 F5
Almont-les-Junies (12) 154 A2
Alos (09) 184 D6
Alos (81) 170 A2
Alos-Sibas-Abense (64) 181 G3
Aloxe-Corton (21) 101 G3
Alpuech (12) 140 D6
Alquines (62) 1 H4
Alrance (12) 154 D6
Alsting (57) 27 G4
Altagène (2A) 207 E2
Alteckendorf (67) 50 D4
Altenach (68) 89 E3
Altenheim (67) 50 C4
Althen-des-Paluds (84) 175 F2
Altiani (2B) 205 F3
Altier (48) 156 C3
Altillac (19) 139 E4
Altkirch (68) 89 F3
Altorf (67) 50 D6
Altrippe (57) 49 G2
Altviller (57) 49 G1
Altwiller (67) 49 H3
Aluze (71) 101 F5
Alvignac (46) 138 D6
Alvimare (76) 18 A3
Alzen (09) 185 G5
Alzi (2B) 205 F2
Alzing (57) 27 E4
Alzon (30) 172 C2
Alzonne (11) 186 D3
Amage (70) 88 A1
Amagne (08) 23 H3
Amagney (25) 87 G6
Amailloux (79) 93 F5
Amance (10) 66 D3
Amance (54) 48 D4
Amance (70) 87 F1
Amancey (25) 103 G3
Amancy (74) 118 D6
Amange (39) 102 D2
Amanlis (35) 57 G4
Amanty (55) 68 C1
Amanvillers (57) 26 B5
Amanzé (71) 115 F4
Amarens (81) 170 A1
Amathay-Vésigneux (25) 103 H3
Amayé-sur-Orne (14) 14 B5
Amayé-sur-Seulles (14) 38 A1
Amazy (58) 83 G6
Ambacourt (88) 69 F2
Ambarès-et-Lagrave (33) 135 F4
Ambax (31) 184 C2
Ambazac (87) 124 C1
Ambel (38) 145 H6
Ambenay (27) 40 B4
Ambérac (16) 122 B2
Ambérieu-en-Bugey (01) 130 D1
Ambérieux (69) 129 H1
Ambérieux-en-Dombes (01) 130 B1
Ambernac (16) 123 E1
Amberre (86) 94 A5
Ambert (63) 128 B5
Ambès (33) 135 F4
Ambeyrac (12) 153 G3
Ambialet (81) 170 D2
Ambiegna (2A) 204 C4
Ambierle (42) 114 D6
Ambiévillers (70) 69 G6
Ambillou (37) 78 C5
Ambillou-Château (49) 77 F6
Ambilly (74) 118 C4
Amblainville (60) 20 B6
Amblans-et-Velotte (70) 87 H2
Ambleny (02) 21 H5
Ambléon (01) 131 F3
Ambleteuse (62) 1 F3
Ambleville (16) 121 H5
Ambleville (95) 41 H1
Amblie (14) 14 B3
Amblimont (08) 24 D2
Ambloy (41) 79 F2
Ambly-Fleury (08) 23 H4
Ambly-sur-Meuse (55) 47 G2
Amboise (37) 79 F5
Ambon (56) 73 E2

Ambonil (26)..........144 B6
Ambonnay (51)..........45 G2
Ambonville (52)..........67 G3
Ambrault (36)..........97 E5
Ambres (81)..........169 H4
Ambricourt (62)..........2 C4
Ambrief (02)..........22 B5
Ambrières (51)..........46 C6
Ambrières-les-Vallées (53)..58 D2
Ambronay (01)..........130 D1
Ambrugeat (19)..........125 G5
Ambrumesnil (76)..........17 G2
Ambrus (47)..........150 C5
Ambutrix (01)..........130 D1
Amécourt (27)..........19 G5
Amel-sur-l'Étang (55)..........25 G6
Amélécourt (57)..........49 E3
Amélie-les-
Bains-Palalda (66)..........200 D4
Amendeuix-Oneix (64)..........181 F1
Amenoncourt (54)..........49 G5
Amenucourt (54)..........41 G1
Ames (62)..........2 C6
Amettes (62)..........2 B6
Amfreville (71)..........116 A2
Ameuvelle (88)..........69 E6
Amfreville (14)..........14 C4
Amfreville (50)..........12 D4
Amfreville-la-Campagne (27)..18 B6
Amfreville-la-Mi-Voie (76)..18 D4
Amfreville-les-Champs (27)..19 E5
Amfreville-les-Champs (76)..17 F4
Amfreville-sous-
les-Monts (27)..........18 D5
Amfreville-sur-Iton (27)..........40 D1
Amfroipret (59)..........9 G2
Amiens (80)..........7 G6
Amifontaine (02)..........23 E4
Amigny (50)..........13 E6
Amigny-Rouy (02)..........22 A3
Amillis (77)..........43 H5
Amilly (28)..........62 A2
Amilly (45)..........64 B6
Amions (42)..........128 D2
Amirat (06)..........178 B2
Ammerschwihr (68)..........71 F4
Ammerzwiller (68)..........89 E2
Amné (72)..........59 H5
Amnéville (57)..........26 B4
Amoncourt (70)..........87 F2
Amondans (25)..........103 G2
Amont-et-Effreney (70)..........88 A1
Amorots-Succos (64)..........181 E1
Amou (40)..........165 G5
Ampilly-le-Sec (21)..........85 E2
Ampilly-les-Bordes (21)..........85 E3
Amplepuis (69)..........129 F1
Amplier (62)..........7 G4
Ampoigné (53)..........76 C1
Amponville (77)..........63 H3
Ampriani (2B)..........205 G2
Ampuis (69)..........130 A5
Ampus (83)..........177 G5
Amuré (79)..........107 G4
Amy (60)..........21 F2
Anais (16)..........122 C3
Anais (17)..........107 E4
Anan (31)..........184 B2
Ance (64)..........181 H3
Anceaumeville (76)..........17 G5
Anceins (61)..........39 H3
Ancelle (05)..........160 C1
Ancemont (55)..........47 F2
Ancenis (44)..........75 F4
Ancerville (55)..........46 D6
Ancerville (57)..........26 D6
Ancerviller (54)..........49 G6
Ancey (21)..........85 H6
Anchamps (08)..........11 E5
Anché (37)..........94 B2
Anché (86)..........108 D3
Anchenoncourt-
et-Chazel (70)..........87 F1
Ancienville (02)..........21 H6
Ancier (70)..........86 D5
Ancinnes (72)..........60 A2
Ancizan (65)..........183 G6
les Ancizes-Comps (63)..126 D2
Ancône (04)..........158 A2
Ancourt (76)..........17 H2
Ancourteville-sur-
Héricourt (76)..........17 E4
Ancretiéville-Saint-Victor (76)..17 G4
Ancretteville-sur-Mer (76)..16 D3
Ancteville (50)..........36 D1
Anctoville (14)..........38 A1
Anctoville-sur-Boscq (50)..35 G2
Ancy (69)..........129 G2
Ancy-le-Franc (89)..........84 B2
Ancy-le-Libre (89)..........84 B3
Ancy-sur-Moselle (57)..........26 B6
Andainville (80)..........6 D6
Andance (07)..........144 A2
Andancette (26)..........144 A2
Andard (49)..........77 E4
Andé (27)..........18 D6
Andechy (80)..........21 E2
Andelain (02)..........22 A3
Andelaroche (03)..........114 C4
Andelarre (70)..........87 F3
Andelarrot (70)..........87 F3
Andelat (15)..........141 E4
Andelnans (90)..........88 C3
Andelot-Blancheville (52)..68 A3
Andelot-en-Montagne (39)..103 F4
Andelot-Morval (39)..........117 F3
Andelu (78)..........41 H3
les Andelys (27)..........19 E6
Andernay (55)..........46 D4
Andernos-les-Bains (33)..134 B6
Anderny (54)..........26 A3
Andert-et-Condon (01)..131 F2
Andeville (60)..........20 B6
Andigné (49)..........76 D2
Andillac (81)..........170 A2
Andilly (17)..........106 D4
Andilly (54)..........48 B4
Andilly (74)..........118 B5
Andilly (95)..........42 C2
Andilly-en-Bassigny (52)..68 B6
Andiran (47)..........150 C6
Andlau (67)..........71 F2
Andoins (64)..........182 C2
Andolsheim (68)..........71 F4
Andon (06)..........178 B3
Andonville (45)..........63 E3
Andornay (70)..........88 B3
Andouillé (53)..........58 C4
Andouillé-Neuville (35)..........57 F1
Andouque (81)..........170 D1
Andrein (64)..........181 G1
Andres (62)..........1 H3
Andrest (65)..........183 E2
Andrésy (78)..........42 B3
Andrezé (49)..........75 G5
Andrezel (77)..........43 F6
Andrézieux-Bouthéon (42)..129 E4
Andryes (89)..........83 F4
Anduze (30)..........173 G1
Anéran-Camors (65)..........183 H6
Anet (28)..........41 F4
Angaïs (64)..........182 C3
Angé (41)..........79 H6
Angeac-Champagne (16)..122 A4
Angeac-Charente (16)..122 A4
Angecourt (08)..........24 C2
Angeduc (16)..........122 A5
Angely (89)..........84 A4
Angeot (90)..........88 D2
Angers (49)..........76 D4
Angerville (14)..........14 D4
Angerville (91)..........63 E3
Angerville-Bailleul (76)..16 D4
Angerville-la-Martel (76)..16 D3
Angerville-l'Orcher (76)..16 D1
Angervilliers (91)..........42 B6
Angeville (82)..........168 C2

Angevillers (57)..........26 B3
Angey (50)..........35 G3
Angicourt (60)..........20 D5
Angiens (76)..........17 E2
Angirey (70)..........86 D4
Angivillers (60)..........20 D6
Anglade (33)..........135 E2
Anglards-de-
Saint-Flour (15)..........141 F4
Anglards-de-Salers (15)..140 A2
Anglars (46)..........153 F1
Anglars-Juillac (46)..........152 B3
Anglars-Nozac (46)..........138 C6
Anglars-Saint-Félix (12)..153 H4
Anglefort (01)..........131 G1
Anglemont (88)..........70 B2
Angles (04)..........177 H2
les Angles (30)..........174 D2
les Angles (65)..........183 E4
les Angles (66)..........199 H3
Angles (81)..........171 E6
les Angles (85)..........106 B2
les Angles-sur-Corrèze (19)..139 E1
Angles-sur-l'Anglin (86)..95 F6
Anglesqueville-
la-Bras-Long (76)..........17 E3
Anglesqueville-l'Esneval (76)..16 B4
Anglet (64)..........164 B6
Angliers (17)..........107 E4
Angliers (86)..........94 A3
Anglure (51)..........45 E6
Anglure-sous-Dun (71)..115 G4
Angluzelles-et-
Courcelles (51)..........45 E6
Angoisse (24)..........124 A6
Angomont (54)..........49 H6
Angos (65)..........183 F3
Angoulême (16)..........122 B4
Angoulins (17)..........106 D5
Angoumé (40)..........164 D4
Angous (64)..........181 G2
Angoustrine-Villeneuve-
des-Escaldes (66)..........199 G3
Angoville (14)..........38 C3
Angoville-au-Plain (50)..13 E4
Angoville-sur-Ay (50)..12 C5
Angres (62)..........8 B1
Angresse (40)..........164 C4
Angrie (49)..........76 B3
Anguerny (14)..........14 B4
Anguilcourt-le-Sart (02)..22 B2
Angy (60)..........20 C5
Anhaux (64)..........180 D3
Anhiers (59)..........8 D1
Aniane (34)..........172 D5
Aniche (59)..........9 E2
Anizy (14)..........14 B4
Anizy-le-Château (02)..22 B4
Anjeux (70)..........87 G1
Anjou (38)..........144 B1
Anjouin (36)..........96 D2
Anjoutey (90)..........88 D2
Anla (65)..........184 A5
Anlezy (58)..........99 G4
Anlhiac (24)..........138 A1
Annay (58)..........82 C4
Annay (62)..........8 B1
Annay-la-Côte (89)..........84 A4
Annay-sur-Serein (89)..........84 A2
Annebault (14)..........15 E4
Annecy (74)..........132 A1
Annecy-le-Vieux (74)..132 B1
Annelles (08)..........23 G4
Annemasse (74)..........118 C4
Annéot (89)..........84 A4
Annepont (17)..........121 E2
Annequin (62)..........2 D6
Annesse-et-Beaulieu (24)..137 E2
Annet-sur-Marne (77)..43 F3
Anneux (59)..........8 D3
Annéville-Ambourville (76)..17 F6
Anneville-en-Saire (50)..13 E2
Anneville-la-Prairie (52)..67 H4
Anneville-sur-Mer (50)..12 C6
Anneville-sur-Scie (76)..17 G2
Anneyron (26)..........144 B2
Annezay (17)..........107 F6
Annezin (62)..........2 D6
Annœullin (59)..........8 C1
Annoire (39)..........102 B4
Annois (02)..........21 H2
Annoisin-Chatelans (38)..130 D3
Annoix (18)..........97 H4
Annonay (07)..........143 H2
Annonville (52)..........68 A2
Annot (04)..........178 A2
Annouville-Vilmesnil (76)..16 C4
Annoux (89)..........84 B3
Annoville (50)..........35 G1
Anor (59)..........10 B5
Anos (64)..........182 C1
Anost (71)..........100 B3
Anould (88)..........70 D3
Anoux (54)..........25 H5
Anoye (64)..........182 D1
Anquetierville (76)..........18 A3
Anrosey (52)..........86 D1
Ansac-sur-Vienne (16)..123 F1
Ansacq (60)..........20 C5
Ansan (32)..........168 A4
Ansauville (54)..........48 A4
Ansauvillers (60)..........20 C3
Anse (69)..........129 H1
Ansignan (66)..........200 C2
Ansost (65)..........183 F1
Ansouis (84)..........176 A4
Anstaing (59)..........3 G5
Antagnac (47)..........150 B4
Anterrieux (15)..........141 F6
Anteuil (25)..........88 B5
Antezant-la-Chapelle (17)..107 H6
Anthé (47)..........151 H4
Anthelupt (54)..........49 E6
Anthenay (51)..........44 D1
Antheny (08)..........10 C6
Antheuil (21)..........101 F2
Antheuil-Portes (60)..........21 E4
Anthien (58)..........83 H6
Anthon (38)..........130 C3
Anthy-sur-Léman (74)..118 D3
Antibes (06)..........195 E4
Antichan (65)..........184 A5
Antichan-de-Frontignes (31)..184 A5
Antignac (15)..........140 A2
Antignac (31)..........197 F1
Antigny (85)..........92 C6
Antigny (86)..........109 H2
Antigny-la-Ville (21)..101 E2
Antilly (57)..........26 C5
Antilly (60)..........43 G1
Antin (65)..........183 G2
Antisanti (2B)..........205 G2
Antist (65)..........183 F4
Antogny-le-Tillac (37)..94 D3
Antoigné (49)..........93 G2
Antoigny (61)..........39 H5
Antonaves (05)..........160 A4
Antony (92)..........42 C5
Antraigues-sur-Volane (07)..157 G1
Antrain (35)..........35 H5
Antran (86)..........94 D4
Antras (09)..........198 C4
Antras (32)..........167 H4
Antrenas (48)..........155 G2
Antugnac (11)..........186 D5
Anvéville (76)..........17 E4
Anville (16)..........122 A2
Anvin (62)..........7 F1
Any-Martin-Rieux (02)..10 C4
Anzat-le-Luguet (63)..141 E1
Anzeling (57)..........26 D4
Anzex (47)..........150 B5
Anzin (59)..........9 F2
Anzin-Saint-Aubin (62)..8 A2
Anzy-le-Duc (71)..........115 E4

Aougny (51)..........44 D1
Aouste (08)..........23 G1
Aouste-sur-Sye (26)..158 C1
Aouze (88)..........69 E2
Apach (57)..........26 D2
Apchat (63)..........141 F1
Apchon (15)..........140 C2
Apinac (42)..........142 D1
Appelle (81)..........170 A5
Appenai-sous-Bellême (61)..60 D2
Appenans (25)..........88 B5
Appenwihr (68)..........71 G5
Appeville (50)..........12 D5
Appeville-Annebault (27)..18 A5
Appietto (2A)..........204 C5
Appilly (60)..........21 H3
Appoigny (89)..........83 F1
Apprieu (38)..........131 E6
Appy (09)..........199 F1
Apremont (01)..........117 G4
Apremont (08)..........24 C6
Apremont (60)..........20 D6
Apremont (70)..........86 C5
Apremont (73)..........131 H5
Apremont (85)..........91 F3
Apremont-la-Forêt (55)..47 H4
Apremont-sur-Allier (18)..98 D4
Aprey (52)..........86 A2
Apt (84)..........176 A3
Arabaux (09)..........185 H5
Arâches-la-Frasse (74)..119 F6
Aragnouet (65)..........196 D1
Aragon (11)..........187 E2
Aramits (64)..........181 H3
Aramon (30)..........174 D3
Aranc (01)..........117 F6
Arancou (64)..........165 E6
Arandas (01)..........131 E2
Arandon (38)..........131 E3
Araujuzon (64)..........181 G1
Araules (43)..........143 E3
Araux (64)..........181 G1
Arbanats (33)..........149 G1
Arbas (31)..........184 C5
Arbecey (70)..........87 E2
Arbellara (2A)..........207 E3
Arbent (01)..........117 G4
Arbéost (65)..........182 C5
Arbérats-Sillègue (64)..181 F1
Arbignieu (01)..........131 F3
Arbigny (01)..........116 C2
Arbigny-sous-Varennes (52)..86 C1
Arbin (73)..........132 A4
Arbis (33)..........149 H1
Arblade-le-Bas (32)..166 C4
Arblade-le-Haut (32)..166 D4
Arbois (39)..........103 E4
Arbonne (64)..........164 B6
Arbonne-la-Forêt (77)..63 H3
Arboras (34)..........172 D4
Arbori (2A)..........204 C4
Arbot (52)..........85 H2
Arbouans (25)..........88 C4
Arboucave (40)..........166 A5
Arbouet-Sussaute (64)..181 F1
Arbourse (58)..........99 E1
Arboussols (66)..........200 C2
l'Arbresle (69)..........129 G2
Arbrissel (35)..........57 H4
Arbus (64)..........182 A2
Arbusigny (74)..........118 C5
Arc-en-Barrois (52)..67 G6
Arc-et-Senans (25)..103 E3
Arc-lès-Gray (70)..........86 C5
Arc-sous-Cicon (25)..104 A2
Arc-sous-Montenot (25)..103 F4
Arc-sur-Tille (21)..........86 A6
Arcachon (33)..........148 B1
Arçais (79)..........107 F3
Arcambal (46)..........152 D3
Arcangues (64)..........164 B6
Arçay (18)..........97 G4
Arçay (86)..........93 H3
Arceau (21)..........86 A5
Arcenant (21)..........101 G2
Arcens (07)..........143 F5
Arces (17)..........120 D4
Arces-Dilo (89)..........65 G4
Arcey (21)..........101 G1
Arcey (25)..........88 B4
Archail (04)..........160 D6
Archamps (74)..........118 C5
Archelange (39)..........102 C2
Arches (15)..........140 A1
Arches (88)..........70 A4
Archettes (88)..........70 A4
Archiac (17)..........121 G4
Archignac (24)..........138 B4
Archignat (03)..........112 C3
Archigny (86)..........94 D6
Archingeay (17)..........121 E1
Archon (02)..........23 E1
Arcinges (42)..........115 F5
Arcins (33)..........134 D2
Arcis-le-Ponsart (51)..22 C6
Arcis-sur-Aube (10)..........66 B1
Arcizac-Adour (65)..........183 E3
Arcizac-Ez-Angles (65)..183 E4
Arcizans-Avant (65)..........182 D5
Arcizans-Dessus (65)..........182 D5
Arçon (25)..........104 A3
Arçonnay (72)..........60 A2
Arconcey (21)..........101 E1
Arconsat (63)..........128 B2
Arconville (10)..........67 E4
les Arcs (83)..........177 H6
Arcueil (94)..........42 D4
Arcy-Sainte-Restitue (02)..22 B6
Arcy-sur-Cure (89)..........83 H4
Ardelles (28)..........61 G2
Ardelu (28)..........62 D3
Ardenais (18)..........112 A1
Ardenay-sur-Mérize (72)..60 C6
Ardengost (65)..........183 G5
Ardentes (36)..........96 D6
Ardes (63)..........127 F6
Ardeuil-et-
Montfauxelles (08)..........24 B6
Ardiège (31)..........184 A4
les Ardillats (69)..........115 H5
Ardilleux (79)..........108 B5
Ardillières (17)..........107 E6
Ardin (79)..........107 G2
Ardizas (32)..........168 C4
Ardoix (07)..........143 H2
Ardon (39)..........103 F5
Ardon (45)..........80 D2
Ardouval (76)..........17 H3
Ardres (62)..........1 H3
Aregno (2B)..........202 C5
Areines (41)..........79 G2
Aren (64)..........181 H2
Arengosse (40)..........165 G2
Arenthon (74)..........118 D5
Arès (33)..........134 B6
Aresches (39)..........103 F4
Aressy (64)..........182 C2
Arette (64)..........181 H3
Arfeuille-Châtain (23)..112 C6
Arfeuilles (03)..........114 C5
Arfons (81)..........186 C1
Argagnon (64)..........165 H6
Argancy (57)..........26 B5
Argançon (10)..........67 E3
Argein (09)..........184 D5
Argelès-Bagnères (65)..183 F4
Argelès-Gazost (65)..........182 D5
Argelès-sur-Mer (66)..........201 G3
Argeliers (11)..........188 A3
Argelliers (34)..........173 E4
Argelos (40)..........165 H5
Argelos (64)..........166 A6
Argelouse (40)..........149 E4
Argences (14)..........14 D5
Argens-Minervois (11)..187 F3
Argent-sur-Sauldre (18)..81 G4
Argentan (61)..........39 E4

Argentat (19)..........139 F3
Argentenay (89)..........84 B2
Argenteuil (95)..........42 C3
Argenteuil-sur-
l'Armançon (89)..........84 B2
Argentière-la-Bessée (05)..147 E6
Argentières (77)..........43 G6
Argentine (73)..........132 C5
Argenton (47)..........150 B4
Argenton-l'Église (79)..93 F3
Argenton-les-Vallées (79)..93 E3
Argenton-Notre-Dame (53)..77 E2
Argenton-sur-Creuse (36)..111 E1
Argentré (53)..........58 D4
Argentré-du-Plessis (35)..58 A5
Argenvières (18)..........98 C2
Argenvilliers (28)..........61 F3
Argers (51)..........46 C2
Arget (64)..........165 H5
Argiésans (90)..........88 C3
Argillières (70)..........86 D3
Argilliers (30)..........174 C2
Argilly (21)..........101 H3
Argis (01)..........117 F6
Argiusta-Moriccio (2A)..207 E1
Argœuves (80)..........7 F5
Argol (29)..........31 E6
Argonay (74)..........132 B1
Argouges (50)..........35 H5
Argoules (80)..........6 D2
Arguel (25)..........103 F2
Arguel (80)..........6 D6
Arguenos (31)..........184 B5
Argut-Dessous (31)..........184 B6
Argy (36)..........96 B4
Arhansus (64)..........181 F2
Aries-Espénan (65)..........183 H2
Arifat (81)..........170 D4
Arignac (09)..........185 G6
Arinthod (39)..........117 F2
Arith (73)..........132 A3
Arjuzanx (40)..........165 F1
Arlanc (63)..........142 C1
Arlay (39)..........102 D5
Arlebosc (07)..........143 H4
Arlempdes (43)..........142 C5
Arles (13)..........174 C5
Arles-sur-Tech (66)..........200 D4
Arleuf (58)..........100 B3
Arleux (59)..........8 D2
Arleux-en-Gohelle (62)..8 B2
Arlos (31)..........184 B6
Armaillé (49)..........76 A2
Armancourt (60)..........21 E5
Armancourt (80)..........21 E2
Armaucourt (54)..........48 D4
Armbouts-Cappel (59)..........2 B2
Armeau (89)..........65 E5
Armendarits (64)..........181 E2
Armenteule (65)..........197 E1
Armentières (59)..........3 E4
Armentières-en-Brie (77)..43 H3
Armentières-sur-Avre (27)..40 B5
Armentières-sur-Ourcq (02)..44 B1
Armentieux (32)..........167 E5
Armes (58)..........83 G5
Armillac (47)..........150 D2
Armissan (11)..........188 B3
Armix (01)..........131 F2
Armous-et-Cau (32)..........167 E5
Armoy (74)..........118 D3
Arnac (15)..........139 H4
Arnac-la-Poste (87)..........110 D4
Arnac-Pompadour (19)..124 B6
Arnac-sur-Dourdou (12)..171 H4
Arnage (72)..........60 A6
Arnancourt (52)..........67 G2
Arnas (69)..........116 B6
Arnave (09)..........185 H6
Arnaville (54)..........26 B6
Arnay-le-Duc (21)..........101 E2
Arnay-sous-Vitteaux (21)..84 D5
Arnayon (26)..........159 E3
Arné (65)..........183 H3
Arnéguy (64)..........180 D3
Arnicourt (08)..........23 G3
Arnières-sur-Iton (27)..40 D2
Arnos (64)..........165 H6
Arnouville-lès-Gonesse (95)..42 D3
Arnouville-lès-Mantes (78)..41 H3
Aroffe (88)..........69 E2
Aromas (39)..........117 F3
Aron (53)..........59 E3
Aroue-Ithorots-Olhaïby (64)..181 F2
Aroz (70)..........87 F3
Arpaillargues-et-
Aureillac (30)..........174 B2
Arpajon (91)..........42 C6
Arpajon-sur-Cère (15)..140 B5
Arpavon (26)..........159 E4
Arpenans (70)..........88 A3
Arpheuilles (18)..........98 A5
Arpheuilles (36)..........95 H4
Arpheuilles-Saint-Priest (03)..112 D5
Arphy (30)..........172 C2
Arquenay (53)..........58 D5
Arques (11)..........187 E5
Arques (12)..........154 D5
les Arques (46)..........152 B2
Arques (62)..........2 B4
Arques-la-Bataille (76)..17 G2
Arquettes-en-Val (11)..187 E4
Arquèves (80)..........7 H4
Arquian (58)..........82 C4
Arracourt (54)..........49 E4
Arradon (56)..........72 D1
Arraincourt (57)..........49 E2
Arrancourt (91)..........63 F2
Arrancy (02)..........22 D4
Arrancy-sur-Crusne (55)..25 G4
Arras (62)..........8 A2
Arras-en-Lavedan (65)..182 D5
Arras-sur-Rhône (07)..144 A3
Arrast-Larrebieu (64)..........181 G2
Arraute-Charritte (64)..181 E1
Arraye-et-Han (54)..........48 D3
Arrayou-Lahitte (65)..........183 E4
Arre (30)..........172 C2
Arreau (65)..........183 G6
Arrelles (10)..........66 C5
Arrembécourt (10)..........67 E1
Arrènes (23)..........111 E6
Arrens-Marsous (65)..........182 C5
Arrentès-de-Corcieux (88)..70 D4
Arrentières (10)..........67 E3
Arrest (80)..........6 C4
Arreux (08)..........11 E6
Arriance (57)..........49 E1
Arricau-Bordes (64)..........166 B6
Arrien (64)..........182 C2
Arrien-en-Bethmale (09)..184 D6
Arrigas (30)..........172 C2
Arrigny (51)..........46 B6
Arro (2A)..........204 C4
Arrodets (65)..........183 G4
Arrodets-Ez-Angles (65)..183 E4
Arromanches-les-Bains (14)..14 A3
Arronnes (03)..........114 B6
Arronville (95)..........42 B1
Arros-de-Nay (64)..........182 C3
Arrosès (64)..........166 C6
Arrou (28)..........61 G5
Arrouède (32)..........184 A2
Arry (57)..........48 C1
Arry (80)..........6 C2
Ars (16)..........121 H4
Ars (23)..........125 E3
Ars-en-Ré (17)..........106 A4
Ars-Laquenexy (57)..........26 C6
Ars-les-Favets (63)..........112 D5
Ars-sur-Formans (01)..........130 A1
Ars-sur-Moselle (57)..........26 B6
Arsac (33)..........135 E3
Arsac-en-Velay (43)..........142 C4
Arsague (40)..........165 G5

Arsans (70)..........86 D5
Arsonval (10)..........67 E3
Arsure-Arsurette (39)..103 G5
les Arsures (39)..........103 E3
Art-sur-Meurthe (54)..........48 D5
Artagnan (65)..........183 E1
Artaise-le-Vivier (08)..........24 C2
Artaix (71)..........115 E4
Artalens-Souin (65)..........182 D5
Artannes-sur-Indre (37)..94 D1
Artannes-sur-Thouet (49)..93 H1
Artas (38)..........130 C5
Artassenx (40)..........166 B3
Artemare (01)..........131 F2
Artemps (02)..........21 H1
Artenay (45)..........62 D5
Arthaz-Pont-
Notre-Dame (74)..........118 C5
Arthel (58)..........99 F1
Arthémonay (26)..........144 C3
Arthenac (17)..........121 G5
Arthenas (39)..........117 F1
Arthès (81)..........170 C2
Arthez-d'Armagnac (40)..166 B2
Arthez-d'Asson (64)..........182 C4
Arthez-de-Béarn (64)..165 H6
Arthezé (72)..........77 G2
Arthies (95)..........41 H2
Arthon (36)..........96 C6
Arthon-en-Retz (44)..........74 A6
Arthonnay (89)..........66 C6
Arthun (42)..........128 D3
Artignosc-sur-Verdon (83)..177 E4
Artigue (31)..........184 A6
Artiguedieu (32)..........167 H5
Artigueloutan (64)..........182 C2
Artiguelouve (64)..........182 B2
Artiguemy (65)..........183 F4
Artigues (09)..........199 F2
Artigues (11)..........200 D1
Artigues (65)..........183 E4
Artigues (83)..........176 D5
les Artigues-de-Lussac (33)..135 H4
Artigues-près-
Bordeaux (33)..........135 F5
Artins (41)..........79 E2
Artix (09)..........185 G4
Artix (64)..........182 A1
Artolsheim (67)..........71 G3
Artonges (02)..........44 C3
Artonne (63)..........127 F2
Artres (59)..........9 F3
Artzenheim (68)..........71 G4
Arudy (64)..........182 B4
Arue (40)..........166 B1
Arvert (17)..........120 B2
Arveyres (33)..........135 G5
Arvieu (12)..........154 C6
Arvieux (05)..........147 F6
Arvigna (09)..........186 A4
Arvillard (73)..........132 B6
Arville (41)..........61 F5
Arville (77)..........63 H4
Arvillers (80)..........21 E1
Arx (40)..........150 B6
Arzacq-Arraziguet (64)..166 A5
Arzal (56)..........73 F2
Arzano (29)..........54 B3
Arzay (38)..........130 C6
Arzembouy (58)..........99 F1
Arzenc-d'Apcher (48)..141 F5
Arzenc-de-Randon (48)..156 B2
Arzens (11)..........186 D3
Arzillières-Neuville (51)..46 B5
Arzon (56)..........72 C2
Arzviller (57)..........50 A4
Asasp-Arros (64)..........182 A3
Ascain (64)..........180 B1
Ascarat (64)..........180 D3
Aschbach (67)..........51 F2
Aschères-le-Marché (45)..63 E5
Asco (2B)..........202 D6
Ascou (09)..........199 G2
Ascoux (45)..........63 F5
Ascros (06)..........178 C2
Asfeld (08)..........23 F4
Aslonnes (86)..........109 E2
Asnan (58)..........83 G6
Asnans-Beauvoisin (39)..102 C4
Asnelles (14)..........14 A3
Asnières (27)..........15 H5
Asnières-en-Bessin (14)..13 G4
Asnières-en-Montagne (21)..84 C3
Asnières-en-Poitou (79)..108 B5
Asnières-la-Giraud (17)..121 F1
Asnières-lès-Dijon (21)..85 H5
Asnières-sous-Bois (89)..83 G4
Asnières-sur-Blour (86)..109 G4
Asnières-sur-Nouère (16)..122 B3
Asnières-sur-Oise (95)..42 D2
Asnières-sur-Saône (01)..116 B3
Asnières-sur-Seine (92)..42 C3
Asnières-sur-Vègre (72)..59 F6
Asnois (58)..........83 G5
Asnois (86)..........109 E5
Aspach (57)..........49 G4
Aspach (68)..........89 E2
Aspach-le-Bas (68)..........89 E2
Aspach-le-Haut (68)..........89 E2
Aspères (30)..........173 G3
Asperjoc (07)..........157 G1
Aspet (31)..........184 C4
Aspin-Aure (65)..........183 G6
Aspin-en-Lavedan (65)..182 D4
Aspiran (34)..........172 C6
Aspremont (05)..........159 H3
Aspremont (06)..........179 F3
les Aspres (61)..........40 A5
Aspres-lès-Corps (05)..146 A6
Aspres-sur-Buëch (05)..159 H2
Aspret-Sarrat (31)..........184 B4
Asprières (12)..........153 G3
Asques (33)..........135 F4
Asques (82)..........168 B2
Asquins (89)..........83 H4
Assac (81)..........170 D2
Assainvillers (80)..........21 E3
Assais-les-Jumeaux (79)..93 H5
Assas (34)..........173 F4
Assat (64)..........182 C2
Assay (37)..........94 B3
Assé-le-Bérenger (53)..59 F4
Assé-le-Boisne (72)..........59 H3
Assé-le-Riboul (72)..........60 A4
Assenay (10)..........66 B4
Assencières (10)..........66 C3
Assenoncourt (57)..........49 G4
Assérac (44)..........73 F3
Assevent (59)..........10 A2
Assevillers (80)..........8 A6
Assier (46)..........153 F2
Assieu (38)..........130 B6
Assignan (34)..........187 G2
Assigny (18)..........81 H5
Assigny (76)..........17 H1
les Assions (07)..........157 E4
Assis-sur-Serre (02)..22 C2
Asson (64)..........182 C3
Asswiller (67)..........50 B3
Astaffort (47)..........168 A1
Astaillac (19)..........139 E5
Asté (65)..........183 F4
Aste-Béon (64)..........182 B4
Astet (07)..........157 E1
Astillé (53)..........58 C5
Astis (64)..........166 B6
Aston (09)..........199 E1
Astugue (65)..........183 F4

Athée (21)..........86 C6
Athée (53)..........58 B6
Athée-sur-Cher (37)..........79 F6
Athesans-Étroitefontaine (70)..88 A3
Athie (21)..........84 C4
Athie (89)..........84 A3
Athienville (54)..........49 E4
Athies (62)..........8 B2
Athies (80)..........8 B6
Athies-sous-Laon (02)..22 D3
Athis (51)..........45 F2
Athis-de-l'Orne (61)..........38 B4
Athis-Mons (91)..........42 D5
Athos-Aspis (64)..........181 F1
Athose (25)..........103 H2
Attainville (95)..........42 D2
Attancourt (52)..........67 G1
les Attaques (62)..........1 H2
Attenschwiller (68)..........89 G3
Attiches (59)..........3 F6
Attichy (60)..........21 G4
Attignat (01)..........116 D4
Attignat-Oncin (73)..........131 G5
Attignéville (88)..........68 D2
Attigny (08)..........24 A4
Attigny (88)..........69 F5
Attilloncourt (57)..........49 E4
Attilly (02)..........8 D6
Attin (62)..........6 C1
Atton (54)..........48 C3
Attray (45)..........63 E5
Attricourt (70)..........86 B4
Atur (24)..........137 F3
Aubagnan (40)..........166 A4
Aubagne (13)..........192 C4
Aubaine (21)..........101 F2
Aubais (30)..........173 H4
Aubarède (65)..........183 F2
Aubas (24)..........138 A3
Aubazat (43)..........141 H3
Aubazines (19)..........138 D3
Aube (57)..........26 C6
Aube (61)..........40 A5
Aubéguimont (76)..........19 G1
Aubenas (07)..........157 G2
Aubenas-les-Alpes (04)..176 C2
Aubenasson (26)..........158 C1
Aubencheul-au-Bac (59)..8 D3
Aubencheul-aux-Bois (02)..9 E5
Aubenton (02)..........10 B6
Aubepierre-Ozouer-
le-Repos (77)..........43 G6
Aubepierre-sur-Aube (52)..85 G1
l'Aubépin (39)..........117 E2
Auberchicourt (59)..........8 D2
Aubercourt (80)..........20 D1
Aubergenville (78)..........42 A3
Aubérive (51)..........23 G6
Auberive (52)..........85 H2
Auberives-en-Royans (38)..144 D3
Auberives-sur-Varèze (38)..130 A6
Aubermesnil-
aux-Érables (76)..........19 F1
Aubermesnil-Beaumais (76)..17 G2
Aubers (59)..........3 E5
Aubertin (64)..........182 A2
Auberville (14)..........14 D3
Auberville-la-Campagne (76)..15 H1
Auberville-la-Manuel (76)..16 D2
Auberville-la-Renault (76)..16 C4
Aubervilliers (93)..........42 D3
Aubeterre (10)..........66 B2
Aubeterre-sur-Dronne (16)..136 C1
Aubeville (16)..........122 A5
Aubevoye (27)..........41 E1
Aubiac (33)..........149 H2
Aubiac (47)..........151 E6
Aubie-et-Espessas (33)..135 F4
Aubière (63)..........127 F3
Aubiet (32)..........168 A5
Aubignan (84)..........175 F1
Aubignas (07)..........157 H3
Aubigné (35)..........57 F1
Aubigné (79)..........108 B5
Aubigné-Racan (72)..........78 B3
Aubigné-sur-Layon (49)..93 E1
Aubignosc (04)..........160 B5
Aubigny (03)..........114 A2
Aubigny (14)..........38 D2
Aubigny (79)..........93 G5
Aubigny (80)..........7 H6
Aubigny (85)..........91 G5
Aubigny-au-Bac (59)..........8 D3
Aubigny-aux-Kaisnes (02)..21 H1
Aubigny-en-Artois (62)..8 A2
Aubigny-en-Laonnois (02)..22 D4
Aubigny-en-Plaine (21)..102 A2
Aubigny-la-Ronce (21)..101 F3
Aubigny-les-Pothées (08)..23 H1
Aubigny-
lès-Sombernon (21)..85 E6
Aubigny-sur-Nère (18)..81 G5
Aubilly (51)..........22 D6
Aubin (12)..........154 A3
Aubin (64)..........166 A6
Aubin-Saint-Vaast (62)..........7 E1
Aubinges (18)..........97 H1
Auboncourt-Vauzelles (08)..23 H3
Aubonne (25)..........104 A3
Aubord (30)..........174 A4
Auboué (54)..........26 A4
Aubous (64)..........166 C5
Aubres (26)..........158 D4
Aubréville (55)..........46 D1
Aubrives (08)..........11 F4
Aubrometz (62)..........7 F3
Aubry-du-Hainaut (59)..........9 F2
Aubry-en-Exmes (61)..........39 F4
Aubry-le-Panthou (61)..........39 F3
Aubure (68)..........71 E3
Aubussargues (30)..........174 A2
Aubusson (23)..........125 G1
Aubusson (61)..........38 B4
Aubusson-d'Auvergne (63)..128 A3
Aubvillers (80)..........20 D2
Auby (59)..........8 C1
Aucaleuc (22)..........34 C5
Aucamville (31)..........169 F4
Aucamville (82)..........168 D3
Aucazein (09)..........184 D5
Aucelon (26)..........158 D2
Aucey-la-Plaine (50)..........35 G5
Auch (32)..........167 H5
Auchel (62)..........2 C6
Auchonvillers (80)..........8 A4
Auchy-au-Bois (62)..........2 C6
Auchy-la-Montagne (60)..20 B3
Auchy-lès-Hesdin (62)..........7 F2
Auchy-les-Mines (62)..........2 D6
Auchy-lez-Orchies (59)..........3 G6
Aucun (65)..........182 D5
Audaux (64)..........181 G1
Audelange (39)..........102 C2
Audeloncourt (52)..........68 B5
Audembert (62)..........1 F3
Audenge (33)..........148 C1
Auderville (50)..........12 A1
Audes (03)..........112 C2
Audeux (25)..........103 F1
Audeville (45)..........63 F3
Audignicourt (02)..........21 H4
Audignies (59)..........9 H2
Audignon (40)..........165 H4
Audigny (02)..........9 G6
Audincourt (25)..........88 C4
Audincthun (62)..........2 B5
Audinghen (62)..........1 F3
Audon (40)..........165 F3
Audouville-la-Hubert (50)..13 E4
Audrehem (62)..........1 H4
Audressein (09)..........184 D5
Audresselles (62)..........1 F3
Audrieu (14)..........14 A4
Audrix (24)..........137 G5
Audruicq (62)..........1 H3
Audun-le-Roman (54)..........26 A3
Audun-le-Tiche (57)..........26 A2
Auenheim (67)..........51 F3
Auffargis (78)..........42 A5
Auffay (76)..........17 G4
Aufferville (77)..........63 H4
Auffreville-Brasseuil (78)..41 H3
Auflance (08)..........25 E2
Auga (64)..........166 B5

Auger-Saint-Vincent (60)..21 F6
Augerans (39)..........102 D3
Augères (23)..........111 F6
Augerolles (63)..........128 A3
Augers-en-Brie (77)..........44 C5
Augerville-la-Rivière (45)..63 G3
Augicourt (70)..........87 E2
Augignac (24)..........123 F4
Augirein (09)..........184 C5
Augisey (39)..........117 F1
Augnat (63)..........127 F6
Augnax (32)..........168 A4
Augny (57)..........26 B6
Auguaise (61)..........39 H4
Augy (02)..........22 B5
Augy (89)..........83 G2
Augy-sur-Aubois (18)..........98 B5
Aujac (17)..........121 G2
Aujac (30)..........156 D4
Aujan-Mournède (32)..183 H1
Aujargues (30)..........173 H4
Aujeurres (52)..........86 A2
Aujols (46)..........152 D4
Aulan (26)..........159 F5
Aulas (30)..........172 D2
Aulhat-Saint-Privat (63)..127 G5
Aullène (2A)..........207 E2
Aulnat (63)..........127 F3
Aulnay (10)..........66 D1
Aulnay (17)..........107 H6
Aulnay (86)..........94 A4
Aulnay-aux-Planches (51)..45 F3
Aulnay-la-Rivière (45)..........63 G4
Aulnay-l'Aître (51)..........46 A4
Aulnay-sous-Bois (93)..........43 E3
Aulnay-sur-Iton (27)..........40 D2
Aulnay-sur-Marne (51)..........45 G2
Aulnay-sur-Mauldre (78)..42 A3
les Aulneaux (72)..........60 B2
Aulnois (88)..........68 D3
Aulnois-en-Perthois (55)..47 E6
Aulnois-sous-Laon (02)..22 C3
Aulnois-sur-Seille (57)..........48 D3
Aulnoy (77)..........43 H4
Aulnoy-lez-Valenciennes (59)..9 F3
Aulnoy-sur-Aube (52)..........85 H2
Aulnoye-Aymeries (59)..........9 H3
Aulon (23)..........111 F5
Aulon (31)..........184 B3
Aulon (65)..........183 G6
Aulos (09)..........199 F1
Ault (80)..........6 B4
Aulus-les-Bains (09)..........198 C2
Aulx-lès-Cromary (70)..........87 G5
Aumagne (17)..........121 G2
Aumale (76)..........19 G2
Aumâtre (80)..........6 D6
Aumelas (34)..........172 D5
Auménancourt (51)..........23 E5
Aumerval (62)..........2 C6
Aumes (34)..........188 D1
Aumessas (30)..........172 C2
Aumetz (57)..........26 A2
Aumeville-Lestre (50)..........13 E3
Aumont (39)..........102 D4
Aumont (80)..........7 E6
Aumont-Aubrac (48)..........155 G1
Aumont-en-Halatte (60)..........20 D6
Aumontzey (88)..........70 C4
Aumur (39)..........102 B3
Aunac (16)..........122 C2
Aunat (11)..........199 H1
Aunay-en-Bazois (58)..........99 H2
Aunay-les-Bois (61)..........39 G6
Aunay-sous-Auneau (28)..62 D2
Aunay-sous-Crécy (28)..........41 E5
Aunay-sur-Odon (14)..........14 A6
Auneau (28)..........62 D2
Auneuil (60)..........20 A5
Aunou-le-Faucon (61)..........39 E5
Aunou-sur-Orne (61)..........39 F6
Auppegard (76)..........17 G3
Aups (83)..........177 F5
Auquainville (14)..........15 F6
Auquemesnil (76)..........6 A5
Auradé (32)..........168 C5
Auradou (47)..........151 G4
Auragne (31)..........185 G1
Auray (56)..........55 G6
Aure (08)..........24 A6
Aurec-sur-Loire (43)..........143 E1
Aureil (87)..........124 C3
Aureilhan (40)..........148 B5
Aureilhan (65)..........183 E3
Aureille (13)..........175 E4
Aurel (26)..........158 C1
Aurel (84)..........159 E6
Aurelle-Verlac (12)..........155 E3
Auremsan (32)..........166 C5
Auriac (11)..........187 E6
Auriac (19)..........139 F2
Auriac (64)..........166 B6
Auriac-du-Périgord (24)..138 A3
Auriac-Lagast (12)..........154 C6
Auriac-l'Église (15)..........141 F2
Auriac-sur-Dropt (47)..........150 C1
Auriac-sur-Vendinelle (31)..169 H6
Auriat (23)..........124 D2
Auribail (31)..........185 F2
Auribeau (84)..........176 B4
Auribeau-sur-Siagne (06)..178 C5
Aurice (40)..........165 H3
Auriébat (65)..........183 E2
Aurières (63)..........126 D3
Aurignac (31)..........184 C3
Aurillac (15)..........140 B5
Aurimont (32)..........168 A5
Auriol (13)..........192 D4
Aurions-Idernes (64)..........166 C6
Auris (38)..........146 A3
Aurons (13)..........191 H2
Auros (33)..........150 A3
Aurouër (03)..........98 D6
Auroux (48)..........156 C1
Aussac (81)..........170 A3
Aussac-Vadalle (16)..........122 C2
Ausseing (31)..........184 D4
Aussevielle (64)..........182 A1
Aussillon (81)..........171 E6
Aussois (73)..........147 E2
Ausson (31)..........184 A4
Aussonce (08)..........23 G5
Aussonne (31)..........169 E5
Aussos (32)..........184 A2
Aussurucq (64)..........181 F3
Autainville (41)..........80 A2
Autechaux (25)..........87 H5
Autechaux-Roide (25)..........88 C5
les Autels (02)..........23 F1
les Autels-Saint-Bazile (14)..39 F2
les Autels-Villevillon (28)..61 F4
Auterive (31)..........185 F2
Auterive (32)..........167 H6
Auterive (82)..........168 C3
Auterrive (64)..........181 G1
Autet (70)..........86 D4
Auteuil (60)..........20 B5
Auteuil (78)..........42 A4
Autevielle-Saint-Martin-
Bideren (64)..........181 F1
Authe (08)..........24 B4
Autheuil (28)..........61 H2
Autheuil (61)..........39 H6
Autheuil-Authouillet (27)..41 E1
Autheuil-en-Valois (60)..........43 H1
Authevernes (27)..........19 G6
Authie (14)..........14 B4
Authie (80)..........7 G4
Authieule (80)..........7 G4
les Authieux (27)..........40 D3
les Authieux-du-Puits (61)..39 G5
les Authieux-Papion (14)..15 E6
Authieux-Ratiéville (76)..18 C3
les Authieux-
sur-Calonne (14)..........15 F4

les Authieux-sur-le-
Port-Saint-Ouen (76) 18 D5
Authiou (58) 99 F1
Authoison (70) 87 G4
Authon (04) 160 C5
Authon (41) 79 F3
Authon-du-Perche (28) 61 F4
Authon-Ébéon (17) 121 G2
Authon-la-Plaine (91) 62 D2
Authou (27) 18 A6
Authuille (80) 8 B5
Authume (39) 102 C2
Authumes (71) 102 B4
Autichamp (26) 158 C1
Autignac (34) 172 B6
Autigny (76) 17 F3
Autigny-la-Tour (88) 68 D2
Autigny-le-Grand (52) 67 H1
Autigny-le-Petit (52) 67 H1
Autingues (62) 1 H3
Autoire (46) 139 E5
Autoreille (70) 87 E5
Autouillet (78) 41 H4
Autrac (43) 141 F1
Autrans (38) 145 F2
Autrèche (37) 79 F4
Autrechêne (90) 88 D3
Autrêches (60) 21 H4
Autrecourt-et-Pourron (08) 24 C3
Autrécourt-sur-Aire (55) 47 E2
Autremencourt (02) 22 D2
Autrepierre (54) 49 G5
Autreppes (02) 10 A5
Autretot (76) 17 E4
Autreville (02) 21 H3
Autreville (88) 69 E1
Autréville-Saint-Lambert (55) 24 D3
Autreville-sur-la-Renne (52) 67 G5
Autreville-sur-Moselle (54) 48 C4
Autrey (54) 69 H1
Autrey (88) 70 B3
Autrey-le-Vay (70) 87 H4
Autrey-lès-Cerre (70) 87 H3
Autrey-lès-Gray (70) 86 C4
Autricourt (21) 67 E6
Autruche (08) 24 C4
Autruy-sur-Juine (45) 63 E3
Autry (08) 24 B6
Autry-Issards (03) 113 G2
Autry-le-Châtel (45) 81 H4
Autun (71) 100 D4
Auty (82) 152 C6
Auvare (06) 178 C1
Auve (51) 46 B2
Auvernaux (91) 63 H1
Auvers (43) 141 H4
Auvers (50) 13 E5
Auvers-le-Hamon (72) 59 F6
Auvers-Saint-Georges (91) 63 F1
Auvers-sous-
Montfaucon (72) 59 H5
Auverse (49) 77 H4
Auvet-et-la-Chapelotte (70) 86 C4
Auvillar (82) 168 B1
Auvillars (14) 15 E4
Auvillars-sur-Saône (21) 102 A3
Auvilliers (76) 19 G1
Auvilliers-en-Gâtinais (45) 63 H6
aux-Aussat (32) 183 G1
Auxais (50) 13 E6
Auxange (39) 102 D2
Auxant (21) 101 F2
Auxelles-Bas (90) 88 C3
Auxelles-Haut (90) 88 C2
Auxerre (89) 83 F2
Auxey-Duresses (21) 101 F3
Auxi-le-Château (62) 7 F3
Auxon (10) 66 A5
Auxon (70) 87 G3
Auxon-Dessous (25) 87 F6
Auxon-Dessus (25) 87 F6
Auxonne (21) 102 B1
Auxy (45) 63 H6
Auxy (71) 100 D4
Auzainvilliers (88) 69 E3
Auzances (23) 126 B1
Auzas (31) 184 C3
Auzat (09) 198 D1
Auzat-la-Combelle (63) 127 G6
Auzay (85) 107 E2
Auzebosc (76) 17 E5
Auzelles (63) 128 A4
Auzers (15) 140 B2
Auzet (04) 160 D4
Auzeville-Tolosane (31) 169 G6
Auzielle (31) 169 G6
Auzits (12) 154 A3
Auzon (43) 141 G1
Auzouer-en-Touraine (37) 79 F4
Auzouville-Auberbosc (76) 16 D4
Auzouville-l'Esneval (76) 17 F4
Auzouville-sur-Ry (76) 19 E4
Auzouville-sur-Saâne (76) 17 F3
Availles-en-Châtellerault (86) 94 D5
Availles-Limouzine (86) 109 G5
Availles-sur-Seiche (35) 58 A5
Availles-Thouarsais (79) 93 G4
Avajan (65) 183 G6
Avallon (89) 84 A4
les Avanchers-Valmorel (73) 132 D5
Avançon (05) 160 C2
Avançon (08) 23 F4
Avanne-Aveney (25) 103 F1
Avant-lès-Marcilly (10) 65 F2
Avant-lès-Ramerupt (10) 66 C2
Avanton (86) 94 B6
Avapessa (2B) 202 C5
Avaray (41) 80 B3
Avaux (08) 23 F4

Avillers-Sainte-Croix (55) 47 H2
Avilley (25) 87 H5
Avilly-Saint-Léonard (60) 43 E1
Avion (62) 8 B1
Avioth (55) 25 E3
Aviré (49) 76 C2
Avirey-Lingey (10) 66 C5
Aviron (27) 40 D2
Avize (51) 45 F3
Avocourt (55) 24 D6
Avoine (37) 94 A1
Avoine (61) 39 E5
Avoise (72) 77 G1
Avolsheim (67) 50 D6
Avon (77) 64 A2
Avon (79) 108 C3
Avon-la-Pèze (10) 65 G2
Avon-les-Roches (37) 94 C2
Avondance (62) 2 A6
Avord (18) 98 A3
Avosnes (21) 85 E6
Avot (21) 85 H3
Avoudrey (25) 104 A1
Avrainville (54) 48 B4
Avrainville (88) 69 G2
Avrainville (91) 63 F1
Avranches (50) 35 H3
Avranville (88) 68 C2
Avrechy (60) 20 C4
Avrecourt (52) 68 C6
Avrée (58) 100 A5
Avremesnil (76) 17 F2
Avressieux (73) 131 G4
Avreuil (10) 66 A5
Avricourt (54) 49 G5
Avricourt (57) 49 G5
Avricourt (60) 21 F2
Avrieux (73) 147 E2
Avrigney-Virey (70) 87 E5
Avrigny (60) 20 D4
Avril (54) 26 A4
Avril-sur-Loire (58) 99 F5
Avrillé (49) 76 D4
Avrillé (85) 91 F6
Avrillé-les-Ponceaux (37) 78 B5
Avrilly (03) 114 D4
Avrilly (27) 40 D4
Avrilly (61) 38 A6
Avroult (62) 2 A5
Avy (17) 121 F4
Awoingt (59) 9 E3
Ax-les-Thermes (09) 199 G2
Axat (11) 200 B1
Axiat (09) 199 F1
Ay (51) 45 F2
Ay-sur-Moselle (57) 26 C4
Ayat-sur-Sioule (63) 113 F6
Aydat (63) 127 E4
Aydie (64) 166 C5
Aydius (64) 182 A5
Aydoilles (88) 70 A3
Ayen (19) 138 B2
Ayencourt (80) 20 D3
Ayette (62) 8 B3
Ayguatébia-Talau (66) 199 F4
Ayguemorte-les-Graves (33) 135 F6
Ayguesvives (31) 185 H1
Ayguetinte (32) 167 G3
Ayherre (64) 180 D1
Ayn (73) 131 G4
Aynac (46) 139 E6
les Aynans (70) 88 A3
Ayrens (15) 140 A4
Ayron (86) 94 A6
Ayros-Arbouix (65) 182 D5
Ayse (74) 118 D5
Ayssènes (12) 171 G1
Aytré (17) 106 D5
les Ayvelles (08) 24 B2
Ayzac-Ost (65) 182 D4
Ayzieu (32) 166 D3
Azannes-et-
Soumazannes (55) 25 F5
Azas (31) 169 G4
Azat-Châtenet (23) 111 F6
Azat-le-Ris (87) 110 B4
Azay-le-Brûlé (79) 108 A3
Azay-le-Ferron (36) 95 G5
Azay-le-Rideau (37) 94 C1
Azay-sur-Cher (37) 79 E6
Azay-sur-Indre (37) 95 F1
Azay-sur-Thouet (79) 93 H6
Azé (41) 79 F1
Azé (53) 76 D1
Azé (71) 116 B3
Azelot (54) 48 D5
Azerables (23) 110 D3
Azerailles (54) 70 B1
Azerat (24) 138 A3
Azérat (43) 141 G1
Azereix (65) 183 E3
Azet (65) 183 G6
Azeville (50) 13 E3
Azillanet (34) 187 G2
Azille (11) 187 G3
Azilone-Ampaza (2A) 205 E6
Azincourt (62) 7 F2
Azolette (69) 115 G5
Azoudange (57) 49 G4
Azur (40) 164 C3
Azy (18) 98 B2
Azy-le-Vif (58) 99 E5
Azy-sur-Marne (02) 44 B2
Azzana (2A) 204 D4

B

Baâlon (55) 25 E4
Baâlons (08) 24 A3
Babeau-Bouldoux (34) 188 A1
Baboeuf (60) 21 G3
Baby (77) 65 E2
Baccarat (54) 70 B1
Baccon (45) 80 B1
Bach (46) 153 E4
Bachant (59) 10 A3
la Bachellerie (24) 138 A3
Bachivillers (60) 20 A6
Bachos (31) 184 A6
Bachy (59) 3 G6
Bacilly (50) 35 G3
Baconnes (51) 45 H1
la Baconnière (53) 58 C4
Bacouël (60) 20 C3
Bacouel-sur-Selle (80) 20 B1
Bacourt (57) 49 E3
Bacquepuis (27) 40 D2
Bacqueville (27) 19 E5
Bacqueville-en-Caux (76) 17 G3
Badailhac (15) 140 C5
Badaroux (48) 156 A3
Badecon-le-Pin (36) 111 F1
Badefols-d'Ans (24) 138 A2
Badefols-sur-Dordogne (24) 137 F5
Baden (56) 72 C1
Badens (11) 187 F3
Badevel (25) 88 D4
Badménil-aux-Bois (88) 70 A2
Badonviller (54) 70 C1
Badonvilliers-
Gérauvilliers (55) 47 H6
Baerendorf (67) 50 A3
Baerenthal (57) 28 C6
la Baffe (88) 70 A3
Baffie (63) 128 C6
Bagard (30) 173 G1
Bagas (33) 150 A1
Bagat-en-Quercy (46) 152 B4
Bâgé-la-Ville (01) 116 C4
Bâgé-le-Châtel (01) 116 C4
Bagert (09) 184 D4
Bages (11) 188 A4
Bages (66) 201 F3
Bagiry (31) 184 B4
Bagnac-sur-Célé (46) 153 H1
Bagneaux (89) 65 F4
Bagneaux-sur-Loing (77) 64 A3

Bagnères-de-Bigorre (65) 183 F4
Bagnères-de-Luchon (31) 197 F1
Bagneux (02) 22 A4
Bagneux (03) 113 G1
Bagneux (36) 96 C2
Bagneux (51) 65 H1
Bagneux (54) 48 B6
Bagneux (92) 42 C4
Bagneux-la-Fosse (10) 66 C6
Bagnizeau (17) 121 G1
Bagnoles (11) 187 E3
Bagnoles-de-l'Orne (61) 38 C6
Bagnols (63) 126 C5
Bagnols (69) 129 G2
Bagnols-en-Forêt (83) 178 B5
Bagnols-les-Bains (48) 156 B3
Bagnols-sur-Cèze (30) 158 A6
Bagnot (21) 102 A3
Baguer-Morvan (35) 35 E5
Baguer-Pican (35) 35 F4
Baho (66) 201 E2
Bahus-Soubiran (40) 166 B4
Baigneaux (28) 62 D5
Baigneaux (33) 135 H6
Baigneaux (41) 79 H2
Baignes (70) 87 F3
Baignes-Sainte-
Radegonde (16) 121 H6
Baigneux-les-Juifs (21) 85 E4
Baignolet (28) 62 B4
Baigts (40) 165 G4
Baigts-de-Béarn (64) 165 F5
Baillargues (34) 173 G5
Baillé (35) 35 H6
Bailleau-Armenonville (28) 62 C1
Bailleau-le-Pin (28) 62 A2
Bailleau-l'Évêque (28) 62 A1
Baillet-en-France (95) 42 C2
Bailleul (59) 2 D4
Bailleul (61) 39 E4
Bailleul (80) 17 E2
Bailleul-aux-Cornailles (62) 7 H2
Bailleul-la-Vallée (27) 15 G4
Bailleul-le-Soc (60) 20 D4
Bailleul-lès-Pernes (62) 2 B6
Bailleul-Neuville (76) 19 E1
Bailleul-Sir-Berthoult (62) 8 B2
Bailleul-sur-Thérain (60) 20 B5
Bailleulmont (62) 8 A3
Bailleulval (62) 8 A3
Bailleval (60) 20 D5
Baillolet (76) 19 E1
Baillou (41) 61 F6
Bailly (60) 21 G4
Bailly (78) 42 B4
Bailly-aux-Forges (52) 67 G1
Bailly-le-Franc (10) 67 E1
Bailly-Romainvilliers (77) 43 G4
Bain-de-Bretagne (35) 57 E5
Bainctun (62) 1 F4
Bains (43) 142 B4
Bains-les-Bains (88) 69 G5
Bains-sur-Oust (35) 56 C6
Bainville-aux-Miroirs (54) 69 G1
Bainville-aux-Saules (88) 69 F3
Bainville-sur-Madon (54) 48 C6
Bairols (06) 178 D1
Bais (35) 57 H4
Bais (53) 59 F3
Baisieux (59) 3 G5
Baissey (52) 86 B1
Baives (59) 10 B4
Baix (07) 158 A1
Baixas (66) 201 E2
Baizieux (80) 7 H5
le Baizil (51) 45 E3
Bajamont (47) 151 F5
Bajonnette (32) 168 A4
Bajus (62) 7 H1
Balacet (09) 184 C6
Baladou (46) 138 C4
Balagny-sur-Thérain (60) 20 C5
Balaguères (09) 184 D6
Balaguier-d'Olt (12) 153 G3
Balaguier-sur-Rance (12) 171 E3
Balaiseaux (39) 102 C3
Balaives-et-Butz (08) 24 B2
Balan (01) 130 C2
Balanod (39) 117 E2
Balansun (64) 165 G5
Balanzac (17) 120 D3
Balaruc-le-Vieux (34) 189 F1
Balaruc-les-Bains (34) 189 F1
Balâtre (80) 21 F2
Balazé (35) 58 A4
Balazuc (07) 157 G3
Balbigny (42) 129 E3
Balbins (38) 130 D6
Balbronn (67) 50 C5
Baldenheim (67) 71 G3
Baldersheim (68) 89 F1
la Baleine (50) 37 E2
Baleix (64) 182 D1
Balesmes-sur-Marne (52) 86 B1
Balesta (31) 184 A3
Baleyssagues (47) 150 C1
Balgau (68) 71 G6
Balham (08) 23 F4
Balignac (82) 168 B2
Balignicourt (10) 66 D1
Bâlines (27) 40 C4
Balinghem (62) 1 H3
Baliracq-Maumusson (64) 166 B5
Baliros (64) 182 C3
Balizac (33) 149 G3
Ballainvilliers (91) 42 C5
Ballaison (74) 118 D3
Ballan-Miré (37) 78 D6
Ballancourt-sur-
Essonne (91) 63 G1
Ballans (17) 121 H2
Ballay (08) 24 B4
Balledent (87) 110 C5
Balleray (58) 99 E3
Balleroy (14) 13 G6
Ballersdorf (68) 89 E3
Balléville (88) 69 E2
Ballon (17) 106 D5
Ballon (72) 60 B4
Ballons (26) 159 G5
Ballore (71) 115 G2
Ballots (53) 58 B6
Balloy (77) 64 D2
Balma (31) 169 F5
la Balme (73) 131 F3
la Balme-de-Sillingy (74) 132 A1
la Balme-de-Thuy (74) 132 B1
la Balme-d'Épy (39) 117 F3
Balnot-la-Grange (10) 66 C6
Balnot-sur-Laignes (10) 66 D5
Balogna (2A) 204 C4
Balot (21) 84 D2
Balsac (12) 154 B4
Balschwiller (68) 89 E2
Balsièges (48) 156 A3
Baltzenheim (68) 71 G4
Balzac (16) 122 B3
Bambiderstroff (57) 49 G1
Ban-de-Laveline (88) 70 D3
Ban-de-Sapt (88) 70 D2
le Ban-Saint-Martin (57) 26 B5
Ban-sur-Meurthe-Clefcy (88) 70 D4
Banassac (48) 155 G4
Banca (64) 180 C3
Bancigny (02) 23 E1
Bancourt (62) 8 C4
Bandol (83) 192 D5
Baneins (01) 116 C5
Baneuil (24) 137 F5
Bangor (56) 72 A2
Banios (65) 183 F4
Banize (23) 125 F2

Bannalec (29) 54 A3
Bannans (25) 103 H4
Bannay (18) 82 B6
Bannay (51) 44 D4
Bannay (57) 27 E5
Banne (07) 157 F4
Bannegon (18) 98 B5
Bannes (46) 139 F6
Bannes (51) 45 E4
Bannes (52) 68 B6
Bannes (53) 59 E6
Banneville-la-Campagne (14) 14 C5
Banneville-sur-Ajon (14) 14 A5
Bannières (81) 169 H5
Bannoncourt (55) 47 G3
Bannogne-Recouvrance (08) 23 E3
Banon (04) 176 A1
Banos (40) 165 H4
Bans (39) 102 D3
Bansat (63) 127 G6
Bantanges (71) 116 D1
Banteux (59) 8 D4
Banthelu (95) 41 H1
Bantheville (55) 24 D5
Bantigny (59) 8 D3
Bantouzelle (59) 8 D4
Bantzenheim (68) 89 G1
Banville (14) 14 B4
Banvillars (90) 88 C3
Banvou (61) 38 B5
Banyuls-dels-Aspres (66) 201 F3
Banyuls-sur-Mer (66) 201 G4
Baon (89) 84 B2
Baons-le-Comte (76) 17 E4
Bapaume (62) 8 B4
Bar (19) 139 E1
Bar-lès-Buzancy (08) 24 C4
le Bar-sur-Loup (06) 178 C4
Bar-sur-Aube (10) 67 E3
Bar-sur-Seine (10) 66 D5
Baracé (49) 77 F3
Baraigne (11) 186 A2
Baraize (36) 111 E2
Baralle (62) 8 C3
Baraqueville (12) 154 B5
Barastre (62) 8 C4
Baratier (05) 161 E2
Barbachen (65) 183 F1
Barbaggio (2B) 203 F4
Barbaira (11) 187 F3
Barbaise (08) 24 A2
Barbas (54) 49 G6
Barbaste (47) 150 D6
Barbazan (31) 184 A5
Barbazan-Debat (65) 183 F3
Barbazan-Dessus (65) 183 F4
Barbechat (44) 75 E4
la Barben (13) 191 H3
Barbentane (13) 174 D3
Barberaz (73) 131 H4
Barberey-Saint-Sulpice (10) 66 A3
Barberier (03) 113 H5
Barbery (14) 14 B6
Barbery (60) 21 E6
Barbeville (14) 13 H5
Barbey (77) 64 C2
Barbey-Seroux (88) 70 C4
Barbezières (16) 122 A1
Barbezieux-
Saint-Hilaire (16) 121 H5
Barbières (26) 144 C4
Barbirey-sur-Ouche (21) 101 F1
Barbizon (77) 63 H2
Barbonne-Fayel (51) 44 D6
le Barboux (25) 104 C2
Barbuise (10) 65 F1
Barby (08) 23 F3
Barby (73) 132 A4
Barc (27) 40 B2
le Barcarès (66) 201 G1
Barcelonne (26) 144 C5
Barcelonne-du-Gers (32) 166 C4
Barcelonnette (04) 161 F3
Barchain (57) 49 H5
Barcillonnette (05) 160 A3
Barcugnan (32) 183 G1
Barcus (64) 181 G3
Barcy (77) 43 G2
Bard (42) 128 D5
Bard-le-Régulier (21) 100 D2
Bard-lès-Époisses (21) 84 C4
Bard-lès-Pesmes (70) 86 D6
la Barde (17) 136 A2
Bardenac (16) 136 A1
Bardigues (82) 168 B1
le Bardon (45) 80 C1
Bardos (64) 164 D6
Bardou (24) 137 F6
Bardouville (76) 17 F6
Barèges (65) 183 E6
Bareilles (65) 183 G6
Barembach (67) 71 E1
Baren (31) 184 A6
Barentin (76) 17 F5
Barenton (50) 37 H6
Barenton-Bugny (02) 22 C2
Barenton-Cel (02) 22 C2
Barenton-sur-Serre (02) 22 C2
Barésia-sur-l'Ain (39) 117 G1
Barfleur (50) 13 E1
Bargème (83) 178 A3
Bargemon (83) 177 H5
Barges (21) 101 H2
Barges (43) 142 C6
Barges (70) 87 E1
Bargny (60) 21 G6
Barie (33) 150 A2
les Barils (27) 40 B4
Barisey-au-Plain (54) 48 B6
Barisey-la-Côte (54) 48 B6
Barisis (02) 22 A3
Barizey (71) 101 F5
Barjac (09) 184 D4
Barjac (30) 157 F5
Barjac (48) 155 H3
Barjols (83) 193 F1
Barjon (21) 85 G3
Barjouville (28) 62 B2
Barles (04) 160 D4
Barlest (65) 182 D3
Barleux (80) 8 C6
Barlin (62) 8 A1
Barly (62) 7 H3
Barly (80) 7 G3
Barmainville (28) 62 D3
Barnas (07) 157 E1
Barnave (26) 159 E1
Barnay (71) 100 D3
Barneville-Carteret (50) 12 B4
Barneville-la-Bertran (14) 15 F3
Barneville-sur-Seine (27) 18 A5
la Baroche-sous-Lucé (61) 38 B6
les Baroches (54) 26 A4
Baromesnil (76) 6 B5
Baron (30) 173 H1
Baron (33) 135 G5
Baron (60) 21 F6
Baron (71) 115 H2
Baron-sur-Odon (14) 14 B5
Barou-en-Auge (14) 39 E2
Baroville (10) 67 E3
le Barp (33) 148 D2
Barquet (27) 40 C2
Barr (67) 71 F1
Barrais-Bussolles (03) 114 C4
Barran (32) 167 G5
Barrancoueu (65) 183 G5
Barras (04) 160 C6
Barraute-Camu (64) 181 F1
Barraux (38) 132 A6
la Barre (39) 102 D1
la Barre (70) 87 H4
Barre (81) 171 E4
la Barre-de-Monts (85) 90 C2

la Barre-de-Semilly (50) 37 G1
la Barre-en-Ouche (27) 40 A3
Barrême (04) 177 G2
Barret (16) 122 A5
Barret-de-Lioure (26) 159 F6
Barret-sur-Méouge (05) 159 H5
Barretaine (39) 103 E5
Barrettali (2B) 203 F2
Barriac-les-Bosquets (15) 139 H5
Barro (16) 108 D6
Barrou (37) 95 E4
le Barroux (84) 158 D6
Barry (65) 183 E3
Barry-d'Islemade (82) 169 E1
Bars (24) 137 H3
Bars (32) 167 F6
Barsac (26) 159 E1
Barsac (33) 149 G2
Barst (57) 27 G5
Bart (25) 88 C4
Bartenheim (68) 89 G3
Barthe (65) 183 H2
la Barthe-de-Neste (65) 183 G4
Bartherans (25) 103 F3
les Barthes (82) 168 D1
Bartrès (65) 182 D4
Barville (27) 15 G5
Barville (61) 60 C1
Barville (88) 69 E2
Barville-en-Gâtinais (45) 63 G5
Barzan (17) 120 D5
Barzun (64) 182 D3
Barzy-en-Thiérache (02) 9 H4
Barzy-sur-Marne (02) 44 C2
Bas-en-Basset (43) 142 D1
Bas-Lieu (59) 10 A4
Bas-et-Lezat (63) 127 G1
Bascons (40) 166 A3
Bascous (32) 167 E3
Baslieux (54) 25 H4
Baslieux-lès-Fismes (51) 22 C5
Baslieux-sous-Châtillon (51) 45 E1
Basly (14) 14 B4
Bassac (16) 122 A4
Bassan (34) 188 B2
Bassanne (33) 150 A2
Basse-Goulaine (44) 74 D5
Basse-Ham (57) 26 C3
Basse-Rentgen (57) 26 C2
la Basse-Vaivre (70) 69 F6
la Bassée (59) 3 E6
Bassemberg (67) 71 F2
Basseneville (14) 14 D4
Bassens (33) 135 F5
Bassens (73) 131 H4
Bassercles (40) 165 G5
Basses (86) 94 A3
Basseux (62) 8 A3
Bassevelle (77) 44 A3
Bassignac (15) 140 A1
Bassignac-le-Bas (19) 139 E4
Bassignac-le-Haut (19) 139 G3
Bassigney (70) 87 G1
Bassilac (24) 137 G3
Bassillon-Vauzé (64) 182 D1
Bassing (57) 49 G3
Bassoles-Aulers (02) 22 A3
Bassoncourt (52) 68 B5
Bassou (89) 83 F1
Bassoues (32) 167 E5
Bassu (51) 46 C3
Bassuet (51) 46 B3
Bassurels (48) 156 B6
Bassussarry (64) 164 C6
Bassy (74) 131 G1
Bastanès (64) 181 G1
Bastelica (2A) 205 E5
Bastelicaccia (2A) 204 C6
Bastennes (40) 165 G4
Bastia (2B) 203 G4
la Bastide (09) 186 A6
la Bastide (83) 178 A4
la Bastide-Clairence (64) 164 C6
la Bastide-de-Besplas (09) 185 E3
la Bastide-
de-Bousignac (09) 186 B5
la Bastide-de-Lordat (09) 185 H4
la Bastide-de-Sérou (09) 185 F5
la Bastide-d'Engras (30) 174 B1
la Bastide-
des-Jourdans (84) 176 B3
la Bastide-du-Salat (09) 184 D4
la Bastide-l'Évêque (12) 153 H4
la Bastide-Pradines (12) 172 A2
la Bastide-Puylaurent (48) 156 D2
la Bastide-Solages (12) 171 E2
la Bastidonne (84) 176 B4
la Bastie (79) 108 B3
la Bataille (79) 108 B5
Bathelémont-
lès-Bauzemont (54) 49 E5
Batilly (54) 26 A5
Batilly (61) 38 C4
Batilly-en-Gâtinais (45) 63 G5
Batilly-en-Puisaye (45) 82 B4
Bats (40) 166 A4
Batsère (65) 183 G4
Battenans-les-Mines (25) 87 H5
Battenans-Varin (25) 88 C6
Battenheim (68) 89 F1
Battexey (88) 69 G2
Battigny (54) 69 E1
Battrans (70) 86 D5
Batz-sur-Mer (44) 73 F4
Batzendorf (67) 51 E4
Baubigny (21) 101 F3
Baubigny (50) 12 B3
la Bauche (73) 131 G5
Baud (56) 55 E4
Baudement (51) 45 E6
Baudemont (71) 115 F4
Baudignan (40) 150 B6
Baudignécourt (55) 47 G6
Baudinard-sur-Verdon (83) 177 F4
Baudoncourt (70) 87 H2
Baudonvilliers (55) 46 D5
Baudre (50) 37 G1
Baudrecourt (52) 67 G2
Baudrecourt (57) 48 D2
Baudreix (64) 182 C3
Baudres (36) 96 B3
Baudreville (28) 62 D3
Baudreville (50) 12 B5
Baudricourt (88) 69 F2
Baudrières (71) 116 C1
Bauduen (83) 177 F4
Baugé (49) 77 G3
Baugy (18) 98 A2
Baugy (60) 21 F3
Baugy (71) 115 E4
Baulay (70) 87 F2
la Baule-Escoublac (44) 73 G4
Baule (45) 80 C2
Baulme-la-Roche (21) 85 F6
Baulne (91) 63 G1
Baulne-en-Brie (02) 44 C3
Baulny (55) 24 C6
Baulon (35) 56 D4
Baulou (09) 185 G5
la Baume (74) 119 E4
la Baume-Cornillane (26) 144 C6
la Baume-de-Transit (26) 158 B4
la Baume-d'Hostun (26) 144 C4
Baume-les-Dames (25) 88 A6
Baume-les-Messieurs (39) 102 D6

Bauné (49) 77 F4
Bauquay (14) 14 A6
Baurech (33) 135 F6
la Baussaine (35) 56 D1
Bauvin (59) 3 E6
les Baux-de-Breteuil (27) 40 B3
les Baux-de-Provence (13) 191 E2
les Baux-Sainte-Croix (27) 40 D3
Bauzemont (54) 49 E5
Bauzy (41) 80 C4
Bavans (25) 88 C4
Bavay (59) 9 H2
Bavelincourt (80) 7 H5
Bavent (14) 14 C4
Baverans (39) 102 D2
Bavilliers (90) 88 C3
Bavinchove (59) 2 C3
Bavincourt (62) 8 A3
Bax (31) 185 F3
Bay (70) 86 D5
Bay-sur-Aube (52) 85 H2
Bayac (24) 137 F6
Bayard-sur-Marne (52) 47 E6
Bayas (33) 135 H3
Baye (29) 54 B4
Baye (51) 44 D4
Bayecourt (88) 70 A2
Bayel (10) 67 F4
Bayencourt (80) 8 A4
Bayenghem-
lès-Éperlecques (62) 2 A3
Bayenghem-
lès-Seninghem (62) 2 A4
Bayers (16) 122 C1
Bayet (03) 113 H4
Bayeux (14) 13 H5
Bayon (54) 69 G1
Bayon-sur-Gironde (33) 135 E3
Bayonne (64) 164 B6
Bayons (04) 160 C4
Bayonville (08) 24 C4
Bayonville-sur-Mad (54) 26 B6
Bayonvillers (80) 8 A6
Bazac (16) 136 B2
Bazaiges (36) 111 E2
Bazailles (54) 25 H4
Bazainville (78) 41 G4
Bazancourt (51) 23 F5
Bazancourt (60) 19 H3
Bazarnes (89) 83 G3
Bazas (33) 149 H3
Bazauges (17) 121 H1
Bazegney (88) 69 G3
Bazeilles (08) 24 C2
Bazeilles-sur-Othain (55) 25 F3
Bazelat (23) 111 E3
Bazemont (78) 42 A3
Bazens (47) 150 D5
Bazentin (80) 8 B5
Bazenville (14) 14 A4
Bazet (65) 183 E3
la Bazeuge (87) 110 B4
Bazian (32) 167 E4
Bazicourt (60) 21 E5
Baziège (31) 185 H1
Bazien (88) 70 B2
Bazillac (65) 183 F2
Bazincourt-sur-Epte (27) 19 G5
Bazincourt-sur-Saulx (55) 47 E5
Bazinghen (62) 1 F3
Bazinval (76) 6 B6
la Bazoche-Gouet (28) 61 F4
Bazoches (58) 83 H5
Bazoches-au-Houlme (61) 38 D4
Bazoches-en-Dunois (28) 62 B5
Bazoches-lès-Bray (77) 64 D2
Bazoches-
les-Gallerandes (45) 63 E4
Bazoches-les-Hautes (28) 62 D4
Bazoches-sur-Guyonne (78) 42 A4
Bazoches-sur-Hoëne (61) 39 H6
Bazoches-sur-le-Betz (45) 64 C4
Bazoches-sur-Vesles (02) 22 C5
la Bazoge (50) 37 F4
la Bazoge (72) 60 A4
la Bazoge-Montpinçon (53) 59 E3
Bazoges-en-Paillers (85) 92 A4
Bazoges-en-Pareds (85) 92 B6
Bazoilles-et-Ménil (88) 69 F3
Bazoilles-sur-Meuse (88) 68 D3
Bazolles (58) 99 G2
Bazoncourt (57) 26 D6
la Bazoque (14) 13 G6
la Bazoque (61) 38 A4
Bazoques (27) 15 H4
Bazordan (65) 183 H3
la Bazouge-de-Chemeré (53) 59 E5
la Bazouge-des-Alleux (53) 58 D3
la Bazouge-du-Désert (35) 58 A1
Bazougers (53) 59 E5
Bazouges-la-Pérouse (35) 35 F6
Bazouges-sur-le-Loir (72) 77 G2
Bazuel (59) 9 F4
Bazugues (32) 183 G1
Bazus (31) 169 F4
Bazus-Aure (65) 183 G6
Bazus-Neste (65) 183 G4
le Béage (07) 142 D6
Béalcourt (80) 7 F3
Béalencourt (62) 7 F2
Béard (58) 99 E5
Beaubec-la-Rosière (76) 19 F2
Beaubery (71) 115 G3
Beaubray (27) 40 C3
Beaucaire (30) 174 C3
Beaucaire (32) 167 G2
Beaucamps-le-Jeune (80) 19 H1
Beaucamps-le-Vieux (80) 6 D6
Beaucamps-Ligny (59) 3 E5
Beaucé (35) 58 A2
Beaucens (65) 182 D5
le Beaucet (84) 175 G2
Beauchalot (31) 184 C4
Beauchamp (95) 42 C2
Beauchamps (50) 35 G2
Beauchamps (80) 6 B5
Beauchamps-
sur-Huillard (45) 63 G6
Beauchastel (07) 144 A6
Beauche (28) 40 C5
Beauchemin (52) 68 B6
Beauchêne (41) 61 F6
Beauchêne (61) 38 A5
Beauchery-Saint-Martin (77) 44 B6
Beauclair (55) 24 D4
Beaucoudray (50) 37 F2
Beaucourt (90) 88 D4
Beaucourt-en-Santerre (80) 20 D1
Beaucourt-sur-l'Ancre (80) 8 A4
Beaucourt-sur-l'Hallue (80) 7 H5
Beaucouzé (49) 76 D4
Beaucroissant (38) 145 E1
Beaudéan (65) 183 F4
Beaudéduit (60) 20 A2
Beaudignies (59) 9 F3
Beaudricourt (62) 7 G2
Beaufai (61) 39 H4
Beaufay (72) 60 B4
Beauficel (50) 37 G4
Beauficel-en-Lyons (27) 19 F4
Beaufin (38) 145 H5
Beaufort (31) 184 D2
Beaufort (34) 187 H2
Beaufort (38) 130 D6
Beaufort (39) 117 F1
Beaufort (59) 9 G3
Beaufort (73) 133 E3
Beaufort-Blavincourt (62) 7 H2
Beaufort-en-Argonne (55) 24 D4
Beaufort-en-Santerre (80) 21 E1
Beaufort-en-Vallée (49) 77 F5
Beaufort-sur-Gervanne (26) 144 C6
Beaufou (85) 91 F3
Beaufour-Druval (14) 15 E4
Beaufremont (88) 68 D3
Beaugas (47) 151 F3
Beaugeay (17) 120 C2
Beaugency (45) 80 B2
Beaugies-sous-Bois (60) 21 G2
Beaujeu (04) 160 D5
Beaujeu (69) 115 H5
Beaujeu-Saint-Vallier-
Pierrejux-et-Quitteur (70) 86 D4
Beaulandais (61) 38 B6
Beaulencourt (62) 8 B4
Beaulieu (07) 157 F4
Beaulieu (14) 37 H3
Beaulieu (15) 126 B6
Beaulieu (21) 85 H2
Beaulieu (25) 88 A5
Beaulieu (34) 173 G4
Beaulieu (36) 110 D3
Beaulieu (38) 145 E2
Beaulieu (43) 142 D3
Beaulieu (58) 99 F6
Beaulieu (61) 39 H5
Beaulieu (63) 127 G6
Beaulieu-en-Argonne (55) 46 D2
Beaulieu-les-Fontaines (60) 21 F2
Beaulieu-lès-Loches (37) 95 F2
Beaulieu-sous-la-Roche (85) 91 F4
Beaulieu-sous-
Parthenay (79) 108 A1
Beaulieu-sur-Dordogne (19) 139 E4
Beaulieu-sur-Layon (49) 76 D6
Beaulieu-sur-Loire (45) 82 B4
Beaulieu-sur-Mer (06) 179 F4
Beaulieu-sur-Oudon (53) 58 B5
Beaulieu-sur-Sonnette (16) 122 D2
Beaulon (03) 114 C1
Beaumais (14) 39 E3
Beaumarchés (32) 167 E5
Beaumat (46) 152 D2
Beaumé (02) 10 B6
la Beaume (05) 159 G2
Beauménil (88) 70 B4
Beaumerie-Saint-Martin (62) 6 D1
Beaumes-de-Venise (84) 158 C6
Beaumesnil (14) 37 G2
Beaumesnil (27) 40 B2
Beaumettes (84) 175 G3
Beaumetz (80) 7 F4
Beaumetz-lès-Aire (62) 2 A6
Beaumetz-lès-Cambrai (62) 8 C4
Beaumetz-lès-Loges (62) 8 A3
Beaumont (07) 157 E4
Beaumont (19) 125 E6
Beaumont (32) 167 F2
Beaumont (43) 141 H1
Beaumont (54) 48 B3
Beaumont (63) 127 E3
Beaumont (74) 118 B5
Beaumont (86) 94 C6
Beaumont (89) 83 F1
Beaumont-
de-Lomagne (82) 168 C3
Beaumont-de-Pertuis (84) 176 C4
Beaumont-du-Gâtinais (77) 63 H4
Beaumont-du-Lac (87) 125 E3
Beaumont-du-Périgord (24) 137 F6
Beaumont-du-Ventoux (84) 158 D6
Beaumont-en-Auge (14) 15 E4
Beaumont-en-Beine (02) 21 H2
Beaumont-en-
Cambrésis (59) 9 F4
Beaumont-en-Diois (26) 159 F2
Beaumont-en-Verdunois (55) 25 E6
Beaumont-en-Véron (37) 94 A1
Beaumont-Hague (50) 12 B1
Beaumont-Hamel (80) 8 A4
Beaumont-la-Ferrière (58) 99 E2
Beaumont-la-Ronce (37) 78 D3
Beaumont-le-Hareng (76) 17 H4
Beaumont-le-Roger (27) 40 B2
Beaumont-les-Autels (28) 61 F3
Beaumont-les-Nonains (60) 20 A5
Beaumont-lès-Randan (63) 127 H1
Beaumont-lès-Valence (26) 144 B5
Beaumont-Monteux (26) 144 B4
Beaumont-
Pied-de-Boeuf (53) 59 E6
Beaumont-Pied-de-Boeuf (72) 78 C2
Beaumont-Sardolles (58) 99 F4
Beaumont-sur-Dême (72) 78 D2
Beaumont-sur-Grosne (71) 101 G6
Beaumont-sur-Lèze (31) 185 F2
Beaumont-sur-Oise (95) 42 C1
Beaumont-sur-Sarthe (72) 60 A4
Beaumont-sur-Vesle (51) 45 G1
Beaumont-
sur-Vingeanne (21) 86 B5
Beaumont-Village (37) 95 G2
Beaumontel (27) 40 B1
Beaumotte-Aubertans (70) 87 G5
Beaumotte-lès-Pin (70) 87 E6
Beaunay (51) 45 E4
Beaune (21) 101 G3
Beaune-d'Allier (03) 113 E4
Beaune-la-Rolande (45) 63 G5
Beaune-sur-Arzon (43) 142 B2
Beaunotte (21) 85 F3
Beaupont (01) 117 E3
Beaupouyet (24) 136 C4
Beaupréau (49) 75 G5
Beaupuy (31) 169 E5
Beaupuy (32) 168 B3
Beaupuy (47) 150 C2
Beaupuy (82) 168 D2
Beauquesne (80) 7 G4
Beaurain (59) 9 F3
Beaurains (62) 8 B3
Beaurains-lès-Noyon (60) 21 G3
Beaurainville (62) 7 E1
Beaurecueil (13) 176 B6
Beauregard (01) 129 H1
Beauregard (46) 153 F4
Beauregard-Baret (26) 144 C4
Beauregard-
de-Terrasson (24) 138 A3
Beauregard-et-Bassac (24) 137 E4
Beauregard-l'Évêque (63) 127 G3
Beauregard-Vendon (63) 127 F1
Beaurepaire (38) 144 C1
Beaurepaire (60) 20 D6
Beaurepaire (76) 16 C3
Beaurepaire (85) 92 A3
Beaurepaire-en-Bresse (71) 102 C6
Beaurepaire-sur-Sambre (59) 9 H4
Beaurevoir (02) 9 E5
Beaurières (26) 159 F2
Beaurieux (02) 22 C5
Beaurieux (59) 10 B3
Beauronne (24) 136 D3
Beausemblant (26) 144 A2
Beausite (55) 47 E2
Beausoleil (06) 179 F3
Beaussac (24) 123 E5
Beaussais (79) 108 A4
Beaussault (76) 19 F2
Beausse (49) 75 H4
le Beausset (83) 192 D4
Beauteville (31) 186 A2
Beautheil (77) 43 H5
Beautiran (33) 149 G1
Beautor (02) 22 A2
Beautot (76) 17 G4
Beauvain (61) 38 C5
Beauvais (60) 20 A4
Beauvais-sur-Matha (17) 121 H2
Beauvais-sur-Tescou (81) 169 G3
Beauval (80) 7 G4
Beauval-en-Caux (76) 17 G3
Beauvallon (26) 144 B5
Beauvau (49) 77 F3
Beauvène (07) 143 G5
Beauvernois (71) 102 C5
Beauvezer (04) 161 F6
Beauville (31) 186 A1
Beauville (47) 151 H4
Beauvilliers (28) 62 C3
Beauvilliers (41) 79 H1
Beauvilliers (89) 84 A5
Beauvoir (50) 35 G4
Beauvoir (60) 20 C3
Beauvoir (77) 43 G6
Beauvoir (89) 83 E1
Beauvoir-de-Marc (38) 130 C5
Beauvoir-en-Lyons (76) 19 F4

Beauvoir-en-Royans (38) 144 D3
Beauvoir-sur-Mer (85) 90 C2
Beauvoir-sur-Niort (79) 107 H5
Beauvoir-Wavans (62) 7 F3
Beauvois (62) 8 D6
Beauvois-en-Cambrésis (59) 9 E4
Beauvois-en-Vermandois (02) 8 D6
Beauvoisin (26) 159 E5
Beauvoisin (30) 174 A4
Beaux (43) 142 D2
Beauzac (43) 142 D2
Beauzelle (31) 169 E5
Beauziac (47) 150 B4
Bébing (57) 49 H4
Beblenheim (68) 71 F4
Bec-de-Mortagne (76) 16 C4
le Bec-Hellouin (27) 18 A6
le Bec-Thomas (27) 18 C6
Beccas (32) 183 F1
Béceleuf (79) 107 G2
Béchamps (54) 25 H6
Bécheresse (16) 122 B5
Béchereche (16) 56 D1
Béchy (57) 48 D2
Bécon-les-Granits (49) 75 H3
Bécordel-Bécourt (80) 8 A2
Bécourt (62) 1 G5
Becquigny (02) 9 F5
Becquigny (80) 21 E2
Bédarieux (34) 172 B5
Bédarrides (84) 175 E1
Beddes (18) 112 A1
Bédéchan (32) 168 B5
Bédée (35) 56 D2
Bédeilhac-et-Aynat (09) 185 G6
Bédeille (09) 184 D4
Bédeille (64) 182 D2
Bedenac (17) 135 G2
Bédoin (84) 158 D6
Bédouès (48) 156 B4
Bedous (64) 182 A5
Béduer (46) 153 G2
Beffes (18) 98 C3
Beffia (39) 117 F2
Beffu-et-le-Morthomme (08)....24 C5
Bégaar (40) 165 F3
Bégadan (33) 120 C6
Béganne (56) 73 H1
Bégard (22) 32 D3
Bègles (33) 135 E5
Bégole (65) 183 G3
Bégrolles-en-Mauges (49) ...75 H6
la Bégude-de-Mazenc (26)....158 C2
Bègues (03) 113 G5
Béguey (33) 149 G1
Béguios (64) 181 E1
Béhagnies (62) 8 B3
Béhasque-Lapiste (64) 181 F1
Béhen (80) 6 D4
Béhencourt (80) 7 H5
Béhéricourt (60) 21 G3
Behonne (55) 47 E4
Béhorléguy (64) 181 E3
Béhoust (78) 41 H4
Behren-lès-Forbach (57)....27 G5
Béhuard (49) 76 D5
Beignon (56) 56 C4
Beillé (72) 60 C5
Beine (89) 83 G2
Beine-Nauroy (51) 23 F6
Beinheim (67) 51 G3
Beire-le-Châtel (21) 86 A5
Beire-le-Fort (21) 102 B1
Beissat (23) 125 H3
Bélâbre (36) 110 B2
Belan-sur-Ource (21) 67 E6
Bélaye (46) 152 B3
Belberaud (31) 169 G6
Belbèse (82) 168 C3
Belbeuf (76) 18 D5
Belbèze-de-Lauragais (31) ...185 G1
Belbèze-en-
  Comminges (31) 184 D4
Belcaire (11) 199 G1
Belcastel (12) 154 A4
Belcastel (81) 169 H5
Belcastel-et-Buc (11) 187 E5
Belcodène (13) 192 C2
Bélesta (09) 186 B6
Bélesta (66) 200 D2
Bélesta-en-Lauragais (31) ...186 A1
Beleymas (24) 137 E4
Belfahy (70) 88 C1
Belfays (25) 88 D6
Belflou (11) 186 A2
Belfonds (61) 39 F6
Belfort (90) 88 D3
Belfort-du-Quercy (46) 152 D5
Belfort-sur-Rebenty (11) ...199 H1
Belgeard (53) 59 E3
Belgentier (83) 193 F4
Belgodère (2B) 202 D5
Belhade (40) 149 F4
Belhomert-Guéhouville (28)...61 G1
le Bélieu (25) 104 C2
Bélignat (01) 130 C2
Bélis (40) 166 A1
Belin-Béliet (33) 148 D2
Bélis (40) 170 D1
Bellac (87) 110 B5
Bellaffaire (04) 160 C3
Bellaing (59) 9 E2
Bellancourt (80) 7 E4
Bellange (57) 49 F3
Bellavilliers (61) 60 C2
le Bellay-en-Vexin (95)....42 A1
Belle-Église (60) 42 C1
Belle-et-Houllefort (62)....1 F4
Belle-Isle-en-Terre (22) 32 C4
Belleau (02) 44 B2
Belleau (54) 48 C4
Bellebat (33) 135 H6
Bellebrune (62) 1 F4
Bellechassagne (19) 125 H4
Bellechaume (89) 65 G5
Bellecombe (73) 118 A4
Bellecombe-en-Bauges (73)..132 B3
Bellecombe-Tarendol (26)....159 E4
Bellefond (21) 85 H5
Bellefond (33) 135 H6
Bellefonds (86) 94 D6
Bellefontaine (39) 118 A3
Bellefontaine (50) 37 G5
Bellefontaine (88) 69 G5
Bellefontaine (95) 42 D2
Bellefosse (67) 71 E1
Bellegarde (30) 174 C4
Bellegarde (32) 184 A1
Bellegarde (45) 63 G6
Bellegarde (81) 170 D1
Bellegarde-du-Razès (11) ...186 C4
Bellegarde-en-Diois (26)....159 F2
Bellegarde-en-Forez (42)....129 E4
Bellegarde-en-Marche (23)...125 H1
Bellegarde-
  Sainte-Marie (31) 168 D5
Bellegarde-
  sur-Valserine (01) 117 H5
Belleherbe (25) 88 B6
Bellemagny (68) 89 E2
Bellême (61) 60 D2
Bellenaves (03) 113 G5
Bellencombre (76) 17 H4
Belleneuve (21) 86 A6
Bellengreville (14) 38 D1
Bellengreville (76) 17 H2
Bellenod-sur-Seine (21) 85 E3
Bellenot-sous-Pouilly (21)...101 E1
Bellentre (73) 133 E4
Belleray (55) 47 F1
Bellerive-sur-Allier (03) 114 A6
Belleroche (42) 115 G5
Belles-Forêts (57) 49 H4
Belleserre (81) 170 B6
Belleu (02) 22 A5
Belleuse (80) 20 B2
Bellevaux (74) 119 E4

Bellevesvre (71) 102 C5
Belleville (54) 48 C4
Belleville (69) 116 B6
Belleville (79) 107 G5
Belleville-en-Caux (76) 17 G4
Belleville-
  Châtillon-sur-Bar (08)....24 B4
Belleville-sur-Loire (18)....82 B4
Belleville-sur-Mer (76) 17 H1
Belleville-sur-Meuse (55)....47 F1
Belleville-sur-Vie (85) 91 G3
Bellevigne-la-Montagne (43)..142 B2
Bellevigny (41) 131 F3
Belleydoux (01) 117 H4
la Bellière (61) 39 E5
la Bellière (76) 19 E3
Bellignat (01) 117 G4
Belligné (44) 76 B4
Bellignies (59) 9 H2
la Belliole (89) 64 D4
Belloc (09) 186 B5
Belloc-Saint-Clamens (32)...183 H1
Bellon (16) 136 B1
Bellonne (62) 8 C2
Bellot (77) 44 B4
Bellou (14) 15 H6
Bellou-en-Houlme (61) 38 B5
Bellou-le-Trichard (61) 60 D3
Bellou-sur-Huisne (61) 61 E2
Belloy (60) 21 E3
Belloy-en-France (95) 42 D2
Belloy-en-Santerre (80) 8 B6
Belloy-Saint-Léonard (80)....6 D6
Belloy-sur-Somme (80) 7 F5
Belluire (17) 121 F5
Belmesnil (76) 17 G3
Belmont (25) 104 A1
Belmont (32) 167 F4
Belmont (38) 131 E5
Belmont (39) 102 D3
Belmont (52) 86 C2
Belmont (67) 71 E1
Belmont (70) 88 A1
Belmont-Bretenoux (46) 139 E5
Belmont-d'Azergues (69) 129 H2
Belmont-de-la-Loire (42) ...115 G5
Belmont-lès-Darney (88) 69 F5
Belmont-Luthézieu (01) 131 F1
Belmont-Sainte-Foi (46) 153 E5
Belmont-sur-Buttant (88) 70 B3
Belmont-sur-Rance (12) ...171 G3
Belmont-sur-Vair (88) 69 E3
Belmont-Tramonet (73) 131 F5
Belmontet (46) 152 A4
Belonchamp (70) 88 B2
Belpech (11) 186 A3
Belrain (55) 47 F3
Belrupt (88) 69 F4
Belrupt-en-Verdunois (55) ...47 G1
Belval (08) 24 A1
Belval (50) 37 E1
Belval (88) 70 C1
Belval-Bois-des-Dames (08)...24 C4
Belval-en-Argonne (51) 46 D3
Belval-sous-Châtillon (51)...45 E1
Belvédère (06) 179 E1
Belvédère-Campomoro (2A)..206 C3
Belvès (24) 137 H6
Belvès-de-Castillon (33) 136 A5
Belvèze (82) 152 A4
Belvèze-du-Razès (11) 186 C4
Belvézet (30) 174 A1
Belvézet (48) 156 C2
Belvianes-et-Cavirac (11)....200 A1
Belvis (11) 199 H1
Belz (56) 54 D6
Bémécourt (27) 40 C4
Bénac (09) 185 G5
Bénac (65) 183 E3
Benagues (09) 185 H4
Benais (37) 78 A6
Bénaix (09) 186 B6
Bénaménil (54) 49 G6
Bénarville (76) 16 D4
Benassay (86) 108 C1
la Benâte (17) 107 G6
Benay (02) 22 A1
Benayes (19) 124 C5
Bendejun (06) 195 F2
Bendorf (68) 89 F4
Bénéjacq (64) 182 C3
Benerville-sur-Mer (14) 15 E3
Bénesse-lès-Dax (40) 165 E4
Bénesse-Maremne (40) 164 C4
Benest (16) 109 F6
Bénestroff (57) 49 G3
Bénesville (76) 17 F3
Benet (85) 107 G3
Beneuvre (21) 85 G3
Bénévent-et-Charbillac (05)..160 D1
Bénévent-l'Abbaye (23) 111 E5
Beney-en-Woëvre (55) 48 A3
Benfeld (67) 71 G2
Bengy-sur-Craon (18) 98 B3
Bénifontaine (62) 8 B1
Béning-lès-Saint-Avold (57)..49 G1
la Bénisson-Dieu (42) 115 E5
Bénivay-Ollon (26) 158 D5
Bennecourt (78) 41 G2
Bennetot (76) 16 D4
Benney (54) 69 G1
Bennwihr (68) 71 F4
Bénodet (29) 53 F4
Benoisey (21) 84 D4
Benoîtville (50) 12 B3
Benon (17) 107 E4
Bénonces (01) 131 E2
Bénouville (14) 14 C4
Bénouville (76) 16 B3
Benque (31) 184 C3
Benque-Dessous-
  et-Dessus (31) 197 F1
Benquet (40) 166 A3
Bentayou-Sérée (64) 182 D1
Bény (01) 117 E4
le Bény-Bocage (14) 37 H2
Bény-sur-Mer (14) 14 B3
Béon (01) 131 G2
Béon (89) 65 F6
Béost (64) 182 B5
Bérat (31) 185 E2
Béraut (32) 167 G2
Berbérust-Lias (65) 182 D4
Berbezit (43) 142 A1
Berbiguières (24) 137 H6
Bercenay-en-Othe (10) 66 A4
Bercenay-le-Hayer (10) 65 G3
Berchères-les-Pierres (28)....62 B2
Berchères-
  Saint-Germain (28) 62 A1
Berchères-sur-Vesgre (28)...41 G4
Berck (62) 6 B1
Bercloux (17) 121 F2
Berd'huis (61) 60 D2
Berdoues (32) 183 G1
Bérelles (59) 10 B3
Bérengeville-
  la-Campagne (27) 40 D1
Berentzwiller (68) 89 G3
Bérenx (64) 165 F6
Béréziat (01) 116 C3
Berfay (72) 61 E5
Berg (67) 50 A3
Berg-sur-Moselle (57) 26 C2
Berganty (46) 153 E3
Bergbieten (67) 50 C6
Bergerac (24) 137 E5
Bergères (10) 67 E4
Bergères-lès-Vertus (51) 45 F3
Bergères-sous-
  Montmirail (51) 44 C4
Bergesserin (71) 115 H3
Bergheim (68) 71 F3
Bergholtz (68) 71 F6
Bergholtzzell (68) 71 F6

Bergicourt (80) 20 A1
Bergnicourt (08) 23 G4
Bergonne (63) 127 F5
Bergouey (40) 165 G4
Bergouey-Viellenave (64)....165 E6
Bergueneuse (62) 2 B6
Bergues (59) 2 C2
Bergues-sur-Sambre (02) 9 G5
Bérig-Vintrange (57) 49 F2
Bérigny (50) 13 G6
Berjou (61) 38 B3
Berlaimont (59) 9 H3
Berlancourt (02) 22 D1
Berlancourt (60) 21 G2
Berlats (81) 171 E4
Berlencourt-le-Cauroy (62)...7 H2
Berles-au-Bois (62) 8 A3
Berles-Monchel (62) 7 H2
la Berlière (08) 24 C3
Berling (57) 50 B4
Berlise (02) 23 F2
Berlou (34) 188 A1
Bermerain (59) 9 F3
Bermeries (59) 9 H2
Bermering (57) 49 F3
Bermesnil (80) 6 D6
Bermicourt (62) 7 G1
Bermont (90) 88 C3
Bermonville (76) 18 A2
Bernac (16) 108 D6
Bernac (81) 170 B2
Bernac-Debat (65) 183 E3
Bernac-Dessus (65) 183 E3
Bernadets (64) 182 C1
Bernadets-Debat (65) 183 G2
Bernadets-Dessus (65) 183 G3
le Bernard (85) 91 F6
la Bernardière (85) 91 H1
Bernardswiller (67) 71 G1
Bernardvillé (67) 71 F2
Bernâtre (80) 7 F3
Bernaville (80) 7 F4
Bernay (27) 15 H5
Bernay-en-Champagne (72)...59 H5
Bernay-en-Ponthieu (80) 6 D2
Bernay-Saint-Martin (17) ...107 G6
Bernay-Vilbert (77) 43 G5
Berné (56) 54 C3
Bernécourt (54) 48 A4
Bernède (32) 166 C4
la Bernerie-en-Retz (44) 73 H6
Bernes (80) 8 D5
Bernes-sur-Oise (95) 42 C1
Bernesq (14) 13 G5
Berneuil (16) 122 A6
Berneuil (17) 121 E4
Berneuil (80) 7 F4
Berneuil (87) 110 B6
Berneuil-en-Bray (60) 20 A5
Berneuil-sur-Aisne (60) 21 G4
Berneval-le-Grand (76) 17 H1
Bernex (74) 119 F3
Bernienville (27) 40 D2
Bernières (76) 16 D3
Bernières-d'Ailly (14) 39 E2
Bernières-le-Patry (14) 38 A4
Bernières-sur-Mer (14) 14 B3
Bernières-sur-Seine (27) 19 E6
Bernieulles (62) 1 G6
Bernin (38) 145 H1
Bernis (30) 174 A4
Bernolsheim (67) 51 E4
Bernon (10) 66 B6
Bernos-Beaulac (33) 149 H4
Bernot (02) 9 F6
Bernouil (89) 84 A1
Bernouville (27) 19 G5
Bernwiller (68) 89 E2
Berny-en-Santerre (80) 8 B6
Berny-Rivière (02) 21 H5
Bérou-la-Mulotière (28) 40 D5
Berrac (32) 167 H1
Berre-les-Alpes (06) 195 F2
Berre-l'Étang (13) 175 G6
Berriac (11) 187 E3
Berric (56) 73 F1
Berrie (86) 93 H2
Berrien (29) 32 A5
Berrieux (02) 22 D4
Berrogain-Larrus (64) 181 G2
Berru (51) 23 F6
Berry-au-Bac (02) 23 E5
Berry-Bouy (18) 97 G2
le Bersac (05) 159 H4
Bersac-sur-Rivalier (87) 110 D6
Bersaillin (39) 102 D4
Bersée (59) 8 D1
Berson (33) 135 E3
Berstett (67) 51 E5
Berstheim (67) 51 E4
Bert (03) 114 C4
Bertangles (80) 7 G5
Bertaucourt-Epourdon (02)...22 A3
Berteaucourt-les-Dames (80)..7 F4
Berteaucourt-
  lès-Thennes (80) 20 D1
Berthecourt (60) 20 B5
Berthegon (86) 94 B4
Berthelange (25) 103 E1
Berthelming (57) 49 H4
Berthen (59) 2 D4
Berthenay (37) 78 C6
Berthenicourt (02) 22 A1
Berthenonville (27) 41 G1
la Berthenoux (36) 97 E6
Berthez (33) 150 A3
Bertholène (12) 154 D4
Berthouville (27) 15 H5
Bertignat (63) 128 B4
Bertignolles (10) 66 D5
Bertincourt (62) 8 C4
Bertoncourt (08) 23 G3
Bertrambois (54) 49 H5
Bertrancourt (80) 7 H4
Bertrange (57) 26 B4
Bertre (81) 170 A5
Bertren (65) 184 A5
Bertreville (76) 16 D3
Bertreville-Saint-Ouen (76)...17 G3
Bertric-Burée (24) 136 D1
Bertrichamps (54) 70 B1
Bertricourt (02) 23 E5
Bertrimont (76) 17 G4
Bertrimoutier (88) 70 D3
Bertry (59) 9 F4
Béru (89) 84 A2
Béruges (86) 108 D1
Bérulle (10) 65 H4
Bérus (72) 60 A2
Berville (76) 17 F4
Berville (95) 42 B1
Berville-en-Roumois (27) 18 B5
Berville-la-Campagne (27)...40 C2
Berville-sur-Mer (27) 15 F2
Berville-sur-Seine (76) 17 F6
Berviller-en-Moselle (57) 27 E4
Berzé-la-Ville (71) 116 A3
Berzé-le-Châtel (71) 116 A3
Berzème (07) 157 H2
Berzieux (51) 46 C1
Berzy-le-Sec (02) 22 A5
la Besace (08) 24 C3
Besain (39) 103 E5
Besançon (25) 103 G1
Bésayes (26) 144 C4
Bescat (64) 182 B4
Bésignan (26) 159 E4
Bésingrand (64) 182 A1
Beslon (50) 37 F3
Besmé (02) 21 H3
Besmont (02) 10 B6
Besnans (70) 87 G5
Besné (44) 73 H3

Besneville (50) 12 C4
Besny-et-Loizy (02) 22 C3
Bessac (16) 122 A6
Bessais-le-Fromental (18)....98 B6
Bessamorel (43) 142 D3
Bessan (34) 188 D2
Bessancourt (95) 42 C2
Bessans (73) 147 G1
Bessas (07) 157 F4
le Bessat (42) 143 G1
Bessay (85) 106 C1
Bessay-sur-Allier (03) 113 H3
Besse (15) 140 A3
Besse (24) 152 B1
Bessé (16) 122 B1
Besse (38) 146 A3
Bessé-sur-Braye (72) 79 E1
Besse-et-
  Saint-Anastaise (63)....127 E5
Bessède-de-Sault (11) 200 A1
Bessèges (30) 157 E5
Bessenay (69) 129 G3
Bessens (82) 169 E3
Besset (09) 186 A4
Bessey (42) 129 H6
Bessey-en-Chaume (21)....101 F2
Bessey-la-Cour (21) 101 F2
Bessey-lès-Cîteaux (21) 102 A2
la Besseyre-Saint-Mary (43)..141 H4
Bessières (31) 169 G3
Bessines (79) 107 G3
Bessines-sur-
  Gartempe (87) 110 D6
Bessins (38) 144 D2
Besson (03) 113 H2
Bessoncourt (90) 88 D3
Bessonies (46) 139 G5
les Bessons (48) 141 G6
Bessuéjouls (12) 154 D3
Bessy (10) 66 B1
Bessy-sur-Cure (89) 83 G3
Bestiac (09) 199 F1
Bétaille (46) 139 E5
Betaucourt (70) 87 E1
Betbèze (65) 183 H2
Betbezer-d'Armagnac (40)...166 C2
Betcave-Aguin (32) 184 A1
Betchat (09) 184 D4
Bétête (23) 111 H3
Béthancourt-en-Valois (60)...21 F6
Béthancourt-en-Vaux (02)...21 H3
Béthelainville (55) 47 E1
Béthemont-la-Forêt (95) 42 C2
Béthencourt (59) 9 F4
Béthencourt-sur-Mer (80) 6 B4
Béthencourt-sur-Somme (80)..21 F1
Bétheniville (51) 23 G5
Bétheny (51) 23 E6
Béthincourt (55) 25 E6
Béthines (86) 110 A2
Béthisy-Saint-Martin (60)....21 F5
Béthisy-Saint-Pierre (60) 21 F5
Bethmale (09) 184 D6
Bethon (51) 44 D5
Béthon (72) 60 A2
Bethoncourt (25) 88 C4
Béthonsart (62) 7 H1
Béthonvilliers (28) 61 F4
Bethonvilliers (90) 88 D2
Béthune (62) 2 D6
Bétignicourt (10) 66 D2
Beton-Bazoches (77) 44 A5
Betoncourt-
  Saint-Pancras (70) 69 G6
Betoncourt-sur-Mance (70)...86 D1
Bétous (32) 166 D3
Betplan (32) 183 F2
Betpouey (65) 183 E6
Bétracq (64) 166 D6
Betschdorf (67) 51 F2
Bettainvillers (54) 26 A3
Bettancourt-la-Ferrée (52)...46 C5
Bettancourt-la-Longue (51)...46 C4
Bettange (57) 26 D4
Bettant (01) 130 D2
Bettborn (57) 50 A4
Bettegney-Saint-Brice (88)...69 G3
Bettelainville (57) 26 C4
Bettembos (80) 19 H1
Bettencourt-Rivière (80) 7 E5
Bettencourt-Saint-Ouen (80)..7 F4
Bettendorf (68) 89 F3
Bettes (65) 183 F4
Betteville (76) 17 E5
Bettignies (59) 10 A2
Betting (57) 49 G1
Betton (35) 57 F2
Betton-Bettonet (73) 132 B5
Bettoncourt (88) 69 F2
Bettrechies (59) 9 G2
Bettviller (57) 50 B1
Bettwiller (67) 50 A3
Betz (60) 43 G1
Betz-le-Château (37) 95 F3
Beugin (62) 7 H1
Beugnâtre (62) 8 B4
Beugneux (02) 22 B6
Beugnies (59) 10 A4
le Beugnon (79) 107 H1
Beugnon (89) 65 H6
Beugny (62) 8 C4
Beuil (06) 161 H6
le Beulay (88) 70 D2
Beulotte-Saint-Laurent (70)...88 B1
Beure (25) 103 F1
Beurey (10) 66 D3
Beurey-Bauguay (21) 100 D1
Beurey-sur-Saulx (55) 46 D4
Beurières (63) 128 B6
Beurizot (21) 84 D6
Beurlay (17) 120 D2
Beurville (52) 67 F3
Beussent (62) 1 G6
Beuste (64) 182 C3
Beutal (25) 88 B4
Beutin (62) 1 F6
Beuvardes (02) 44 C1
Beuvezin (54) 69 E2
Beuvillers (14) 15 F5
Beuvillers (54) 26 A3
Beuvrages (59) 9 F2
Beuvraignes (80) 21 F2
Beuvron (58) 83 F6
Beuvron-en-Auge (14) 14 D4
Beuvry (62) 2 D6
Beuvry-la-Forêt (59) 9 E1
Beux (57) 48 D2
Beuxes (86) 94 A2
Beuzec-Cap-Sizun (29) 52 D2
Beuzeville (27) 15 G3
Beuzeville-au-Plain (50) 13 E4
Beuzeville-la-Bastille (50)....13 E4
Beuzeville-la-Grenier (76)....16 C4
Beuzeville-la-Guérard (76)...16 D3
Beuzevillette (76) 16 D4
Bévenais (38) 131 E6
Beveuge (70) 88 A4
Béville-le-Comte (28) 62 C2
Bévillers (59) 9 F4
Bevons (04) 160 A5
Bévy (21) 101 G1
Bey (01) 116 C4
Bey (71) 101 H5
Bey-sur-Seille (54) 49 E4
Beychac-et-Caillau (33) 135 G5
Beylongue (40) 165 G2
Beynac (87) 124 A3
Beynac-et-Cazenac (24)....138 A5
Beynat (19) 139 E3
Beynes (04) 177 G2
Beynes (78) 42 A4
Beynost (01) 130 C2
le Bez (81) 171 E5
Bez-et-Esparon (30) 172 D2
Bézac (09) 185 G4
Bezalles (77) 44 A5
Bézancourt (76) 19 F4
Bezange-la-Grande (54) 49 E4
Bezange-la-Petite (57) 49 F4
Bezannes (51) 23 E6
Bézaudun-les-Alpes (06)....195 E2
Bézaudun-sur-Bîne (26) 158 D2
Bezaumont (54) 48 C3
Bèze (21) 86 A5
Bézenac (24) 137 H5
Bézenet (03) 113 E4
Bézéril (32) 168 B6
Béziers (34) 188 C2
Bezinghem (62) 1 G5
Bezins-Garraux (31) 184 A5
la Bezole (11) 186 C5
Bezolles (32) 167 F3
Bezons (95) 42 C3
Bezonvaux (55) 25 F6
Bezouce (30) 174 B3
Bézouotte (21) 86 B5
Bézu-la-Forêt (27) 19 G4
Bézu-le-Guéry (02) 44 A2
Bézu-Saint-Éloi (27) 19 G5
Bézu-Saint-Germain (02)....44 C1
Bézues-Bajon (32) 184 A1
Biache-Saint-Vaast (62) 8 C2
Biaches (80) 8 C6
Bians-les-Usiers (25) 103 H3
Biard (86) 109 E1
Biarne (39) 102 C2
Biarre (80) 21 F2
Biarritz (64) 164 C6
Biarrotte (40) 164 C5
Biars-sur-Cère (46) 139 E5
Bias (40) 148 A5
Bias (47) 151 F4
Biaudos (40) 164 C5
Bibiche (57) 26 D3
Biblisheim (67) 51 F3
Bibost (69) 129 G3
Bichancourt (02) 21 H3
Biches (58) 99 G3
Bickenholtz (57) 50 A4
Bicqueley (54) 48 B6
Bidache (64) 165 E5
Bidarray (64) 180 D3
Bidart (64) 164 A6
Bidestroff (57) 49 F3
Biding (57) 49 G1
Bidon (07) 157 H4
Bidos (64) 182 A3
Biécourt (88) 69 E3
Biederthal (68) 89 G4
Bief (25) 88 C6
Bief-des-Maisons (39) 103 G5
Bief-du-Fourg (39) 103 G5
Biefmorin (39) 102 D4
Biefvillers-lès-Bapaume (62)...8 B4
Bielle (64) 182 B4
Biencourt (80) 6 C5
Biencourt-sur-Orge (55) 47 F6
Bienville (60) 21 F5
Bienville-la-Petite (54) 49 F5
Bienvillers-au-Bois (62) 8 A3
Biermes (08) 23 G4
Biermont (60) 21 E3
Bierné (53) 77 E1
Bierne (59) 2 C2
Bierre-lès-Semur (21) 84 C5
Bierry-les-
  Belles-Fontaines (89) 84 B4
Biert (09) 185 F6
Bierville (76) 17 H5
Biesheim (68) 71 G5
Biesles (52) 68 A5
Bietlenheim (67) 51 E4
Bieujac (33) 149 H2
Bieuxy (02) 22 A4
Biéville (50) 37 H1
Biéville-Beuville (14) 14 C4
Biéville-Quétiéville (14) 39 E1
Bièvres (02) 22 D4
Bièvres (08) 24 D3
Bièvres (91) 42 C5
Biffontaine (88) 70 B3
Biganos (33) 148 C1
Bignac (16) 122 B3
Bignan (56) 55 F4
Bignay (17) 121 F2
la Bigne (14) 38 A2
Bignicourt (08) 23 H4
Bignicourt-sur-Marne (51)....46 B5
Bignicourt-sur-Saulx (51) 46 C5
le Bignon (44) 74 D6
le Bignon-du-Maine (53) 58 D6
le Bignon-Mirabeau (45) 64 B4
Bignoux (86) 109 F1
Bigorno (2B) 203 F6
la Bigottière (53) 58 C3
Biguglia (2B) 203 G4
Bihorel (76) 18 D4
Bihucourt (62) 8 B4
Bilhac (19) 139 E4
Bilhères (64) 182 B4
Bilia (2A) 206 D3
Bilieu (38) 131 F6
Billancelles (28) 61 H1
Billancourt (80) 21 F2
les Billanges (87) 124 D1
les Billaux (33) 135 H4
Billé (35) 57 H2
Billecul (39) 103 G5
Billère (64) 182 B2
Billey (21) 102 C2
Billezois (03) 114 B5
Billiat (01) 117 H5
Billième (73) 131 G3
Billière (31) 197 F1
Billiers (56) 73 F2
Billio (56) 55 G4
Billom (63) 127 G3
Billy (03) 114 A4
Billy (14) 38 D1
Billy (41) 80 A6
Billy-Berclau (62) 3 E6
Billy-Chevannes (58) 99 F3
Billy-le-Grand (51) 45 G1
Billy-lès-Chanceaux (21)....85 E4
Billy-Montigny (62) 8 C1
Billy-sous-Mangiennes (55)...25 G5
Billy-sur-Aisne (02) 22 A5
Billy-sur-Oisy (58) 83 F5
Billy-sur-Ourcq (02) 22 A6
Biltzheim (68) 71 F5
Bilwisheim (67) 51 E4
Bimont (62) 1 G6
Binarville (51) 24 C6
Binas (41) 80 A1
Bindernheim (67) 71 H2
Binges (21) 86 A6
Binic (22) 33 H3
Bining (57) 50 B1
Biniville (50) 12 D4
Binos (31) 184 A5
Binson-et-Orquigny (51) 45 E1
Bio (46) 138 D6
Biol (38) 131 E5
la Biolle (73) 131 H3
Biollet (63) 126 C1
Bion (50) 37 G5
Bioncourt (57) 49 E4
Bionville (54) 70 C1
Bionville-sur-Nied (57) 49 E1
Biot (06) 195 E4
le Biot (74) 119 F4
Bioule (82) 169 F1
Bioussac (16) 108 D6
Biozat (03) 113 H6
Birac (16) 122 A5
Birac (33) 149 H3
Birac-sur-Trec (47) 150 C3

Biran (32) 167 G4
Biras (24) 137 E1
Biriatou (64) 180 A1
Birieux (01) 130 B1
Birkenwald (67) 50 C5
Biron (17) 121 F4
Biron (24) 151 G2
Biron (64) 165 G6
Biscarrosse (40) 148 B3
Bischheim (67) 51 E5
Bischholtz (67) 50 D3
Bischoffsheim (67) 50 D6
Bischwihr (68) 71 G4
Bischwiller (67) 51 F4
Bisel (68) 89 F4
Bisinchi (2B) 203 F6
Bislée (55) 47 H2
Bissert (67) 49 H2
Bisseuil (51) 45 F2
Bissey-la-Côte (21) 67 E6
Bissey-la-Pierre (21) 84 D1
Bissey-sous-Cruchaud (71)..101 F6
Bissières (14) 39 E1
Bissezeele (59) 2 C3
Bissy-la-Mâconnaise (71)....116 B2
Bissy-sous-Uxelles (71) 116 A1
Bissy-sur-Fley (71) 101 F6
Bisten-en-Lorraine (57) 27 E5
Bistroff (57) 49 F2
Bitche (57) 50 C1
Bitry (58) 82 D5
Bitry (60) 21 G4
Bitschhoffen (67) 51 E3
Bitschwiller-lès-Thann (68)...89 E1
Bivès (32) 168 B3
Biviers (38) 145 G2
Biville (50) 12 B2
Biville-la-Baignarde (76) 17 G3
Biville-la-Rivière (76) 17 F3
Biville-sur-Mer (76) 17 H1
Bivilliers (61) 60 D1
Bizanet (11) 187 H4
Bizanos (64) 182 B2
Bize (52) 86 D2
Bize (65) 183 H4
Bize-Minervois (11) 187 H3
Bizeneuille (03) 112 D3
Biziat (01) 116 C5
Bizonnes (38) 131 E6
le Bizot (25) 104 C2
les Bizots (71) 100 D6
Bizou (61) 61 E1
Bizous (65) 183 H4
Blacé (69) 116 A6
Blacourt (60) 19 H4
Blacqueville (76) 17 F5
Blacy (51) 46 A4
Blacy (89) 84 B4
Blaesheim (67) 51 E6
Blagnac (31) 169 E5
Blagny (08) 24 D2
Blagny-sur-Vingeanne (21)...86 B5
Blaignac (33) 150 A2
Blaignan (33) 134 D1
Blain (44) 74 B3
Blaincourt-lès-Précy (60) 20 C6
Blaincourt-sur-Aube (10) 66 D2
Blainville-Crevon (76) 17 H5
Blainville-sur-l'Eau (54) 49 E6
Blainville-sur-Mer (50) 36 D1
Blainville-sur-Orne (14) 14 C4
Blairville (62) 8 B3
Blaise-sous-Arzillières (51)...46 B5
Blaison-Gohier (49) 77 F5
Blaisy (52) 67 G4
Blaisy-Bas (21) 85 F6
Blaisy-Haut (21) 85 F6
Blajan (31) 184 A3
Blamont (25) 88 C5
Blâmont (54) 49 H6
Blan (81) 170 B6
le Blanc (36) 110 B1
le Blanc-Mesnil (93) 42 D3
Blancafort (18) 81 H4
Blancey (21) 84 D6
Blancfossé (60) 20 B2
Blanche-Église (57) 49 F4
Blanchefosse-et-Bay (08) 23 F1
Blancherupt (67) 71 E1
Blandainville (28) 61 H3
Blandas (30) 172 C3
Blandin (38) 131 E5
Blandouet (53) 59 F5
Blandy (77) 64 B1
Blandy (91) 63 F3
Blangermont (62) 7 F2
Blangerval-Blangermont (62)..7 F2
Blangy-le-Château (14) 15 F4
Blangy-sous-Poix (80) 20 A1
Blangy-sur-Bresle (76) 6 C5
Blangy-sur-Ternoise (62) 7 F1
Blangy-Tronville (80) 7 H6
Blannay (89) 83 H4
Blanot (21) 100 D1
Blanot (71) 116 A2
Blanquefort (32) 168 A5
Blanquefort (33) 135 E4
Blanquefort-
  sur-Briolance (47) 151 H2
Blanzac (43) 142 C3
Blanzac (87) 110 B5
Blanzac-lès-Matha (17) 121 G2
Blanzac-Porcheresse (16)....122 B5
Blanzaguet-
  Saint-Cybard (16) 122 C5
Blanzat (63) 127 E2
Blanzay (86) 108 D4
Blanzay-sur-Boutonne (17)...107 H5
Blanzée (55) 47 G1
Blanzy (71) 100 D6
Blanzy-la-Salonnaise (08)....23 G4
Blanzy-lès-Fismes (02) 22 C5
Blargies (60) 19 G2
Blarians (25) 87 F6
Blaringhem (59) 2 B4
Blars (46) 153 F2
Blaru (78) 41 F2
Blasimon (33) 136 A6
Blaslay (86) 94 B5
Blassac (43) 141 H3
Blaudeix (23) 111 H5
Blausasc (06) 195 F2
Blauvac (84) 175 G1
Blauzac (30) 174 B2
Blavignac (48) 141 G5
Blavozy (43) 142 C4
Blay (14) 13 G5
Blaye (33) 135 E3
Blaye-les-Mines (81) 170 C1
Blaymont (47) 151 G4
Blaziert (32) 167 G2
Blécourt (52) 67 G2
Blécourt (59) 8 D3
Bleigny-le-Carreau (89) 83 G2
Blémerey (54) 49 G6
Blémerey (88) 69 F2
Blendecques (62) 2 B4
Bléneau (89) 82 C3
Blennes (77) 64 C3
Blénod-lès-
  Pont-à-Mousson (54) 48 C3
Blénod-lès-Toul (54) 48 B6
Bléquin (62) 1 H5
Blérancourt (02) 21 H3
Bléré (37) 79 F6
Bléruais (35) 56 C2
Blésignac (33) 135 G6
Blesle (43) 141 F1
Blesmes (02) 44 C2
Blessac (23) 125 G1
Blessonville (52) 67 G5
Blessy (62) 2 B5
Blet (18) 98 B4
Bletterans (39) 102 C6
Bleurville (88) 69 E5
Bleury (28) 62 C1
Blevaincourt (88) 68 D4
Blèves (72) 60 B1
Blicourt (60) 20 A3
Blienschwiller (67) 71 F2

Blies-Ébersing (57) 27 H5
Blies-Guersviller (57) 27 H5
Bliesbruck (57) 28 A5
Blieux (04) 177 G2
Blignicourt (10) 66 D2
Bligny (10) 67 E4
Bligny (51) 45 E1
Bligny-le-Sec (21) 85 F5
Bligny-lès-Beaune (21) 101 G3
Bligny-sur-Ouche (21) 101 F2
Blincourt (60) 21 E5
Blingel (62) 7 F1
Blis-et-Born (24) 137 G2
Blismes (58) 100 A1
Blodelsheim (68) 71 G6
Blois (41) 79 H4
Blois-sur-Seille (39) 102 D5
Blomac (11) 187 F3
Blomard (03) 113 F4
Blombay (08) 23 H1
Blond (87) 110 A5
Blondefontaine (70) 87 E1
Blonville-sur-Mer (14) 15 E3
Blosseville (76) 17 E2
Blosville (50) 13 E4
Blot-l'Église (63) 113 F6
Blotzheim (68) 89 G3
Blou (49) 77 G5
Blousson-Sérian (32) 167 E6
la Bloutière (50) 37 F3
Bloye (74) 131 H2
Bluffy (74) 132 B2
Blumeray (52) 67 F3
Blussangeaux (25) 88 B5
Blussans (25) 88 B5
Blye (39) 117 G1
Blyes (01) 130 D2
le Bô (14) 38 C3
Bobigny (93) 42 D3
Bobital (22) 34 C5
le Bocasse (76) 17 G5
Bocé (49) 77 G4
Bocognano (2A) 205 E4
Bocquegney (88) 69 G3
Bocquencé (61) 39 H4
le Bodéo (22) 33 G5
Bodilis (29) 31 G3
Boé (47) 151 F6
Boëcé (61) 60 C1
Boëge (74) 118 D4
Boeil-Bezing (64) 182 C3
Boën (42) 128 D3
Bœrsch (67) 50 D6
Boeschepe (59) 2 D3
Boeseghem (59) 2 B5
Bösenbiesen (67) 71 G3
Boëssé-le-Sec (72) 60 D4
Boësses (45) 63 G4
Bœurs-en-Othe (89) 65 G5
Boffles (62) 7 F3
Boffres (07) 143 H5
Bogève (74) 118 D4
Bogny-sur-Meuse (08) 11 H6
Bogy (07) 144 A2
Bohain-en-Vermandois (02)...9 F5
Bohal (56) 56 A5
Bohars (29) 30 D4
Bohas-Meyriat-Rignat (01)...117 F5
Boigneville (91) 63 G3
Boigny-sur-Bionne (45) 81 E1
Boinville-en-Mantois (78) ...41 H3
Boinville-en-Woëvre (55) 25 G6
Boinville-le-Gaillard (78) 62 D2
Boinvilliers (78) 41 G3
Boiry-Becquerelle (62) 8 B3
Boiry-Notre-Dame (62) 8 C2
Boiry-Saint-Martin (62) 8 A3
Boiry-Sainte-Rictrude (62) 8 A3
le Bois (73) 132 D5
Bois-Anzeray (27) 40 A2
Bois-Arnault (27) 40 B4
Bois-Bernard (62) 8 C1
Bois-Colombes (92) 42 C3
Bois-d'Amont (39) 118 B1
Bois-d'Arcy (78) 42 B4
Bois-d'Arcy (89) 83 G4
Bois-de-Céné (85) 90 D2
Bois-de-Champ (88) 70 C3
Bois-de-Gand (39) 102 C5
Bois-de-la-Pierre (31) 185 E2
Bois-d'Ennebourg (76) 17 H6
le Bois-d'Oingt (69) 129 G2
Bois-Grenier (59) 3 E4
Bois-Guilbert (76) 19 E3
Bois-Guillaume (76) 18 D4
le Bois-Hellain (27) 15 G4
Bois-Héroult (76) 19 E3
Bois-Herpin (91) 63 F2
Bois-Himont (76) 17 E5
Bois-Jérôme-
  Saint-Ouen (27) 41 G1
Bois-le-Roi (27) 40 D3
Bois-le-Roi (77) 64 A1
Bois-lès-Pargny (02) 22 C2
Bois-l'Évêque (76) 17 H6
Bois-Normand-
  près-Lyre (27) 40 B3
le Bois-Plage-en-Ré (17) 106 B4
le Bois-Robert (76) 17 G2
Bois-Sainte-Marie (71) 115 F4
Boisbergues (80) 7 F3
Boisbreteau (16) 135 H1
Boiscommun (45) 63 G5
Boisdinghem (62) 2 A4
Boisdon (77) 44 A5
Boisemont (27) 19 F6
Boisemont (95) 42 B2
Boisgasson (28) 61 F5
Boisgervilly (35) 56 C2
Boisjean (62) 6 C1
le Boisle (80) 7 E2
Boismé (79) 93 E5
Boismont (54) 25 H4
Boismont (80) 6 D4
Boismorand (45) 82 A2
Boisney (27) 40 B1
Boisredon (17) 135 F1
Boisroger (50) 36 D1
Boissay (76) 19 E3
Boisse (24) 151 F1
Boisse-Penchot (12) 153 H2
Boisseau (41) 80 A2
Boisseaux (45) 62 D3
Boissède (31) 184 B2
Boissei-la-Lande (61) 39 F5
Boisseron (34) 173 G4
Boisset (15) 139 H5
Boisset (34) 187 F2
Boisset (43) 142 D1
Boisset-et-Gaujac (30) 173 G2
Boisset-lès-Montrond (42)....129 E4
Boisset-les-Prévanches (27)..41 E3
Boisset-Saint-Priest (42) 129 E5
Boissets (78) 41 G4
Boissettes (77) 64 A1
Boisseuil (87) 124 B2
Boisseuilh (24) 138 A1
Boissey (01) 116 C3
Boissey (14) 39 F2
Boissey-le-Châtel (27) 18 B6
Boissezon (81) 170 D6
Boissia (39) 117 H1
la Boissière (14) 15 E6
la Boissière (27) 41 F3
la Boissière (34) 173 E4
la Boissière (39) 117 G3
la Boissière (53) 76 C1
la Boissière-
  de-Montaigu (85) 92 A3
la Boissière-des-Landes (85)..91 G5
la Boissière-du-Doré (44) 75 E5
la Boissière-École (78) 41 G5
la Boissière-en-Gâtine (79)...107 H1
la Boissière-sur-Èvre (49)....75 G4

Boissières (30) 174 A4
Boissières (46) 152 C2
Boissise-la-Bertrand (77) 63 H1
Boissise-le-Roi (77) 63 H1
Boissy-aux-Cailles (77) 63 H3
Boissy-en-Drouais (28) 41 E5
Boissy-Fresnoy (60) 43 H2
Boissy-la-Rivière (91) 63 F2
Boissy-l'Aillerie (95) 42 B2
Boissy-Lamberville (27) 15 H5
Boissy-le-Bois (60) 19 H6
Boissy-le-Châtel (77) 44 A4
Boissy-le-Cutté (91) 63 F2
Boissy-le-Repos (51) 44 D4
Boissy-le-Sec (91) 63 E1
Boissy-lès-Perche (28) 40 C5
Boissy-Maugis (61) 61 E2
Boissy-Mauvoisin (78) 41 G3
Boissy-Saint-Léger (94) 43 E5
Boissy-sous-Saint-Yon (91) ...63 E1
Boistrudan (35) 57 G4
Boisville-la-Saint-Père (28) ...62 C2
Boisyvon (50) 37 F4
Boitron (61) 39 G6
Boitron (77) 44 A3
Bolandoz (25) 103 G3
Bolazec (29) 32 B4
Bolbec (76) 15 G1
Bollène (84) 158 B5
la Bollène-Vésubie (06) 179 F1
Bolleville (50) 12 C5
Bolleville (76) 15 H1
Bollezeele (59) 3 H4
Bollwiller (68) 71 F6
Bologne (52) 67 H4
Bolozon (01) 117 F5
Bolquère (66) 199 H4
Bombon (77) 43 G6
Bommes (33) 149 G2
Bommiers (36) 97 E5
Bompas (09) 185 H6
Bompas (66) 201 F2
Bomy (62) 3 G5
Bongheat (63) 127 H3
le Bonhomme (68) 71 E4
Bonifacio (2A) 207 F5
Bonlier (60) 20 B4
Bonlieu (39) 117 H1
Bonlieu-sur-Roubion (26) ...158 B2
Bonloc (64) 180 D1
Bonnac (09) 185 G4
Bonnac (15) 141 F2
Bonnac-la-Côte (87) 124 B1
Bonnal (25) 87 H4
Bonnard (89) 83 F1
Bonnat (23) 111 G4
Bonnaud (39) 117 F1
Bonnay (25) 87 F6
Bonnay (71) 116 A2
Bonnay (80) 7 H5
Bonne (74) 118 D5
Bonnecourt (52) 68 B6
Bonnée (45) 81 G2
Bonnefamille (38) 130 C4
Bonnefoi (61) 39 H6
Bonnefond (19) 125 F5
Bonnefont (65) 183 G3
Bonnefontaine (39) 103 E5
Bonnegarde (40) 165 G5
Bonneil (02) 44 B2
Bonnelles (78) 42 B6
Bonnemain (35) 35 E5
Bonnemaison (14) 14 A6
Bonnencontre (21) 102 A2
Bonnes (16) 122 D4
Bonnes (86) 109 G1
Bonnesvalyn (02) 44 B1
Bonnet (55) 68 B1
Bonnétable (72) 60 C4
Bonnétage (25) 104 C1
Bonnetan (33) 135 F5
Bonneuil (16) 121 H4
Bonneuil (60) 110 C3
Bonneuil-en-France (95) ...42 D3
Bonneuil-en-Valois (60) ...21 H6
Bonneuil-les-Eaux (60) ...20 B2
Bonneuil-Matours (86) ...94 D6
Bonneuil-sur-Marne (94) ...43 E4
Bonneval (28) 62 A4
Bonneval (43) 142 B1
Bonneval (73) 133 G6
Bonneval-sur-Arc (73) ...133 G6
Bonnevaux (25) 103 H5
Bonnevaux (30) 157 F4
Bonnevaux (74) 119 F3
Bonnevaux-le-Prieuré (25) ...103 G2
Bonneveau (41) 79 F2
Bonnevent-Velloreille (70) ...87 E5
la Bonneville (50) 12 D4
Bonneville (16) 122 A2
Bonneville (74) 118 D6
Bonneville (80) 7 G4
Bonneville-Aptot (27) 18 A6
Bonneville-et-Saint-Avit-
de-Fumadières (24) 136 B5
Bonneville-la-Louvet (14) ...15 G4
la Bonneville-sur-Iton (27) ...40 D2
Bonneville-sur-Touques (14) ...5 E3
Bonnières (60) 21 H5
Bonnières (62) 7 G3
Bonnières-sur-Seine (78) 41 G2
Bonnieux (84) 175 H3
Bonningues-lès-Ardres (62) ...3 E4
Bonningues-lès-Calais (62) ...1 G3
Bonnoeil (14) 38 C2
Bonnoeuvre (44) 75 F2
Bonnut (64) 165 G5
Bonny-sur-Loire (45) 82 B2
Bono (56) 55 E6
Bonrepos (65) 183 G3
Bonrepos-Riquet (31) 169 G5
Bonrepos-sur-
Aussonnelle (31) 168 D6
Bons-en-Chablais (74) 118 D4
Bons-Tassilly (14) 38 D2
Bonsecours (76) 18 D1
Bonsmoulins (61) 39 H5
Bonson (06) 195 E1
Bonson (42) 129 E5
Bonvillard (73) 132 C4
Bonvillaret (73) 132 C4
Bonviller (54) 49 E5
Bonvillers (60) 20 B4
Bonvillet (88) 69 F5
Bony (02) 8 D5
Bonzac (33) 135 H4
Bonzée (55) 47 G1
Boô-Silhen (65) 182 D4
Boofzheim (67) 71 H2
Boos (40) 165 E2
Boos (76) 18 D1
Bootzheim (67) 71 G3
Boqueho (22) 33 F4
Bor-et-Bar (12) 153 G4
Boran-sur-Oise (60) 42 D1
Borce (64) 182 A5
Bord-Saint-Georges (23) ...112 B4

Bordeaux (33) 135 E5
Bordeaux-en-Gâtinais (45) ...63 H5
Bordeaux-Saint-Clair (76) ...16 C3
Bordères (64) 182 C3
Bordères-et-
Lamensans (40) 166 B3
Bordères-Louron (65) 183 G6
Bordères-sur-l'Échez (65) ...183 E2
les Bordes (36) 97 E3
les Bordes (45) 81 G2
les Bordes (65) 183 F3
les Bordes (71) 101 H4
les Bordes (89) 65 E5
les Bordes-Aumont (10) ...66 B4
Bordes-de-Rivière (31) ...184 A4
la Bordes-sur-Arize (09) ...185 F4
les Bordes-sur-Lez (09) ...184 D6
Bordezac (30) 157 E5
Bords (17) 120 D1
Borée (07) 143 E5
Boresse-et-Martron (17) ...136 A1
Borest (60) 43 F1
Borey (70) 87 H3
Borgo (2B) 203 G5
Bormes-les-Mimosas (83) ...193 H5
le Born (31) 169 F3
le Born (48) 156 B2
Bornambusc (76) 16 C4
Bornay (39) 117 F1
Borne (07) 156 D2
Borne (43) 142 B3
Bornel (60) 42 C1
Boron (90) 88 D3
Borre (59) 3 H5
Borrèze (24) 138 C4
Bors (Canton de Baignes-
Sainte-Radegonde) (16) ...135 H1
Bors (Canton de Montmoreau-
Saint-Cybard) (16) 136 A2
Bort-les-Orgues (19) 126 B6
Bort-l'Étang (63) 127 H3
Borville (54) 69 H1
le Bosc (09) 185 G5
le Bosc (34) 172 C4
Bosc-Bénard-Commin (27) ...18 B5
Bosc-Bénard-Crescy (27) ...18 B5
Bosc-Bérenger (76) 17 H4
Bosc-Bordel (76) 19 E3
Bosc-Édeline (76) 19 E3
Bosc-Guérard-
Saint-Adrien (76) 18 D3
Bosc-Hyons (76) 19 G4
Bosc-le-Hard (76) 17 H4
Bosc-Mesnil (76) 19 E3
le Bosc-Renoult (61) 39 G3
Bosc-Renoult-en-Ouche (27) ...40 B3
Bosc-Renoult-
en-Roumois (27) 18 A5
le Bosc-Roger-
en-Roumois (27) 18 B5
Bosc-Roger-sur-Buchy (76) ...19 E3
Boscamnant (17) 136 A3
Bosdarros (64) 182 B3
Bosgouet (27) 18 B5
Bosguérard-
de-Marcouville (27) 18 B5
Bosjean (71) 102 B5
Bosmie-l'Aiguille (87) 124 A3
Bosmont-sur-Serre (02) 22 D2
Bosmoreau-les-Mines (23) ...125 E1
Bosnormand (27) 18 B5
Bosquentin (27) 19 F4
Bosquel (80) 20 B1
Bosroger (23) 125 H1
Bossancourt (10) 67 E3
Bossay-sur-Claise (37) 95 F5
la Bosse (25) 104 C2
la Bosse (72) 60 D4
la Bosse-de-Bretagne (35) ...57 F5
Bosséval-et-Briancourt (08) ...24 B2
Bossey (74) 118 C5
Bossieu (38) 130 C6
Bossugan (33) 136 A6
Bossus-lès-Rumigny (08) ...10 B6
Bost (03) 114 B5
Bostens (40) 166 B2
Bosville (76) 17 E3
Botans (90) 88 C3
Botmeur (29) 31 H5
Botsorhel (29) 32 B4
les Bottereaux (27) 40 B4
Botz-en-Mauges (49) 75 G4
Bou (45) 81 E1
Bouafle (78) 42 A3
Bouafles (27) 19 E6
Bouan (09) 199 H1
Bouaye (44) 74 B6
Boubers-lès-Hesmond (62) ...1 H6
Boubers-sur-Canche (62) ...7 F2
Boubiers (60) 42 A1
Boucagnères (32) 167 H5
Boucau (64) 164 B5
Boucé (03) 114 A4
Boucé (61) 39 E5
le Bouchage (16) 109 E4
le Bouchage (38) 131 E4
Bouchain (59) 9 E3
Bouchamps-lès-Craon (53) ...76 B1
le Bouchaud (03) 114 D5
Bouchavesnes-Bergen (80) ...8 C5
Bouchemaine (49) 76 D5
Boucheporn (57) 49 F1
Bouchet (26) 158 B4
le Bouchet (74) 132 D1
le Bouchet-
Saint-Nicolas (43) 142 B5
Bouchevilliers (27) 19 G4
Bouchoir (80) 21 E1
Bouchon (80) 7 F4
le Bouchon-sur-Saulx (55) ...47 E6
les Bouchoux (39) 117 H4
Bouchy-Saint-Genest (51) ...44 C6
Bouclans (25) 87 H6
Boucoiran-et-Nozières (30) ...173 H2
Bouconville (08) 24 B5
Bouconville-sur-Madt (55) ...47 H4
Bouconville-Vauclair (02) ...22 D4
Bouconvillers (60) 19 H6
Boucq (54) 48 A4
Boudes (63) 127 F6
Boudeville (76) 17 F3
Boudou (82) 168 C1
Boudrac (31) 183 H3
Boudreville (21) 67 E4
Boudy-de-Beauregard (47) ...151 F2
Boué (02) 9 G5
Boueilh-
Boueilho-Lasque (64) 166 B5
Bouelles (76) 19 F3
Bouër (72) 60 D5
Bouessay (53) 77 F1
Bouesse (36) 111 F1
Bouëx (16) 122 D4
la Bouëxière (35) 57 G2
Bouffémont (95) 42 D2
Boufféré (85) 91 H2
Bouffignereux (02) 22 D5
Boufflers (80) 7 E3
Bougainville (80) 7 F6
Bougarber (64) 182 B1
Bouges-le-Château (36) 96 C3
Bougey (70) 86 D2
Bougival (78) 42 C4
Bouglainval (28) 41 F6
Bougligny (77) 63 H4
Bouglon (47) 150 B4
Bougneau (17) 121 F4
Bougnon (70) 87 F2
Bougon (79) 108 B4

Bougue (40) 166 B2
Bouguenais (44) 74 C5
Bougy (14) 14 A5
Bougy-lez-Neuville (45) ...63 E5
Bouhans (71) 102 B5
Bouhans-et-Feurg (70) ...86 C4
Bouhans-lès-Lure (70) ...87 H2
Bouhans-lès-
Montbozon (70) 87 H4
Bouhet (17) 107 E5
Bouhy (58) 82 D4
Bouilh-devant (65) 183 F2
Bouilh-Péreuilh (65) 183 F2
Bouilhonnac (11) 187 E3
Bouillac (12) 153 H2
Bouillac (24) 137 H6
Bouillac (82) 168 C3
la Bouilladisse (13) 192 C4
Bouillancourt-en-Séry (80) ...6 C5
Bouillancourt-la-Bataille (80) ...20 D2
Bouillancy (60) 43 G2
Bouilland (21) 101 G2
Bouillargues (30) 174 B3
la Bouille (76) 18 B5
Bouillé-Courdault (85) 107 F3
Bouillé-Loretz (79) 93 F2
Bouillé-Ménard (49) 76 B2
Bouillé-Saint-Paul (79) ...93 F3
la Bouillie (22) 34 A4
le Bouillon (61) 39 F6
Bouillon (64) 166 A6
Bouillonville (54) 48 A3
Bouilly (10) 66 A4
Bouilly (51) 45 E1
Bouilly-en-Gâtinais (45) ...63 F5
Bouin (79) 108 C5
Bouin (85) 90 C1
Bouin-Plumoison (62) ...7 E1
Bouisse (11) 187 E5
Bouix (21) 84 D1
Boujailles (25) 103 G4
Boujan-sur-Libron (34) 188 C2
Boulages (10) 45 E6
Boulancourt (77) 63 G4
Boulaur (32) 168 A5
le Boulay (37) 79 G3
Boulay-les-Barres (45) ...62 C6
Boulay-les-Ifs (53) 59 G2
le Boulay-Morin (27) 41 E2
Boulay-Moselle (57) 26 D5
la Boulaye (71) 100 C6
Boulazac (24) 137 F2
Boulbon (13) 174 D3
Boulc (26) 159 G1
Boule-d'Amont (66) 200 D3
Bouleternère (66) 200 D3
Bouleurs (77) 43 G4
Bouleuse (51) 22 C6
Bouliac (33) 135 F5
Boulieu-lès-Annonay (07) ...143 H2
Bouligneux (01) 116 C6
Bouligney (70) 69 G6
Bouligny (55) 25 H6
Boulin (65) 183 F2
Boullarre (60) 43 H1
le Boullay-les-
Deux-Églises (28) 41 E6
le Boullay-les-Trouxe (28) ...41 E6
le Boullay-Mivoye (28) 41 E6
le Boullay-Thierry (28) 41 E6
Boulleville (27) 15 G3
Bouloc (31) 169 F4
Bouloc (82) 152 A5
Boulogne (85) 91 H4
Boulogne-Billancourt (92) ...42 C4
Boulogne-la-Grasse (60) ...20 D2
Boulogne-sur-Gesse (31) ...184 A2
Boulogne-sur-Helpe (59) ...9 H4
Boulogne-sur-Mer (62) ...1 F4
Bouloire (72) 60 D6
Boulon (14) 14 B6
Boulot (70) 87 F6
le Boulou (66) 201 E4
Boult (70) 87 F5
Boult-aux-Bois (08) 24 B4
Boult-sur-Suippe (51) ...23 F5
Boulzicourt (08) 24 A2
Boumourt (64) 166 A6
Bouniagues (24) 137 E6
le Boupère (85) 92 B5
Bouquehault (62) 1 H3
Bouquelon (27) 16 D6
Bouquemaison (80) ...7 F3
Bouquemont (55) 47 G2
Bouquetot (27) 18 B5
Bouqueval (95) 42 D2
Bouranton (10) 66 B3
Bouray-sur-Juine (91) ...63 F1
Bourbach-le-Bas (68) ...88 D1
Bourbach-le-Haut (68) ...88 D1
Bourberain (21) 86 B5
Bourbévelle (70) 69 E6
Bourbon-Lancy (71) ...114 C1
Bourbon-l'Archambault (03) ...113 F1
Bourbonne-les-Bains (52) ...68 D6
la Bourboule (63) 126 C5
Bourbourg (59) 3 F3
Bourbriac (22) 33 E4
Bourcefranc-le-Chapus (17) ...120 B2
Bourcia (39) 117 F3
Bourcq (08) 24 A4
Bourdainville (76) 17 G4
Bourdalat (40) 166 C3
Bourdeau (73) 131 G3
Bourdeaux (26) 158 C2
Bourdeilles (24) 137 E1
le Bourdeix (24) 123 E4
Bourdelles (33) 150 B2
Bourdenay (10) 65 G2
le Bourdet (79) 107 G4
Bourdettes (64) 182 C3
Bourdic (30) 174 A2
la Bourdinière-
Saint-Loup (28) 62 A3
Bourdon (80) 7 F5
Bourdonnay (57) 49 G4
Bourdonné (78) 41 H5
la Bourdonnie (02) 10 A6
Bouresches (02) 44 B2
Bouresse (86) 109 G3
Bouret-sur-Canche (62) ...7 F2
Boureuilles (55) 24 C6
Bourg (33) 135 F3
le Bourg (46) 153 F1
Bourg (52) 86 C2
Bourg-Achard (27) 18 B5
Bourg-Archambault (86) ...110 A3
Bourg-Argental (42) 143 H1
Bourg-Beaudouin (27) ...19 E4
Bourg-Blanc (29) 30 D4
Bourg-Bruche (67) 71 E2
Bourg-Charente (16) 121 H3
Bourg-de-Bigorre (65) ...183 F4
Bourg-de-Péage (26) ...144 C4
Bourg-de-Sirod (39) ...103 G5
Bourg-de-Thizy (69) 115 G6
Bourg-des-Comptes (35) ...57 E4
Bourg-des-Maisons (24) ...136 D1
le Bourg-d'Iré (49) 76 B2
le Bourg-d'Oisans (38) ...146 A3
Bourg-d'Oueil (31) 183 H6
Bourg-Dun (76) 17 F2
Bourg-en-Bresse (01) ...116 D4
Bourg-et-Comin (02) ...22 C5
Bourg-Fidèle (08) 10 D5
Bourg-la-Reine (92) 42 D4
Bourg-Lastic (63) 126 C4
Bourg-le-Comte (71) ...115 E4
Bourg-le-Roi (72) 60 A3
Bourg-lès-Valence (26) ...144 B4
Bourg-l'Évêque (49) 76 B3

Bourg-Madame (66) 199 G4
le Bourg-Saint-Andéol (07) ...158 A4
le Bourg-Saint-Léonard (61) ...39 F4
Bourg-Saint-Maurice (73) ...133 F4
le Bourg-sous-Châtelet (90) ...88 D2
Bourg-sous-Châtelet (90) ...88 D2
Bourgaltroff (57) 49 G3
Bourganeuf (23) 125 E2
Bourgbarré (35) 57 F4
Bourgeauville (14) 15 E4
le Bourget (93) 42 D3
le Bourget-du-Lac (73) ...131 H4
Bourget-en-Huile (73) ...132 B5
Bourgheim (67) 71 G1
Bourghelles (59) 3 G5
Bourgnac (24) 136 D4
Bourgneuf (17) 106 D4
Bourgneuf (73) 132 B4
Bourgneuf-en-Mauges (49) ...75 H4
le Bourgneuf-la-Forêt (53) ...58 B4
Bourgogne (51) 23 E5
Bourgoin-Jallieu (38) ...130 D4
Bourgon (53) 58 B4
la Bourgonce (88) 70 C2
Bourgougnague (47) ...150 D2
Bourgtheroulde-Infreville (27) ...18 B5
Bourguébus (14) 38 D1
Bourgueil (37) 78 A6
Bourguenolles (50) 36 D2
Bourguignon (25) 88 C5
Bourguignon-
lès-Conflans (70) 87 G1
Bourguignon-
lès-la-Charité (70) 87 F3
Bourguignon-lès-Morey (70) ...86 D2
Bourguignon-
sous-Coucy (02) 21 H3
Bourguignon-
sous-Montbavin (02) ...22 B3
Bourgvilain (71) 116 A3
Bourideys (33) 149 G4
Bouriège (11) 186 C5
Bourigeole (11) 186 C5
Bourlens (47) 151 H4
Bourlon (62) 8 D4
Bourmont (52) 68 C4
Bournainville-Faverolles (27) ...15 H6
Bournan (37) 95 E3
Bournand (86) 93 H3
Bournazel (12) 154 A3
Bournazel (81) 170 B1
Bournel (47) 151 F2
Bourneau (85) 107 F2
Bournel (47) ... .151 F2
Bournezeau (85) 92 A6
Bourniquel (24) 137 F5
Bournois (25) 88 A4
Bournoncle-
Saint-Pierre (43) 141 G1
Bournonville (62) 1 G4
Bournos (64) 166 A6
Bourogne (90) 88 D3
Bourran (47) 151 E4
Bourré (41) 79 H6
Bourréac (65) 183 E4
Bourret (82) 168 D2
Bourriot-Bergonce (40) ...149 H6
Bourron-Marlotte (77) ...64 A4
Bourrou (24) 137 E4
Bourrouillan (32) 166 D3
Bours (62) 7 G1
Bours (65) 183 E2
Boursault (51) 45 E2
Boursay (41) 61 F5
Bourscheid (57) ....49 H4 ... 27 H6
Bourseul (22) 34 B5
Bourseville (80) 6 B4
Boursières (70) 87 G3
Boursies (59) 8 D4
Boursin (62) 1 G4
Boursonne (60) 43 H1
Bourth (27) 40 C4
Bourthes (62) 1 G5
Bourville (76) 17 F3
Boury-en-Vexin (60) ...19 H6
Bousbach (57) 27 G5
Bousbecque (59) 3 F4
le Bouscat (33) 135 E5
Bousies (59) 9 G4
Bousignies (59) 9 E2
Bousignies-sur-Roc (59) ...10 A2
le Bousquet (11) 200 A2
le Bousquet-d'Orb (34) ...172 C4
Boussac (12) 154 B5
Boussac (23) 112 B4
la Boussac (35) 35 F5
Boussac (46) 153 F2
Boussac-Bourg (23) 112 B3
Boussais (79) 93 F4
Boussan (31) 184 B3
Boussay (37) 95 F5
Boussay (44) 91 H1
Bousse (57) 26 C4
Bousse (72) 77 H2
Bousselange (21) 102 B3
Boussenac (09) 185 F6
Boussens (31) 184 C3
Bousseraucourt (70) ...69 E6
Boussès (47) 150 C6
Bousseviller (57) 28 A5
Boussey (21) 85 E6
Boussicourt (80) 20 D2
Boussières (25) 103 F1
Boussières-en-Cambrésis (59) ...9 F3
Boussières-sur-Sambre (59) ...9 H3
Boussois (59) 10 A2
Boussy (74) 131 H1
Boussy-Saint-Antoine (91) ...43 E5
Boust (57) 26 C2
Boustroff (57) 49 F2
Bout-du-Pont-de-Larn (81) ...187 G1
Boutancourt (08) 24 B2
Boutavent (60) 19 H2
la Bouteille (02) 10 B6
Bouteilles-
Saint-Sébastien (24) 136 C1
Boutenac (11) 187 H4
Boutenac-Touvent (17) ...120 D5
Boutencourt (60) 19 H5
Boutervilliers (91) 63 E2
Bouteville (16) 122 A4
Boutiers-Saint-Trojan (16) ...121 G3
Boutigny (77) 43 H3
Boutigny-Prouais (28) ...41 F4
Boutigny-sur-Essonne (91) ...63 G2
Bouttencourt (80) 6 C5
Boutteville (50) 13 E4
Boutx (31) 184 A5
Bouvaincourt-
sur-Bresle (80) 6 B5
Bouvancourt (51) 22 D5
Bouvante (26) 144 D4
Bouvelinghem (62) 3 E4
Bouvellemont (08) 24 A3
Bouverans (25) 103 H4
Bouvesse-Quirieu (38) ...131 E3
Bouvières (26) 158 C3
Bouvignies (59) 9 E2
Bouvigny-Boyeffles (62) ...8 B1
Bouville (28) 62 B3
Bouville (76) 17 G4
Bouville (91) 63 F3
Bouvincourt-en-
Vermandois (80) 8 C6
Bouvines (59) 3 G6
Bouvresse (60) 19 G2
Bouvron (44) 74 B3
Bouvron (54) 48 A4
Boux-sous-Salmaise (21) ...85 E5
Bouxières-aux-Bois (88) ...69 G3
Bouxières-aux-Chênes (54) ...48 D4
Bouxières-aux-Dames (54) ...48 C4

Bouxières-
sous-Froidmont (54) 48 C3
Bouxurulles (88) 69 G2
Bouxwiller (67) 50 C3
Bouxwiller (68) 89 F4
Bouy (51) 46 A1
Bouy-Luxembourg (10) ...66 C2
Bouy-sur-Orvin (10) ...65 F2
le Bouyssou (46) 153 G1
Bouzais (18) 97 H6
Bouzancourt (52) 67 G3
Bouzanville (54) 69 F2
Bouze-lès-Beaune (21) ...101 G3
Bouzel (63) 127 G3
Bouzemont (88) 69 G3
Bouzeron (71) 101 G4
Bouzic (24) 152 B1
Bouziès (46) 153 E3
Bouzigues (34) 189 F1
Bouzillé (49) 75 F5
Bouzin (31) 184 B3
Bouzincourt (80) 8 A4
Bouzon-Gellenave (32) ...166 D4
Bouzonville (57) 27 E4
Bouzonville-aux-Bois (45) ...63 F5
Bouzy (51) 45 H2
Bouzy-la-Forêt (45) ...81 H1
Bovée-sur-Barboure (55) ...47 G5
Bovel (35) 56 D4
Bovelles (80) 7 F6
Boves (80) 7 G6
Boviolles (55) 47 G5
Boyaval (62) 2 B6
Boyelles (62) 8 B3
Boyer (42) 115 G6
Boyer (71) 116 B2
Boyeux-Saint-Jérôme (01) ...117 F6
Boynes (45) 63 G5
Boz (01) 116 C3
Bozas (07) 143 H4
Bozel (73) 133 E5
Bozouls (12) 154 D3
Brabant-en-Argonne (55) ...47 E1
Brabant-le-Roi (55) 46 D4
Brabant-sur-Meuse (55) ...25 E6
Brach (33) 134 C3
Brachay (52) 67 G3
Braches (80) 20 D2
Brachy (76) 17 F3
Bracieux (41) 80 B4
Bracon (39) 103 F4
Bracquemont (76) 17 G2
Bracquetuit (76) 17 H4
Bradiancourt (76) 19 E2
Braffais (50) 37 E4
Bragassargues (30) ...173 G2
Bragayrac (31) 168 C6
Brageac (15) 139 H3
Bragelogne-Beauvoir (10) ...66 C6
Bragny-sur-Saône (71) ...101 H4
Braillans (25) 87 F6
Brailly-Cornehotte (80) ...7 E3
Brain (21) 84 D5
Brain-sur-Allonnes (49) ...77 H6
Brain-sur-l'Authion (49) ...77 E5
Brain-sur-Longuenée (49) ...76 C3
Brainans (39) 102 D4
Braine (02) 22 B5
Brains (44) 74 B5
Brains-sur-Gée (72) ...59 H6
Brains-sur-les-Marches (53) ...58 A6
Brainville (50) 36 D1
Brainville (54) 48 A2
Brainville-sur-Meuse (52) ...68 C4
Braisnes (60) 21 G4
Braize (03) 98 B6
Bralleville (54) 69 F2
Bram (11) 186 C3
Bramans (73) 147 F2
Brametot (76) 17 F3
Bramevaque (65) 184 A5
Bran (17) 121 G6
Branceilles (19) 139 E4
Brancourt-en-Laonnois (02) ...22 B4
Brancourt-le-Grand (02) ...9 E5
Brandérion (56) 54 D5
Brandeville (55) 25 E4
Brandivy (56) 55 F5
Brando (2B) 203 G3
Brandon (71) 116 A3
Brandonnet (12) 153 H4
Brandonvillers (51) ...46 A6
Branges (02) 22 C5
Branges (71) 102 A5
Brangues (38) 131 E4
Brannay (89) 64 D4
Branne (25) 88 B5
Branne (33) 135 H5
Branoux-les-Taillades (30) ...156 D5
Brans (39) 102 D1
Bransat (03) 113 H4
Branscourt (51) 22 D6
Bransles (77) 64 B4
Brantes (84) 159 E5
Brantigny (88) 69 G3
Brantôme (24) 137 E1
Branville (14) 14 D4
Branville-Hague (50) ...12 B1
Braquis (55) 25 G6
Bras (83) 193 E3
Bras-d'Asse (04) 177 E2
Bras-sur-Meuse (55) ...25 E6
Brasc (12) 171 E2
Braslou (37) 94 B3
Brasparts (29) 31 H5
Brassac (09) 185 G5
Brassac (81) 170 D5
Brassac (82) 151 H5
Brassac-les-Mines (63) ...127 G6
Brassempouy (40) 165 G5
Brasseuse (60) 21 E6
Brassy (58) 100 A1
Brassy (80) 7 F6
Braud-et-Saint-Louis (33) ...135 E1
Brauvilliers (55) 47 E6
Braux (04) 178 A2
Braux (10) 46 A6
Braux (21) 84 D5
Braux-le-Châtel (52) ...67 G4
Braux-Saint-Remy (51) ...46 C2
Braux-Sainte-Cohière (51) ...46 C1
Brax (31) 168 D5
Brax (47) 151 E5
Bray (27) 40 D1
Bray (71) 116 A2
Bray-Dunes (59) 2 C1
Bray-en-Val (45) 81 G2
Bray-et-Lû (95) 41 H1
Bray-lès-Mareuil (80) ...7 E4
Bray-Saint-Christophe (02) ...21 H1
Bray-sur-Seine (77) ...64 D2
Bray-sur-Somme (80) ...8 B5
Braye (02) 22 A5
Braye-en-Laonnois (02) ...22 C4
Braye-en-Thiérache (02) ...23 G1
Braye-sous-Faye (37) ...94 B3
Braye-sur-Maulne (37) ...78 B4
Brazey-en-Morvan (21) ...100 D2
Brazey-en-Plaine (21) ...102 A2
Bréal-sous-Montfort (35) ...56 D3
Bréal-sous-Vitré (35) ...58 A4
Bréançon (95) 42 B1
Bréau (77) 64 B1
Bréau-et-Salagosse (30) ...172 D2
Bréauté (76) 16 C4
Bréban (51) 46 B6
Brebières (62) 8 C3
Brebotte (90) 88 D3
Brécé (35) 57 G3
Brécé (53) 58 B2
Brécey (50) 37 E5
Brech (56) 55 E5
Brechainville (88) 68 B2
Bréchamps (28) 41 F5
Bréchaumont (68) 89 E3
Brèches (37) 78 C4
Breconchaux (25) 87 H6

Brectouville (50) 37 G2
Brécy (02) 44 B1
Brécy (18) 98 A3
Brécy-Brières (08) 24 B4
la Brède (33) 149 F1
Brée (53) 59 E3
la Brée-les-Bains (17) 106 B6
Brégnier-Cordon (01) ...131 F4
Brégy (60) 43 G2
Bréhain (54) 49 E6
Bréhain-la-Ville (54) 26 A2
Bréhal (50) 36 C2
Bréhan (56) 55 G3
Bréhand (22) 33 H5
Bréhémont (37) 78 B6
Bréhéville (55) 25 E5
Breidenbach (57) 28 B5
Breil (49) 78 A4
le Breil-sur-Mérize (72) ...60 C5
Breil-sur-Roya (06) ...179 G2
la Breille-les-Pins (49) ...77 H6
Breilly (80) 7 F5
Breistroff-la-Grande (57) ...26 C2
Breitenau (67) 71 F2
Breitenbach (67) 71 F2
Breitenbach-Haut-Rhin (68) ...71 E5
Brélès (29) 30 C4
Brélidy (22) 33 E3
Brem-sur-Mer (85) ...90 D5
Bréménil (54) 49 H6
Brêmes (62) 1 H3
Brémoncourt (54) 69 G1
Bremondans (25) 104 A1
Brémontier-Merval (76) ...19 F4
Brémur-et-Vaurois (21) ...85 E2
Bren (26) 144 B3
Brenac (11) 186 C6
Brenas (34) 172 B5
Brenat (63) 127 G5
Brénaz (01) 131 G1
Brenelle (02) 22 B5
Brengues (46) 153 F2
Brennes (52) 86 B1
Brennilis (29) 31 H5
Brénod (01) 117 G5
Brenon (83) 177 H3
Brenouille (60) 20 D5
Brenoux (48) 156 B4
Brens (01) 131 G2
Brens (81) 170 A3
Brenthonne (74) 118 D4
Breny (02) 44 B1
la Bréole (04) 160 D3
Brères (25) 103 F2
Bréry (39) 102 D6
Bresdon (17) 121 H2
les Bréseux (25) 88 D6
Bresilley (70) 102 D1
Brésis (30) 156 D4
Bresle (80) 7 H5
Bresles (60) 20 C4
Bresnay (03) 113 H3
Bresolettes (61) 40 C6
la Bresse (88) 70 C5
Bressey-sur-Tille (21) ...86 A6
Bressieux (38) 144 D1
Bressolles (01) 130 D1
Bressolles (03) 113 H3
Bressols (82) 169 E1
Bresson (38) 145 G3
Bressuire (79) 92 D4
Brest (29) 30 D4
Brestot (27) 18 A5
Bretagne (36) 96 D3
Bretagne (90) 88 D3
Bretagne-d'Armagnac (32) ...167 E2
Bretagne-de-Marsan (40) ...166 A3
Bretagnolles (27) 41 F3
Breteau (45) 82 C3
Breteil (35) 56 D2
Bretenière (21) 86 A6
la Bretenière (25) 88 C5
la Bretenière (39) 102 D2
Bretenières (39) 102 D4
Bretenoux (46) 139 E5
Breteuil (27) 40 C4
Breteuil (60) 20 B3
Brethel (61) 39 H5
Brethenay (52) 67 H4
le Brethon (03) 112 D1
Bretigney (25) 88 B4
Bretigney-Notre-Dame (25) ...88 B6
Bretignolles (79) 92 D4
Bretignolles-sur-Mer (85) ...90 D5
Brétigny (21) 86 A5
Brétigny (27) 18 A6
Brétigny (60) 21 G3
Brétigny-sur-Orge (91) ...42 D6
Bretoncelles (61) 61 E2
la Bretonnière-la-Claye (85) ...91 H6
Bretonvillers (25) 104 C1
Brette (26) 158 C2
Brette-les-Pins (72) ...60 B6
Bretten (68) 89 E3
Brettes (16) 108 C6
Bretteville (50) 12 D2
Bretteville-du-
Grand-Caux (76) 16 C4
Bretteville-le-Rabet (14) ...38 D1
Bretteville-l'Orgueilleuse (14) ...14 B4
Bretteville-Saint-Laurent (76) ...17 F3
Bretteville-sur-Ay (50) ...12 C5
Bretteville-sur-Dives (14) ...39 E1
Bretteville-sur-Laize (14) ...14 C6
Bretteville-sur-Odon (14) ...14 B5
Brettnach (57) 27 E4
Bretx (31) 168 D4
Breuches (70) 87 H1
Breuchotte (70) 88 A1
Breugnon (58) 83 E5
le Breuil (03) 114 C5
le Breuil (51) 45 E2
le Breuil (69) 129 G2
le Breuil (71) 101 E5
Breuil (80) 21 E2
le Breuil-Bernard (79) ...92 D5
Breuil-Bois-Robert (78) ...41 H3
le Breuil-en-Auge (14) ...15 E5
le Breuil-en-Bessin (14) ...13 G5
Breuil-la-Réorte (17) ...107 F5
Breuil-le-Sec (60) 20 D4
Breuil-le-Vert (60) 20 D4
Breuil-Magné (17) 106 D6
le Breuil-sur-Couze (63) ...127 G6
Breuilaufa (87) 110 B6
Breuilh (24) 137 F4
Breuillet (17) 120 B3
Breuillet (91) 42 C6
Breuilpont (27) 41 F2
Breurey-lès-Faverney (70) ...87 G2
Breuschwickersheim (67) ...51 E5
Breuvannes-
en-Bassigny (52) 68 C5
Breuvery-sur-Coole (51) ...45 H4
Breuville (50) 12 C3
Breux (55) 25 E3
Breux-Jouy (91) 63 F1
Breux-sur-Avre (27) 40 D4
Brévainville (41) 61 H6
Bréval (78) 41 G3
Brévands (50) 13 F4
Brevans (39) 102 C2
le Brévedent (14) 15 F5
Bréviandes (10) 66 B3
la Brévière (14) 39 F2
Bréville (16) 121 H3
Bréville-les-Monts (14) ...14 C4
Bréville-sur-Mer (50) ...36 C3
Brévillers (62) 7 F2
Brévillers (80) 7 G3
Brevilliers (70) 88 C3
Brévilly (08) 24 D2
Brévonnes (10) 66 D2
Bréxent-Énocq (62) 6 C1

Brey-et-Maison-
du-Bois (25) 103 H5
Brézé (49) 93 H3
Bréziers (05) 160 C3
Brézilhac (11) 186 C4
Brézins (38) 144 D1
Brezolles (28) 40 D5
Brezons (15) 140 D5
Briançon (05) 147 E5
Briançonnet (06) 178 B2
Brianny (21) 84 D5
Briant (71) 115 F4
Briantes (36) 111 H1
Briare (45) 82 A3
Briarres-sur-Essonne (45) ...63 G4
Brias (62) 7 G1
Briastre (59) 9 F4
Briatexte (81) 170 A4
Bricon (52) 67 G5
Briconville (28) 62 A1
Bricquebec (50) 12 C3
Bricquebosq (50) 12 B3
Bricqueville (14) 13 G5
Bricqueville-la-Blouette (50) ...36 C1
Bricqueville-sur-Mer (50) ...36 C2
Bricy (45) 62 C6
Brides-les-Bains (73) ...132 D5
la Bridoire (73) 131 G4
Bridoré (37) 95 G5
Brie (02) 22 B4
Brie (09) 185 G3
Brie (16) 122 C3
Brie (35) 57 F4
Brie (79) 93 H4
Brie (80) 8 C6
Brie-Comte-Robert (77) ...43 E5
Brié-et-Angonnes (38) ...145 G3
Brie-sous-Barbezieux (16) ...122 A6
Brie-sous-Chalais (16) ...136 A1
Brie-sous-Matha (17) ...121 H3
Brie-sous-Mortagne (17) ...120 D5
Briec (29) 53 G2
Brielles (35) 58 A4
Brienne (71) 116 C1
Brienne-la-Vieille (10) ...66 D2
Brienne-le-Château (10) ...66 D2
Brienne-sur-Aisne (08) ...23 F4
Briennon (42) 115 E5
Brienon-sur-Armançon (89) ...65 G5
Brières-les-Scellés (91) ...63 F2
Brieuil-sur-Chizé (79) ...108 A5
Brieulles-sur-Bar (08) ...24 B4
Brieulles-sur-Meuse (55) ...24 D5
Brieux (61) 39 E4
Briey (54) 26 A5
Briffons (63) 126 C4
Brignac (34) 172 D5
Brignac (56) 55 H2
Brignac-la-Plaine (19) ...138 C3
Brignais (69) 129 H4
Brignancourt (95) 42 A1
Brigné (49) 93 F1
Brignemont (31) 168 C4
Brignogan-Plage (29) ...31 F2
Brignoles (83) 193 E3
Brignon (30) 174 A2
le Brignon (43) 142 C4
la Brigue (06) 163 F6
Brignoud (38) 145 H2
Briis-sous-Forges (91) ...42 B6
Brillac (16) 109 H6
la Brillanne (04) 176 D2
Brillecourt (10) 66 C1
Brillevast (50) 12 D2
Brillon (59) 9 E2
Brillon-en-Barrois (55) ...47 E5
Brimeux (62) 6 D1
Brimont (51) 23 E5
Brin-sur-Seille (54) ...48 D4
Brinay (18) 97 F2
Brinay (58) 99 H4
Brinckheim (68) 89 G3
Bringolo (22) 33 F4
Brinon-sur-Beuvron (58) ...99 F1
Brinon-sur-Sauldre (18) ...81 F4
Briod (39) 102 D6
Briollay (49) 77 E4
Brion (01) 117 G5
Brion (36) 96 C4
Brion (38) 144 D1
Brion (48) 155 H1
Brion (71) 100 D4
Brion (86) 109 H3
Brion (89) 65 E4
Brion-près-Thouet (79) ...93 G2
Brion-sur-Ource (21) ...85 E1
la Brionne (23) 111 F5
Briord (01) 131 E2
Briosne-lès-Sables (72) ...60 C4
Briou (41) 80 B2
Brioude (43) 141 H2
Brioux-sur-Boutonne (79) ...108 A5
Briouze (61) 38 C4
Briquemesnil-Floxicourt (80) ...7 F6
Briquenay (08) 24 B4
Briscous (64) 164 C6
Brison-Saint-Innocent (73) ...131 H3
Brissac (34) 173 E3
Brissac-Quincé (49) ...77 E6
Brissarthe (49) 77 E3
Brissay-Choigny (02) ...22 A2
Brissy-Hamégicourt (02) ...22 A2
la Brit-la-Gaillarde (19) ...138 C2
Brives (36) 97 F5
Brives-Charensac (43) ...142 C4
Brives-sur-Charente (17) ...121 F3
Brivezac (19) 139 E4
Brix (50) 12 C3
Brixey-aux-Chanoines (55) ...68 B2
Brizambourg (17) 121 F2
Brizay (37) 94 B2
Brizeaux (55) 46 D2
Brizon (74) 118 D6
le Broc (06) 195 E2
Broc (49) 78 A3
le Broc (63) 127 G6
Brocas (40) 166 A1
Brochon (21) 101 H1
Brocourt (80) 7 E6
Brocourt-en-Argonne (55) ...47 E1
Broglie (27) 40 B1
Brognard (25) 88 C4
Brognon (08) 10 C5
Brognon (21) 86 B5
Broin (21) 102 A2
Broindon (21) 101 H2
Broissia (39) 117 F3
Brombos (60) 19 H2
Bromeilles (45) 63 H4
Brommat (12) 140 C6
Bromont-Lamothe (63) ...126 D3
Bron (69) 130 B3
Bronvaux (57) 26 B5
Broons (22) 34 B6
la Broque (67) 70 D1
Broquiès (12) 171 E2
Broquiers (60) 19 H2
Brossac (16) 136 A1
Brossainc (07) 143 H1
Brossay (49) 93 F1
la Brosse-Montceaux (77) ...64 C3
Brosses (89) 83 G4
Brosville (27) 18 D6
Brotte-lès-Luxeuil (70) ...87 H1
Brotte-lès-Ray (70) ...86 D3
Brou (28) 61 F4
Brou-sur-Chantereine (77) ...43 E3
Brouains (50) 37 F4
Broualan (35) 35 F5
Brouay (14) 14 A4
Brouchaud (24) 137 H2
Brouchy (80) 21 G2

Brouck (57) 49 E1
Brouckerque (59) 2 B2
Brouderdorff (57) 50 A5
Broué (28) 41 F5
Brouennes (55) 25 E3
le Brouilh-Monbert (32) 167 G4
Brouilla (66) 201 F3
Brouillet (51) 22 D6
Brouqueyran (33) 149 H3
la Brousse (17) 121 G1
Brousse (23) 126 B1
Brousse (63) 127 H4
Brousse (81) 170 B4
Brousse-le-Château (12) 171 F2
Brousses-et-Villaret (11) 186 D2
Brousseval (52) 67 G1
Broussey-en-Blois (55) 47 G5
Broussey-Raulecourt (55) 47 H4
Broussy-le-Grand (51) 45 E4
Broussy-le-Petit (51) 45 E4
Broût-Vernet (03) 113 H5
Brouvelieures (88) 70 B3
Brouville (54) 70 B1
Brouviller (57) 50 A4
Brouy (91) 63 F3
Brouzet-lès-Alès (30) 157 F6
Brouzet-lès-Quissac (30) 173 G3
les Brouzils (85) 91 H2
Broxeele (59) 2 B3
Broye (71) 100 D4
Broye-Aubigney-Montseugny (70) 86 C6
Broye-les-Loups-et-Verfontaine (70) 86 B5
Broyes (51) 44 D5
Broyes (60) 20 D3
Broze (81) 170 A2
Brû (88) 70 B2
Bruailles (71) 117 E1
Bruay-la-Buissière (62) 2 C6
Bruay-sur-l'Escaut (59) 9 F1
Bruc-sur-Aff (35) 56 C5
Brucamps (80) 7 E4
Bruch (47) 150 D5
Brucheville (50) 13 E4
Brucourt (14) 14 D4
Brue-Auriac (83) 193 E1
Bruebach (68) 89 F2
Brueil-en-Vexin (78) 41 H2
Bruère-Allichamps (18) 97 H5
la Bruère-sur-Loir (72) 78 B3
la Bruffière (85) 92 A3
Brugairolles (11) 186 C4
le Brugeron (63) 128 B3
Bruges (33) 135 E5
Bruges-Capbis-Mifaget (64) 182 C3
Brugheas (03) 114 A6
Brugnac (47) 151 E3
Brugnens (32) 168 A3
Brugny-Vaudancourt (51) 45 E2
la Bruguière (30) 174 B1
Bruguières (31) 169 F4
Bruille-lez-Marchiennes (59) 9 E2
Bruille-Saint-Amand (59) 4 B6
Bruis (05) 159 F3
Brûlain (79) 108 A4
les Brulais (35) 56 C4
Brulange (57) 49 E2
la Brûlatte (53) 58 B4
Bruley (54) 48 A5
Brullemail (61) 39 G5
Brullioles (69) 129 G3
Brûlon (72) 59 G6
Brumath (67) 51 E4
Brumetz (02) 44 A2
Brunehamel (02) 23 F1
Brunelles (28) 61 F3
les Brunels (11) 186 C1
Brunembert (62) 1 G4
Brunémont (59) 8 D2
Brunet (04) 177 E2
Bruniquel (82) 169 G1
Brunoy (91) 43 E5
Brunstatt (68) 89 F2
Brunville (76) 17 H1
Brunvillers-la-Motte (60) 20 D3
Brusque (12) 171 H4
le Brusquet (04) 160 D6
Brussey (70) 87 E6
Brussieu (69) 129 G3
Brusson (51) 46 B5
Brusvily (22) 34 C6
Brutelles (80) 6 B4
Bruville (54) 26 A5
Brux (86) 108 D4
la Bruyère (70) 88 A1
Bruyères (88) 70 B3
Bruyères-et-Montbérault (02) 22 C3
Bruyères-le-Châtel (91) 42 C6
Bruyères-sur-Fère (02) 44 B1
Bruyères-sur-Oise (95) 42 D1
Bruys (02) 22 B6
Bruz (35) 57 E3
Bry (59) 9 G2
Bry-sur-Marne (94) 43 E4
Bû (28) 41 F4
le Bû-sur-Rouvres (14) 38 D2
Buais (50) 37 G6
Buanes (40) 166 A4
Bubertré (61) 40 A6
Bubry (56) 54 D3
Buc (78) 42 B4
Buc (90) 88 C3
Bucamps (60) 20 C3
Bucéels (14) 14 A4
Bucey-en-Othe (10) 65 H3
Bucey-lès-Gy (70) 87 E5
Bucey-lès-Traves (70) 87 F3
Buchelay (78) 41 G3
Buchères (10) 66 B4
Buchy (57) 48 D2
Buchy (76) 19 E3
Bucilly (02) 10 B6
Bucquoy (62) 8 A4
Bucy-le-Long (02) 22 A5
Bucy-le-Roi (45) 62 D5
Bucy-lès-Cerny (02) 22 B3
Bucy-lès-Pierrepont (02) 22 D2
Bucy-Saint-Liphard (45) 62 C6
Budelière (23) 112 C5
Buding (57) 26 C3
Budling (57) 26 C3
Budos (33) 149 G2
Bué (18) 82 B6
Bueil (27) 41 F3
Bueil-en-Touraine (37) 78 D3
Buellas (01) 116 D5
Buethwiller (68) 89 E2
Buffard (25) 103 E3
Buffières (71) 115 H3
Buffignécourt (70) 87 F1
Buffon (21) 84 C3
Bugarach (11) 187 E6
Bugard (65) 183 G2
Bugeat (19) 125 F4
Bugnein (64) 181 G1
Bugnicourt (59) 8 D2
Bugnières (52) 67 H6
Bugny (25) 104 A3
le Bugue (24) 137 G5
Buhl (67) 51 F2
Buhl (68) 71 E6
Buhl-Lorraine (57) 50 A4
Buhy (95) 41 H1
Buicourt (60) 19 H3
Buigny-l'Abbé (80) 7 E4
Buigny-lès-Gamaches (80) 6 C5
Buigny-Saint-Maclou (80) 6 D3
Buire (02) 10 B6
Buire-au-Bois (62) 7 F2
Buire-Courcelles (80) 8 C6
Buire-le-Sec (62) 6 D1
Buire-sur-l'Ancre (80) 8 A5
Buironfosse (02) 9 H5
le Buis (87) 110 C6
Buis-les-Baronnies (26) 159 E5
Buis-sur-Damville (27) 40 D4
Buissard (05) 160 C1
la Buisse (38) 145 F1
la Buissière (38) 132 A6
le Buisson (48) 155 G2
le Buisson (51) 46 C4
Buisson (84) 158 C5
le Buisson-de-Cadouin (24) 137 G5
Buissoncourt (54) 48 D5
Buissy (62) 8 C3
Bujaleuf (87) 124 D3
Bulan (65) 183 F4
Bulat-Pestivien (22) 32 D5
Bulcy (58) 98 D1
Buléon (56) 55 G4
Bulgnéville (88) 69 E4
Bulhon (63) 127 G2
Bullainville (28) 62 B4
Bulle (25) 103 H4
Bullecourt (62) 8 C3
Bulles (60) 20 C4
Bulligny (54) 48 A6
Bullion (78) 42 B6
Bullou (28) 61 H3
Bully (42) 128 D2
Bully (69) 129 G2
Bully (76) 19 E2
Bully-les-Mines (62) 8 B1
Bulson (08) 24 C2
Bult (88) 70 B3
Bun (65) 182 D5
Buncey (21) 85 E2
Buneville (62) 7 G2
Buno-Bonnevaux (91) 63 G2
Bunus (64) 181 E2
Bunzac (16) 122 D3
Buoux (84) 175 H3
Burbach (67) 50 A3
la Burbanche (01) 131 F2
Burbure (62) 2 C6
Burcin (38) 131 E6
Burcy (14) 37 H3
Burcy (77) 63 H4
Burdignes (42) 143 G2
Burdignin (74) 118 D4
Bure (55) 68 B1
Buré (61) 60 C1
Bure-les-Templiers (21) 85 G2
Burelles (02) 22 D1
Bures (54) 49 F5
Bures (61) 39 G6
Bures-en-Bray (76) 19 E1
Bures-les-Monts (14) 37 G2
Bures-sur-Yvette (91) 42 C5
le Buret (53) 59 E6
Burey (27) 40 C2
Burey-en-Vaux (55) 47 H6
Burey-la-Côte (55) 68 D1
Burg (65) 183 G3
Burgalays (31) 184 A6
Burgaronne (64) 181 G1
le Burgaud (31) 168 D3
Burgille (25) 87 E6
Burgnac (87) 124 A3
Burgy (71) 116 B2
Burie (17) 121 G2
Buriville (54) 49 G6
Burlats (81) 170 D5
Burlioncourt (57) 49 F3
Burnand (71) 116 A1
Burnevillers (25) 88 D5
Burnhaupt-le-Bas (68) 89 E2
Burnhaupt-le-Haut (68) 89 E2
Buros (64) 182 C1
Burosse-Mendousse (64) 166 C6
Burret (09) 185 G5
Bursard (61) 39 F6
Burthecourt-aux-Chênes (54) 48 D6
Burtoncourt (57) 26 D4
Bury (60) 20 C5
Burzet (07) 157 F1
Burzy (71) 115 H1
Bus (62) 8 C4
Bus-la-Mésière (80) 21 E2
Bus-lès-Artois (80) 7 H4
Bus-Saint-Rémy (27) 41 G1
Buschwiller (68) 89 G3
Busigny (59) 9 F5
Busloup (41) 79 G1
Busnes (62) 2 C5
Busque (81) 170 A4
Bussac (24) 137 E2
Bussac-Forêt (17) 135 G2
Bussac-sur-Charente (17) 121 E2
Bussang (88) 70 C6
le Busseau (79) 107 G1
Busseaut (21) 85 E2
Busséol (63) 127 G4
Busserolles (24) 123 F4
Busserotte-et-Montenaille (21) 85 G3
Busset (03) 114 B6
Bussiares (02) 44 A2
la Bussière (45) 82 A2
la Bussière (86) 109 H1
Bussière-Badil (24) 123 E4
Bussière-Boffy (87) 109 H6
Bussière-Dunoise (23) 111 F4
Bussière-Galant (87) 123 H4
Bussière-Nouvelle (23) 126 A1
Bussière-Poitevine (87) 110 A4
Bussière-Saint-Georges (23) 112 A3
la Bussière-sur-Ouche (21) 101 F1
Bussières (21) 85 G3
Bussières (42) 129 E2
Bussières (63) 112 D6
Bussières (70) 87 F6
Bussières (71) 116 A3
Bussières (77) 44 A3
Bussières (89) 84 B5
Bussières-et-Pruns (63) 127 F1
Busson (52) 68 B3
Bussu (80) 8 C5
Bussunarits-Sarrasquette (64) 181 E3
Bussus-Bussuel (80) 7 E4
Bussy (18) 98 A4
Bussy (60) 21 G3
Bussy-Albieux (42) 128 D3
Bussy-en-Othe (89) 65 F6
Bussy-la-Pesle (21) 85 F6
Bussy-la-Pesle (58) 99 F1
Bussy-le-Château (51) 46 A2
Bussy-le-Grand (21) 85 E4
Bussy-le-Repos (51) 46 C3
Bussy-le-Repos (89) 64 D5
Bussy-lès-Daours (80) 7 H6
Bussy-lès-Poix (80) 20 A1
Bussy-Lettrée (51) 45 G4
Bussy-Saint-Georges (77) 43 F4
Bussy-Saint-Martin (77) 43 F4
Bust (67) 50 B3
Bustanico (2B) 205 F2
Bustince-Iriberry (64) 181 E3
Buswiller (67) 50 D3
Busy (25) 103 F1
Buthiers (70) 87 F6
Buthiers (77) 63 G3
Butot (76) 17 G4
Butot-Vénesville (76) 16 D3
Butry-sur-Oise (95) 42 C2
Butteaux (89) 65 H6
Butten (67) 28 A6
Buverchy (80) 21 G2
Buvilly (39) 103 E4
la Buxerette (36) 111 F2
Buxerolles (21) 85 G2
Buxerolles (86) 109 E1
Buxeuil (10) 66 D5
Buxeuil (36) 96 C2
Buxeuil (86) 95 E3
Buxières-d'Aillac (36) 111 F1
Buxières-lès-Clefmont (52) 68 B5
Buxières-les-Mines (03) 113 F2
Buxières-lès-Villiers (52) 67 H5
Buxières-sous-les-Côtes (55) 47 H3
Buxières-sous-Montaigut (63) 113 E5
Buxières-sur-Arce (10) 66 D5
Buxy (71) 101 F6
Buysscheure (59) 2 B3
Buzan (09) 184 C5
Buzançais (36) 96 A4
Buzancy (02) 22 A5
Buzancy (08) 24 C4
Buzeins (12) 155 E4
Buzet-sur-Baïse (47) 150 D5
Buzet-sur-Tarn (31) 169 G4
Buziet (64) 182 B3
Buzignargues (34) 173 G4
Buzon (65) 183 F1
Buzy (64) 182 B3
Buzy-Darmont (55) 47 H1
By (25) 103 F3
Byans-sur-Doubs (25) 103 E2

C

Cabanac (65) 183 F2
Cabanac-Cazaux (31) 184 B5
Cabanac-et-Villagrains (33) 149 F2
Cabanac-Séguenville (31) 168 C3
la Cabanasse (66) 200 A4
Cabanès (12) 154 A6
Cabanès (81) 170 A4
le Cabanial (31) 170 A6
les Cabannes (09) 199 F1
Cabannes (13) 175 F3
les Cabannes (81) 170 A1
Cabara (33) 135 H5
Cabariot (17) 120 D1
Cabas-Loumassès (32) 184 A2
Cabasse (83) 193 G2
Cabestany (66) 201 F2
Cabidos (64) 166 A5
Cabourg (14) 14 D4
Cabrerets (46) 153 E3
Cabrerolles (34) 172 A6
Cabrespine (11) 187 E2
Cabrières (30) 174 B3
Cabrières (34) 172 C6
Cabrières-d'Aigues (84) 176 A3
Cabrières-d'Avignon (84) 175 G3
Cabriès (13) 192 B2
Cabris (06) 178 C4
Cachan (94) 42 D4
Cachen (40) 166 A1
Cachy (80) 7 H6
Cadalen (81) 170 B3
Cadarcet (09) 185 G5
Cadarsac (33) 135 G5
Cadaujac (33) 135 F6
Cadéac (65) 183 G6
Cadeilhan (32) 168 A3
Cadeilhan-Trachère (65) 196 D1
Cadeillan (32) 184 C1
Cademène (25) 103 G2
Caden (56) 73 G1
Cadenet (84) 175 H4
Caderousse (84) 174 D1
la Cadière-d'Azur (83) 192 D4
la Cadière-et-Cambo (30) 173 F2
Cadillac (33) 149 G1
Cadillac-en-Fronsadais (33) 135 G4
Cadillon (64) 166 C6
Cadix (81) 171 E2
Cadolive (13) 192 C3
Cadours (31) 168 C4
Cadrieu (46) 153 F3
Caen (14) 14 B4
Caëstre (59) 2 D4
Caffiers (62) 1 G3
Cagnac-les-Mines (81) 170 C2
Cagnano (2B) 203 G2
Cagnes-sur-Mer (06) 195 E3
Cagnicourt (62) 8 C3
Cagnoncles (59) 9 E3
Cagnotte (40) 165 E5
Cagny (14) 38 D1
Cagny (80) 7 G6
Cahagnes (14) 38 A1
Cahagnolles (14) 13 H6
Cahaignes (27) 19 F6
Cahan (61) 38 C3
Caharet (65) 183 G3
Cahon (80) 6 C4
Cahors (46) 152 C3
Cahus (46) 139 F5
Cahuzac (11) 186 A3
Cahuzac (47) 151 E1
Cahuzac (81) 186 C1
Cahuzac-sur-Adour (32) 166 D5
Cahuzac-sur-Vère (81) 170 A2
Caignac (31) 185 H2
le Cailar (30) 174 A5
Cailhau (11) 186 C4
Cailhavel (11) 186 C4
Cailla (11) 200 A1
Caillac (46) 152 C3
Caillavet (32) 167 F4
Caille (06) 178 B3
la Caillère-Saint-Hilaire (85) 92 B6
Cailleville (76) 17 E2
Caillouël-Crépigny (02) 21 H3
Caillouet-Orgeville (27) 41 E2
Cailloux-sur-Fontaines (69) 130 A2
Cailly (76) 17 H5
Cailly-sur-Eure (27) 41 E1
la Caine (14) 14 A6
Cairanne (84) 158 C5
le Caire (04) 160 B4
Cairon (14) 14 B4
Caisnes (60) 21 G3
Caissargues (30) 174 B4
Caix (80) 21 E1
Caixas (66) 200 D3
Caixon (65) 183 E1
Cajarc (46) 153 F3
Calacuccia (2B) 204 D2
Calais (62) 1 G2
Calamane (46) 152 C3
Calan (56) 54 C4
Calanhel (22) 32 C5
Calavanté (65) 183 F3
Calcatoggio (2A) 204 C5
Calce (66) 201 E2
Calenzana (2B) 202 C6
Calès (24) 137 F5
Calès (46) 138 C6
Calignac (47) 150 D6
Caligny (61) 38 B4
Callac (22) 32 C5
Callas (83) 177 H5
Callen (40) 149 F4
Callengeville (76) 19 F1
Calleville (27) 18 A6
Calleville-les-Deux-Églises (76) 17 G4
Callian (32) 167 F5
Callian (83) 178 B5
Calmeilles (66) 200 D3
Calmels-et-le-Viala (12) 171 G2
la Calmette (30) 174 A2
Calmont (12) 154 B5
Calmont (31) 185 H2
Calmoutier (70) 87 G3
Caloire (42) 129 E6
Calonges (47) 150 C4
Calonne-Ricouart (62) 2 C6
Calonne-sur-la-Lys (62) 2 D5
Calorguen (22) 34 D5
la Calotterie (62) 1 F6
Caluire-et-Cuire (69) 130 A3
Calvi (2B) 202 B5
Calviac (46) 139 G5
Calviac-en-Périgord (24) 138 B5
Calvignac (46) 153 E3
Calvinet (15) 154 B1
Calvisson (30) 173 H4
Calzan (09) 186 A5
Camalès (65) 183 E1
Camarade (09) 185 E4
Camarès (12) 171 G3
Camaret-sur-Aigues (84) 158 B6
Camaret-sur-Mer (29) 30 D5
Camarsac (33) 135 G5
Cambayrac (46) 152 B4
la Cambe (14) 13 F4
Cambernard (31) 185 E1
Cambernon (50) 37 E1
Cambes (33) 135 F6
Cambes (46) 153 G2
Cambes (47) 150 D2
Cambes-en-Plaine (14) 14 B4
Cambia (2B) 205 F2
Cambiac (31) 169 H6
Cambieure (11) 186 C4
Camblain-Châtelain (62) 2 C6
Camblain-l'Abbé (62) 8 A1
Camblanes-et-Meynac (33) 135 F6
Cambligneul (62) 8 A1
Cambo-les-Bains (64) 180 C1
Cambon (81) 170 C3
Cambon-et-Salvergues (34) 171 G5
Cambon-lès-Lavaur (81) 170 A5
Camboulazet (12) 154 B5
Camboulit (46) 153 G2
Cambounès (81) 171 E5
Cambounet-sur-le-Sor (81) 170 B6
le Cambout (22) 55 H3
Cambrai (59) 8 D3
Cambremer (14) 15 E5
Cambrin (62) 2 D6
Cambron (80) 6 D4
Cambronne-lès-Clermont (60) 20 C5
Cambronne-lès-Ribécourt (60) 21 F4
Camburat (46) 153 G2
Came (64) 164 D6
Camélas (66) 200 D3
Camelin (02) 21 H3
Camembert (61) 39 F3
Cametours (50) 37 E1
Camiac-et-Saint-Denis (33) 135 G6
Camiers (62) 1 F5
Camiran (33) 150 A1
Camjac (12) 154 B6
Camlez (22) 32 D2
les Cammazes (81) 186 C1
Camoël (56) 73 F2
Camon (09) 186 B5
Camon (80) 7 G6
Camors (56) 55 E4
Camou-Cihigue (64) 181 F3
Camous (65) 183 G5
Campagna-de-Sault (11) 199 H1
Campagnac (12) 155 F4
Campagnac (81) 170 A1
Campagnac-lès-Quercy (24) 152 B1
Campagnan (34) 172 D6
Campagne (24) 137 G5
Campagne (34) 173 G4
Campagne (40) 165 H2
Campagne (60) 21 G2
Campagne-d'Armagnac (32) 166 D3
Campagne-lès-Boulonnais (62) 1 H5
Campagne-lès-Guines (62) 1 G3
Campagne-lès-Hesdin (62) 6 D1
Campagne-lès-Wardrecques (62) 2 B4
Campagne-sur-Arize (09) 185 F4
Campagne-sur-Aude (11) 186 D6
Campagnolles (14) 37 G3
Campan (65) 183 F5
Campana (2B) 205 F1
Campandré-Valcongrain (14) 14 A6
Camparan (65) 183 G6
Campbon (44) 74 A3
Campeaux (14) 37 G2
Campeaux (60) 19 G3
Campel (35) 56 D4
Campénéac (56) 56 B4
Campestre-et-Luc (30) 172 C2
Campet-et-Lamolère (40) 165 H2
Camphin-en-Carembault (59) 3 F6
Camphin-en-Pévèle (59) 3 G5
Campi (2B) 205 G2
Campigneulles-les-Grandes (62) 6 C1
Campigneulles-les-Petites (62) 6 D1
Campigny (14) 13 H5
Campigny (27) 15 H3
Campile (2B) 203 F6
Campistrous (65) 183 G3
Campitello (2B) 203 F5
Camplong (34) 172 A5
Camplong-d'Aude (11) 187 G4
Campneuseville (76) 6 C6
Campo (2A) 205 E6
Campôme (66) 200 B2
Campouriez (12) 154 C1
Campoussy (66) 200 C2
Campremy (60) 20 C3
Camprond (50) 37 E1
Camps-en-Amiénois (80) 7 E6
Camps-la-Source (83) 193 F3
Camps-Saint-Mathurin-Léobazel (19) 139 F4
Camps-sur-l'Agly (11) 187 E6
Camps-sur-l'Isle (33) 136 A4
Campsas (82) 169 E3
Campsegret (24) 137 E5
Campuac (12) 154 C2
Campugnan (33) 135 E2
Campuzan (65) 183 H2
Camurac (11) 199 G1
Canale-di-Verde (2B) 205 G2
Canals (82) 169 E3
Canaples (80) 7 F4
Canappeville (27) 40 D1
Canapville (14) 15 E3
Canapville (61) 39 G3
Canari (2B) 203 F2
Canaules-et-Argentières (30) 173 G2
Canavaggia (2B) 203 F6
Canaveilles (66) 200 B4
Cancale (35) 35 E3
Canchy (14) 13 G5
Canchy (80) 6 D3
Cancon (47) 151 F2
Candas (80) 7 G4
Candé (49) 76 B3
Candé-sur-Beuvron (41) 79 H4
Candes-Saint-Martin (37) 94 A1
Candillargues (34) 173 H5
Candor (60) 21 F3
Candresse (40) 165 E4
Canehan (76) 6 A5
Canéjan (33) 135 E6
Canens (31) 185 F3
Canenx-et-Réaut (40) 166 A1
Canet (11) 187 H3
Canet (34) 172 D5
Canet-de-Salars (12) 154 D5
Canet-en-Roussillon (66) 201 G2
Canettemont (62) 7 G2
Cangey (37) 79 G5
Caniac-du-Causse (46) 153 E2
Canihuel (22) 33 E6
Canilhac (48) 155 G4
Canisy (50) 37 F1
Canlers (62) 2 A6
Canly (60) 21 E5
Cannectancourt (60) 21 F3
Cannelle (2A) 204 C5
Cannes (06) 195 E4
Cannes-Écluse (77) 64 C2
Cannes-et-Clairan (30) 173 H3
Cannessières (80) 6 D5
le Cannet (06) 178 D5
Cannet (32) 166 D5
le Cannet-des-Maures (83) 193 H2
Canny-sur-Matz (60) 21 F3
Canny-sur-Thérain (60) 19 G3
Canohès (66) 201 E2
la Canourgue (48) 155 G4
Canouville (76) 16 D3
Cantaing-sur-Escaut (59) 8 D4
Cantaous (65) 183 H4
Cantaron (06) 195 F2
Canté (09) 185 G3
Canteleu (76) 17 G6
Canteleux (62) 7 G3
Canteloup (14) 39 E1
Canteloup (50) 13 E2
Cantenac (33) 135 E3
Cantenay-Épinard (49) 76 D4
Cantiers (27) 19 F6
Cantigny (80) 20 D2
Cantillac (24) 123 E6
Cantin (59) 8 D2
Cantoin (12) 140 D6
Cantois (33) 149 H1
Canville-la-Rocque (50) 12 C4
Canville-les-Deux-Églises (76) 17 F3
Cany-Barville (76) 18 A1
Caorches-Saint-Nicolas (27) 15 H5
Caouënnec-Lanvézéac (22) 32 D2
Caours (80) 6 D4
Cap-d'Ail (06) 179 F3
Capbreton (40) 164 B4
Capdenac (46) 153 G2
Capdenac-Gare (12) 153 G2
Capdrot (24) 151 H1
la Capelle (02) 10 A5
Capelle (59) 9 F3
la Capelle-Balaguier (12) 153 G4
la Capelle-Bleys (12) 153 H5
la Capelle-Bonance (12) 155 F4
la Capelle-et-Masmolène (30) 174 C1
Capelle-Fermont (62) 8 A2
la Capelle-lès-Boulogne (62) 1 F4
Capelle-les-Grands (27) 15 G6
Capelle-lès-Hesdin (62) 7 E2
Capendu (11) 187 F3
Capens (31) 185 E2
Capestang (34) 188 B2
Capian (33) 135 G6
Capinghem (59) 3 F5
Caplong (33) 136 B6
Capoulet-et-Junac (09) 199 E1
Cappel (57) 49 G1
Cappelle-Brouck (59) 2 A2
Cappelle-en-Pévèle (59) 3 G6
Cappelle-la-Grande (59) 2 B2
Cappy (80) 8 B6
Captieux (33) 149 H4
Capvern (65) 183 G4
Caragoudes (31) 169 G6
Caraman (31) 169 H6
Caramany (66) 200 D2
Carantec (29) 31 H2
Carantilly (50) 37 F1
Carayac (46) 153 F3
Carbay (49) 57 H6
Carbes (81) 170 C5
Carbini (2A) 207 F3
Carbon-Blanc (33) 135 F5
Carbonne (31) 185 E2
Carbuccia (2A) 204 D5
Carcagny (14) 14 A4
Carcanières (09) 200 A2
Carcans (33) 134 B3
Carcarès-Sainte-Croix (40) 165 G3
Carcassonne (11) 187 E3
Carcen-Ponson (40) 165 G2
Carcès (83) 177 F6
Carcheto-Brustico (2B) 205 G2
Cardaillac (46) 153 G1
Cardan (33) 149 G1
Cardeilhac (31) 184 B3
Cardesse (64) 182 A2
Cardet (30) 173 H1
Cardo-Torgia (2A) 204 D6
Cardonnette (80) 7 G5
le Cardonnois (80) 20 D3
Cardonville (14) 13 F4
Cardroc (35) 56 D1
Carelles (53) 58 C2
Carency (62) 8 A1
Carennac (46) 139 E5
Carentan (50) 13 E5
Carentoir (56) 56 C5
Cargèse (2A) 204 B4
Cargiaca (2A) 207 E2
Carhaix-Plouguer (29) 32 B6
Carignan (08) 24 D2
Carignan-de-Bordeaux (33) 135 F5
Carisey (89) 83 H1
Carla-Bayle (09) 185 F4
Carla-de-Roquefort (09) 186 A5
le Carlaret (09) 185 H4
Carlat (15) 140 B5
Carlencas-et-Levas (34) 172 B5
Carlepont (60) 21 G4
Carling (57) 27 F5
Carlipa (11) 186 C2
Carlucet (46) 152 D1
Carlus (81) 170 B3
Carlux (24) 138 B5
Carly (62) 1 F5
Carmaux (81) 170 C1
Carnac (56) 72 B1
Carnac-Rouffiac (46) 152 B4
Carnas (30) 173 G3
la Carneille (61) 38 C4
Carnet (50) 35 H5
Carnetin (77) 43 F3
Carneville (50) 12 D1
Carnières (59) 9 E3
Carnin (59) 3 F6
Carnoët (22) 32 B5
Carnoules (83) 193 G3
Carnoux-en-Provence (13) 192 C4
Carnoy (80) 8 B5
Caro (56) 56 B5
Caro (64) 180 D3
Carolles (50) 35 G3
Caromb (84) 158 D6
Carpentras (84) 175 F1
Carpineto (2B) 205 G2
Carpiquet (14) 14 B4
Carquebut (50) 13 E4
Carquefou (44) 74 D4
Carqueiranne (83) 193 F5
Carrépuis (80) 21 F2
Carrère (64) 166 B6
Carresse-Cassaber (64) 165 E6
Carrières-sous-Poissy (78) 42 B3
Carrières-sur-Seine (78) 42 C3
Carros (06) 195 E2
Carrouges (61) 38 D6
Carry-le-Rouet (13) 191 H5
Cars (33) 135 E3
les Cars (87) 123 H4
Carsac-Aillac (24) 138 B6
Carsac-de-Gurson (24) 136 B4
Carsan (30) 157 H5
Carsix (27) 40 B1
Carspach (68) 89 E3
Cartelègue (33) 135 E2
Carticasi (2B) 205 F2
Cartignies (59) 9 H4
Cartigny (80) 8 C6
Cartigny-l'Épinay (14) 13 F5
Carves (24) 137 H6
Carville (14) 37 H3
Carville-la-Folletière (76) 17 E5
Carville-Pot-de-Fer (76) 17 E3
Carvin (62) 3 F6
Casabianca (2B) 203 G6
Casaglione (2A) 204 C4
Casalabriva (2A) 206 D2
Casalta (2B) 203 G6
Casamaccioli (2B) 204 D2
Casanova (2B) 205 E3
Cascastel-des-Corbières (11) 187 G5
Casefabre (66) 200 D3
Caseneuve (84) 176 A3
Cases-de-Pène (66) 201 E1
Casevecchie (2B) 205 G3
Cassagnabère-Tournas (31) 184 B3
Cassagnas (48) 156 C5
la Cassagne (24) 138 B4
Cassagne (31) 184 C4
Cassagnes (46) 152 A2
Cassagnes (66) 200 D2
Cassagnes-Bégonhès (12) 154 C6
Cassagnoles (30) 173 H2
Cassagnoles (34) 187 G2
la Cassaigne (11) 186 B3
Cassaigne (32) 167 F2
Cassaignes (11) 186 D6
Cassaniouze (15) 154 B1
Cassel (59) 2 C3
Cassen (40) 165 F3
Casseneuil (47) 151 F3
les Cassés (11) 186 B1
Casseuil (33) 150 A2
Cassignas (47) 151 G5
Cassis (13) 192 C4
Casson (44) 74 D3
Cassuéjouls (12) 154 D1
Cast (29) 53 F1
Castagnac (31) 185 F3
Castagnède (31) 184 C4
Castagnède (64) 165 E6
Castagniers (06) 195 F2
Castaignos-Souslens (40) 165 G5
Castandet (40) 166 B3
Castanet (12) 154 A5
Castanet (81) 170 B2
Castanet (82) 153 G5
Castanet-le-Haut (34) 171 H5
Castanet-Tolosan (31) 169 F6
Castans (11) 187 F1
Casteide-Cami (64) 182 A1
Casteide-Candau (64) 165 H6
Casteide-Doat (64) 183 E1
Casteil (66) 200 C4
Castel-Sarrazin (40) 165 G5
Castelbajac (65) 183 G3
Castelbiague (31) 184 C5
Castelculier (47) 151 F6
Castelferrus (82) 168 D2
Castelfranc (46) 152 B3
Castelgaillard (31) 184 C2
Castelginest (31) 169 F4
Casteljaloux (47) 150 B4
Castella (47) 151 F4
Castellane (04) 177 H3
Castellar (06) 195 G2
le Castellard-Melan (04) 160 C5
Castellare-di-Casinca (2B) 203 G6
Castellare-di-Mercurio (2B) 205 F2
le Castellet (04) 176 D2
le Castellet (83) 192 D4
Castellet (84) 176 A3
Castellet-lès-Sausses (04) 178 B1
Castello-di-Rostino (2B) 203 F6
Castelmary (12) 154 A6
Castelmaurou (31) 169 F5
Castelmayran (82) 168 C1
Castelmoron-d'Albret (33) 150 B1
Castelmoron-sur-Lot (47) 151 E4
Castelnau-Barbarens (32) 168 A5
Castelnau-Chalosse (40) 165 F4
Castelnau-d'Anglès (32) 167 F5
Castelnau-d'Arbieu (32) 168 A3
Castelnau-d'Aude (11) 187 G3
Castelnau-d'Auzan (32) 167 E2
Castelnau-de-Brassac (81) 171 E5
Castelnau-de-Guers (34) 188 D1
Castelnau-de-Lévis (81) 170 B2
Castelnau-de-Mandailles (12) 155 E3
Castelnau-de-Médoc (33) 134 D3
Castelnau-de-Montmiral (81) 169 H2
Castelnau-d'Estrétefonds (31) 169 E4
Castelnau-Durban (09) 185 F5
Castelnau-le-Lez (34) 173 F5
Castelnau-Magnoac (65) 183 H2
Castelnau-Montratier (46) 152 C5
Castelnau-Pégayrols (12) 155 E6
Castelnau-Picampeau (31) 184 D2
Castelnau-Rivière-Basse (65) 166 D5
Castelnau-sur-Gupie (47) 150 C2
Castelnau-sur-l'Auvignon (32) 167 G2
Castelnau-Tursan (40) 166 A4
Castelnau-Valence (30) 174 A2
Castelnaud-de-Gratecambe (47) 151 F3
Castelnaud-la-Chapelle (24) 138 A6
Castelnaudary (11) 186 B2
Castelnavet (32) 167 E4
Castelner (40) 165 H5
Castelnou (66) 201 E3
Castelreng (11) 186 C5
Castels (24) 137 H5
Castelsagrat (82) 151 H6
Castelsarrasin (82) 168 D1
Castelvieilh (65) 183 F2
Castelviel (33) 150 A1
le Castéra (31) 168 D5
Castéra-Bouzet (82) 168 B2
Castéra-Lanusse (65) 183 G3
Castéra-Lectourois (32) 167 H2
Castéra-lou (65) 183 F2
Castéra-Loubix (64) 183 E1
Castéra-Verduzan (32) 167 G3
Castéra-Vignoles (31) 184 B2
Castéras (09) 185 F4
Casterets (65) 184 A2
Castéron (32) 168 B3
Castet (64) 182 B4
Castet-Arrouy (32) 168 A2
Castetbon (64) 181 G1
Castétis (64) 165 G6
Castetnau-Camblong (64) 181 G2
Castetner (64) 165 G6
Castetpugon (64) 166 C5
Castets (40) 164 D2
Castets-en-Dorthe (33) 150 A2
Castex (09) 185 F3
Castex (32) 183 G1
Castex-d'Armagnac (32) 166 C3
Casties-Labrande (31) 184 D2
Castifao (2B) 203 E6
Castiglione (2B) 205 E1
Castillon (06) 195 G2
Castillon (14) 13 H6
Castillon (65) 183 F4
Castillon (Canton d'Arthez-de-Béarn) (64) 165 H6
Castillon (Canton de Lembeye) (64) 166 C6
Castillon-de-Castets (33) 150 A2
Castillon-de-Larboust (31) 197 F1
Castillon-de-Saint-Martory (31) 184 C4
Castillon-Debats (32) 167 E4
Castillon-du-Gard (30) 174 C2
Castillon-en-Auge (14) 15 E6
Castillon-en-Couserans (09) 184 D6
Castillon-la-Bataille (33) 136 A5
Castillon-Massas (32) 167 H4
Castillon-Savès (32) 168 C5
Castillonnès (47) 151 F1
Castilly (14) 13 F5
Castin (32) 167 H4
Castineta (2B) 203 F6
Castirla (2B) 205 E2
Castres (02) 21 H1
Castres (81) 170 C5
Castres-Gironde (33) 149 G1
Castries (34) 173 G5
le Cateau-Cambrésis (59) 9 F4
le Catelet (02) 9 E5
le Catelier (76) 18 D1
Catenay (76) 19 E3
Catenoy (60) 20 D5
Cateri (2B) 202 C5
Cathervielle (31) 197 F1
Catheux (60) 20 B2
Catigny (60) 21 F2
Catillon-Fumechon (60) 20 C4
Catillon-sur-Sambre (59) 9 G4
Catllar (66) 200 C3
Catonvielle (32) 168 C5
Cattenières (59) 9 E4
Cattenom (57) 26 C3
Catteville (50) 12 C4
Catus (46) 152 C2
Catz (50) 13 E5
Caubeyres (47) 150 C5
Caubiac (31) 168 C4
Caubios-Loos (64) 182 B1
Caubon-Saint-Sauveur (47) 150 C2
Caubous (31) 183 H6
Caubous (65) 183 H3
Caucalières (81) 170 D6
la Cauchie (62) 8 A3
Cauchy-à-la-Tour (62) 2 C6
Caucourt (62) 8 A1
Caudan (56) 54 C5
Caudebec-en-Caux (76) 17 E5
Caudebec-lès-Elbeuf (76) 18 C5
Caudebronde (11) 187 E2
Caudecoste (47) 151 F6
Caudeval (11) 186 B4
Caudiès-de-Conflent (66) 200 A3
Caudiès-de-Fenouillèdes (66) 200 B1
Caudrot (33) 150 A2
Caudry (59) 9 F4
Cauffry (60) 20 D5
Caugé (27) 40 D2
Caujac (31) 185 G2
Caulaincourt (02) 8 D6
le Caule-Sainte-Beuve (76) 19 F1
Caulières (80) 19 H1
Caullery (59) 9 E4
Caulnes (22) 56 C1
Caumont (02) 21 H2
Caumont (09) 184 D5
Caumont (27) 18 B5
Caumont (32) 166 C4
Caumont (33) 150 B1
Caumont (62) 7 E2
Caumont (82) 168 C1
Caumont-l'Éventé (14) 37 H1
Caumont-sur-Durance (84) 175 E3
Caumont-sur-Garonne (47) 150 C3
Caumont-sur-Orne (14) 38 B2
Cauna (40) 165 H3
Caunay (79) 108 C4
Cauneille (40) 165 E5
Caunes-Minervois (11) 187 F2
la Caunette (34) 187 H2
Caunette-sur-Lauquet (11) 187 E5
Caunettes-en-Val (11) 187 F4
Caupenne (40) 165 G4
Caupenne-d'Armagnac (32) 166 D3
la Caure (51) 45 E3
Caurel (22) 55 E1
Caurel (51) 23 F5
Cauro (2A) 204 D6
Cauroir (59) 9 E3
Cauroy (08) 23 H5
Cauroy-lès-Hermonville (51) 23 E5
le Causé (82) 168 C3
Cause-de-Clérans (24) 137 E5
Caussade (82) 152 D6
Caussade-Rivière (65) 166 D6
Causse-Bégon (30) 172 C1
Causse-de-la-Selle (34) 173 E4
Causse-et-Diège (12) 153 G3
Caussens (32) 167 G2
Causses-et-Veyran (34) 188 B1
Caussiniojouls (34) 172 B6
Caussols (06) 178 C3
Caussou (09) 199 F1
Cauterets (65) 182 D6
Cauverville-en-Roumois (27) 18 A5
Cauvicourt (14) 38 D2
Cauvignac (33) 150 A3
Cauvigny (60) 20 B5
Cauville (14) 38 B2
Cauville-sur-Mer (76) 15 E1
Caux (34) 172 C6
Caux-et-Sauzens (11) 186 D3
Cauzac (47) 151 G5
Cavagnac (46) 138 D4
Cavaillon (84) 175 F3
Cavalaire-sur-Mer (83) 194 A4
la Cavalerie (12) 172 B2
Cavan (22) 32 D3
Cavanac (11) 187 E4
Cavarc (47) 151 F1
Caveirac (30) 174 A3
Caves (11) 188 A6
Cavignac (33) 135 G3
Cavigny (50) 13 F6
Cavillargues (30) 174 C1
Cavillon (80) 7 F6
Cavron-Saint-Martin (62) 7 E1
Caychax (09) 199 F1
Cayeux-en-Santerre (80) 21 E1
Cayeux-sur-Mer (80) 6 B3
le Caylar (34) 172 C3
Caylus (82) 153 E5
Cayrac (82) 169 F1
Cayres (43) 142 B5
Cayriech (82) 152 D5
le Cayrol (12) 154 D2
Cayrols (15) 139 H6
Cazac (31) 184 C2
Cazalis (33) 149 G4
Cazalis (40) 165 G5
Cazalrenoux (11) 186 B3
Cazals (46) 152 B2
Cazals (82) 153 E6
Cazals-des-Baylès (09) 186 B4
Cazaril-Laspènes (31) 197 F1
Cazaril-Tambourès (31) 183 H3
Cazarilh (65) 184 A5
Cazats (33) 149 H3
Cazaubon (32) 166 D2
Cazaugitat (33) 150 B1
Cazaunous (31) 184 B5
Cazaux (09) 185 G4
Cazaux-d'Anglès (32) 167 F5
Cazaux-debat (65) 183 G6
Cazaux-Fréchet-Anéran-Camors (65) 183 G6
Cazaux-Layrisse (31) 184 A6
Cazaux-Savès (32) 168 C6
Cazaux-Villecomtal (32) 183 F1
Cazavet (09) 184 D5
Cazeaux-de-Larboust (31) 197 F1
Cazedarnes (34) 188 B1
Cazenave-Serres-et-Allens (09) 199 F1
Cazeneuve (32) 167 E2
Cazeneuve-Montaut (31) 184 C3
Cazères (31) 184 D3
Cazères-sur-l'Adour (40) 166 B3
Cazes-Mondenard (82) 152 B5
Cazevieille (34) 173 F4
Cazideroque (47) 151 H4
Cazilhac (11) 187 E3
Cazilhac (34) 173 E2
Cazillac (46) 138 D4
Cazoulès (24) 138 C5
Cazouls-d'Hérault (34) 172 D6
Cazouls-lès-Béziers (34) 188 B2
Ceaucé (61) 58 D1
Ceaulmont (36) 111 E2
Céaux (50) 35 H4
Céaux-d'Allègre (43) 142 B3
Ceaux-en-Couhé (86) 108 D3
Ceaux-en-Loudun (86) 94 B3
Cébazan (34) 188 A1
Cébazat (63) 127 F2
Ceffonds (52) 67 F1
Ceignes (01) 117 F5
Ceilhes-et-Rocozels (34) 172 A4
Ceillac (05) 161 G1
Ceilloux (63) 127 H4
Ceintrey (54) 69 F1
la Celette (18) 112 C1
la Celle (03) 113 E5
la Celle (18) 97 H5
Cellé (41) 79 E1
la Celle (63) 126 B2
la Celle (83) 193 F3
la Celle-Condé (18) 97 F5
la Celle-Dunoise (23) 111 F4
la Celle-en-Morvan (71) 100 C3
la Celle-Guenand (37) 95 F4
la Celle-les-Bordes (78) 42 A6
Celle-Lévescault (86) 108 D3
la Celle-Saint-Avant (37) 94 D3
la Celle-Saint-Cloud (78) 42 C4
la Celle-Saint-Cyr (89) 65 E6
la Celle-sous-Chantemerle (51) 44 D6
la Celle-sous-Gouzon (23) 112 A5
la Celle-sous-Montmirail (02) 44 C4
la Celle-sur-Loire (58) 82 C5
la Celle-sur-Morin (77) 43 G4
la Celle-sur-Nièvre (58) 99 E1
Cellefrouin (16) 122 D2
Celles (09) 185 H6

Celles (15) 141 E3
Celles (17) 121 G4
Celles (24) 136 D1
Celles (34) 172 C5
Celles-en-Bassigny (52) 68 C6
Celles-lès-Condé (02) 44 C2
Celles-sur-Aisne (02) 22 B5
Celles-sur-Belle (79) 108 A4
Celles-sur-Durolle (63) 128 A2
Celles-sur-Ource (10) 66 D5
Celles-sur-Plaine (88) 70 C1
la Cellette (23) 111 H3
la Cellette (63) 112 D6
Cellettes (16) 122 C2
Cellettes (41) 80 A4
le Cellier (44) 75 E4
Cellier-du-Luc (07) 156 D1
Cellieu (42) 129 G5
Cellule (63) 127 F1
Celon (36) 110 D2
Celoux (15) 141 G3
Celsoy (52) 86 C1
Cély (77) 63 H2
Cemboing (70) 87 E1
Cempuis (60) 20 A2
Cénac (33) 135 F6
Cénac-et-Saint-Julien (24) 138 A6
Cenans (70) 87 G5
Cendras (30) 157 E6
le Cendre (63) 127 F3
Cendrecourt (70) 87 E1
Cendrey (25) 87 G5
Cendrieux (24) 137 G4
Cénevières (46) 153 E3
Cenne-Monestiés (11) 186 C2
Cenon (33) 135 F5
Cenon-sur-Vienne (86) 94 D5
Censeau (39) 103 G5
Censerey (21) 100 D1
Censy (89) 84 B3
les Cent-Acres (76) 18 D1
Centrès (12) 154 B6
Centuri (2B) 203 F1
Cenves (69) 116 A4
Cépet (31) 169 F4
Cépie (11) 186 D4
Cepoy (45) 64 A5
Céran (32) 168 A3
Cérans-Foulletourte (72) 78 A1
Cerbère (66) 201 H4
Cerbois (18) 97 F2
Cercié (69) 116 A5
Cercier (74) 118 B6
Cercles (24) 136 D1
Cercottes (45) 62 D6
Cercoux (17) 135 H3
le Cercueil (61) 39 E6
Cercy-la-Tour (58) 99 G5
Cerdon (01) 117 F6
Cerdon (45) 81 G3
Cère (40) 166 A1
Céré-la-Ronde (37) 95 H1
Cerelles (37) 78 D4
Cérences (50) 35 H1
Céreste (04) 176 B3
Céret (66) 201 E4
Cerfontaine (59) 10 A2
le Cergne (42) 115 G5
Cergy (95) 42 B2
Cérilly (03) 113 E1
Cérilly (21) 84 D1
Cérilly (89) 65 G4
Cerisé (61) 60 A1
Cerisières (52) 67 H3
Cerisiers (89) 65 F5
Cerisy (80) 8 A6
Cerisy-Belle-Étoile (61) 38 A4
Cerisy-Buleux (80) 6 D5
Cerisy-la-Forêt (50) 13 G6
Cerisy-la-Salle (50) 37 E2
Cerizay (79) 92 D4
Cérizols (09) 184 D4
Cerizy (02) 22 A1
la Cerlangue (76) 15 G2
Cernans (39) 103 F4
Cernay (14) 15 F6
Cernay (28) 61 H2
Cernay (68) 89 E1
Cernay (86) 94 B5
Cernay-en-Dormois (51) 24 B6
Cernay-la-Ville (78) 42 A5
Cernay-l'Église (25) 88 C6
Cernay-lès-Reims (51) 23 F6
Cerneux (77) 44 B5
Cernex (74) 118 B6
Cerniébaud (39) 103 G5
Cernion (08) 23 G1
Cernon (39) 117 G3
Cernon (51) 45 H4
Cernoy (60) 20 D4
Cernoy-en-Berry (45) 82 A4
Cernusson (49) 93 E1
Cerny (91) 63 G1
Cerny-en-Laonnois (02) 22 C4
Cerny-lès-Bucy (02) 22 B3
Céron (71) 114 D4
Cérons (33) 149 G1
Cerqueux (14) 15 G6
les Cerqueux (49) 92 D3
les Cerqueux-sous-Passavant (49) 93 E2
Cerre-lès-Noroy (70) 87 H3
Cers (34) 188 C2
Cersay (79) 93 F2
Cerseuil (02) 22 B5
Cersot (71) 101 F6
Certilleux (88) 68 D3
Certines (01) 117 E5
Cervens (74) 118 D4
Cervières (05) 147 F5
Cervières (42) 128 B2
Cerville (54) 48 D5
Cervione (2B) 205 G2
Cervon (58) 99 H1
Cerzat (43) 141 H3
Cesancey (39) 117 F1
Césarches (73) 132 C3
Césarville-Dossainville (45) 63 F3
Cescau (09) 184 D6
Cescau (64) 182 B1
Cesny-aux-Vignes (14) 39 E1
Cesny-Bois-Halbout (14) 14 B6
Cessac (33) 135 H6
Cessales (31) 186 A1
Cesse (55) 24 D3
Cessenon-sur-Orb (34) 188 B1
Cessens (73) 131 H2
Cesseras (34) 187 G2
Cesset (03) 113 G4
Cesseville (27) 40 C1
Cessey (25) 103 F2
Cessey-sur-Tille (21) 86 A6
Cessières (02) 22 B3
Cessieu (38) 131 E5
Cesson (77) 63 H1
Cesson-Sévigné (35) 57 F3
Cessoy-en-Montois (77) 64 D1
Cessy (01) 118 B3
Cessy-les-Bois (58) 82 D6
Cestas (33) 135 E6
Cestayrols (81) 170 B2
Ceton (61) 61 E4
Cette-Eygun (64) 182 A5
Cevins (73) 132 D4
Ceyras (34) 172 D5
Ceyrat (63) 127 E3
Ceyreste (13) 192 C4
Ceyroux (23) 111 E6
Ceyssac (43) 142 C4
Ceyssat (63) 126 D3
Ceyzériat (01) 117 E5
Ceyzérieu (01) 131 G2
Cézac (33) 135 F3
Cézac (46) 152 C4
Cezais (85) 107 F1
Cézan (32) 167 G3
Cezay (42) 128 C3
Cézens (15) 140 D4
Cézia (39) 117 G3
Cézy (89) 65 E6
Chabanais (16) 123 F2
la Chabanne (03) 128 B1
Chabestan (05) 159 H3
Chabeuil (26) 144 B5
Chablis (89) 83 H2
Châbons (38) 131 E6
Chabottes (05) 160 C1
Chabournay (86) 94 B6
Chabrac (16) 123 F1
Chabreloche (63) 128 B2
Chabrignac (19) 138 B1
Chabrillan (26) 158 C1
Chabris (36) 96 C1
Chacé (49) 93 H1
Chacenay (10) 66 D5
Chacrise (02) 22 B5
Chadeleuf (63) 127 F5
Chadenac (17) 121 F5
Chadenet (48) 156 B3
Chadrac (43) 142 C4
Chadron (43) 142 C5
Chadurie (16) 122 B5
le Chaffal (26) 144 D5
le Chaffaut-Saint-Jurson (04) 177 F1
Chaffois (25) 103 H4
Chagey (70) 88 C3
Chagnon (42) 129 G5
Chagny (08) 24 A3
Chagny (71) 101 F4
Chahaignes (72) 78 C2
Chahains (61) 38 D6
Chaignay (21) 85 H5
Chaignes (27) 41 F2
Chail (79) 108 B4
Chaillac (36) 110 C3
Chaillac-sur-Vienne (87) 123 G2
Chailland (53) 58 C3
Chaillé-les-Marais (85) 106 D2
Chaillé-sous-les-Ormeaux (85) 91 G5
Chailles (41) 79 H4
Chaillevette (17) 120 C3
Chaillevois (02) 22 B4
Chailley (89) 65 G5
Chaillon (55) 47 H3
Chailloué (61) 39 F5
Chailly-en-Bière (77) 63 H2
Chailly-en-Brie (77) 43 H4
Chailly-en-Gâtinais (45) 63 H6
Chailly-lès-Ennery (57) 26 C4
Chailly-sur-Armançon (21) 101 E1
Chainaz-les-Frasses (74) 132 A3
Chaînée-des-Coupis (39) 102 C4
Chaingy (45) 80 C1
Chaintré (71) 116 B4
Chaintreaux (77) 64 B4
Chaintrix-Bierges (51) 45 F3
la Chaise (10) 67 E2
la Chaise-Baudouin (50) 37 F4
la Chaise-Dieu (43) 142 B1
Chaise-Dieu-du-Theil (27) 40 B4
Chaix (85) 107 E2
la Chaize-Giraud (85) 90 D4
la Chaize-le-Vicomte (85) 91 H4
Chalabre (11) 186 B5
Chalagnac (24) 137 F3
Chalain-d'Uzore (42) 128 D4
Chalain-le-Comtal (42) 129 E4
Chalaines (55) 47 H6
Chalais (16) 136 B1
Chalais (36) 110 C2
Chalais (86) 94 A3
Chalamont (01) 130 C1
Chalampé (68) 89 G1
Chalancey (52) 85 H3
Chalancon (26) 159 E3
Chalandray (86) 93 H6
Chalandry (02) 22 C2
Chalandry-Elaire (08) 24 B2
le Chalange (61) 39 G6
le Chalard (87) 124 A5
Chalautre-la-Grande (77) 65 F1
Chalautre-la-Petite (77) 65 E1
Chalaux (58) 84 A6
Chaleins (01) 116 B6
Chaleix (24) 123 G5
Chalencon (07) 143 G5
les Chalesmes (39) 103 G6
Châlette-sur-Loing (45) 64 A6
Chalette-sur-Voire (10) 66 D2
Chaley (01) 131 E1
Chalèze (25) 87 F6
Chalezeule (25) 87 F6
Chaliers (15) 141 F5
Chalifert (77) 43 F3
Chaligny (54) 48 C5
Chalinargues (15) 141 E3
Chalindrey (52) 86 B2
Chalivoy-Milon (18) 98 B5
Challain-la-Potherie (49) 76 B3
Challans (85) 90 D2
Challement (58) 83 G6
Challerange (08) 24 B5
Challes (72) 60 C6
Challes-la-Montagne (01) 117 F5
Challes-les-Eaux (73) 132 A5
Challet (28) 62 A1
Challex (01) 118 B5
Challignac (16) 122 A6
Challonges (74) 118 A6
Challuy (58) 98 D4
Chalmaison (77) 64 D1
Chalmazel (42) 128 C4
Chalmoux (71) 114 D1
Chalo-Saint-Mars (91) 63 E2
le Chalon (26) 144 C3
Chalon-sur-Saône (71) 101 G5
Chalonnes-sous-le-Lude (49) 78 A4
Chalonnes-sur-Loire (49) 76 C5
Châlons (38) 130 B6
Châlons-du-Maine (53) 58 D4
Châlons-en-Champagne (51) 45 H3
Châlons-sur-Vesle (51) 23 E6
Châlonvillars (70) 88 C3
Chalou-Moulineux (91) 63 E2
Chaltrait (51) 45 E3
Chalus (63) 127 F6
Châlus (87) 123 H4
Chalvignac (15) 139 H2
Chalvraines (52) 68 B3
Chamadelle (33) 136 A3
Chamagne (88) 69 G2
Chamagnieu (38) 130 C4
Chamalières (63) 127 E3
Chamalières-sur-Loire (43) 142 D2
Chamaloc (26) 145 E6
Chamant (60) 21 E6
Chamarande (91) 63 F1
Chamarandes-Choignes (52) 68 A5
Chamaret (26) 158 B4
la Chamba (42) 128 B3
Chambain (21) 85 G2
Chambeire (21) 86 A6
Chambellay (49) 76 D2
Chambéon (42) 129 E4
Chambérat (03) 112 B3
Chamberaud (23) 111 H6
Chamberet (19) 125 E5
Chambéria (39) 117 G2
Chambéry (73) 131 H4
Chambeugle (89) 82 C1
Chambezon (43) 141 G1
Chambilly (71) 115 E4
Chamblac (27) 40 A2
Chamblanc (21) 102 A3
Chamblay (39) 103 E3
Chambles (42) 129 E6
Chamblet (03) 112 D4
Chambley-Bussières (54) 26 A6
Chambly (60) 42 C1
Chambœuf (21) 101 G1
Chambœuf (42) 129 F5
Chambois (61) 39 F4
Chambolle-Musigny (21) 101 H2
le Chambon (07) 143 F6
Chambon (17) 107 E5
Chambon (18) 97 G5
Chambon (30) 157 E5
Chambon (37) 95 E5
le Chambon-Feugerolles (42) 129 F6
Chambon-la-Forêt (45) 63 F5
Chambon-le-Château (48) 142 B5
Chambon-Sainte-Croix (23) 111 F3
Chambon-sur-Cisse (41) 79 H4
Chambon-sur-Dolore (63) 128 A5
Chambon-sur-Lac (63) 126 D5
le Chambon-sur-Lignon (43) 143 F4
Chambon-sur-Voueize (23) 112 C5
Chambonas (07) 157 E4
Chambonchard (23) 112 C5
la Chambonie (42) 128 B3
Chamborand (23) 111 E5
Chambord (27) 40 A3
Chambord (41) 80 B3
Chamboret (87) 124 A1
Chamborigaud (30) 156 D5
Chambornay-lès-Bellevaux (70) 87 G5
Chambornay-lès-Pin (70) 87 E6
Chambors (60) 19 H6
Chambost-Allières (69) 129 G1
Chambost-Longessaigne (69) 129 F3
Chamboulive (19) 125 E6
Chambourcy (78) 42 B3
Chambourg-sur-Indre (37) 95 F2
Chambray (27) 41 E2
Chambray-lès-Tours (37) 78 D6
la Chambre (73) 132 C6
Chambrecy (51) 45 E1
les Chambres (50) 35 H3
Chambretaud (85) 92 B3
Chambrey (57) 49 E4
Chambroncourt (52) 68 B2
Chambry (02) 22 C3
Chambry (77) 43 G2
Chaméane (63) 127 H5
Chamelet (69) 129 G1
Chamery (51) 45 F1
Chamesey (25) 104 C1
Chamesol (25) 88 C5
Chamesson (21) 85 E2
Chameyrat (19) 138 D2
Chamigny (77) 44 A3
Chamilly (71) 101 F4
Chammes (53) 59 F5
Chamole (39) 103 E4
Chamonix-Mont-Blanc (74) 133 F1
Chamouillac (17) 135 F1
Chamouille (02) 22 C4
Chamouilley (52) 46 D6
Chamousset (73) 132 B4
Chamoux (89) 83 G5
Chamoux-sur-Gelon (73) 132 B5
Chamoy (10) 66 A5
le Champ-de-la-Pierre (61) 38 D6
Champ-d'Oiseau (21) 84 C4
Champ-Dolent (27) 40 D3
Champ-du-Boult (14) 37 G4
Champ-Haut (61) 39 G5
Champ-Laurent (73) 132 B5
Champ-le-Duc (88) 70 B3
le Champ-près-Froges (38) 145 H1
le Champ-Saint-Père (85) 91 G6
Champ-sur-Barse (10) 66 D4
Champ-sur-Drac (38) 145 G3
Champ-sur-Layon (49) 76 D6
Champagnac (15) 140 A1
Champagnac (17) 121 G6
Champagnac-de-Belair (24) 123 F6
Champagnac-la-Noaille (19) 139 F1
Champagnac-la-Prune (19) 139 F2
Champagnac-la-Rivière (87) 123 G3
Champagnac-le-Vieux (43) 141 H1
Champagnat (23) 125 H1
Champagnat (71) 117 E2
Champagnat-le-Jeune (63) 127 H6
Champagne (07) 144 A2
Champagne (17) 120 D2
Champagne (28) 41 G5
Champagné (72) 60 B5
Champagne-au-Mont-d'Or (69) 130 A3
Champagne-en-Valromey (01) 131 F1
Champagne-et-Fontaine (24) 122 C6
Champagné-le-Sec (86) 108 D5
Champagné-les-Marais (85) 106 D3
Champagne-Mouton (16) 122 D1
Champagné-Saint-Hilaire (86) 109 E3
Champagne-sur-Loue (39) 103 E3
Champagne-sur-Oise (95) 42 C1
Champagne-sur-Seine (77) 64 B2
Champagne-sur-Vingeanne (21) 86 B5
Champagne-Vigny (16) 122 B5
Champagneux (73) 131 F4
Champagney (25) 103 F1
Champagney (39) 102 C1
Champagney (70) 88 B2
Champagnier (38) 145 G3
Champagnole (39) 103 F5
Champagnolles (17) 121 E5
Champagny (21) 85 F5
Champagny-en-Vanoise (73) 133 E5
Champagny-sous-Uxelles (71) 116 A1
Champallement (58) 99 F1
Champanges (74) 119 E3
Champaubert (51) 44 D4
Champcella (05) 147 E6
Champcenest (77) 44 B5
Champcerie (61) 38 D4
Champcervon (50) 35 H2
Champcevinel (24) 137 F2
Champcevrais (89) 82 C2
Champcey (50) 35 G3
Champclause (43) 143 E4
Champcueil (91) 63 G1
Champdeniers-Saint-Denis (79) 107 H2
Champdeuil (77) 43 F6
Champdieu (42) 128 D4
Champdivers (39) 102 C3
Champdolent (17) 120 D1
Champdor (01) 117 G6
Champdôtre (21) 102 B2
Champdray (88) 70 B4
Champeau-en-Morvan (21) 100 C1
Champeaux (35) 57 H2
Champeaux (50) 35 G3
les Champeaux (61) 39 F3
Champeaux (77) 43 F6
Champeaux-et-la-Chapelle-Pommier (24) 123 E5
Champeaux-sur-Sarthe (61) 39 H6
Champeix (63) 127 F5
Champenard (27) 41 E1
la Champenoise (36) 96 D4
Champenoux (54) 48 D4
Champéon (53) 59 E2
Champétières (63) 128 B5
Champey (70) 88 B3
Champey-sur-Moselle (54) 48 C3
Champfleur (72) 60 A2
Champfleury (10) 45 F6
Champfleury (51) 23 E6
Champforgeuil (71) 101 G5
Champfrémont (53) 59 H2
Champfromier (01) 117 H5
Champgenéteux (53) 59 F3
Champguyon (51) 44 C4
Champhol (28) 62 B1
Champien (80) 21 F2
Champier (38) 130 D6
Champigné (49) 76 D3
Champignelles (89) 82 C2
Champigneul-Champagne (51) 45 G3
Champigneul-sur-Vence (08) 24 A2
Champigneulle (08) 24 C5
Champigneulles (54) 48 C4
Champigneulles-en-Bassigny (52) 68 C4
Champignol-lez-Mondeville (10) 67 E4
Champignolles (21) 101 E3
Champignolles (27) 40 B3
Champigny (51) 23 E6
Champigny (89) 64 D3
Champigny-en-Beauce (41) 79 H3
Champigny-la-Futelaye (27) 41 E4
Champigny-le-Sec (86) 94 A6
Champigny-lès-Langres (52) 86 B1
Champigny-sous-Varennes (52) 86 D1
Champigny-sur-Aube (10) 66 B1
Champigny-sur-Marne (94) 43 E4
Champigny-sur-Veude (37) 94 B2
Champillet (36) 111 H2
Champillon (51) 45 F2
Champis (07) 143 H4
Champlan (91) 42 C5
Champlat-et-Boujacourt (51) 45 E1
Champlay (89) 65 F6
Champlecy (71) 115 F2
Champlemy (58) 99 F1
Champlin (08) 10 C6
Champlin (58) 99 F1
Champlitte (70) 86 C3
Champlive (25) 87 G6
Champlost (89) 65 G5
Champmillon (16) 122 B4
Champmotteux (91) 63 G3
Champnétery (87) 124 D2
Champneuville (55) 25 E6
Champniers (16) 122 C3
Champniers (86) 109 E4
Champniers-et-Reilhac (24) 123 F4
Champoléon (05) 146 C6
Champoly (42) 128 C2
Champosoult (61) 39 F3
Champougny (55) 47 H6
Champoulet (45) 82 C3
Champoux (25) 87 G6
Champrenault (21) 85 F5
Champrepus (50) 35 H2
Champrond (72) 61 E5
Champrond-en-Gâtine (28) 61 G2
Champrond-en-Perchet (28) 61 F3
Champrougier (39) 102 D4
Champs (02) 21 H3
Champs (61) 40 A6
Champs (63) 113 G6
les Champs-de-Losque (50) 13 E6
les Champs-Géraux (22) 34 D5
Champs-Romain (24) 123 F5
Champs-sur-Marne (77) 43 E4
Champs-sur-Tarentaine-Marchal (15) 126 B6
Champs-sur-Yonne (89) 83 G2
Champsac (87) 123 H3
Champsanglard (23) 111 G4
Champsecret (61) 38 B6
Champseru (28) 62 C1
Champsevraine (52) 86 C2
Champtercier (04) 160 C6
Champteussé-sur-Baconne (49) 76 D3
Champtocé-sur-Loire (49) 75 H3
Champtoceaux (49) 75 E4
Champtonnay (70) 86 D5
Champvallon (89) 65 E6
Champvans (39) 102 C2
Champvans (70) 86 C5
Champvans-les-Moulins (25) 103 F1
Champvert (58) 99 G5
Champvoisy (51) 44 D1
Champvoux (58) 98 D2
Chamrousse (38) 145 H3
Chamvres (89) 65 E6
Chanac (48) 155 H3
Chanac-les-Mines (19) 139 E2
Chanaleilles (43) 141 H5
Chanas (38) 144 A1
Chanat-la-Mouteyre (63) 127 E2
Chanay (01) 117 H6
Chanaz (73) 131 G2
Chançay (37) 79 E5
Chancé (35) 57 G3
Chanceaux (21) 85 F4
Chanceaux-près-Loches (37) 95 F2
Chanceaux-sur-Choisille (37) 78 D5
Chancelade (24) 137 F2
Chancenay (52) 46 D5
Chancey (70) 86 D6
Chancia (39) 117 G3
Chandai (61) 40 B4
Chandolas (07) 157 F4
Chandon (42) 115 F5
Chanéac (07) 143 F5
Chaneins (01) 116 B6
Chânes (71) 116 B4
le Change (24) 137 G2
Changé (53) 58 C4
Change (71) 101 F4
Changé (72) 60 B6
Changey (52) 68 B6
Changis-sur-Marne (77) 43 H3
Changy (42) 114 D5
Changy (51) 46 B4
Changy (71) 115 F3
Chaniat (43) 141 H1
Chaniers (17) 121 F3
Channay (21) 84 C1
Channay-sur-Lathan (37) 78 B4
Channes (10) 66 C6
Chanonat (63) 127 F4
Chanos-Curson (26) 144 B3
Chanousse (05) 159 G4
Chanoy (52) 68 A6
Chanoz-Châtenay (01) 116 C5
Chanteau (45) 62 D6
Chantecoq (45) 64 C5
Chantecorps (79) 108 B2
Chanteheux (54) 49 F6
Chanteix (19) 138 D1
Chantelle (03) 113 G4
Chanteloup (27) 40 D3
Chanteloup (35) 57 F4
Chanteloup (50) 35 G1
Chanteloup (79) 93 E5
Chanteloup-en-Brie (77) 43 F4
Chanteloup-les-Bois (49) 92 D2
Chanteloup-les-Vignes (78) 42 B3
Chantelouve (38) 146 A4
Chantemerle (51) 44 D6
Chantemerle-les-Blés (26) 144 B3
Chantemerle-lès-Grignan (26) 158 B4
Chantemerle-sur-la-Soie (17) 107 F6
Chantenay-Saint-Imbert (58) 99 E6
Chantenay-Villedieu (72) 59 G6
Chantepie (35) 57 F3
Chantérac (24) 136 D2
Chanteraine (55) 47 F5
Chanterelle (15) 140 D1
Chantes (70) 87 E3
Chantesse (38) 145 E2
Chanteuges (43) 142 A4
Chantillac (16) 135 H1
Chantilly (60) 42 D1
Chantonnay (85) 92 A6
Chantraine (88) 69 H4
Chantraines (52) 68 A4
Chantrans (25) 103 G3
Chantrigné (53) 59 E2
Chanu (61) 38 A4
Chanville (57) 49 E2
Chanzeaux (49) 76 D6
Chaon (41) 81 F4
Chaouilley (54) 69 F1
Chaource (10) 66 B5
Chaourse (02) 23 E2
Chapaize (71) 116 A1
Chapareillan (38) 132 A5
Chapdes-Beaufort (63) 126 D2
Chapdeuil (24) 136 D1
Chapeau (03) 114 B2
Chapeiry (74) 132 A2
Chapelaine (51) 46 A6
la Chapelaude (03) 112 C3
la Chapelle (03) 114 B6
la Chapelle (08) 24 C1
la Chapelle (16) 122 B2
la Chapelle (73) 132 C6
la Chapelle-Achard (85) 91 E5
la Chapelle-Agnon (63) 128 A4
la Chapelle-Anthenaise (53) 58 D4
la Chapelle-au-Mans (71) 114 D1
la Chapelle-au-Moine (61) 38 B5
la Chapelle-au-Riboul (53) 59 F2
la Chapelle-Aubareil (24) 138 A4
la Chapelle-aux-Bois (88) 69 H5
la Chapelle-aux-Brocs (19) 138 D3
la Chapelle-aux-Chasses (03) 99 G6
la Chapelle-aux-Choux (72) 78 B3
la Chapelle-aux-Filtzméens (35) 35 E6
la Chapelle-aux-Lys (85) 92 D6
la Chapelle-aux-Naux (37) 78 C6
la Chapelle-aux-Saints (19) 139 E4
la Chapelle-Baloue (23) 111 E3
la Chapelle-Basse-Mer (44) 75 E5
la Chapelle-Bâton (79) 108 A2
la Chapelle-Bâton (86) 109 E5
la Chapelle-Bayvel (27) 15 G4
la Chapelle-Bertin (43) 142 A2
la Chapelle-Bertrand (79) 93 G6
la Chapelle-Biche (61) 38 A5
la Chapelle-Blanche (22) 56 C1
la Chapelle-Blanche (73) 132 A5
la Chapelle-Blanche-Saint-Martin (37) 95 E2
la Chapelle-Bouëxic (35) 56 D4
la Chapelle-Caro (56) 56 A5
la Chapelle-Cécelin (50) 37 F4
la Chapelle-Chaussée (35) 57 E1
la Chapelle-Craonnaise (53) 58 B6
la Chapelle-d'Abondance (74) 119 G3
la Chapelle-d'Alagnon (15) 140 D3
la Chapelle-d'Aligné (72) 77 F2
la Chapelle-d'Andaine (61) 38 B6
la Chapelle-d'Angillon (18) 81 G6
la Chapelle-d'Armentières (59) 3 E5
la Chapelle-d'Aunainville (28) 62 D2
la Chapelle-d'Aurec (43) 143 E1
la Chapelle-de-Bragny (71) 116 B1
la Chapelle-de-Brain (35) 56 D6
la Chapelle-de-Guinchay (71) 116 B5
la Chapelle-de-la-Tour (38) 131 E4
la Chapelle-de-Mardore (69) 115 G6
la Chapelle-de-Surieu (38) 130 B6
Chapelle-des-Bois (25) 118 B1
la Chapelle-des-Fougeretz (35) 57 E2
la Chapelle-des-Marais (44) 73 G3
la Chapelle-des-Pots (17) 121 F3
la Chapelle-devant-Bruyères (88) 70 C4
Chapelle-d'Huin (25) 103 G4
la Chapelle-du-Bard (38) 132 A6
la Chapelle-du-Bois (72) 60 D4
la Chapelle-du-Bois-des-Faulx (27) 40 D1
la Chapelle-du-Bourgay (76) 18 D1
la Chapelle-du-Châtelard (01) 116 C6
la Chapelle-du-Genêt (49) 75 G5
la Chapelle-du-Lou (35) 56 D2
la Chapelle-du-Mont-de-France (71) 115 H3
la Chapelle-du-Mont-du-Chat (73) 131 H3
la Chapelle-du-Noyer (28) 61 H5
la Chapelle-en-Juger (50) 37 F1
la Chapelle-en-Lafaye (42) 128 D6
la Chapelle-en-Serval (60) 43 E1
la Chapelle-en-Valgaudémar (05) 146 B5
la Chapelle-en-Vercors (26) 145 E4
la Chapelle-en-Vexin (95) 41 H1
la Chapelle-Enchérie (41) 79 H2
la Chapelle-Engerbold (14) 38 B3
la Chapelle-Erbrée (35) 58 A4
la Chapelle-Faucher (24) 137 F1
la Chapelle-Felcourt (51) 46 C2
la Chapelle-Forainvilliers (28) 41 F5
la Chapelle-Fortin (28) 40 C5
la Chapelle-Gaceline (56) 56 C5
la Chapelle-Gaudin (79) 93 F4
la Chapelle-Gaugain (72) 78 D2
la Chapelle-Gauthier (27) 39 H2
la Chapelle-Gauthier (77) 64 B1
la Chapelle-Geneste (43) 142 B1
la Chapelle-Glain (44) 75 F1
la Chapelle-Gonaguet (24) 137 E2
la Chapelle-Grésignac (24) 122 D6
Chapelle-Guillaume (28) 61 F5
la Chapelle-Hareng (27) 15 G5
la Chapelle-Haute-Grue (14) 39 F2
la Chapelle-Hermier (85) 91 E4
la Chapelle-Heulin (44) 75 E5
la Chapelle-Hugon (18) 98 C4
la Chapelle-Hullin (49) 76 A2
la Chapelle-Huon (72) 79 E1
la Chapelle-Iger (77) 43 H6
la Chapelle-Janson (35) 58 B2
la Chapelle-la-Reine (77) 63 H3
la Chapelle-Lasson (51) 45 E6
la Chapelle-Launay (44) 74 A3
la Chapelle-Laurent (15) 141 G3
la Chapelle-lès-Luxeuil (70) 87 H2
la Chapelle-Marcousse (63) 127 F6
la Chapelle-Montabourlet (24) 122 D6
la Chapelle-Montbrandeix (87) 123 G4
la Chapelle-Monthodon (02) 44 D2
la Chapelle-Montligeon (61) 60 D1
la Chapelle-Montlinard (18) 98 C2
la Chapelle-Montmartin (41) 96 C1
la Chapelle-Montmoreau (24) 123 F6
la Chapelle-Montreuil (86) 108 D1
la Chapelle-Moulière (86) 94 D6
la Chapelle-Moutils (77) 44 B4
la Chapelle-Naude (71) 116 D1
la Chapelle-Neuve (22) 32 C4
la Chapelle-Neuve (56) 55 F4
la Chapelle-Onzerain (45) 62 B5
la Chapelle-Orthemale (36) 96 B5
la Chapelle-Palluau (85) 91 F3
la Chapelle-Pouilloux (79) 108 C5
la Chapelle-près-Sées (61) 39 F6
la Chapelle-Rablais (77) 64 C1
la Chapelle-Rainsouin (53) 59 E4
la Chapelle-Rambaud (74) 118 C6
la Chapelle-Réanville (27) 41 F2
la Chapelle-Rousselin (49) 75 H5
Chapelle-Royale (28) 61 G4
la Chapelle-Saint-André (58) 83 E5
la Chapelle-Saint-Aubert (35) 57 H1
la Chapelle-Saint-Aubin (72) 60 A5
la Chapelle-Saint-Étienne (79) 92 D6
la Chapelle-Saint-Florent (49) 75 G4
la Chapelle-Saint-Fray (72) 60 A4
la Chapelle-Saint-Géraud (19) 139 F4
la Chapelle-Saint-Jean (24) 138 A2
la Chapelle-Saint-Laud (49) 77 F3
la Chapelle-Saint-Laurent (79) 93 E5
la Chapelle-Saint-Laurian (36) 96 D3
la Chapelle-Saint-Luc (10) 66 B3
la Chapelle-Saint-Martial (23) 111 G6
la Chapelle-Saint-Martin (73) 131 G4
la Chapelle-Saint-Martin-en-Plaine (41) 80 A3
la Chapelle-Saint-Maurice (74) 132 B3
la Chapelle-Saint-Mesmin (45) 80 D1
la Chapelle-Saint-Ouen (76) 19 E3
la Chapelle-Saint-Quillain (70) 87 E4
la Chapelle-Saint-Rémy (72) 60 C5
la Chapelle-Saint-Sauveur (44) 76 B4
la Chapelle-Saint-Sauveur (71) 102 B5
la Chapelle-Saint-Sépulcre (45) 64 B6
la Chapelle-Saint-Sulpice (77) 64 D1
la Chapelle-Saint-Ursin (18) 97 G3
la Chapelle-Souëf (61) 60 D3
la Chapelle-sous-Brancion (71) 116 B2
la Chapelle-sous-Dun (71) 115 F4
la Chapelle-sous-Orbais (51) 44 D3
la Chapelle-sous-Uchon (71) 100 C5
Chapelle-Spinasse (19) 139 G1
la Chapelle-sur-Aveyron (45) 82 B1
la Chapelle-sur-Chézy (02) 44 B3
la Chapelle-sur-Coise (69) 129 G4
la Chapelle-sur-Dun (76) 17 F2
la Chapelle-sur-Erdre (44) 74 D4
la Chapelle-sur-Furieuse (39) 103 F3
la Chapelle-sur-Loire (37) 94 B1
la Chapelle-sur-Oreuse (89) 65 E3
la Chapelle-sur-Oudon (49) 75 H1
la Chapelle-sur-Usson (63) 127 H6
la Chapelle-Taillefert (23) 111 G6
la Chapelle-Thècle (71) 116 D1
la Chapelle-Thémer (85) 107 E1
la Chapelle-Thireuil (79) 107 G1
la Chapelle-Thouarault (35) 57 E2
la Chapelle-Urée (50) 37 F5
Chapelle-Vallon (10) 66 B2
la Chapelle-Vaupelteigne (89) 83 H1
la Chapelle-Vendômoise (41) 79 H3
la Chapelle-Vicomtesse (41) 61 G6
la Chapelle-Viel (61) 40 A5
la Chapelle-Villars (42) 129 H6
Chapelle-Viviers (86) 109 G2
Chapelle-Voland (39) 102 C5
la Chapelle-Yvon (14) 15 G6
les Chapelles (73) 133 E4
les Chapelles-Bourbon (77) 43 G5
Chapelon (45) 63 H5
la Chapelotte (18) 81 H6
Chapet (78) 42 A3
Chapois (39) 103 F4
Chaponnay (69) 130 B4
Chaponost (69) 129 H3
Chappes (03) 113 F3
Chappes (08) 23 G3
Chappes (10) 66 C4
Chappes (63) 127 F2
Chaptelat (87) 124 B2
Chaptuzat (63) 113 G6
Charancieu (38) 131 F5
Charantonnay (38) 130 C5
Charavines (38) 131 E6
Charbogne (08) 24 A4
Charbonnat (71) 100 C5
Charbonnier-les-Mines (63) 127 G6
Charbonnières (28) 61 F4
Charbonnières (71) 116 B3
Charbonnières-les-Bains (69) 129 H3
Charbonnières-les-Sapins (25) 103 H2
Charbonnières-les-Varennes (63) 127 E2
Charbonnières-les-Vieilles (63) 127 E1
Charbuy (89) 83 F2
la Charce (26) 159 F3
Charcé-Saint-Ellier-sur-Aubance (49) 77 E5
Charcenne (70) 87 E5
Charchigné (53) 59 F2
Charchilla (39) 117 H2
Charcier (39) 117 H1
Chard (23) 126 B1
Chardeny (08) 24 A4
Chardogne (55) 47 E4
Chardonnay (71) 116 B2
Chareil-Cintrat (03) 113 G4
Charencey (21) 85 E5
Charency (39) 103 F5
Charency-Vezin (54) 25 F4
Charens (26) 159 F2
Charensat (63) 126 C1
Charentay (69) 116 A6
Charentenay (89) 83 F3
Charentilly (37) 78 D5
Charenton-du-Cher (18) 98 A6
Charenton-le-Pont (94) 42 D4
Charentonnay (18) 98 C2
Charette (38) 130 D2
Charette-Varennes (71) 102 B4
Charey (54) 48 B2
Charézier (39) 117 H1
Chargé (37) 79 F5
Chargey-lès-Gray (70) 86 C4
Chargey-lès-Port (70) 87 F2
Chariez (70) 87 F3
Charigny (21) 84 D5
la Charité-sur-Loire (58) 98 D2
Charix (01) 117 G5
Charlas (31) 184 B3
Charleval (13) 191 H2
Charleval (27) 19 E5
Charleville (51) 44 D4
Charleville-Mézières (08) 24 A1
Charleville-sous-Bois (57) 26 D5
Charlieu (42) 115 F5
Charly (18) 98 B4
Charly (69) 130 A4
Charly-Oradour (57) 26 C5
Charly-sur-Marne (02) 44 B3
Charmant (16) 122 C5
Charmauvillers (25) 88 D6
Charmé (16) 122 B1
la Charme (39) 102 D4
le Charme (45) 82 C2
la Charmée (71) 101 G6
Charmeil (03) 114 A5
le Charmel (02) 44 C1
Charmensac (15) 141 F2
Charmentray (77) 43 F3
Charmes (02) 22 A2
Charmes (03) 113 H6
Charmes (21) 86 B5
Charmes (52) 68 B6
Charmes (88) 69 G2
Charmes-en-l'Angle (52) 67 G2
Charmes-la-Côte (54) 48 A6
Charmes-la-Grande (52) 67 G2
Charmes-Saint-Valbert (70) 86 D2
Charmes-sur-l'Herbasse (26) 144 B3
Charmes-sur-Rhône (07) 144 A5
Charmoille (25) 88 B6
Charmoille (70) 87 F3
Charmois (54) 49 E6
Charmois (90) 88 D3
Charmois-devant-Bruyères (88) 70 A4
Charmois-l'Orgueilleux (88) 69 G4
Charmont (51) 46 C3
Charmont (95) 41 H1
Charmont-en-Beauce (45) 63 E4
Charmont-sous-Barbuise (10) 66 B2
les Charmontois (51) 46 D3
Charmoy (10) 65 G2
Charmoy (71) 100 D5
Charmoy (89) 65 F6
Charnas (07) 143 H1
Charnat (63) 127 H1
Charnay (25) 103 F2
Charnay (69) 129 H2
Charnay-lès-Chalon (71) 102 A4
Charnay-lès-Mâcon (71) 116 B4
Charnècles (38) 145 F1
Charnizay (37) 95 F4
Charnod (39) 117 F3
Charnois (08) 11 F4
Charnoz-sur-Ain (01) 130 D2
Charny (21) 84 D6
Charny (77) 43 F3
Charny (89) 82 D1
Charny-le-Bachot (10) 66 A1
Charny-sur-Meuse (55) 25 E6
Charolles (71) 115 F3
Charols (26) 158 C2
Charonville (28) 61 H3
Charost (18) 97 F3
Charpentry (55) 24 C6
Charpey (26) 144 C5
Charpont (28) 41 F5
Charquemont (25) 104 D1
Charrais (86) 94 B6
Charraix (43) 142 A4
Charras (16) 122 D5
Charray (28) 61 H6
Charre (64) 181 G2
Charrecey (71) 101 F5
Charrey-sur-Saône (21) 102 A2
Charrey-sur-Seine (21) 66 D6
Charrin (58) 99 G5
Charritte-de-Bas (64) 181 G2
Charron (17) 106 D3
Charron (23) 112 C6
Charroux (03) 113 G5
Charroux (86) 109 E5
Chars (95) 42 A1
Charsonville (45) 62 B6
Chartainvilliers (28) 62 B1
Chartèves (02) 44 C2
la Chartre-sur-le-Loir (72) 78 D2
Chartrené (49) 77 G4
Chartres (28) 62 B2
Chartres-de-Bretagne (35) 57 E3
Chartrettes (77) 64 A1
Chartrier-Ferrière (19) 138 C3
Chartronges (77) 44 A5
Chartuzac (17) 135 F1
Charvieu-Chavagneux (38) 130 C3
Charvonnex (74) 132 B1
Chas (63) 127 G3
Chaserey (10) 66 B6
Chasnais (85) 91 H6
Chasnans (25) 103 H2
Chasnay (58) 99 E1
Chasné-sur-Illet (35) 57 F1
Chaspinhac (43) 142 C3
Chaspuzac (43) 142 B4
la Chassagne (39) 102 C4
Chassagne (63) 127 E5
Chassagne-Montrachet (21) 101 F4
Chassagne-Saint-Denis (25) 103 G2
Chassagnes (43) 142 A2
Chassagny (69) 129 H4
Chassaignes (24) 136 C2
Chassal (39) 117 H3
Chassant (28) 61 G3
Chassé (72) 60 B1
Chasse-sur-Rhône (38) 130 A5
Chasseguey (50) 37 F5
Chasselas (71) 116 A4
Chasselay (38) 144 D2
Chasselay (69) 130 A2
Chassemy (02) 22 B5
Chassenard (03) 114 D3
Chasseneuil (36) 110 D1
Chasseneuil-du-Poitou (86) 94 C6
Chasseneuil-sur-Bonnieure (16) 122 D2
Chassenon (16) 123 F2
Chasseradès (48) 156 C2
Chassey (21) 84 D5
Chassey-Beaupré (55) 68 B1
Chassey-le-Camp (71) 101 F4
Chassey-lès-Montbozon (70) 87 H4
Chassey-lès-Scey (70) 87 F3
Chassiecq (16) 122 D1
Chassiers (07) 157 F2
Chassieu (69) 130 B3
Chassignelles (89) 84 B2
Chassignieu (38) 131 E5
Chassignolles (36) 111 G2
Chassignolles (43) 127 H6
Chassigny (52) 86 B2
Chassigny-sous-Dun (71) 115 F4
Chassillé (72) 59 G5
Chassors (16) 121 H3
Chassy (18) 98 B3
Chassy (71) 115 E1
Chassy (89) 83 E1
le Chastang (19) 139 E3
Chastanier (48) 156 C1
Chasteaux (19) 138 C3
Chastel (43) 141 G3
Chastel-Arnaud (26) 158 D1
Chastel-Nouvel (48) 156 A2
Chastel-sur-Murat (15) 140 D3
Chastellux-sur-Cure (89) 84 A5
Chastreix (63) 126 C5
la Châtaigneraie (85) 92 C6
Chatain (86) 109 E6
Châtaincourt (28) 41 E5
Châtas (88) 70 D2
Château (71) 115 H3
Château-Arnoux-Saint-Auban (04) 160 B6
Château-Bernard (38) 145 F4
Château-Bréhain (57) 49 E3
Château-Chalon (39) 102 D5
Château-Chervix (87) 124 B4
Château-Chinon (Campagne) (58) 100 A3
Château-Chinon (Ville) (58) 100 A3
le Château-d'Almenêches (61) 39 F5
Château-des-Prés (39) 118 A2
le Château-d'Oléron (17) 120 B1
Château-d'Olonne (85) 91 E6
Château-du-Loir (72) 78 C3
Château-Gaillard (01) 130 D1
Château-Garnier (86) 109 E4
Château-Gontier (53) 76 D1
Château-Guibert (85) 91 H5
Château-la-Vallière (37) 78 B4
Château-l'Abbaye (59) 4 B6
Château-Landon (77) 64 A4
Château-Larcher (86) 109 E3
Château-l'Évêque (24) 137 F2
Château-l'Hermitage (72) 78 A2
Château-Porcien (08) 23 F3
Château-Renard (45) 64 C6
Château-Renault (37) 79 F4
Château-Rouge (57) 27 E4
Château-Salins (57) 49 E4
Château-sur-Allier (03) 98 D5
Château-sur-Cher (63) 112 C6
Château-sur-Epte (27) 19 G6
Château-Thébaud (44) 74 D6
Château-Thierry (02) 44 B2
Château-Verdun (09) 199 F1
Château-Ville-Vieille (05) 147 F6
Château-Voué (57) 49 F3
Châteaubernard (16) 121 G3
Châteaubleau (77) 43 H6
Châteaubourg (07) 144 A4
Châteaubourg (35) 57 G3
Châteaubriant (44) 57 G6
Châteaudouble (26) 144 C5
Châteaudouble (83) 177 H5
Châteaudun (28) 61 H5
Châteaufort (04) 160 B5
Châteaufort (78) 42 B5
Châteaugay (63) 127 F2
Châteaugiron (35) 57 G3
Châteaulin (29) 53 G1
Châteaumeillant (18) 112 A2
Châteauneuf (21) 101 F1
Châteauneuf (42) 129 H5
Châteauneuf (71) 115 F5
Châteauneuf (73) 132 B5
Châteauneuf (85) 90 D2
Châteauneuf-de-Bordette (26) 158 D4
Châteauneuf-de-Chabre (05) 160 A5
Châteauneuf-de-Gadagne (84) 175 E2
Châteauneuf-de-Galaure (26) 144 B2
Châteauneuf-de-Randon (48) 156 B2
Châteauneuf-de-Vernoux (07) 143 H5
Châteauneuf-d'Entraunes (06) 161 G6

Châteauneuf-d'Ille-et-Vilaine (35) 36 A5
Châteauneuf-d'Oze (05) 160 A3
Châteauneuf-du-Faou (29) 53 H1
Châteauneuf-du-Pape (84) 175 E1
Châteauneuf-du-Rhône (26) 158 A1
Châteauneuf-en-Thymerais (28) 41 E6
Châteauneuf-Grasse (06) 178 C4
Châteauneuf-la-Forêt (87) 124 D3
Châteauneuf-le-Rouge (13) 176 B6
Châteauneuf-les-Bains (63) 126 D1
Châteauneuf-les-Martigues (13) 191 H5
Châteauneuf-Miraval (04) 159 H6
Châteauneuf-sur-Charente (16) 122 A4
Châteauneuf-sur-Cher (18) 97 G5
Châteauneuf-sur-Isère (26) 144 B4
Châteauneuf-sur-Loire (45) 81 F1
Châteauneuf-sur-Sarthe (49) 77 E2
Châteauneuf-Val-de-Bargis (58) 99 E1
Châteauneuf-Val-Saint-Donat (04) 160 B6
Châteauneuf-Villevieille (06) 195 F3
Châteauponsac (87) 110 C5
Châteauredon (04) 177 F1
Châteaurenard (13) 175 E3
Châteauroux (36) 96 C5
Châteauroux-les-Alpes (05) 161 F1
Châteauvert (83) 177 E6
Châteauvieux (05) 160 B3
Châteauvieux (41) 96 A1
Châteauvieux (83) 178 A3
Châteauvieux-les-Fossés (25) 103 H2
Châteauvilain (38) 130 D5
Châteauvillain (52) 67 G5
le Châtel (73) 146 C1
Châtel (74) 119 G4
Châtel-Censoir (89) 83 G4
Chatel-Chéhéry (08) 24 C5
Châtel-de-Joux (39) 117 H2
Châtel-de-Neuvre (03) 113 H3
Châtel-Gérard (89) 84 B3
Châtel-Montagne (03) 114 C6
Châtel-Moron (71) 101 F5
Châtel-Saint-Germain (57) 26 B5
Châtel-sur-Moselle (88) 69 H2
Châtelaillon-Plage (17) 106 C6
Châtelain (53) 76 D1
la Châtelaine (39) 103 E4
Châtelais (49) 76 A1
Châtelard (23) 126 B1
le Châtelard (73) 132 B3
Châtelaudren (22) 33 F4
Châtelay (39) 103 E3
Châtelblanc (25) 103 G6
Châteldon (63) 127 H1
le Châtelet (18) 112 B1
le Châtelet-en-Brie (77) 64 B1
le Châtelet-sur-Meuse (52) 68 C6
le Châtelet-sur-Retourne (08) 23 G4
Châtelguyon (63) 127 E2
les Châtelets (28) 40 C5
le Chateley (39) 102 D4
Châtelguyon (63) 127 E2
le Châtelier (51) 46 A6
Châtelneuf (21) 101 E1
Châtelraould-
Saint-Louvent (51) 46 A5
Châtelus (03) 114 C5
Châtelus (38) 145 E3
Châtelus-le-Marcheix (23) 124 D1
Châtelus-Malvaleix (23) 111 H4
Châtenay (01) 116 D6
Châtenay (28) 62 D2
Châtenay (38) 144 D3
Châtenay (71) 115 G4
Châtenay-en-France (95) 42 D2
Châtenay-Mâcheron (52) 86 B1
Châtenay-Malabry (92) 42 C5
Châtenay-sur-Seine (77) 64 D2
Châtenay-Vaudin (52) 86 B1
Chatenet (17) 121 H6
le Châtenet-en-Dognon (87) 124 C2
Châteney (70) 87 H2
Châtenois (67) 71 F3
Châtenois (70) 87 G2
Châtenois (88) 69 E3
Châtenois-les-Forges (90) 88 C3
Châtenoy (45) 81 G1
Châtenoy (77) 64 A4
Châtenoy-en-Bresse (71) 101 G5
Châtenoy-le-Royal (71) 101 G5
Châtignac (16) 136 A1
Chatignonville (91) 62 D2
Châtillon (03) 113 G2
Châtillon (39) 103 E6
Châtillon (69) 129 H2
Châtillon (86) 108 D3
Châtillon (92) 42 C4
Châtillon-Coligny (45) 82 B2
Châtillon-en-Bazois (58) 99 G3
Châtillon-en-Diois (26) 159 F1
Châtillon-en-Dunois (28) 61 H4
Châtillon-en-Michaille (01) 117 H5
Châtillon-en-Vendelais (35) 58 A3
Châtillon-Guyotte (25) 87 G6
Châtillon-la-Borde (77) 64 B1
Châtillon-la-Palud (01) 130 D1
Châtillon-le-Duc (25) 87 F6
Châtillon-le-Roi (45) 63 E4
Châtillon-lès-Sons (02) 22 C1
Châtillon-Saint-Jean (26) 144 C3
Châtillon-sous-les-Côtes (55) 47 G1
Châtillon-sur-Broué (51) 67 E1
Châtillon-sur-Chalaronne (01) 116 C5
Châtillon-sur-Cher (41) 96 A1
Châtillon-sur-Cluses (74) 119 E5
Châtillon-sur-Colmont (53) 58 D2
Châtillon-sur-Indre (36) 95 H3
Châtillon-sur-Lison (25) 103 F2
Châtillon-sur-Loire (45) 82 A4
Châtillon-sur-Marne (51) 44 D1
Châtillon-sur-Morin (51) 44 C5
Châtillon-sur-Oise (02) 22 B1
Châtillon-sur-Saône (88) 69 E6
Châtillon-sur-Seine (21) 85 E1
Châtillon-sur-Thouet (79) 93 G6
Châtin (58) 100 A2
Chatonrupt-
Sommermont (52) 67 H1
Chatou (78) 42 B4
la Châtre (36) 111 H1
la Châtre-Langlin (36) 110 D3
Châtres (10) 65 H1
Châtres (24) 138 A2
Châtres (77) 43 F6
Châtres-la-Forêt (53) 59 E4
Châtres-sur-Cher (41) 96 D1
Châtrices (51) 46 D2
Chattancourt (55) 25 E6
Chatte (38) 144 D3
Chatuzange-le-Goubet (26) 144 C4
Chaucenne (25) 87 F6
Chauchailles (48) 141 F6
Chauché (85) 91 H3
le Chauchet (23) 112 B6
Chauchigny (10) 66 A2
Chauconin-
Neufmontiers (77) 43 G3
Chaudebonne (26) 159 E3

Chaudefonds-sur-Layon (49) 76 C6
la Chaze-de-Peyre (48) 155 G1
Chaudefontaine (25) 87 G6
Chaudefontaine (51) 46 C1
Chaudenay (52) 86 B2
Chaudenay (71) 101 G4
Chaudenay-la-Ville (21) 101 F2
Chaudenay-le-Château (21) 101 F2
Chaudeney-sur-Moselle (54) 48 B5
Chaudes-Aigues (15) 141 E6
Chaudeyrac (48) 156 C2
Chaudeyrolles (43) 143 E5
la Chaudière (26) 158 D2
Chaudon (28) 41 F5
Chaudon-Norante (04) 177 G2
Chaudrey (10) 66 C1
Chaudron-en-Mauges (49) 76 B6
Chaudun (02) 22 A5
Chauffailles (71) 115 G5
Chauffayer (05) 146 A6
Chauffecourt (88) 69 F2
Chauffour-lès-Bailly (10) 66 C4
Chauffour-Notre-Dame (72) 60 A6
Chaugey (21) 85 G2
Chaulgnes (58) 98 D2
Chaulhac (48) 141 G5
Chaulieu (50) 37 H4
la Chaulme (63) 128 C6
Chaulnes (80) 21 F1
Chaum (31) 184 A5
Chaumard (58) 100 A2
la Chaume (21) 85 F1
Chaume-et-Courchamp (21) 86 B4
Chaume-les-Baigneux (21) 85 E3
Chaumeil (19) 125 F6
Chaumercenne (70) 86 D6
Chaumergy (39) 102 C4
Chaumes-en-Brie (77) 43 G5
Chaumesnil (10) 67 E2
Chaumont (18) 98 B5
Chaumont (52) 67 H5
Chaumont (61) 39 G4
Chaumont (74) 118 A6
Chaumont (89) 64 D3
Chaumont-
devant-Damvillers (55) 25 F5
Chaumont-en-Vexin (60) 19 H6
Chaumont-la-Ville (52) 68 D4
Chaumont-le-Bois (21) 67 E6
Chaumont-le-Bourg (63) 128 B6
Chaumont-Porcien (08) 23 F2
Chaumont-sur-Aire (55) 47 F3
Chaumont-sur-Loire (41) 79 G5
Chaumont-sur-Tharonne (41) 80 D4
Chaumontel (95) 42 D1
Chaumot (58) 99 E1
Chaumot (89) 64 D5
Chaumousey (88) 69 H4
Chaumoux-Marcilly (18) 98 B2
Chaumussay (37) 95 F3
la Chaumusse (39) 118 A1
Chaumuzy (51) 45 E1
Chaunac (17) 121 G6
Chaunay (86) 108 D4
Chauny (02) 21 H3
Chauray (79) 107 H3
Chauriat (63) 127 G3
la Chaussade (23) 125 H1
la Chaussaire (49) 75 F5
Chaussan (69) 129 H4
la Chaussée (76) 17 G3
la Chaussée (86) 94 A4
la Chaussée-d'Ivry (28) 41 F3
la Chaussée-Saint-Victor (41) 80 A3
la Chaussée-sur-Marne (51) 46 A4
la Chaussée-Tirancourt (80) 7 F5
Chaussenac (15) 139 H3
Chaussenans (39) 103 E5
Chausseterre (42) 128 C2
Chaussin (39) 102 C3
Chaussoy-Epagny (80) 20 C2
Chaussy (45) 63 E4
Chaussy (95) 41 H1
le Chautay (18) 98 C4
Chauvac-
Laux-Montaux (26) 159 G4
Chauvé (44) 74 A5
Chauvency-le-Château (55) 25 E3
Chauvency-Saint-Hubert (55) 25 E3
Chauvigné (35) 57 H1
Chauvigny (86) 109 G1
Chauvigny-du-Perche (41) 61 G1
Chauvincourt-
Provemont (27) 19 G6
Chauvirey-la-Châtel (70) 86 D2
Chauvirey-le-Vieil (70) 86 D2
Chauvoncourt (55) 47 G3
Chauvry (95) 42 C2
Chaux (21) 101 G2
la Chaux (25) 104 A3
la Chaux (61) 38 D6
la Chaux (71) 102 B5
Chaux (90) 88 C2
Chaux-Champagny (39) 103 E4
Chaux-des-Crotenay (39) 103 F6
Chaux-des-Prés (39) 118 A2
la Chaux-du-Dombief (39) 118 A1
la Chaux-en-Bresse (39) 102 C5
Chaux-la-Lotière (70) 87 F4
Chaux-lès-Clerval (25) 88 A4
Chaux-lès-Passavant (25) 104 A1
Chaux-lès-Port (70) 87 F2
Chaux-Neuve (25) 103 G6
Chauzon (07) 157 F3
Chavagnac (15) 140 D3
Chavagnac (24) 138 B3
Chavagne (35) 57 E3
Chavagnes (49) 77 E6
Chavagnes-en-Paillers (85) 91 H2
Chavagnes-les-Redoux (85) 92 B5
Chavaignes (49) 77 H4
Chavanat (23) 125 G1
Chavanatte (90) 89 E3
Chavanay (42) 129 H6
Chavanges (10) 67 E1
Chavaniac-Lafayette (43) 142 B3
Chavannaz (74) 118 A6
la Chavanne (73) 132 A5
Chavannes (18) 97 G5
Chavannes (26) 144 B3
les Chavannes-
en-Maurienne (73) 132 C6
Chavannes-les-Grands (90) 88 D3
Chavannes-sur-l'Étang (68) 88 D3
Chavannes-
sur-Reyssouze (01) 116 C3
Chavannes-sur-Suran (01) 117 F4
Chavanod (74) 132 A2
Chavanoz (38) 130 C3
Chavaroux (63) 127 G2
la Chavatte (80) 21 E1
Chaveignes (37) 94 C3
Chavelot (88) 69 H3
Chavenay (78) 42 B4
Chavençon (60) 42 B1
Chavenon (03) 113 F3
Chavéria (39) 117 G2
Chaveroche (19) 125 H5
Chaveyriat (01) 116 C4
Chavignon (02) 22 B4
Chavigny (02) 22 A4
Chavigny (54) 48 C5
Chavigny-Bailleul (27) 41 E3
Chavin (36) 111 E2
Chavonne (02) 22 C5
Chavornay (01) 131 G1
Chavot-Courcourt (51) 45 E2
Chavoy (50) 35 H3
Chavroches (03) 114 B3
le Chay (17) 120 D3
Chay (25) 103 F3

Chazay-d'Azergues (69) 129 H2
Chazé-Henry (49) 76 A2
Chazé-sur-Argos (49) 76 B3
Chazeaux (07) 157 F2
Chazelet (36) 110 D2
Chazelles (16) 122 D4
Chazelles (15) 141 G3
Chazelles (43) 141 H4
Chazelles-sur-Albe (54) 49 G6
Chazelles-sur-Lavieu (42) 128 D5
Chazelles-sur-Lyon (42) 129 F4
Chazemais (03) 112 C2
Chazeuil (21) 86 A4
Chazeuil (58) 99 F1
Chazey-Bons (01) 131 F2
Chazey-sur-Ain (01) 130 D2
Chazilly (21) 101 E2
Chazot (25) 88 B6
Chécy (45) 81 E1
Chédigny (37) 95 G1
Chef-Boutonne (79) 108 B5
Chef-du-Pont (50) 12 D4
Chef-Haut (88) 69 F2
Cheffes (49) 77 E3
Cheffois (85) 92 C6
Cheffreville-Tonnencourt (14) 15 F6
le Chefresne (50) 37 F3
Chéhéry (08) 24 B2
Cheillé (37) 94 C1
Cheilly-lès-Maranges (71) 101 F4
Chein-Dessus (31) 184 C4
Cheissoux (87) 124 D2
Cheix (03) 127 F1
Cheix-en-Retz (44) 74 B5
Chélan (32) 184 A2
Chelers (62) 7 H1
Chélieu (38) 131 E5
Chelle-debat (65) 183 F2
Chelle-Spou (65) 183 F4
Chelles (21) 86 C6
Chelles (60) 21 G5
Chelles (77) 43 E4
Chelun (35) 57 H5
Chemaudin (25) 103 F1
Chemazé (53) 76 C1
Chemellier (49) 77 F6
Chemenot (39) 102 D3
Chémeré (44) 74 A6
Chémeré-le-Roi (53) 59 E6
Chémery (18) 97 H5
Chémery-les-Deux (57) 26 D4
Chémery-sur-Bar (08) 24 B3
Chemilla (39) 117 G3
Chemillé (49) 75 H6
Chemillé-sur-Dême (37) 78 D3
Chemillé-sur-Indrois (37) 95 H2
Chemilly (03) 113 H2
Chemilly (70) 87 F3
Chemilly-sur-Serein (89) 83 H2
Chemilly-sur-Yonne (89) 83 F1
Chemin (39) 102 B3
le Chemin (51) 46 D2
Chemin-d'Aisey (21) 144 A3
Cheminas (07) 144 A3
Cheminon (51) 46 C4
Cheminot (57) 48 C3
Chemiré-en-Charnie (72) 59 G5
Chemiré-le-Gaudin (72) 59 H6
Chemiré-sur-Sarthe (49) 77 E2
Chenac-Saint-Seurin-
d'Uzet (17) 120 D5
Chenailler-Mascheix (19) 139 E4
la Chenalotte (25) 104 C2
Chénas (69) 116 A5
Chenaud (24) 136 B2
Chenay (51) 23 E6
Chenay (72) 60 A3
Chenay (79) 108 C3
Chenay-le-Châtel (71) 114 D5
le Chêne (10) 66 B1
Chêne-Arnoult (89) 82 C1
Chêne-Bernard (39) 102 C4
Chêne-en-Semine (74) 118 A6
Chêne-Sec (39) 102 C5
Chenebier (70) 88 B3
Chenecey-Buillon (25) 103 F2
Cheneché (86) 94 B5
Chenedollé (14) 38 A3
Chénedouit (61) 38 C4
Chênehutte-
Trèves-Cunault (49) 77 G6
Chénelette (69) 115 H5
Chénérailles (23) 112 A6
Chenereilles (42) 128 D6
Chenereilles (43) 143 E3
Chenevelles (86) 94 D6
Chenevières (54) 49 F6
Chenevrey-et-Morogne (70) 86 D6
Cheney (89) 84 A1
Chenicourt (54) 48 D4
Chenières (54) 25 G3
Chéniers (23) 111 F3
Chéniers (51) 45 G3
Chenillé-Changé (49) 76 D3
Cheniménil (88) 70 B4
Chennebrun (27) 40 C4
Chennegy (10) 65 H4
Chennevières-
lès-Louvres (95) 43 E2
Chennevières-
sur-Marne (94) 43 E4
Chenois (57) 49 E2
Chenoise (77) 44 A6
Chenommet (16) 122 C1
Chenon (16) 122 C2
Chenonceaux (37) 79 F6
Chenou (77) 64 A4
Chenôve (21) 85 H6
Chenôves (71) 101 F6
Chens-sur-Léman (74) 118 D3
Chenu (72) 78 C3
Cheny (89) 83 F1
Chepniers (17) 135 G6
Chepoix (60) 20 C2
la Cheppe (51) 46 A2
Cheppes-la-Prairie (51) 46 A3
Cheppy (55) 24 D6
Cheptainville (91) 63 F1
Chepy (51) 46 A3
Chépy (80) 6 C4
Chérac (17) 121 F3
Chérancé (53) 76 D1
Chérancé (72) 59 H3
Chéraute (64) 181 G2
Cherbonnières (17) 121 G1
Cherbourg-Octeville (50) 12 C2
Chérence (95) 41 G2
Chérencé-le-Héron (50) 37 F4
Chérencé-le-Roussel (50) 37 G5
les Chéres (69) 129 H2
Chérence (17) 107 H5
le Chéreil (50) 37 G3
Chéreng (59) 3 G5
Chérêt (02) 22 C3
Chériennes (62) 7 E2
Chérier (42) 128 C1
Chérigné (79) 108 B5
le Chérioux (92) 42 C5
Chérisay (72) 60 A2
Chérisey (57) 48 C2
Cherisy (28) 41 F5
Chérisy (62) 8 C3
Chérizet (71) 116 A3
Chermignac (17) 121 E3
Chermisey (88) 68 D3
Chermizy-Ailles (02) 22 C3
Chéronnac (87) 123 F3
Chéroy (89) 64 D4
Cherré (72) 60 D4
Cherré (49) 77 F2
Cherrueix (35) 35 F4
Cherval (24) 122 D5
Cherveix-Cubas (24) 138 A1
Cherves (86) 93 H6
Cherves-Châtelars (16) 123 F2
Cherves-Richemont (16) 121 G2

Chervettes (17) 107 F6
Cherveux (79) 107 H2
Chervey (10) 66 D5
Cherville (51) 45 F2
Chéry (18) 97 E2
Chéry-Chartreuve (02) 22 C6
Chéry-lès-Pouilly (02) 22 C2
Chéry-lès-Rozoy (02) 23 F2
Chesley (10) 66 B6
le Chesnay (78) 42 B4
Chesnois-Auboncourt (08) 23 H3
Chesny (57) 48 C2
Chessenaz (74) 118 A6
Chessy (69) 129 G2
Chessy (77) 43 F4
Chessy-les-Prés (10) 65 H6
Cheu (89) 65 H6
Cheust (65) 183 E4
Cheux (14) 14 A5
Chevagnes (03) 114 B1
Chevagny-
les-Chevrières (71) 116 B4
Chevagny-sur-Guye (71) 115 H2
Chevaigné (35) 57 F2
Chevaigné-du-Maine (53) 59 F1
le Chevain (72) 60 A2
Cheval-Blanc (84) 175 F3
Chevaline (74) 132 B3
la Chevallerais (44) 74 C3
Chevanceaux (17) 135 H1
Chevannay (21) 85 E5
Chevannes (21) 85 G6
Chevannes (45) 64 B5
Chevannes (89) 83 F2
Chevannes (91) 63 G1
Chevannes-Changy (58) 99 F1
Chevennes (02) 22 D1
Chevenon (58) 99 E4
Chevenoz (74) 119 F3
Cheverny (41) 80 A4
Cheveuges (08) 24 C2
Chevières (08) 24 C5
Chevigney (70) 86 D5
Chevigney-lès-Vercel (25) 104 A1
Chevigney-sur-l'Ognon (25) 87 E6
Chevigny (39) 102 B2
Chevigny-en-Valière (21) 101 G3
Chevigny-Saint-Sauveur (21) 85 H6
Chevillard (01) 117 G5
Chevillé (72) 59 G6
Chevillon (52) 67 G2
Chevillon (89) 82 D2
Chevillon-sur-Huillard (45) 81 H1
la Chevillotte (25) 103 H2
Chevilly (45) 62 D5
Chevilly-Larue (94) 42 D5
Chevinay (69) 129 G3
Chevincourt (60) 21 F4
Cheviré-le-Rouge (49) 77 F3
Chevrainvilliers (77) 64 A4
Chevreaux (39) 117 F2
Chevregny (02) 22 C4
Chèvremont (90) 88 D3
la Chèvrerie (16) 108 C6
Chevresis-Monceau (02) 22 B1
Chevreuse (78) 42 B5
Chèvreville (50) 37 G6
Chèvreville (60) 43 G1
Chevrier (74) 118 A5
Chevrières (38) 144 D2
Chevrières (42) 129 F5
Chevrières (60) 21 E5
Chevroches (58) 83 F5
la Chevrolière (44) 74 C6
Chevrotaine (39) 103 F6
Chevroux (01) 116 C3
Chevroz (25) 87 F6
Chevru (77) 44 A5
Chevry (01) 118 B4
Chevry (50) 37 F2
Chevry-Cossigny (77) 43 F5
Chevry-en-Sereine (77) 64 C3
Chevry-sous-le-Bignon (45) 64 A4
Chey (79) 108 C4
Cheylade (15) 140 C2
le Cheylard (07) 143 G5
le Cheylard-l'Évêque (48) 156 C1
le Cheylas (38) 132 A6
Cheyssieu (38) 130 A6
Chezal-Benoît (18) 97 F5
la Chèze (22) 55 H2
Chèze (65) 182 D6
Chezelle (03) 113 G6
Chezelles (36) 96 B4
Chezelles (37) 94 C3
Chèzeneuve (38) 130 D5
Chézery-Forens (01) 118 A4
Chèzes (43) 141 H4
Chezy (03) 114 A1
Chézy (02) 44 B2
Chézy-en-Orxois (02) 44 A1
Chézy-sur-Marne (02) 44 B3
Chiatra (2B) 205 G2
Chiché (79) 93 E5
Chichée (89) 83 H2
Chichery (89) 83 F1
Chichey (51) 45 E5
Chichilianne (38) 145 F6
le Chillou (79) 93 G5
Chilhac (43) 141 H3
Chillac (16) 122 A6
Chille (39) 117 F1
Chilleurs-aux-Bois (45) 63 E5
Chilly (08) 10 D6
Chilly (74) 118 A6
Chilly (80) 21 E1
Chilly-le-Vignoble (39) 102 C6
Chilly-Mazarin (91) 42 D5
Chilly-sur-Salins (39) 103 F4
Chimilin (38) 131 F4
Chindrieux (73) 131 G2
Chinon (37) 94 B2
Chipilly (80) 8 A6
Chirac (16) 123 F1
Chirac (48) 155 G3
Chirac-Bellevue (19) 125 H5
Chirassimont (42) 129 E2
Chirat-l'Église (03) 113 G4
Chiré-en-Montreuil (86) 94 A6
Chirens (38) 131 F6
Chirmont (80) 20 C2
Chirols (07) 157 F1
Chiroubles (69) 116 A5
Chiry-Ourscamp (60) 21 G3
Chis (65) 183 F2
Chisa (2B) 205 F5
Chissay-en-Touraine (41) 79 G6
Chisséaux (37) 79 F6
Chisseria (39) 117 G3
Chissey-en-Morvan (71) 100 C2
Chissey-lès-Mâcon (71) 116 A2
Chissey-sur-Loue (39) 103 E3
Chitenay (41) 79 H4
Chitray (36) 110 D1
Chitry (89) 83 G2
Chitry-les-Mines (58) 99 G2
Chives (17) 108 B6
Chivres (21) 102 A3
Chivres-en-Laonnois (02) 22 D2
Chivres-Val (02) 22 B5
Chivy-lès-Étouvelles (02) 22 C3

Choisey (74) 118 B6
Choisy-au-Bac (60) 21 F4
Choisy-en-Brie (77) 44 A5
Choisy-la-Victoire (60) 20 D4
Choisy-le-Roi (94) 42 D5
Cholet (49) 92 C2
Cholonge (38) 145 G4
Choloy-Ménillot (54) 48 A5
Chomelix (43) 142 C2
Chomérac (07) 158 A1
le Chomette (43) 141 H2
Chonas-l'Amballan (38) 130 A6
Chonville-Malaumont (55) 47 G4
Chooz (08) 11 F1
Choqueuse-les-Bénards (60) 20 A2
Choranche (38) 145 E3
Chorey-les-Beaune (21) 101 G3
Chorges (05) 160 D2
Chouain (14) 14 A4
Chouday (36) 97 F4
Choue (41) 61 F5
Chougny (58) 99 H3
Chouilly (51) 45 F2
Chouppes (86) 94 A5
Chourgnac (24) 137 H2
Choussy (41) 79 H6
Chouvigny (03) 113 F5
Choux (39) 117 H4
les Choux (45) 82 A2
Chouy (02) 44 A1
Chouzé-sur-Loire (37) 94 A1
Chouzelot (25) 103 F2
Choye (70) 86 D5
Chozeau (38) 130 C3
Chuelles (45) 82 C1
Chuffilly-Roche (08) 24 A4
Chuignes (80) 8 A6
Chuignolles (80) 8 A6
Chuisnes (28) 61 H2
Chusclan (30) 158 A6
Chuyer (42) 129 H6
Chuzelles (38) 130 A4
Ciadoux (31) 184 B3
Ciamannacce (2A) 205 E5
Ciboure (64) 180 B1
Cideville (76) 17 F4
Ciel (71) 101 H4
Cier-de-Luchon (31) 184 A5
Cier-de-Rivière (31) 184 A4
Cierges (02) 44 C1
Cierges-sous-
Montfaucon (55) 24 D5
Cierp-Gaud (31) 184 A6
Cierrey (27) 41 E2
Cierzac (17) 121 G4
Cieurac (46) 152 D4
Cieutat (65) 183 F4
Cieux (87) 123 H1
Ciez (58) 82 D5
Cigogné (37) 95 F1
Cilly (02) 22 D2
Cinais (37) 94 B2
Cindré (03) 114 B4
Cinq-Mars-la-Pile (37) 78 C6
Cinqueux (60) 20 D5
Cintegabelle (31) 185 G2
Cintheaux (14) 38 D2
Cintray (27) 40 C4
Cintray (28) 62 B2
Cintré (35) 56 D3
Cintrey (70) 86 D2
la Ciotat (13) 192 C5
Cipières (06) 178 C3
Ciral (61) 59 G1
Ciran (37) 95 F3
Circourt (88) 69 F3
Circourt-sur-Mouzon (88) 68 D3
Ciré-d'Aunis (17) 107 E6
Cirès (31) 183 H6
Cires-lès-Mello (60) 20 C6
Cirey (21) 87 G5
Cirey-lès-Mareilles (52) 68 A4
Cirey-sur-Blaise (52) 67 F3
Cirey-sur-Vezouze (54) 49 H6
Cirfontaines-en-Azois (52) 67 G5
Cirfontaines-en-Ornois (52) 68 B2
Cirières (79) 92 D4
Ciron (36) 110 C1
Ciry-le-Noble (71) 115 F1
Ciry-Salsogne (02) 22 B5
Cisai-Saint-Aubin (61) 39 G4
Cisery (89) 84 B4
Cissac-Médoc (33) 134 D2
Cissé (86) 94 B6
Cisternes-la-Forêt (63) 126 C3
Cistrières (43) 142 A1
Citerne (80) 6 D5
Citers (70) 87 H2
Citey (70) 87 E4
Citou (11) 187 F2
Citry (77) 44 B3
Civaux (86) 109 G2
Civens (42) 129 E3
Civières (27) 19 F6
Civrac-de-Blaye (33) 135 F3
Civrac-en-Médoc (33) 134 C1
Civrac-sur-Dordogne (33) 136 A5
Civray (18) 97 F4
Civray-de-Touraine (37) 79 F6
Civray-sur-Esves (37) 95 E3
Civrieux (01) 130 A1
Civrieux-d'Azergues (69) 129 H2
Civry (89) 83 E3
Civry-en-Montagne (21) 85 F6
Civry-la-Forêt (78) 41 G4
Cizancourt (80) 8 B6
Cizay-la-Madeleine (49) 93 G1
Cize (01) 117 F5
Cize (39) 103 F5
Cizely (58) 99 F3
Cizos (65) 183 H2
Clacy-et-Thierret (02) 22 B3
Cladech (24) 137 H6
Claira (66) 201 F2
Clairac (47) 150 D4
Clairavaux (23) 125 G3
Clairefontaine-
en-Yvelines (78) 42 A6
Clairegoutte (70) 88 B3
Clairfayts (59) 10 B3
Clairfontaine (02) 10 A5
Clairmarais (62) 2 B4
Clairoix (60) 21 F4
Clairvaux-d'Aveyron (12) 154 B4
Clairvaux-les-Lacs (39) 117 H1
Clairy-Saulchoix (80) 7 F6
Clais (76) 19 F1
Claix (16) 122 B5
Claix (38) 145 G3
Clam (17) 121 F5
Clamanges (51) 45 G4
Clamart (92) 42 C4
Clamecy (02) 22 A4
Clamecy (58) 83 F5
Clamensane (04) 160 B4
Clamerey (21) 84 D5
Clans (06) 162 C6
Clans (70) 87 F3
Clansayes (26) 158 B4
le Claon (55) 46 D1
le Clapier (12) 172 A3
Clapiers (34) 173 F5
Clara (66) 200 C3
Clarac (31) 183 H3
Clarac (65) 183 F3
Claracq (64) 166 B6
Clarafond-Arcine (74) 118 A5
Clarbec (14) 15 E4
Clarens (65) 183 G3
Clarensac (30) 174 A3
Claret (04) 160 B5
Claret (34) 173 F3
Clarques (62) 2 B5
Clary (59) 9 E4
Classun (40) 166 A4
Clasville (76) 17 E2

le Clat (11) 200 A1
Claudon (88) 69 F5
le Claux (15) 140 C3
Clavans-
en-Haut-Oisans (38) 146 B3
Clavé (79) 108 B2
Claveisolles (69) 115 H6
Clavette (17) 106 D5
Claville (27) 40 D2
Claville-Motteville (76) 17 H5
Clavy-Warby (08) 23 H2
Claye-Souilly (77) 43 F3
Clayes (35) 57 E2
les Clayes-sous-Bois (78) 42 B4
la Clayette (71) 115 G4
Clayeures (54) 69 H1
Cléby (53) 38 D6
Cléden-Cap-Sizun (29) 52 C2
Cléden-Poher (29) 32 B6
Cléder (29) 31 G2
Clèdes (40) 166 B5
Cleebourg (67) 51 F2
Clefmont (52) 68 C5
les Clefs (74) 132 C2
Cléguer (56) 54 C4
Cléguérec (56) 55 E1
Clelles (38) 145 F5
Clémencey (21) 101 G1
Clémensat (63) 127 F5
Clémery (54) 48 C3
Clémont (18) 81 F4
Clénay (21) 85 H5
Clenleu (62) 1 G6
Cléon (76) 18 C5
Cléon-d'Andran (26) 158 C2
Cleppé (42) 129 E4
Clérac (17) 135 H2
Cléré-du-Bois (36) 95 G4
Cléré-les-Pins (37) 78 B5
Cléré-sur-Layon (49) 93 F2
Clères (76) 17 H4
Clérey (10) 66 B4
Clérey-la-Côte (88) 68 D2
Clérey-sur-Brenon (54) 69 F1
Clergoux (19) 139 F2
Clérieux (26) 144 B3
les Clérimois (89) 65 F4
le Clerjus (88) 69 H5
Clerlande (63) 127 F2
Clermain (71) 115 H3
Clermont (09) 184 D4
Clermont (40) 165 G4
Clermont (60) 20 C5
Clermont (74) 131 H1
Clermont-Créans (72) 77 H2
Clermont-
de-Beauregard (24) 137 E4
Clermont-Dessous (47) 150 D5
Clermont-d'Excideuil (24) 137 H1
Clermont-en-Argonne (55) 46 D1
Clermont-Ferrand (63) 127 F3
Clermont-les-Fermes (02) 23 E2
Clermont-Savès (32) 168 C5
Clermont-Soubiran (47) 151 G6
Clermont-sur-Lauquet (11) 187 E5
Cléron (25) 103 G2
Clerques (62) 1 H3
Clerval (25) 88 A5
Cléry (21) 86 C6
Cléry (73) 132 C4
Cléry-en-Vexin (95) 42 A1
Cléry-le-Grand (55) 24 D5
Cléry-le-Petit (55) 24 D5
Cléry-Saint-André (45) 80 C2
Cléry-sur-Somme (80) 8 B5
Clesles (51) 65 H1
Clessé (71) 116 B3
Clessé (79) 93 E5
Clessy (71) 115 E2
Cléty (62) 2 A5
Cleurie (88) 70 B5
Cleuville (76) 17 E3
Cléville (14) 14 D5
Cléville (76) 16 D4
Clévilliers (28) 62 A1
Cleyrac (33) 136 A6
Cleyzieu (01) 131 E2
Clézentaine (88) 70 A2
Clichy (92) 42 C3
Clichy-sous-Bois (93) 43 E3
Climbach (67) 51 F1
Clinchamp (52) 68 B4
Clion (17) 121 F6
Clion (36) 95 H5
Cliousclat (26) 158 B1
Cliponville (76) 17 E4
Cliron (08) 24 A1
Clis (44) 73 F4
la Clisse (17) 120 D3
Clisson (44) 75 E6
Clitourps (50) 12 D2
Clohars-Carnoët (29) 54 B5
Clohars-Fouesnant (29) 53 G3
le Cloître-Pleyben (29) 31 H6
le Cloître-
Saint-Thégonnec (29) 32 A4
Clomot (21) 101 E2
Clonas-sur-Varèze (38) 130 A6
Clos-Fontaine (77) 43 H6
la Clotte (17) 135 H3
Clouange (57) 26 B4
Cloué (86) 108 D2
les Clouzeaux (85) 91 G4
Cloyes-sur-le-Loir (28) 61 H5
Cloyes-sur-Marne (51) 46 B5
Clucy (39) 103 F3
Clugnat (23) 111 H4
Cluis (36) 111 F2
Clumanc (04) 177 G1
Cluny (71) 116 A3
la Clusaz (74) 132 C1
la Cluse (05) 160 A1
la Cluse-et-Mijoux (25) 104 A4
les Cluses (66) 201 F4
Cluses (74) 119 E6
Clussais-la-Pommeraie (79) 108 C5
Clux (71) 102 A4
Coadout (22) 33 E5
Coaraze (06) 195 F1
Coarraze (64) 182 C3
Coat-Méal (29) 30 D3
Coatascorn (22) 32 D3
Coatréven (22) 32 D2
Cobonne (26) 144 C6
Cobrieux (59) 3 G6
la Cochère (61) 39 F5
Cocheren (57) 27 G5
Coclois (10) 66 C1
Cocquerel (80) 7 E4
Cocumont (47) 150 B4
Cocurès (48) 156 B4
Codalet (66) 200 C3
Codognan (30) 174 A4
Codolet (30) 158 A6
Coësmes (35) 57 G5
Coëtlogon (22) 55 H2
Coëtmieux (22) 33 H5
Cœuvres-et-Valsery (02) 21 H5
Coëx (85) 90 D3
Coggia (2A) 204 C4
Coglès (35) 35 H6
Cogna (39) 117 H1
Cognac (16) 121 H3
Cognac-la-Forêt (87) 123 H2
Cognat-Lyonne (03) 113 H6
Cogners (72) 78 D1
Cognet (38) 145 G5
Cognières (70) 87 H4
Cognin (73) 131 H4
Cognin-les-Gorges (38) 145 E2
Cognocoli-Monticchi (2A) 206 D2
Cogny (18) 98 A5
Cogny (69) 129 G1

le Cogolin (83) 194 A4
Cohade (43) 141 G1
Cohennoz (73) 132 D3
Cohiniac (22) 33 F5
Cohons (52) 86 B2
Coiffy-le-Bas (52) 68 D6
Coiffy-le-Haut (52) 68 D6
Coigneux (80) 7 H4
Coignières (78) 42 A5
Coigny (50) 12 C5
Coimères (33) 149 H3
Coin-lès-Cuvry (57) 26 B6
Coin-sur-Seille (57) 26 B6
Coinces (45) 62 C6
Coinches (88) 70 D3
Coincourt (54) 49 F5
Coincy (02) 44 B1
Coincy (57) 26 C5
Coings (36) 96 C4
Coirac (33) 149 H1
Coise (69) 129 G4
Coise-Saint-Jean-
Pied-Gauthier (73) 132 B5
Coiserette (39) 117 H3
Coisevaux (70) 88 B3
Coisia (39) 117 G4
Coisy (80) 7 G5
Coivert (17) 107 H6
Coivrel (60) 20 D3
Coizard-Joches (51) 45 E4
Colayrac-Saint-Cirq (47) 151 E5
Colembert (62) 1 G4
Coligny (01) 117 E3
Coligny (39) 102 C4
Collan (89) 83 H1
la Collancelle (58) 99 G2
Collandres (15) 140 C2
Collandres-Quincarnon (27) 40 C2
Collanges (63) 127 F6
Collat (43) 142 A2
la Colle-sur-Loup (06) 195 E3
Collégien (77) 43 F4
Collemiers (89) 64 D4
Colleret (59) 10 B3
le Collet-de-Dèze (48) 156 D5
Colletot (27) 15 H3
Colleville (76) 16 D3
Colleville-Montgomery (14) 14 C4
Colleville-sur-Mer (14) 13 G4
Collias (30) 174 B2
Colligis-Crandelain (02) 22 C4
Colligny (57) 26 C5
Colline-Beaumont (62) 6 C2
Collioure (66) 201 G4
Collobrières (83) 193 H4
Collonge-en-Charollais (71) 115 H1
Collonge-la-Madeleine (71) 101 E3
Collonges (01) 118 A5
Collonges-
au-Mont-d'Or (69) 130 A3
Collonges-la-Rouge (19) 138 D4
Collonges-lès-Bévy (21) 101 G2
Collonges-
lès-Premières (21) 102 B1
Collonges-sous-Salève (74) 118 C5
Collongues (06) 178 C2
Collongues (65) 183 F2
Collorec (29) 32 A6
Collorgues (30) 174 A2
Colmar (68) 71 F4
Colmars (04) 161 F5
Colmen (57) 27 E3
Colméry (58) 83 E6
Colmesnil-Manneville (76) 17 G2
Colmey (54) 25 G4
Colmier-le-Bas (52) 85 G2
Colmier-le-Haut (52) 85 G2
Colognac (30) 173 F1
Cologne (32) 168 C4
Colomars (06) 195 F2
la Colombe (41) 80 A1
la Colombe (50) 37 F3
Colombé-la-Fosse (10) 67 F3
Colombé-le-Sec (10) 67 F3
Colombelles (14) 14 C4
Colombes (92) 42 C3
Colombey-les-Belles (54) 69 E1
Colombey-
les-Deux-Églises (52) 67 F4
Colombier (03) 113 G4
Colombier (21) 101 F2
Colombier (24) 137 E5
Colombier (42) 143 H1
Colombier (70) 87 H3
Colombier-
en-Brionnais (71) 115 G3
Colombier-Fontaine (25) 88 B4
Colombier-le-Cardinal (07) 143 H2
Colombier-le-Jeune (07) 143 H4
Colombier-le-Vieux (07) 143 H3
Colombier-Saugnieu (69) 130 C3
Colombières (14) 13 F5
Colombières-sur-Orb (34) 171 H6
Colombiers (17) 121 F4
Colombiers (18) 97 H6
Colombiers (34) 188 B2
Colombiers (61) 60 A1
Colombiers (86) 94 C5
Colombiers-du-Plessis (53) 58 C2
Colombiers-sur-Seulles (14) 14 A3
Colombiès (12) 154 A4
Colombotte (70) 87 H3
Colomby (50) 12 D4
Colomby-sur-Thaon (14) 14 B4
Colomiers (31) 169 E5
Colomieu (01) 131 F3
Colonard-Corubert (61) 60 D2
Colondannes (23) 111 E4
Colonfay (02) 9 H6
Colonne (39) 102 D4
Colonzelle (26) 158 B4
Colpo (56) 55 F5
Colroy-la-Grande (88) 71 E2
Colroy-la-Roche (67) 71 E1
Coltainville (28) 62 B1
Coltines (15) 141 E3
Coly (24) 138 B3
Combaillaux (34) 173 F5
Combas (30) 173 H3
la Combe-de-Lancey (38) 145 H2
Combeaufontaine (70) 87 F2
Combefa (81) 170 B1
Comberanche-
et-Épeluche (24) 136 C2
Comberjon (70) 87 G3
Comberouger (82) 168 C3
Combertault (21) 101 G3
les Combes (25) 104 B2
Combes (34) 172 A5
Comblanchien (21) 101 G2
Combles (80) 8 B5
Combles-en-Barrois (55) 47 F5
Comblessac (35) 56 C5
Combleux (45) 81 E1
Comblot (61) 60 D1
Combloux (74) 133 E2
Combon (27) 40 C1
Combourg (35) 35 E6
Combourtillé (35) 57 H2
Combovin (26) 144 C5
Combrailles (63) 126 C2
Combrand (79) 92 D4
Combray (14) 38 C2
Combre (42) 115 F6
Combres (28) 61 F3
Combres-
sous-les-Côtes (55) 47 H2
Combressol (19) 125 G6
Combret (12) 171 F3
Combreux (45) 81 G1
Combrimont (88) 70 D3
Combrit (29) 53 F3
Combronde (63) 127 E1
Combs-la-Ville (77) 43 E6
la Comelle (71) 100 C4

Comiac (46) 139 F5
Comigne (11) 187 F4
Comines (59) 3 F4
Commana (29) 31 H5
Commarin (21) 101 F1
Commeaux (61) 38 D4
Commelle (38) 130 D6
Commelle-Vernay (42) 128 D1
Commenailles (39) 102 C5
Commenchon (02) 21 H2
Commensacq (40) 148 D5
Commentry (03) 112 D4
Commeny (95) 42 A1
Commequiers (85) 90 D3
Commer (53) 58 D3
Commercy (55) 47 H4
Commerveil (72) 60 C3
Commes (14) 13 H5
Communailles-en-Montagne (39) 103 G5
Communay (69) 130 A4
Compains (63) 127 E6
Compainville (76) 19 F2
Compans (77) 43 F3
le Compas (23) 126 B1
Compertrix (51) 45 H3
Compeyre (12) 155 F6
Compiègne (60) 21 F4
Compigny (89) 65 E2
Compolibat (12) 153 H4
la Compôte (73) 132 B3
Comprégnac (12) 171 H1
Compreignac (87) 124 B1
Comps (26) 158 D2
Comps (30) 174 C3
Comps (33) 135 E3
Comps-la-Grand-Ville (12) 154 C5
Comps-sur-Artuby (83) 177 H4
la Comté (62) 7 H1
Comus (11) 199 G1
Conan (41) 79 H2
Conand (01) 131 E2
Conat (66) 200 B3
Conca (2A) 207 G2
Concarneau (29) 53 G4
Concevreux (02) 22 D5
Concèze (19) 138 B1
Conches-en-Ouche (27) 40 C3
Conches-sur-Gondoire (77) 43 F4
Conchez-de-Béarn (64) 166 C5
Conchil-le-Temple (62) 6 C1
Conchy-les-Pots (60) 21 E3
Conchy-sur-Canche (62) 7 F2
Concorès (46) 152 C1
Concoret (56) 56 B3
Concots (46) 153 E4
Concoules (30) 156 D4
Concourson-sur-Layon (49) 93 F1
Concremiers (36) 110 B1
Concressault (18) 81 H5
Concriers (41) 80 A2
Condac (16) 108 D6
Condal (71) 117 E2
Condamine (01) 117 G5
Condamine (39) 102 C6
la Condamine-Châtelard (04) 161 G3
Condat (15) 140 C1
Condat (46) 138 D4
Condat-en-Combraille (63) 126 B2
Condat-lès-Montboissier (63) 127 H5
Condat-sur-Ganaveix (19) 124 D6
Condat-sur-Trincou (24) 123 F6
Condat-sur-Vézère (24) 138 A3
Condat-sur-Vienne (87) 124 B3
Condé (36) 97 E4
Condé-en-Brie (02) 44 C2
Condé-Folie (80) 7 E5
Condé-lès-Autry (08) 24 B6
Condé-lès-Herpy (08) 23 F3
Condé-Northen (57) 26 D5
Condé-Sainte-Libiaire (77) 43 G3
Condé-sur-Aisne (02) 22 B5
Condé-sur-Huisne (61) 61 F2
Condé-sur-Ifs (14) 39 E2
Condé-sur-Iton (27) 40 C4
Condé-sur-l'Escaut (59) 9 G1
Condé-sur-Marne (51) 45 G2
Condé-sur-Noireau (14) 38 B3
Condé-sur-Risle (27) 15 H3
Condé-sur-Sarthe (61) 60 A2
Condé-sur-Seulles (14) 14 A4
Condé-sur-Suippe (02) 23 E4
Condé-sur-Vesgre (78) 41 G5
Condé-sur-Vire (50) 37 G1
Condeau (61) 61 E2
Condécourt (95) 42 A2
Condeissiat (01) 116 D5
Condéon (16) 121 H6
Condes (39) 117 G3
Condes (52) 67 H4
Condette (62) 1 F5
Condezaygues (47) 151 H3
Condillac (26) 158 B2
Condom (32) 167 G2
Condom-d'Aubrac (12) 155 E2
Condorcet (26) 158 D4
Condren (02) 22 A2
Condrieu (69) 130 A6
Conflandey (70) 87 F2
Conflans-en-Jarnisy (54) 48 A1
Conflans-Sainte-Honorine (78) 42 B3
Conflans-sur-Anille (72) 61 E6
Conflans-sur-Lanterne (70) 87 G1
Conflans-sur-Loing (45) 64 B6
Conflans-sur-Seine (51) 65 G1
Confolens (16) 109 G6
Confolent-Port-Dieu (19) 126 B5
Confort (01) 117 H5
Confort-Meilars (29) 53 E2
Confracourt (70) 87 E3
Confrançon (01) 116 D4
Congé-sur-Orne (72) 60 B4
Congénies (30) 173 H4
Congerville-Thionville (91) 63 E2
Congis-sur-Thérouanne (77) 43 G2
Congrier (53) 76 A1
Congy (51) 45 E4
Conie-Molitard (28) 62 A5
Conilhac-Corbières (11) 187 G3
Conilhac-de-la-Montagne (11) 186 D5
Conjux (73) 131 G2
Conlie (72) 59 H4
Conliège (39) 102 D6
Connac (12) 171 F2
Connangles (43) 142 A1
Connantray-Vaurefroy (51) 45 F5
Connantre (51) 45 E5
Connaux (30) 174 C1
Conne-de-Labarde (24) 137 E6
Connelles (27) 18 D6
Connerré (72) 60 C5
Connezac (24) 123 E5
Connigis (02) 44 C2
Conquereuil (44) 74 C1
Conques (12) 154 B2
Conques-sur-Orbiel (11) 187 E3
le Conquet (29) 30 C5
Conqueyrac (30) 173 F2
Cons-la-Grandville (54) 25 G4
Cons-Sainte-Colombe (74) 132 C3
Consac (17) 121 E6
Ségudes (06) 195 E2
Consenvoye (55) 25 E5
Consigny (52) 68 B4
Consolation-Maisonnettes (25) 104 B1
Contalmaison (80) 8 B5
Contamine-Sarzin (74) 118 B6
Contamine-sur-Arve (74) 118 D5
les Contamines-Montjoie (74) 133 E2
Contault (51) 46 C3
Contay (80) 7 H5
Conte (39) 103 G5
Contes (06) 195 F2
Contes (62) 7 E1
Contescourt (02) 21 H1
Contest (53) 58 D3
Conteville (14) 38 D1
Conteville (27) 15 G2
Conteville (60) 20 A2
Conteville (76) 19 G2
Conteville (80) 7 F3
Conteville-en-Ternois (62) 7 G1
Conteville-lès-Boulogne (62) 1 F4
Conthil (57) 49 F3
Contigné (49) 77 E2
Contigny (03) 113 H3
Contilly (72) 60 C2
Continvoir (37) 78 A5
Contoire (80) 20 D2
Contrazy (09) 185 E4
Contré (17) 108 A6
Contre (80) 20 B1
Contréglise (70) 87 F1
Contremoulins (76) 16 C3
Contres (18) 97 H5
Contres (41) 80 A5
Contreuve (08) 24 A5
Contrevoz (01) 131 F2
Contrexéville (88) 69 E4
Contrières (50) 36 D2
Contrisson (55) 46 D4
Conty (80) 20 B1
Contz-les-Bains (57) 26 C2
Conzieu (01) 131 F3
Coole (51) 45 H5
Coolus (51) 45 H3
la Copechagnière (85) 91 G3
Copponex (74) 118 B6
Coquainvilliers (14) 15 F4
Coquelles (62) 1 G2
la Coquille (24) 123 H5
Corancez (28) 62 B2
Corancy (58) 100 B2
Coray (29) 53 H2
Corbara (2B) 202 C5
Corbarieu (82) 169 E2
Corbas (69) 130 B4
Corbehem (62) 8 C2
Corbeil (51) 46 A6
Corbeil-Cerf (60) 20 B6
Corbeil-Essonnes (91) 43 E6
Corbeilles (45) 63 H5
Corbel (73) 131 G6
Corbelin (38) 131 F4
Corbenay (70) 69 H6
Corbeny (02) 22 D4
Corbère (66) 200 D2
Corbère-Abères (64) 166 C6
Corbère-les-Cabanes (66) 200 D2
Corberon (21) 101 H3
Corbès (30) 173 G1
Corbie (80) 7 H6
la Corbière (70) 88 A1
Corbières (04) 176 C4
Corbières (11) 186 B5
Corbigny (58) 99 H1
Corbon (14) 15 E5
Corbon (61) 60 D1
Corbonod (01) 131 G1
Corbreuse (91) 62 D1
Corcelle-Mieslot (25) 87 G5
Corcelles (01) 117 G6
Corcelles-en-Beaujolais (69) 116 A5
Corcelles-Ferrières (25) 103 E1
Corcelles-les-Arts (21) 101 G4
Corcelles-lès-Cîteaux (21) 102 A2
Corcelles-les-Monts (21) 85 G6
Corcieux (88) 70 C4
Corcondray (25) 103 E1
Corconne (30) 173 G3
Corcoué-sur-Logne (44) 91 F1
Corcy (02) 21 H6
Cordéac (38) 145 H5
Cordebugle (14) 15 G5
Cordelle (42) 128 D1
Cordemais (44) 74 B4
Cordes-sur-Ciel (81) 170 A1
Cordes-Tolosannes (82) 168 D2
Cordesse (71) 100 D3
Cordey (14) 38 D3
Cordon (74) 133 E1
Cordonnet (70) 87 F5
Coren (15) 141 F4
Corenc (38) 145 G2
Corent (63) 127 F4
Corféllix (51) 44 D4
Corgengoux (21) 101 H3
Corgnac-sur-l'Isle (24) 123 G6
Corgoloin (21) 101 G2
Corignac (17) 135 G2
Corlay (22) 33 E6
Corlier (01) 117 F6
Cormainville (28) 62 B4
Cormaranche-en-Bugey (01) 131 F1
Cormatin (71) 116 A2
Corme-Écluse (17) 120 D4
Corme-Royal (17) 120 D3
Cormeilles (27) 15 G4
Cormeilles (60) 20 B2
Cormeilles-en-Parisis (95) 42 C3
Cormeilles-en-Vexin (95) 42 B1
Cormelles-le-Royal (14) 14 C5
Cormenon (41) 61 F6
Cormeray (41) 80 A5
Cormery (37) 95 F1
Cormes (72) 61 E4
Cormicy (51) 22 D5
le Cormier (27) 41 E3
Cormolain (14) 37 H1
Cormont (62) 1 F5
Cormontreuil (51) 23 E6
Cormoranche-sur-Saône (01) 116 B4
Cormost (10) 66 B4
Cormot-le-Grand (21) 101 F4
Cormoyeux (51) 45 E1
Cormoz (01) 117 E2
Corn (46) 153 F2
Cornac (46) 139 F5
Cornant (89) 64 D5
Cornas (07) 144 A4
Cornay (08) 24 C5
Corné (49) 77 F4
Cornebarrieu (31) 169 E5
Corneilhan (34) 188 C1
Corneilla-de-Conflent (66) 200 B3
Corneilla-del-Vercol (66) 201 F3
Corneilla-la-Rivière (66) 201 E2
Corneillan (32) 166 C4
Corneuil (27) 40 D3
Corneville-la-Fouquetière (27) 40 B2
Corneville-sur-Risle (27) 15 H3
Cornier (74) 118 D5
Cornil (19) 138 D2
Cornillac (26) 159 F3
Cornille (24) 137 F2
Cornillé (35) 57 H3
Cornillé-les-Caves (49) 77 F4
Cornillon (30) 157 H5
Cornillon-Confoux (13) 191 G3
Cornillon-en-Trièves (38) 145 G5
Cornillon-sur-l'Oule (26) 159 E3
Cornimont (88) 70 C6
Cornod (39) 117 G4
Cornot (70) 87 E3
la Cornuaille (49) 76 B4
Cornus (12) 172 B3
Cornusse (18) 98 B4
Corny (27) 19 E6
Corny-Machéroménil (08) 23 H3
Corny-sur-Moselle (57) 26 B6
Coron (49) 92 D2
Corpe (85) 91 H6
Corpeau (21) 101 F4
Corpoyer-la-Chapelle (21) 85 E4
Corps (38) 146 A5
Corps-Nuds (35) 57 F4
Corquilleroy (45) 64 A5
Corquoy (18) 97 G4
Corrano (2A) 205 E6
Corravillers (70) 70 B6
Corre (70) 69 F6
Corrençon-en-Vercors (38) 145 F4
Correns (83) 177 E6
Corrèze (19) 139 F1
Corribert (51) 44 D3
Corrobert (51) 44 C3
Corrombles (21) 84 C4
Corronsac (31) 185 G1
Corroy (51) 45 E5
Corsaint (21) 84 C4
Corsavy (66) 200 D4
Corscia (2B) 204 D2
Corsept (44) 73 H4
Corseul (22) 34 C5
Cortambert (71) 116 A2
Corte (2B) 205 E2
Cortevaix (71) 116 A2
Cortrat (45) 82 B1
les Corvées-les-Yys (28) 61 G2
Corveissiat (01) 117 F4
Corvol-d'Embernard (58) 99 F1
Corvol-l'Orgueilleux (58) 83 E5
Corzé (49) 77 E4
Cos (09) 185 G5
Cosges (39) 102 C5
Coslédaà-Lube-Boast (64) 166 B6
Cosmes (53) 58 C6
Cosnac (19) 138 D3
Cosne-Cours-sur-Loire (58) 82 C5
Cosne-d'Allier (03) 113 E2
Cosnes-et-Romain (54) 25 G3
Cosqueville (50) 12 D1
Cossaye (58) 99 F6
Cossé-d'Anjou (49) 92 D1
Cossé-en-Champagne (53) 59 F6
Cossé-le-Vivien (53) 58 B6
Cossesseville (14) 38 C3
Cosswiller (67) 50 C5
Costa (2B) 202 D5
Costaros (43) 142 C5
les Costes (05) 146 A6
les Costes-Gozon (12) 171 G2
la Côte (70) 88 B2
la Côte-d'Aime (73) 133 E4
la Côte-d'Arbroz (74) 119 F4
la Côte-en-Couzan (42) 128 B3
la Côte-Saint-André (38) 130 D6
le Coteau (42) 115 E6
Côtebrune (25) 87 H6
les Côtes-d'Arey (38) 130 A6
les Côtes-de-Corps (38) 145 H5
Coti-Chiavari (2A) 206 C2
Cotignac (83) 193 G1
Cottance (42) 129 E3
Cottenchy (80) 20 C1
Cottévrard (76) 17 H4
Cottun (14) 13 H5
la Couarde (79) 108 B3
la Couarde-sur-Mer (17) 106 B4
Couargues (18) 98 C1
Coubert (77) 43 F5
Coubeyrac (33) 136 B6
Coubisou (12) 154 D3
Coubjours (24) 138 B2
Coublanc (52) 86 C3
Coublanc (71) 115 F5
Coublevie (38) 145 F1
Coublucq (64) 166 B6
Coubon (43) 142 C4
Coubron (93) 43 E3
Couches (71) 101 E4
Couchey (21) 101 H1
la Coucourde (26) 158 B2
Coucouron (07) 142 D6
Coucy (08) 23 H4
Coucy-la-Ville (02) 22 A3
Coucy-le-Château-Auffrique (02) 22 A4
Coucy-lès-Eppes (02) 22 D3
Couddes (41) 80 A6
Coudehard (61) 39 F4
Coudekerque-Branche (59) 2 B1
Coudekerque-Village (59) 2 C2
Coudes (63) 127 F4
Coudeville-sur-Mer (50) 35 G1
Coudons (11) 186 C6
Coudoux (13) 191 H3
Coudray (27) 19 F5
le Coudray (28) 62 B2
Coudray (45) 63 G3
Coudray (53) 76 D1
Coudray-au-Perche (28) 61 F3
le Coudray-Macouard (49) 93 G1
le Coudray-Montceaux (91) 63 H1
Coudray-Rabut (14) 15 F3
le Coudray-Saint-Germer (60) 19 H4
le Coudray-sur-Thelle (60) 20 B5
la Coudre (79) 93 E3
Coudreceau (28) 61 F2
Coudrecieux (72) 60 D6
Coudres (27) 41 E4
Coudroy (45) 81 G1
Coudun (60) 21 F4
Coudures (40) 166 A4
Coueilles (31) 184 C2
Couëron (44) 74 C5
Couesmes (37) 78 B4
Couesmes-Vaucé (53) 58 D1
Couffé (44) 75 E3
Couffoulens (11) 186 D4
Couffy (41) 96 B1
Couffy-sur-Sarsonne (19) 126 A4
Couflens (09) 198 B1
Coufouleux (81) 169 H3
Couhé (86) 108 D4
Couilly-Pont-aux-Dames (77) 43 G4
Couin (62) 7 H4
Couiza (11) 186 D6
Couladère (31) 184 D3
Coulaines (72) 60 B5
Coulandon (03) 113 H2
Coulangeron (89) 83 F3
Coulanges (03) 114 D2
Coulanges (41) 79 H4
Coulanges-la-Vineuse (89) 83 G3
Coulanges-lès-Nevers (58) 99 E3
Coulanges-sur-Yonne (89) 83 F4
Coulans-sur-Gée (72) 59 H5
Coulaures (24) 137 H1
Couleuvre (03) 98 C6
Coulevon (70) 87 G3
Coulgens (16) 122 C2
Coulimer (61) 60 C1
Coullemelle (80) 20 C2
Coullemont (62) 7 H3
Coullons (45) 81 H3
Coulmer (61) 39 G4
Coulmier-le-Sec (21) 84 D2
Coulmiers (45) 62 C6
Coulobres (34) 188 C1
Coulogne (62) 1 G2
Couloisy (60) 21 G5
Coulombiers (72) 60 A3
Coulombiers (86) 108 D2
Coulombs (14) 14 A4
Coulombs (28) 41 G6
Coulombs-en-Valois (77) 43 H2
Coulomby (62) 1 H4
Coulommes (77) 43 G3
Coulommes-et-Marqueny (08) 24 A4
Coulommes-la-Montagne (51) 23 E6
Coulommiers (77) 43 H4
Coulommiers-la-Tour (41) 79 G2
Coulon (79) 107 G3
Coulonces (14) 37 G3
Coulonces (61) 39 E4
la Couloche (61) 38 B5
Coulongé (72) 78 A3
Coulonges (16) 122 B2
Coulonges (17) 121 G4
Coulonges (86) 110 B3
Coulonges-Cohan (02) 22 C6
Coulonges-les-Sablons (61) 61 F2
Coulonges-sur-l'Autize (79) 107 G2
Coulonges-sur-Sarthe (61) 60 C1
Coulonges-Thouarsais (79) 93 F4
Coulonvillers (80) 7 E4
Couloumé-Mondebat (32) 167 E5
Coulounieix-Chamiers (24) 137 F2
Coulours (89) 65 G4
Couloutre (58) 82 D5
Coulouvray-Boisbenâtre (50) 37 F4
Coulvain (14) 38 A2
Coulx (47) 151 E3
Coume (57) 27 E4
Counozouls (11) 200 A2
Coupelle-Neuve (62) 2 A6
Coupelle-Vieille (62) 2 A6
Coupesarte (14) 15 E6
Coupetz (51) 45 H4
Coupéville (51) 46 B3
Coupiac (12) 171 F2
Coupray (52) 67 G6
Coupru (02) 44 A2
Couptrain (53) 59 F1
Coupvray (77) 43 F3
Couquèques (33) 120 D6
Cour-Cheverny (41) 80 A4
Cour-et-Buis (38) 130 B6
Cour-l'Évêque (52) 67 G6
la Cour-Marigny (45) 81 H1
Cour-Saint-Maurice (25) 88 C6
Cour-sur-Loire (41) 80 A3
Courances (91) 63 H2
Courant (17) 107 G6
Courban (21) 85 F1
la Courbe (61) 38 D4
Courbehaye (28) 62 B4
Courbépine (27) 15 H5
Courbes (02) 22 B2
Courbesseaux (54) 49 E5
Courbette (39) 117 G1
Courbeveille (53) 58 C5
Courbevoie (92) 42 C3
Courbiac (47) 152 A4
Courbillac (16) 121 H3
Courboin (02) 44 C3
Courbouzon (39) 102 D6
Courbouzon (41) 80 B3
Courçais (03) 112 C2
Courçay (37) 95 F1
Courceboeufs (72) 60 B4
Courcelette (80) 8 B4
Courcelles (17) 121 F1
Courcelles (25) 103 F2
Courcelles (45) 63 G5
Courcelles (54) 69 F2
Courcelles (58) 83 E5
Courcelles (90) 89 E4
Courcelles-au-Bois (80) 8 A4
Courcelles-Chaussy (57) 49 E1
Courcelles-de-Touraine (37) 78 B4
Courcelles-en-Barrois (55) 47 G4
Courcelles-en-Bassée (77) 64 C2
Courcelles-en-Montagne (52) 86 A1
Courcelles-Epayelles (60) 21 E3
Courcelles-Frémoy (21) 84 B5
Courcelles-la-Forêt (72) 77 H2
Courcelles-le-Comte (62) 8 B3
Courcelles-lès-Gisors (60) 19 G6
Courcelles-lès-Lens (62) 8 C1
Courcelles-lès-Montbard (21) 84 D4
Courcelles-lès-Montbéliard (25) 88 C4
Courcelles-lès-Semur (21) 84 C5
Courcelles-Sapicourt (51) 22 D6
Courcelles-sous-Châtenois (88) 68 D3
Courcelles-sous-Moyencourt (80) 20 A1
Courcelles-sous-Thoix (80) 20 A2
Courcelles-sur-Aire (55) 47 E3
Courcelles-sur-Blaise (52) 67 G2
Courcelles-sur-Nied (57) 48 D1
Courcelles-sur-Seine (27) 41 F1
Courcelles-sur-Vesles (02) 22 C5
Courcelles-sur-Viosne (95) 42 B2
Courcelles-sur-Voire (10) 66 D1
Courcemain (51) 45 E6
Courcemont (72) 60 B4
Courcerac (17) 121 G2
Courcerault (61) 60 D2
Courceroy (10) 65 E2
Courchamp (77) 44 B6
Courchamps (02) 44 A1
Courchamps (49) 93 G1
Courchapon (25) 103 E1
Courchaton (70) 88 A4
Courchelettes (59) 8 C2
Courcité (53) 59 G3
Courcival (72) 60 C3
Courcôme (16) 122 B1
Courçon (17) 107 E4
Courcoué (37) 94 C3
Courcouronnes (91) 42 D6
Courcoury (17) 121 F3
Courcuire (70) 87 E6
Courcy (14) 39 E2
Courcy (50) 37 E1
Courcy (51) 23 E5
Courcy-aux-Loges (45) 63 F5
Courdemanche (27) 41 E4
Courdemanche (72) 78 D1
Courdemanges (51) 46 A5
Courdimanche (95) 42 B2
Courdimanche-sur-Essonne (91) 63 G2
Couret (31) 184 B4
Courgains (72) 60 B3
Courgeac (16) 122 B6
Courgenard (72) 61 E4
Courgenay (89) 65 F3
Courgent (78) 41 G3
Courgeon (61) 60 D1
Courgeoût (61) 60 C1
Courgis (89) 83 H2
Courgivaux (51) 44 C5
Courgoul (63) 127 E5
Courjeonnet (51) 45 E4
Courlac (16) 136 B1
Courlandon (51) 22 C5
Courlans (39) 102 C6
Courlaoux (39) 102 C6
Courlay (79) 93 E5
Courléon (49) 78 A5
Courlon (21) 85 G3
Courlon-sur-Yonne (89) 64 D3
Courmangoux (01) 117 E3
Courmas (51) 45 E1
Courmelles (02) 22 A5
Courmemin (41) 80 B5
Courménil (61) 39 G4
Courmes (06) 178 D3
Courmont (02) 44 C1
Courmont (70) 88 B3
Cournanel (11) 186 D5
la Courneuve (93) 42 D3
Courniou (34) 187 G1
Cournols (63) 127 E4
Cournon (56) 56 C6
Cournon-d'Auvergne (63) 127 F3
Cournonsec (34) 173 E6
Cournonterral (34) 173 E6
la Couronne (16) 122 B4
Courouvre (55) 47 F3
Courpalay (77) 43 G6
Courpiac (33) 135 H6
Courpière (63) 128 A3
Courpignac (17) 135 F1
Courquetaine (77) 43 F5
Courrensan (32) 167 F3
Courrières (62) 8 C1
Courris (81) 170 D2
Courry (30) 157 E5
Cours (46) 152 D3
Cours (47) 151 E4
le Cours (56) 55 H6
Cours (79) 107 H2
Cours-de-Monségur (33) 150 C1
Cours-de-Pile (24) 137 E5
Cours-la-Ville (69) 115 G6
Cours-les-Bains (33) 150 B4
Cours-les-Barres (18) 98 D3
Coursac (24) 137 E3
Coursan (11) 188 B3
Coursan-en-Othe (10) 65 H5
Coursegoules (06) 195 E2
Courset (62) 1 G5
Courseulles-sur-Mer (14) 14 B3
Courson (14) 37 F3
Courson-les-Carrières (89) 83 F4
Courson-Monteloup (91) 42 B6
Courtacon (77) 44 B5
Courtagnon (51) 45 E1
Courtalain (28) 61 G5
Courtaoult (10) 65 H6
Courtauly (11) 186 C5
Courtavon (68) 89 E4
Courtefontaine (25) 88 D6
Courtefontaine (39) 103 E2
Courteilles (27) 40 C5
Courteix (19) 126 A4
Courtelevant (90) 89 E4
Courtemanche (80) 20 D2
Courtemaux (45) 64 C5
Courtémont (51) 46 C1
Courtemont-Varennes (02) 44 C2
Courtempierre (45) 64 A5
Courtenay (38) 131 E3
Courtenay (45) 64 C5
Courtenot (10) 66 C4
Courteranges (10) 66 C3
Courteron (10) 66 D6
Courtes (01) 116 D2
Courtesoult-et-Gatey (70) 86 D3
Courtetain-et-Salans (25) 88 A6
la Courtète (11) 186 C4
Courteuil (60) 43 E1
Courthézon (84) 175 E1
Courthiézy (51) 44 C2
Courties (32) 167 E5
Courtieux (60) 21 G5
Courtillers (72) 77 F1
Courtils (50) 35 H4
la Courtine (23) 125 H4
Courtisols (51) 46 A2
Courtivron (21) 85 G4
Courtoin (89) 64 D5
Courtois-sur-Yonne (89) 65 E4
Courtomer (61) 39 G6
Courtomer (77) 43 G6
Courtonne-la-Meurdrac (14) 15 F5
Courtonne-les-Deux-Églises (14) 15 G5
Courtrizy-et-Fussigny (02) 22 D3
Courtry (77) 43 E3
Courvaudon (14) 14 A6
Courvières (25) 103 G4
Courville (51) 22 C6
Courville-sur-Eure (28) 61 H2
Courzieu (69) 129 G3
Cousance (39) 117 E2
Cousances-les-Forges (55) 47 E6
Cousances-lès-Triconville (55) 47 F4
Cousolre (59) 10 B3
Coussa (09) 185 H4
Coussac-Bonneval (87) 124 B5
Coussan (65) 183 F3
Coussay (86) 94 B4
Coussay-les-Bois (86) 95 E5
Coussegrey (10) 66 A6
Coussergues (12) 155 E4
Coussey (88) 68 D2
Coust (18) 98 A6
Coustaussa (11) 186 D6
Coustouge (11) 187 G5
Coustouges (66) 200 D5
Coutances (50) 36 D1
Coutansouze (03) 113 F5
Coutarnoux (89) 84 A4
Coutençon (77) 64 C2
Coutens (09) 186 A4
Couterne (61) 59 F1
Couternon (21) 86 A6
Couteuges (43) 141 H2
Coutevroult (77) 43 G4
Couthenans (70) 88 C3
Couthures-sur-Garonne (47) 150 B3
Coutiches (59) 8 D1
Coutières (79) 108 B2
Coutouvre (42) 115 F6
Coutras (33) 135 H3
Couture (16) 122 C1
la Couture (62) 2 D5
la Couture (85) 91 H6
la Couture-Boussey (27) 41 F3
Couture-d'Argenson (79) 108 B6
Couture-sur-Loir (41) 78 D2
Couturelle (62) 7 H3
Coutures (24) 136 D1
Coutures (33) 150 B1
Coutures (49) 77 F5
Coutures (82) 168 C2
Couvains (50) 13 F6
Couvains (61) 40 A4
la Couvertoirade (12) 172 C3
Couvertpuis (55) 47 F6
Couvignon (10) 67 E4
Couville (50) 12 C2
Couvonges (55) 46 D4
Couvrelles (02) 22 B5
Couvron-et-Aumencourt (02) 22 B2
Couvrot (51) 46 B5
Coux (07) 157 H1
Coux (17) 135 G1
Coux-et-Bigaroque (24) 137 G6
Couy (18) 98 B2
la Couyère (35) 57 G5
Couze-et-Saint-Front (24) 137 F6
Couzeix (87) 124 B2
Couziers (37) 94 A2
Couzon (03) 113 G1
Couzon-au-Mont-d'Or (69) 130 A2
Couzou (46) 138 D6
Cox (31) 168 C4
Coye-la-Forêt (60) 42 D1
Coyecques (62) 2 A5
Coyolles (02) 21 G6
Coyrière (39) 118 A3
Coyron (39) 117 G2
Coyviller (54) 48 D6
Cozes (17) 120 D4
Cozzano (2A) 205 E5
Crach (56) 72 C1
Crachier (38) 130 D5
Crain (89) 83 F4
Craincourt (57) 48 D3
Craintilleux (42) 129 E5
Crainvilliers (88) 69 E4
Cramaille (02) 22 B6
Cramans (39) 103 E3
Cramant (51) 45 F3
Cramchaban (17) 107 F4
Craménil (61) 38 C4
Cramoisy (60) 20 C6
Cramont (80) 7 E4
Crampagna (09) 185 H5
Cran-Gevrier (74) 132 A1
Crancey (10) 65 G1
Crançot (39) 102 D6
Crandelles (15) 140 A5
Crannes-en-Champagne (72) 59 H6
Crans (01) 130 C1
Crans (39) 103 F6
Cransac (12) 154 A3
Crantenoy (54) 69 G1
Cranves-Sales (74) 118 D5
Craon (53) 76 B1
Craon (86) 93 H5
Craonne (02) 22 D4
Craonnelle (02) 22 D4
Crapeaumesnil (60) 21 F2
Craponne (69) 129 H3
Craponne-sur-Arzon (43) 142 C1
Cras (38) 145 E2
Cras (46) 152 D2
Cras-sur-Reyssouze (01) 116 D4
Crastatt (67) 50 C5
Crastes (32) 168 A4
Crasville (27) 18 C6
Crasville (50) 13 E3
Crasville-la-Mallet (76) 17 E3
Crasville-la-Rocquefort (76) 17 F3
la Crau (83) 193 F5
Cravanche (90) 88 C3
Cravans (17) 121 E4
Cravant (45) 80 B2
Cravant (89) 83 G3
Cravant-les-Côteaux (37) 94 C2
Cravencères (32) 166 D4
Cravent (78) 41 F2
Crayssac (46) 152 C3
Craywick (59) 2 B2
Crazannes (17) 121 E2
Cré (72) 77 G3
Créances (50) 12 C6
Créancey (21) 101 E1
Crécey-sur-Tille (21) 85 H4
la Crèche (79) 108 A3
Crêches-sur-Saône (71) 116 B4
Créchets (65) 184 A5
Créchy (03) 114 A4
Crécy-au-Mont (02) 22 A4
Crécy-Couvé (28) 41 E5
Crécy-en-Ponthieu (80) 6 D3
Crécy-la-Chapelle (77) 43 G4
Crécy-sur-Serre (02) 22 C2
Crédin (56) 55 G3
Crégols (46) 153 E3
Crégy-lès-Meaux (77) 43 G3
Créhange (57) 49 F1
Créhen (22) 34 C4
Creil (60) 20 D6
Creissan (34) 188 A2
Creissels (12) 172 A1
Crémarest (62) 1 G4
Cremeaux (42) 128 C2
Crémery (80) 21 F1
Crémieu (38) 130 D3
Crempigny-Bonneguête (74) 131 H1
Cremps (46) 152 D4
Crenans (39) 117 H2
Creney-près-Troyes (10) 66 B3
Crennes-sur-Fraubée (53) 59 F2
Créon (33) 135 G6
Créon-d'Armagnac (40) 166 C1
Créot (71) 101 F4
Crépand (21) 84 C3
Crépey (54) 69 E1
Crépol (26) 144 C2
Crépon (14) 14 A3
Crépy (02) 22 B3
Crépy (62) 2 A6
Crépy-en-Valois (60) 21 F6
Créquy (62) 1 H6
le Crès (34) 173 G5
Cresancey (70) 86 D5
Crésantignes (10) 66 A4
les Cresnays (50) 37 F4
Crespian (30) 173 H3
Crespières (78) 42 A3
Crespin (12) 154 A6
Crespin (59) 9 G1
Crespin (81) 170 D1
Crespinet (81) 170 D2
Crespy-le-Neuf (10) 67 E2
Cressac-Saint-Genis (16) 122 B6
Cressanges (03) 113 G3
Cressat (23) 111 H5
la Cresse (12) 155 F6
Cressé (17) 121 H1
Cressensac (46) 138 C4
Cresserons (14) 14 C3
Cresseveuille (14) 15 E4
Cressia (39) 117 F2
Cressin-Rochefort (01) 131 G3
Cressonsacq (60) 20 D4
Cressy (76) 17 H3
Cressy-Omencourt (80) 21 F2
Cressy-sur-Somme (71) 100 A6
Crest (26) 158 C1
le Crest (63) 127 F4
Crest-Voland (73) 132 D2
Creste (63) 127 E5
le Crestet (07) 143 H4
Crestet (84) 158 D5
Crestot (27) 18 C6
Créteil (94) 42 D4
Cretteville (50) 12 D4
Creully (14) 14 A3
la Creuse (70) 87 H3
Creuse (80) 7 F6
le Creusot (71) 101 E5
Creutzwald (57) 27 F4
Creuzier-le-Neuf (03) 114 A5
Creuzier-le-Vieux (03) 114 A5
Crevans-et-la-Chapelle-lès-Granges (70) 88 B4
Crevant (36) 111 G2
Crevant-Laveine (63) 127 G2
Créváchamps (54) 48 D6
Crèvecœur-en-Auge (14) 15 E5
Crèvecoeur-en-Brie (77) 43 G5
Crèvecœur-le-Grand (60) 20 A3
Crèvecœur-le-Petit (60) 20 D3
Crèvecœur-sur-l'Escaut (59) 9 E4
Creveney (70) 87 H2
Crévic (54) 49 E5
Crevin (35) 57 F4
Crévoux (05) 161 F2
Creys-Mépieu (38) 131 E3
Creyssac (24) 137 E1
Creysse (24) 137 E5
Creysse (46) 138 D5
Creysseilles (07) 143 G6
Creyssensac-et-Pissot (24) 137 F3
Crézançay-sur-Cher (18) 97 G5
Crézancy (02) 44 C2
Crézancy-en-Sancerre (18) 82 A6
Crézières (79) 108 B5
Crézilles (54) 48 B6
Cricquebœuf (14) 16 B6
Cricqueville-en-Auge (14) 14 D4
Cricqueville-en-Bessin (14) 13 F4
Criel-sur-Mer (76) 6 A5
Crillon (60) 19 H3
Crillon-le-Brave (84) 158 D6
Crimolois (21) 102 A1
Crion (54) 49 E5
la Crique (76) 17 H4
Criquebeuf-en-Caux (76) 16 C3
Criquebeuf-la-Campagne (27) 18 C6
Criquebeuf-sur-Seine (27) 18 C5
Criquetot-le-Mauconduit (76) 16 D3
Criquetot-l'Esneval (76) 16 B4
Criquetot-sur-Longueville (76) 17 G3
Criquetot-sur-Ouville (76) 17 F4
Criquiers (76) 19 G2
Crisenoy (77) 43 F6
Crisolles (60) 21 G3
Crissay-sur-Manse (37) 94 C2
Crissé (72) 59 H4
Crissey (39) 102 C2
Crissey (71) 101 G5
Cristinacce (2A) 204 C3
Cristot (14) 14 A4
Criteuil-la-Magdeleine (16) 121 H5
Critot (76) 17 H4
Croce (2B) 203 G6
Crochte (59) 2 B2
Crocicchia (2B) 203 F6
Crocq (23) 126 A2
le Crocq (60) 20 B3
Crocy (14) 39 E3
Crœttwiller (67) 51 G2
Croignon (33) 135 G5
Croisances (43) 142 A5
Croisette (62) 7 G2
le Croisic (44) 73 E4
la Croisille (27) 40 C2
la Croisille-sur-Briance (87) 124 D4
Croisilles (14) 14 B6
Croisilles (28) 41 F5
Croisilles (61) 39 G4
Croisilles (62) 8 B3
Croismare (54) 49 F6
Croissanville (14) 39 E1
Croissy-Beaubourg (77) 43 F4
Croissy-sur-Celle (60) 20 B2
Croissy-sur-Seine (78) 42 B4
le Croisty (56) 54 C2
Croisy (18) 98 B4
Croisy-sur-Andelle (76) 19 E4
Croisy-sur-Eure (27) 41 F2
Croix (59) 3 G4
Croix (90) 88 D4
la Croix-aux-Bois (08) 24 B4
la Croix-aux-Mines (88) 70 D3
la Croix-Avranchin (50) 35 H4
la Croix-Blanche (47) 151 F5
Croix-Caluyau (59) 9 G4
Croix-Chapeau (17) 106 D5
la Croix-Comtesse (17) 107 G5
la Croix-de-la-Rochette (73) 132 B5
la Croix-du-Perche (28) 61 G3
la Croix-en-Brie (77) 43 H6
la Croix-en-Champagne (51) 46 B2
Croix-en-Ternois (62) 7 G1
la Croix-en-Touraine (37) 79 F6
Croix-Fonsommes (02) 9 E6
la Croix-Helléan (56) 55 H4
Croix-Mare (76) 17 F5
Croix-Moligneaux (80) 21 G1
la Croix-Saint-Leufroy (27) 41 E1
la Croix-sur-Gartempe (87) 110 A5
la Croix-sur-Ourcq (02) 44 B1
la Croix-sur-Roudoule (06) 178 C1
la Croix-Valmer (83) 194 B4
Croixanvec (56) 55 F2
Croixdalle (76) 19 E1
la Croixille (53) 58 B3
Croixrault (80) 20 A1
Croizet-sur-Gand (42) 129 E2
Crolles (38) 145 H1
Crollon (50) 35 H4
Cromac (87) 110 C3
Cromary (70) 87 F5
Cronat (71) 99 H6
Cronce (43) 141 G3
la Cropte (53) 59 E6
Cropus (76) 18 D1
Cros (30) 173 F2
le Cros (34) 172 C3
Cros (63) 126 B6
Cros-de-Géorand (07) 142 D6
Cros-de-Montvert (15) 139 G4
Cros-de-Ronesque (15) 140 C5
Crosey-le-Grand (25) 88 A5
Crosey-le-Petit (25) 88 A5
Crosmières (72) 77 G2
Crosne (91) 42 D5
Crossac (44) 73 H3
Crosses (18) 98 A3
Crosville-la-Vieille (27) 40 C1
Crosville-sur-Douve (50) 12 D4
Crosville-sur-Scie (76) 17 G3
Crotelles (37) 79 E4
Crotenay (39) 103 E5
Croth (27) 41 F4
le Crotoy (80) 6 C3
Crots (05) 161 E2
Crottes-en-Pithiverais (45) 63 E5
Crottet (01) 116 B4
le Crouais (35) 56 C2
Crouay (14) 13 H5
la Croupte (14) 15 F6
Crouseilles (64) 166 C6
Croutelle (86) 109 E2
les Croûtes (10) 65 H6
Croutoy (60) 21 G5
Crouttes (61) 39 F3
Crouttes-sur-Marne (02) 44 A3
Crouy (02) 22 A5
Crouy-en-Thelle (60) 20 C6
Crouy-Saint-Pierre (80) 7 F5
Crouy-sur-Cosson (41) 80 B3
Crouy-sur-Ourcq (77) 43 H2
le Crouzet (25) 103 G6
Crouzet-Migette (25) 103 G3
la Crouzille (63) 112 D5
Crouzilles (37) 94 C2
Crozant (23) 111 E3
Croze (23) 125 G3
Crozes-Hermitage (26) 144 A3
Crozet (01) 118 B4
le Crozet (42) 114 D5
les Crozets (39) 117 H2
Crozon (29) 30 D6
Crozon-sur-Vauvre (36) 111 G2
Cruas (07) 158 B1
Crucey-Villages (28) 40 D5
Crucheray (41) 79 G2
Cruéjouls (12) 155 E3
Cruet (73) 132 A5
Crugey (21) 101 F2
Crugny (51) 22 D6
Cruguel (56) 55 H4
Cruis (04) 176 C1
Crulai (61) 40 A5
Crupies (26) 158 D2
Crupilly (02) 9 H6
Cruscades (11) 187 H3
Cruseilles (74) 118 B6
Crusnes (54) 26 A2
Cruviers-Lascours (30) 173 H2
Crux-la-Ville (58) 99 G2
Cruzille (71) 116 B2
Cruzilles-lès-Mépillat (01) 116 B4
Cruzy (34) 188 A2
Cruzy-le-Châtel (89) 84 C1
Cry (89) 84 C3
Cubelles (43) 142 A4
Cubières (48) 156 C3
Cubières-sur-Cinoble (11) 187 E6
Cubiérettes (48) 156 C3
Cubjac (24) 137 G2
Cublac (19) 138 B3
Cublize (69) 129 F1
Cubnezais (33) 135 F3
Cubrial (25) 87 H4
Cubry (25) 88 A4
Cubry-lès-Faverney (70) 87 G1
Cubzac-les-Ponts (33) 135 F4
Cucharmoy (77) 44 A6
Cuchery (51) 45 E1
Cucq (62) 1 F6
Cucugnan (11) 200 D1
Cucuron (84) 176 A4
Cudos (33) 149 H4
Cudot (89) 64 D6
Cuébris (06) 178 D2
Cuélas (32) 183 H2
Cuers (83) 193 F4
Cuffies (02) 22 A5
Cuffy (18) 98 D4
Cugand (85) 91 H1
Cuges-les-Pins (13) 192 D4
Cugnaux (31) 169 E6
Cugney (70) 86 D5
Cugny (02) 21 H2
Cuguen (35) 35 F5
Cuguron (31) 183 H4
Cuhon (86) 94 A5
Cuignières (60) 20 D4
Cuigy-en-Bray (60) 19 H4
Cuillé (53) 58 A5
Cuinchy (62) 2 D6
Cuincy (59) 8 C1
le Cuing (31) 184 A4
Cuinzier (42) 115 F5
Cuirieux (02) 22 D2
Cuiry-Housse (02) 22 B6
Cuiry-lès-Chaudardes (02) 22 D5
Cuiry-lès-Iviers (02) 23 F1
Cuis (51) 45 F2
Cuise-la-Motte (60) 21 G5
Cuiseaux (71) 117 E2
Cuiserey (21) 86 B5
Cuisery (71) 116 C1
Cuisia (39) 117 F2
Cuisles (51) 44 D1
Cuissai (61) 59 H1
Cuissy-et-Geny (02) 22 C4
Cuisy (55) 24 D6
Cuisy (77) 43 F2
Cuisy-en-Almont (02) 21 H4
Culan (18) 112 B2
Culètre (21) 101 E2
Culey-le-Patry (14) 38 B2
Culhat (63) 127 G2
Culin (38) 130 D5
Culles-les-Roches (71) 116 A1
Cully (14) 14 A4
Culmont (52) 86 B1
Culoz (01) 131 G2
Cult (70) 86 D6
Cultures (48) 155 H3
Cumières (51) 45 E2
Cumières-le-Mort-Homme (55) 25 E6

Cumiès (11)........186 A2
Cumont (82)........168 B3
Cunac (81)........170 C2
Cuncy-lès-Varzy (58)........83 F6
Cunèges (24)........136 D6
Cunel (55)........24 D5
Cunelières (90)........88 D3
Cunfin (10)........67 E5
Cunlhat (63)........128 A4
Cuon (49)........77 G4
Cuperly (51)........45 H2
Cuq (47)........168 A1
Cuq (81)........170 B5
Cuq-Toulza (81)........170 A6
Cuqueron (64)........182 A2
Curac (16)........136 B1
Curan (12)........155 E6
Curbans (04)........160 B3
Curbigny (71)........115 G4
Curçay-sur-Dive (86)........93 H3
Curchy (80)........21 H3
Curciat-Dongalon (01)........116 D2
Curcy-sur-Orne (14)........14 A6
Curdin (71)........115 E1
Curel (04)........159 G6
Curel (52)........67 H1
Curemonte (19)........139 E4
Cures (72)........59 H5
Curgies (59)........9 G2
Curgy (71)........100 D3
Curienne (73)........132 A4
Curières (12)........155 E2
Curis-au-Mont-d'Or (69)........130 C2
Curley (21)........101 G1
Curlu (80)........8 B5
Curmont (52)........67 G3
Curnier (26)........159 E4
Cursan (33)........135 G6
Curtafond (01)........116 D4
Curtil-Saint-Seine (21)........85 G5
Curtil-sous-Buffières (71)........115 H3
Curtil-sous-Burnand (71)........116 A1
Curtil-Vergy (21)........101 G2
Curvalle (81)........171 E2
Curzay-sur-Vonne (86)........108 C2
Curzon (85)........91 G6
Cusance (25)........88 A6
Cuse-et-Adrisans (25)........87 H4
Cusey (52)........86 B3
Cussac (15)........141 E4
Cussac (87)........123 G3
Cussac-Fort-Médoc (33)........134 D3
Cussac-sur-Loire (43)........142 C4
Cussangy (10)........66 B6
Cussay (37)........95 E3
Cusset (03)........114 A5
Cussey-les-Forges (21)........85 H3
Cussey-sur-Lison (25)........103 F2
Cussey-sur-l'Ognon (25)........87 F6
Cussy (14)........13 H5
Cussy-en-Morvan (71)........100 C2
Cussy-la-Colonne (21)........101 F3
Cussy-le-Châtel (21)........101 E2
Cussy-les-Forges (89)........84 B5
Custines (54)........48 C4
Cusy (74)........132 A3
Cutry (02)........21 H5
Cutry (54)........25 H4
Cuts (60)........21 G3
Cuttoli-Corticchiato (2A)........204 D5
Cuttura (39)........117 H3
Cuvat (74)........132 A1
Cuve (70)........69 G6
Cuvergnon (60)........43 H1
Cuverville (14)........14 C4
Cuverville (27)........19 E5
Cuverville (76)........16 B4
Cuverville-sur-Yères (76)........6 B5
Cuves (50)........37 F4
Cuves (52)........68 B5
Cuvier (39)........103 G5
Cuvillers (59)........9 E3
Cuvilly (60)........21 E3
Cuvry (57)........26 B6
Cuxac-Cabardès (11)........186 D2
Cuxac-d'Aude (11)........188 A3
Cuy (60)........21 F3
Cuy (89)........65 E3
Cuy-Saint-Fiacre (76)........19 G3
Cuzac (46)........154 A2
Cuzance (46)........138 C4
Cuzieu (01)........131 F2
Cuzieu (42)........129 E4
Cuzion (36)........111 E2
Cuzorn (47)........151 H2
Cuzy (71)........100 B5
Cys-la-Commune (02)........22 C5
Cysoing (59)........3 G5

Dabo (57)........50 B5
Dachstein (67)........50 D6
Dadonville (45)........63 F4
Daglan (24)........152 B1
Dagneux (01)........130 C2
Dagny (77)........44 A5
Dagny-Lambercy (02)........23 E1
Dagonville (55)........47 F4
la Daguenière (49)........77 E5
Dahlenheim (67)........50 D5
Daignac (33)........135 G6
Daigny (08)........24 C2
Daillancourt (52)........67 G3
Daillecourt (52)........68 C5
Dainville (62)........8 A3
Dainville-Bertheléville (55)........68 C2
Daix (21)........85 G6
Dalem (57)........27 E4
Dalhain (57)........49 F3
Dalhunden (67)........51 F4
Dallet (63)........127 F3
Dallon (02)........21 H1
Dalou (09)........185 H5
Dalstein (57)........26 D3
Daluis (06)........178 B1
Damas-aux-Bois (88)........69 H2
Damas-et-Bettegney (88)........69 G3
Damazan (47)........150 C4
Dambach (67)........28 C6
Dambach-la-Ville (67)........71 F2
Dambelin (25)........88 B5
Dambenois (25)........88 C4
Dambenoît-lès-Colombe (70)........87 H2
Damblain (88)........68 D5
Damblainville (14)........14 D6
Dambron (28)........62 D5
Dame-Marie (27)........40 D4
Dame-Marie (61)........60 C2
Dame-Marie-les-Bois (37)........79 F4
Damelevières (54)........49 E6
Daméraucourt (60)........19 H2
Damery (51)........45 E2
Damery (80)........21 E2
Damgan (56)........73 E2
Damiatte (81)........170 B5
Damigny (61)........60 A1
Damloup (55)........25 F6
Dammard (02)........44 A1
Dammarie (28)........62 B4
Dammarie-en-Puisaye (45)........82 B3
Dammarie-les-Lys (77)........64 A1
Dammarie-sur-Loing (45)........82 B2
Dammarie-sur-Saulx (55)........47 F6
Dammartin-en-Goële (77)........43 F2
Dammartin-en-Serve (78)........41 G3
Dammartin-
   lès-Templiers (25)........87 H6
Dammartin-Marpain (39)........102 D1
Dammartin-sur-Meuse (52)........68 C6
Dammartin-sur-Tigeaux (77)........43 G4
Damousies (59)........10 A3
Damparis (39)........102 C2
Dampierre (10)........66 C1
Dampierre (14)........37 H2

Dampierre (39)........103 E2
Dampierre (52)........68 B6
Dampierre-au-Temple (51)........45 H2
Dampierre-en-Bray (76)........19 G3
Dampierre-en-Bresse (71)........102 B5
Dampierre-en-Burly (45)........81 H1
Dampierre-en-Crot (18)........81 H5
Dampierre-en-Graçay (18)........97 E2
Dampierre-en-Montagne (21)........85 E5
Dampierre-et-Flée (21)........86 B5
Dampierre-le-Château (51)........46 C2
les Damps (27)........18 D5
Dampierre-Saint-Nicolas (76)........17 H2
Dampierre-sous-Bois (25)........82 D5
Dampierre-sous-Brou (28)........61 G4
Dampierre-sur-Avre (28)........40 D4
Dampierre-
   sur-Boutonne (17)........107 H6
Dampierre-sur-Doubs (25)........88 C4
Dampierre-sur-Linotte (70)........87 G4
Dampierre-sur-Moivre (51)........46 A3
Dampierre-sur-Salon (70)........86 D3
Dampjoux (25)........88 C5
Dampleux (02)........21 H6
Dampmart (77)........43 F3
Dampniat (19)........138 D3
Damprichard (25)........88 D6
Dampsmesnil (27)........41 G1
Dampvalley-
   lès-Colombe (70)........87 G3
Dampvalley-
   Saint-Pancras (70)........69 G6
Dampvitoux (54)........48 A2
Damrémont (52)........68 D6
Damville (27)........40 D3
Damvillers (55)........25 F5
Damvix (85)........107 F3
Dancé (42)........128 D2
Dancé (61)........61 E2
Dancevoir (52)........67 G6
Dancourt (76)........6 B6
Dancourt-Popincourt (80)........21 E2
Dancy (28)........62 A4
Danestal (14)........15 E4
Dangé-Saint-Romain (86)........94 D4
Dangeau (28)........61 H4
Dangers (28)........62 A1
Dangeul (72)........60 A3
Dangolsheim (67)........50 C6
Dangu (27)........19 G6
Dangy (50)........37 F1
Danizy (02)........22 B2
Danjoutin (90)........88 C3
Danne-et-Quatre-Vents (57)........50 B4
Dannelbourg (57)........50 B4
Dannemarie (25)........88 D5
Dannemarie (68)........89 E3
Dannemarie (78)........41 G5
Dannemarie-sur-Crête (25)........103 F1
Dannemoine (89)........84 A1
Dannemois (91)........63 H2
Dannes (62)........1 F5
Dannevoux (55)........24 D5
Danvou-la-Ferrière (14)........38 A2
Danzé (41)........79 F1
Daon (53)........76 D2
Daoulas (29)........31 F5
Darazac (19)........139 G3
Darbonnay (39)........102 D5
Darbres (07)........157 H2
Darcey (21)........85 E4
Dardenac (33)........135 G6
Dardez (27)........41 E2
Dardilly (69)........129 H3
Dareizé (69)........129 G2
Dargies (60)........20 A2
Dargnies (80)........6 B4
Dargoire (42)........129 H5
Darmannes (52)........68 A4
Darnac (87)........110 A4
Darnétal (76)........18 D4
Darnets (19)........125 G6
Darney (88)........69 F4
Darney-aux-Chênes (88)........68 D3
Darnieulles (88)........69 H4
Darois (21)........85 G5
Darvault (77)........64 A3
Darvoy (45)........81 F1
Dasle (25)........88 D4
Daubensand (67)........71 H2
Daubeuf-la-Campagne (27)........18 C6
Daubeuf-près-Vatteville (27)........19 E6
Daubeuf-Serville (76)........16 D4
Daubèze (33)........135 H6
Dauendorf (67)........50 D3
Daumazan-sur-Arize (09)........185 F4
Daumeray (49)........77 F2
Dauphin (04)........176 C2
Dausse (47)........151 G4
Daux (31)........169 E4
Dauzat-sur-Vodable (63)........127 F1
Davayat (63)........127 F1
Davayé (71)........116 B4
Davejean (11)........187 F5
Davenescourt (80)........20 D2
Davézieux (07)........143 H2
Davignac (19)........125 H6
Davron (78)........42 A4
Dax (40)........165 E4
Deauville (14)........15 E3
Débats-Rivière-d'Orpra (42)........128 C3
Decazeville (12)........154 A2
Dechy (59)........8 D2
Décines-Charpieu (69)........130 B3
Decize (58)........99 F5
Dégagnac (46)........152 C1
Degré (72)........60 A5
Dehault (72)........60 D4
Dehéries (59)........9 E5
Deinbert (67)........28 A6
Deinvillers (88)........70 A2
Delain (70)........86 D4
Delettes (62)........2 A5
Delincourt (60)........19 H6
Delle (90)........88 D4
Delme (57)........49 E3
Delouze-Rosières (55)........47 G6
le Déluge (60)........20 B5
Delut (55)........25 F4
Deluz (25)........87 G6
Demandolx (04)........178 A2
Demange-aux-Eaux (55)........47 G6
Demangevelle (70)........69 F6
Demi-Quartier (74)........133 E1
la Demie (70)........87 G3
Démouville (14)........14 C4
Dému (32)........167 E4
Démuin (80)........20 D1
Denain (59)........9 E2
Dénat (81)........170 C3
Denazé (53)........76 D1
Denée (49)........76 D5
Denestanville (76)........17 H3
Deneuille-lès-Chantelle (03)........113 G4
Deneuille-les-Mines (03)........113 E3
Deneuvre (54)........70 B1
Denève (54)........70 B1
Dénezé-sous-Doué (49)........93 G1
Dénezé-sous-le-Lude (49)........78 A4
Denezières (39)........117 H1
Denicé (69)........129 H1
Denier (62)........7 H2
Denipaire (88)........70 D2
Dennebrœucq (62)........2 A5
Denney (90)........88 C3
Denneville (50)........12 C4
Dennemont (78)........41 G2
Denonville (28)........62 D2
Denting (57)........27 E4
Déols (36)........96 C5
Derbamont (88)........69 G3
Dercé (86)........94 B4
Derchigny (76)........17 H2

Dercy (02)........22 C2
Dernacueillette (11)........187 F6
Dernancourt (80)........8 A5
Derval (44)........74 C1
Désaignes (07)........143 G4
Désandans (25)........88 B4
Descartes (37)........95 E3
le Deschaux (39)........102 C4
le Désert (14)........37 H3
Désertines (03)........112 D3
Désertines (53)........58 C1
les Déserts (73)........132 A4
Déservillers (25)........103 G3
Desges (43)........141 H4
Desingy (74)........118 A6
Desmonts (45)........63 H4
Desnes (39)........102 C5
Desseling (57)........49 G4
Dessenheim (68)........71 G5
Dessia (39)........117 F3
Destord (88)........70 B3
la Destrousse (13)........192 C3
Destry (57)........49 F2
Desvres (62)........1 G5
Détain-et-Bruant (21)........101 G2
Détrier (73)........132 A6
le Détroit (14)........38 C3
Dettey (71)........100 C5
Dettwiller (67)........50 C4
Deuil-la-Barre (95)........42 D3
Deuillet (02)........22 A2
Deûlémont (59)........3 F4
Deux-Chaises (03)........113 F3
Deux-Évailles (53)........59 E4
Les Deux-Fays (39)........102 C4
Deux-Jumeaux (14)........13 G4
Deux-Verges (15)........141 E5
les Deux-Villes (08)........24 D2
Deuxville (54)........49 E5
Devay (58)........99 G5
Devecey (25)........87 F6
Devesset (07)........143 F4
Déville (61)........41 G6
Déville-lès-Rouen (76)........17 G6
Devrouze (71)........102 A5
Deycimont (88)........70 B3
Deyme (31)........185 G1
Deyvillers (88)........70 A3
le Dézert (50)........13 F5
Dezize-lès-Maranges (71)........101 F4
D'Huison-Longueville (91)........63 G2
Dhuisy (77)........44 A2
Dhuizel (02)........22 C5
Dhuizon (41)........80 C4
Diancey (21)........100 D2
Diane-Capelle (57)........49 H4
Diant (77)........64 C3
Diarville (54)........69 F2
Dicy (89)........82 D1
Didenheim (68)........89 F2
Die (26)........145 E6
Diebling (57)........49 H1
Diebolsheim (67)........71 H2
Diedendorf (67)........50 A3
Dieffenbach-lès-Wœrth (67)........51 E2
Dieffenthal (67)........71 F2
Dieffmatten (68)........89 E2
Dième (69)........129 F1
Diemeringen (67)........50 B2
Diémoz (38)........130 C4
Diénay (21)........85 H4
Dienne (86)........109 F2
Dienné (86)........109 F2
Diennes-Aubigny (58)........99 G4
Dienville (10)........66 D3
Dieppe (76)........17 G2
Dieppe-sous-
   Douaumont (55)........25 F6
Dierre (37)........79 F6
Dierrey-Saint-Julien (10)........65 H3
Dierrey-Saint-Pierre (10)........65 H3
Diesen (57)........27 E5
Dietwiller (68)........89 G2
Dieudonné (60)........20 B6
Dieue-sur-Meuse (55)........47 G2
Dieulefit (26)........158 C3
Dieulivol (33)........150 C1
Dieulouard (54)........48 C4
Dieupentale (82)........169 E3
Dieuze (57)........49 G3
Diéval (62)........7 H1
Diffembach-lès-Hellimer (57)........49 G2
Diges (89)........83 E3
Digna (39)........117 F2
Dignac (16)........122 C5
la Digne-d'Amont (11)........186 C5
la Digne-d'Aval (11)........186 D5
Digne-les-Bains (04)........160 C6
Dignonville (88)........70 A3
Digny (28)........61 G1
Digoin (71)........114 D2
Digoine (71)........12 D1
Digosville (50)........12 D2
Dijon (21)........85 H6
Dimancheville (45)........63 G3
Dimbsthal (67)........50 C5
Diménchaux (59)........10 A3
Dimont (59)........10 A3
Dinan (22)........34 D5
Dinard (35)........34 D3
Dinéault (29)........31 F6
Dingé (35)........35 E6
Dingsheim (67)........51 E5
Dingy-en-Vuache (74)........118 A5
Dingy-Saint-Clair (74)........132 B1
Dinozé (88)........70 A3
Dinsac (87)........110 C5
Dinsheim-sur-Bruche (67)........50 C6
Dinteville (52)........67 F5
Dio-et-Valquières (34)........172 B5
Dionay (38)........144 D2
Dions (30)........174 A2
Diou (03)........114 C2
Diou (36)........97 E3
Dirac (16)........122 C4
Dirinon (29)........31 F5
Dirol (58)........83 G6
Dissangis (89)........84 A4
Dissay (86)........94 C6
Dissay-sous-Courcillon (72)........78 C3
Dissé-sous-Ballon (72)........60 B3
Dissé-sous-le-Lude (72)........78 A3
Distré (49)........93 G1
Distroff (57)........26 C3
Diusse (64)........166 C5
Divajeu (26)........158 C1
Dives (60)........21 F3
Dives-sur-Mer (14)........14 D4
Divion (62)........7 H1
Divonne-les-Bains (01)........118 C3
Dixmont (89)........65 E4
Dizimieu (38)........130 D3
Dizy (51)........45 F2
Dizy-le-Gros (02)........23 E3
Doazit (40)........165 H4
Doazon (64)........165 H6
Docelles (88)........70 B4
Dœuil-sur-le-Mignon (17)........107 G5
Dognen (64)........181 H2
Dogneville (88)........70 A3
Dohem (62)........2 A4
Dohis (02)........23 F2
Doignies (59)........8 C4
Doingt (80)........8 C5
Doissat (24)........152 A1
Doissin (38)........131 E5
Doix (85)........107 F2
Doizieux (42)........129 G6
Dol-de-Bretagne (35)........35 E4
Dolaincourt (88)........68 D3
Dolancourt (10)........67 E3
Dolcourt (54)........69 E1
Dole (39)........102 D2
Dolignon (02)........23 E2

Dolleren (68)........88 D1
Dollon (72)........60 D5
Dollot (89)........64 C4
Dolmayrac (47)........151 F4
Dolo (22)........34 B6
Dolomieu (38)........131 E4
Dolus-d'Oléron (17)........120 A1
Dolus-le-Sec (37)........95 F2
Dolving (57)........50 A4
Dom-le-Mesnil (08)........24 B2
Domagné (35)........57 G3
Domaize (63)........128 A4
Domalain (35)........57 H4
la Dornac (24)........138 B3
Domancy (74)........133 E1
Domarin (38)........130 D4
Domart-en-Ponthieu (80)........7 F4
Domart-sur-la-Luce (80)........20 D1
Domats (89)........64 C5
Domazan (30)........174 D2
Dombasle-
   devant-Darney (88)........69 F4
Dombasle-en-Argonne (55)........47 E1
Dombasle-en-Xaintois (88)........69 F3
Dombasle-sur-Meurthe (54)........49 E5
Domblans (39)........102 D5
Dombras (55)........25 F4
Dombrot-le-Sec (88)........69 E4
Dombrot-sur-Vair (88)........69 E3
Domecy-sur-Cure (89)........83 H5
Domecy-sur-le-Vault (89)........83 H5
Doméliers (60)........20 B2
Domène (38)........145 H2
Domérat (03)........112 C3
Domesmont (80)........7 F4
Domessargues (30)........173 H2
Domessin (73)........131 G5
Domèvre-en-Haye (54)........48 B4
Domèvre-sous-Montfort (88)........69 F3
Domèvre-sur-Avière (88)........69 H3
Domèvre-sur-Durbion (88)........70 A2
Domèvre-sur-Vezouze (54)........49 G6
Domeyrat (43)........141 H2
Domeyrot (23)........112 A4
Domezain-Berraute (64)........181 F1
Domfaing (88)........70 B3
Domfessel (67)........50 A2
Domfront (60)........20 D3
Domfront (61)........38 A6
Domfront-
   en-Champagne (72)........59 H4
Domgermain (54)........48 A5
la Dominelais (35)........57 E6
Dominois (80)........6 D2
Domjean (50)........37 G2
Domjevin (54)........49 G6
Domjulien (88)........69 F3
Domléger-Longvillers (80)........7 F3
Domloup (35)........57 F3
Dommarie-Eulmont (54)........69 F2
Dommartemont (54)........48 D5
Dommartin (01)........116 C3
Dommartin (25)........103 H4
Dommartin (58)........100 A2
Dommartin (69)........129 H2
Dommartin (80)........20 C1
Dommartin-aux-Bois (88)........69 G4
Dommartin-Dampierre (51)........46 C2
Dommartin-la-Chaussée (54)........26 A6
Dommartin-la-Montagne (55)........47 H2
Dommartin-le-Coq (10)........66 C1
Dommartin-le-Franc (52)........67 G2
Dommartin-
   le-Saint-Père (52)........67 G2
Dommartin-
   lès-Cuiseaux (71)........117 E2
Dommartin-
   lès-Remiremont (88)........70 B5
Dommartin-lès-Toul (54)........48 B5
Dommartin-lès-Vallois (88)........69 F4
Dommartin-Lettrée (51)........45 H4
Dommartin-
   sous-Amance (54)........48 D4
Dommartin-sous-Hans (51)........46 C1
Dommartin-sur-Vraine (88)........69 E2
Dommartin-Varimont (51)........46 C2
Dommary-Baroncourt (55)........25 G5
Domme (24)........138 A6
Dommery (08)........23 H3
Dommiers (02)........21 H5
Domnom-lès-Dieuze (57)........49 G3
Domont (95)........42 D2
Dompaire (88)........69 G3
Dompcevrin (55)........47 G3
Dompierre (60)........21 E3
Dompierre (61)........38 B5
Dompierre (88)........70 A2
Dompierre-aux-Bois (55)........47 G2
Dompierre-Becquincourt (80)........8 B6
Dompierre-du-Chemin (35)........58 A3
Dompierre-en-Morvan (21)........84 C5
Dompierre-les-Églises (87)........110 D4
Dompierre-les-Ormes (71)........115 H3
Dompierre-les-Tilleuls (25)........103 H4
Dompierre-
   sous-Sanvignes (71)........115 F1
Dompierre-sur-Authie (80)........7 E2
Dompierre-sur-Besbre (03)........114 C2
Dompierre-
   sur-Chalaronne (01)........116 C5
Dompierre-
   sur-Charente (17)........121 F3
Dompierre-sur-Helpe (59)........10 A4
Dompierre-sur-Héry (58)........99 G1
Dompierre-sur-Mer (17)........106 D4
Dompierre-sur-Mont (39)........117 G1
Dompierre-sur-Nièvre (58)........99 E1
Dompierre-sur-Veyle (01)........116 D6
Dompierre-sur-Yon (85)........91 G4
Dompnac (07)........157 E3
Domprel (25)........104 B1
Dompremy (51)........46 C5
Domprix (54)........25 H5
Domps (87)........125 E4
Domptail (88)........70 B1
Domptail-en-l'Air (54)........69 F1
Domptin (02)........44 B2
Domqueur (80)........7 F4
Domremy-la-Canne (55)........25 G5
Domrémy-la-Pucelle (88)........68 D2
Domrémy-Landéville (52)........67 H3
Domsure (01)........117 E3
Domvallier (88)........69 F3
Domvast (80)........7 E3
Don (59)........3 E5
Donazac (11)........186 C4
Donchery (08)........24 B2
Doncières (88)........70 A2
Doncourt-aux-Templiers (55)........47 H1
Doncourt-lès-Conflans (54)........26 A5
Doncourt-lès-Longuyon (54)........25 G4
Doncourt-sur-Meuse (52)........68 C5
Dondas (47)........151 G5
Donges (44)........73 G4
Donjeux (52)........67 H3
Donjeux (57)........49 E3
le Donjon (03)........114 C3
Donnay (14)........38 C2
Donnazac (81)........170 A1
Donnelay (57)........49 F4
Donnemain-
   Saint-Mamès (28)........62 A5
Donnemarie-Dontilly (77)........64 D1
Donnement (10)........66 D1
Donnenheim (67)........50 D4
Donnery (45)........81 F1
Donnezac (33)........135 F2
Dontreix (23)........126 B1
Dontrien (51)........23 G6
Donville-les-Bains (50)........35 G2
Donzac (33)........150 A2
Donzac (82)........151 G6
Donzacq (40)........165 G4
Le Donzeil (23)........111 H6
Donzenac (19)........138 C2
Donzère (26)........158 A4
Donzy (58)........82 C6
Donzy-le-National (71)........116 A3
Donzy-le-Pertuis (71)........116 B2

Doranges (63)........128 A6
Dorans (90)........88 C3
Dorat (63)........127 H2
le Dorat (87)........110 B4
Dorceau (61)........61 E2
Dordives (45)........64 A4
Dore-l'Église (63)........142 B1
la Dorée (53)........58 B1
Dorengt (02)........9 G5
Dorlisheim (67)........50 D6
Dormans (51)........44 D2
Dormelles (77)........64 B3
la Dornac (24)........138 B3
Dornas (07)........143 F5
Dornecy (58)........83 G5
Dornes (58)........99 F6
Dornot (57)........26 B6
Dorres (66)........199 G4
Dortan (01)........117 G3
Dosches (10)........66 C3
Dosnon (10)........45 G6
Dossenheim-
   Kochersberg (67)........50 D5
Dossenheim-sur-Zinsel (67)........50 D3
Douadic (36)........95 G6
Douai (59)........8 D2
Douains (27)........41 F2
Douarnenez (29)........53 E2
Douaumont (55)........25 F6
Doubs (25)........104 A4
Doucelles (72)........60 A3
Douchapt (24)........136 D2
Douchy (02)........21 H1
Douchy (45)........82 C2
Douchy-les-Ayette (62)........8 B3
Douchy-les-Mines (59)........9 E2
Doucier (39)........117 H1
Doucy-en-Bauges (73)........132 B3
Doudeauville (62)........1 G5
Doudeauville (76)........19 G3
Doudeauville-en-Vexin (27)........19 F5
Doudelainville (80)........6 D5
Doudeville (76)........17 E3
Doudrac (47)........151 F1
Doue (77)........44 A3
Doué-la-Fontaine (49)........93 F1
Douelle (46)........152 C3
le Douhet (17)........121 F2
Douillet (72)........59 H3
Douilly (80)........21 H1
Doulaincourt-Saucourt (52)........68 A3
Doulcon (55)........24 D4
Doulevant-le-Château (52)........67 G2
Doulevant-le-Petit (52)........67 G2
Doulezon (33)........136 A6
Le Doulieu (59)........2 D4
Doumely-Bégny (08)........23 G2
Doumy (64)........166 B6
Dounoux (88)........69 H4
Dourbies (30)........172 C1
Dourdain (35)........57 H2
Dourdan (91)........63 E1
Dourges (62)........8 C1
Dourgne (81)........186 B1
Douriez (62)........6 D1
Dourlers (59)........10 A3
le Dourn (81)........171 E1
Dournazac (87)........123 G4
Dournon (39)........103 F3
Dours (65)........183 F2
Doussard (74)........132 B3
Doussay (86)........94 B5
Douvaine (74)........118 D3
Douville (24)........137 E4
Douville-en-Auge (14)........15 E3
Douville-sur-Andelle (27)........19 E5
Douvrend (76)........6 A6
Douvres (01)........130 D1
Douvres-la-Délivrande (14)........14 B3
Douvrin (62)........3 E6
Doux (08)........23 H4
Doux (79)........93 H5
Douy (28)........62 A5
Douy-la-Ramée (77)........43 G2
Douzains (47)........151 E2
la Douze (24)........137 G4
Douzens (11)........187 F3
Douville (24)........137 E4
Douzy (08)........24 C2
Doville (50)........12 C4
Doye (39)........103 G5
Doyet (03)........113 E3
Dozulé (14)........14 D4
Dracé (69)........116 B5
Draché (37)........94 D3
Dracy (89)........83 E2
Dracy-le-Fort (71)........101 G5
Dracy-lès-Couches (71)........101 E4
Dracy-Saint-Loup (71)........100 D3
Dragey-Ronthon (50)........35 G3
Draguignan (83)........177 H5
Draillant (74)........119 E3
Drain (49)........75 F4
Draix (04)........160 D6
Draize (08)........23 G2
Drambon (21)........86 B5
Dramelay (39)........117 F2
Drancy (93)........42 D3
Draveil (91)........42 D5
Drée (21)........85 F6
Drefféac (44)........74 A2
Drémil-Lafage (31)........169 G5
le Drennec (29)........31 E3
Dreuil-lès-Amiens (80)........7 G5
Dreuilhe (09)........186 A5
Dreux (28)........41 F4
Drevant (18)........97 H6
Dricourt (08)........23 H5
Driencourt (80)........8 C5
Drincham (59)........2 B3
Drocourt (62)........8 C1
Drocourt (78)........41 H2
Droisy (27)........40 D3
Droisy (74)........131 H1
Droiturier (03)........114 C5
Droizy (02)........22 B6
Drom (01)........117 F4
Dromesnil (80)........7 E6
Drosay (76)........17 E3
Drosnay (51)........46 C6
Droué (41)........61 F4
Droue-sur-Drouette (28)........41 G6
Drouges (35)........57 H5
Drouilly (51)........46 A4
Droupt-Saint-Basile (10)........66 A1
Droupt-Sainte-Marie (10)........66 A1
Drouville (54)........49 E5
Drouvin-le-Marais (62)........7 H1
Droux (87)........110 B5
Droyes (52)........67 E1
Drubec (14)........15 E4
Drucat (80)........6 D4
Drucourt (27)........15 G5
Drudas (31)........168 D4
Druelle (12)........154 B4
Drugeac (15)........140 B3
Druillat (01)........117 E5
Drulhe (12)........153 H3
Drulingen (67)........50 B3
Drumettaz-Clarafond (73)........131 H4
Drusenheim (67)........51 F4
Druval (14)........15 E4
Druy-Parigny (58)........99 F5
Druye (37)........78 C6
Druyes-les-Belles-
   Fontaines (89)........83 F4
Dry (45)........80 C2
Duault (22)........32 C5
Ducey (50)........35 H4
Duclair (76)........17 F6
Ducy-Sainte-Marguerite (14)........14 A4
Duerne (69)........129 G4
Duesme (21)........85 F3
Duffort (32)........183 G1
Dugny (93)........42 D3
Dugny-sur-Meuse (55)........47 F1

Duhort-Bachen (40)........166 B4
Duilhac-sous-
   Peyrepertuse (11)........187 F6
Duingt (74)........132 B2
Duisans (62)........8 A2
Dullin (73)........131 G5
Dumes (40)........165 H4
Dun (09)........186 A5
Dun-le-Palestel (23)........111 E4
Dun-le-Poëlier (36)........96 C1
Dun-les-Places (58)........100 A1
Dun-sur-Auron (18)........98 A4
Dun-sur-Grandry (58)........99 H3
Dun-sur-Meuse (55)........24 D5
Duneau (72)........60 D4
Dunes (82)........168 A2
Dunet (36)........110 C2
Dung (25)........88 C4
Dunière-sur-Eyrieux (07)........143 H6
Dunières (43)........143 E2
Dunkerque (59)........2 B1
Duntzenheim (67)........50 D4
Duran (32)........167 H5
Durance (47)........150 C5
Duranus (06)........179 E1
Duranville (27)........15 H5
Duras (47)........150 D1
Duravel (46)........152 A3
Durban (32)........167 H6
Durban-Corbières (11)........187 H5
Durban-sur-Arize (09)........185 F5
Durbans (46)........153 E1
Durcet (61)........38 C5
Durdat-Larequille (03)........112 D4
Dureil (72)........77 G2
Durenque (12)........171 F1
Durfort (09)........185 H2
Durfort (81)........186 B2
Durfort-et-Saint-Martin-
   de-Sossenac (30)........173 G2
Durfort-Lacapelette (82)........152 A6
Durlinsdorf (68)........89 F4
Durmenach (68)........89 F4
Durmignat (63)........113 E5
Durnes (25)........103 H2
Durningen (67)........50 D5
Durrenbach (67)........51 E3
Durrenentzen (68)........71 G4
Durstel (67)........50 B3
Durtal (49)........77 G3
Durtol (63)........127 E3
Dury (02)........21 H1
Dury (62)........8 C3
Dury (80)........7 G6
Dussac (24)........123 H6
Duttlenheim (67)........50 D6
Duvy (60)........21 F6
Duzey (55)........25 G5
Dye (89)........83 H1
Dyo (71)........115 F3

E

Eancé (35)........57 H5
Eaubonne (95)........42 C3
Eaucourt-sur-Somme (80)........6 D4
Eaunes (31)........185 F1
Eaux-Bonnes (64)........182 B5
Eaux-Puiseaux (10)........65 H5
Eauze (32)........167 E3
Ébaty (21)........101 G4
Ebblinghem (59)........2 B4
Eberbach-Seltz (67)........51 G2
Ebersheim (67)........71 G2
Ebersmunster (67)........71 G2
Ébersviller (57)........26 D4
Éblange (57)........26 D4
Ébouleau (02)........22 D2
Ébréon (16)........122 B1
Ébreuil (03)........113 G6
l'Écaille (08)........23 G4
Écaillon (59)........8 D2
Écalles-Alix (76)........17 F4
Écaquelon (27)........18 A5
Écardenville-
   la-Campagne (27)........40 C1
Écardenville-sur-Eure (27)........41 E1
Écausseville (50)........12 D3
Écauville (27)........40 D1
Eccica-Suarella (2A)........204 C6
Échalas (69)........129 H5
Échallat (16)........122 A3
Échallon (01)........117 H4
Échalot (21)........85 F4
Échandelys (63)........128 A5
Échannay (21)........101 F1
Écharcon (91)........42 D6
Échassières (03)........113 F5
Échauffour (61)........39 G5
Échavanne (70)........88 C2
Échay (25)........103 F3
Échebrune (17)........121 F4
l'Échelle (08)........23 H1
l'Échelle-Saint-Aurin (80)........21 E2
les Échelles (73)........131 G6
Échemines (10)........65 H2
Échemiré (49)........77 G4
Échenans (25)........88 B4
Échenans-sous-
   Mont-Vaudois (70)........88 B3
Échenay (52)........68 A2
Échenevex (01)........118 B3
Échenon (21)........102 B2
Échenoz-la-Méline (70)........87 G3
Échenoz-le-Sec (70)........87 G4
Échevannes (21)........86 A5
Échevannes (25)........103 H2
Échevis (26)........145 E3
Échevronne (21)........101 G2
Échigey (21)........102 A2
Échillais (17)........120 C2
Échilleuses (45)........63 G4
Echinghen (62)........1 F4
Échiré (79)........107 H3
Échirolles (38)........145 G3
Échouboulains (77)........64 C2
Échourgnac (24)........136 C3
Eckartswiller (67)........50 C4
Eckbolsheim (67)........51 E5
Eckwersheim (67)........51 E4
Éclaibes (59)........10 A3
Éclaires (51)........46 D2
Éclance (10)........67 E3
Éclans-Nenon (39)........102 D2
Éclaron-Braucourt-
   Sainte-Livière (52)........46 D6
Eclassan (07)........144 A3
Écleux (39)........103 E3
Éclimeux (62)........7 F1
Eclose (38)........130 D5
Éclusier-Vaux (80)........8 B5
Écluzelles (28)........41 F5
Écly (08)........23 F3
Écoche (42)........115 F5
Écoivres (62)........7 G2
École (73)........132 B4
École-Valentin (25)........87 F6
Écollemont (51)........46 D6
Écommoy (72)........78 B2
Écoquenéauville (50)........13 E4
Écorcei (61)........39 G5
Écorches (61)........39 E3
Écordal (08)........24 A3
Écorpain (72)........60 D5
Écos (27)........41 G1
Écot (25)........88 C4
Écot-la-Combe (52)........68 B4
Écotay-l'Olme (42)........128 D5
Écouché (61)........38 D4
Écouen (95)........42 D2
Écouflant (49)........76 D4
Écouis (27)........19 E5
Écourt-Saint-Quentin (62)........8 C3
Écoust-Saint-Mein (62)........8 C4

Écoviez (55)........25 F3
l'Écouvotte (25)........87 G6
Écoyeux (17)........121 F2
Ecquedecques (62)........2 C6
Ecques (62)........2 A5
Ecquevilly (78)........42 A3
Écrainville (76)........16 C4
Écrammeville (14)........13 G5
Écretteville-lès-Baons (76)........17 F4
Écretteville-sur-Mer (76)........16 D3
Écrille (39)........117 G2
Écromagny (70)........88 A1
Écrosnes (28)........62 C1
Écrouves (54)........48 A5
Ectot-l'Auber (76)........17 F4
Ectot-lès-Baons (76)........17 F4
Écueil (51)........45 E1
Écueillé (36)........96 B2
Écuélin (59)........10 A3
Écuelle (70)........86 C4
Écuelles (71)........102 A4
Écuelles (77)........64 B3
Écues (49)........76 D3
Écuillé (49)........76 D3
Écuires (62)........6 D1
Écuisses (71)........101 E5
Éculleville (50)........12 B1
Écully (69)........130 A3
Écuras (16)........123 E4
Écurat (17)........121 E2
Écurcey (25)........88 C5
Écurey-en-Verdunois (55)........25 E5
Écurie (62)........8 A2
Écury-le-Repos (51)........45 F4
Écury-sur-Coole (51)........45 H3
Écutigny (21)........101 F2
Écuvilly (60)........21 G2
Édern (29)........53 G2
Édon (16)........122 D5
les Éduts (17)........108 A6
Eecke (59)........2 C4
Effiat (63)........113 H6
Effincourt (52)........67 H2
Effry (02)........9 H6
Égat (66)........199 H4
Égleny (89)........83 E2
Égletons (19)........125 G6
Égligny (77)........64 D2
Eglingen (68)........89 E2
l'Église-aux-Bois (19)........125 E4
Église-Neuve-d'Issac (24)........136 D4
Égliseneuve-
   d'Entraigues (63)........126 C5
Égliseneuve-des-Liards (63)........127 H5
Égliseneuve-
   près-Billom (63)........127 G3
Églisolles (63)........128 C6
les Églisottes-
   et-Chalaures (33)........136 A3
Égly (91)........42 D6
Égreville (77)........64 B4
Égriselles-le-Bocage (89)........64 D5
Égry (45)........63 G5
Éguelshardt (57)........28 C6
Eguenigue (90)........88 D2
Éguilles (13)........192 D2
Éguilly (21)........84 D6
Éguilly-sous-Bois (10)........67 E4
Eguisheim (68)........71 F5
Éguzon-Chantôme (36)........111 E3
Éhuns (70)........87 H2
Eichhoffen (67)........71 F2
Eincheville (57)........49 F2
Einvaux (54)........69 H1
Einville-au-Jard (54)........49 E5
Eix (55)........25 F6
Élan (08)........24 B2
Élancourt (78)........42 A4
Elbach (68)........89 E3
Elbeuf (76)........18 C5
Elbeuf-en-Bray (76)........19 G4
Elbeuf-sur-Andelle (76)........19 E4
Elcourt (60)........20 B1
Élesmes (59)........10 A2
Életot (76)........16 D3
Éleu-dit-Leauwette (62)........8 B1
Élincourt (59)........9 E4
Élincourt-
   Sainte-Marguerite (60)........21 F3
Élise-Daucourt (51)........46 C2
Éliotcourt (76)........19 G3
Ellon (14)........13 H6
Elne (66)........201 F3
Éloise (74)........118 A5
Éloyes (88)........70 B4
Elsenheim (67)........71 G4
Elven (56)........55 H6
Elzange (57)........26 C3
Émagny (25)........87 E6
Émalleville (27)........40 D1
Émance (78)........62 C1
Émanville (27)........40 D1
Émanville (76)........17 F4
Embermesnil (54)........49 G6
Embres-
   et-Castelmaure (11)........187 H6
Embreville (80)........6 B5
Embrun (05)........161 E2
Embry (62)........7 E1
Émerainville (77)........43 F4
Émerchicourt (59)........8 D2
Émeringes (69)........116 B4
Éméville (60)........21 G6
Émiéville (14)........14 C5
Emlingen (68)........89 F3
Emmerin (59)........3 E5
Émondeville (50)........13 E3
Empeaux (31)........168 D6
Empuré (16)........108 C6
Empury (58)........83 H6
Encausse (32)........168 C4
Encausse-les-Thermes (31)........184 B4
Enchastrayes (04)........161 E4
Enchenberg (57)........28 B6
Encourtiech (09)........185 E5
Endoufielle (32)........168 C6
Énencourt-le-Sec (60)........19 H5
Énencourt-Léage (60)........19 H5
Enfonvelle (52)........69 E6
Engayrac (47)........151 G5
Engente (10)........67 E3
Engenville (45)........63 F4
Enghien-les-Bains (95)........42 D3
Engins (38)........145 F2
Englancourt (02)........9 H6
Englebelmer (80)........8 A4
Englefontaine (59)........9 G3
Englesqueville-
   la-Percée (14)........13 G4
Englos (59)........3 E5
Engomer (09)........184 D5
Enguinegatte (62)........2 B5
Engwiller (67)........50 D3
Ennemain (80)........8 C6
Ennery (57)........26 C4
Ennery (95)........42 C2
Ennetières-en-Weppes (59)........3 E5
Ennevelin (59)........3 F5
Ennezat (63)........127 F2
Ennordres (18)........81 G5
Enquin-les-Mines (62)........2 B5
Enquin-sur-Baillons (62)........1 G5
Ens (65)........196 D1
Ensigné (79)........108 A5
Ensisheim (68)........71 F6
Ensuès-la-Redonne (13)........191 H5
Entrages (04)........160 C6
Entraigues (38)........146 A3
Entraigues (63)........127 G2
Entraigues-
   sur-la-Sorgue (84)........175 E2

227

Entrains-sur-Nohain (58)....83 E5
Entrammes (53)....58 D5
Entrange (57)....26 B3
Entraunes (06)....161 G5
Entraygues-sur-Truyère (12)..154 C2
Entre-deux-Eaux (88)....70 D3
Entre-deux-Guiers (38)..131 G6
Entre-deux-Monts (39)..103 F6
Entrecasteaux (83)....193 G1
Entrechaux (84)....158 D5
Entremont (74)....132 C1
Entremont-le-Vieux (73)..131 H6
Entrepierres (04)....160 B5
Entrevaux (04)....178 B2
Entrevennes (04)....177 E2
Entrevernes (74)....132 B2
Entzheim (67)....50 D6
Enval (63)....127 E2
Enveitg (66)....199 G4
Envermeu (76)....17 H2
Envronville (76)....17 E4
Éourres (05)....159 H5
Eoux (31)....184 C2
Épagne (10)....66 D2
Épagne-Épagnette (80)....6 D4
Épagny (21)....21 H4
Épagny (74)....132 A1
Épagny (02)....21 G4
Épaignes (27)....15 E4
Épaney (14)....38 D3
Épannes (79)....107 G4
Éparcy (02)....10 B6
les Éparges (55)....47 H2
Épargnes (17)....120 D4
les Éparres (38)....130 D6
Épaumesnil (80)....6 D6
Épaux-Bézu (02)....44 B1
Épeautrolles (28)....62 A3
Épécamps (80)....7 F4
Épégard (27)....40 C1
Épehy (80)....8 D5
Épeigné-les-Bois (37)....95 G1
Épeigné-sur-Dême (37)....78 D3
Épénancourt (80)....21 F1
Épenède (16)....109 F6
Épenouse (25)....104 A1
Épenoy (25)....104 A2
Épense (51)....46 C3
Épercieux-Saint-Paul (42)..129 E3
Éperlecques (62)....2 A3
Épernay (51)....45 F2
Épernay-sous-Gevrey (21)..101 H2
Épernon (28)....41 G6
Éperrais (61)....60 D2
Épersy (73)....131 H3
Épertully (71)....101 G5
les Épesses (85)....92 C4
Épeugney (25)....103 G2
Épfig (67)....71 G2
Épiais-lès-Louvres (95)....43 E2
Épiais-Rhus (95)....42 B1
Épieds (02)....44 B2
Épieds (27)....41 F3
Épieds (49)....93 H2
Épieds-en-Beauce (45)....80 B2
Épierre (73)....132 C5
Épiez-sur-Chiers (54)....25 F4
Épiez-sur-Meuse (55)....47 H6
Épinac (71)....101 E3
Épinal (88)....70 A3
Épinay (27)....40 A2
Épinay-Champlâtreux (95)..42 D2
l'Épinay-le-Comte (61)....58 C1
Épinay-sous-Sénart (91)....43 E5
Épinay-sur-Duclair (76)....17 F5
Épinay-sur-Odon (14)....38 A2
Épinay-sur-Orge (91)....42 D5
Épinay-sur-Seine (93)....42 D3
l'Épine (05)....159 G3
l'Épine (51)....46 A3
l'Épine-aux-Bois (02)....44 C3
Épineau-les-Voves (89)....65 F6
Épineu-le-Chevreuil (72)..59 G5
Épineuil (89)....84 A1
Épineuil-le-Fleuriel (18)..112 H2? H2
Épineuse (60)....20 D5
Épineux-le-Seguin (53)....59 F6
Épiniac (35)....35 F5
Épinonville (55)....24 D6
Épinouze (26)....144 B1
Épinoy (62)....8 D3
Épiry (58)....99 H2
Épisy (77)....64 B3
Épizon (52)....68 B2
Éplessier (80)....20 A1
Éply (54)....48 C4
Époisses (21)....84 B4
Épône (78)....41 H3
Épothémont (10)....67 E2
Épouville (76)....14 C4
Époye (51)....23 F5
Eppe-Sauvage (59)....10 B4
Eppes (02)....22 C3
Eppeville (80)....21 G1
Épping (57)....28 B5
Épretot (76)....15 G1
Épreville (76)....14 D3
Épreville-en-Lieuvin (27)..15 H4
Épreville-en-Roumois (27)..18 A5
Épreville-
   près-le-Neubourg (27)....40 C1
Épron (14)....14 B4
Eps (62)....7 G1
Épuisay (41)....79 F1
Équancourt (80)....8 C5
Équemauville (14)....16 B6
Équennes-Éramecourt (80)..20 A2
Équeurdreville-
   Hainneville (50)....12 C2
Équevilley (70)....87 G2
Équevillon (39)....103 F5
Équihen-Plage (62)....1 F4
Équilly (50)....35 H2
Équirre (62)....7 G1
Éragny (95)....42 B2
Éragny-sur-Epte (60)....19 G5
Eraines (14)....38 D2
Éraville (16)....122 A4
Erbajolo (2B)....205 F2
Erbéviller-sur-Amezule (54)..49 E4
Erbray (44)....75 E1
Erbrée (35)....58 A4
Ercé (09)....185 G6
Ercé-en-Lamée (35)....57 F5
Ercé-près-Liffré (35)....57 G1
Erceville (45)....63 E4
Erches (80)....21 E2
Erchin (59)....8 D3
Erching (57)....28 B5
Erckartswiller (67)....50 C3
Ercourt (80)....6 C4
Ercuis (60)....20 C6
Erdeven (56)....54 C6
Éréac (22)....56 B1
Ergersheim (67)....50 D6
Ergnies (80)....7 F4
Ergny (62)....1 H5
Ergué-Gabéric (29)....53 G3
Érin (62)....7 F1
Éringes (21)....84 D4
Éringhem (59)....2 A3
Érize-la-Brûlée (55)....47 F4
Érize-la-Petite (55)....47 F3
Érize-Saint-Dizier (55)....47 F4
Erlon (02)....22 C2
Erloy (02)....9 G5
Ermenonville (60)....43 F1
Ermenonville-la-Grande (28)..62 A3
Ermenonville-la-Petite (28)..62 A3
Ermenouville (76)....17 F3
Ermont (95)....42 C2
Ernée (53)....58 C3
Ernemont-Boutavent (60)....19 H3
Ernemont-la-Villette (76)..19 G4
Ernemont-sur-Buchy (76)....19 E3
Ernes (14)....38 D2
Ernestviller (57)....49 H1

Erneville-aux-Bois (55)....47 G5
Ernolsheim-Bruche (67)....50 D6
Ernolsheim-
   lès-Saverne (67)....50 C4
Erny-Saint-Julien (62)....2 B5
Érôme (26)....144 A3
Érondelle (80)....6 D4
Érone (2B)....205 F1
Éroudeville (50)....12 D3
Erp (09)....185 G5
Erquery (60)....20 D4
Erquinghem-le-Sec (59)....3 E5
Erquinghem-Lys (59)....3 E4
Erquinvillers (60)....20 D4
Erquy (22)....34 A3
Err (66)....199 H4
Erre (59)....9 E2
Errevet (70)....88 C2
Errouville (54)....26 A3
Ersa (2B)....203 F1
Erstein (67)....71 H1
Erstroff (57)....49 G2
Ervauville (45)....64 C5
Ervillers (62)....8 B3
Ervy-le-Châtel (10)....65 H5
Esbareich (65)....183 H5
Esbarres (21)....102 B2
Esbly (77)....43 F3
Esboz-Brest (70)....88 A1
Escala (65)....183 G4
Escalans (40)....166 D2
l'Escale (04)....160 B6
Escales (11)....187 G3
Escalles (62)....1 F2
Escalquens (31)....169 G6
Escames (60)....19 H3
Escamps (46)....153 E4
Escamps (89)....83 F2
Escandolières (12)....154 A3
Escanecrabe (31)....184 C3
Escardes (51)....44 C5
l'Escarène (06)....195 G2
Escarmain (59)....9 F3
Escassefort (47)....150 C2
Escatalens (82)....168 D2
Escaudain (59)....9 E2
Escaudes (33)....149 H4
Escaudœuvres (59)....8 D3
Escaunets (65)....182 D2
Escautpont (59)....9 G2
Escazeaux (82)....168 C3
Eschau (67)....51 E6
Eschbach (67)....51 E3
Eschbach-au-Val (68)....71 E5
Eschbourg (67)....50 C3
Eschentzwiller (68)....89 G2
Escherange (57)....26 B3
Esches (60)....20 B6
Eschwiller (67)....50 B3
Esclagne (09)....186 A5
Esclainvillers (80)....20 C2
Esclandes (48)....156 A1
Esclassan-Labastide (32)..184 A1
Esclauzels (46)....152 D4
Esclavelles (76)....19 E2
Esclavolles-Lurey (51)....65 H1
Escles (88)....69 G4
Escles-Saint-Pierre (60)..19 H1
Esclottes (47)....150 C1
Escobecques (59)....3 E5
Escœuilles (62)....1 H4
Escoire (24)....137 G2
Escolives-
   Sainte-Camille (89)..83 G3
Escombres-
   et-le-Chesnois (08)....24 D2
Escondeaux (65)....183 F2
Esconnets (65)....183 F4
Escorailles (15)....140 A3
Escornebœuf (32)....168 B5
Escorpain (28)....41 E5
Escos (64)....165 G6
Escosse (09)....185 G4
Escot (64)....182 A4
Escots (65)....183 F4
Escou (64)....182 A3
Escoubès (64)....182 C1
Escoubès-Pouts (65)....183 E4
Escoulis (31)....184 D4
Escouloubre (11)....200 A2
Escource (40)....148 C5
Escoussans (33)....149 H1
Escoussens (81)....170 C6
Escout (64)....182 A3
Escoutoux (63)....128 A3
Escoville (14)....14 C4
Escragnolles (06)....178 B4
Escrennes (45)....63 F5
Escrignelles (45)....82 B2
Escroux (81)....171 F4
Escueillens-et-Saint-Just-
   de-Bélengard (11)....186 C4
Escurès (65)....166 C6
Escurolles (03)....113 H5
Eslettes (76)....17 G5
Esley (88)....69 F3
Eslourenties-Daban (64)..182 D2
Esmans (77)....64 C3
Esmery-Hallon (80)....21 G2
Esmoulières (70)....88 B1
Esmoulins (70)....86 C5
Esnandes (17)....106 D4
Esnans (25)....87 H5
Esnes (59)....9 E4
Esnes-en-Argonne (55)....24 D6
Esnon (89)....65 F6
Esnouveaux (52)....68 B4
Espagnac (19)....139 F2
Espagnac-
   Sainte-Eulalie (46)....153 F2
Espalais (82)....168 B1
Espalem (43)....141 F1
Espalion (12)....154 D3
Espaly-Saint-Marcel (43)..142 C4
Espanès (31)....185 G1
Espaon (32)....184 C1
Esparron (05)....160 A3
Esparron (31)....184 B2
Esparron (83)....193 E1
Esparron-de-Verdon (04)..177 E3
Esparros (65)....183 G5
Esparsac (82)....168 B2
Espartignac (19)....124 D6
Espas (32)....167 E3
Espaubourg (60)....19 H4
Espèche (65)....183 F4
Espéchède (64)....182 C2
Espédaillac (46)....153 E2
Espelette (64)....180 C1
Espeluche (26)....158 B3
Espenel (26)....159 E1
Espérausses (81)....171 E5
Espéraza (11)....186 D5
Esperce (31)....185 F2
Espère (46)....152 C3
Espès-Undurein (64)....181 G2
Espeyrac (12)....154 C2
Espeyroux (46)....139 F6
Espezel (11)....199 H1
Espiells (47)....150 D4
Espiens (47)....150 D6
Espiet (33)....135 G6
Espinas (82)....153 F6
Espinasse (15)....141 E5
Espinasse (63)....112 D6
Espinasse-Vozelle (03)....113 H5
Espinasses (05)....160 C3
Espinchal (63)....140 D2
Espira-de-Conflent (66)..199 G4
Espira-de-l'Agly (66)....201 E1
Espirat (63)....127 G3
Espiute (64)....181 F1
Esplantas (43)....142 A5
Esplas (09)....185 G3
Esplas-de-Sérou (09)....185 F5
Espoey (64)....182 C2
Espondeilhan (34)....188 C1
Esprels (70)....87 H3
Esquay-Notre-Dame (14)..14 A5
Esquay-sur-Seulles (14)....14 A4
Esquéhéries (02)....9 G5

Esquelbecq (59)....2 C3
Esquennoy (60)....20 C2
Esquerchin (59)....8 C1
Esquerdes (62)....2 A4
Esquièze-Sère (65)....183 E6
Esquiule (64)....181 H2
les Essards (16)....136 B2
les Essards (17)....120 D2
les Essards (37)....94 A1
les Essards-
   Taignevaux (39)....102 C4
Essarois (21)....85 E2
Essars (62)....2 D5
les Essarts (27)....40 D3
les Essarts (41)....79 E2
les Essarts (85)....91 H3
les Essarts-le-Roi (78)....42 A4
les Essarts-le-Vicomte (51)..44 D5
les Essarts-
   lès-Sézanne (51)....44 D5
Essay (61)....60 C1
Esse (16)....109 G6
Essé (35)....57 H4
Essegney (88)....69 G2
les Esseintes (33)....150 A2
Essert (90)....88 C3
Essert-Romand (74)....119 F5
Essertaux (80)....20 B1
Essertenne (71)....101 E6
Essertenne-et-Cecey (70)..86 C5
Essertines-
   en-Châtelneuf (42)....128 D4
Essertines-en-Donzy (42)..129 F3
Esserts-Blay (73)....132 D4
Esserval-Combe (39)....103 G5
Esserval-Tartre (39)....103 G5
Essey (21)....101 E1
Essey-et-Maizerais (54)....48 A3
Essey-la-Côte (54)....69 H1
Essey-les-Nancy (54)....48 D5
Essia (39)....117 F1
Essigny-le-Grand (02)....22 A1
Essigny-le-Petit (02)....9 E6
Essises (02)....44 B3
Essômes-sur-Marne (02)....44 B2
Esson (14)....38 B2
Essoyes (10)....67 E5
les Estables (43)....143 E5
Estables (48)....156 A1
Establet (26)....159 E3
Estadens (31)....184 C4
Estagel (66)....201 E1
Estaing (12)....154 C2
Estaing (65)....183 E6
Estaires (59)....3 E5
Estal (46)....139 F5
Estampes (32)....183 G2
Estampures (65)....183 F2
Estancarbon (31)....184 B4
Estandeuil (63)....127 H4
Estang (32)....166 D3
Estarvielle (65)....197 F1
Estavar (66)....199 H4
Esteil (63)....127 G6
Esténos (31)....184 A5
Estensan (65)....197 E1
Estérençuby (64)....181 E5
Esternay (51)....44 C5
Esterre (65)....183 E6
Estevelles (62)....3 E6
Estéziargues (30)....174 C2
Estialescq (64)....182 A2
Estibeaux (40)....165 F5
Estigarde (40)....166 C1
Estillac (47)....151 E6
Estipouy (32)....183 G1
Estirac (65)....166 D6
Estissac (10)....65 H3
Estivals (19)....138 C4
Estivareilles (03)....112 D3
Estivareilles (42)....128 D6
Estivaux (19)....138 C1
Estoher (66)....199 G4
Estos (64)....182 A3
Estoublon (04)....177 F2
Estouches (91)....63 F4
Estourmel (59)....9 E4
Estouteville-Écalles (76)..19 E3
Estouy (45)....63 G5
Estrablin (38)....130 B5
Estramiac (32)....168 B3
Estrebay (08)....10 B6
Estrébœuf (80)....6 C3
l'Estréchure (30)....173 F1
Estrée (62)....1 G6
Estrée-Blanche (62)....2 B5
Estrée-Cauchy (62)....8 A1
Estrée-Wamin (62)....7 G2
Estréelles (62)....1 G6
Estrées (02)....8 D6
Estrées (59)....8 D2
Estrées-Deniécourt (80)....21 E1
Estrées-la-Campagne (14)..38 D2
Estrées-lès-Crécy (80)....7 E3
Estrées-Mons (80)....8 C6
Estrées-Saint-Denis (60)..21 E4
Estrées-sur-Noye (80)....20 C1
Estrennes (88)....69 F2
Estreux (59)....9 G2
Estrun (59)....9 E3
Estry (14)....37 H3
Esves-le-Moutier (37)....95 F3
Esvres (37)....79 E6
Eswars (59)....9 E3
Étable (73)....132 B4
Étables (07)....143 H3
Étables-sur-Mer (22)....33 H3
Étagnac (16)....123 F2
Étaimpuis (76)....17 H4
Étain (55)....25 G6
Étaing (62)....8 C3
Étainhus (76)....15 G1
Étais (21)....84 D3
Étais-la-Sauvin (89)....83 E4
Étalans (25)....103 H2
Étalante (21)....85 F3
Étalle (08)....23 H2
Étalleville (76)....17 F4
Étalon (80)....21 F2
Étalondes (76)....6 B5
Étampes (91)....63 F3
Étampes-sur-Marne (02)....44 B2
l'Étang-Bertrand (50)....12 C4
l'Étang-la-Ville (78)....42 B3
Étang-sur-Arroux (71)....100 C4
l'Étang-Vergy (21)....101 G2
les Étangs (57)....26 D5
Étaples (62)....1 F6
Étaule (89)....84 A4
Étaules (21)....85 H6
Étaules (17)....120 B3
Étauliers (33)....135 E2
Étaux (74)....118 D6
Étaves-et-Bocquiaux (02)..9 F5
Étavigny (60)....43 G1
Etcharry (64)....181 F1
Etchebar (64)....181 G3
Éteignières (08)....10 D5
Éteimbes (68)....88 D2
Étel (56)....54 C6
Ételfay (80)....20 D2
Étercy (74)....132 A2
Éternoz (25)....103 G3
Éterpigny (62)....8 C3
Éterpigny (80)....8 C6
Éterville (14)....14 B5
Étévaux (21)....86 B5
Eth (59)....9 G2
Étienville (50)....12 D4
Étigny (89)....65 E4
les Étilleux (28)....61 E3
Étinehem (80)....8 A6
Étival (39)....117 G2
Étival-Clairefontaine (88)..70 C2
Étival-lès-le-Mans (72)....60 A6
Étivey (89)....84 B4
Étobon (70)....88 C3
Étoges (51)....45 E3
l'Étoile (39)....102 D6
l'Étoile (80)....7 E5

l'Étoile-Saint-Cyrice (05)..159 G4
Étoile-sur-Rhône (26)....144 B6
Éton (55)....25 G5
Étormay (21)....85 E4
Étouars (24)....123 E4
Étourvy (10)....66 C6
Étoutteville (76)....17 E4
Étouvans (25)....88 C4
Étouvelles (02)....22 C3
Étouvy (14)....37 H3
Étrabonne (25)....103 E1
Étrappe (25)....88 B4
l'Étrat (42)....129 F5
Étray (25)....104 A2
Étréaupont (02)....10 A6
Étréchet (36)....96 D5
Étréchy (18)....98 B2
Étréchy (51)....45 E3
Étréchy (91)....63 F1
Étréham (14)....13 H5
Étreillers (02)....21 H1
Étréjust (80)....6 D6
Étrelles (35)....58 A5
Étrelles-et-la-
   Montbleuse (70)....87 E5
Étrelles-sur-Aube (10)....65 H1
Étrembières (74)....118 C5
Étrépagny (27)....19 F5
Étrepigney (39)....102 D2
Étrépigny (08)....24 B2
Étrépilly (77)....43 G2
Étrepy (51)....46 C4
Étretat (76)....16 B3
Étreux (02)....9 G5
Étreval (54)....69 E1
Étréville (27)....18 A5
Étrez (01)....116 D3
Étriac (16)....122 A5
Étriché (49)....77 E2
Étricourt-Manancourt (80)..8 C5
Étrigny (71)....116 B1
Étrochey (21)....85 E1
Étrœungt (59)....10 A4
Étroussat (03)....113 G5
Étrun (62)....8 B2
Étsaut (64)....182 A5
Ettendorf (67)....50 D3
Etting (57)....28 A5
Étueffont (90)....88 D2
Étupes (25)....88 C4
Éturqueraye (27)....18 A5
Étusson (79)....93 E3
Étuz (70)....87 F5
Etzling (57)....27 G4
Eu (76)....6 B4
Euffigneix (52)....67 H4
Eugénie-les-Bains (40)....166 B4
Euilly-et-Lombut (08)....24 D2
Eulmont (54)....48 D4
Eup (31)....184 A5
Eurre (26)....144 B6
Eurville-Bienville (52)....46 D6
Eus (66)....199 G3
Euvezin (54)....48 A3
Euville (55)....47 H4
Euvy (51)....45 F5
Evaillé (72)....78 D1
Évans (39)....103 E1
Évaux-et-Ménil (88)....69 G2
Évaux-les-Bains (23)....112 C5
Ève (60)....43 F2
Évecquemont (78)....42 A2
Évenos (83)....193 E5
Évergnicourt (02)....23 E4
Everly (77)....64 D2
Évette-Salbert (90)....88 C2
Éveux (69)....129 H3
Évian-les-Bains (74)....119 F3
Évigny (08)....24 A1
Évillers (25)....103 H3
Évin-Malmaison (62)....8 C1
Évires (74)....118 D6
Évisa (2A)....204 C4
Évosges (01)....131 E1
Évran (22)....34 D6
Évrange (57)....26 B2
Évrecy (14)....14 A5
Èvres (55)....47 E2
Évreux (27)....40 D2
Évricourt (60)....21 F3
Évriguet (56)....56 A2
Évron (53)....59 E4
Évry (89)....65 F4
Évry (91)....42 D6
Évry-Grégy-sur-Yerre (77)..43 F5
Excenevex (74)....118 D3
Excideuil (24)....137 H1
Exermont (08)....24 C5
Exideuil (16)....123 F3
Exincourt (25)....88 C4
Exireuil (79)....108 B3
Exmes (61)....39 F4
Exoudun (79)....108 B3
Expiremont (17)....135 G1
Eybens (38)....145 G2
Eybouleuf (87)....124 C2
Eyburie (19)....124 D6
Eycheil (09)....185 F5
Eydoche (38)....130 D6
Eygalayes (26)....159 F4
Eygaliers (26)....159 E4
Eygalières (13)....175 E3
Eygliers (05)....161 F1
Eygluy-Escoulin (26)....144 C6
Eyguians (05)....159 H4
Eyguières (13)....175 E4
Eygurande (19)....126 B4
Eygurande-
   et-Gardedeuil (24)....136 B3
Eyjeaux (87)....124 C3
Eyliac (24)....137 G3
Eymet (24)....150 D1
Eymeux (26)....144 C3
Eymoutiers (87)....125 E3
Eyne (66)....199 G5
Eynesse (33)....136 B5
Eyragues (13)....174 D3
Eyrans (33)....135 F2
Eyrein (19)....139 F1
Eyres-Moncube (40)....165 H4
Eyroles (26)....159 E3
Eysines (33)....135 E5
Eysson (25)....104 B1
Eysus (64)....182 A4
Eyvirat (24)....137 F1
Eywiller (67)....50 B3
Eyzahut (26)....158 C2
Eyzerac (24)....137 F2
les Eyzies-de-
   Tayac-Sireuil (24)....137 H5
Eyzin-Pinet (38)....130 B5
Ézanville (95)....42 D2
Èze (06)....195 F2
Ézy-sur-Eure (27)....41 E4

F

Fa (11)....186 D6
Fabas (09)....185 E4
Fabas (31)....184 D3
Fabas (82)....169 E2
Fabras (07)....157 F1
Fabrègues (34)....173 F6
Fabrezan (11)....187 G4
Faches-Thumesnil (59)....3 F5
Fâchin (58)....100 B3
la Fage-Montivernoux (48)..155 H1
la Fage-Saint-Julien (48)..141 H6
le Faget (31)....170 A6
Faget-Abbatial (32)....168 A5
Fagnières (51)....45 H3
Fagnon (08)....24 A1

Fahy-lès-Autrey (70)....86 C4
Failly (57)....26 C5
Faimbe (25)....88 B4
Fain-lès-Montbard (21)....84 D4
Fain-lès-Moutiers (21)....84 C4
Fains (27)....41 F2
Fains-la-Folie (28)....62 C4
Fains-Véel (55)....47 E4
Faissault (08)....23 H3
Fajac-en-Val (11)....187 E4
Fajac-la-Relenque (11)....186 A3
Fajoles (46)....138 B6
Fajolles (82)....168 C2
la Fajolle (11)....199 G1
Falaise (08)....24 B5
Falaise (14)....38 D3
Falck (57)....27 E4
Faleyras (33)....135 G6
Falga (31)....186 B1
le Falgoux (15)....140 C3
Falicon (06)....195 F2
Falkwiller (68)....89 E2
Fallencourt (76)....6 C6
Fallerans (25)....104 A2
Falleron (85)....91 E2
Falletans (39)....102 D2
la Faloise (80)....20 C2
Fals (47)....168 A1
Falvy (80)....21 F1
Famars (59)....9 F2
Famechon (62)....7 H4
Famechon (80)....20 A2
Fameck (57)....26 B4
Familly (14)....39 G3
Fampoux (62)....8 B2
Fanjeaux (11)....186 C3
Fanlac (24)....137 H3
le Faou (29)....31 F6
le Faouët (22)....33 F3
le Faouët (56)....54 B3
Faramans (01)....130 C2
Faramans (38)....130 C6
Farbus (62)....8 B2
Farceaux (27)....19 F5
la Fare-en-Champsaur (05)..160 B2
la Fare-les-Oliviers (13)..191 H3
Farébersviller (57)....49 G1
Fareins (01)....116 C6
Faremoutiers (77)....43 H4
les Farges (24)....138 A3
Farges-Allichamps (18)....97 G5
Farges-en-Septaine (18)....98 A3
Farges-lès-Chalon (71)....101 G5
Farges-lès-Mâcon (71)....116 B2
Fargues (33)....149 H2
Fargues (40)....166 A4
Fargues (46)....152 C5
Fargues-Saint-Hilaire (33)..135 F5
Fargues-sur-Ourbise (47)..150 C5
la Farlède (83)....193 F5
Farnay (42)....129 G5
Farschviller (57)....49 G1
Fatines (72)....60 B5
Fatouville-Grestain (27)..16 C6
le Fau (15)....140 C3
Fau-de-Peyre (48)....155 H1
Fauch (81)....170 C3
Faucigny (74)....118 D5
Faucogney-et-la-Mer (70)..88 A1
Faucompierre (88)....70 B4
Faucon (84)....158 D5
Faucon-
   de-Barcelonnette (04)..161 F3
Faucon-du-Caire (04)....160 B4
Faucoucourt (02)....22 B3
Faudoas (82)....168 C3
le Fauga (31)....185 F1
Faugères (07)....157 F2
Faugères (34)....172 B5
Fauguernon (14)....15 F5
Fauguerolles (47)....150 C4
Fauillet (47)....150 C3
le Faulq (14)....15 F5
Faumont (59)....8 D1
Fauquembergues (62)....2 A5
la Faurie (05)....159 H2
Faurilles (24)....137 F6
Fauroux (82)....151 H5
Faussergues (81)....171 E1
la Faute-sur-Mer (85)....106 B3
Fauverney (21)....102 A1
Fauville (27)....41 E2
Fauville-en-Caux (76)....17 E3
Faux (08)....23 H4
Faux (24)....137 E5
Faux-Fresnay (51)....45 E5
Faux-la-Montagne (23)....125 F3
Faux-Mazuras (23)....125 E2
Faux-Vésigneul (51)....45 H4
Faux-Villecerf (10)....65 G3
Favalello (2B)....205 F2
Favars (19)....138 D2
Faveraye-Mâchelles (49)..93 F1
Faverdines (18)....112 B1
Faverelles (45)....82 C4
Faverges (74)....132 C2
Faverges-de-la-Tour (38)..131 E4
Faverney (70)....87 F2
Faverois (90)....88 D3
Faverolles (02)....21 H4
Faverolles (15)....141 F5
Faverolles (28)....41 F5
Faverolles (36)....96 A4
Faverolles (52)....85 H1
Faverolles (61)....38 C5
Faverolles (80)....21 E2
Faverolles-et-Coëmy (51)..22 D6
Faverolles-la-Campagne (27)..40 D2
Faverolles-lès-Lucey (21)..85 G2
Faverolles-sur-Cher (41)..79 G6
la Favière (39)....103 G5
Favières (28)....61 H1
Favières (54)....69 E2
Favières (77)....43 G4
Favières (80)....6 C3
Favresse (51)....46 C4
Favreuil (62)....8 B4
Favrieux (78)....41 G3
le Favril (27)....15 G5
le Favril (28)....61 F2
le Favril (59)....9 G4
Fay (61)....39 G5
le Fay (71)....117 E1
Fay (72)....60 A6
Fay (80)....21 E1
Fay-aux-Loges (45)....81 F1
Fay-de-Bretagne (44)....74 B3
Fay-en-Montagne (39)....103 E5
Fay-le-Clos (26)....144 B2
Fay-les-Étangs (60)....19 H6
Faÿ-lès-Nemours (77)....64 A3
le Fay-Saint-Quentin (60)..20 C4
Fay-sur-Lignon (43)....143 F4
Faycelles (46)....153 G2
Faye (41)....79 G3
Faye-d'Anjou (49)....77 F6
Faye-l'Abbesse (79)....93 E4
Faye-la-Vineuse (37)....94 C3
Faye-sur-Ardin (79)....107 G2
Fayence (83)....178 B5
Fayet (02)....8 D6
Fayet (12)....171 H2
Fayet-le-Château (63)....127 H4
Fayet-Ronaye (63)....128 A6
Fayl-Billot (52)....86 D2
Faymont (70)....88 B3
Faymoreau (85)....107 F2
Fays (52)....67 F2
Fays (88)....70 B3
Fays-la-Chapelle (10)....66 A4

Fayssac (81)....170 B2
Féas (64)....181 H3
Febvin-Palfart (62)....2 B5
Fécamp (76)....16 C3
Féchain (59)....8 D3
Fèche-l'Église (90)....88 D4
Fécocourt (54)....69 F2
Fédry (70)....87 F3
Fégréac (44)....74 A1
Feigères (74)....118 C6
Feignies (59)....10 A2
Feillens (01)....116 B3
Feings (61)....60 D1
Feings (41)....80 A5
Feins (35)....57 F1
Feins-en-Gâtinais (45)....82 B2
Feissons-sur-Isère (73)....132 D4
Feissons-sur-Salins (73)..132 D5
le Fel (12)....154 C2
Fel (61)....39 F4
Felce (2B)....205 G2
Feldbach (68)....89 F4
Feldkirch (68)....71 F6
Feliceto (2B)....202 D5
Félines (07)....143 H1
Félines (43)....142 B2
Félines-Minervois (34)....187 F2
Félines-sur-Rimandoule (26)..158 C2
Félines-Termenès (11)....187 F5
Felleries (59)....10 A4
Fellering (68)....88 D1
Felletin (23)....125 H2
Felluns (66)....200 C2
Felon (90)....88 D2
Felzins (46)....153 H2
Fenain (59)....9 E2
Fénay (21)....101 H1
Fendeille (11)....186 B3
Fénery (79)....93 F6
Fénétrange (57)....49 H3
Feneu (49)....76 D3
Féneyrols (82)....153 F6
Fénols (81)....170 C3
le Fenouiller (85)....90 D4
Fenouillet (31)....169 F5
Fenouillet (66)....200 B2
Fenouillet-du-Razès (11)..186 C4
Fépin (08)....11 E5
Fercé (44)....57 F6
Fercé-sur-Sarthe (72)....59 H6
Ferdrupt (88)....70 C6
la Fère (02)....22 A2
Fère-Champenoise (51)....45 F5
Fère-en-Tardenois (02)....44 A1
Fèrebrianges (51)....45 E4
la Férée (08)....23 G1
Férel (56)....73 F2
Ferfay (62)....2 C6
Féricy (77)....64 B2
Férin (59)....8 D2
Fermanville (50)....12 D1
la Fermeté (58)....99 E4
Ferney-Voltaire (01)....118 B4
Fernoël (63)....126 B3
Férolles (45)....81 F2
Férolles-Attilly (77)....43 E5
Féron (59)....10 A4
Ferques (62)....1 G3
Ferrals-les-Corbières (11)..187 G4
Ferrals-les-Montagnes (34)..187 G1
Ferran (11)....186 C4
Ferrassières (26)....159 F5
le Ferré (35)....35 H5
les Ferres (06)....195 E2
Ferrensac (47)....151 F2
Ferrere (65)....183 H5
Ferrette (68)....89 F4
Ferreux-Quincey (10)....65 G2
Ferrière-et-Lafolie (52)....67 G2
la Ferrière (22)....55 H2
la Ferrière (37)....79 E3
la Ferrière (38)....146 A1
la Ferrière-Airoux (86)....109 F3
la Ferrière-au-Doyen (61)..39 H5
la Ferrière-aux-Étangs (61)..38 B5
la Ferrière-Béchet (61)....39 F6
la Ferrière-Bochard (61)..59 H2
la Ferrière-Duval (14)....38 A3
la Ferrière-en-Parthenay (79)..93 G6
la Ferrière-Harang (14)....37 H2
la Ferrière-
   sur-Risle (27)....40 B2
Ferrières (17)....107 E5
Ferrières (50)....37 F5
Ferrières (54)....69 F1
Ferrières (60)....21 E4
Ferrières (65)....183 E4
Ferrières (80)....7 F6
Ferrières (81)....171 F4
Ferrières-en-Bray (76)....19 G4
Ferrières-en-Brie (77)....43 F4
Ferrières-Haut-Clocher (27)..40 C2
Ferrières-la-Verrerie (61)..39 G6
Ferrières-le-Lac (25)....88 C6
Ferrières-les-Bois (25)....103 E1
Ferrières-lès-Ray (70)....87 E3
Ferrières-lès-Scey (70)....87 F3
Ferrières-les-Verreries (34)..173 F3
Ferrières-Poussarou (34)..187 H1
Ferrières-Saint-Hilaire (27)..40 A2
Ferrières-Saint-Mary (15)..141 F3
Ferrières-sur-Ariège (09)..185 H6
Ferrières-sur-Sichon (03)..114 B6
Ferrussac (43)....142 A3
Fertans (25)....103 G3
la Ferté (39)....102 C4
Ferté-Hauterive (03)....114 A3
la Ferté-Imbault (41)....80 D6
la Ferté-Loupière (89)....83 E1
la Ferté-Macé (61)....38 C6
la Ferté-Milon (02)....43 H1
la Ferté-Saint-Aubin (45)..81 E3
la Ferté-Saint-Cyr (41)....80 C3
la Ferté-Saint-Samson (76)..19 F3
la Ferté-sous-Jouarre (77)..43 H3
la Ferté-Vidame (28)....40 C6
la Ferté-Villeneuil (28)....61 H5
Fertrève (58)....99 G4
Fervaches (50)....37 F2
Fervaques (14)....39 F2
Fescamps (80)....21 E2
Fesches-le-Châtel (25)....88 C4
Fesmy-le-Sart (02)....9 G4
Fesques (76)....19 F1
Fessanvilliers-
   Mattanvilliers (28)....40 D5
Fessenheim (68)....71 G6
Fessenheim-le-Bas (67)....50 D5
les Fessey (70)....88 A1
Fessevillers (25)....88 C6
Festalemps (24)....136 C2
Festes-et-Saint-André (11)..186 C5
Festieux (02)....22 D3
Festigny (51)....44 D2
Festigny (89)....83 F4
Festubert (62)....3 E5
Féternes (74)....119 E3
Fétigny (39)....117 F2
Feucherolles (78)....42 B3
Feuchy (62)....8 B2
Feugarolles (47)....150 D5

Feugères (50)....12 D6
Feuges (10)....66 B2
Feuguerolles (27)....40 D1
Feuguerolles-Bully (14)....14 A5
Feuilla (11)....188 A6
Feuillade (16)....122 D4
la Feuillade (24)....138 C3
la Feuillée (29)....31 H5
Feuillères (80)....8 B5
la Feuillie (50)....12 D5
la Feuillie (76)....19 F4
Feule (25)....88 C5
Feuquières (60)....19 H2
Feuquières-en-Vimeu (80)..6 C4
Feurs (42)....129 E3
Feusines (36)....111 H2
Feux (18)....98 B1
Fèves (57)....26 B5
Féy (57)....26 B6
Fey-en-Haye (54)....48 B3
Feyt (19)....126 B3
Feytiat (87)....124 B3
Feyzin (69)....130 A4
Fiac (81)....170 A4
Ficaja (2B)....203 G6
Ficheux (62)....8 B3
Fichous-Riumayou (64)....166 A6
le Fidelaire (27)....40 C3
le Fied (39)....103 E5
le Fief-Sauvin (49)....75 G5
Fieffes-Montrelet (80)....7 F4
Fiefs (62)....2 C6
Fiennes (62)....1 G3
Fienvillers (80)....7 F4
Fierville-Bray (14)....38 D1
Fierville-les-Mines (50)....12 C4
Fierville-les-Parcs (14)....15 F4
le Fieu (33)....136 A3
Fieulaine (02)....9 F6
Fieux (47)....167 F1
Figanières (83)....177 H5
Figari (2A)....207 F4
Figarol (31)....184 C4
Fignévelle (88)....69 E6
Fignières (80)....20 D2
Filain (02)....22 B4
Filain (70)....87 G4
Fillé (72)....78 A1
Fillières (54)....25 H4
Fillinges (74)....118 D5
Fillols (66)....199 G4
Filstroff (57)....27 E3
Fiménil (88)....70 B4
Finestret (66)....199 G3
Finhan (82)....168 D3
les Fins (25)....104 C2
Fins (80)....8 C5
Fiquefleur-Équainville (27)..16 B6
Firbeix (24)....123 H4
Firfol (14)....15 F5
Firmi (12)....154 A3
Firminy (42)....129 F6
Fislis (68)....89 G4
Fitou (11)....188 A6
Fitz-James (60)....20 D5
Fix-Saint-Geneys (43)....142 B3
Fixem (57)....26 C2
Fixin (21)....101 H1
Flacey (21)....86 A5
Flacey (28)....62 A4
Flacey-en-Bresse (71)....117 E1
la Flachère (38)....131 H6
Flachères (38)....131 E5
Flacourt (78)....41 G3
Flacy (89)....65 F4
Flagey (25)....103 G3
Flagey (52)....86 A2
Flagey-Echézeaux (21)....101 H2
Flagey-lès-Auxonne (21)..102 C2
Flagey-Rigney (25)....87 G5
Flagnac (12)....154 A2
Flagy (70)....87 G3
Flagy (71)....116 A2
Flagy (77)....64 B3
Flaignes-Havys (08)....23 G1
Flainval (54)....49 E5
Flamanville (50)....12 A3
Flamanville (76)....17 F4
Flamarens (32)....168 A2
la Flamengrie (02)....10 A5
la Flamengrie (59)....10 A2
Flamets-Frétils (76)....19 F1
Flammerans (21)....102 C1
Flammerécourt (52)....67 G3
Flancourt-Catelon (27)....18 A5
Flangebouche (25)....104 B2
Flassan (84)....158 C6
Flassans-sur-Issole (83)..193 G3
Flassigny (55)....25 F4
Flastroff (57)....27 E3
Flat (63)....127 F5
Flaucourt (80)....8 B6
Flaugeac (24)....137 E6
Flaugnac (46)....152 C5
Flaujac-Gare (46)....153 E1
Flaujac-Poujols (46)....152 D4
Flaujagues (33)....136 A5
Flaumont-Waudrechies (59)..10 A4
Flavacourt (60)....19 H5
Flaviac (07)....157 G1
Flavignac (87)....124 A3
Flavignerot (21)....101 G1
Flavigny (18)....98 B3
Flavigny (51)....45 F3
Flavigny-le-Grand-
   et-Beaurain (02)....9 G6
Flavigny-sur-Moselle (54)..48 D6
Flavigny-sur-Ozerain (21)..85 E4
Flavin (12)....154 C5
Flavy-le-Martel (02)....21 H2
Flavy-le-Meldeux (60)....21 G2
Flaxlanden (68)....89 F2
Flayat (23)....126 A3
Flayosc (83)....177 H6
Fléac (16)....122 B4
Fléac-sur-Seugne (17)....121 F5
la Flèche (72)....77 H2
Fléchin (62)....2 B5
Fléchy (60)....20 C3
Flée (21)....84 D5
Flée (72)....78 C2
Fleigneux (08)....24 C2
Fleisheim (57)....50 A4
le Fleix (24)....136 C5
Fleix (86)....109 H2
Fléré-la-Rivière (36)....95 G3
Flers (61)....38 B4
Flers (62)....7 G3
Flers (80)....8 A4
Flers-en-Escrebieux (59)..8 D2
Flers-sur-Noye (80)....20 C2
Flesquières (59)....8 D4
Flétrange (57)....49 F1
Flêtre (59)....2 D4
Fleurac (16)....122 C3
Fleurac (24)....137 H4
Fleurance (32)....168 A3
Fleurat (23)....111 F4
Fleurbaix (62)....3 E5
Fleuré (61)....39 F5
Fleuré (86)....109 F2
Fleurey (25)....88 C6
Fleurey-lès-Faverney (70)..87 F2
Fleurey-lès-Lavoncourt (70)..86 D3
Fleurey-lès-Saint-Loup (70)..88 A1
Fleurey-sur-Ouche (21)....85 G6
Fleurie (69)....116 A4
Fleuriel (03)....113 F4
Fleurieu-sur-Saône (69)..130 A2
Fleurieux-sur-
   l'Arbresle (69)....129 H2
Fleurigné (35)....58 A2
Fleurines (60)....20 D6
Fleurville (71)....116 B2

Fleury (02)...21 H6
Fleury (11)...188 B3
Fleury (57)...37 E3
Fleury (60)...26 C6
Fleury (62)...20 A6
Fleury (80)...20 B1
Fleury-devant-Douaumont (55)...25 D6
Fleury-en-Bière (77)...63 H2
Fleury-la-Forêt (27)...19 E4
Fleury-la-Montagne (71)...115 E5
Fleury-la-Rivière (51)...45 E2
Fleury-la-Vallée (89)...83 F1
Fleury-les-Aubrais (45)...62 D6
Fleury-Mérogis (91)...42 D6
Fleury-sur-Andelle (27)...19 E5
Fleury-sur-Loire (58)...99 E5
Fleury-sur-Orne (14)...14 B5
Fléville (08)...24 C5
Fléville-devant-Nancy (54)...48 D5
Fléville-Lixières (54)...25 H6
Flévy (57)...26 C4
Flexanville (78)...41 H4
Flexbourg (67)...50 C6
Fley (71)...101 F6
Fleys (89)...83 H2
Flez-Cuzy (58)...83 G6
Fligny (08)...10 C6
Flin (54)...70 B1
Flines-lès-Mortagne (59)...4 B6
Flines-lez-Raches (59)...8 D1
Flins-Neuve-Église (78)...41 G4
Flins-sur-Seine (78)...42 A3
Flipou (27)...18 D5
Flirey (54)...48 A3
Flixecourt (80)...7 F5
Flize (08)...24 B2
la Flocellière (85)...92 C4
Flocourt (57)...26 D6
Flocques (76)...6 A5
Flogny-la-Chapelle (89)...65 H6
Floing (08)...24 C2
Floirac (17)...120 D5
Floirac (33)...135 F5
Floirac (46)...134 B5
Florac (48)...156 B5
Florange (57)...26 B3
Florémont (88)...69 G2
Florensac (34)...187 H2
Florent-en-Argonne (51)...46 D1
Florentia (39)...117 F3
Florentin (81)...170 B3
Florentin-la-Capelle (12)...154 C2
Floressas (46)...152 A3
Florimont (90)...89 E4
Florimont-Gaumier (24)...152 B1
Florinhem (62)...2 A6
la Flotte (17)...106 B4
Flottemanville (50)...12 D3
Flottemanville-Hague (50)...12 B2
Floudès (33)...150 A2
Floure (11)...187 F3
Flourens (31)...169 G5
Floursies (59)...10 A3
Floyon (59)...9 H4
Flumet (73)...132 D2
Fluquières (02)...21 H1
Fluy (80)...7 F6
Foameix-Ornel (55)...25 G6
Foce (2A)...207 E3
Focicchia (2B)...205 F3
Fœcy (18)...97 F2
le Fœil (22)...33 F5
Foisches (08)...11 F4
Foissac (12)...153 G3
Foissac (30)...174 A1
Foissiat (01)...116 D3
Foissy (21)...101 E2
Foissy-lès-Vézelay (89)...83 H5
Foissy-sur-Vanne (89)...65 F4
Foix (09)...185 H5
Folcarde (31)...186 A1
Foléembray (02)...22 A3
Folgensbourg (68)...89 G3
le Folgoët (29)...31 F3
la Folie (14)...13 G5
Folies (80)...21 E1
Folkling (57)...27 G5
Follainville-Dennemont (78)...41 H2
Folles (87)...110 D5
Folleville (27)...17 H4
Folleville (80)...20 C2
Folligny (50)...35 H2
Folschviller (57)...49 F1
Fomerey (88)...69 H3
Fomperron (79)...108 B2
Fonbeauzard (31)...169 F5
Foncegrive (21)...86 A3
Fonches-Fonchette (80)...21 F1
Foncine-le-Bas (39)...103 G6
Foncine-le-Haut (39)...103 G6
Foncquevillers (62)...8 A4
Fondamente (12)...172 A3
Fondettes (37)...78 D5
Fondremand (70)...87 F4
Fongrave (47)...151 E4
Fonroque (24)...151 E1
Fons (07)...157 G2
Fons (30)...173 H3
Fons (46)...153 E1
Fons-sur-Lussan (30)...157 G6
Fonsommes (02)...9 E6
Fonsorbes (31)...168 D6
Font-Romeu-Odeillo-Via (66)...199 H4
Fontain (25)...103 G1
Fontaine (10)...67 H4
Fontaine (38)...145 G2
Fontaine (90)...88 D3
Fontaine-au-Bois (59)...9 G4
Fontaine-au-Pire (59)...9 E4
Fontaine-Bellenger (27)...41 E1
Fontaine-Bonneleau (60)...20 B2
Fontaine-Chaalis (60)...43 F1
Fontaine-Chalendray (17)...121 H1
Fontaine-Couverte (53)...58 A6
Fontaine-de-Vaucluse (84)...175 G2
Fontaine-Denis-Nuisy (51)...44 D6
Fontaine-en-Bray (76)...19 E2
Fontaine-en-Dormois (51)...24 B6
Fontaine-Française (21)...86 B4
Fontaine-Guérin (49)...77 G4
Fontaine-Henry (14)...14 B3
Fontaine-Heudebourg (27)...41 E1
Fontaine-la-Gaillarde (89)...65 E4
Fontaine-la-Guyon (28)...61 H1
Fontaine-la-Louvet (27)...15 G5
Fontaine-la-Mallet (76)...15 E1
Fontaine-la-Rivière (91)...63 F3
Fontaine-la-Soret (27)...40 B1
Fontaine-l'Abbé (27)...40 B1
Fontaine-Lavaganne (60)...20 A3
Fontaine-le-Bourg (76)...17 H5
Fontaine-le-Comte (86)...109 E1
Fontaine-le-Dun (76)...17 F3
Fontaine-le-Pin (14)...38 D2
Fontaine-le-Port (77)...64 B1
Fontaine-le-Puits (73)...132 D5
Fontaine-le-Sec (80)...6 D5
Fontaine-les-Bassets (61)...39 E3
Fontaine-lès-Boulans (62)...2 A6
Fontaine-lès-Cappy (80)...8 B6
Fontaine-lès-Clercs (02)...21 H1
Fontaine-lès-Clerval (25)...88 A5
Fontaine-les-Coteaux (41)...79 E2
Fontaine-lès-Croisilles (62)...8 C3
Fontaine-lès-Dijon (21)...85 H6
Fontaine-les-Grès (10)...66 A2
Fontaine-lès-Hermans (62)...2 B6
Fontaine-lès-Luxeuil (70)...87 H1
Fontaine-les-Ribouts (28)...41 E5
Fontaine-lès-Vervins (02)...10 A5
Fontaine-l'Étalon (62)...7 F3
Fontaine-Mâcon (10)...65 F2
Fontaine-Milon (49)...77 F4

Fontaine-Notre-Dame (02)...9 F4
Fontaine-Notre-Dame (59)...8 D3
Fontaine-Raoul (41)...61 G6
Fontaine-Saint-Lucien (60)...20 B4
la Fontaine-Saint-Martin (72)...77 H2
Fontaine-Simon (28)...61 G1
Fontaine-sous-Jouy (27)...41 E2
Fontaine-sous-Montdidier (80)...20 D2
Fontaine-sous-Préaux (76)...17 H6
Fontaine-sur-Ay (51)...45 F2
Fontaine-sur-Maye (80)...7 E3
Fontaine-sur-Somme (80)...7 E5
Fontaine-Uterte (02)...9 E6
Fontainebleau (77)...64 A2
Fontainebrux (39)...102 C6
Fontaines (71)...101 G5
Fontaines (85)...107 E2
Fontaines (89)...83 E3
Fontaines-d'Ozillac (17)...121 G6
Fontaines-en-Duesmois (21)...85 E3
Fontaines-en-Sologne (41)...80 B4
Fontaines-les-Sèches (21)...84 C2
Fontaines-Saint-Clair (55)...25 E5
Fontaines-Saint-Martin (69)...130 A2
Fontaines-sur-Marne (52)...67 H1
Fontaines-sur-Saône (69)...130 A2
Fontains (77)...64 C1
Fontan (06)...179 G1
Fontanès (30)...173 H3
Fontanès (34)...173 F4
Fontanès (42)...129 F5
Fontanès (48)...142 B6
Fontanès-de-Sault (11)...199 H1
Fontanes-du-Causse (46)...153 E1
Fontanges (15)...140 B3
Fontangy (21)...84 D6
Fontanières (23)...112 C6
Fontanil-Cornillon (38)...145 F2
Fontannes (43)...141 H1
Fontans (48)...155 H1
Fontarèches (30)...174 B1
Fontclaireau (16)...122 C2
Fontcouverte (11)...187 G4
Fontcouverte (17)...121 F2
Fontcouverte-la-Toussuire (73)...146 C2
la Fontelaye (76)...17 F4
Fontenai-les-Louvets (61)...59 H1
Fontenai-sur-Orne (61)...39 E5
Fontenailles (77)...64 C1
Fontenailles (89)...83 F3
Fontenay (27)...19 F6
Fontenay (36)...96 C3
Fontenay (50)...37 G5
Fontenay (71)...115 F1
Fontenay (76)...15 F1
Fontenay (88)...70 A3
Fontenay-aux-Roses (92)...42 C4
Fontenay-de-Bossery (10)...65 F2
Fontenay-en-Parisis (95)...42 D2
Fontenay-le-Comte (85)...107 F2
Fontenay-le-Fleury (78)...42 B4
Fontenay-le-Marmion (14)...14 B5
Fontenay-le-Pesnel (14)...14 A4
Fontenay-le-Vicomte (91)...63 G1
Fontenay-lès-Briis (91)...42 C6
Fontenay-Mauvoisin (78)...41 G3
Fontenay-près-Chablis (89)...83 H1
Fontenay-près-Vézelay (89)...83 H5
Fontenay-Saint-Père (78)...41 H2
Fontenay-sous-Bois (94)...42 D4
Fontenay-sous-Fouronnes (89)...83 G3
Fontenay-sur-Conie (28)...62 C4
Fontenay-sur-Eure (28)...62 A2
Fontenay-sur-Loing (45)...64 B5
Fontenay-sur-Mer (50)...13 E3
Fontenay-sur-Vègre (72)...59 G6
Fontenay-Torcy (60)...19 G3
Fontenay-Trésigny (77)...43 G5
Fontenelle (21)...86 B4
Fontenelle (90)...89 E3
la Fontenelle (35)...35 G5
la Fontenelle (41)...61 F5
Fontenelle (02)...9 H6
Fontenelle-Montby (25)...88 A5
les Fontenelles (25)...104 C1
Fontenermont (14)...37 F3
Fontenet (17)...121 F1
Fontenille (16)...122 C1
Fontenille-Saint-Martin-d'Entraigues (79)...108 B5
Fontenilles (31)...168 D6
Fontenois-la-Ville (70)...69 G6
Fontenois-lès-Montbozon (70)...87 G4
Fontenotte (25)...87 H5
Fontenouilles (89)...82 C1
Fontenoy (02)...21 H5
Fontenoy (89)...83 E3
Fontenoy-la-Joûte (54)...70 B1
Fontenoy-le-Château (88)...69 G6
Fontenoy-sur-Moselle (54)...48 B5
Fontenu (39)...103 E6
Fonteny (57)...49 E3
Fonters-du-Razès (11)...186 B3
Fontès (34)...172 C6
Fontet (33)...150 B2
Fontette (10)...67 E4
Fontevraud-l'Abbaye (49)...94 A1
Fontgombault (36)...95 F6
Fontguenaud (36)...96 H1
Fontienne (04)...176 D1
Fontiers-Cabardès (11)...186 D2
Fontiès-d'Aude (11)...187 E3
Fontjoncouse (11)...187 H5
Fontoy (57)...26 A3
Fontpédrouse (66)...199 H4
Fontrabiouse (66)...199 H3
Fontrailles (65)...183 G2
Fontvannes (10)...65 H3
Fontvieille (13)...191 E2
Forbach (57)...27 G4
Forcalqueiret (83)...193 F3
Forcalquier (04)...176 C2
la Force (11)...186 C3
la Force (24)...136 C5
Forcé (53)...58 D5
Forcelles-Saint-Gorgon (54)...69 F1
Forcelles-sous-Gugney (54)...69 F2
Forceville (80)...7 H5
Forceville-en-Vimeu (80)...6 D5
Forcey (52)...68 B4
Forciolo (2A)...205 E6
la Forclaz (74)...119 E3
Forest-en-Cambrésis (59)...9 F4
Forest-l'Abbaye (80)...6 D3
la Forest-Landerneau (29)...31 F4
Forest-Montiers (80)...6 D3
Forest-Saint-Julien (05)...160 C1
Forest-sur-Marque (59)...3 G5
Foreste (02)...21 G1
la Forestière (51)...44 C6
la Forêt-Auvray (61)...38 C4
la Forêt-de-Tessé (16)...108 C6
la Forêt-du-Parc (27)...41 E3
la Forêt-du-Temple (23)...111 G3
la Forêt-Fouesnant (29)...53 G3
la Forêt-le-Roi (91)...63 E1
la Forêt-Sainte-Croix (91)...63 F2
la Forêt-sur-Sèvre (79)...92 D5
Forfry (77)...43 G2
la Forge (88)...70 B5
Forges (17)...107 E5
Forges (19)...138 D2
Forges (49)...93 H1
Forges (56)...56 A4
les Forges (79)...108 C1
les Forges (88)...69 H4
Forges-la-Forêt (35)...57 H5
Forges-les-Bains (91)...42 B6
Forges-les-Eaux (76)...19 F3
Forges-sur-Meuse (55)...25 E6
Forgues (31)...184 D1
la Forie (63)...128 B5

Forléans (21)...84 C5
Formentin (14)...15 E4
Formerie (60)...19 G2
Formigny (14)...13 G5
Formiguères (66)...199 H3
Fornex (09)...185 E3
Fors (79)...107 H4
Forstfeld (67)...51 G3
Forstheim (67)...51 E3
Fort-du-Plasne (39)...118 A1
Fort-Louis (67)...51 G3
Fort-Mahon-Plage (80)...6 C2
Fort-Mardyck (59)...2 B1
Fort-Moville (27)...15 G3
Fortan (41)...79 G3
Fortel-en-Artois (62)...7 G3
la Forteresse (38)...145 E1
Fortschwihr (68)...71 G4
Fos (31)...184 B6
Fos (34)...172 B6
Fos-sur-Mer (13)...191 F4
le Fossat (09)...185 F3
Fossé (08)...24 C4
Fossé (41)...79 H3
Fosse (66)...200 C1
le Fossé (76)...19 F3
la Fosse-Corduan (10)...65 G2
la Fosse-de-Tigné (49)...93 F1
Fossemagne (24)...137 H3
Fossemanant (80)...20 B1
les Fosses (79)...107 H5
Fossès (95)...43 E2
Fossès-et-Baleyssac (33)...150 B2
Fosseuse (60)...20 B6
Fosseux (62)...7 H3
Fossieux (57)...48 D3
Fossoy (02)...44 C2
Foucarmont (76)...6 A6
Foucart (76)...15 H1
Foucaucourt-en-Santerre (80)...8 B6
Foucaucourt-Hors-de-Nesle (80)...6 C6
Foucaucourt-sur-Thabas (55)...47 E2
Fouchécourt (70)...87 E1
Fouchécourt (88)...69 E5
Foucherans (25)...103 G2
Foucherans (39)...102 C2
Fouchères (10)...66 C4
Fouchères (89)...64 D4
Fouchères-aux-Bois (55)...47 F6
Foucherolles (45)...64 C5
Fouchy (67)...71 E2
Foucrainville (27)...41 E3
Fouday (67)...71 E1
Fouencamps (80)...20 C1
Fouesnant (29)...53 G4
Foufflin-Ricametz (62)...7 G2
Foug (54)...48 A5
Fougaron (31)...184 C5
Fougax-et-Barrineuf (09)...186 B6
Fougeré (49)...77 G3
Fougeré (85)...91 H4
Fougères (35)...58 A2
Fougères-sur-Bièvre (41)...79 H5
les Fougerêts (56)...56 B6
Fougerolles (36)...111 G2
Fougerolles (70)...70 A6
Fougerolles-du-Plessis (53)...58 B1
Fougueyrolles (24)...136 B5
la Fouillade (12)...153 G5
Fouilleuse (60)...20 D4
Fouilloux (60)...160 B3
la Fouillouse (42)...129 F5
le Fouilloux (17)...135 H2
Fouilloy (60)...19 H2
Fouilloy (80)...8 A6
Fouju (77)...43 G6
Foulain (52)...68 A5
Foulangues (60)...20 C6
Foulayronnes (47)...151 F5
Foulbec (27)...15 F3
Foulcrey (57)...49 G5
Fouleix (24)...137 F4
Foulenay (39)...102 C4
Fouligny (57)...49 E1
Foulognes (14)...13 G6
Fouquebrune (16)...122 C5
Fouquenies (60)...20 A4
Fouquereuil (62)...2 D6
Fouquerolles (60)...20 B4
Fouquescourt (80)...21 E1
Fouqueure (16)...122 B2
Fouqueville (27)...18 B6
Fouquières-lès-Béthune (62)...2 D6
Fouquières-lès-Lens (62)...8 C1
Four (38)...130 C4
Fouras (17)...106 D6
Fourbanne (25)...87 H6
Fourcatier-et-Maison-Neuve (25)...104 A5
Fourcès (32)...167 F2
Fourchambault (58)...98 D3
Fourches (14)...39 E3
Fourcigny (80)...19 H1
Fourdrain (02)...22 B3
Fourdrinoy (80)...7 F6
Fourg (25)...103 E2
Fourges (27)...41 G1
les Fourgs (39)...104 A4
Fourilles (03)...113 G4
Fourmagnac (46)...153 G1
Fourmetot (27)...15 H3
Fourmies (59)...10 A5
Fournaudin (89)...65 F4
Fournaux (42)...129 E1
Fournaux (50)...37 G2
Fournaux-le-Val (14)...38 D3
Fournels (48)...141 F6
Fournès (30)...174 C2
Fournes-Cabardès (11)...187 E2
Fournes-en-Weppes (59)...3 E5
le Fournet (14)...15 E4
Fournet-Blancheroche (25)...104 D1
Fournets-Luisans (25)...104 B2
Fourneville (14)...15 F3
Fournival (60)...20 C4
Fournols (63)...128 A5
Fournols (46)...153 F2
Fournoulès (15)...154 A1
Fouronnes (89)...83 F3
Fourques (30)...174 C4
Fourques (66)...201 E3
Fourques-sur-Garonne (47)...150 C3
Fourqueux (78)...42 B3
Fourquevaux (31)...169 G6
Fours (33)...135 E2
Fours (58)...99 H5
Fours-en-Vexin (27)...41 G1
Fourtou (11)...187 F6
Foussais-Payré (85)...107 F1
Foussemagne (90)...88 D3
le Fousseret (31)...184 D2
Foussignac (16)...122 A3
Fouvent-Saint-Andoche (70)...86 D3
Fouzilhon (34)...172 B6
Foville (57)...48 D3
Fox-Amphoux (83)...193 F1
la Foye-Monjault (79)...107 G4
Fozières (34)...172 C5
Fozzano (2A)...207 E2
Fragnes (71)...101 G5
Frahier-et-Chatebier (70)...88 C3
Fraignot-et-Vesvrotte (21)...85 G3
Fraillicourt (08)...23 F2
Fraimbois (54)...49 F6
Frain (88)...69 E4
Fraisans (39)...103 E2
Fraisnes-en-Saintois (54)...69 F2
Fraisse (24)...136 C5
Fraisse-Cabardès (11)...186 D2
Fraissé-des-Corbières (11)...187 H5
Fraisse-sur-Agout (34)...171 G5
Fraisses (42)...129 E6
Fraissines (81)...171 E2
Fraissinet-de-Fourques (48)...156 A6

Fraissinet-de-Lozère (48)...156 B4
Fraize (88)...70 D3
Fralignes (10)...66 C4
la Framboisière (28)...40 C6
Framecourt (62)...7 G2
Framerville-Rainecourt (80)...8 A6
Framicourt (80)...6 C5
Framont (70)...86 C4
Frampas (52)...67 E1
Francalmont (70)...87 G1
Francaltroff (57)...49 G2
Francarville (31)...169 H5
Francastel (60)...20 B3
Françay (41)...79 G3
Francazal (31)...184 D5
Francescas (47)...167 G1
Francheleins (01)...116 B6
Franchesse (03)...113 F1
Francheval (08)...24 C2
Franchevelle (70)...88 A2
la Francheville (08)...24 A1
Francheville (21)...85 G5
Francheville (27)...40 C4
Francheville (39)...102 C5
Francheville (51)...46 A3
Francheville (54)...48 B4
Francheville (61)...39 E5
Francheville (69)...129 H3
Francières (60)...21 E4
Francières (80)...7 E4
Francillon (36)...96 B4
Francillon-sur-Roubion (26)...158 D2
Francilly-Selency (02)...8 D6
Francin (73)...132 A5
Franclens (74)...118 A6
Françon (31)...184 C3
Franconville (54)...69 H1
Franconville (95)...42 C3
Francoulès (46)...152 D3
Francourt (70)...86 D3
Francourville (28)...62 C2
Francs (33)...136 A4
Francueil (37)...79 G6
Franey (25)...103 E1
Frangy (74)...118 A6
Frangy-en-Bresse (71)...102 B6
Franken (68)...89 F3
Franleu (80)...6 C4
Franois (25)...103 F1
Franqueville (02)...22 D1
Franqueville (27)...40 C2
Franqueville (80)...7 E4
Franqueville-Saint-Pierre (76)...18 D4
Frans (01)...130 A1
Fransart (80)...21 F1
Fransèches (23)...125 G1
Fransu (80)...7 F4
Fransures (80)...20 B2
Franvillers (80)...7 H6
Franxault (21)...102 B3
Frapelle (88)...70 D2
Fraquelfing (57)...49 H5
Fraroz (39)...103 G5
Frasnay-Reugny (58)...99 G3
Frasne (25)...103 H4
Frasne-le-Château (70)...87 E4
Frasnes-lès-Meulières (39)...102 C1
la Frasnée (39)...117 H1
le Frasnois (39)...103 F6
Frasnoy (59)...9 G2
Frasseto (2A)...205 E6
Frauenberg (57)...49 H1
Frausseilles (81)...170 A1
Fravaux (10)...67 E4
le Fraysse (81)...170 D3
Frayssinet (46)...152 D2
Frayssinet-le-Gélat (46)...152 B2
Frayssinhes (46)...139 F5
Frazé (28)...61 G3
Fréauville (76)...19 E1
Frebécourt (88)...68 D2
Frébuans (39)...102 C6
le Frêche (40)...166 C2
Fréchède (65)...183 F1
Fréchencourt (80)...7 H5
Fréchendets (65)...183 F4
le Fréchet (31)...184 C3
Fréchet-Aure (65)...183 G5
Fréchou (47)...167 F1
Fréchou-Fréchet (65)...183 F3
Frécourt (52)...68 B5
Frédéric-Fontaine (70)...88 B3
la Frédière (17)...121 F2
Frédille (36)...96 B3
Frégimont (47)...151 E5
Frégouville (32)...168 B5
Fréhel (22)...34 B3
Freigné (49)...76 C3
Freissinières (05)...147 E6
la Freissinouse (05)...160 B2
Freistroff (57)...26 D4
Freix-Anglards (15)...140 A4
Fréjairolles (81)...170 C3
Fréjeville (81)...170 C5
Fréjus (83)...178 B6
Fréland (68)...71 E4
Frelinghien (59)...3 F4
Frémainville (95)...42 A2
Frémécourt (95)...42 B1
Fréménil (54)...49 G6
Frémeréville-sous-les-Côtes (55)...47 H4
Frémery (57)...49 E3
Frémestroff (57)...49 G2
Frémicourt (62)...8 B4
Fremifontaine (88)...70 B3
Frémontiers (80)...20 A1
Frémonville (54)...49 H6
la Frénaye (76)...15 H2
Frencq (62)...1 G5
Frenelle-la-Grande (88)...69 F2
Frenelle-la-Petite (88)...69 F2
Frênes (61)...38 A4
Freneuse (76)...18 C5
Freneuse (78)...41 G2
Freneuse-sur-Risle (27)...18 A6
Freney (73)...147 E2
le Freney-d'Oisans (38)...146 B3
Fréniches (60)...21 G2
Frénois (21)...85 G4
Frénois (88)...69 E3
Frénouville (14)...14 C5
Frépillon (95)...42 C2
Fresles (76)...19 E1
la Fresnaie-Fayel (61)...39 F4
la Fresnais (35)...35 E4
Fresnay (10)...67 E2
Fresnay-en-Retz (44)...90 C1
Fresnay-le-Comte (28)...62 B3
Fresnay-le-Gilmert (28)...62 A1
Fresnay-le-Long (76)...17 G4
Fresnay-le-Samson (61)...39 F3
Fresnay-l'Évêque (28)...62 D3
Fresnay-sur-Sarthe (72)...59 H3
la Fresnaye-sur-Chédouet (72)...60 A2
le Fresne (27)...40 D2
le Fresne (51)...46 A3
le Fresne-Camilly (14)...14 A4
Fresne-Cauverville (27)...15 G4
Fresné-la-Mère (14)...39 E2
Fresne-l'Archevêque (27)...19 E5
Fresne-le-Plan (76)...18 D4
Fresne-Léguillon (60)...20 A6
Fresne-lès-Reims (51)...23 F5
le Fresne-Poret (50)...37 H4
Fresnes (02)...21 H4
Fresnes (21)...84 D3
Fresnes (41)...80 A5
Fresnes (89)...84 A2
Fresnes (94)...42 D5

Fresnes-au-Mont (55)...47 G3
Fresnes-en-Saulnois (57)...49 E3
Fresnes-en-Tardenois (02)...44 C1
Fresnes-en-Woëvre (55)...47 H1
Fresnes-lès-Montauban (62)...8 C2
Fresnes-Mazancourt (80)...8 B6
Fresnes-sur-Apance (52)...69 E6
Fresnes-sur-Escaut (59)...9 F1
Fresnes-sur-Marne (77)...43 F3
Fresnes-Tilloloy (80)...6 D5
Fresney (27)...41 E3
Fresney-le-Puceux (14)...14 B5
Fresney-le-Vieux (14)...14 B6
Fresnicourt-le-Dolmen (62)...8 A1
Fresnières (60)...21 F3
Fresnois-la-Montagne (54)...25 G3
Fresnoy (62)...7 F2
Fresnoy-Andainville (80)...6 D6
Fresnoy-au-Val (80)...7 E6
Fresnoy-en-Chaussée (80)...20 D1
Fresnoy-en-Gohelle (62)...8 C2
Fresnoy-en-Thelle (60)...20 C6
Fresnoy-Folny (76)...6 B6
Fresnoy-la-Rivière (60)...21 F6
Fresnoy-le-Château (10)...66 C4
Fresnoy-le-Grand (02)...9 E5
Fresnoy-le-Luat (60)...21 F6
Fresnoy-lès-Roye (80)...21 F2
Frespech (47)...151 G5
Fresquiennes (76)...17 G5
Fressac (30)...173 G2
Fressain (59)...8 D2
Fressancourt (02)...22 B2
Fresse (70)...88 B2
Fresse-sur-Moselle (88)...70 C6
Fresselines (23)...111 F3
Fressenneville (80)...6 C4
Fressies (59)...8 D3
Fressin (62)...7 F1
Fressines (79)...108 A3
la Frestoy-Vaux (60)...21 E3
Fresville (50)...12 D4
Fréterive (73)...132 B4
Fréteval (41)...79 H2
Fréthun (62)...1 G2
Fretigney-et-Velloreille (70)...87 F3
Frétigny (28)...61 F2
Fretin (59)...3 G6
Frétoy (77)...44 B4
Frétoy-le-Château (60)...21 G2
la Frette (38)...131 E5
la Frette (71)...116 C1
la Frette-sur-Seine (95)...42 C3
Frettecuisse (80)...6 D6
Frettemeule (80)...6 C5
Fretterans (71)...102 B4
le Frety (08)...23 G1
Freulleville (76)...17 H3
Frévent (62)...7 G2
Fréville (76)...17 F5
Fréville (88)...68 D3
Fréville-du-Gâtinais (45)...63 G5
Frévillers (62)...7 H1
Frévin-Capelle (62)...8 A2
Freybouse (57)...49 G2
Freycenet-la-Cuche (43)...142 D5
Freycenet-la-Tour (43)...142 D5
Freychenet (09)...185 H6
Freyming-Merlebach (57)...49 G1
Freyssenet (07)...157 H1
Friaize (28)...61 G2
Friardel (14)...15 F6
Friaucourt (80)...6 B5
Friauville (54)...26 A5
Fribourg (57)...49 G4
Fricamps (80)...20 A1
Frichemesnil (76)...17 G4
Fricourt (80)...8 A5
Fridefont (15)...141 E5
Friedolsheim (67)...50 C4
Frières-Faillouël (02)...21 H2
Friesen (68)...89 E3
Friesenheim (67)...71 H1
Friville-Escarbotin (80)...6 B4
Frizon (88)...69 H3
Froberville (76)...16 C3
Frocourt (60)...20 A5
Frœningen (68)...89 F2
Frœschwiller (67)...51 E2
Froges (38)...145 H1
Frohen-sur-Authie (80)...7 F3
Frohmuhl (67)...50 B3
Froideconche (70)...87 H1
Froidefontaine (90)...88 D3
Froidestrées (02)...10 A5
Froideterre (70)...88 A2
Froidevaux (25)...88 B6
Froideville (39)...102 C5
Froidfond (85)...91 E2
Froidmont-Cohartille (02)...22 C3
Froidos (55)...47 E2
Froissy (60)...20 B3
Frôlois (21)...85 E4
Frolois (54)...48 C6
Fromelennes (08)...11 F4
Fromelles (59)...3 E5
Fromental (87)...110 D5
Fromentières (51)...44 D3
Fromentières (53)...76 D1
Fromeréville-les-Vallons (55)...47 F1
Fromezey (55)...25 G6
Fromont (77)...63 H3
Fromy (08)...24 D3
Froncles (52)...67 H3
Fronsac (31)...184 A5
Fronsac (33)...135 G4
Frontenac (33)...135 H6
Frontenac (46)...153 G3
Frontenard (71)...102 A4
Frontenas (69)...129 H1
Frontenaud (71)...117 E2
Frontenay (39)...102 D5
Frontenay-Rohan-Rohan (79)...107 G4
Frontenex (73)...132 C4
Frontignan (34)...189 F1
Frontignan-de-Comminges (31)...184 A5
Frontignan-Savès (31)...184 C1
Fronton (31)...169 F3
Frontonas (38)...130 D4
Fronville (52)...67 H3
Frossay (44)...74 A5
Frotey-lès-Lure (70)...88 A3
Frotey-lès-Vesoul (70)...87 G3
Frouard (54)...48 C4
Frouville (95)...42 C1
Frouzins (31)...169 E6
Froville (54)...69 H1
Froyelles (80)...7 E3
Frozes (86)...94 A6
Frucourt (80)...6 D5
Frugerès-les-Mines (43)...141 G1
Fruges (62)...2 A6
Frugières-le-Pin (43)...141 H2
Fruncé (28)...61 H2
Fry (76)...19 F3
Fuans (25)...104 B2
Fublaines (77)...43 G3
le Fugeret (04)...178 A1
Fuilla (66)...200 B3
Fuissé (71)...116 B4
Fuligny (10)...67 E3
Fulleren (68)...89 E3
Fultot (76)...17 F3
Fulvy (89)...84 B2
Fumay (08)...11 E5
Fumel (47)...151 H3
Fumichon (14)...15 G5
Furchhausen (67)...50 C4
Furdenheim (67)...50 D5
Furiani (2B)...203 G4
Furmeyer (05)...160 A2
Fussey (21)...101 G2
Fussy (18)...97 G2
Fustérouau (32)...166 D4
Fustignac (31)...184 C2

Futeau (55)...46 D2
Fuveau (13)...192 C3
Fyé (72)...60 A3

G

Gaas (40)...165 E5
Gabarnac (33)...149 H2
Gabarret (40)...166 D2
Gabaston (64)...182 C1
Gabat (64)...181 F1
Gabian (34)...172 B6
Gabillou (24)...137 H2
Gabre (09)...185 F4
Gabriac (12)...154 D3
Gabriac (48)...156 C6
Gabrias (48)...156 A3
Gacé (61)...39 G4
la Gacilly (56)...56 C6
Gâcogne (58)...100 A1
Gadancourt (95)...42 A2
Gadencourt (27)...41 F3
Gaël (35)...56 B3
Gageac-et-Rouillac (24)...136 C6
Gagnac-sur-Cère (46)...139 F5
Gagnac-sur-Garonne (31)...169 E4
Gagnières (30)...157 E5
Gagny (93)...43 E4
Gahard (35)...57 F1
Gailhan (30)...173 G3
Gaillac (81)...170 A3
Gaillac-d'Aveyron (12)...155 E4
Gaillac-Toulza (31)...185 G3
Gaillagos (65)...182 C5
Gaillan-en-Médoc (33)...120 C6
Gaillard (74)...118 C5
Gaillardbois-Cressenville (27)...19 F5
la Gaillarde (76)...17 F2
Gaillefontaine (76)...19 F2
Gaillères (40)...166 B2
Gaillon (27)...41 E1
Gaillon-sur-Montcient (78)...42 A2
Gainneville (76)...15 F2
Gaja-et-Villedieu (11)...186 D4
Gaja-la-Selve (11)...186 A3
Gajac (33)...150 A3
Gajan (09)...184 D4
Gajan (30)...174 A3
Gajoubert (87)...109 H5
Galametz (62)...7 F2
Galan (65)...183 G3
Galapian (47)...150 D5
Galargues (34)...173 G4
Galéria (2B)...204 B1
Galey (09)...184 C5
Galez (65)...183 G3
Galfingue (68)...89 E2
Galgan (12)...153 H3
Galgon (33)...135 G4
Galiax (32)...166 D4
Galié (31)...184 A5
Galinagues (11)...199 H1
Gallardon (28)...62 C1
Gallargues-le-Montueux (30)...173 H4
le Gallet (60)...20 B3
Galluis (78)...41 H4
Gamaches (80)...6 B5
Gamaches-en-Vexin (27)...19 F6
Gamarde-les-Bains (40)...165 F4
Gamarthe (64)...181 E3
Gambais (78)...41 G4
Gambaiseuil (78)...41 H5
Gan (64)...182 B3
Ganac (09)...185 G5
Ganagobie (04)...176 D1
Gancourt-Saint-Étienne (76)...19 G3
Gandelain (61)...59 H1
Gandelu (02)...44 A2
Gandrange (57)...26 B4
Ganges (34)...173 E2
Gannat (03)...113 G6
Gannay-sur-Loire (03)...99 G6
Gannes (60)...20 C3
Gans (33)...150 A3
Ganties (31)...184 B4
Ganzeville (76)...16 C3
Gap (05)...160 B2
Gapennes (80)...7 E3
Gâprée (61)...60 B1
Garac (31)...168 D4
Garancières (78)...41 H4
Garancières-en-Beauce (28)...62 D2
Garancières-en-Drouais (28)...41 E4
Garanou (09)...199 F1
Garat (16)...122 D4
Garcelles-Secqueville (14)...14 C5
Garches (92)...42 C4
Garchizy (58)...98 D3
Garchy (58)...98 C1
Gardanne (13)...192 B3
la Garde (04)...177 H3
la Garde (38)...146 A3
la Garde (83)...193 F5
la Garde-Adhémar (26)...158 B4
la Garde-Freinet (83)...194 A3
Gardefort (18)...98 B1
Gardegan-et-Tourtirac (33)...136 A5
Gardères (65)...182 D2
Gardes-le-Pontaroux (16)...122 C5
Gardie (11)...186 D4
Gardonne (24)...136 C5
Gardouch (31)...185 H1
Garein (40)...165 H1
Garencières (27)...41 E3
la Garenne-Colombes (92)...42 C3
Garennes-sur-Eure (27)...41 F3
Garéoult (83)...193 F4
Garentreville (77)...63 H4
Garéoult...
Garganvillar (82)...168 C2
Gargas (31)...169 F4
Gargas (84)...175 H2
Gargenville (78)...41 H2
Garges-lès-Gonesse (95)...42 D3
Gargilesse-Dampierre (36)...111 F2
Garidech (31)...169 G4
Gariès (82)...168 C3
Garigny (18)...98 C3
Garin (31)...197 F1
Garindein (64)...181 F3
Garlan (29)...32 A3
Garlède-Mondebat (64)...166 B6
Garlin (64)...166 B6
le Garn (30)...157 G5
la Garnache (85)...90 D2
Garnat-sur-Engièvre (03)...114 B1
Garnay (28)...41 E5
Garnerans (01)...116 B5
Garons (30)...174 B4
Garos (64)...166 A6
Garravet (32)...184 B1
Garrebourg (57)...50 B4
Garrevaques (81)...170 A6
Garrey (40)...165 F4
le Garric (81)...170 C2
Garrigues (34)...173 G3
Garrigues (81)...169 H4
Garrigues-Sainte-Eulalie (30)...174 A2
Garris (64)...181 F1
Garrosse (40)...165 F1
Gars (06)...178 C2
Gartempe (23)...111 F5
Gas (28)...62 B1
Gasny (27)...41 G2
Gasques (82)...151 G6
Gassin (83)...194 A3
Gastes (40)...148 B4
Gastines (53)...58 A6
Gastins (77)...43 H6
Gasville-Oisème (28)...62 B2
Gatey (39)...102 C4
Gathemo (50)...37 G4
Gatteville-le-Phare (50)...13 E1
Gattières (06)...195 E2
Gatuzières (48)...156 A6

Gaubertin (45)...63 G5
la Gaubretière (85)...92 B3
Gauchin-Légal (62)...8 A1
Gauchin-Verloingt (62)...7 G1
Gauchy (02)...22 A1
Gauciel (27)...41 E2
la Gaudaine (28)...61 E3
la Gaude (06)...195 E3
Gaudechart (60)...20 A3
Gaudent (65)...184 A5
Gaudiempré (62)...7 H3
Gaudiès (09)...186 A3
Gaudonville (32)...168 B3
Gaudreville-la-Rivière (27)...40 D3
Gaugeac (24)...151 G1
Gaujac (30)...174 C1
Gaujac (32)...167 H2
Gaujac (47)...150 B3
Gaujacq (40)...165 G4
Gaujan (32)...184 B1
le Gault-Perche (41)...61 F5
le Gault-Saint-Denis (28)...62 B3
le Gault-Soigny (51)...44 C4
Gauré (31)...169 G5
Gauriac (33)...135 E3
Gauriaguet (33)...135 G3
Gaussan (65)...183 H3
Gausson (22)...33 G6
Gauville (61)...40 A4
Gauville (80)...19 H1
Gauville-la-Campagne (27)...40 D2
Gavarnie (65)...196 B5
Gavarret-sur-Aulouste (32)...167 H4
Gavaudun (47)...151 G2
Gavignano (2B)...203 F6
Gavisse (57)...26 C2
Gavray (50)...35 H1
le Gâvre (44)...74 C2
Gavrelle (62)...8 C2
Gâvres (56)...54 C6
Gavrus (14)...14 A5
Gayan (65)...183 E2
Gaye (51)...45 E5
Gayon (64)...166 C6
Gazaupouy (32)...167 G1
Gazave (65)...183 G4
Gazax-et-Baccarisse (32)...167 E4
Gazeran (78)...41 H5
Geaune (40)...166 B4
Geay (17)...120 D2
Geay (79)...93 F4
Gèdre (65)...196 B5
Gée (49)...77 F5
Gée-Rivière (32)...166 C4
Geffosses (50)...12 C6
Géfosse-Fontenay (14)...13 F4
Gehée (36)...96 B3
Geishouse (68)...70 D6
Geispitzen (68)...89 G2
Geispolsheim (67)...51 E6
Geiswasser (68)...71 H5
Geiswiller (67)...50 D4
Gélacourt (54)...70 B1
Gélannes (10)...65 G2
Gélaucourt (54)...69 E1
Gellainville (28)...62 B2
Gellenoncourt (54)...49 E5
Gelles (63)...126 D3
Gellin (25)...103 H5
Gelos (64)...182 B2
Geloux (40)...165 H1
Gelucourt (57)...49 F4
Gémage (61)...60 D2
Gemaingoutte (88)...70 D3
Gembrie (65)...184 A5
Gemeaux (21)...85 H5
Gémenos (13)...192 C4
Gémigny (45)...62 C6
Gémil (31)...169 G4
Gemmelaincourt (88)...69 E3
Gémonval (25)...88 B4
Gémonville (54)...69 E2
Gémozac (17)...121 E4
Genac (16)...122 B2
Genainville (95)...41 H1
Genas (69)...130 B3
Génat (09)...199 E1
Genay (21)...84 C5
Genay (69)...130 A2
Gençay (86)...109 E3
Gendreville (88)...68 D3
Gendrey (39)...102 D1
Génébrières (82)...169 F2
Genech (59)...3 G6
Génelard (71)...115 F1
Générac (30)...174 B4
Générac (33)...135 F2
Générargues (30)...173 G1
Générest (65)...183 H5
Generville (11)...186 B3
Geneslay (61)...59 F2
le Genest-Saint-Isle (53)...58 C4
Genestelle (07)...157 G1
la Genête (71)...116 C2
la Genêtouze (17)...136 A2
la Genêtouze (85)...91 G4
Genêts (50)...35 G3
les Genettes (61)...40 A5
Geneuille (25)...87 F6
la Genevraie (61)...39 G5
la Genevraye (77)...64 A3
Genevreuille (70)...87 H2
Genevrey (70)...87 H2
Genevrières (52)...86 C2
Gennes (25)...103 G1
Gennes (49)...77 F5
Gennes-Ivergny (62)...7 F2
Gennes-sur-Glaize (53)...76 D1
Gennes-sur-Seiche (35)...58 A5
Genneteil (49)...77 H4
Gennetines (03)...114 A1
Genneton (79)...93 F3
Genneville (14)...15 F3
Gennevilliers (92)...42 C3
Genod (39)...117 F3
Génolhac (30)...156 D5
Génos (31)...197 E1
Génos (65)...197 E1
Genouillac (16)...123 E2
Genouillac (23)...111 H3
Genouillé (17)...107 F5
Genouillé (86)...108 D4
Genouilleux (01)...116 B5
Genouilly (18)...97 E2
Genouilly (71)...115 H1
Gensac (33)...136 B5
Gensac (65)...183 E1
Gensac (82)...168 C2
Gensac-de-Boulogne (31)...184 A3
Gensac-la-Pallue (16)...121 H4
Gensac-sur-Garonne (31)...184 D3
Genté (16)...121 G4
Gentelles (80)...20 C1
Gentilly (94)...42 D4
Gentioux-Pigerolles (23)...125 F4
Genvry (60)...21 G2
Georfans (70)...88 A4
Géovreisset (01)...117 G5
Géovreissiat (01)...117 G5
Ger (50)...37 G5
Ger (64)...182 D2
Ger (65)...182 D4
Geraise (39)...103 F4
Gérardmer (88)...70 C5
Géraudot (10)...66 C3
Gerbaix (73)...131 G4
Gerbamont (88)...70 C5

Gerbécourt (57) 49 E3
Gerbécourt-
et-Haplemont (54)........69 F1
Gerbépal (88) 70 C4
Gerberoy (60) 19 H3
Gerbéviller (54) 70 A1
Gercourt-et-Drillancourt (55) ...25 E5
Gercy (02) 22 D1
Gerde (65) 183 F4
Gerderest (64) 182 D1
Gère-Bélesten (64) 182 B4
Gergny (02) 10 A6
Gergueil (21) 101 G1
Gergy (71) 101 H4
Gerland (21) 101 H2
Germ (65) 197 E1
Germagnat (01) 117 F4
Germagny (71) 101 F6
Germaine (02) 21 H1
Germaine (51) 45 F1
Germaines (52) 86 B2
Germainville (28) 41 F5
Germainvilliers (52) 68 D4
Germay (52) 68 B2
Germéfontaine (25) 104 B1
Germenay (58) 99 G1
Germigney (17) 121 G4
Germigney (39) 102 E3
Germigny (70) 86 C5
Germignonville (28) 62 C4
Germigny (51) 22 D6
Germigny (89) 65 H6
Germigny-des-Prés (45) 81 H1
Germigny-l'Évêque (77) ...43 G3
Germigny-l'Exempt (98) 98 C4
Germigny-
sous-Coulombs (77) 44 A2
Germigny-sur-Loire (58) ...98 D3
Germignon (51) 46 A4
Germiny (51) 48 B6
Germisay (52) 67 H2
Germolles-sur-Grosne (71) ...115 H4
Germond-Rouvre (79) 107 H2
Germont (08) 24 B4
Germonville (54) 69 G2
Germs-sur-l'Oussouet (65) ...183 E4
Gernelle (08) 24 B1
Gernicourt (02) 22 D5
Géronce (64) 181 H2
Gerponville (76) 16 D3
Gerrots (14) 15 E4
Gerstheim (67) 71 H1
Gertwiller (67) 71 G1
Geruge (39) 117 F1
Gervais (54) 44 A3
Gerville (76) 16 C4
Géry (54) 47 F4
Gerzat (63) 127 F2
Gesnes (54) 59 E4
Gesnes-en-Argonne (55) ...24 D5
Gesnes-le-Gandelin (72) ...59 H2
Gespunsart (08) 24 B1
Gestas (64) 181 G1
Gesté (49) 75 F5
Gestel (56) 54 C5
Gestiès (09) 199 E1
Gesvres (09) 59 H3
Gesvres-le-Chapitre (77) ...43 G2
Gétigné (44) 75 E6
les Gets (74) 119 F5
Geu (65) 182 D4
Geudertheim (67) 51 E4
Géus-d'Arzacq (64) 165 H6
Géus-d'Oloron (64) 181 H2
Gévezé (35) 57 E2
Gevigney-et-Mercey (70) ...87 E2
Geville (55) 47 H4
Gevingey (39) 117 F1
Gevresin (25) 103 G3
Gevrey-Chambertin (21) ...101 H1
Gevrolles (21) 67 F6
Gevry (39) 102 C3
Gex (01) 118 B3
Geyssans (26) 144 C3
Gez (65) 182 D5
Gez-Ez-Angles (65) 183 E4
Gézaincourt (80) 7 G4
Gézier-et-Fontenelay (70) ...87 E6
Gézoncourt (54) 48 B4
Ghisonaccia (2B) 205 G5
Ghisoni (2B) 205 F4
Ghissignies (59) 9 G3
Ghyvelde (59) 2 C1
Giat (63) 126 B3
Gibeaumeix (54) 48 A6
Gibel (31) 185 H2
Gibercourt (02) 22 A2
Giberville (14) 14 C4
Gibles (71) 115 G4
Gibourne (17) 121 G1
Gibret (40) 165 H4
le Gicq (17) 121 H1
Gidy (45) 62 D6
Giel-Courteilles (61) 38 D4
Gien (45) 82 A3
Gien-sur-Cure (58) 100 B2
Gières (38) 145 G2
la Giettaz (73) 132 D2
Giéville (50) 37 G2
Gièvres (41) 96 C1
Giey-sur-Aujon (52) 85 H1
Giez (74) 132 B3
Gif-sur-Yvette (91) 42 B5
Giffaumont-
Champaubert (51) 67 F1
Gigean (34) 173 E6
Gignac (34) 172 D5
Gignac (46) 138 C4
Gignac (84) 176 B2
Gignac-la-Nerthe (13) ...190 D3
Gignat (63) 127 F6
Gignéville (88) 69 E4
Gigney (88) 69 H3
Gigny (39) 117 F2
Gigny (89) 84 C2
Gigny-Bussy (51) 46 C6
Gigny-sur-Saône (71) 101 H6
Gigondas (84) 158 C6
Gigors (04) 160 C3
Gigors-et-Lozeron (26) ...144 C6
Gigouzac (46) 152 C2
Gijounet (81) 171 E4
Gildwiller (68) 89 E2
Gilette (06) 195 E2
Gilhac-et-Bruzac (07) ...143 H5
Gilhoc-sur-Ormèze (07) ...143 H4
Gillancourt (52) 67 G3
Gillaumé (52) 68 B1
Gilles (28) 41 F3
Gilley (25) 104 B2
Gilley (52) 86 D3
Gillois (39) 103 G5
Gillonnay (38) 130 D6
Gilly-lès-Cîteaux (21) 101 H2
Gilly-sur-Isère (73) 132 C4
Gilly-sur-Loire (71) 114 C2
Gilocourt (60) 21 F6
Gimat (82) 168 C2
Gimbrède (32) 168 A1
Gimeaux (63) 127 F1
Gimécourt (55) 47 F3
Gimel-les-Cascades (19) ...139 E1
Gimeux (16) 121 G4
la Gimond (42) 129 F5
Gimont (32) 168 B5
Gimouille (58) 98 D4
Ginai (61) 39 F4
Ginals (82) 153 F6
Ginasservis (83) 176 D3
Ginchy (80) 8 B5
Gincla (11) 200 B1
Gincrey (55) 25 G6
Gindou (46) 152 B2
Ginestas (11) 187 H3
Ginestet (24) 136 D5
Gingsheim (67) 50 D4
Ginoles (11) 186 C6
Ginouillac (46) 152 D1
Gintrac (46) 138 D5
Giocatojo (2B) 203 F6

Gionges (51) 45 F3
Giou-de-Mamou (15) 140 B5
Gioux (23) 125 G3
Gipcy (03) 113 F2
Girac (46) 139 E5
Girancourt (88) 69 G4
Giraumont (54) 26 A5
Giraumont (60) 21 F5
Girauvoisin (55) 47 H4
Gircourt-lès-Viéville (88) ...69 G2
Girecourt-sur-Durbion (88) ...70 A3
Giremoutiers (77) 43 H4
Girgols (15) 140 B4
Giriviller (54) 70 A1
Girmont (88) 69 H3
Girmont-Val-d'Ajol (88) ...70 A6
Girolles (45) 64 A5
Girolles (89) 83 H4
Giromagny (90) 88 D2
Giron (01) 117 H4
Gironcourt-sur-Vraine (88) ...69 E3
Gironde-sur-Dropt (33) ...150 A2
Gironville (77) 63 H4
Gironville-sur-Essonne (91) ...63 G2
le Girouard (85) 91 E5
Giroussens (81) 169 H4
Giroux (36) 96 D3
Giry (58) 99 F1
Gisay-la-Coudre (27) 40 A3
Giscaro (32) 168 A5
Giscos (33) 149 H5
Gisors (27) 19 G6
Gissac (12) 171 H3
Gissey-le-Vieil (21) 84 D6
Gissey-sous-Flavigny (21) ...85 E4
Gissey-sur-Ouche (21) ...101 G1
Giuncaggio (2A) 205 G3
Giuncheto (2A) 206 D3
Givardon (18) 98 B5
Givarlais (03) 112 D2
Givenchy-en-Gohelle (62) ...8 B2
Givenchy-le-Noble (62) 7 H2
Givenchy-lès-la-Bassée (62) ...2 D6
Giverny (27) 41 G2
Giverville (27) 15 H4
Givet (08) 11 G4
Givonne (08) 24 C2
Givors (69) 130 A5
Givraines (45) 63 G4
Givrand (85) 90 D4
Givrauval (55) 47 F5
le Givre (85) 91 G6
Givrezac (17) 121 E4
Givron (08) 23 G3
Givry (08) 23 H4
Givry (71) 101 H5
Givry (89) 83 H4
Givry-en-Argonne (51) ...46 C3
Givry-lès-Loisy (51) 45 E3
Givrycourt (57) 49 H3
Gizaucourt (51) 46 C2
Gizay (86) 109 F2
Gizeux (37) 78 A5
Gizia (39) 117 F2
Gizy (02) 22 D3
la Glacerie (50) 12 C2
Glageon (59) 10 B4
Glaignes (60) 21 F6
Glaine-Montaigut (63) ...127 G3
Glaire (08) 24 C2
le Glaizil (05) 146 A6
Glamondans (25) 87 H6
Gland (02) 44 C2
Gland (89) 84 C2
Glandage (26) 159 G1
Glandon (87) 123 H4
Glanes (46) 139 F5
Glanges (87) 124 C4
Glanon (21) 102 A3
Glanville (14) 15 E4
Glatens (82) 168 C3
Glatigny (50) 12 C5
Glatigny (57) 26 C5
Glatigny (60) 19 H4
Glay (25) 88 D5
Gleizé (69) 129 H1
Glénac (56) 56 C6
Glénat (15) 139 H5
Glénay (79) 93 F4
Glénic (23) 111 G5
Glennes (02) 22 C5
Glénouze (86) 93 H3
Glère (25) 88 D5
Glicourt (76) 17 H2
Glisolles (27) 40 C2
Glisy (80) 7 G6
Glomel (22) 54 C1
Glonville (54) 70 A1
Glos (14) 15 F5
Glos-la-Ferrière (61) 40 A4
Glos-sur-Risle (27) 18 A6
Gluiras (07) 143 G5
Glun (07) 144 A4
Glux-en-Glenne (58) 100 B3
Goas (82) 168 D3
la Godefroy (50) 35 H3
Godenvillers (60) 20 D3
Goderville (76) 16 C4
Godisson (61) 39 G5
la Godivelle (63) 141 E1
Godoncourt (88) 68 D5
Goerlingen (67) 50 A4
Goersdorf (67) 51 E2
Goès (64) 182 A3
Goetzenbruck (57) 50 C2
Goeulzin (59) 8 D2
Gœuy (56) 56 B4
Gognies-Chaussée (59) ...10 A2
la Gohannière (50) 37 E4
Gohory (28) 61 H4
Goin (57) 48 C2
Goincourt (60) 20 A4
Golancourt (60) 21 G2
Golbey (88) 69 G3
Goldbach-Altenbach (68) ...71 E6
Golfech (82) 168 B2
Golinhac (12) 154 C3
Golleville (50) 12 C3
Gombergean (41) 79 G3
Gomené (22) 56 A2
Gomer (64) 182 C2
Gomelange (57) 26 D4
Gometz-la-Ville (91) 42 B5
Gometz-le-Châtel (91) ...42 B5
Gomiécourt (62) 8 B4
Gommecourt (62) 8 A5
Gommecourt (78) 41 G2
Gommegnies (59) 9 G3
Gommenec'h (22) 33 E3
Gommersdorf (68) 89 E3
Gommerville (28) 62 D3
Gommerville (76) 16 C1
Gomméville (21) 66 D6
Gomont (08) 23 F3
Goncelin (38) 145 H4
Goncourt (52) 68 C3
Gond-Pontouvre (16) 122 C4
Gondecourt (59) 8 D1
Gondenans-les-Moulins (25) ...87 H4
Gondenans-Montby (25) ...88 A4
Gondeville (16) 122 A4
Gondrecourt-Aix (54) 25 H6
Gondrecourt-le-Château (55) ...68 C1
Gondreville (45) 64 A5
Gondreville (54) 48 B5
Gondreville (60) 21 G6
Gondrexange (57) 49 G5
Gondrexon (54) 49 G5
Gondrin (32) 167 E3
les Gonds (17) 121 F3
Gonesse (95) 42 D3
Gonez (65) 183 F3
Gonfaron (83) 192 A4
Gonfreville (50) 12 D5
Gonfreville-Caillot (76) ...16 C4

Gonfreville-l'Orcher (76) ...15 F2
la Gonfrière (61) 39 H4
Gonnehem (62) 2 C5
Gonnelieu (59) 8 D4
Gonnetot (76) 17 F3
Gonneville (50) 12 D2
Gonneville-en-Auge (14) ...14 C4
Gonneville-la-Mallet (76) ...16 B4
Gonneville-sur-Honfleur (14) ...15 F3
Gonneville-sur-Mer (14) ...14 D4
Gonneville-sur-Scie (76) ...17 G3
Gonsans (25) 103 H1
Gontaud-de-Nogaret (47) ...150 D3
la Gonterie-Boulouneix (24) ...123 E6
Gonzeville (76) 17 F3
Goos (40) 165 F4
Gorbio (06) 195 G2
Gorcy (54) 25 G3
Gordes (84) 175 G2
Gorenflos (80) 7 F4
Gorges (44) 75 E6
Gorges (50) 12 D5
Gorges (80) 7 F4
la Gorgue (59) 2 D5
Gorhey (88) 69 G4
Gornac (33) 150 A1
Gorniès (34) 173 E3
Gorre (87) 123 H3
Gorrevod (01) 116 C3
Gorron (53) 58 C2
Gorses (46) 139 F6
Gorze (57) 26 A6
Gosnay (62) 2 C6
Gosné (35) 57 G1
Gosselming (57) 49 H4
Gotein-Libarrenx (64) ...181 G3
Gottenhouse (67) 50 C4
Gottesheim (67) 50 C4
Gouaix (77) 65 E1
Goualade (33) 150 A4
Gouarec (22) 54 D1
Gouaux (65) 183 G6
Gouaux-de-Larboust (31) ...197 E1
Gouaux-de-Luchon (31) ...184 A6
Gouberville (50) 13 E1
Goudargues (30) 157 G5
Goudelancourt-
lès-Berrieux (02) 22 D4
Goudelancourt-
lès-Pierrepont (02) 22 D2
Goudelin (22) 33 F3
Goudet (43) 142 C5
Goudex (31) 184 C2
Goudon (65) 183 F5
Goudourville (82) 151 H6
Gouesnach (29) 53 F3
Gouesnières (35) 35 E4
Gouesnou (29) 31 E4
Gouex (86) 109 G3
Gouézec (29) 53 G1
Gougenheim (67) 50 D4
Gouhelans (70) 87 H4
Gouhenans (70) 88 A3
Goujounac (46) 152 B2
la Goulafrière (27) 39 H3
Goulet (61) 38 D5
Goulien (29) 52 D2
Goulier (09) 199 E1
Goulles (19) 139 G4
les Goulles (21) 85 G6
Goult (84) 175 G3
Goulven (29) 31 F2
Goumois (25) 88 D6
Goupillières (14) 14 B5
Goupillières (27) 40 B1
Goupillières (76) 17 F5
Goupillières (78) 41 H3
Gouraincourt (55) 25 H5
le Gouray (22) 34 A6
Gourbera (40) 165 E3
Gourbesville (50) 12 D4
Gourbit (09) 199 F1
Gourchelles (60) 20 A1
Gourdan-Polignan (31) ...184 A4
Gourdièges (15) 140 D4
Gourdon (06) 178 C4
Gourdon (07) 157 G1
Gourdon (46) 152 C1
Gourdon (71) 115 G1
Gourdon-Murat (19) 125 F5
Gourfaleur (50) 37 F1
Gourgançon (51) 45 F6
Gourgé (79) 93 G5
Gourgeon (70) 87 E2
Gourgue (65) 183 F5
Gourhel (56) 56 A4
Gourin (56) 54 B2
Gourlizon (29) 53 E2
Gournay (36) 111 F1
Gournay-en-Bray (76) ...19 G4
Gournay-le-Guérin (27) ...40 B4
Gournay-Loizé (79) 108 B5
Gournay-sur-Aronde (60) ...21 E4
Gournay-sur-Marne (93) ...43 E4
les Gourreaux (42) 114 A2
Gours (33) 136 A5
Gourvieille (11) 186 A3
Gourville (16) 122 A2
Gourvillette (17) 121 H1
Goussaincourt (55) 68 B1
Goussainville (28) 41 G4
Goussainville (95) 42 D3
Goussancourt (02) 44 D1
Gousse (40) 165 F3
Goussonville (78) 41 H3
Gout-Rossignol (24) 122 D6
la Goutelle (63) 126 C2
Goutevernisse (31) 185 E3
Goutrens (12) 154 B3
Gouts (40) 165 G3
Goutz (32) 168 A3
Gouttières (27) 40 B2
Gouttières (63) 113 E6
Goutz (32) 168 A3
Gouvernes (77) 43 F4
Gouves (62) 8 A3
Gouvets (50) 37 F2
Gouvieux (60) 20 D6
Gouville (27) 40 C2
Gouville-sur-Mer (50) ...36 D1
Gouvix (14) 14 C6
Goux (32) 166 D5
Goux-lès-Dambelin (25) ...88 C4
Goux-les-Usiers (25) 103 H3
Goux-sous-Landet (25) ...103 F2
Gouy (02) 9 E5
Gouy (76) 18 D5
Gouy-en-Artois (62) 8 A3
Gouy-en-Ternois (62) 7 G2
Gouy-les-Groseillers (60) ...20 B2
Gouy-Saint-André (62) 7 E1
Gouy-Servins (62) 8 A2
Gouy-sous-Bellonne (62) ...8 C2
Gouzangrez (95) 42 A1
Gouzeaucourt (59) 8 D4
Gouzens (31) 185 E3
Gouzon (23) 112 A5
Goven (35) 57 E3
Goviller (54) 69 F1
Goxwiller (67) 71 G1
Goyencourt (80) 21 E2
Goyrans (31) 185 F1
Gozon (12) 169 H1
Grabels (34) 173 F5
Graçay (18) 96 D3
Grâce-Uzel (22) 55 G1
Gracay (18) 96 D2
Grâces (22) 33 E4
Gradignan (33) 135 E6
Graffigny-Chemin (52) ...68 C4
Gragnague (31) 169 G5
Graignes-Mesnil-Angot (50) ...13 E5
Grailhen (65) 183 G6
Graimbouville (76) 15 G1
Graincourt-
lès-Havrincourt (62) 8 D4
Grainville (27) 19 E5
Grainville-la-Teinturière (76) ...17 E3
Grainville-Langannerie (14) ...38 D2

Grainville-sur-Odon (14) ...14 A5
Grainville-sur-Ry (76) 17 H6
Grainville-Ymauville (76) ...16 C4
le Grais (61) 38 C5
Graissac (12) 140 D6
Graissessac (34) 172 A5
Graix (42) 143 G1
Gramat (46) 153 F1
Gramazie (11) 186 C4
Grambois (84) 176 B4
Grammond (42) 129 F5
Grammont (70) 88 A4
Gramond (12) 154 A5
Gramont (82) 167 H3
Granace (2A) 207 E3
Grancey-le-Château-
Neuville (21) 85 H3
Grancey-sur-Ource (21) ...67 E6
Granchain (27) 40 A2
Grand (88) 68 B2
le Grand-Abergement (01) ...117 G6
Grand-Auverné (44) 75 F2
le Grand-Bornand (74) ...132 C1
Grand-Bourg (23) 111 E5
Grand-Brassac (24) 136 D1
Grand-Camp (27) 15 H6
Grand-Camp (76) 15 H1
le Grand-Celland (50) 37 F5
Grand-Champ (56) 55 F5
Grand-Charmont (25) 88 C4
le Grand-Combe (30) 157 E6
Grand-Corent (01) 117 F5
Grand-Couronne (76) 18 C5
Grand-Croix (42) 129 G5
Grand-Failly (54) 25 F4
Grand-Fayt (59) 9 H4
le Grand-Fort-Philippe (59) ...2 A2
Grand-Fougeray (35) 57 E6
le Grand-Laviers (80) 6 D4
le Grand-Lemps (38) 131 E6
le Grand-Lucé (72) 79 F1
Grand-Madieu (16) 122 D1
le Grand-Pressigny (37) ...95 E4
le Grand-Quevilly (17) ...17 G6
Grand-Rozoy (02) 22 A6
Grand-Rullecourt (62) 7 H3
Grand-Serre (26) 144 C2
Grand-Verly (02) 9 G5
le Grand-Village-Plage (17) ...120 B1
Grandcamp-Maisy (14) ...13 F4
Grandchamp (08) 23 G2
Grandchamp (52) 86 B2
Grandchamp (72) 60 B3
Grandchamp (78) 41 G5
Grandchamp (89) 82 D3
Grandchamp-le-Château (14) ...14 C5
Grandchamps-
des-Fontaines (44) 74 C4
Grand'Combe-
Châteleu (25) 104 B3
Grand'Combe-
des-Bois (25) 104 D2
Grandcourt (76) 6 B6
Grandcourt (80) 8 A4
la Grande-Fosse (88) 70 D2
la Grande-Motte (34) 173 H6
la Grande-Paroisse (77) ...64 B2
la Grande-Résie (70) 86 C6
la Grande-Rivière (39) ...118 A1
la Grande-Verrière (71) ...100 C4
Grandcourt (77) 87 E3
la Grande-Verrière (71) ...100 C4
les Grandes-Armoises (08) ...24 B3
les Grandes-Chapelles (10) ...66 A2
les Grandes-Loges (51) ...45 H2
les Grandes-Ventes (76) ...17 H3
Grandeyrolles (63) 127 E5
Grandfontaine (25) 103 F1
Grandfontaine (67) 71 E1
Grandfontaine-
sur-Creuse (25) 104 A1
Grandfresnoy (60) 21 E5
Grandham (08) 24 B5
Grandjean (17) 121 F2
Grand'Landes (85) 91 F3
Grandlup-et-Fay (02) 22 C2
Grandpré (08) 24 B5
Grandpuits-
Bailly-Carrois (77) 43 G6
Grandrieu (48) 142 A6
Grandrieux (02) 23 F2
Grandrif (63) 128 B5
Grandris (69) 115 H6
Grandrû (60) 21 G3
Grandrupt (88) 70 D2
Grandrupt-de-Bains (88) ...69 F5
les Grands-Chézeaux (87) ...110 D3
Grandsaigne (19) 125 F5
Grandval (63) 128 A5
Grandvals (48) 155 F1
Grandvaux (71) 115 F2
Grandvelle-
et-le-Perrenot (70) 87 F4
Grandvillars (90) 88 D3
la Grandville (08) 24 B1
Grandville (10) 45 G6
Grandvillers (88) 70 B3
Grandvillers-aux-Bois (60) ...21 E4
Grandvilliers (27) 40 D3
Grandvilliers (60) 20 A2
Grane (26) 158 C1
Granès (11) 186 D6
la Grange (25) 88 B6
Grange-de-Vaivre (39) ...103 E3
Grangermont (45) 63 G4
les Granges (10) 66 B5
Granges (71) 101 F6
les Granges-d'Ans (24) ...138 A2
Granges-la-Ville (70) 88 B3
Granges-le-Bourg (70) ...88 B3
les Granges-le-Roi (91) ...63 E1
Granges-les-Beaumont (26) ...144 B3
Granges-Narboz (25) 104 A4
Granges-sur-Aube (51) ...45 E6
Granges-sur-Lot (47) 151 E4
Granges-sur-Vologne (88) ...70 C4
les Grangettes (25) 104 A4
Grangues (14) 14 D4
Granier (73) 133 E4
Granieu (38) 131 F4
Grans (13) 191 H3
Granville (50) 35 G2
Granzay-Gript (79) 107 G4
Gras (07) 157 H3
les Gras (25) 104 B3
Grassac (16) 122 D4
Grasse (06) 178 C4
Grassendorf (67) 50 D3
Grateloup-
Saint-Gayrand (47) 150 D3
Gratens (31) 185 E2
Gratentour (31) 169 F4
Gratibus (80) 20 D2
Gratot (50) 36 D1
Gratreuil (51) 24 A6
Grattepanche (80) 20 C1
le Gratteris (25) 103 G1
Grattery (70) 87 G3
le Grau-du-Roi (30) 173 H6
les Graulges (24) 122 D5
Graulhet (81) 170 A4
Grauves (51) 45 F3
Graval (76) 19 F3
la Grave (05) 146 C3
Gravelines (59) 2 A1
Gravelotte (57) 26 A5
Graveron-Sémerville (27) ...40 C1
Graves-Saint-Amant (16) ...122 A4
Graveson (13) 174 D3
Gravières (07) 157 E4
Gravigny (27) 40 D2
Gravon (77) 64 D2
Gray (70) 86 C5
Gray-la-Ville (70) 86 C5
Grayan-et-l'Hôpital (33) ...120 B5
Graye-et-Charnay (39) ...117 F2

Graye-sur-Mer (14) 14 B3
Grayssas (47) 151 G6
Grazac (31) 185 G2
Grazac (43) 143 E2
Grazac (81) 169 G3
Grazay (53) 59 E3
Gréalou (46) 153 F3
Gréasque (13) 192 C2
Grébault-Mesnil (80) 6 C5
Grécourt (80) 21 F2
Gredisans (39) 102 C2
la Grée-Saint-Laurent (56) ...56 A3
Grézac (17) 120 D4
le Grez (72) 59 F4
Gréez-sur-Roc (72) 61 E4
Greffeil (11) 187 E4
Grèges (76) 17 G2
Grémecey (57) 49 E4
Grémévillers (60) 19 H3
Gremilly (55) 25 F5
Grémonville (76) 17 E4
Grenade (31) 169 E4
Grenade-sur-l'Adour (40) ...166 A3
Grenant (52) 86 C2
Grenant-
lès-Sombernon (21) 101 F1
Grenay (38) 130 C4
Grenay (62) 2 D6
Grendelbruch (67) 50 C6
Greneville-en-Beauce (45) ...63 E4
Grenier-Montgon (43) ...141 F2
Gréning (57) 49 G2
Grenoble (38) 145 G2
Grenois (58) 83 F6
Grentheville (14) 38 D1
Grentzingen (68) 89 F3
Greny (76) 6 B6
Gréolières (06) 178 C3
Gréoux-les-Bains (04) ...176 D3
Grépiac (31) 185 G1
le Grès (31) 168 D4
le Grès-de-Longroi (28) ...62 C2
le Grès-de-Veliure (85) ...107 E3
Grésigny-Sainte-Reine (21) ...84 D4
la Gresle (42) 115 F6
Gresse-en-Vercors (38) ...145 F4
Gressey (78) 41 G4
Gresswiller (67) 50 C6
Gressy (77) 43 F3
Grésy-sur-Aix (73) 131 H3
Grésy-sur-Isère (73) 132 B4
Gretz-Armainvilliers (77) ...43 F5
Greucourt (70) 87 F3
Greuville (76) 17 F3
Greux (88) 68 B3
la Grève-sur-Mignon (17) ...107 F4
Grévillers (62) 8 A4
Gréville-Hague (50) 12 B1
Grevilly (71) 116 B2
Grez (60) 20 A2
le Grez (72) 59 G4
Grez-en-Bouère (53) 77 E1
Grez-Neuville (49) 76 D3
Grez-sur-Loing (77) 64 A3
Grézac (17) 120 D4
Grézels (46) 152 A3
Grèzes (24) 138 B3
Grèzes (43) 141 H5
Grèzes (46) 153 F2
Grèzes (48) 155 H3
Grézet-Cavagnan (47) ...150 C4
Grézian (65) 183 G6
Grézieu-la-Varenne (69) ...129 H3
Grézieu-le-Marché (69) ...129 F4
Grézieux-le-Fromental (42) ...129 E4
Grézillac (33) 135 H5
Grézillé (49) 77 F5
Grézolles (42) 128 C2
Gricourt (02) 9 E6
Grièges (01) 116 B4
Gries (67) 51 E4
Griesbach-au-Val (68) ...71 E5
Griesheim-
près-Molsheim (67) 50 D6
Griesheim-sur-Souffel (67) ...51 E5
Grignan (26) 158 C4
Grigneuseville (76) 17 H4
Grignois (33) 137 E3
Grignon (21) 84 D4
Grignon (73) 132 C4
Grignoncourt (88) 69 E6
Grigny (62) 7 E1
Grigny (69) 130 A4
Grigny (91) 42 D6
la Grigonnais (44) 74 C2
Grillon (84) 158 C4
Grilly (01) 118 B3
Grimaucourt-en-Woëvre (55) ...47 G1
Grimaucourt-
près-Sampigny (55) 47 G4
Grimaud (83) 194 A4
la Grimaudière (86) 93 H5
Grimault (89) 84 A3
Grimbosq (14) 14 B5
Grimesnil (50) 36 D2
Grimonviller (54) 69 F2
Grincourt-lès-Pas (62) 7 H4
Grindorff-Bizing (57) 27 E3
la Gripperie-
Saint-Symphorien (17) ...120 C2
Grippon (54) 69 G2
Griscourt (54) 48 B4
Griselles (21) 84 C1
Griselles (45) 64 B5
Grisolles (02) 44 B1
Grisolles (82) 169 E3
Grisy-les-Plâtres (95) 42 B2
Grisy-Suisnes (77) 43 F5
Grisy-sur-Seine (77) 65 E2
Grives (24) 137 H6
Grivesnes (80) 20 D2
Grivillers (80) 21 E2
Grivy-Loisy (08) 24 A4
Groffliers (62) 6 C1
la Groise (59) 9 G4
Groises (18) 98 B1
Groissiat (01) 117 G4
Groisy (74) 118 C6
Grois (76) 19 E5
Grolejac (24) 138 B6
Gron (18) 98 B2
Gron (89) 65 E4
Gronard (02) 22 D1
Gros-Chastang (19) 139 F2
Gros-Réderching (57) 28 A5
le Gros-Theil (27) 18 B6
Grosbliederstroff (57) 27 G5
Grosbois (25) 87 H6
Grosbois-en-Montagne (21) ...85 E6
Grosbois-lès-Tichey (21) ...102 B3
Grosbreuil (85) 91 E5
les Groseillers (79) 107 H1
Groslay (95) 42 D3
Groslée (01) 131 F3
Grosley-sur-Risle (27) ...40 B2
Grosmagny (90) 88 D2
Grosne (90) 88 D3
Grospierres (07) 157 F4
Grosrouvre (78) 41 H4
Grosrouvres (54) 48 A4
Grossa (2A) 206 D3
Grosseto-Prugna (2A) ...204 D6
Grossœuvre (27) 40 D2
Grossouvre (18) 98 C4
Grostenquin (57) 49 G2
Grosville (50) 12 B3
Grouches-Luchuel (80) ...7 G4
Grougis (02) 9 F5
la Groutte (18) 97 H6
Grozon (39) 102 D4
Gruchet-le-Valasse (76) ...15 H1
Gruchet-Saint-Siméon (76) ...17 F2
Grues (85) 106 C3
Gruey-lès-Surance (88) ...69 G5
Gruffy (74) 132 A2
Grugé-l'Hôpital (49) 76 B2
Grugies (02) 9 E6
Grugny (76) 17 H4
Gruissan (11) 188 B4
Grumesnil (76) 19 G3
Grun-Bordas (24) 137 E4
Grundviller (57) 27 G5
Gruny (80) 21 E2
Grury (71) 100 B6

Guizerix (65) 183 H2
Gujan-Mestras (33) 148 C1
Gumbrechtshoffen (67) ...50 D3
Gumery (10) 65 F2
Gumiane (26) 159 E3
Gumières (42) 128 D5
Gumond (19) 139 F2
Gundershoffen (67) 50 D3
Gundolsheim (68) 71 F6
Gungwiller (67) 50 A3
Gunsbach (68) 71 E5
Gunstett (67) 51 E2
Guntzviller (57) 50 B4
Guny (02) 22 A4
Guran (31) 184 A6
Gurat (16) 122 C6
Gurcy-le-Châtel (77) 64 D2
Gurgy (89) 83 G1
Gurgy-la-Ville (21) 85 F1
Gurgy-le-Château (21) ...85 G1
Gurmençon (64) 182 A3
Gurs (64) 181 H2
Gurunhuel (22) 32 D4
Gury (60) 21 F3
Gussainville (55) 47 H1
Gussignies (59) 9 G2
Guyancourt (78) 42 B4
Guyans-Durnes (25) 103 H2
Guyans-Vennes (25) 104 B2
Guyencourt (02) 22 D5
Guyencourt-Saulcourt (80) ...8 D5
Guyencourt-sur-Noye (80) ...20 C1
la Guyonnière (85) 91 H2
Guyonvelle (52) 86 D1
Guzargues (34) 173 G4
Gy (70) 87 E5
Gy-en-Sologne (41) 80 B6
Gy-les-Nonains (45) 64 B6
Gy-l'Évêque (89) 83 F3
Gye (54) 48 B6
Gyé-sur-Seine (10) 66 D5

H

Habarcq (62) 8 A2
Habas (40) 165 H5
Habère-Lullin (74) 118 D4
Habère-Poche (74) 119 E4
l'Habit (27) 41 F4
Hablainville (54) 49 G6
Hableville (61) 38 D4
Habloville (61) 38 D4
Haboudange (57) 49 F3
Habsheim (68) 89 G2
Hachan (65) 183 H2
Hâcourt (52) 68 C4
Hacqueville (27) 19 F6
Hadancourt-
le-Haut-Clocher (60) ...42 A1
Hadigny-les-Verrières (88) ...69 H2
Hadol (88) 70 A4
Haegen (67) 50 C4
Hagécourt (88) 69 G3
Hagen (57) 26 B2
Hagenbach (68) 89 E2
Hagenthal-le-Bas (68) ...89 G4
Hagenthal-le-Haut (68) ...89 G4
Haget (32) 183 F1
Hagetaubin (64) 165 H6
Hagetmau (40) 165 H4
Hagéville (54) 26 A5
Hagnéville-et-Roncourt (88) ...68 D3
Hagondange (57) 26 B4
Haguenau (67) 51 E3
Haigneville (54) 69 H1
la Haie-Fouassière (44) ...74 D6
la Haie-Traversaine (53) ...59 E2
les Haies (69) 129 H5
Haigneville (54) 69 H1
Haillainville (88) 70 A2
Haillicourt (62) 2 C6
Haims (86) 110 A2
Hainvillers (60) 21 E3
Haironville (55) 47 E5
Haisnes (62) 2 D6
Haleine (61) 58 D1
Halinghen (62) 6 C1
Hallencourt (80) 7 E5
Hallennes-lez-Haubourdin (59) ...3 F5
Hallering (57) 27 E5
les Halles (69) 129 F3
Halles-sous-les-Côtes (55) ...24 D4
Hallignicourt (52) 46 C6
Hallines (62) 2 B4
la Hallotière (76) 19 F4
Halloville (54) 70 A1
Halloy (60) 20 A2
Halloy (62) 7 H3
Halloy-lès-Pernois (80) ...7 F4
Hallu (80) 21 F1
Halluin (59) 3 G4
Halsou (64) 180 C1
Halstroff (57) 27 E3
le Ham (50) 12 D3
le Ham (53) 59 F2
Ham-en-Artois (62) 2 C5
Ham-les-Moines (08) 24 A1
Ham-sous-Varsberg (57) ...27 F5
Ham-sur-Meuse (08) 11 F4
Hamars (14) 14 A6
Hambach (57) 27 H5
Hambers (53) 59 F3
Hamblain-les-Prés (62) ...8 B3
Hambye (50) 37 E2
le Hamel (60) 20 A3
le Hamel (80) 20 B1
Hamel (59) 8 D3
Hamelet (80) 20 B1
Hamelin (50) 37 F6
Hames-Boucres (62) 2 C3
Hammeville (54) 69 F1
Hamonville (54) 48 A4
Hampigny (10) 67 E2
Hampont (57) 49 F3
Han-devant-Pierrepont (54) ...25 G4
Han-lès-Juvigny (55) 25 F4
Han-sur-Meuse (55) 47 G3
Han-sur-Nied (57) 49 E2
Hanc (79) 108 C5
Hanches (28) 41 G6
Hancourt (80) 8 D6
Handschuheim (67) 50 D5
Hangard (80) 20 C1
Hangenbieten (67) 51 E5
Hangest-en-Santerre (80) ...20 D1
Hangest-sur-Somme (80) ...7 F5
Hangviller (57) 50 B4
Hannaches (60) 19 H4
Hannapes (02) 9 G5
Hannappes (08) 23 F1
Hannescamps (62) 8 A4
Hannocourt (57) 49 F2
Hannogne-Saint-Martin (08) ...24 B2
Hannogne-Saint-Rémy (08) ...23 F3
Hannonville-
sous-les-Côtes (55) 47 H2
le Hanouard (76) 17 E3
Hans (51) 46 B1
Hantay (59) 3 E6
Hanvec (29) 31 F5
Hanviller (57) 28 B5
Hanvoile (60) 19 H4
Haplincourt (62) 8 C4
Happencourt (02) 21 H1
Happonvilliers (28) 61 G3
Haramont (02) 21 G6
Haraucourt (08) 24 B2
Haraucourt (54) 49 E5
Haraucourt-sur-Seille (57) ...49 F4
Haravesnes (62) 7 E2
Haravilliers (95) 42 B1

230

Harbonnières (80) 8 A6
Harbouey (54) 49 H6
Harcanville (76) 17 E3
Harchéchamp (88) 68 D2
Harcigny (02) 23 E1
Harcourt (27) 40 B1
Harcy (08) 11 E6
Hardancourt (88) 70 A2
Hardanges (53) 59 F2
Hardecourt-aux-Bois (80) 8 B5
Hardencourt-Cocherel (27) 41 E2
Hardifort (59) 3 G3
Hardinghen (62) 1 G3
Hardinvast (50) 12 C2
Hardivillers (60) 20 B3
Hardivillers-en-Vexin (60) 19 H5
Hardricourt (78) 42 A2
la Harengère (27) 18 C6
Haréville (88) 69 F4
Harfleur (76) 15 F2
Hargarten-aux-Mines (57) 27 E4
Hargeville (78) 41 H3
Hargicourt (02) 20 D2
Hargicourt (80) 20 D2
Hargnies (08) 11 F5
Hargnies (59) 9 H3
Harly (02) 20 A1
Harmonville (88) 69 E1
la Harmoye (22) 33 E6
Harnes (62) 8 C1
Harol (88) 69 G4
Haroué (54) 69 G1
Harponville (80) 7 H5
Harprich (57) 49 F2
Harquency (27) 19 F6
Harreberg (57) 50 B5
Harréville-les-Chanteurs (52) 68 C3
Harricourt (08) 24 C4
Harsault (88) 69 G5
Harskirchen (67) 50 A2
Hartennes-et-Taux (02) 22 A4
Hartmannswiller (68) 71 E6
Hartzviller (57) 50 A5
Harville (55) 47 H1
Hary (02) 23 E1
Haselbourg (57) 50 B5
Hasnon (59) 9 F2
Hasparren (64) 180 D1
Haspelschiedt (57) 28 C5
Haspres (59) 9 F3
Hastingues (40) 164 D5
Hatrize (54) 26 A5
Hatten (67) 51 F2
Hattencourt (80) 21 F1
Hattenville (76) 16 D4
Hattigny (57) 49 H5
Hattmatt (67) 50 C4
Hattstatt (68) 71 F5
Hauban (65) 183 F4
Haubourdin (59) 3 F5
Haucourt (02) 9 G4
Haucourt (62) 8 C3
Haucourt (76) 19 G2
Haucourt-en-Cambrésis (59) 9 E4
Haucourt-Moulaine (54) 25 H3
Haudainville (55) 47 F1
Haudiomont (55) 47 G1
Haudivillers (60) 20 B4
Haudonville (54) 70 A1
Haudrecy (08) 24 A1
Haudricourt (76) 19 G2
Haulchin (59) 9 F2
Haulies (32) 168 A6
Haulmé (08) 11 F6
Haumont-près-Samogneux (55) 25 E6
Hauriet (40) 165 G4
Hausgauen (68) 89 F3
Haussez (76) 19 G3
Haussignémont (51) 46 C5
Haussimont (51) 45 G5
Haussonville (54) 48 D6
Haussy (59) 9 F4
Haut-Clocher (57) 49 H4
le Haut-Corlay (22) 33 E6
Haut-de-Bosdarros (64) 182 C3
Haut-du-Them-Château-Lambert (70) 88 B1
Haut-Lieu (59) 10 A4
Haut-Loquin (62) 1 H4
Haut-Mauco (40) 165 H3
Hautaget (65) 183 H4
Hautbos (60) 19 H2
Haute-Amance (52) 86 D1
Haute-Avesnes (62) 8 A2
la Haute-Beaume (05) 159 G2
la Haute-Chapelle (61) 38 A6
Haute-Épine (60) 20 A3
Haute-Goulaine (44) 74 D5
Haute-Isle (95) 41 G2
Haute-Kontz (57) 26 C2
la Haute-Maison (77) 43 H4
Haute-Rivoire (69) 129 F3
Haute-Vigneulles (57) 27 E5
Hautecloque (62) 7 G2
Hautecour (39) 117 H1
Hautecour (73) 132 D5
Hautecourt-Romanèche (01) 117 F5
Hautefage (19) 139 F3
Hautefage-la-Tour (47) 151 G4
Hautefaye (24) 123 E5
Hautefeuille (77) 43 G5
Hautefond (71) 115 F3
Hautefontaine (60) 21 G5
Hautefort (24) 138 A2
Hauteluce (73) 132 D3
Hautepierre-le-Châtelet (25) 103 H2
Hauterive (03) 114 A6
Hauterive (61) 60 B1
Hauterive (89) 83 G1
Hauterive-la-Fresse (25) 104 A3
Hauterives (26) 144 B2
Hauteroche (21) 85 E4
Hautes-Duyes (04) 160 C5
les Hautes-Rivières (08) 11 F6
Hautesvignes (47) 150 D3
Hauteville (02) 87 G1
Hauteville (08) 44 A1
Hauteville (51) 67 F6
Hauteville (62) 23 G3
Hauteville (73) 131 H4
Hauteville (51) 46 C6
la Hauteville (78) 41 G5
Hauteville-la-Guichard (50) 13 G6
Hauteville-lès-Dijon (21) 85 G6
Hauteville-Lompnes (01) 131 F1
Hauteville-sur-Fier (74) 131 H1
Hauteville-sur-Mer (50) 36 C2
Haution (02) 9 H6
Hautmont (59) 10 A3
Hautmougey (88) 69 G5
Hautot-l'Auvray (76) 17 E3
Hautot-Saint-Sulpice (76) 17 E4
Hautot-sur-Mer (76) 17 G2
Hautot-sur-Seine (76) 18 C5
les Hauts-de-Chée (55) 47 E3
Hauteville-Bocage (50) 12 D4
Hautvillers (51) 45 E1
Hautvillers-Ouville (80) 6 D3
Hauville (27) 18 A5
Hauviné (08) 23 G5
Haux (33) 135 G6
Haux (64) 181 G4
Havange (57) 26 B3
Havelu (28) 41 G4
Haveluy (59) 9 F2
Havernas (80) 7 F4
Haverskerque (59) 2 C5
le Havre (76) 15 E2
Havrincourt (62) 8 D4
le Haÿ-les-Roses (94) 42 D4
Hayange (57) 26 B3
Haybes (08) 11 F5
la Haye (76) 19 E4
la Haye (88) 69 H3
la Haye-Aubrée (27) 18 A5
la Haye-Bellefond (50) 37 E2

la Haye-de-Calleville (27) 18 B6
la Haye-de-Routot (27) 17 E6
la Haye-d'Ectot (50) 12 B4
la Haye-du-Puits (50) 12 C5
la Haye-du-Theil (27) 18 B6
la Haye-le-Comte (27) 18 D6
la Haye-Malherbe (27) 18 C6
la Haye-Pesnel (50) 35 H2
la Haye-Saint-Sylvestre (27) 40 A3
les Hayes (41) 79 E2
Hayes (57) 26 D5
Haynecourt (59) 8 D3
les Hays (39) 102 C4
Hazebrouck (59) 2 C4
Hazembourg (57) 49 H2
le Heaulme (95) 42 B1
Héauville (50) 12 B3
Hébécourt (27) 19 G5
Hébécourt (80) 20 C1
Hébécrevon (50) 37 F1
Héberville (76) 17 E3
Hébuterne (62) 8 A4
Hèches (65) 183 G5
Hecken (68) 89 E2
Hecmanville (27) 40 A1
Hécourt (27) 41 F3
Hécourt (60) 19 G3
Hecq (59) 9 G4
Hectomare (27) 18 B6
Hédauville (80) 8 A4
Hédé (35) 57 E1
Hégenheim (68) 89 G3
Heidolsheim (67) 71 G3
Heidwiller (68) 89 F2
Heiligenberg (67) 50 C6
Heiligenstein (67) 71 F1
Heillecourt (54) 48 D5
Heilles (60) 20 C5
Heilly (80) 7 H5
Heiltz-le-Hutier (51) 46 C5
Heiltz-le-Maurupt (51) 46 C4
Heiltz-l'Évêque (51) 46 C4
Heimersdorf (68) 89 F3
Heimsbrunn (68) 89 E2
Heining-lès-Bouzonville (57) 27 E3
Heippes (55) 47 F2
Heiteren (68) 71 G6
Heiwiller (68) 89 F3
Hélesmes (59) 9 F2
Hélette (64) 180 D2
Helfaut (62) 2 B4
Helfrantzkirch (68) 89 G3
Helléan (56) 56 A4
Hellering-lès-Fénétrange (57) 50 A4
Helleville (50) 12 B2
Hellimer (57) 49 G2
Héloup (61) 59 H2
Helstroff (57) 27 E5
Hem (59) 3 G5
Hem-Hardinval (80) 7 G3
Hem-Lenglet (59) 8 D3
Hem-Monacu (80) 8 C5
Hémevez (50) 12 D3
Hémévillers (60) 21 E4
Héming (57) 49 H4
Hémilly (57) 27 E5
Hémonstoir (22) 55 F2
Hénaménil (54) 49 F5
Hénanbihen (22) 34 B4
Hénansal (22) 34 A4
Hendaye (64) 180 A1
Hendecourt-lès-Cagnicourt (62) 8 C3
Hendecourt-lès-Ransart (62) 8 B3
Hénencourt (80) 7 H5
Henflingen (68) 89 F3
Hengoat (22) 33 E2
Hengwiller (67) 50 C5
Hénin-Beaumont (62) 8 C1
Hénin-sur-Cojeul (62) 8 B3
Héninel (62) 8 B3
Hennebont (56) 54 D5
Hennecourt (88) 69 G3
Hennemont (55) 47 H1
Henneveux (62) 1 G4
Hennezel (88) 69 F5
Hénon (22) 33 H5
Hénonville (60) 20 A6
Hénouville (76) 17 F6
Henrichemont (18) 81 H6
Henridorff (57) 50 B4
Henriville (57) 49 G1
Hénu (62) 7 H3
Henvic (29) 31 H3
Hérange (57) 50 B4
Herbault (41) 79 G3
Herbécourt (80) 8 B5
les Herbelles (62) 2 A5
l'Herbergement (85) 91 G2
Herbéviller (54) 49 G6
Herbeuval (08) 25 E3
Herbeuville (55) 47 H2
Herbeville (78) 42 A3
Herbéville (54) 49 G6
Herbeys (38) 145 G3
les Herbiers (85) 92 B4
Herbignac (44) 73 G3
Herbinghen (62) 1 G3
Herbisse (10) 45 G6
Herbitzheim (67) 27 H6
Herblay (95) 42 C3
Herbsheim (67) 71 H2
Hercé (53) 58 C1
Herchies (60) 20 A4
la Hérelle (60) 20 C3
Hérenguerville (50) 36 D2
Hérépian (34) 172 A5
Hères (65) 166 D5
la Hérie (02) 10 A6
le Hérie-la-Viéville (02) 22 C1
Hériménil (54) 49 E6
Hérimoncourt (25) 88 D5
Hérin (59) 9 F2
Hérissart (80) 7 G4
Hérisson (03) 112 D2
Herleville (80) 8 B6
la Herlière (62) 7 H3
Herlies (59) 3 E5
Herlin-le-Sec (62) 7 G2
Herly (62) 1 G5
Herly (80) 21 F1
l'Herm (09) 185 H6
Herm (40) 164 D3
Hermanville (76) 17 F3
Hermanville-sur-Mer (14) 14 C4
les Hermaux (48) 155 H3
Hermaville (62) 8 A2
Hermé (77) 65 E1
Hermelange (57) 50 A5
Hermelinghen (62) 1 G3
l'Hermenault (85) 107 E1
Herment (63) 126 B3
Hermeray (78) 41 G6
Hermes (60) 20 B5
Hermeville (76) 15 F1
Herméville-en-Woëvre (55) 25 G6
Hermies (62) 8 D4
Hermillon (73) 146 C1
Hermin (62) 7 H1

Hérouville-Saint-Clair (14) 14 C4
Hérouvillette (14) 14 C4
Herpelmont (88) 70 B4
Herpont (51) 46 B2
Herpy-l'Arlésienne (08) 23 F3
Herqueville (27) 18 D5
Herqueville (50) 12 A1
Herré (40) 166 D1
Herrère (64) 182 A3
Herrin (59) 3 F5
Herrlisheim (67) 51 F4
Herrlisheim-près-Colmar (68) 71 F5
Hersbach (67) 71 E1
Herserange (54) 25 H3
Hersin-Coupigny (62) 8 A1
Hertzing (57) 49 H5
Hervelinghen (62) 1 F3
Hervilly (80) 8 D6
Héry (58) 99 G1
Héry (89) 83 G1
Héry-sur-Alby (74) 132 A2
Herzeele (59) 2 D3
Hesbécourt (80) 8 D6
Hescamps (80) 19 H2
Hesdigneul-lès-Béthune (62) 2 D6
Hesdigneul-lès-Boulogne (62) 1 F5
Hesdin (62) 7 E2
Hesdin-l'Abbé (62) 1 F4
Hésingue (68) 89 G3
Hesmond (62) 7 E1
Hesse (57) 50 A5
Hessenheim (67) 71 G3
Hestroff (57) 26 D4
Hestrud (59) 10 B3
Hestrus (62) 7 G1
Hétomesnil (60) 20 A3
Hettange-Grande (57) 26 B3
Hettenschlag (68) 71 F5
Heubécourt-Haricourt (27) 41 G1
Heuchin (62) 2 B6
Heucourt-Croquoison (80) 6 D6
Heudebouville (27) 18 D6
Heudicourt (27) 19 G5
Heudicourt (80) 8 D6
Heudicourt-sous-les-Côtes (55) 47 H3
Heudreville-en-Lieuvin (27) 15 H4
Heudreville-sur-Eure (27) 41 E1
Heugas (40) 165 E4
Heugleville-sur-Scie (76) 17 G3
Heugnes (36) 96 A3
Heugon (61) 39 H4
Heugueville-sur-Sienne (50) 36 D1
Heuilley-Cotton (52) 86 B2
Heuilley-le-Grand (52) 86 C2
Heuilley-sur-Saône (21) 86 C6
Heuland (14) 15 E4
Heume-l'Église (63) 126 C3
la Heunière (27) 41 F2
Heuqueville (27) 19 E5
Heuqueville (76) 16 B4
Heuringhem (62) 2 B4
Heurteauville (76) 17 F6
Heurtevent (14) 15 E6
Heussé (50) 37 G6
Heutrégiville (51) 23 G5
Heuzecourt (80) 7 F3
Hévilliers (55) 47 F6
Heyrieux (38) 130 C4
Hézecques (62) 2 A6
le Hézo (56) 73 E1
Hibarette (65) 183 E3
Hières-sur-Amby (38) 130 D3
Hierges (08) 11 F4
Hiermont (80) 7 F3
Hiers-Brouage (17) 120 C2
Hiersac (16) 122 A4
Hiesse (16) 109 F6
Hiesville (50) 13 E4
Hiéville (14) 39 E2
Higuères-Souye (64) 182 C1
Hiis (65) 183 E3
Hilbesheim (57) 50 A4
Hillion (22) 33 H4
Hilsenheim (67) 71 G2
Hilsprich (57) 49 H2
Hinacourt (02) 22 A1
Hinckange (57) 26 D5
Hindisheim (67) 71 H1
Hindlingen (68) 89 E3
Hinges (62) 2 D5
le Hinglé (22) 34 C6
Hinsbourg (67) 50 B3
Hinsingen (67) 49 H2
Hinx (40) 165 E4
Hipsheim (67) 71 H1
Hirel (35) 35 E4
Hirschland (67) 50 A3
Hirsingue (68) 89 F3
Hirson (02) 10 B6
Hirtzbach (68) 89 F3
Hirtzfelden (68) 71 G6
His (31) 184 C4
Hitte (65) 183 F3
Hochfelden (67) 50 D4
Hochstatt (68) 89 F2
Hochstett (67) 51 E4
Hocquigny (50) 35 H2
Hocquinghen (62) 1 G3
Hodenc-en-Bray (60) 19 H4
Hodenc-l'Évêque (60) 20 B5
Hodeng-au-Bosc (76) 6 C6
Hodeng-Hodenger (76) 19 F3
Hodent (95) 41 H1
Hœdic (56) 72 C3
Hœnheim (67) 51 E5
Hœrdt (67) 51 E4
Hœville (54) 49 E5
Hoffen (67) 51 F2
les Hogues (27) 19 E4
la Hoguette (14) 38 D2
Hohatzenheim (67) 50 D4
Hohengœft (67) 50 D5
Hohfrankenheim (67) 50 D4
Hohrod (68) 71 E5
le Hohwald (67) 71 E1
Holacourt (57) 49 E2
Holling (57) 26 D4
Holnon (02) 20 D1
Holque (59) 2 A3
Holtzheim (67) 51 E6
Holtzwihr (68) 71 F4
Holving (57) 49 H2
Hombleux (80) 21 G2
Homblières (02) 9 E6
Hombourg (68) 89 G1
Hombourg-Budange (57) 26 C4
Hombourg-Haut (57) 49 G1
l'Hôme-Chamondot (61) 40 B6
Homécourt (54) 26 A4
Hommarting (57) 50 B4
Hommert (57) 50 B5
Hommes (37) 78 B5
le Hommet-d'Arthenay (50) 13 F6
Homps (11) 187 F3
Homps (32) 168 A3
Hon-Hergies (59) 9 H2
Hondainville (60) 20 C5
Hondeghem (59) 2 C4
Hondevilliers (77) 44 B3
Hondouville (27) 18 C6
Hondschoote (59) 2 D2
Honfleur (14) 15 F3
Honguemare-Guenouville (27) 18 B5
Honnechy (59) 9 F5
Honnecourt-sur-Escaut (59) 8 D5
l'Honor-de-Cos (82) 152 C6
Honskirch (57) 49 H2
Hontanx (40) 166 B3
Hôpital (57) 49 G1
l'Hôpital-Camfrout (29) 31 F5
l'Hôpital-d'Orion (64) 165 F6
l'Hôpital-du-Grosbois (25) 103 H1
l'Hôpital-le-Grand (42) 129 E5
l'Hôpital-le-Mercier (71) 115 E3
l'Hôpital-Saint-Blaise (64) 181 G2
l'Hôpital-Saint-Lieffroy (25) 88 A5
l'Hôpital-sous-Rochefort (42) 128 C3

les Hôpitaux-Neufs (25) 104 A5
les Hôpitaux-Vieux (25) 104 A5
Horbourg-Wihr (68) 71 F4
Hordain (59) 9 E3
la Horgne (08) 24 A2
Horgues (65) 183 E3
l'Horme (42) 129 G5
Hornaing (59) 9 E2
Hornoy-le-Bourg (80) 6 D6
le Horps (53) 59 E2
Horsarrieu (40) 165 H4
Horville-en-Ornois (55) 68 B1
l'Hosmes (27) 40 D4
l'Hospitalet (04) 176 D1
l'Hospitalet-du-Larzac (12) 172 B2
l'Hospitalet-près-l'Andorre (09) 199 F3
Hosta (64) 181 E3
Hoste (57) 49 G1
Hostens (33) 149 E3
Hostiaz (01) 131 F2
Hostun (26) 144 D4
l'Hôtellerie (14) 15 F4
l'Hôtellerie-de-Flée (49) 76 C2
Hotonnes (01) 117 H6
Hotot-en-Auge (14) 14 D5
Hottot-les-Bagues (14) 14 A5
Hottviller (57) 50 C1
la Houblonnière (14) 15 E5
les Houches (74) 133 F1
Houchin (62) 2 D6
Houdain (62) 7 H1
Houdain-lez-Bavay (59) 9 H2
Houdan (78) 41 G4
Houdancourt (60) 21 E4
Houdelaincourt (55) 47 G6
Houdelmont (54) 48 C6
Houdemont (54) 48 D5
Houdetot (76) 17 E3
Houdilcourt (08) 23 F4
Houdreville (54) 69 F1
Houécourt (88) 69 E3
Houeillès (47) 150 B5
Houetteville (27) 18 D6
Houéville (88) 68 D2
Houeydets (65) 183 G3
le Houga (32) 166 C3
Houilles (78) 42 C3
Houlbec-Cocherel (27) 41 F2
Houlbec-près-le-Gros-Theil (27) 18 B6
Houldizy (08) 24 A1
Houlette (16) 121 H3
Houlgate (14) 14 D3
Houlle (62) 2 A3
le Houlme (76) 17 G5
l'Houmeau (17) 106 C4
Hounoux (11) 186 B4
Houplin-Ancoisne (59) 3 F5
Houplines (59) 3 E4
Houppeville (76) 17 G5
Houquetot (76) 15 G1
Hourc (65) 183 F2
Hourges (51) 22 D6
Hours (64) 182 D3
Hourtin (33) 134 B2
Houry (02) 22 D1
Houssay (41) 79 F2
Houssay (53) 58 D6
la Houssaye (27) 40 C2
la Houssaye-Béranger (76) 17 G4
la Houssaye-en-Brie (77) 43 G5
le Housseau-Brétignolles (53) 59 E1
Houssen (68) 71 F4
Housseras (88) 70 B2
Housset (02) 22 C1
la Houssière (88) 70 C3
la Houssoye (60) 19 H5
Houtaud (25) 104 A4
Houtkerque (59) 2 D3
Houtteville (50) 12 D5
Houville-en-Vexin (27) 19 E5
Houville-la-Branche (28) 62 C2
Houvin-Houvigneul (62) 7 G2
Houx (28) 41 G6
Hoymille (59) 2 C2
Huanne-Montmartin (25) 87 H5
Hubersent (62) 1 F5
Hubert-Folie (14) 14 C5
Huberville (50) 12 D3
Huby-Saint-Leu (62) 7 E1
Huchenneville (80) 6 D5
Huclier (62) 7 G1
Hucqueliers (62) 1 G5
Hudimesnil (50) 35 G2
Hudiviller (54) 49 E5
Huelgoat (29) 32 A5
Huest (27) 41 E2
Huêtre (45) 62 C6
Huez (38) 146 A3
Hugier (70) 86 D6
Hugleville-en-Caux (76) 17 F4
Huillé (49) 77 F3
Huilliécourt (52) 68 C4
Huilly-sur-Seille (71) 116 C1
Huiron (51) 46 A5
Huismes (37) 94 B1
Huisnes-sur-Mer (50) 35 G4
Huisseau-en-Beauce (41) 79 F2
Huisseau-sur-Cosson (41) 80 A3
Huisseau-sur-Mauves (45) 80 C1
l'Huisserie (53) 58 C5
Hulluch (62) 3 E6
Hultehouse (57) 50 B4
Humbauville (51) 46 A6
Humbécourt (52) 46 C6
Humbercamps (62) 7 H3
Humbercourt (80) 7 G3
Humberville (52) 68 B3
Humbligny (18) 98 A1
Humerœuille (62) 7 F1
Humes-Jorquenay (52) 86 A1
Humières (62) 7 F1
Hunawihr (68) 71 F3
Hundling (57) 49 H1
Hundsbach (68) 89 F3
Huningue (68) 89 G2
Hunspach (67) 51 F2
Hunting (57) 26 C2
Huparlac (12) 154 D1
Huppy (80) 6 D5
Hurbache (88) 70 C2
Hure (33) 150 B2
Hures-la-Parade (48) 155 H5
Huriel (03) 112 C3
Hurigny (71) 116 B3
Hurtières (38) 146 A1
Hurtigheim (67) 51 E5
Husseren-les-Châteaux (68) 71 F5
Husseren-Wesserling (68) 70 D6
Hussigny-Godbrange (54) 25 H3
Husson (50) 37 G6
Huttendorf (67) 51 E4
Huttenheim (67) 71 H2
Hyds (03) 113 E4
Hyémondans (25) 88 B5
Hyencourt-le-Grand (80) 21 F1
Hyenville (50) 36 D2
Hyères (83) 193 G5
Hyet (70) 87 F4
Hyèvre-Magny (25) 88 A5
Hyèvre-Paroisse (25) 88 A5
Hymont (88) 69 F3

I

Ibarrolle (64) 181 E3
Ibigny (57) 49 H5
Ibos (65) 183 E2
Ichtratzheim (67) 51 F6
Ichy (77) 63 H4
Idaux-Mendy (64) 181 F3

Idrac-Respaillès (32) 167 G6
Idron (64) 182 C2
Ids-Saint-Roch (18) 97 F6
Iffendic (35) 56 D2
les Iffs (35) 57 E1
Ifs (14) 14 B5
les Ifs (76) 16 D3
Igé (61) 60 D2
Igé (71) 116 B3
Ignaucourt (80) 20 D1
Igney (54) 49 G5
Igney (88) 69 G2
Ignol (18) 98 B4
Igny (70) 86 D5
Igny (91) 42 C5
Igny-Comblizy (51) 44 D2
Igon (64) 182 C3
Igornay (71) 100 D3
Igoville (27) 18 D5
Iguerande (71) 115 E5
Iholdy (64) 181 E2
Île-aux-Moines (56) 72 D1
l'Île-Bouchard (37) 94 C2
Île-d'Aix (17) 106 C6
Île-de-Batz (29) 31 H2
Île-de-Bréhat (22) 33 F1
Île-de-Sein (29) 52 B2
l'Île-d'Elle (85) 107 E3
Île-d'Houat (56) 72 C3
l'Île-d'Yeu (85) 90 A3
Île-Molène (29) 30 A4
l'Île-Rousse (2B) 202 D5
l'Île-Saint-Denis (93) 42 D3
Île-Tudy (29) 53 F4
Ilharre (64) 181 E2
Ilhat (09) 186 A6
les Ilhes (11) 187 E2
Ilhet (65) 183 G5
Ilheu (65) 184 A5
Illange (57) 26 B3
Illartein (09) 184 D5
Illats (33) 149 G2
Ille-sur-Têt (66) 200 D3
Illeville-sur-Montfort (27) 18 A5
Illfurth (68) 89 F2
Illhaeusern (68) 71 G3
Illiat (01) 116 B5
Illier-et-Laramade (09) 199 E1
Illiers-Combray (28) 61 H3
Illiers-l'Évêque (27) 41 E4
Illies (59) 3 E5
Illifaut (22) 56 B2
Illkirch-Graffenstaden (67) 51 E6
Illois (76) 19 G2
Illoud (52) 68 C4
Illy (08) 24 C1
Illzach (68) 89 F1
Ilonse (06) 178 D1
Imbleville (76) 17 F4
Imécourt (08) 24 C5
Imling (57) 49 H4
Imphy (58) 99 E4
Inaumont (08) 23 G3
Incarville (27) 18 D6
Incheville (76) 6 B5
Inchy (59) 9 F4
Inchy-en-Artois (62) 8 D4
Incourt (62) 7 F1
Indevillers (25) 88 D5
Indre (44) 74 C5
Ineuil (18) 97 G5
les Infournas (05) 160 B1
Ingenheim (67) 50 D4
Ingersheim (68) 71 F4
Inghem (62) 2 B5
Inglange (57) 26 C3
Ingolsheim (67) 51 F2
Ingouville (76) 17 E2
Ingrandes (36) 110 A4
Ingrandes (49) 75 H4
Ingrandes-de-Touraine (37) 78 B6
Ingrannes (45) 63 F6
Ingré (45) 80 D1
Inguiniel (56) 54 D3
Ingwiller (67) 50 C3
Injoux-Génissiat (01) 117 H6
Innenheim (67) 71 E1
Innimond (01) 131 F3
Inor (55) 24 D3
Insming (57) 49 G2
Insviller (57) 49 H3
Intraville (76) 17 H2
Intres (07) 143 F4
Intville-la-Guétard (45) 63 F3
Inval-Boiron (80) 6 D6
Inxent (62) 1 F6
Inzinzac-Lochrist (56) 54 D4
Ippécourt (55) 47 F2
Ippling (57) 49 H1
Irai (61) 40 B5
Irais (79) 93 G4
Irancy (89) 83 G3
Iré-le-Sec (55) 25 E4
Irigny (69) 130 A4
Irissarry (64) 180 D2
Irles (80) 8 B4
Irodouër (35) 56 D1
Iron (02) 9 G6
Irouléguy (64) 180 D3
Irreville (27) 41 E1
Irvillac (29) 31 F5
Is-en-Bassigny (52) 68 B6
Is-sur-Tille (21) 85 H4
Isbergues (62) 2 C5
Isches (88) 69 E6
Isdes (45) 81 F3
Isenay (58) 99 G5
Isigny-le-Buat (50) 37 F5
Isigny-sur-Mer (14) 13 F5
Island (89) 83 H5
Isle (87) 124 B3
l'Isle-Adam (95) 42 C2
l'Isle-Arné (32) 168 A5
Isle-Aubigny (10) 66 C1
Isle-Aumont (10) 66 B4
l'Isle-Bouzon (32) 168 A2
l'Isle-d'Abeau (38) 130 D4
l'Isle-de-Noé (32) 167 G5
l'Isle-d'Espagnac (16) 122 B4
l'Isle-en-Dodon (31) 184 C1
l'Isle-Jourdain (32) 168 C5
l'Isle-Jourdain (86) 109 F3
l'Isle-Saint-Georges (33) 135 F6
l'Isle-sur-la-Sorgue (84) 175 F2
l'Isle-sur-le-Doubs (25) 88 B5
l'Isle-sur-Marne (51) 46 B6
l'Isle-sur-Serein (89) 84 A4
les Isles-Bardel (14) 38 C2
Isles-les-Meldeuses (77) 43 H2
Isles-lès-Villenoy (77) 43 G3
les Islettes (55) 46 D2
Isneauville (76) 17 G5
Isola (06) 161 H6
Isolaccio-di-Fiumorbo (2B) 205 F5
Isômes (52) 86 B3
Ispagnac (48) 156 A4
Ispoure (64) 180 D3
Isques (62) 1 F4
Issac (24) 136 D4
Issamoulenc (07) 143 G5
Issancourt-et-Rumel (08) 24 B1
Issanlas (07) 142 D4
Issans (25) 88 C4
les Issards (09) 186 A4
Issarlès (07) 142 D5
Issé (44) 74 D1
Issel (11) 186 C2
Issendolus (46) 153 F1
Issenhausen (67) 50 D3
Issenheim (68) 71 E6
Issepts (46) 153 G1
Isserpent (03) 114 B5
Isserteaux (63) 127 G4

Issigeac (24) 151 F1
Issirac (30) 157 G5
Issoire (63) 127 G5
Issor (64) 181 H4
Issou (78) 41 H3
Issoudun (36) 97 E3
Issoudun-Létrieix (23) 112 A6
Issus (31) 185 G1
Issy-les-Moulineaux (92) 42 C4
Issy-l'Évêque (71) 100 B6
Istres (13) 191 G4
les Istres-et-Bury (51) 45 F3
Isturits (64) 181 E1
Itancourt (02) 22 A1
Iteuil (86) 109 E2
Itterswiller (67) 71 F1
Itteville (91) 63 G1
Itxassou (64) 180 C1
Itzac (81) 170 A1
Ivergny (62) 7 G3
Iverny (77) 43 F2
Iviers (02) 23 F1
Iville (27) 40 C1
Ivors (60) 43 H1
Ivory (39) 103 F4
Ivoy-le-Pré (18) 81 H6
Ivrey (39) 103 F3
Ivry-en-Montagne (21) 101 F3
Ivry-la-Bataille (27) 41 F3
Ivry-le-Temple (60) 20 A6
Ivry-sur-Seine (94) 42 D4
Iwuy (59) 9 E3
Izaourt (65) 184 A5
Izaut-de-l'Hôtel (31) 184 B5
Izaux (65) 183 G4
Izé (53) 59 F3
Izeaux (38) 145 E1
Izel-lès-Équerchin (62) 8 C2
Izel-lès-Hameaux (62) 7 G2
Izenave (01) 117 F6
Izernore (01) 117 G4
Izeron (38) 145 E3
Izeste (64) 182 B3
Izeure (21) 102 A2
Izier (21) 86 A6
Izieu (01) 131 F3
Izon (33) 135 G4
Izon-la-Bruisse (26) 159 G5
Izotges (32) 166 D5

J

Jablines (77) 43 F3
Jabreilles-les-Bordes (87) 124 C1
Jabrun (15) 141 E5
Jacob-Bellecombette (73) 131 H5
Jacou (34) 173 F5
Jacque (65) 183 F2
Jagny-sous-Bois (95) 42 D2
Jaignes (77) 43 H3
Jaillans (26) 144 C4
la Jaille-Yvon (49) 76 D2
Jaillon (54) 48 B4
Jailly (58) 99 F2
Jailly-les-Moulins (21) 85 E5
Jainvillotte (88) 68 D3
Jalesches (23) 111 H4
Jaleyrac (15) 140 A2
Jaligny-sur-Besbre (03) 114 B3
Jallais (49) 75 G5
Jallanges (21) 102 A3
Jallans (28) 62 A4
Jallaucourt (57) 49 E3
Jallerange (25) 103 E1
Jalognes (18) 98 B2
Jalogny (71) 116 A3
Jâlons (51) 45 F3
Jambles (71) 101 F5
Jambville (78) 42 A2
Jaméricourt (60) 19 H5
Jametz (55) 25 E4
Janailhac (87) 124 B4
Janaillat (23) 111 F6
Jancigny (21) 86 B5
Jandun (08) 24 A2
Janneyrias (38) 130 C3
Jans (44) 74 C1
Janville (14) 14 D5
Janville (28) 62 D4
Janville (60) 21 F4
Janville-sur-Juine (91) 63 G1
Janvilliers (51) 44 D3
Janvry (51) 22 D6
Janvry (91) 42 C6
Janzé (35) 57 F4
Jarcieu (38) 144 B1
Jard-sur-Mer (85) 106 A3
Jardin (38) 130 B5
Jardres (86) 109 G1
Jargeau (45) 81 E2
Jarjayes (05) 160 C3
Jarménil (88) 70 A4
Jarnac (16) 122 A4
Jarnac-Champagne (17) 121 G4
Jarnages (23) 111 H5
la Jarne (17) 106 D5
Jarnioux (69) 129 G1
Jarnosse (42) 115 F5
Jarny (54) 26 A5
Jarret (65) 183 E4
la Jarrie (17) 107 E5
la Jarrie-Audouin (17) 107 G5
Jarrie (38) 145 G3
Jarrier (73) 146 C1
Jars (18) 82 A5
Jarsy (73) 132 B3
Jarville-la-Malgrange (54) 48 D5
Jarzé (49) 77 F3
Jas (42) 129 E4
Jasney (70) 87 H2
Jassans-Riottier (01) 116 B6
Jasseines (10) 66 C1
Jasseron (01) 117 E4
Jasses (64) 181 H2
Jatxou (64) 180 C1
Jau-Dignac-et-Loirac (33) 120 C6
Jaucourt (10) 67 E3
la Jaudonnière (85) 92 B6
Jaudrais (28) 41 E6
Jaujac (07) 157 F2
Jauldes (16) 122 C3
Jaulges (89) 83 H1
Jaulgonne (02) 44 C2
Jaulnay (37) 94 C4
Jaulnes (77) 65 E2
Jaulny (54) 48 B2
Jaulzy (60) 21 G5
Jaunac (07) 143 F5
Jaunay-Clan (86) 94 C6
Jaure (24) 137 E4
Jausiers (04) 161 F3
Jaux (60) 21 F5
Jauzé (72) 60 C4
Javaugues (43) 141 H2
Javené (35) 57 H2
Javerdat (87) 123 H1
Javerlhac-et-la-Chapelle-Saint-Robert (24) 123 E5
Javernant (10) 66 A4
la Javie (04) 160 D5
Javols (48) 155 H1
Javrezac (16) 121 H3
Javron-les-Chapelles (53) 59 F2
Jax (43) 142 A3
Jaxu (64) 181 E3
Jayac (24) 138 B4
Jayat (01) 116 D3
Jazeneuil (86) 108 D2
Jazennes (17) 121 E4
Jeancourt (02) 8 D6
Jeandelaincourt (54) 48 D3
Jeandelize (54) 48 A1
Jeanménil (88) 70 B2
Jeansagnière (42) 128 C3
Jeantes (02) 23 E1

Jebsheim (68) 71 G4
Jegun (32) 167 G4
la Jemaye (24) 136 D2
Jenlain (59) 9 G3
Jenzat (03) 113 G5
Jésonville (88) 69 F4
Jessains (10) 67 E3
Jetterswiller (67) 50 C5
Jettingen (68) 89 F3
Jeu-les-Bois (36) 96 B6
Jeu-Maloches (36) 96 A3
Jeufosse (78) 41 G2
Jeugny (10) 66 B4
Jeumont (59) 10 B2
Jeurre (39) 117 H3
Jeux-lès-Bard (21) 84 C4
Jeuxey (88) 70 A3
Jevoncourt (54) 69 F2
Jezainville (54) 48 C3
Jézeau (65) 183 G6
Joannas (07) 157 F2
Job (63) 128 B4
Jobourg (50) 12 A1
Joch (66) 200 C3
Jœuf (54) 26 A4
Joganville (50) 12 D3
Joigny (89) 65 F6
Joigny-sur-Meuse (08) 11 F6
Joinville (52) 67 H2
Joinville-le-Pont (94) 42 D4
Joiselle (51) 44 C5
Jolimetz (59) 9 G3
Jolivet (54) 49 F5
Jonage (69) 130 B3
Joncels (34) 172 B4
la Jonchère (85) 91 G6
la Jonchère-Saint-Maurice (87) 124 C1
Jonchères (26) 159 F2
Joncherey (90) 89 E4
Jonchery (52) 67 H4
Jonchery-sur-Suippe (51) 46 A1
Jonchery-sur-Vesle (51) 22 D6
Joncourt (02) 9 E6
Joncreuil (10) 67 E1
Joncy (71) 115 H1
Jonquerets-de-Livet (27) 15 H6
Jonquerettes (84) 175 E2
Jonquery (51) 45 E1
Jonquières (11) 187 G5
Jonquières (34) 172 D5
Jonquières (60) 21 E5
Jonquières (81) 170 C5
Jonquières (84) 158 C6
Jonquières-Saint-Vincent (30) 174 C3
Jons (69) 130 C3
Jonval (08) 24 B3
Jonvelle (70) 69 E6
Jonville-en-Woëvre (55) 48 A1
Jonzac (17) 121 G6
Jonzier-Épagny (74) 118 B6
Jonzieux (42) 143 F1
Joppécourt (54) 25 H4
Jort (14) 39 E2
Josat (43) 142 A2
Joserand (63) 127 F1
Josnes (41) 80 B2
Josse (40) 164 D4
Josselin (56) 55 H3
Jossigny (77) 43 F4
Jou-sous-Monjou (15) 140 C5
Jouac (87) 110 C3
Jouaignes (02) 22 B5
Jouancy (89) 84 A3
Jouars-Pontchartrain (78) 42 A4
Jouaville (54) 26 A6
Joucas (84) 175 G2
Joucou (11) 199 H1
Joudes (71) 117 E2
Joudreville (54) 25 H5
Joué-du-Bois (61) 38 D6
Joué-du-Plain (61) 38 D5
Joué-en-Charnie (72) 59 G5
Joué-l'Abbé (72) 60 B4
Joué-lès-Tours (37) 78 D6
Joué-sur-Erdre (44) 75 E3
Jouet-sur-l'Aubois (18) 98 C3
Jouey (21) 101 E2
Jougne (25) 104 A5
Jouhe (39) 102 C2
Jouhet (86) 109 H2
Jouillat (23) 111 H4
Jouques (13) 176 B5
Jouqueviel (81) 153 H6
Jourgnac (87) 124 A3
Journans (01) 117 F4
Journet (86) 110 A2
Journiac (24) 137 G4
Journy (62) 1 H4
Jours-en-Vaux (21) 101 E3
Jours-lès-Baigneux (21) 85 E3
Joussé (86) 109 F4
Jouvençon (71) 116 C1
Joux (69) 129 F2
Joux-la-Ville (89) 83 H4
Jouy (28) 62 B1
Jouy (89) 64 D4
Jouy-aux-Arches (57) 26 B6
Jouy-en-Argonne (55) 47 E1
Jouy-en-Josas (78) 42 C5
Jouy-en-Pithiverais (45) 63 E5
Jouy-le-Châtel (77) 43 H5
Jouy-le-Moutier (95) 42 B2
Jouy-le-Potier (45) 80 C2
Jouy-lès-Reims (51) 45 E1
Jouy-Mauvoisin (78) 41 G3
Jouy-sous-Thelle (60) 20 A5
Jouy-sur-Eure (27) 41 E2
Jouy-sur-Morin (77) 44 B4
Joyeuse (07) 157 F3
Joyeux (01) 130 C2
Joze (63) 127 G2
Jozerand (63) 127 F1
Jû-Belloc (32) 166 D5
Juaye-Mondaye (14) 13 H6
Jubainville (88) 68 D1
la Jubaudière (49) 75 H6
Jublains (53) 59 E3
le Juch (29) 53 F2
Jugazan (33) 135 H6
Jugeals-Nazareth (19) 138 D3
Jugon-les-Lacs (22) 34 B5
Jugy (71) 116 B1
Juicq (17) 121 F2
Juif (71) 102 A6
Juignac (16) 122 B6
Juigné-des-Moutiers (44) 75 F1
Juigné-sur-Loire (49) 77 E5
Juigné-sur-Sarthe (72) 77 F1
Juignettes (27) 40 A3
Juillac (19) 138 B1
Juillac (32) 167 E6
Juillac (33) 136 A6
Juillac-le-Coq (16) 121 H4
Juillaguet (16) 122 C5
Juillan (65) 183 E3
Juillé (16) 122 C1
Juillé (72) 60 A3
Juillé (79) 108 B5
Juillenay (21) 84 C6
Juilles (32) 168 B5
Juilley (50) 35 H4
Juilly (21) 84 D5
Juilly (77) 43 F2
Jujols (66) 200 B3
Jujurieux (01) 117 F5
Julianges (48) 141 G5
Juliénas (69) 116 A5
Julienne (16) 121 H3
Jullianges (43) 142 B1
Jullié (69) 116 A4
Jullouville (50) 35 G2
Jully (89) 84 B2
Jully-lès-Buxy (71) 101 F6
Jully-sur-Sarce (10) 66 C5
Julos (65) 183 E4
Julvécourt (55) 47 E2

231

Jumeauville (78) ... 41 H3
Jumeaux (63) ... 127 G6
Jumel (80) ... 20 C1
Jumelles (27) ... 41 E3
la Jumellière (49) ... 76 C6
Jumencourt (02) ... 22 A4
Jumièges (76) ... 17 E6
Jumigny (02) ... 22 C4
Jumilhac-le-Grand (24) ... 123 H5
Junas (30) ... 173 H4
Junay (89) ... 84 A1
Juncalas (65) ... 183 E4
Jungholtz (68) ... 71 E6
Junhac (15) ... 154 B1
les Junies (46) ... 152 B3
Junville (08) ... 23 G5
Jupilles (72) ... 78 C2
Jurançon (64) ... 182 B2
Juranville (45) ... 63 H5
Juré (42) ... 128 C2
Jurignac (16) ... 122 A5
Jurques (14) ... 38 A2
Jurvielle (31) ... 197 E1
Jury (57) ... 48 D1
Juscorps (79) ... 107 H4
Jusix (47) ... 150 B2
Jussac (15) ... 140 A4
Jussarupt (88) ... 70 B4
Jussas (17) ... 135 G1
Jussecourt-Minecourt (51) ... 46 C4
Jussey (70) ... 87 E1
Jussy (02) ... 21 H3
Jussy (57) ... 26 B5
Jussy (89) ... 83 G3
Jussy-Champagne (18) ... 98 A3
Jussy-le-Chaudrier (18) ... 98 C2
Justian (32) ... 167 F3
Justine-Herbigny (08) ... 23 F3
Justiniac (09) ... 185 G3
Jutigny (77) ... 64 D1
Juvaincourt (88) ... 69 F2
Juvancourt (10) ... 67 F5
Juvanzé (10) ... 67 E3
Juvardeil (49) ... 77 E1
Juvelize (57) ... 49 F4
Juvignac (34) ... 173 H5
Juvigné (53) ... 58 B3
Juvignies (60) ... 20 B3
Juvigny (02) ... 22 A4
Juvigny (51) ... 45 H1
Juvigny (74) ... 118 C2
Juvigny-en-Perthois (55) ... 47 E6
Juvigny-le-Tertre (50) ... 37 G5
Juvigny-sous-Andaine (61) ... 38 B6
Juvigny-sur-Loison (55) ... 25 E4
Juvigny-sur-Orne (61) ... 39 E5
Juvigny-sur-Seulles (14) ... 14 A5
Juville (57) ... 48 D3
Juvinas (07) ... 157 F1
Juvincourt-et-Damary (02) ... 22 D4
Juvisy-sur-Orge (91) ... 42 D5
Juvrecourt (54) ... 49 F4
Juxue (64) ... 181 F2
Juzanvigny (10) ... 67 E2
Juzennecourt (52) ... 67 G4
Juzes (31) ... 186 A1
Juzet-de-Luchon (31) ... 197 F1
Juzet-d'Izaut (31) ... 184 B5
Juziers (78) ... 42 A2

K

Kalhausen (57) ... 27 H6
Kaltenhouse (67) ... 51 E3
Kanfen (57) ... 26 B2
Kappelen (68) ... 89 F2
Kappelkinger (57) ... 49 H2
Katzenthal (68) ... 71 F4
Kauffenheim (67) ... 51 G3
Kaysersberg (68) ... 71 F4
Kédange-sur-Canner (57) ... 26 C3
Keffenach (67) ... 51 F2
Kembs (68) ... 89 G2
Kemplich (57) ... 26 D3
Kerbach (57) ... 27 G5
Kerbors (22) ... 33 E1
Kerfot (22) ... 33 F2
Kerfourn (56) ... 55 F3
Kergloff (29) ... 32 B6
Kergrist (56) ... 55 F2
Kergrist-Moëlou (22) ... 32 C6
Kerien (22) ... 32 D5
Kerlaz (29) ... 31 E2
Kerling-lès-Sierck (57) ... 26 C3
Kerlouan (29) ... 31 E2
Kermaria-Sulard (22) ... 32 D2
Kermoroc'h (22) ... 33 E3
Kernascléden (56) ... 54 C3
Kernilis (29) ... 31 E3
Kernouës (29) ... 31 E3
Kerpert (22) ... 32 C5
Kerprich-aux-Bois (57) ... 49 H4
Kersaint-Plabennec (29) ... 31 E4
Kertzfeld (67) ... 71 G2
Kervignac (56) ... 54 D4
Keskastel (67) ... 27 H6
Kesseldorf (67) ... 51 G3
Kienheim (67) ... 50 D4
Kiffis (68) ... 89 F4
Killem (59) ... 3 G2
Kilstett (67) ... 51 F4
Kindwiller (67) ... 50 D3
Kingersheim (68) ... 89 F1
Kintzheim (67) ... 71 F3
Kirchberg (68) ... 88 D1
Kirchheim (67) ... 50 D4
Kirrberg (67) ... 50 A3
Kirrwiller (67) ... 50 D3
Kirsch-lès-Sierck (57) ... 26 D2
Kirschnaumen (57) ... 26 D3
Kirviller (57) ... 49 H4
Klang (57) ... 26 D3
Kleingœft (67) ... 50 C5
Knœringue (68) ... 89 G3
Knœrsheim (67) ... 50 C5
Knutange (57) ... 26 B3
Kœnigsmacker (57) ... 26 C3
Kœstlach (68) ... 89 F4
Kœtzingue (68) ... 89 G2
Kœur-la-Grande (55) ... 47 G4
Kœur-la-Petite (55) ... 47 G4
Kogenheim (67) ... 71 G2
Kolbsheim (67) ... 50 D5
Krautergersheim (67) ... 71 G1
Krautwiller (67) ... 51 E4
le Kremlin-Bicêtre (94) ... 42 D4
Kriegsheim (67) ... 51 E4
Kruth (68) ... 70 D6
Kunheim (68) ... 71 G4
Kuntzig (57) ... 26 C3
Kurtzenhouse (67) ... 51 E4
Kuttolsheim (67) ... 50 D5
Kutzenhausen (67) ... 51 F2

L

Laá-Mondrans (64) ... 165 G6
Laas (32) ... 167 E4
Laas (45) ... 63 F5
Laàs (64) ... 181 G1
Labalme (01) ... 117 F6
Labarde (33) ... 135 E4
Labaroche (68) ... 71 E4
Labarrère (32) ... 167 E2
Labarthe (32) ... 167 H4
Labarthe (82) ... 152 B5
Labarthe-Bleys (81) ... 170 A1
Labarthe-Inard (31) ... 184 A4
Labarthe-Rivière (31) ... 184 A4
Labarthe-sur-Lèze (31) ... 185 G1
Labassère (65) ... 183 E4
Labastide (65) ... 183 G4
Labastide-Beauvoir (31) ... 185 H1

Labastide-
 Castel-Amouroux (47) ... 150 C4
Labastide-Cézéracq (64) ... 182 A1
Labastide-Chalosse (40) ... 165 H5
Labastide-Clermont (31) ... 184 D2
Labastide-d'Anjou (11) ... 186 B2
Labastide-d'Armagnac (40) ... 166 C2
Labastide-de-Lévis (81) ... 170 B2
Labastide-de-Penne (82) ... 152 D5
Labastide-de-Virac (07) ... 157 G4
Labastide-Dénat (81) ... 170 C3
Labastide-
 du-Haut-Mont (46) ... 139 G6
Labastide-du-Temple (82) ... 168 D1
Labastide-du-Vert (46) ... 152 B3
Labastide-en-Val (11) ... 187 F4
Labastide-
 Esparbairenque (11) ... 187 E2
Labastide-Gabausse (81) ... 170 B1
Labastide-Marnhac (46) ... 152 C4
Labastide-Monréjeau (64) ... 182 A1
Labastide-Murat (46) ... 152 D2
Labastide-Paumès (31) ... 184 C2
Labastide-Rouairoux (81) ... 187 G1
Labastide-
 Saint-Georges (81) ... 170 A4
Labastide-Saint-Pierre (82) ... 169 E2
Labastide-Saint-Sernin (31) ... 169 F4
Labastide-Savès (32) ... 168 C6
Labastide-
 sur-Bésorgues (07) ... 157 F1
Labastide-Villefranche (64) ... 165 E6
Labastidette (31) ... 185 E1
Labathude (46) ... 153 G1
Labatie-d'Andaure (07) ... 143 G4
Labatmale (64) ... 182 D3
Labatut (09) ... 185 G3
Labatut (40) ... 165 E5
Labatut (64) ... 183 E1
Labatut-Rivière (65) ... 166 D6
Labbeville (95) ... 42 C1
Labeaume (07) ... 157 F3
Labécède-Lauragais (11) ... 186 C2
Labège (31) ... 169 F6
Labégude (07) ... 157 G2
Labéjan (32) ... 167 G6
Labenne (40) ... 164 B5
Labergement-
 du-Navois (25) ... 103 G3
Labergement-Foigney (21) ... 102 B1
Labergement-
 lès-Auxonne (21) ... 102 C2
Labergement-
 lès-Seurre (21) ... 102 A3
Labergement-
 Sainte-Marie (25) ... 103 H5
Laberlière (60) ... 21 E3
Labescau (33) ... 150 A3
Labesserette (15) ... 154 B1
Labessette (63) ... 126 B5
Labessière-Candeil (81) ... 170 B4
Labets-Biscay (64) ... 181 F1
Labeuville (55) ... 48 A1
Labeuvrière (62) ... 2 C6
Labeyrie (64) ... 165 G6
Lablachère (07) ... 157 F3
Laboissière-en-Santerre (80) ... 21 E2
Laboissière-en-Thelle (60) ... 20 B6
Laborde (65) ... 183 G4
Laborel (26) ... 159 G5
Labosse (60) ... 19 H5
Labouheyre (40) ... 148 C5
Laboulbène (81) ... 170 C4
Laboule (07) ... 157 E2
Labouquerie (24) ... 137 F6
Labourgade (82) ... 168 D2
Labourse (62) ... 2 D6
Laboutarie (81) ... 170 B4
Labretonie (47) ... 150 D3
Labrihe (32) ... 168 B4
Labrit (40) ... 149 F6
Labroquère (31) ... 184 A4
Labrosse (45) ... 63 G4
Labrousse (15) ... 140 B5
Labroye (62) ... 7 E2
Labruguière (81) ... 170 C6
Labruyère (21) ... 102 A3
Labruyère (60) ... 20 D5
Labruyère-Dorsa (31) ... 185 G1
Labry (54) ... 26 A5
Laburgade (46) ... 152 D4
Lac-des-Rouges-
 Truites (39) ... 118 B1
le Lac-d'Issarlès (07) ... 142 D6
Lacabarède (81) ... 187 F1
Lacadée (64) ... 165 G6
Lacajunte (40) ... 166 A5
Lacalm (12) ... 140 D6
Lacam-d'Ourcet (46) ... 139 F6
Lacanau (33) ... 134 B4
Lacanche (21) ... 101 E3
Lacapelle-Barrès (15) ... 140 C5
Lacapelle-Biron (47) ... 151 H2
Lacapelle-Cabanac (46) ... 152 A3
Lacapelle-del-Fraisse (15) ... 140 A5
Lacapelle-Livron (82) ... 153 E5
Lacapelle-Marival (46) ... 153 F1
Lacapelle-Pinet (81) ... 170 D1
Lacapelle-Ségalar (81) ... 170 B1
Lacapelle-Viescamp (15) ... 139 H5
Lacarre (64) ... 181 E3
Lacarry-Arhan-Charritte-
 de-Haut (64) ... 181 F4
Lacassagne (65) ... 183 F2
Lacaugne (31) ... 185 E2
Lacaune (81) ... 171 E4
Lacaussade (47) ... 151 G3
Lacave (09) ... 184 D5
Lacave (46) ... 138 D5
Lacaze (81) ... 171 E4
Lacenas (69) ... 129 H1
Lacépède (47) ... 151 E4
Lachaise (16) ... 121 H6
Lachalade (55) ... 46 D1
Lachambre (57) ... 49 G1
Lachamp (48) ... 155 H2
Lachamp-Raphaël (07) ... 143 F6
Lachapelle (47) ... 150 C2
Lachapelle (54) ... 70 C1
Lachapelle (80) ... 20 A1
Lachapelle (82) ... 168 B2
Lachapelle-aux-Pots (60) ... 19 H4
Lachapelle-Auzac (46) ... 138 C5
Lachapelle-en-Blaisy (52) ... 67 G4
Lachapelle-Graillouse (07) ... 142 D6
Lachapelle-Saint-Pierre (60) ... 20 B6
Lachapelle-
 sous-Aubenas (07) ... 157 G2
Lachapelle-
 sous-Chanéac (07) ... 143 F5
Lachapelle-sous-Chaux (90) ... 88 D2
Lachapelle-
 sous-Gerberoy (60) ... 19 H3
Lachapelle-
 sous-Rougemont (90) ... 88 D2
Lachassagne (69) ... 129 H1
Lachau (26) ... 159 G5
Lachaussée (55) ... 48 A2
Lachaussée-
 du-Bois-d'Écu (60) ... 20 B3
Lachaux (63) ... 128 A1
Lachelle (60) ... 21 E4
Lachy (51) ... 44 D5
Lacollonge (90) ... 88 D2
Lacombe (11) ... 186 D1
Lacommande (64) ... 182 A2
Lacoste (34) ... 172 C5
Lacoste (84) ... 175 H3
Lacougotte-Cadoul (81) ... 169 H5
Lacour (82) ... 152 C4
Lacour-d'Arcenay (21) ... 84 C3
Lacourt (09) ... 185 E5
Lacourt-Saint-Pierre (82) ... 169 E2
Lacq (64) ... 182 A1
Lacquy (40) ... 166 B2
Lacres (62) ... 1 F5
Lacroisille (81) ... 186 A1
Lacroix-Barrez (12) ... 140 C4
Lacroix-Falgarde (31) ... 169 F6

Lacroix-Saint-Ouen (60) ... 21 F5
Lacroix-sur-Meuse (55) ... 47 G2
Lacropte (24) ... 137 G4
Lacrost (71) ... 116 C1
Lacrouzette (81) ... 170 D5
Lacs (36) ... 111 H1
Ladapeyre (23) ... 111 H4
Ladaux (33) ... 149 H1
Ladern-sur-Lauquet (11) ... 187 E4
Ladevèze-Rivière (32) ... 167 E5
Ladevèze-Ville (32) ... 166 D6
Ladignac-le-Long (87) ... 124 A5
Ladignac-
 sur-Rondelles (19) ... 139 E3
Ladinhac (15) ... 154 B1
Ladirat (46) ... 139 F6
Ladiville (16) ... 122 A5
Ladoix-Serrigny (21) ... 101 G3
Ladon (45) ... 63 H6
Ladoye-sur-Seille (39) ... 103 E5
Laduz (89) ... 83 E1
Lafage (11) ... 186 B3
Lafage-sur-Sombre (19) ... 139 G2
Lafare (84) ... 158 D6
Lafarre (07) ... 143 G3
Lafarre (43) ... 142 D4
Lafat (23) ... 111 E4
Lafauche (52) ... 68 C3
Laféline (03) ... 113 G3
Laferté-sur-Amance (52) ... 86 D1
Laferté-sur-Aube (52) ... 67 F5
Lafeuillade-en-Vézie (15) ... 140 B6
Laffaux (02) ... 22 B4
Laffite-Toupière (31) ... 184 C3
Laffrey (38) ... 145 G4
Lafitole (65) ... 183 E1
Lafitte (82) ... 168 D2
Lafitte-sur-Lot (47) ... 150 D4
Lafitte-Vigordane (31) ... 185 E2
Lafox (47) ... 151 F6
Lafrançaise (82) ... 152 B6
Lafraye (60) ... 20 B4
Lagamas (34) ... 172 C5
Lagarde (09) ... 186 B5
Lagarde (31) ... 185 H2
Lagarde (32) ... 167 F2
Lagarde (57) ... 49 G5
Lagarde (65) ... 183 E2
Lagarde-d'Apt (84) ... 176 A2
Lagarde-Enval (19) ... 139 E3
Lagarde-Hachan (32) ... 183 H1
Lagarde-Paréol (84) ... 158 B5
Lagarde-sur-le-Né (16) ... 121 H5
Lagardelle (46) ... 152 B3
Lagardelle-sur-Lèze (31) ... 185 F1
Lagardère (32) ... 167 F3
Lagardiolle (81) ... 170 B6
Lagarrigue (47) ... 150 D5
Lagarrigue (81) ... 170 C5
Lageon (79) ... 93 G5
Lagery (51) ... 22 C6
Lagesse (10) ... 66 B6
Lagleygeolle (19) ... 139 F3
Laglorieuse (40) ... 166 B2
Lagnes (84) ... 175 G3
Lagney (54) ... 48 A5
Lagnicourt-Marcel (62) ... 8 C3
Lagnieu (01) ... 130 D2
Lagny (60) ... 21 G3
Lagny-le-Sec (60) ... 43 F2
Lagny-sur-Marne (77) ... 43 F4
Lagor (64) ... 181 H1
Lagorce (07) ... 157 G3
Lagorce (33) ... 135 H3
Lagord (17) ... 106 C4
Lagos (64) ... 182 C3
Lagrâce-Dieu (31) ... 185 F2
Lagrand (05) ... 159 H4
Lagrange (40) ... 166 D2
Lagrange (65) ... 183 G4
Lagrange (90) ... 88 D2
Lagrasse (11) ... 187 G4
Lagraulet-du-Gers (32) ... 167 F3
Lagraulet-Saint-Nicolas (31) ... 168 C3
Lagraulière (19) ... 138 D1
Lagrave (81) ... 170 B3
Lagruère (47) ... 150 C4
Laguenne (19) ... 139 E2
Laguépie (82) ... 153 G6
Laguian-Mazous (32) ... 183 F1
Laguinge-Restoue (64) ... 181 F4
Laguiole (12) ... 140 D6
Lagupie (47) ... 150 C2
Lahage (31) ... 184 D1
Lahas (32) ... 168 B6
Lahaymeix (55) ... 47 F3
Lahayville (55) ... 48 A3
Lahitère (31) ... 185 E3
Lahitte (32) ... 168 A5
Lahitte-Toupière (65) ... 166 D6
Lahonce (64) ... 164 C6
Lahontan (64) ... 165 F6
Lahosse (40) ... 165 G4
Lahourcade (64) ... 182 A1
Lahoussoye (80) ... 7 H5
Laifour (08) ... 11 H6
la Laigne (17) ... 107 F4
Laigné (53) ... 76 C1
Laigné-en-Belin (72) ... 78 B1
Laignelet (35) ... 58 A2
Laigneville (60) ... 20 D6
Laillé (35) ... 57 E4
Lailly (89) ... 65 F4
Lailly-en-Val (45) ... 80 C2
Laimont (55) ... 46 D4
Lainsecq (89) ... 82 D3
Laines-aux-Bois (10) ... 66 A4
Lains (39) ... 117 F3
Lainville-en-Vexin (78) ... 41 H2
Laire (25) ... 88 B3
Laires (62) ... 2 B6
Lairière (11) ... 187 F5
Lairoux (85) ... 91 H6
Laissac (12) ... 154 D4
Laissaud (73) ... 132 A6
Laissey (25) ... 87 G6
Laître-sous-Amance (54) ... 48 D4
Laives (71) ... 116 B1
Laix (54) ... 25 H4
Laizé (71) ... 116 B3
Laize-la-Ville (14) ... 14 B6
Laizy (71) ... 100 C4
Lajo (48) ... 141 H6
Lajoux (39) ... 118 A3
Lalacelle (61) ... 59 G1
Lalande (89) ... 83 E3
Lalande-de-Pomerol (33) ... 135 H4
Lalande-en-Son (60) ... 19 H5
Lalandelle (60) ... 19 H5
Lalandusse (47) ... 151 E2
Lalanne (32) ... 168 A4
Lalanne (65) ... 184 A2
Lalanne-Arqué (32) ... 184 A2
Lalanne-Trie (65) ... 183 G2
Lalaye (67) ... 71 E2
Lalbenque (46) ... 152 D4
Laleu (61) ... 59 H2
Laleu (80) ... 20 D1
Lalevade-d'Ardèche (07) ... 157 F2
Lalheue (71) ... 116 B1
Lalinde (24) ... 137 F5
Lalizolle (03) ... 113 F5
Lallaing (59) ... 8 D1
Lalleu (35) ... 57 F6
Lalleyriat (01) ... 117 H5
Lalley (38) ... 145 G6
Lalobbe (08) ... 23 G2
Lalœuf (54) ... 69 E1
Lalongue (64) ... 182 C1
Lalonquette (64) ... 166 B6
Laloubère (65) ... 183 E3
Lalouret-Laffiteau (31) ... 184 B3

Lalouvesc (07) ... 143 G3
Laluque (40) ... 165 E2
Lama (2B) ... 203 E5
Lamadeleine-
 Val-des-Anges (90) ... 88 D2
Lamagdelaine (46) ... 152 D3
Lamagistère (82) ... 151 G6
Lamaguère (32) ... 168 A6
Lamaids (03) ... 112 C4
Lamalou-les-Bains (34) ... 172 A5
Lamancine (52) ... 67 H4
Lamanère (66) ... 200 C5
Lamanon (13) ... 191 G2
Lamarche (88) ... 68 D5
Lamarche-sur-Saône (21) ... 102 C1
Lamargelle (21) ... 85 F4
Lamarque (33) ... 135 E4
Lamarque-Pontacq (65) ... 182 D3
Lamarque-Rustaing (65) ... 183 G2
Lamasquère (31) ... 185 E1
Lamastre (07) ... 143 G4
Lamath (54) ... 49 E6
Lamative (46) ... 139 G5
Lamayou (64) ... 183 E2
Lamazère (32) ... 167 G5
Lamazière-Basse (19) ... 139 G1
Lamazière-Haute (19) ... 126 A4
Lambach (57) ... 50 C1
Lamballe (22) ... 34 A5
Lambersart (59) ... 3 F5
Lamberville (50) ... 37 H1
Lamberville (76) ... 17 G3
Lambesc (13) ... 175 H5
Lamblore (28) ... 40 C6
Lambres (62) ... 2 B5
Lambres-lez-Douai (59) ... 8 D2
Lambrey (70) ... 87 E2
Lambruisse (04) ... 177 G1
Laméac (65) ... 183 F2
Lamécourt (60) ... 20 D4
Lamelouze (30) ... 156 D6
Lamenay-sur-Loire (58) ... 99 G5
Lamérac (16) ... 121 H6
Lametz (08) ... 24 A3
Lamillarié (81) ... 170 C3
Lammerville (76) ... 17 G3
Lamnay (72) ... 61 E5
Lamongerie (19) ... 124 D5
Lamontélarié (81) ... 171 F5
Lamontgie (63) ... 127 G6
Lamontjoie (47) ... 167 H1
Lamonzie-Montastruc (24) ... 137 E5
Lamonzie-Saint-Martin (24) ... 136 D5
Lamorlaye (60) ... 42 D1
Lamorville (55) ... 47 G2
Lamothe (40) ... 165 H3
Lamothe (43) ... 141 H2
Lamothe-Capdeville (82) ... 169 E1
Lamothe-Cassel (46) ... 152 D2
Lamothe-Cumont (82) ... 168 B3
Lamothe-en-Blaisy (52) ... 67 G3
Lamothe-Fénelon (46) ... 138 C6
Lamothe-Goas (32) ... 167 H3
Lamothe-Landerron (33) ... 150 B2
Lamothe-Montravel (24) ... 136 B5
Lamotte-Beuvron (41) ... 81 E4
Lamotte-Brebière (80) ... 7 G6
Lamotte-Buleux (80) ... 6 D3
Lamotte-du-Rhône (84) ... 158 A5
Lamotte-Warfusée (80) ... 8 A6
Lamouilly (55) ... 24 D4
Lamoura (39) ... 118 A3
Lampaul-Guimiliau (29) ... 31 G4
Lampaul-Plouarzel (29) ... 30 C4
Lampaul-Ploudalmézeau (29) ... 30 D3
Lampertheim (67) ... 51 E4
Lampertsloch (67) ... 29 E6
Lamure-sur-Azergues (69) ... 115 H6
Lanans (25) ... 88 A5
Lanarce (07) ... 156 D1
Lanarvily (29) ... 31 E3
Lanas (07) ... 157 G3
Lancé (41) ... 79 G3
Lanchères (80) ... 6 B3
Lanches-Saint-Hilaire (80) ... 7 F4
Lanchy (02) ... 21 G2
Lancié (69) ... 116 A5
Lancieux (22) ... 34 C4
Lancôme (41) ... 79 G3
Lançon (08) ... 24 B6
Lançon (65) ... 183 G6
Lançon-Provence (13) ... 191 H3
Lancrans (01) ... 118 A5
Landange (57) ... 49 H5
Landas (59) ... 9 E1
Landaul (56) ... 55 E5
Landaville (88) ... 68 D3
Landavran (35) ... 57 H2
la Lande-Chasles (49) ... 77 G4
la Lande-d'Airou (50) ... 37 E3
la Lande-de-Fronsac (33) ... 135 G4
la Lande-de-Goult (61) ... 39 E6
la Lande-de-Lougé (61) ... 38 D6
la Lande-Patry (61) ... 38 B4
la Lande-Saint-Léger (27) ... 15 H4
la Lande-Saint-Siméon (61) ... 38 C4
la Lande-sur-Drôme (14) ... 37 H1
la Lande-sur-Eure (61) ... 40 C6
Landéan (35) ... 58 A1
Landebaëron (22) ... 33 E3
Landébia (22) ... 34 B4
Landécourt (54) ... 69 H1
la Landec (22) ... 34 C4
Landéda (29) ... 30 D3
Landéhen (22) ... 34 A4
Landeleau (29) ... 54 A1
Landelles (28) ... 41 E6
Landelles-et-Coupigny (14) ... 37 G3
Landemont (49) ... 75 F5
Landepéreuse (27) ... 15 H6
Landerneau (29) ... 31 F4
Landeronde (85) ... 91 F4
Landerrouat (33) ... 136 B6
Landerrouet-sur-Ségur (33) ... 150 B1
Landersheim (67) ... 50 D4
Landes (17) ... 107 G6
les Landes-Genusson (85) ... 92 A3
Landes-le-Gaulois (41) ... 79 G3
Landes-sur-Ajon (14) ... 14 A5
Landes-Vieilles-
 et-Neuves (76) ... 19 G1
Landévant (56) ... 54 D5
Landévennec (29) ... 31 F5
Landevieille (85) ... 90 D4
Landeyrat (15) ... 140 D2

Lanet (11) ... 187 F5
Laneuvelle (52) ... 68 D6
Laneuvelotte (54) ... 48 D4
Laneuveville-aux-Bois (54) ... 49 F5
Laneuveville-
 derrière-Foug (54) ... 48 A5
Laneuveville-
 devant-Bayon (54) ... 69 G1
Laneuveville-
 devant-Nancy (54) ... 48 D5
Laneuveville-en-Saulnois (57) ... 49 E4
Laneuveville-lès-Lorquin (57) ... 49 G5
Laneuville-au-Pont (51) ... 46 C2
Laneuville-au-Rupt (55) ... 47 G4
Laneuville-sur-Meuse (55) ... 24 D4
Lanfains (22) ... 33 F6
Lanfroicourt (54) ... 48 D4
Langan (35) ... 57 E1
Langast (22) ... 55 H1
Langatte (57) ... 49 H4
Langé (36) ... 96 B3
Langeac (43) ... 142 A3
Langeais (37) ... 78 C6
Langensoultzbach (67) ... 51 E2
Langeron (58) ... 98 D5
Langesse (45) ... 82 A2
Langey (28) ... 61 G5
Langlade (30) ... 174 A3
Langley (88) ... 69 G2
Langoat (22) ... 32 D2
Langoëlan (56) ... 54 D2
Langogne (48) ... 156 C1
Langoiran (33) ... 149 H1
Langolen (29) ... 53 H2
Langon (33) ... 149 H2
Langon (35) ... 56 D6
Langon (41) ... 96 D1
le Langon (85) ... 107 E2
Langonnet (56) ... 54 B2
Langourla (22) ... 34 A6
Langres (52) ... 86 B1
Langrolay-sur-Rance (22) ... 36 A6
Langrune-sur-Mer (14) ... 14 B3
Languédias (22) ... 34 C5
Languenan (22) ... 34 C5
Langueux (22) ... 33 G4
Languevoisin-Quiquery (80) ... 21 F1
Languidic (56) ... 54 D4
Languimberg (57) ... 49 G4
Langy (03) ... 114 A4
Lanhélin (35) ... 35 E5
Lanhères (55) ... 25 G6
Lanhouarneau (29) ... 31 F3
Lanildut (29) ... 30 C4
Laning (57) ... 49 G2
Laniscat (22) ... 33 E6
Laniscourt (02) ... 22 B3
Lanleff (22) ... 33 F2
Lanloup (22) ... 33 F2
Lanmérin (22) ... 32 D2
Lanmeur (29) ... 32 B2
Lanmodez (22) ... 33 E1
Lanne (65) ... 183 E3
Lanne-en-Barétous (64) ... 181 G3
Lanne-Soubiran (32) ... 166 D3
Lannéanou (29) ... 32 B3
Lannebert (22) ... 33 F2
Lannecaube (64) ... 182 C1
Lannédern (29) ... 31 H6
Lannemaignan (32) ... 166 C2
Lannemezan (65) ... 183 G4
Lannepax (32) ... 167 F3
Lanneplaà (64) ... 165 G6
Lannes (47) ... 167 H1
Lanneuffret (29) ... 31 F4
Lannilis (29) ... 30 D3
Lannion (22) ... 32 C2
Lannoy (59) ... 3 G5
Lannoy-Cuillère (60) ... 19 G3
Lannux (32) ... 166 C5
Lano (2B) ... 205 F1
Lanobre (15) ... 126 B6
Lanouaille (24) ... 124 A6
Lanouée (56) ... 55 H3
Lanoux (09) ... 185 F3
Lanquais (24) ... 137 F6
Lanques-sur-Rognon (52) ... 68 B5
Lanquetot (76) ... 15 H1
Lanrelas (22) ... 56 B1
Lanrigan (35) ... 35 F6
Lanrivain (22) ... 32 D6
Lanrivoaré (29) ... 30 D4
Lanrodec (22) ... 33 F4
Lans (71) ... 101 H6
Lans-en-Vercors (38) ... 145 F3
Lansac (33) ... 135 G3
Lansac (65) ... 183 F3
Lansac (66) ... 200 C1
Lansargues (34) ... 173 H5
Lanslebourg-
 Mont-Cenis (73) ... 147 F1
Lanslevillard (73) ... 147 G1
Lanta (31) ... 185 H1
Lantabat (64) ... 181 E2
Lantages (10) ... 66 C5
Lantan (18) ... 98 A4
Lantéfontaine (54) ... 26 A4
Lantenay (01) ... 117 G6
Lantenay (21) ... 85 F6
Lantenne-Vertière (25) ... 103 E1
Lantenot (70) ... 88 A2
la Lanterne-
 et-les-Armonts (70) ... 88 A1
Lanteuil (19) ... 138 D3
Lanthenans (25) ... 88 B5
Lanthes (21) ... 102 B3
Lantheuil (14) ... 14 B4
Lantic (22) ... 33 F3
Lantignié (69) ... 116 A5
Lantillac (56) ... 55 G3
Lantilly (21) ... 84 D4
Lanton (33) ... 134 B6
Lantosque (06) ... 179 E1
Lantriac (43) ... 142 D4
Lanty (58) ... 100 A5
Lanty-sur-Aube (52) ... 67 E5
Lanuéjols (30) ... 155 H5
Lanuéjols (48) ... 156 A3
Lanuéjouls (12) ... 153 H3
Lanvallay (22) ... 34 D5
Lanvaudan (56) ... 54 D4
Lanvellec (22) ... 32 C3
Lanvénégen (56) ... 54 B3
Lanvéoc (29) ... 31 E5
Lanvollon (22) ... 33 F3
Lanzac (46) ... 138 C5
Laon (02) ... 22 C3
Laons (28) ... 41 E4
Lapalisse (03) ... 114 B4
Lapalud (84) ... 158 A5
Lapan (18) ... 97 G4
Lapanouse (12) ... 155 E4
Lapanouse-de-Cernon (12) ... 172 A2
Laparade (47) ... 150 D4
Laparrouquial (81) ... 170 B1
Lapège (09) ... 199 E1
Lapenche (82) ... 152 D5
Lapenne (09) ... 186 A4
Lapenty (50) ... 37 G6
Laperche (47) ... 150 D3
Lapeyre (65) ... 183 G2
Lapeyrère (31) ... 185 F2
Lapeyrouse (01) ... 130 B1
Lapeyrouse (63) ... 113 E5
Lapeyrouse-Fossat (31) ... 169 F4
Lapeyrouse-Mornay (26) ... 144 B1
Lapeyrugue (15) ... 154 B1
Lapleau (19) ... 139 G2
Laplume (47) ... 151 E5
Lapoutroie (68) ... 71 E4
Lapouyade (33) ... 135 G3
Lappion (02) ... 23 E4
Laprade (11) ... 186 D1
Laprade (16) ... 136 C2
la Laupie (26) ... 158 B2
Laprugne (03) ... 128 C1
Laps (63) ... 127 G4
Lapte (43) ... 143 E2
Lapugnoy (62) ... 2 C6

Laquenexy (57) ... 48 D1
Laqueuille (63) ... 126 C4
Laragne-Montéglin (05) ... 160 A4
Larajasse (69) ... 129 G4
Laramière (46) ... 153 F4
Laran (65) ... 183 H3
Larbey (40) ... 165 G4
Larbont (09) ... 185 F5
Larbroye (60) ... 21 G3
Larcan (31) ... 184 B3
Larcat (09) ... 199 E1
Larçay (37) ... 79 E6
Larceveaux-Arros-Cibits (64) ... 181 E2
Larchamp (53) ... 58 B2
Larchamp (61) ... 38 B5
Larchant (77) ... 63 H4
Larche (04) ... 161 G3
Larche (19) ... 138 C3
le Larderet (39) ... 103 F5
Lardier-et-Valença (05) ... 160 B3
Lardiers (04) ... 176 C1
le Lardin-Saint-Lazare (24) ... 138 A3
Lardy (91) ... 63 F1
Larée (32) ... 166 D2
Laréole (31) ... 168 C4
Largeasse (79) ... 93 E6
Largentière (07) ... 157 F3
Largillay-Marsonnay (39) ... 117 G1
Largitzen (68) ... 89 E3
Largny-sur-Automne (02) ... 21 G6
Larians-et-Munans (70) ... 87 G5
Larivière (90) ... 88 D2
Larivière-Arnoncourt (52) ... 68 C5
Larmor-Baden (56) ... 72 C1
Larmor-Plage (56) ... 54 C5
Larnage (26) ... 144 A3
Larnagol (46) ... 153 E3
Larnas (07) ... 158 A3
Larnat (09) ... 199 E1
Larnaud (39) ... 102 C6
Larnod (25) ... 103 F1
Laroche-près-Feyt (19) ... 126 B4
Laroche-Saint-Cydroine (89) ... 65 F6
Larochemillay (58) ... 100 B5
Larodde (63) ... 126 B5
Laroin (64) ... 182 B2
Laronxe (54) ... 49 F6
Laroque (33) ... 149 H1
Laroque (34) ... 173 E2
Laroque-de-Fa (11) ... 187 F5
Laroque-des-Albères (66) ... 201 F4
Laroque-des-Arcs (46) ... 152 D3
Laroque-d'Olmes (09) ... 186 B5
Laroque-Timbaut (47) ... 151 F5
Laroquebrou (15) ... 139 H5
Laroquevieille (15) ... 140 B4
Larouillies (59) ... 10 A5
Larra (31) ... 168 D4
Larrau (64) ... 181 F4
Larrazet (82) ... 168 D2
Larré (56) ... 55 H5
Larré (61) ... 60 A1
Larressingle (32) ... 167 F3
Larressore (64) ... 180 D1
Larret (70) ... 86 D3
Larreule (64) ... 165 H6
Larreule (65) ... 183 E1
Larrey (21) ... 84 D2
Larribar-Sorhapuru (64) ... 181 F2
Larrivière (40) ... 166 B3
Larrivoire (39) ... 117 H3
Larroque (31) ... 184 A3
Larroque (65) ... 183 H2
Larroque (81) ... 169 H1
Larroque-Engalin (32) ... 167 H2
Larroque-Saint-Sernin (32) ... 167 G3
Larroque-sur-l'Osse (32) ... 167 F2
Larroque-Toirac (46) ... 153 F3
Lartigue (32) ... 168 A6
Lartigue (33) ... 149 H3
Laruns (64) ... 182 B4
Laruscade (33) ... 135 G3
Larzac (24) ... 137 H6
Larzicourt (51) ... 46 B6
Lasalle (30) ... 173 F1
Lasbordes (11) ... 186 C2
Lascabanes (46) ... 152 B4
Lascaux (19) ... 138 D1
Lascazères (65) ... 166 D6
Lascelle (15) ... 140 B4
Lasclaveries (64) ... 182 C1
Lasfaillades (81) ... 171 E5
Lasgraisses (81) ... 170 B3
Laslades (65) ... 183 F3
Lassales (65) ... 183 H3
Lassay-les-Châteaux (53) ... 59 E2
Lassay-sur-Croisne (41) ... 80 B6
Lasse (49) ... 77 H4
Lasse (64) ... 180 D2
Lasséran (32) ... 167 H5
Lasserade (32) ... 166 D5
Lasserre (09) ... 185 E4
Lasserre (31) ... 168 D4
Lasserre (47) ... 167 H2
Lasserre-de-Prouille (11) ... 186 B3
Lasseube (64) ... 182 A3
Lasseube-Propre (32) ... 167 H6
Lasseubetat (64) ... 182 A3
Lassicourt (10) ... 66 D2
Lassigny (60) ... 21 F3
Lasson (14) ... 14 B4
Lasson (89) ... 65 G5
Lassouts (12) ... 155 E3
Lassur (09) ... 199 F1
Lassy (14) ... 38 A3
Lassy (35) ... 56 D4
Lassy (95) ... 42 D2
Lastic (15) ... 141 F3
Lastic (63) ... 126 C3
Lastours (11) ... 187 E2
Lataule (60) ... 21 E3
le Latet (39) ... 103 G5
la Latette (39) ... 103 G5
Lathuile (74) ... 132 B2
Lathus-Saint-Rémy (86) ... 110 A3
Latillé (86) ... 108 D1
Latilly (02) ... 44 B1
Latoue (31) ... 184 B3
Latouille-Lentillac (46) ... 139 F5
Latour (31) ... 185 F3
Latour-Bas-Elne (66) ... 201 G3
Latour-de-Carol (66) ... 198 D3
Latour-de-France (66) ... 200 C1
Latour-en-Woëvre (55) ... 48 A1
Latrape (31) ... 185 F2
Latrecey-
 Ormoy-sur-Aube (52) ... 67 F6
Latresne (33) ... 135 F6
Latrille (40) ... 166 B5
Latronche (19) ... 139 G2
Latronquière (46) ... 139 G6
Lattainville (60) ... 19 H6
Lattes (34) ... 173 H6
Lattre-Saint-Quentin (62) ... 8 A3
Lau-Balagnes (65) ... 182 D4
Laubach (67) ... 51 E3
Laubert (48) ... 156 B2
les Laubies (48) ... 156 A1
Laubressel (10) ... 66 C3
Laubrières (53) ... 58 B6
Laucourt (80) ... 21 E2
Laudrefang (57) ... 49 G1
Laudun-l'Ardoise (30) ... 174 D1
Laugnac (47) ... 151 F5
Laujuzan (32) ... 166 C3
Laulne (50) ... 12 C5
Laumesfeld (57) ... 26 D3
Launac (31) ... 168 D4
Launaguet (31) ... 169 F5
Launay (27) ... 40 B1
Launay-Villiers (53) ... 58 B4
Launois-sur-Vence (08) ... 23 H2
Launstroff (57) ... 26 D2
la Laupie (26) ... 158 B2
Laurabuc (11) ... 186 B3
Laurac (11) ... 186 B3
Laurac-en-Vivarais (07) ... 157 F3
Lauraët (32) ... 167 F2
Lauraguel (11) ... 186 D4
Laure-Minervois (11) ... 187 E3
Laurède (40) ... 165 G3
Laurenan (22) ... 55 H1
Laurens (34) ... 172 B6
Lauresses (46) ... 139 G6
Lauret (34) ... 173 F3
Lauret (40) ... 166 B5
Laurie (15) ... 141 F2
Laurière (87) ... 110 D6
Lauris (84) ... 175 H4
Lauroux (34) ... 172 B4
Laussonne (43) ... 142 D4
Laussou (47) ... 151 G2
Lautenbach (68) ... 71 E6
Lautenbachzell (68) ... 71 E6
Lauterbourg (67) ... 51 G2
Lauthiers (86) ... 109 G1
Lautignac (31) ... 184 D1
Lautrec (81) ... 170 C4
Lauw (68) ... 88 D2
Lauwin-Planque (59) ... 8 C1
Lauzach (56) ... 73 E1
Lauzerte (82) ... 152 A5
Lauzerville (31) ... 169 G6
Lauzès (46) ... 152 D2
le Lauzet-Ubaye (04) ... 161 E3
Lauzun (47) ... 151 E2
Lavacquerie (60) ... 20 B2
Laval (38) ... 145 H2
Laval (53) ... 58 C5
Laval-Atger (48) ... 142 B6
Laval-d'Aix (26) ... 159 F2
Laval-d'Aurelle (07) ... 156 D2
Laval-de-Cère (46) ... 139 F5
Laval-en-Brie (77) ... 64 C2
Laval-en-Laonnois (02) ... 22 C4
Laval-le-Prieuré (25) ... 104 B1
Laval-Morency (08) ... 10 D6
Laval-Pradel (30) ... 157 E6
Laval-Roquecézière (12) ... 171 F4
Laval-Saint-Roman (30) ... 157 H5
Laval-sur-Doulon (43) ... 142 A1
Laval-sur-Luzège (19) ... 139 G2
Laval-sur-Tourbe (51) ... 46 B1
Laval-sur-Vologne (88) ... 70 B4
Lavalade (24) ... 151 G1
Lavaldens (38) ... 145 H4
Lavalette (11) ... 186 D3
Lavalette (31) ... 169 G5
Lavalette (34) ... 172 A5
Lavallée (55) ... 47 F4
Lavancia-Epercy (39) ... 117 G3
le Lavandou (83) ... 193 H5
Lavangeot (39) ... 102 D2
Lavannes (51) ... 23 E5
Lavans-lès-
 Saint-Claude (39) ... 117 H3
Lavans-Quingey (25) ... 103 E2
Lavans-sur-Valouse (39) ... 117 G3
Lavans-Vuillafans (25) ... 103 H2
Lavaqueresse (02) ... 9 G5
Lavardac (47) ... 150 D6
Lavardens (32) ... 167 H4
Lavardin (41) ... 79 F2
Lavardin (72) ... 60 A5
Lavaré (72) ... 60 D5
Lavars (38) ... 145 G5
Lavastrie (15) ... 141 E5
Lavatoggio (2B) ... 202 C5
Lavau (10) ... 66 B3
Lavau (89) ... 82 C4
Lavau-sur-Loire (44) ... 73 H4
Lavaudieu (43) ... 142 A2
Lavaufranche (23) ... 112 A4
Lavault-de-Frétoy (58) ... 100 B3
Lavault-Sainte-Anne (03) ... 112 D4
Lavaur (24) ... 151 G1
Lavaur (81) ... 169 H5
Lavaurette (82) ... 153 E5
Lavausseau (86) ... 108 C1
Lavaveix-les-Mines (23) ... 111 H5
Lavazan (33) ... 150 A3
Laveissenet (15) ... 140 D3
Laveissière (15) ... 140 D3
Lavelanet (09) ... 186 B5
Lavelanet-
 de-Comminges (31) ... 184 D2
Laveline-
 devant-Bruyères (88) ... 70 B4
Laveline-du-Houx (88) ... 70 B4
Lavenay (72) ... 78 D1
Laventie (62) ... 3 E4
Laveraët (32) ... 167 E6
Lavercantière (46) ... 152 C2
Laverdines (18) ... 98 B2
Lavergne (46) ... 139 E5
Lavergne (47) ... 150 D2
Lavernat (72) ... 78 D2
Lavernay (25) ... 103 E1
Lavernhe (12) ... 155 E5
Lavernose-Lacasse (31) ... 185 E1
Lavernoy (52) ... 68 B6
Laverrière (60) ... 20 A2
Laversine (02) ... 21 H5
Laversines (60) ... 20 B4
Lavérune (34) ... 173 H5
Laveyron (26) ... 144 A2
Laveyrune (07) ... 156 C1
Laveyssière (24) ... 137 E5
Lavieu (42) ... 129 E5
Laviéville (80) ... 8 A5
Lavigerie (15) ... 140 C3
Lavignac (87) ... 123 H4
Lavigney (70) ... 87 E2
Lavigny (39) ... 102 D5
Lavillatte (07) ... 156 C1
Laville-aux-Bois (52) ... 68 A4
Lavilledieu (07) ... 157 G2
Lavilleneuve (52) ... 68 B5
Lavilleneuve-au-Roi (52) ... 67 H4
Lavilletertre (60) ... 42 B1
Laviolle (07) ... 157 F1
Laviron (25) ... 88 B6
Lavit (82) ... 168 C2
Lavoncourt (70) ... 87 E3
Lavours (01) ... 131 F1
Lavoûte-Chilhac (43) ... 141 H3
Lavoûte-sur-Loire (43) ... 142 C3
Lavoux (86) ... 109 F1
Lavoye (55) ... 47 E2
Lawarde-
 Mauger-l'Hortoy (80) ... 20 C2
Laxou (54) ... 48 C5
Lay (42) ... 129 E2
Lay-Lamidou (64) ... 181 H2
Lay-Saint-Christophe (54) ... 48 D4
Lay-Saint-Rémy (54) ... 48 A5
Laye (05) ... 160 B2
Laymont (32) ... 184 D1
Layrac (47) ... 151 F6
Layrac-sur-Tarn (31) ... 169 F3
Layrisse (65) ... 183 E3
Lays-sur-le-Doubs (71) ... 102 C4
Laz (29) ... 53 H1
Lazenay (18) ... 97 E3
Lazer (05) ... 160 A4
Léalvillers (80) ... 7 G4
Léaupartie (14) ... 15 E4
Léaz (01) ... 118 A5
Lebetain (90) ... 89 E3
Lebeuville (54) ... 69 G1
Lebiez (62) ... 1 H6
Leboulin (32) ... 167 H5
Lebreil (46) ... 152 B4
Lebucquière (62) ... 8 C4
Lecci (2A) ... 207 G3
Lecelles (59) ... 9 E1
Lecey (52) ... 86 C1
Lechâtelet (21) ... 102 A3
Léchelle (62) ... 8 C4
Léchelle (77) ... 44 C6
la Léchère (73) ... 132 D5
les Lèches (24) ... 136 D4

Lécluse (59) 8 C2
Lécousse (35) 58 A2
Lecques (30) 173 G3
Lect (39) 117 G3
Lectoure (32) 167 H2
Lécumberry (64) 181 E3
Lécussan (31) 183 H1
Lédas-et-Penthiès (81) 170 D1
Lédat (47) 151 F3
Lédenon (30) 174 C2
Lédergues (12) 171 E1
Lederzeele (59) 2 B3
Ledeuix (64) 181 H1
Lédignan (30) 173 H2
Ledinghem (62) 1 H3
Ledringhem (59) 2 C3
Lée (64) 182 C2
Leers (59) 5 E4
Lées-Athas (64) 181 H5
Lefaux (62) 1 F5
Leffard (14) 38 C3
Leffincourt (08) 23 H5
Leffonds (52) 67 H6
Leffrinckoucke (59) 2 D1
Leforest (62) 8 D1
Lège (31) 184 A6
Lège-Cap-Ferret (33) 134 B5
Légéville-et-Bonfays (88) 69 G4
Léglantiers (60) 20 D4
Légna (39) 117 G3
Légny (69) 129 G2
Léguevin (31) 168 D5
Léguillac-de-Cercles (24) 123 E6
Léguillac-de-l'Auche (24) 137 E2
Lehaucourt (02) 24 A1
Léhon (22) 34 C6
Leigné-les-Bois (86) 95 E5
Leigné-sur-Usseau (86) 94 C4
Leignes-sur-Fontaine (86) 109 H2
Leigneux (42) 128 C3
Leimbach (68) 89 E1
Leintrey (54) 49 G5
Lélex (01) 118 A4
Lelin-Lapujolle (32) 166 C4
Lelling (57) 49 F2
Lemainville (54) 69 G1
Lembach (67) 51 E2
Lemberg (57) 50 C2
Lembeye (64) 166 C6
Lembras (24) 137 E5
Lemé (02) 22 H6
Lème (64) 166 A6
Leménil-Mitry (54) 69 G1
Lémeré (37) 94 B2
Lemmecourt (88) 68 D3
Lemmes (55) 47 F2
Lempaut (81) 170 B6
Lempdes (63) 127 F3
Lempdes-sur-Allagnon (43) 141 G1
Lemps (07) 144 A3
Lemps (26) 159 F4
Lempty (63) 127 G2
Lempzours (24) 137 G1
Lemud (57) 48 D2
Lemuy (39) 103 F4
Lénault (14) 38 A3
Lenax (03) 114 C4
Lencloître (86) 94 B5
Lencouacq (40) 149 G6
Lengelsheim (57) 50 C1
Lengronne (50) 35 H1
Lenharrée (51) 45 H3
Léning (57) 49 G2
Lennon (29) 53 H1
Lenoncourt (54) 48 D5
Lens (62) 8 B1
Lens-Lestang (26) 144 C1
Lent (01) 116 D5
Lent (39) 103 F5
Lentigny (42) 128 D2
Lentillac-du-Causse (46) 153 E2
Lentillac-Saint-Blaise (46) 153 H1
Lentillères (07) 157 F2
Lentilles (10) 67 E1
Lentilly (69) 129 H3
Lentiol (38) 144 C1
Lento (2B) 203 F5
Léobard (46) 152 C1
Léogeats (33) 149 G2
Léognan (33) 135 E6
Léojac (82) 169 F2
Léon (40) 164 C2
Léoncel (26) 144 C5
Léotoing (43) 141 F1
Léouville (45) 63 E4
Lépanges-sur-Vologne (88) 70 B4
Lépaud (23) 112 C4
Lépin-le-Lac (73) 131 G5
Lépinas (23) 111 G6
Lépine (62) 6 D1
Léron-les-Vallées (08) 23 H1
Lepuix (90) 88 C2
Lepuix-Neuf (90) 89 E4
Léran (09) 186 B5
Lercoul (09) 199 E1
Léré (18) 82 A4
Léren (64) 165 E6
Lérigneux (42) 128 C4
Lerm-et-Musset (33) 150 A4
Lerné (37) 94 B2
Lérouville (55) 47 G4
Lerrain (88) 69 G4
Léry (21) 85 F4
Léry (27) 18 D5
Lerzy (02) 10 A6
Lesbœufs (80) 8 B4
Lesbois (53) 58 C1
Lescar (64) 182 A1
Leschaux (74) 132 B3
Leschelle (02) 9 H5
Lescheraines (73) 132 A3
Leschères (39) 117 H2
Leschères-sur-le-Blaiseron (52) 67 G3
Lescherolles (77) 44 B5
Lescheroux (01) 116 D3
Lesches (77) 43 F3
Lesches-en-Diois (26) 159 F2
Lescouët-Gouarec (22) 54 D2
Lescousse (09) 185 G4
Lescout (81) 170 B6
Lescun (64) 181 G5
Lescuns (31) 184 D3
Lescure (09) 185 E5
Lescure-d'Albigeois (81) 170 C2
Lescure-Jaoul (12) 153 H4
Lescurry (65) 183 F2
Lesdain (59) 9 E4
Lesdins (02) 9 E6
Lesges (02) 22 C5
Lesgor (40) 165 F2
Lésignac-Durand (16) 123 F2
Lésigny (77) 43 E5
Lésigny (86) 95 F6
le Leslay (22) 33 F5
Lesme (71) 114 C1
Lesménils (54) 48 C3
Lesmont (10) 66 D2
Lesparre-Médoc (33) 134 C1
Lesparrou (09) 186 B6
Lesperon (07) 158 D2
Lespéron (40) 165 E1
Lespesses (62) 2 C5
Lespielle (64) 166 C6
Lespignan (34) 188 B3
Lespinasse (31) 169 E5
Lespinassière (11) 187 F1
Lespiteau (31) 184 B4
Lespouey (65) 183 F3
Lespourcy (64) 182 C1
Lespugue (31) 184 A3
Lesquerde (66) 200 C2
Lesquielles-Saint-Germain (02) 9 G5
Lesquin (59) 3 G5

Lessac (16) 109 G6
Lessard-en-Bresse (71) 102 A5
Lessard-et-le-Chêne (14) 15 E5
Lessard-le-National (71) 101 G4
Lessay (50) 12 C5
Lesse (57) 49 E2
Lesseux (88) 70 D3
Lessy (57) 26 B5
Lestanville (76) 17 F3
Lestelle-Saint-Martory (31) 184 C4
Lesterps (16) 109 H6
Lestiac-sur-Garonne (33) 149 G1
Lestiou (41) 80 B2
Lestrade-et-Thouels (12) 171 F1
Lestre (50) 12 D3
Lestrem (62) 2 D5
Létanne (08) 24 D3
Lételon (03) 112 D1
Léthuin (28) 62 D2
Letia (2A) 204 C3
Létra (69) 129 G1
Létricourt (54) 48 D3
Letteguives (27) 19 E4
Lettret (05) 160 B3
Leubringhen (62) 1 F3
Leuc (11) 187 E4
Leucamp (15) 140 B6
Leucate (11) 188 B6
Leugny (86) 94 D6
Leugny (89) 83 E3
Leuhan (29) 54 A2
Leuilly-sous-Coucy (02) 22 A4
Leulinghem (62) 2 A4
Leulinghen-Bernes (62) 1 F3
Leurville (52) 68 B3
Leury (02) 22 A4
Leutenheim (67) 51 G3
Leuville-sur-Orge (91) 42 C6
Leuvrigny (51) 44 D2
le Leuy (40) 165 H3
Leuze (02) 10 B6
Levainville (28) 62 C2
Leval (59) 9 H3
Leval (90) 88 D2
Levallois-Perret (92) 42 C3
Levaré (53) 58 C1
Levécourt (52) 68 C4
Levens (06) 195 F1
Levergies (02) 9 E6
Levernois (21) 101 G3
Lèves (28) 62 B1
les Lèves-et-Thoumeyragues (33) 136 B6
Levesville-la-Chenard (28) 62 D3
Levet (18) 97 G5
Levie (2A) 207 E2
Levier (25) 103 G4
Lévignac (31) 168 D5
Lévignac-de-Guyenne (47) 150 C2
Lévignacq (40) 164 D1
Lévignen (60) 43 G1
Lévigny (10) 67 F3
Lévis (89) 83 E3
Lévis-Saint-Nom (78) 42 A5
Levoncourt (55) 47 F4
Levoncourt (68) 89 E4
Levroux (36) 96 C3
Lewarde (59) 8 D2
Lexy (54) 25 G3
Ley (57) 49 F5
Leychert (09) 185 H5
Leyme (46) 139 F6
Leymen (68) 89 G4
Leyment (01) 130 D1
Leynes (71) 116 A4
Leynhac (15) 154 A1
Leyr (54) 48 D4
Leyrieu (38) 130 D3
Leyritz-Moncassin (47) 150 C4
Leyssard (01) 117 F5
Leyvaux (15) 141 F1
Leyviller (57) 49 F2
Lez (31) 184 B6
Lez-Fontaine (59) 10 B3
Lézan (30) 173 G2
Lézardrieux (22) 33 E2
Lézat (39) 118 A2
Lézat-sur-Lèze (31) 185 F2
Lezay (79) 108 C4
Lezennes (59) 3 G5
Lézéville (52) 68 B2
Lézey (57) 49 F4
Lézignan (65) 183 E4
Lézignan-Corbières (11) 187 H3
Lézignan-la-Cèbe (34) 172 C6
Lézigné (49) 77 F3
Lézigneux (42) 128 D4
Lézinnes (89) 84 B2
Lezoux (63) 127 G2
Lhéraule (60) 19 H4
Lherm (31) 185 E1
Lherm (46) 152 B3
Lhéry (51) 45 E1
Lhez (65) 183 F3
Lhommaizé (86) 109 G2
Lhomme (72) 78 D2
l'Hôpital (57) 27 H5
Lhor (57) 49 G3
Lhospitalet (46) 152 C4
Lhoumois (79) 93 G6
Lhuis (01) 131 F3
Lhuître (10) 45 G6
Lhuys (02) 22 C5
Liac (65) 183 E1
Liancourt (60) 20 D5
Liancourt-Fosse (80) 21 F1
Liancourt-Saint-Pierre (60) 19 H6
Liart (08) 10 C6
Lias (32) 168 D6
Lias-d'Armagnac (32) 166 D3
Liausson (34) 172 C5
Libaros (65) 183 G3
Libercourt (62) 3 F6
Libermont (60) 21 G2
Libourne (33) 135 G5
Licey-sur-Vingeanne (21) 86 B4
Lichans-Sunhar (64) 181 G4
Lichères (16) 122 C1
Lichères-près-Aigremont (89) 83 H3
Lichères-sur-Yonne (89) 83 G4
Lichos (64) 181 G2
Lichtenberg (67) 50 C2
Licourt (80) 21 F1
Licq-Athérey (64) 181 G4
Licques (62) 1 H3
Licy-Clignon (02) 44 B1
Lidrezing (57) 49 F3
Liebenswiller (68) 89 G4
Liebsdorf (68) 89 F4
Liebvillers (25) 88 C5
Liederschiedt (57) 50 D1
Lieffrans (70) 87 F4
le Liège (37) 95 G1
Liéhon (57) 26 C6
Liencourt (62) 7 H3
Lieoux (31) 184 B3
Lièpvre (68) 71 F3
Liéramont (80) 8 C5
Liercourt (80) 7 E4
Lières (62) 2 C5
Liergues (69) 129 G2
Liernais (21) 100 D1
Liernolles (03) 114 C3
Lierval (02) 22 C4
Lierville (60) 42 A1
Lies (65) 183 F4
Liesle (25) 103 E2
Liesse-Notre-Dame (02) 22 D3
Liessies (59) 10 B4
Liesville-sur-Douve (50) 12 D4
Liettres (62) 2 B5
Lieu-Saint-Amand (59) 9 E3
Lieuche (06) 178 C1

Lieucourt (70) 86 D6
Lieudieu (38) 130 C6
Lieurac (09) 186 A5
Lieuran-Cabrières (34) 172 C5
Lieuran-lès-Béziers (34) 188 C1
Lieuron (35) 56 D5
Lieusaint (50) 12 D3
Lieusaint (77) 43 E6
Lieutadès (15) 140 D6
Lieuvillers (60) 20 D4
Liévans (70) 87 H3
Liévin (62) 8 A1
Liez (02) 22 A2
Liez (85) 107 F3
Liézey (88) 70 C4
Liffol-le-Grand (88) 68 C3
Liffol-le-Petit (52) 68 C3
Liffré (35) 57 F2
Ligardes (32) 167 G1
Ligescourt (80) 6 D2
Liginiac (19) 126 A6
Liglet (86) 110 B2
Lignac (36) 110 D2
Lignairolles (11) 186 B4
Lignan-de-Bazas (33) 149 H3
Lignan-de-Bordeaux (33) 135 F6
Lignan-sur-Orb (34) 188 B2
Lignareix (19) 125 H4
Ligné (16) 122 B1
Ligné (44) 75 E3
Lignères (61) 39 G5
Lignereuil (62) 7 H2
Lignerolles (03) 112 D4
Lignerolles (21) 85 G1
Lignerolles (27) 41 E4
Lignerolles (36) 112 A2
Lignerolles (61) 40 A6
Lignéville (88) 69 E4
Ligneyrac (19) 138 D4
Lignières (10) 66 A5
Lignières (18) 97 F6
Lignières (41) 79 H2
Lignières (80) 21 E2
Lignières-Châtelain (80) 19 H1
Lignières-de-Touraine (37) 78 C6
Lignières-en-Vimeu (80) 6 D6
Lignières-la-Carelle (72) 60 B2
Lignières-Orgères (53) 38 D6
Lignières-Sonneville (16) 121 H4
Lignières-sur-Aire (55) 47 F4
Lignol (56) 54 D3
Lignol-le-Château (10) 67 F4
Lignon (51) 46 B6
Lignorelles (89) 83 H2
Lignou (61) 38 D5
Ligny-en-Barrois (55) 47 F5
Ligny-en-Brionnais (71) 115 F4
Ligny-en-Cambrésis (59) 9 F4
Ligny-le-Châtel (89) 83 H1
Ligny-lès-Aire (62) 2 C5
Ligny-Saint-Flochel (62) 7 H2
Ligny-sur-Canche (62) 7 G2
Ligny-Thilloy (62) 8 B4
Ligré (37) 94 B2
Ligron (72) 77 H2
Ligsdorf (68) 89 F4
Ligueil (37) 95 E2
Ligueux (24) 137 G1
Ligueux (33) 136 C6
Liguge (86) 109 E2
Lihons (80) 21 E1
Lihus (60) 20 A3
les Lilas (93) 42 D3
Lilhac (31) 184 B3
Lille (59) 3 F5
Lillebonne (76) 15 H1
Lillemer (35) 35 E4
Lillers (62) 2 C5
Lilly (27) 19 F4
Limalonges (79) 108 D5
Limans (04) 176 C2
Limanton (58) 99 H3
Limas (69) 129 H2
Limay (78) 41 H2
Limbrassac (09) 186 A5
Limé (02) 22 C5
Limeil-Brévannes (94) 43 E5
Limendous (64) 182 D2
Limeray (37) 79 F5
Limersheim (67) 71 H1
Limerzel (56) 73 G1
Limésy (76) 17 F4
Limetz-Villez (78) 41 G2
Limeuil (24) 137 G5
Limeux (18) 97 F3
Limeux (80) 7 E5
Limey-Remenauville (54) 48 B3
Limeyrat (24) 137 H3
Limoges (87) 124 A2
Limoges-Fourches (77) 43 F6
Limogne-en-Quercy (46) 153 E3
Limoise (03) 98 D6
Limon (58) 99 F3
Limonest (69) 130 A2
Limont-Fontaine (59) 10 A3
Limony (07) 144 A1
Limours (91) 42 B5
Limousis (11) 187 F2
Limoux (11) 186 D5
la Limouzinière (44) 91 F1
Limpiville (76) 16 C3
Linac (46) 153 H1
Linard (23) 111 G3
Linards (87) 124 C3
Linars (16) 122 B4
Linas (91) 42 C5
Linay (08) 24 D3
Linazay (86) 108 D5
Lindebeuf (76) 17 F3
le Lindois (16) 123 E3
Lindre-Basse (57) 49 G4
Lindre-Haute (57) 49 G4
Linexert (70) 88 A2
Lingé (36) 95 G4
Lingeard (50) 37 G5
Lingèvres (14) 13 H6
Linghem (62) 2 C5
Lingolsheim (67) 51 E5
Lingreville (50) 35 G1
Linguizzetta (2B) 205 G2
Linières-Bouton (49) 77 H5
Liniers (86) 109 F1
Liniez (36) 96 C3
Linsdorf (68) 89 G4
Linselles (59) 3 F4
Linthal (68) 71 E6
Linthelles (51) 45 E5
Linthes (51) 45 E5
Lintot (76) 15 H1
Lintot-les-Bois (76) 17 G3
Linxe (40) 164 D2
Liny-devant-Dun (55) 24 D4
Linzeux (62) 7 F2
Liocourt (57) 48 D3
Liorac-sur-Louyre (24) 137 E4
Liouc (30) 173 G3
Liourdres (19) 139 E5
Lioux (84) 176 A2
Lioux-les-Monges (23) 126 B3
Liposthey (40) 148 D4
Lipsheim (67) 51 E6
Lirac (30) 174 D1
Liré (49) 75 F4
Lirey (10) 66 B4
Liron (30) 173 F1
Lironville (54) 48 B3
Liry (08) 24 A5
Lisbourg (62) 2 B6
Lisieux (14) 15 F5
Lisle (24) 137 E1
Lisle (41) 79 G2

Lisle-en-Barrois (55) 47 E3
Lisle-en-Rigault (55) 46 D5
Lisle-sur-Tarn (81) 169 H3
Lislet (02) 23 E2
Lison (14) 13 F5
Lisores (14) 39 F3
Lisors (27) 19 F5
Lissac (09) 185 G3
Lissac (43) 142 B3
Lissac-et-Mouret (46) 153 G2
Lissac-sur-Couze (19) 138 C3
Lissay-Lochy (18) 97 G4
Lisse-en-Champagne (51) 46 B4
Lisses (91) 42 D6
Lisseuil (63) 113 F6
Lissey (55) 25 E4
Lissieu (69) 129 H2
Lissy (77) 43 F6
Listrac-de-Durèze (33) 136 A6
Listrac-Médoc (33) 134 D3
Lit-et-Mixe (40) 164 D1
Lithaire (50) 12 C5
Litteau (14) 13 G6
Littenheim (67) 50 C4
Litz (60) 20 C4
Livaie (61) 59 H1
Livarot (14) 15 F6
Liverdun (54) 48 C4
Liverdy-en-Brie (77) 43 F5
Livernon (46) 153 F2
Livers-Cazelles (81) 170 B1
Livet (53) 58 D5
Livet-en-Saosnois (72) 60 B2
Livet-et-Gavet (38) 145 H3
la Livinière (34) 187 G2
Livilliers (95) 42 B2
Livinhac-le-Haut (12) 154 A2
la Livinière (34) 187 G2
Livré-la-Touche (53) 58 B6
Livré-sur-Changeon (35) 57 H2
Livron (64) 182 D3
Livron-sur-Drôme (26) 144 A6
Livry (14) 38 A1
Livry (58) 98 D5
Livry-Gargan (93) 43 E3
Livry-Louvercy (51) 45 H1
Livry-sur-Seine (77) 64 A1
Lixhausen (67) 50 D4
Lixheim (57) 50 A4
Lixing-lès-Rouhling (57) 27 G5
Lixing-lès-Saint-Avold (57) 49 G2
Lixy (89) 64 C4
Lizac (82) 168 D1
Lizant (86) 108 D6
Lizeray (36) 96 D3
Lizières (23) 111 E5
Lizine (25) 103 F2
Lizines (77) 64 D1
Lizio (56) 55 H4
Lizos (65) 183 F2
Lizy (02) 22 B3
Lizy-sur-Ourcq (77) 43 H2
la Llagonne (66) 200 A4
Llauro (66) 201 E3
Llo (66) 199 H4
Llupia (66) 201 E3
Lobsann (67) 51 E2
Loc-Brévalaire (29) 31 E3
Loc-Eguiner (29) 31 G4
Loc-Eguiner-Saint-Thégonnec (29) 31 H4
Loc-Envel (22) 32 C4
Locarn (22) 32 C6
Loché-sur-Indrois (37) 95 G2
Loches (37) 95 F2
Loches-sur-Ource (10) 66 D5
le Locheur (14) 14 A5
Lochieu (01) 131 G1
Lochwiller (67) 50 D4
Locmalo (56) 54 D2
Locmaria (56) 72 B4
Locmaria-Berrien (29) 32 A4
Locmaria-Grand-Champ (56) 55 F5
Locmaria-Plouzané (29) 30 D4
Locmariaquer (56) 72 C1
Locmélar (29) 31 G4
Locminé (56) 55 F4
Locmiquélic (56) 54 C5
Locoal-Mendon (56) 55 E6
Locon (62) 2 D5
Loconville (60) 19 H6
Locquénolé (29) 32 A3
Locquignol (59) 9 G3
Locquirec (29) 32 B2
Locronan (29) 53 F2
Loctudy (29) 53 F4
Locunolé (29) 54 B3
Loddes (03) 114 C4
Lodes (31) 184 A3
Lodève (34) 172 C4
Lods (25) 103 H3
Lœuilley (70) 86 C5
Lœuilly (80) 20 B1
Loffre (59) 8 D2
la Loge (10) 66 D3
la Loge-aux-Chèvres (10) 66 D3
Loge-Fougereuse (85) 92 D6
la Loge-Pomblin (10) 66 B5
Logelheim (68) 71 F5
les Loges (14) 37 H2
les Loges (52) 86 B1
les Loges (76) 16 B4
les Loges-en-Josas (78) 42 B5
les Loges-Marchis (50) 37 F6
les Loges-Margueron (10) 66 B5
les Loges-Saulces (14) 38 D3
les Loges-sur-Brécey (50) 37 F5
Lognes (77) 43 E4
Logny-Bogny (08) 23 G1
Logny-lès-Aubenton (02) 23 F1
Logonna-Daoulas (29) 31 E5
Logrian-Florian (30) 173 G2
Logron (28) 61 H4
Loguivy-Plougras (22) 32 C4
Lohéac (35) 56 D4
Lohitzun-Oyhercq (64) 181 F2
Lohr (67) 50 C3
Lohuec (22) 32 C4
Loigné-sur-Mayenne (53) 76 C1
Loigny-la-Bataille (28) 62 C4
Loiré (49) 76 B3
Loire-les-Marais (17) 107 E5
Loiré-sur-Nie (17) 121 H1
Loiron (53) 58 C5
Loisail (61) 60 D1
Loisey-Culey (55) 47 F4
Loisia (39) 117 F2
Loisieux (73) 131 G4
Loisin (74) 118 D3
Loison (55) 25 F5
Loison-sous-Lens (62) 8 B1
Loison-sur-Créquoise (62) 7 E1
Loisy (54) 48 C3
Loisy (71) 116 C1
Loisy-en-Brie (51) 45 E4
Loisy-sur-Marne (51) 46 B4
Loivre (51) 23 E5
Loix (17) 106 B4
Lolif (50) 35 H3
Lolme (24) 151 G1
Lombard (25) 103 E2
Lombard (39) 102 D4
Lombers (81) 170 C4
Lombez (32) 168 B6
Lombia (64) 182 C1
Lombrès (65) 183 H4
Lombreuil (45) 64 A5
Lombron (72) 60 C5
Lommerange (57) 26 A3
Lommoye (78) 41 G3
Lomné (65) 183 G4
Lomont (70) 88 B3
Lomont-sur-Crête (25) 88 B5
Lompnas (01) 131 F2
Lompnieu (01) 131 F1
Lompret (59) 3 F5
la Londe (76) 18 C5
la Londe-les-Maures (83) 193 G6
Londigny (16) 108 D6

Londinières (76) 6 B6
Long (80) 7 E4
Longages (31) 185 E2
Longaulnay (35) 56 D1
Longavesnes (80) 8 C5
Longchamp (21) 102 A1
Longchamp (52) 68 B4
Longchamp (88) 70 A3
Longchamp-sous-Châtenois (88) 69 E3
Longchamps (27) 19 F5
Longchamps-sur-Aire (55) 47 F3
Longchaumois (39) 118 A2
Longcochon (39) 103 G5
Longeau-Percey (52) 86 B2
Longeault (21) 102 A1
Longeaux (55) 47 F5
Longechaux (25) 104 A1
Longechenal (38) 130 D6
Longecourt-en-Plaine (21) 102 A1
Longecourt-lès-Culêtre (21) 101 E2
Longemaison (25) 104 B2
Longepierre (71) 102 B4
Longes (69) 129 H5
Longessaigne (69) 129 F3
Longevelle (70) 88 A3
Longevelle-lès-Russey (25) 104 C1
Longevelle-sur-Doubs (25) 88 B4
Longèves (17) 106 D4
Longèves (85) 107 E2
Longeville (25) 103 H3
la Longeville (25) 104 B3
Longeville-en-Barrois (55) 47 F5
Longeville-lès-Metz (57) 26 B5
Longeville-lès-Saint-Avold (57) 49 F1
Longeville-sur-la-Laines (52) 67 E2
Longeville-sur-Mer (85) 106 B2
Longeville-sur-Mogne (10) 66 B4
Longevilles-Mont-d'Or (25) 104 A5
Longfossé (62) 1 G5
le Longeron (49) 92 B3
Longjumeau (91) 42 C5
Longlaville (54) 25 H2
Longmesnil (76) 19 F3
Longnes (72) 59 H5
Longnes (78) 41 G3
Longny-au-Perche (61) 61 E1
Longperrier (77) 43 F2
Longpont (02) 44 A1
Longpont-sur-Orge (91) 42 C6
Longpré-le-Sec (10) 66 D4
Longpré-les-Corps-Saints (80) 7 E5
Longraye (14) 13 H6
Longré (16) 108 C6
Longroy (76) 6 C5
Longsols (10) 66 C2
Longué-Jumelles (49) 77 G6
Longueau (80) 7 G6
Longuefuye (53) 76 D1
Longueil (76) 17 F2
Longueil-Annel (60) 21 F4
Longueil-Sainte-Marie (60) 21 E5
Longuenesse (62) 2 A4
Longuenoë (61) 59 H1
Longuerue (76) 17 H5
Longues-sur-Mer (14) 13 H5
Longuesse (95) 42 A2
Longueval (80) 8 B5
Longueval-Barbonval (02) 22 C5
Longueville (14) 13 G5
Longueville (47) 150 C3
la Longueville (59) 9 H2
Longueville (77) 64 C1
Longueville-sur-Aube (10) 66 A2
Longueville-sur-Scie (76) 17 H3
Longuevillette (80) 7 G4
Longuyon (54) 25 F4
Longvic (21) 85 H6
Longvillers (14) 14 A6
Longvillers (62) 1 G6
Longvilliers (78) 42 B6
Longwé (08) 24 B4
Longwy (54) 25 H3
Longwy-sur-le-Doubs (39) 102 C3
Lonlay-l'Abbaye (61) 38 A6
Lonlay-le-Tesson (61) 38 C6
Lonnes (16) 122 C1
Lonny (08) 24 A1
Lonrai (61) 60 A2
Lons (64) 182 B2
Lons-le-Saunier (39) 102 D6
Lonzac (17) 121 G4
le Lonzac (19) 125 E5
Looberghe (59) 2 B3
Loon-Plage (59) 2 A2
Loos (59) 3 F5
Loos-en-Gohelle (62) 8 B1
Looze (89) 65 F6
Lopérec (29) 31 G6
Loperhet (29) 31 E5
Lopigna (2A) 204 C4
Loqueffret (29) 31 H5
Lor (02) 23 E3
Loray (25) 104 B1
Lorcières (15) 141 F4
Lorcy (45) 63 H5
Lordat (09) 199 F1
Loré (61) 58 C1
Lorentzen (67) 50 B2
Loreto-di-Casinca (2B) 205 G1
Loreto-di-Tallano (2A) 207 E2
Lorette (42) 129 G5
le Loreur (50) 35 H2
Loreux (41) 81 E3
le Loroux (35) 58 B2
le Loroux-Bottereau (44) 75 E5
Lorp-Sentaraille (09) 184 D5
Lorquin (57) 49 H5
Lorrez-le-Bocage-Préaux (77) 64 B3
Lorris (45) 82 A1
Lorry-lès-Metz (57) 26 B5
Lorry-Mardigny (57) 48 C2
Lortet (65) 183 G4
Loscouët-sur-Meu (22) 56 B2
Losne (21) 102 B2
Losse (40) 150 A6
Lostanges (19) 139 E4
Lostroff (57) 49 G3
Lothey (29) 53 G2
Lottinghen (62) 1 G4
le Lou-du-Lac (35) 56 D2
Louailles (72) 77 F2
Louan-Villegruis-Fontaine (77) 44 C6
Louannec (22) 32 D2
Louans (37) 95 E1
Louargat (22) 32 D4
Louâtre (02) 44 A1
Loubajac (65) 182 D3
Loubaresse (07) 157 E2
Loubaresse (15) 141 F5
Loubaut (09) 185 F3
Loubédat (32) 166 C3
Loubens (09) 185 H4
Loubens (33) 150 A1
Loubens-Lauragais (31) 169 H6

Loubers (81) 170 A1
Loubersan (32) 167 G6
Loubès-Bernac (47) 136 C6
Loubeyrat (63) 127 E1
Loubieng (64) 181 G1
la Loubière (12) 154 C4
Loubières (09) 185 H5
Loubigné (79) 108 B6
Loubillé (79) 108 B6
Loubressac (46) 139 E5
Loucé (61) 39 E5
Loucelles (14) 14 A4
Louchats (33) 149 F2
Louches (62) 1 H3
Louchy-Montfand (03) 113 H4
Loucrup (65) 183 E4
Loudéac (22) 55 F2
Loudenvielle (65) 197 E1
Loudervielle (65) 197 E1
Loudes (43) 142 B3
Loudet (31) 184 A3
Loudrefing (57) 49 G3
Loudun (86) 94 A3
Loué (72) 59 H6
Louer (40) 165 F3
Louesme (21) 85 F1
Louestault (37) 78 D3
Loueuse (60) 19 H3
Louey (65) 183 E3
Lougé-sur-Maire (61) 38 D5
Lougratte (47) 151 F2
Lougres (25) 88 B4
Louhans (71) 116 D1
Louhossoa (64) 180 C1
Louignac (19) 138 B2
Louin (79) 93 G5
Louisfert (44) 75 E1
Loulans-Verchamp (70) 87 G4
Loulay (17) 107 G6
Loulle (39) 103 F6
la Loupe (28) 61 F2
Loupeigne (02) 22 C5
Loupershouse (57) 49 H1
Loupes (33) 135 F5
Loupfougères (53) 59 F2
Loupia (11) 186 D5
Loupiac (12) 154 B3
Loupiac (33) 149 H1
Loupiac (46) 138 C5
Loupiac (81) 169 H3
Loupiac-de-la-Réole (33) 150 B2
Loupian (34) 189 F1
Louplande (72) 59 H6
Loupmont (55) 47 H3
Louppy-le-Château (55) 46 D4
Louppy-sur-Loison (55) 25 E4
la Louptière-Thénard (10) 65 E2
Lourches (59) 9 E3
Lourde (31) 184 A5
Lourdes (65) 182 D4
Lourdios-Ichère (64) 181 H4
Lourdoueix-Saint-Michel (36) 111 F3
Lourdoueix-Saint-Pierre (23) 111 F3
Lourenties (64) 182 C2
Loures-Barousse (65) 184 A5
Louresse-Rochemenier (49) 77 F6
Lourmais (35) 35 F5
Lourmarin (84) 175 H4
Lournand (71) 116 A2
Lourouer-Saint-Laurent (36) 111 H1
le Louroux (37) 95 E1
le Louroux-Béconnais (49) 76 B3
Louroux-Bourbonnais (03) 113 E2
Louroux-de-Beaune (03) 113 E4
Louroux-de-Bouble (03) 113 F5
Louroux-Hodement (03) 112 D3
Lourquen (40) 165 G4
Lourties-Monbrun (32) 183 H1
Loury (45) 63 F5
Louslitges (32) 167 E5
Loussous-Débat (32) 167 E5
Loutehel (35) 56 C4
Loutzviller (57) 28 B5
Louvagny (14) 39 E3
Louvaines (49) 76 C2
Louvatange (39) 103 E1
Louveciennes (78) 42 B4
Louvemont (52) 67 F1
Louvemont-Côte-du-Poivre (55) 25 E6
Louvencourt (80) 7 H4
Louvergny (08) 24 B3
le Louverot (39) 102 D6
Louversey (27) 40 C2
Louvetot (76) 17 E5
Louvie-Juzon (64) 182 A4
Louvie-Soubiron (64) 182 A5
la Louvière-Lauragais (11) 186 A3
Louvières (14) 13 G5
Louvières (52) 68 A5
Louvières-en-Auge (61) 39 E4
Louviers (27) 18 D6
Louvigné (53) 58 D5
Louvigné-de-Bais (35) 57 G4
Louvigné-du-Désert (35) 58 A1
Louvignies-Quesnoy (59) 9 G3
Louvigny (14) 14 B5
Louvigny (57) 48 C2
Louvigny (64) 165 H5
Louvigny (72) 60 A3
Louvil (59) 3 G5
Louville-la-Chenard (28) 62 C3
Louvilliers-en-Drouais (28) 41 E5
Louvilliers-lès-Perche (28) 40 D6
Louvois (51) 45 G1
Louvrechy (80) 20 C2
Louvroil (59) 10 A2
Louye (27) 41 F4
Louzac-Saint-André (16) 121 G3
Louze (52) 67 E2
Louzignac (17) 121 H2
Louzouer (45) 64 A5
Louzy (79) 93 G3
Lovagny (74) 132 A2
Loyat (56) 56 A3
la Loye (39) 102 D3
Loye-sur-Arnon (18) 112 B1
la Loyère (71) 101 G5
Loyettes (01) 130 C3
Lozanne (69) 129 H2
Lozay (17) 107 G6
Loze (82) 153 E4
Lozinghem (62) 2 C5
Lozon (50) 13 E6
Lozzi (2B) 204 D2
Luant (36) 96 B6

Lubécourt (57) 49 E3
Lubersac (19) 138 C1
Lubey (54) 25 H5
Lubilhac (43) 141 F2
Lubine (88) 70 D2
Lublé (37) 78 B4
Lubret-Saint-Luc (65) 183 F2
Luby-Betmont (65) 183 G2
Luc (48) 156 D1
le Luc (83) 192 A4
Luc-Armau (64) 182 C1
Luc-en-Diois (26) 159 E1
Luc-la-Primaube (12) 154 C4
Luc-sur-Aude (11) 187 E5
Luc-sur-Mer (14) 14 B4
Luc-sur-Orbieu (11) 187 H3
Lucarré (64) 182 C1
Luçay-le-Libre (36) 96 D3
Luçay-le-Mâle (36) 96 A2
Lucbardez-et-Bargues (40) 166 B2
Lucciana (2B) 203 G6
Lucé (28) 62 B2
Lucé (61) 38 B6
Lucé-sous-Ballon (72) 60 B4
Luceau (72) 78 C2
Lucelle (68) 89 F5
Lucenay (69) 129 H2
Lucenay-le-Duc (21) 85 E3
Lucenay-lès-Aix (58) 99 F6
Lucenay-l'Évêque (71) 100 C3
Lucéram (06) 195 G1
la Lucerne-d'Outremer (50) 35 H2
Lucey (21) 85 F1
Lucey (54) 48 A5
Lucey (73) 131 G3
Lucgarier (64) 182 B2
Luchapt (86) 109 H4
Luchat (17) 120 D3
Luché-Pringé (72) 78 A2
Luché-sur-Brioux (79) 108 B5
Luché-Thouarsais (79) 93 F4
Lucheux (80) 7 G3
Luchy (60) 20 B3
Lucinges (74) 118 D4
Lucmau (33) 149 G4
Luçon (85) 106 C2
Lucq-de-Béarn (64) 181 H2
Lucquy (08) 24 A3
le Lude (72) 78 A3
Ludes (51) 45 G1
Ludesse (63) 127 F4
Ludiès (09) 185 H4
Ludon-Médoc (33) 135 E4
Ludres (54) 48 C5
Lüe (40) 148 C5
Lué-en-Baugeois (49) 77 F4
Luemschwiller (68) 89 F3
Lugagnac (46) 153 E3
Lugagnan (65) 182 D4
Lugaignac (33) 135 H5
Lugan (12) 154 A3
Lugan (81) 169 H4
Lugarde (15) 140 C2
Lugasson (33) 135 H6
Lugny (02) 23 E1
Lugny (71) 116 B2
Lugny-Bourbonnais (18) 98 A4
Lugny-Champagne (18) 98 B2
Lugny-lès-Charolles (71) 115 F3
Lugo-di-Nazza (2B) 205 F4
Lugon-et-l'Île-du-Carnay (33) 135 G4
Lugos (33) 148 D3
Lugrin (74) 119 F2
Lugy (62) 2 B6
le Luhier (25) 104 C1
Luigné (49) 77 F6
Luigny (28) 61 G3
Luisant (28) 62 B2
Luisetaines (77) 64 C2
Luitré (35) 58 A3
Lullin (74) 119 E4
Lully (74) 118 D4
Lumbin (38) 145 H1
Lumbres (62) 2 A4
Lumeau (28) 62 C5
Lumes (08) 24 B1
Lumigny-Nesles-Ormeaux (77) 43 G5
Lumio (2B) 202 C5
Lunac (12) 153 H5
Lunan (46) 153 G2
Lunas (24) 136 D4
Lunas (34) 172 A4
Lunax (31) 184 B2
Lunay (41) 79 F2
Luneau (03) 114 D3
Lunegarde (46) 153 E1
Lunel (34) 173 H5
Lunel-Viel (34) 173 H5
Luneray (76) 17 F2
Lunery (18) 97 F5
Luneville (54) 49 E6
le Luot (50) 35 H3
Lupcourt (54) 48 D6
Lupé (42) 143 H1
Lupersat (23) 126 A1
Lupiac (32) 167 E4
Luplanté (28) 62 A3
Luppé-Violles (32) 166 C4
Luppy (57) 48 D2
Lupsault (16) 108 C6
Lupstein (67) 50 D4
Luquet (65) 182 D2
Lurais (36) 95 F6
Luray (28) 41 F5
Lurbe-Saint-Christau (64) 181 H3
Lurcy (01) 116 B5
Lurcy-le-Bourg (58) 99 F2
Lurcy-Lévis (03) 98 C6
Luré (42) 128 C2
Lure (70) 88 A2
Lureuil (36) 95 G6
Luri (2B) 203 F2
Luriecq (42) 128 D6
Lurs (04) 176 C2
Lury-sur-Arnon (18) 97 E2
Lus-la-Croix-Haute (26) 159 H1
Lusanger (44) 74 D1
Lusans (25) 87 G6
Luscan (31) 184 A5
Lusignac (24) 136 C1
Lusignan (86) 108 D2
Lusignan-Petit (47) 151 E5
Lusigny (03) 114 A2
Lusigny-sur-Barse (10) 66 C3
Lusigny-sur-Ouche (21) 101 F2
Lussac (16) 123 E2
Lussac (17) 121 F5
Lussac (33) 135 H5
Lussac-les-Châteaux (86) 109 G2
Lussac-les-Églises (87) 110 B3
Lussagnet (40) 166 B3
Lussagnet-Lusson (64) 182 B1
Lussan (30) 174 A1
Lussan (32) 168 A5
Lussan-Adeilhac (31) 184 C2
Lussant (17) 120 D1
Lussas (07) 157 G2
Lussas-et-Nontronneau (24) 123 E5
Lussat (23) 112 B5
Lussat (63) 127 G2
Lussault-sur-Loire (37) 79 F5
Lusse (88) 70 D2
Lusseray (79) 108 B5
Lustar (65) 183 G2
Luthenay-Uxeloup (58) 98 D5
Lutilhous (65) 183 G4
Luttange (57) 26 C4
Luttenbach-près-Munster (68) 71 E5
Lutter (68) 89 G4
Lutterbach (68) 89 F2
Lutz-en-Dunois (28) 62 A5
Lutzelbourg (57) 50 B4
Lutzelhouse (67) 71 E1
Luvigny (88) 70 C1
Lux (21) 86 A5
Lux (31) 186 A2
Lux (71) 101 G6
Luxé (16) 122 C2
Luxe-Sumberraute (64) 181 E1
Luxémont-et-Villotte (51) 46 C5
Luxeuil-les-Bains (70) 87 H2
Luxey (40) 149 E5
Luxiol (25) 87 H5
Luz-Saint-Sauveur (65) 197 E1
Luzancy (77) 44 A2
Luzarches (95) 42 D1
Luzay (79) 93 F4
Luzé (37) 94 C3
Luze (70) 88 C2
Luzech (46) 152 B3

Luzenac (09) ... 199 F1
Luzeret (36) ... 110 D2
la Luzerne (50) ... 13 F6
Luzillat (63) ... 127 G1
Luzillé (37) ... 95 G1
Luzinay (38) ... 130 B4
Luzoir (02) ... 10 A6
Luzy (58) ... 100 B5
Luzy-Saint-Martin (55) ... 24 D3
Luzy-sur-Marne (52) ... 68 A5
Ly-Fontaine (02) ... 22 A2
Lyaud (74) ... 119 E3
Lye (36) ... 96 B1
Lynde (59) ... 2 C4
Lyoffans (70) ... 88 B3
Lyon (69) ... 130 A3
Lyons-la-Forêt (27) ... 19 F4
Lys (58) ... 83 G6
Lys (64) ... 182 B3
Lys-lez-Lannoy (59) ... 3 G5
Lys-Saint-Georges (36) ... 111 G1

M

Maast-et-Violaine (02) ... 22 B6
Maâtz (52) ... 86 B3
Mably (42) ... 115 E6
Macau (33) ... 135 E4
Macaye (64) ... 180 D1
Macé (61) ... 39 F5
Macey (10) ... 66 A3
Macey (50) ... 35 G4
Machault (08) ... 23 H5
Machault (77) ... 64 B1
Maché (85) ... 91 E3
Machecoul (44) ... 91 E1
Machemont (60) ... 21 F4
Macheren (57) ... 27 F4
Machézal (42) ... 129 E2
Machiel (80) ... 6 D2
Machilly (74) ... 118 D4
la Machine (58) ... 99 F4
Machy (10) ... 66 B4
Machy (80) ... 6 D2
Mackenheim (67) ... 71 G3
Mackwiller (67) ... 50 B2
Maclas (42) ... 143 H1
Macogny (02) ... 44 A1
Mâcon (71) ... 116 B4
Maconcourt (88) ... 69 E2
Maconge (21) ... 101 E1
Macornay (39) ... 102 D6
Mâcot-la-Plagne (73) ... 133 E4
Macqueville (17) ... 121 H2
Macquigny (02) ... 9 F6
Madaillan (47) ... 151 E5
Madecourt (88) ... 69 F3
Madegney (88) ... 69 G3
la Madeleine-sous-Montreuil (62) ... 1 F6
la Madeleine (59) ... 3 F3
la Madeleine-Bouvet (61) ... 61 F1
la Madeleine-de-Nonancourt (27) ... 41 E4
la Madeleine-sur-Loing (77) ... 64 A4
la Madeleine-Villefrouin (41) ... 80 A2
Madic (15) ... 141 E1
Madière (09) ... 185 G4
Madirac (33) ... 135 F6
Madiran (65) ... 166 D5
Madonne-et-Lamerey (88) ... 69 F3
Madranges (19) ... 125 E6
Madré (53) ... 59 F1
Madriat (63) ... 127 F6
Maël-Carhaix (22) ... 32 C6
Maël-Pestivien (22) ... 32 D5
Maennolsheim (67) ... 50 D4
Maffliers (95) ... 42 D2
Maffrécourt (51) ... 42 D2
Magalas (34) ... 188 C1
la Magdeleine-sur-Tarn (31) ... 169 F3
la Magdeleine (16) ... 108 C6
le Mage (61) ... 61 E1
Magenta (51) ... 45 F2
les Mages (30) ... 153 H6
Magescq (40) ... 164 D3
Magland (74) ... 119 F6
Magnac-Bourg (87) ... 124 C4
Magnac-Laval (87) ... 110 B5
Magnac-Lavalette-Villars (16) ... 122 C5
Magnac-sur-Touvre (16) ... 122 C4
Magnan (82) ... 166 C3
Magnant (10) ... 66 D4
Magnanville (78) ... 41 G3
Magnas (32) ... 168 A3
Magnat-l'Étrange (23) ... 125 H3
Magné (79) ... 107 G3
Magné (86) ... 109 E3
Magnet (03) ... 114 B5
Magneux (51) ... 22 D5
Magneux (52) ... 67 G1
Magneux-Haute-Rive (42) ... 129 E4
Magneville (50) ... 12 C3
Magnicourt (10) ... 66 D1
Magnicourt-en-Comte (62) ... 7 H1
Magnicourt-sur-Canche (62) ... 7 F2
Magnien (21) ... 101 E2
Magnières (54) ... 70 A1
Magnieu (01) ... 131 G2
les Magnils-Reigniers (85) ... 91 H6
Magnivray (70) ... 88 A2
Magnoncourt (70) ... 69 G6
le Magnoray (70) ... 87 F4
Magny (28) ... 61 H1
le Magny (36) ... 89 H5
Magny (68) ... 89 E3
le Magny (88) ... 69 G6
Magny (89) ... 84 A5
Magny-Châtelard (25) ... 103 H1
Magny-Cours (58) ... 98 D4
Magny-Danigon (70) ... 88 B3
Magny-en-Bessin (14) ... 14 A3
Magny-en-Vexin (95) ... 41 H1
Magny-Fouchard (10) ... 67 E3
Magny-Jobert (70) ... 88 B3
Magny-la-Campagne (14) ... 39 F2
Magny-la-Fosse (02) ... 9 E5
Magny-la-Ville (21) ... 84 D5
Magny-Lambert (21) ... 85 E3
Magny-le-Désert (61) ... 38 C6
Magny-le-Freule (14) ... 39 E1
Magny-le-Hongre (77) ... 43 F4
Magny-lès-Aubigny (21) ... 102 A3
Magny-les-Hameaux (78) ... 42 B5
Magny-lès-Jussey (70) ... 87 F1
Magny-lès-Villers (21) ... 101 G2
Magny-Lormes (58) ... 84 A5
Magny-Montarlot (21) ... 102 B3
Magny-Saint-Médard (21) ... 86 A5
Magny-Vernois (70) ... 88 A3
Magoar (22) ... 33 E5
Magrie (11) ... 186 D6
Magrin (81) ... 169 H4
Magstatt-le-Bas (68) ... 89 G3
Magstatt-le-Haut (68) ... 89 G3
Mahalon (29) ... 52 C2
Méhéri (61) ... 39 H5
Maîche (25) ... 88 C5
Maidières (54) ... 48 B3
Maignaut-Tauzia (32) ... 167 G3
Maigné (72) ... 78 A1
Maignelay-Montigny (60) ... 20 D3
Mailhac (11) ... 187 H2
Mailhac-sur-Benaize (87) ... 110 C4
Mailholas (31) ... 185 E3
Maillane (13) ... 175 E3
Maillas (40) ... 149 H5
Maillat (01) ... 117 G4
Maillé (37) ... 94 D3
Maillé (85) ... 107 G2
Maillé (86) ... 94 A6
Maillebois (28) ... 40 D6

la Maillenaye-sur-Seine (76) ... 17 E6
Maillères (40) ... 166 A1
Mailleroncourt-Saint-Pancras (70) ... 69 G6
Maillet (03) ... 112 D2
Maillet (36) ... 111 F1
Mailley-et-Chazelot (70) ... 87 F4
Maillezais (85) ... 107 F3
Maillot (89) ... 65 E4
Mailly (71) ... 115 E4
Mailly-Champagne (51) ... 45 F1
Mailly-la-Ville (89) ... 83 G4
Mailly-le-Camp (10) ... 45 G5
Mailly-le-Château (89) ... 83 G4
les Maillys (21) ... 102 B2
Maimbeville (60) ... 20 B5
Maincy (77) ... 64 A1
Maine-de-Boixe (16) ... 122 C2
Mainfonds (16) ... 122 B5
Maing (59) ... 9 G2
Mainneville (27) ... 19 G5
Mainsat (23) ... 112 B6
Maintenay (62) ... 6 D2
Maintenon (28) ... 41 F6
Mainvillers (57) ... 27 E6
Mainvilliers (28) ... 61 H3
Mainvilliers (45) ... 63 F3
Mainxe (16) ... 121 H4
Mainzac (16) ... 123 E6
Mairé (86) ... 95 E4
Mairé-Levescault (79) ... 108 C5
Mairieux (59) ... 10 A2
Mairy (08) ... 24 C2
Mairy-Mainville (54) ... 25 H5
Mairy-sur-Marne (51) ... 45 H3
Maisey-le-Duc (21) ... 85 E1
Maisières-Notre-Dame (25) ... 87 G6
Maisnières (80) ... 6 C5
le Maisnil (59) ... 3 E5
Maisnil (62) ... 7 G2
Maisnil-lès-Ruitz (62) ... 8 B2
Maisod (39) ... 117 G2
Maison-des-Champs (10) ... 67 E3
la Maison-Dieu (58) ... 83 G5
Maison-Feyne (23) ... 111 F3
Maison-Maugis (61) ... 61 E1
Maison-Ponthieu (80) ... 7 E3
Maison-Roland (80) ... 7 E3
Maison-Rouge (77) ... 64 D1
Maisoncelle (62) ... 7 F2
Maisoncelle-et-Villers (08) ... 24 C3
Maisoncelle-Saint-Pierre (60) ... 20 B3
Maisoncelle-Tuilerie (60) ... 20 B3
Maisoncelles (52) ... 67 G4
Maisoncelles (72) ... 79 E1
Maisoncelles-en-Gâtinais (77) ... 64 A4
Maisoncelles-la-Jourdan (14) ... 37 H4
Maisoncelles-Pelvey (14) ... 38 A1
Maisoncelles-sur-Ajon (14) ... 14 A6
Maisonnais (18) ... 112 A1
Maisonnais-sur-Tardoire (87) ... 123 F3
Maisonnay (79) ... 108 B3
Maisonnisses (23) ... 111 G3
Maisons (11) ... 187 G6
Maisons (14) ... 13 H5
Maisons (28) ... 62 D2
Maisons-Alfort (94) ... 42 D4
Maisons-du-Bois-Lièvremont (25) ... 104 A3
Maisons-en-Champagne (51) ... 46 A5
Maisons-Laffitte (78) ... 42 C3
Maisons-lès-Chaource (10) ... 66 B6
Maisons-lès-Soulaines (10) ... 67 F3
Maisonsgoutte (67) ... 71 E2
Maisontiers (79) ... 93 F5
Maisse (91) ... 63 G2
Maissemy (02) ... 8 D6
Maixe (54) ... 49 E5
Maizeray (55) ... 47 H1
Maizeroy (57) ... 49 E1
Maizery (57) ... 27 E6
Maizet (14) ... 14 B5
Maizey (55) ... 47 G3
Maizicourt (80) ... 7 F3
Maizières (14) ... 14 B5
Maizières (52) ... 67 H1
Maizières (54) ... 48 C6
Maizières (62) ... 7 H2
Maizières (70) ... 87 F3
Maizières-la-Grande-Paroisse (10) ... 65 H1
Maizières-lès-Brienne (10) ... 67 E2
Maizières-lès-Metz (57) ... 26 C5
Maizières-lès-Vic (57) ... 49 G4
Maizières-sur-Amance (52) ... 86 C1
Maizilly (42) ... 115 G5
Maizy (02) ... 22 C5
Majastres (04) ... 177 F2
Malabat (32) ... 183 F1
la Malachère (70) ... 87 G4
Malafretaz (01) ... 116 D4
Malaincourt (88) ... 68 D3
Malaincourt-sur-Meuse (52) ... 68 C4
Malakoff (92) ... 42 C4
Malancourt (55) ... 24 D6
Malandry (08) ... 24 C3
Malange (39) ... 102 D1
Malans (25) ... 103 G3
Malans (70) ... 102 C2
Malansac (56) ... 56 B6
Malarce-sur-la-Thines (07) ... 157 E3
Malataverne (26) ... 158 A3
Malaucène (84) ... 158 A4
Malaucourt-sur-Seille (54) ... 48 D3
Malaunay (76) ... 17 G5
Malause (82) ... 168 C1
Malaussanne (64) ... 166 A5
Malaussène (06) ... 178 C2
Malauzat (63) ... 127 F3
Malaville (16) ... 122 A5
Malavillers (54) ... 26 A4
Malay (71) ... 116 A3
Malay-le-Grand (89) ... 65 E4
Malay-le-Petit (89) ... 65 E4
Malbo (15) ... 140 C4
Malbosc (07) ... 157 E4
Malbouhans (70) ... 88 B2
Malbouzon (48) ... 155 H1
Malbrans (25) ... 103 G2
Malbuisson (25) ... 104 A5
Mâle (61) ... 61 E2
Malegoude (09) ... 186 A4
Malemort-du-Comtat (84) ... 158 B6
Malemort-sur-Corrèze (19) ... 138 D2
la Malène (48) ... 155 H5
Malesherbes (45) ... 63 G3
Malestroit (56) ... 56 A5
Maletable (61) ... 40 B6
Maleville (12) ... 153 H4
Malguénac (56) ... 55 E2
la Malhoure (22) ... 34 A5
Malicorne (03) ... 113 E4
Malicorne (89) ... 82 D2
Malicorne-sur-Sarthe (72) ... 77 G1
Maligny (21) ... 101 G2
Maligny (89) ... 83 H2
Malijai (04) ... 177 E1
Malincourt (59) ... 9 E4
Malintrat (63) ... 127 F3
Malissard (26) ... 144 B5
Mallefougasse-Augès (04) ... 176 D1
Malleloy (54) ... 48 C4
Mallemoisson (04) ... 177 E1
Mallemort (13) ... 175 H4
Malléon (09) ... 185 H5
Malleret (23) ... 126 A3
Malleret-Boussac (23) ... 112 A4
Mallerey (39) ... 117 E1
Malleval (42) ... 143 G1
Malleval-en-Vercors (38) ... 145 E3

Malleville-les-Grès (76) ... 16 D2
Malleville-sur-le-Bec (27) ... 18 A6
Mallièville (85) ... 26 C2
Malling (57) ... 26 C2
Malloué (14) ... 37 G2
la Malmaison (02) ... 23 E3
Malmerspach (68) ... 88 D1
Malmy (51) ... 46 C1
Malons-et-Elze (30) ... 157 E4
Malouy (27) ... 15 H5
Malpart (80) ... 20 D2
Malpas (25) ... 103 H4
Malras (11) ... 186 D4
Malrevers (43) ... 142 C3
Malroy (57) ... 26 C5
Maltat (71) ... 99 H4
Maltot (14) ... 14 B5
Malval (23) ... 111 G3
Malvalette (43) ... 143 E1
Malves-en-Minervois (11) ... 187 E3
Malvezie (31) ... 184 A5
Malvières (43) ... 142 B1
Malviès (11) ... 186 D4
Malville (44) ... 73 H4
Malzéville (54) ... 48 C5
le Malzieu-Forain (48) ... 141 G5
le Malzieu-Ville (48) ... 141 G5
Mamers (72) ... 60 C2
Mametz (62) ... 2 B5
Mametz (80) ... 8 B5
Mamey (54) ... 48 A3
Mamirolle (25) ... 103 G1
Manas (26) ... 158 C2
Manas-Bastanous (32) ... 183 G1
Manaurie (24) ... 137 H4
Mance (54) ... 26 A4
la Mancelière (28) ... 40 D5
la Mancellière-sur-Vire (50) ... 37 G1
Mancenans (25) ... 88 A4
Mancenans-Lizerne (25) ... 88 C6
Mancey (71) ... 116 B1
Manchecourt (45) ... 63 G4
Mancieulles (54) ... 26 A4
Mancioux (31) ... 184 C3
Mancy (51) ... 45 E3
Mandacou (24) ... 137 G6
Mandailles-Saint-Julien (15) ... 140 C4
Mandelieu-la-Napoule (06) ... 178 C5
Manderen (57) ... 26 D2
Mandeville (27) ... 18 C6
Mandeville-en-Bessin (14) ... 13 G5
Mandray (88) ... 70 C2
Mandres (27) ... 40 C5
Mandres-aux-Quatre-Tours (54) ... 48 A4
Mandres-en-Barrois (55) ... 68 B3
Mandres-la-Côte (52) ... 68 B5
Mandres-les-Roses (94) ... 43 E5
Mandres-sur-Vair (88) ... 69 E3
Manduel (30) ... 174 B3
Mane (04) ... 176 C2
Mane (31) ... 184 C4
Manéglise (76) ... 15 F5
Manéhouville (76) ... 17 G2
Manent-Montané (32) ... 184 A2
Manerbe (14) ... 15 F5
Mangiennes (55) ... 25 G5
Manglieu (63) ... 127 H5
Mangonville (54) ... 69 G1
Manhac (12) ... 154 B5
Manheulles (55) ... 47 H1
Manhoué (57) ... 48 D3
Manicamp (02) ... 21 H3
Manigod (74) ... 132 C2
Manin (62) ... 7 H2
Maninghen-Henne (62) ... 1 F4
Maniquerville (76) ... 16 C4
Manlay (21) ... 100 D2
Manneville-ès-Plains (76) ... 17 E2
Manneville-la-Goupil (76) ... 15 F4
Manneville-la-Pipard (14) ... 15 F4
Manneville-la-Raoult (27) ... 15 F4
Manneville-sur-Risle (27) ... 15 H3
Mannevillette (76) ... 15 E4
Mano (40) ... 149 E3
le Manoir (14) ... 14 A3
le Manoir (27) ... 18 D5
Manois (52) ... 68 B4
Manom (57) ... 26 C4
Manoncourt-en-Vermois (54) ... 48 D6
Manoncourt-en-Woëvre (54) ... 48 B4
Manonville (54) ... 48 B4
Manonviller (54) ... 49 F5
Manosque (04) ... 176 D3
Manot (16) ... 123 F1
Manou (28) ... 61 E1
le Mans (72) ... 60 A6
Mansac (19) ... 138 C3
Mansan (65) ... 183 F2
Mansat-la-Courrière (23) ... 125 E1
Mansempuy (32) ... 168 A3
Mansencôme (32) ... 167 F3
Manses (09) ... 186 A4
Mansigné (72) ... 78 A2
Mansle (16) ... 122 C2
Manso (2B) ... 204 C2
Mansonville (82) ... 168 B1
Manspach (68) ... 89 E3
Mant (40) ... 166 A5
Mantallot (22) ... 32 D3
Mantenay-Montlin (01) ... 116 D3
Mantes-la-Jolie (78) ... 41 H3
Mantes-la-Ville (78) ... 41 H3
Mantet (66) ... 200 B4
Manteyer (05) ... 160 A2
Manthelan (37) ... 95 E2
Manthelon (27) ... 40 D3
Manthes (26) ... 144 B2
Mantilly (61) ... 37 H6
Mantoche (70) ... 86 C5
Mantry (39) ... 102 D6
Manvieux (14) ... 14 A3
Many (57) ... 27 E6
Manzac-sur-Vern (24) ... 137 E3
Manzat (63) ... 127 E1
Manziat (01) ... 116 C3
Marac (52) ... 68 A5
Marainville-sur-Madon (54) ... 69 F1
Marainviller (54) ... 49 F5
aux Marais (60) ... 20 A4
le Marais-la-Chapelle (14) ... 39 E3
Marais-Vernier (27) ... 15 F3
Marambat (32) ... 167 F3
Marandeuil (21) ... 86 B5
Marange-Silvange (57) ... 26 B4
Marange-Zondrange (57) ... 27 E5
Marans (17) ... 106 D3
Marans (49) ... 75 H1
Maransin (33) ... 135 G3
Marant (62) ... 1 F6
Maranville (52) ... 67 G5
Maranwez (08) ... 23 G2
Marast (70) ... 88 A4
Marat (63) ... 128 B4
Maraussan (34) ... 188 A4
Maravat (32) ... 168 A3
Maray (41) ... 96 D1
Maraye-en-Othe (10) ... 65 H4

Marcellaz-Albanais (74) ... 132 A2
Marcellois (21) ... 85 E6
Marcellus (47) ... 150 B3
Marcenais (33) ... 135 G3
Marcenat (03) ... 114 A5
Marcenat (15) ... 140 D1
Marcenay (21) ... 85 E2
Marcenod (42) ... 129 G5
Marcey-les-Grèves (50) ... 35 H3
Marchainville (61) ... 40 B6
Marchais (02) ... 22 D3
Marchais-Beton (89) ... 82 C2
Marchais-en-Brie (02) ... 44 C4
Marchamp (01) ... 131 F3
Marchastel (15) ... 140 C2
Marchastel (48) ... 155 F2
Marchaux (25) ... 87 G6
la Marche (58) ... 98 D2
Marché-Allouarde (80) ... 21 F1
Marchélepot (80) ... 21 F1
Marchemaisons (61) ... 60 B2
Marchémoret (77) ... 43 F2
Marchenoir (41) ... 80 D3
Marcheprime (33) ... 148 D1
Marches (26) ... 144 C4
les Marches (73) ... 132 A5
Marcheseuil (21) ... 100 D2
Marchésieux (50) ... 13 E6
Marcheville (28) ... 61 H4
Marchéville-en-Woëvre (55) ... 47 H1
Marchezais (28) ... 41 F4
Marchiennes (59) ... 9 F2
Marciac (32) ... 167 F6
Marcieu (38) ... 145 G5
Marcieux (73) ... 131 G4
Marcigny (71) ... 115 F4
Marcigny-sous-Thil (21) ... 84 D5
Marcilhac-sur-Célé (46) ... 153 E2
Marcillac (33) ... 135 F2
Marcillac-la-Croisille (19) ... 139 G2
Marcillac-la-Croze (19) ... 139 E4
Marcillac-Lanville (16) ... 122 B3
Marcillac-Saint-Quentin (24) ... 138 A4
Marcillac-Vallon (12) ... 154 B3
Marcillat (03) ... 113 F2
Marcillat-en-Combraille (03) ... 112 D5
Marcillé-la-Ville (53) ... 59 F3
Marcillé-Raoul (35) ... 35 F6
Marcillé-Robert (35) ... 57 G4
Marcilloles (38) ... 144 C1
Marcilly (02) ... 44 C1
Marcilly (50) ... 37 G3
Marcilly (77) ... 43 G2
Marcilly-d'Azergues (69) ... 129 H3
Marcilly-en-Bassigny (52) ... 68 C6
Marcilly-en-Beauce (41) ... 79 F2
Marcilly-en-Gault (41) ... 81 E5
Marcilly-en-Villette (45) ... 81 F2
Marcilly-et-Dracy (21) ... 85 E4
Marcilly-la-Campagne (27) ... 41 E4
Marcilly-la-Gueurce (71) ... 115 H3
Marcilly-le-Châtel (42) ... 128 D4
Marcilly-le-Hayer (10) ... 65 G3
Marcilly-lès-Buxy (71) ... 101 G6
Marcilly-Ogny (21) ... 100 D1
Marcilly-sur-Eure (27) ... 41 E4
Marcilly-sur-Maulne (37) ... 78 B4
Marcilly-sur-Seine (51) ... 65 H1
Marcilly-sur-Tille (21) ... 85 H4
Marcilly-sur-Vienne (37) ... 94 D3
Marck (62) ... 2 A2
Marckolsheim (67) ... 71 G3
Marclopt (42) ... 129 E4
Marcoing (59) ... 9 E4
Marcolès (15) ... 140 A6
Marcollin (38) ... 144 C1
Marcols-les-Eaux (07) ... 143 G6
Marçon (72) ... 78 D2
Marconne (62) ... 7 E1
Marconnelle (62) ... 7 E1
Marcorignan (11) ... 187 H3
Marcoussis (91) ... 42 C6
Marcoux (04) ... 177 E1
Marcoux (42) ... 128 D3
Marcq (08) ... 24 C5
Marcq (78) ... 42 A4
Marcq-en-Barœul (59) ... 3 F5
Marcq-en-Ostrevent (59) ... 9 E2
Marcy (02) ... 9 F6
Marcy (58) ... 99 F2
Marcy (69) ... 129 H2
Marcy-l'Étoile (69) ... 129 H3
Marcy-sous-Marne (02) ... 44 B3
Mardeuil (51) ... 45 E2
Mardié (45) ... 81 H1
Mardilly (61) ... 39 G4
Mardor (52) ... 86 A1
Mardore (69) ... 115 G6
Mareau-aux-Bois (45) ... 63 E5
Mareau-aux-Prés (45) ... 80 D1
Mareil-en-Champagne (72) ... 59 G6
Mareil-en-France (95) ... 42 D2
Mareil-le-Guyon (78) ... 42 B4
Mareil-Marly (78) ... 42 B3
Mareil-sur-Loir (72) ... 77 H2
Mareil-sur-Mauldre (78) ... 42 A3
Mareilles (52) ... 68 B4
Marenla (62) ... 1 F6
Marennes (17) ... 120 B2
Marennes (69) ... 130 B4
Maresché (72) ... 60 A4
Maresches (59) ... 9 G2
Maresquel-Ecquemicourt (62) ... 7 E1
Marest (62) ... 7 G1
Marest-Dampcourt (02) ... 21 H3
Marest-sur-Matz (60) ... 21 E4
Marestaing (32) ... 168 C4
Marestmontiers (80) ... 20 D2
Maresville (62) ... 1 F6
les Marêts (77) ... 44 C3
Maretz (59) ... 9 E5
Mareugheol (63) ... 127 F6
Mareuil (16) ... 122 C3
Mareuil (24) ... 122 D6
Mareuil-Caubert (80) ... 7 E4
Mareuil-en-Brie (51) ... 45 E3
Mareuil-en-Dôle (02) ... 44 C1
Mareuil-la-Motte (60) ... 21 E3
Mareuil-le-Port (51) ... 45 E2
Mareuil-lès-Meaux (77) ... 43 G3
Mareuil-sur-Arnon (18) ... 97 F5
Mareuil-sur-Ay (51) ... 45 F2
Mareuil-sur-Cher (41) ... 79 H6
Mareuil-sur-Lay-Dissais (85) ... 91 H5
Mareuil-sur-Ourcq (60) ... 43 H1
Marey (88) ... 69 E4
Marey-lès-Fussey (21) ... 101 G2
Marey-sur-Tille (21) ... 85 H3
Marfaux (51) ... 45 E1
Marfontaine (02) ... 22 C2
Margaux (33) ... 135 E4
Margencel (74) ... 118 D3
Margency (95) ... 42 D3
Margerides (19) ... 126 A5
Margerie-Chantagret (42) ... 128 D5
Margerie-Hancourt (51) ... 66 B1
Margès (26) ... 144 C3
Margival (02) ... 22 B4
le Margnès (81) ... 171 F5
Margny (08) ... 24 C2
Margny (51) ... 45 E1
Margny-aux-Cerises (60) ... 21 F2
Margny-lès-Compiègne (60) ... 21 E4
Margny-sur-Matz (60) ... 21 E3
Margon (28) ... 60 D2
Margon (34) ... 188 C2
Margouët-Meymes (32) ... 167 E5
Margueray (50) ... 37 F2
Marguerittes (30) ... 174 B3
Margueron (33) ... 136 C6
Marguestau (32) ... 166 D4
Margut (08) ... 24 D3
Mariac (07) ... 143 F5
Marignac (17) ... 121 G4
Marignac (31) ... 184 A5
Marignac (82) ... 168 B2

Marignac-en-Diois (26) ... 145 E6
Marignac-Lasclares (31) ... 184 D3
Marignac-Laspeyres (31) ... 184 C3
Marignana (2A) ... 204 C3
Marignane (13) ... 191 H4
Marigné (49) ... 76 D2
Marigné-Laillé (72) ... 78 B2
Marigné-Peuton (53) ... 76 C1
Marignier (74) ... 119 E5
Marignieu (01) ... 131 G2
Marigny (03) ... 113 H1
Marigny (39) ... 103 E6
Marigny (50) ... 37 F1
Marigny (51) ... 45 E6
Marigny (71) ... 101 F6
Marigny (79) ... 107 H4
Marigny-Brizay (86) ... 94 B5
Marigny-Chemereau (86) ... 108 D2
Marigny-en-Orxois (02) ... 44 A2
Marigny-le-Cahouët (21) ... 85 E5
Marigny-le-Châtel (10) ... 65 G3
Marigny-l'Église (58) ... 84 B6
Marigny-lès-Reullée (21) ... 101 H3
Marigny-les-Usages (45) ... 81 G1
Marigny-Marmande (37) ... 94 D4
Marigny-Saint-Marcel (74) ... 131 H2
Marigny-sur-Yonne (58) ... 99 H2
Marillac-le-Franc (16) ... 123 E3
Marillet (85) ... 107 G1
Marimbault (33) ... 149 H3
Marimont-lès-Bénestroff (57) ... 49 G3
Marines (95) ... 42 B1
Maringes (42) ... 129 G4
Maringues (63) ... 127 G2
Mariol (03) ... 114 B6
Marions (33) ... 150 A3
Marizy (71) ... 115 G1
Marizy-Sainte-Geneviève (02) ... 44 A1
Marle (02) ... 22 D2
Marlemont (08) ... 23 G1
Marlenheim (67) ... 50 D5
Marlens (74) ... 132 C3
Marlers (80) ... 19 H1
Marles-en-Brie (77) ... 43 G5
Marles-les-Mines (62) ... 2 C6
Marles-sur-Canche (62) ... 1 F6
Marlhes (42) ... 143 F2
Marliac (31) ... 185 G3
Marliens (21) ... 102 A1
Marlieux (01) ... 116 D6
Marly (57) ... 26 C6
Marly (59) ... 9 G2
Marly-Gomont (02) ... 10 A6
Marly-la-Ville (95) ... 43 E2
Marly-le-Roi (78) ... 42 B4
Marly-sous-Issy (71) ... 100 A5
Marly-sur-Arroux (71) ... 115 F1
Marmagne (18) ... 97 G2
Marmagne (21) ... 100 D1
Marmagne (71) ... 101 E5
Marmande (47) ... 150 B3
Marmanhac (15) ... 140 B4
Marmeaux (89) ... 84 B4
Marminiac (46) ... 152 B1
Marmont-Pachas (47) ... 167 H1
Marmouillé (61) ... 39 F5
Marmoutier (67) ... 50 C5
Marnac (24) ... 137 H5
Marnand (69) ... 115 G6
Marnans (38) ... 144 D1
Marnaves (81) ... 170 A1
Marnay (70) ... 87 E5
Marnay (71) ... 101 H5
Marnay (86) ... 109 E2
Marnay-sur-Marne (52) ... 68 A5
Marnay-sur-Seine (10) ... 65 H1
Marnaz (74) ... 119 E5
la Marne (44) ... 91 E1
Marnes (79) ... 93 H4
Marnes-la-Coquette (92) ... 42 C4
Marnézia (39) ... 117 G1
Marnhagues-et-Latour (12) ... 172 B3
Marnoz (39) ... 103 E3
Marœuil (62) ... 8 A2
Maroilles (59) ... 10 A4
la Marolle-en-Sologne (41) ... 80 D4
Marolles (14) ... 15 F5
Marolles (41) ... 79 H3
Marolles (51) ... 46 B4
Marolles (60) ... 21 H6
Marolles-en-Beauce (91) ... 63 F3
Marolles-en-Brie (94) ... 43 E4
Marolles-en-Brie (77) ... 44 A4
Marolles-en-Hurepoix (91) ... 63 F1
Marolles-les-Bailly (10) ... 66 D4
Marolles-lès-Braults (72) ... 60 B3
Marolles-lès-Saint-Calais (72) ... 61 E6
Marolles-sous-Lignières (10) ... 66 A4
Marolles-sur-Seine (77) ... 64 C3
Marols (42) ... 128 D5
Maromme (76) ... 17 G6
Mâron (36) ... 96 C5
Maron (54) ... 48 C5
Maroncourt (88) ... 69 F3
Marpaps (40) ... 166 A5
Marpent (59) ... 10 B2
Marpiré (35) ... 57 G2
Marquaix (80) ... 8 D5
Marquay (24) ... 138 A4
Marquay (62) ... 7 H1
Marquefave (31) ... 185 E3
Marquéglise (60) ... 21 E4
Marquein (11) ... 186 A3
Marquerie (65) ... 183 F2
Marques (76) ... 19 G1
Marquette-en-Ostrevant (59) ... 9 E3
Marquette-lez-Lille (59) ... 3 F5
Marquigny (08) ... 23 H3
Marquillies (59) ... 3 E6
Marquion (62) ... 8 D3
Marquise (62) ... 1 F3
Marquivillers (80) ... 21 E2
Marquixanes (66) ... 200 C3
Marray (37) ... 78 D4
la Marre (39) ... 103 E5
Mars (07) ... 143 E4
les Mars (23) ... 126 A2
Mars (30) ... 156 D4
Mars-la-Tour (54) ... 26 A6
Mars-sous-Bourcq (08) ... 24 A4
Mars-sur-Allier (58) ... 98 C4
Marsa (11) ... 200 A1
Marsac (16) ... 122 B3
Marsac (23) ... 111 E6
Marsac (65) ... 183 F2
Marsac (82) ... 168 A3
Marsac-en-Livradois (63) ... 128 B5
Marsac-sur-Don (44) ... 74 C2
Marsac-sur-l'Isle (24) ... 137 E2
Marsainvilliers (45) ... 63 F4
Marsais (17) ... 107 F5
Marsais-Sainte-Radégonde (85) ... 107 E1
Marsal (57) ... 49 F4
Marsal (81) ... 170 D2
Marsalès (24) ... 137 H6
Marsan (32) ... 167 H5
Marsaneix (24) ... 137 F3
Marsangis (51) ... 45 E6
Marsangy (89) ... 65 E5
Marsannay-la-Côte (21) ... 101 H1
Marsannay-le-Bois (21) ... 86 A6
Marsanne (26) ... 158 B2
Marsas (33) ... 135 G3
Marsas (65) ... 183 F3
Marsat (63) ... 127 F3
Marsaz (26) ... 144 B3
Marseillan (32) ... 167 H6
Marseillan (34) ... 188 D3
Marseillan (65) ... 183 F2
Marseille (13) ... 192 A5
Marseille-en-Beauvaisis (60) ... 20 A3

Maubec (38) ... 130 D5
Maubec (82) ... 168 B3
Maubec (84) ... 175 G3
Maubert-Fontaine (08) ... 10 A6
Maubeuge (59) ... 10 A2
Maubourguet (65) ... 166 D6
Mauchamps (91) ... 63 F1
Maucomble (76) ... 19 G4
Maucor (64) ... 182 C1
Maucourt (60) ... 21 F1
Maucourt (80) ... 21 F1
Maucourt-sur-Orne (55) ... 25 F6
Maudétour-en-Vexin (95) ... 41 H2
Mauguio (34) ... 173 G5
Maulan (55) ... 47 F3
Maulay (86) ... 94 B3
Maulde (59) ... 9 G1
Maule (78) ... 42 A3
Mauléon (79) ... 92 C3
Mauléon-Barousse (65) ... 184 A5
Mauléon-d'Armagnac (32) ... 166 C2
Mauléon-Licharre (64) ... 181 G2
Maulers (60) ... 20 B3
Maulette (78) ... 41 G4
Maulévrier-Sainte-Gertrude (76) ... 17 E5
Maulichères (32) ... 166 D4
Maumusson (44) ... 75 F3
Maumusson (82) ... 168 B2
Maumusson-Laguian (32) ... 166 C5
Mauny (76) ... 18 B5
Maupas (10) ... 66 C3
Maupas (32) ... 166 C3
Maupertuis (95) ... 37 F2
Maupertus-sur-Mer (50) ... 12 D2
Mauprévoir (86) ... 109 F3
Mauquenchy (76) ... 19 F4
Mauran (31) ... 184 D3
Maure (64) ... 182 D1
Maure-de-Bretagne (35) ... 56 D4
Maurecourt (78) ... 42 B2
Mauregard (95) ... 43 E2
Mauregny-en-Haye (02) ... 22 D4
Maureilhan (34) ... 188 A4
Maureilhas-las-Illas (66) ... 201 E4
Mauremont (31) ... 185 H1
Maurens (24) ... 136 D5
Maurens (31) ... 185 H1
Maurens (32) ... 168 A4
Maurens-Scopont (81) ... 169 H5
Maurepas (78) ... 42 A5
Maurepas (80) ... 8 C5
Mauressac (31) ... 185 F3
Mauressargues (30) ... 173 H2
Maureville (31) ... 169 G6
Mauriac (15) ... 140 A2
Mauriac (33) ... 136 C6
Maurines (15) ... 141 E5
Maurois (59) ... 9 F4
Mauron (56) ... 56 C3
Mauroux (32) ... 168 B2
Mauroux (46) ... 152 A3
Maurrin (40) ... 166 B3
Maurs (15) ... 153 H1
Maurupt-le-Montois (51) ... 46 C5
Maury (66) ... 200 D1
Mausoléo (2B) ... 202 D6
Maussac (19) ... 125 G6
Maussane-les-Alpilles (13) ... 191 G2
Maussans (70) ... 87 G5
Mautes (23) ... 126 A1
Mauvages (55) ... 47 H6
Mauvaisin (31) ... 185 G2
Mauves (07) ... 144 A4
Mauves-sur-Huisne (61) ... 60 D1
Mauves-sur-Loire (44) ... 75 E4
Mauvezin (31) ... 185 G1
Mauvezin (32) ... 168 A4
Mauvezin (65) ... 183 G4
Mauvezin-d'Armagnac (40) ... 166 C2
Mauvezin-de-Prat (09) ... 184 D5
Mauvezin-de-Sainte-Croix (09) ... 185 E4
Mauvezin-sur-Gupie (47) ... 150 B2
Mauvières (36) ... 110 B1
Mauvilly (21) ... 85 F3
Maux (58) ... 99 H3
Mauzac (31) ... 185 F2
Mauzac-et-Grand-Castang (24) ... 137 F5
Mauzé-sur-le-Mignon (79) ... 107 F4
Mauzé-Thouarsais (79) ... 93 F3
Mauzens-et-Miremont (24) ... 137 H4
Mauzun (63) ... 127 H4
Maves (41) ... 80 A2
Mavilly-Mandelot (21) ... 101 F3
la Maxe (57) ... 26 C5
Maxent (35) ... 56 C4
Maxéville (54) ... 48 C5
Maxey-sur-Meuse (88) ... 68 D1
Maxey-sur-Vaise (55) ... 68 C1
Maxilly-Léman (74) ... 119 F3
Maxilly-sur-Saône (21) ... 86 B6
Maxou (46) ... 152 D3
Maxstadt (57) ... 27 G5
May-en-Multien (77) ... 43 H2
le May-sur-Èvre (49) ... 75 H6
May-sur-Orne (14) ... 14 B5
Mayac (24) ... 137 G2
Mayenne (53) ... 59 E3
Mayet (72) ... 78 B2
le Mayet-de-Montagne (03) ... 114 B6
le Mayet-d'École (03) ... 114 A5
Maynal (39) ... 117 E1
les Mayons (83) ... 193 H3
Mayot (02) ... 22 B2
Mayrac (46) ... 138 D5
Mayran (12) ... 154 B4
Mayrègne (31) ... 183 H5
Mayres (07) ... 157 E1
Mayres (63) ... 128 B6
Mayres-Savel (38) ... 145 G5
Mayreville (11) ... 186 A4
Mayrinhac-Lentour (46) ... 139 E5
Mayronnes (11) ... 187 F5
Maysel (60) ... 20 D5
Mazamet (81) ... 170 D6
Mazan (84) ... 158 B6
Mazan-l'Abbaye (07) ... 157 E1
Mazangé (41) ... 79 F1
Mazaugues (83) ... 192 D4
Mazaye (63) ... 126 D3
Mazé (49) ... 77 F5
le Mazeau (85) ... 107 F3
Mazeirat (23) ... 111 G5
Mazeley (88) ... 69 G3
Mazerat-Aurouze (43) ... 142 A2
Mazeray (17) ... 121 F1
Mazères (09) ... 185 H3
Mazères (33) ... 149 H3
Mazères-de-Neste (65) ... 183 H4
Mazères-Lezons (64) ... 182 B2
Mazères-sur-Salat (31) ... 184 C4
Mazerier (03) ... 113 H5
Mazerolles (16) ... 123 E2
Mazerolles (17) ... 121 E4
Mazerolles (40) ... 166 B2
Mazerolles (64) ... 166 A5
Mazerolles (65) ... 183 G3
Mazerolles (86) ... 109 H2
Mazerolles-du-Razès (11) ... 186 C4
Mazerolles-le-Salin (25) ... 103 F1
Mazerulles (54) ... 49 E4
Mazet-Saint-Voy (43) ... 143 E3
Mazeuil (86) ... 94 A5
Mazeyrat-d'Allier (43) ... 142 A3
Mazeyrolles (24) ... 152 A1
la Mazière-aux-Bons-Hommes (23) ... 126 A2
Mazières (16) ... 123 E3
Mazières-de-Touraine (37) ... 78 C5
Mazières-en-Gâtine (79) ... 108 A2
Mazières-en-Mauges (49) ... 92 C2
Mazille (71) ... 115 H3

Mazingarbe (62) 2 D6
Mazingarbe (62) 2 B5
Mazinghien (59) 9 G4
Mazion (33) 135 E2
Mazirat (03) 112 C6
Mazirot (88) 68 A2
le Mazis (80) 6 D6
Mazoires (63) 127 E6
Mazouau (65) 183 G4
Mazuby (11) 199 H1
les Mazures (08) 11 E6
Mazzola (2B) 205 F2
Méailles (04) 178 A1
Méallet (15) 140 A2
Méasnes (23) 111 F3
Meaucé (28) 61 F1
Méaudre (38) 145 F3
la Meauffe (50) 13 F6
la Méaugon (22) 33 G4
Méasnon (03) 112 D1
Méaulte (80) 8 A6
Méaulte (50) 15 G3
Meaux (77) 43 G3
Meaux-la-Montagne (69) 115 G6
Meauzac (82) 169 E1
Mece (35) 57 H2
Mechmont (46) 152 C2
Mécleuves (57) 26 C6
Mecquignies (59) 9 H2
Mécrin (55) 47 G4
Mécringes (51) 44 C4
Médan (78) 42 B3
Médavy (61) 39 F5
Medeyrolles (63) 128 B6
Médière (25) 88 C4
Médillac (16) 136 B2
Médis (17) 120 C4
Médréac (35) 56 C1
le Mée (28) 62 A6
Mée (53) 76 C1
le Mée-sur-Seine (77) 64 A1
Les Mées (04) 176 D1
Mées (40) 165 E4
les Mées (72) 60 B3
Mégange (57) 26 D4
Megève (74) 133 E2
Mégevette (74) 119 E4
Mégrit (22) 34 B6
Méharicourt (80) 21 E1
Méharin (64) 181 E1
Méhers (41) 80 A6
Méhoncourt (54) 69 H1
Méhoudin (61) 59 F1
Mehun-sur-Yèvre (18) 97 F1
la Meignanne (49) 76 D4
Meigné (49) 93 G1
Meigné-le-Vicomte (49) 78 A4
Meignes (57) 64 D1
Meigneux (80) 20 A1
Meigneux (77) 64 D1
Meilhac (87) 124 A3
Meilhan (32) 184 B1
Meilhan (40) 165 G2
Meilhan-sur-Garonne (47) 150 B2
Meilhards (19) 124 D5
Meilhaud (63) 127 F5
Meillac (35) 35 E6
Meillant (18) 97 H5
Meillard (03) 113 H1
le Meillard (80) 7 F3
la Meilleraie-Tillay (85) 92 C5
Meilleray (77) 44 B4
la Meilleraye-
  de-Bretagne (44) 75 E2
Meillerie (74) 119 F2
Meillers (03) 113 G2
Meillon (64) 182 C2
Meillonnas (01) 117 E4
Meilly-sur-Rouvres (21) 101 E1
Meisenthal (57) 50 C2
Meistratzheim (67) 71 G1
le Meix (21) 85 G3
le Meix-Saint-Epoing (51) 44 D5
le Meix-Tiercelin (51) 45 H6
Méjannes-le-Clap (30) 157 G5
Méjannes-lès-Alès (30) 173 H1
Mela (2A) 207 E2
Mélagues (12) 171 H4
Mélamare (76) 15 G1
Melay (49) 92 D1
Melay (52) 87 E2
Melay (71) 115 E5
le Mêle-sur-Sarthe (61) 60 C1
Mélecey (70) 88 A4
Melesse (35) 57 F2
Melgven (29) 53 H3
Mélicocq (60) 21 F4
Mélicourt (27) 39 H3
Méligny-le-Grand (55) 47 G5
Méligny-le-Petit (55) 47 G5
Melin (70) 87 F2
Melincourt (70) 87 F1
Mélisey (70) 88 B2
Mélisey (89) 84 B5
Meljac (12) 154 B6
Mellac (29) 54 B4
Mellé (35) 58 A1
Melle (79) 108 B4
Mellecey (71) 101 F5
Melleran (79) 108 C5
Melleray (72) 61 E5
Melleroy (45) 82 B5
Melles (31) 184 B6
Melleville (76) 6 B5
Mellionnec (56) 54 D1
Mello (60) 20 C6
Meloisey (21) 101 F3
Melrand (56) 55 E3
Melsheim (67) 50 D4
Melun (77) 64 A1
Melve (04) 160 B4
Melz-sur-Seine (77) 65 E1
Membrey (70) 86 D3
la Membrolle-
  sur-Choisille (37) 78 D5
la Membrolle-
  sur-Longuenée (49) 76 D3
Membrolles (41) 62 A6
Méménil (88) 70 B3
Memmelshoffen (67) 51 F2
le Mémont (25) 104 C1
Menades (89) 83 H5
Ménarmont (88) 70 B1
Menars (41) 80 A3
Menat (63) 113 E6
Menaucourt (55) 47 F5
Mencas (62) 2 A6
Menchhoffen (67) 50 C3
Mende (48) 156 A3
Mendionde (64) 180 D1
Menditte (64) 181 F3
Mendive (64) 181 E3
Ménéac (56) 56 A2
Ménerbes (84) 175 G3
Ménerval (76) 19 G3
Ménerville (78) 41 G3
Ménesble (21) 85 G2
Méneslies (80) 6 B4
Ménesplet (24) 136 B4
Ménesqueville (27) 19 E5
Ménessaire (21) 100 C2
Menestreau (58) 83 E5
Ménestreau-en-Villette (45) 81 F3
Menet (15) 140 B2
Menetou-Couture (18) 98 C3
Menetou-Râtel (18) 82 B6
Menetou-Salon (18) 97 H1
Menetou-sur-Nahon (36) 96 C1
Ménétréol-
  sous-Sancerre (18) 82 B6
Ménétréol-sur-Sauldre (18) 81 F5
Ménétréols-sous-Vatan (36) 96 D3
Ménétreuil (71) 116 D1
Ménétreux-le-Pitois (21) 84 D4
Ménétrol (63) 127 F2
Menétru-le-Vignoble (39) 102 D5
Menétrux-en-Joux (39) 117 H1
Menglon (26) 159 F1
Ménigoute (79) 108 C2
Ménil (53) 76 D1

le Ménil (88) 70 C6
Ménil-Annelles (08) 23 H4
Ménil-aux-Bois (55) 47 G4
le Ménil-Bérard (61) 39 H5
le Ménil-Broût (61) 60 B1
le Ménil-Ciboult (61) 37 H4
le Ménil-de-Briouze (61) 38 C5
Ménil-en-Xaintois (88) 69 E3
Ménil-Erreux (61) 60 A1
le Ménil-Froger (61) 39 G5
Ménil-Gondouin (61) 38 C4
le Ménil-Guyon (61) 39 G6
Ménil-Hermei (61) 38 C4
Ménil-Hubert-en-Exmes (61) 39 G4
Ménil-Hubert-sur-Orne (61) 38 C3
Ménil-la-Horgne (55) 47 G5
Ménil-la-Tour (54) 48 A4
Ménil-Lépinois (08) 23 G5
le Ménil-Scelleur (61) 38 D6
Ménil-sur-Belvitte (88) 70 B2
Ménil-sur-Saulx (55) 47 E6
le Ménil-Vicomte (61) 39 G4
Ménil-Vin (61) 38 C3
Ménilles (27) 41 F2
la Ménitré (49) 77 F5
Mennecy (91) 63 G1
Mennessis (02) 22 A2
Mennetou-sur-Cher (41) 96 D1
Menneval (27) 15 H5
Menneville (62) 2 D4
Menneville (02) 23 E4
Mennevret (02) 9 G5
Ménnouveaux (52) 68 B5
Ménoire (19) 139 E3
Menomblet (85) 92 D5
Menoncourt (90) 88 D2
Ménonval (76) 19 F1
Menotey (39) 102 C2
Menou (58) 83 E6
Menouville (95) 42 B1
le Menoux (36) 111 E2
Menoux (70) 87 F1
Mens (38) 145 G6
Mensignac (24) 137 E2
Menskirch (57) 26 D3
Mentheville (76) 16 C4
Menthon-Saint-Bernard (74) 132 B2
Menthonnex-
  en-Bornes (74) 118 C6
Menthonnex-
  sous-Clermont (74) 131 H1
Mentières (15) 141 F4
Menton (06) 195 H2
Mentque-Nortbécourt (62) 1 H3
Menucourt (95) 42 B2
les Menus (61) 61 F1
Menville (31) 168 D5
Méobecq (36) 96 A6
Méolans-Revel (04) 161 E3
Méon (49) 78 A4
Méounes-
  lès-Montrieux (83) 193 E4
Mer (41) 80 B3
Méracq (64) 166 A6
Méral (53) 58 B6
Méras (09) 185 F3
Mercatel (62) 8 B3
Mercenac (09) 184 D5
Merceuil (21) 101 G4
Mercey (27) 41 F2
Mercey-le-Grand (25) 103 E1
Mercey-sur-Saône (70) 86 D4
Mercin-et-Vaux (02) 22 A5
Merck-Saint-Liévin (62) 2 A5
Merckeghem (59) 2 B3
Mercœur (19) 139 F4
Mercœur (43) 141 G2
Mercuer (07) 157 G2
Mercuès (46) 152 C3
Mercurey (71) 101 F5
Mercury (73) 132 C3
Mercus-Garrabet (09) 185 H6
Mercy (03) 114 B2
Mercy (89) 66 A2
Mercy-le-Bas (54) 25 H4
Mercy-le-Haut (54) 25 H4
Merdrignac (22) 56 A2
Méré (89) 83 H1
Méré (78) 41 H4
Méreau (18) 97 E2
Méréaucourt (80) 19 H2
Méréglise (28) 61 H3
Mérélessart (80) 6 D5
Mérens (32) 167 H4
Mérens-les-Vals (09) 199 G3
Merenvielle (31) 168 D5
Méreuil (05) 159 H4
Méréville (54) 48 C6
Méréville (91) 63 F3
Merey (27) 41 E2
Mérey-sous-Montrond (25) 103 G2
Mérey-Vieilley (25) 87 F6
Merfy (51) 23 E5
Mergey (10) 66 A2
Meria (2B) 203 G2
Mérial (11) 199 H1
Méricourt (62) 8 C1
Méricourt (78) 41 G2
Méricourt-en-Vimeu (80) 7 E6
Méricourt-l'Abbé (80) 7 H5
Méricourt-sur-Somme (80) 8 A6
Mériel (95) 42 C2
Mérifons (34) 172 B5
Mérignac (33) 135 E5
Mérignac (17) 135 H2
Mérignac (16) 136 B3
Mérignas (33) 136 A6
Mérignat (01) 117 F6
Mérignies (59) 3 G6
Mérigny (36) 110 A1
Mérigon (09) 185 E4
Mérilheu (65) 183 F4
Mérillac (22) 56 A2
Mérinchal (23) 126 B2
Mérindol (84) 175 G4
Mérindol-les-Oliviers (26) 158 C5
Mérinville (45) 64 C5
le Mériot (10) 65 E1
Merkwiller-Pechelbronn (67) 51 F2
Merlas (38) 131 F6
la Merlatière (85) 91 H3
Merlaut (51) 46 B4
Merle-Leignec (42) 128 D6
Merléac (22) 33 F6
le Merlerault (61) 39 G5
Merles (82) 168 C1
Merles-sur-Loison (55) 25 F5
Merlevenez (56) 54 D5
Merlieux-et-
  Fouquerolles (02) 22 B4
Merlimont (62) 6 C1
Merlines (19) 126 B4
Mernel (35) 56 D4
Mérobert (91) 63 E2
Mérona (39) 117 G1
Mérouville (28) 62 D3
Meroux (90) 88 D3
Merpins (16) 121 G3
Merrey (52) 68 C5
Merrey-sur-Arce (10) 66 C5
Merri (61) 39 E3
Merris (59) 2 D4
Merry-la-Vallée (89) 83 E1
Merry-Sec (89) 83 F3
Merry-sur-Yonne (89) 83 G4
Mers-les-Bains (80) 6 B4
Mers-sur-Indre (36) 111 G1
Merschweiller (57) 26 D2
Mersuay (70) 87 G2
Merten (57) 27 E4
Mertrud (52) 67 G2
Mertzen (68) 89 E3
Mertzwiller (67) 51 E3
Méru (60) 20 B6
Merval (02) 22 D5
Mervans (71) 102 A5
Mervent (85) 107 F1

Mervilla (31) 169 F6
Merville (31) 169 E4
Merville (59) 2 D5
Merville-
  Franceville-Plage (14) 14 C4
Merviller (54) 70 B1
Merxheim (68) 71 F6
Méry (73) 131 H4
Méry-Corbon (14) 39 E1
Méry-ès-Bois (18) 81 G5
Méry-la-Bataille (60) 21 E3
Méry-Prémecy (51) 22 D6
Méry-sur-Cher (18) 97 E1
Méry-sur-Marne (77) 44 A3
Méry-sur-Oise (95) 42 C2
Méry-sur-Seine (10) 65 H1
le Merzer (22) 33 E3
Mésandans (25) 87 H5
Mésanger (44) 75 F3
Mésangueville (76) 19 F3
Mescoules (24) 136 D6
le Mesge (80) 7 E5
Mésigny (74) 132 A1
Meslan (56) 54 C2
Mesland (41) 79 G4
Meslay-du-Maine (53) 59 E6
Meslay-le-Grenet (28) 62 A2
Meslay-le-Vidame (28) 62 A3
Meslières (25) 88 D5
Meslin (22) 33 H5
Mesmay (25) 103 E2
Mesmont (08) 23 G3
Mesmont (21) 85 F6
Mesnac (16) 121 G2
Mesnard-la-Barotière (85) 92 A4
Mesnay (39) 103 E4
les Mesneux (51) 23 E6
la Mesnière (61) 60 C1
Mesnières-en-Bray (76) 19 E1
le Mesnil (50) 12 B4
le Mesnil-Adelée (50) 37 G5
le Mesnil-Amand (50) 35 H1
le Mesnil-Amelot (77) 43 E2
le Mesnil-Amey (50) 37 F1
le Mesnil-au-Grain (14) 14 A6
le Mesnil-au-Val (50) 12 C2
le Mesnil-Aubert (50) 35 H1
le Mesnil-Aubry (95) 42 D2
le Mesnil-Auzouf (14) 38 A2
le Mesnil-Bacley (14) 15 E6
le Mesnil-Benoist (14) 37 G2
Mesnil-Bruntel (80) 8 C6
le Mesnil-Caussois (14) 37 G3
Mesnil-Clinchamps (14) 37 G3
le Mesnil-Conteville (60) 20 A2
le Mesnil-Domqueur (80) 7 E4
Mesnil-Follemprise (76) 17 H3
le Mesnil-Fuguet (27) 40 D2
le Mesnil-Garnier (50) 35 H1
le Mesnil-Germain (14) 15 F6
le Mesnil-Gilbert (50) 37 G4
le Mesnil-Guillaume (14) 15 F5
le Mesnil-Hardray (27) 40 C3
le Mesnil-Herman (50) 37 F2
Mesnil-la-Comtesse (10) 66 B1
le Mesnil-le-Roi (78) 42 B3
Mesnil-Lettre (10) 66 B2
le Mesnil-Lieubray (76) 19 F3
Mesnil-Martinsart (80) 8 A4
le Mesnil-Mauger (76) 19 F2
le Mesnil-Mauger (14) 39 E2
le Mesnil-Opac (50) 37 F2
le Mesnil-Ozenne (50) 37 E5
Mesnil-Panneville (76) 17 F5
le Mesnil-Patry (14) 14 A4
le Mesnil-Rainfray (50) 37 G5
Mesnil-Raoul (76) 18 D4
le Mesnil-Réaume (76) 6 B5
le Mesnil-Robert (14) 37 G3
le Mesnil-Rogues (50) 35 H2
le Mesnil-Rousset (27) 40 A3
le Mesnil-Rouxelin (50) 13 F6
le Mesnil-Saint-Denis (78) 42 A5
le Mesnil-Saint-Firmin (60) 20 D2
Mesnil-Saint-Georges (80) 20 D2
le Mesnil-Saint-Laurent (02) 22 A1
le Mesnil-Saint-Nicaise (80) 21 F1
le Mesnil-Saint-Père (10) 66 C3
le Mesnil-Sellières (10) 66 C3
le Mesnil-Simon (14) 15 E5
le Mesnil-Simon (28) 41 F4
le Mesnil-
  sous-Jumièges (76) 17 F6
le Mesnil-sous-Vienne (27) 19 G5
le Mesnil-sur-Blangy (14) 15 F4
le Mesnil-sur-Bulles (60) 20 D3
le Mesnil-sur-Estrée (27) 41 E4
le Mesnil-sur-Oger (51) 45 F3
le Mesnil-Théribus (60) 20 A5
le Mesnil-Thomas (28) 40 D6
le Mesnil-Tôve (50) 37 G4
le Mesnil-Véneron (50) 13 F5
Mesnil-Verclives (27) 19 E5
le Mesnil-Vigot (50) 13 E6
le Mesnil-Villeman (50) 35 H2
le Mesnil-Villement (14) 38 C3
le Mesnilbus (50) 12 D6
le Mesnildot (50) 13 E4
Mesnois (39) 117 G1
les Mesnuls (78) 42 A5
Mespaul (29) 31 G3
Mesplède (64) 165 G6
Mesples (03) 112 B3
Mespuits (91) 63 F3
Mesquer (44) 73 F3
Messac (17) 121 G6
Messac (35) 57 E5
Messanges (21) 101 G2
Messanges (40) 164 C2
Messas (45) 80 B2
Messé (79) 108 D5
Messei (61) 38 B5
Messein (54) 48 C6
Messeix (63) 126 B5
Messemé (86) 94 A3
Messery (74) 118 C3
Messey-sur-Grosne (71) 116 A1
Messia-sur-Sorne (39) 102 D6
Messigny-et-Vantoux (21) 85 H5
Messimy (69) 129 H4
Messimy-sur-Saône (01) 116 B6
Messincourt (08) 24 D2
Messon (10) 66 A3
Messy (77) 43 F3
Mesterrieux (33) 150 A1
Mestes (19) 126 A5
Mesves-sur-Loire (58) 98 C1
Mesvres (71) 100 C4
Métabief (25) 104 A5
les Métairies (16) 121 H3
Métairies-Saint-Quirin (57) 50 A5
Méteren (59) 2 D4
Méthamis (84) 175 G1
Métigny (80) 7 E5
Metting (57) 50 B4
Mettray (37) 78 D5
Metz (57) 26 B5
Metz-en-Couture (62) 8 C4
Metz-le-Comte (58) 83 G5
Metz-Robert (10) 66 B5
Metz-Tessy (74) 132 A1
Metzeral (68) 71 E5
Metzeresche (57) 26 C4
Metzervisse (57) 26 C3
Metzing (57) 49 H1
Meucon (56) 55 G6

Meudon (92) 42 C4
Meuilley (21) 101 G2
Meulan (78) 42 A2
Meulers (76) 17 H2
Meulles (14) 39 G2
Meulson (21) 85 F3
Meunet-Planches (36) 97 E5
Meunet-sur-Vatan (36) 96 D3
Meung-sur-Loire (45) 80 C2
Meurcé (72) 60 B3
Meurchin (62) 3 E6
Meurcourt (70) 87 G2
la Meurdraquière (50) 35 H2
Meures (52) 67 H4
Meursac (17) 120 D3
Meursanges (21) 101 H3
Meursault (21) 101 G3
Meurville (10) 67 E4
Meusnes (41) 96 B1
Meussia (39) 117 H2
Meuvaines (14) 14 A3
Meux (17) 121 G5
le Meux (60) 21 E5
Meuzac (87) 124 C5
Mévoisins (28) 62 B1
Mévouillon (26) 159 F5
Mexy (54) 25 H3
Mey (57) 26 C5
Meyenheim (68) 71 F6
Meylan (38) 145 G2
Meymac (19) 125 G6
Meynes (30) 174 C3
Meyrals (24) 137 H5
Meyrannes (30) 157 E5
Meyrargues (13) 176 B5
Meyras (07) 157 F1
Meyreuil (13) 176 B6
Meyrié (38) 130 D5
Meyrieu-les-Étangs (38) 130 D5
Meyrieux-Trouet (73) 131 G4
Meyrignac-l'Église (19) 125 E6
Meyronne (46) 138 D5
Meyronnes (04) 161 G3
Meyrueis (48) 156 A6
Meys (69) 129 F4
Meyssac (19) 138 D4
Meysse (07) 158 A2
Meyssies (38) 130 C6
Meythet (74) 132 A1
la Meyze (87) 124 B4
Meyzieu (69) 130 B3
Mézangers (53) 59 E3
Mèze (34) 189 E1
Mézel (04) 177 E2
Mézel (63) 127 G3
Mézens (81) 169 G4
Mézeray (72) 77 H1
Mézères (43) 142 D3
Mézériat (01) 116 C4
Mézerolles (80) 7 F3
Mézerville (11) 186 A3
Mézidon-Canon (14) 39 E1
la Mézière (35) 57 E2
Mézières-au-Perche (28) 61 H3
Mézières-en-Brenne (36) 95 H5
Mézières-en-Drouais (28) 41 F5
Mézières-en-Gâtinais (45) 64 A5
Mézières-en-Santerre (80) 20 D1
Mézières-en-Vexin (27) 41 F1
Mézières-lez-Cléry (45) 80 C2
Mézières-sous-Lavardin (72) 59 H4
Mézières-sur-Couesnon (35) 57 G1
Mézières-sur-Issoire (87) 110 A5
Mézières-sur-Oise (02) 22 A1
Mézières-sur-Ponthouin (72) 60 B4
Mézières-sur-Seine (78) 41 H3
Mézilhac (07) 143 F6
Mézilles (89) 82 D4
Mézin (47) 167 F1
Méziré (90) 88 D3
Mézos (40) 148 B4
Mézy-Moulins (02) 44 C2
Mézy-sur-Seine (78) 42 A2
Mhère (58) 100 A1
Mialet (24) 123 G5
Mialet (30) 173 G1
Mialos (64) 166 A6
Miannay (80) 6 C4
Michaugues (58) 99 G1
Michelbach (68) 89 E2
Michelbach-le-Bas (68) 89 G3
Michelbach-le-Haut (68) 89 G3
Michery (89) 64 D3
Midrevaux (88) 68 C2
Mièges (39) 103 G5
Miélan (32) 183 G1
Miellin (70) 88 B2
Miermaigne (28) 61 F3
Miers (46) 138 D5
Miéry (39) 103 E5
Mietesheim (67) 51 E3
Mieussy (74) 119 E5
Mieuxcé (61) 60 A2
Migé (89) 83 F3
Migennes (89) 65 F6
Miglos (09) 199 E1
Mignaloux-Beauvoir (86) 109 F1
Mignavillers (70) 88 A3
Migné (36) 96 A6
Migné-Auxances (86) 109 E1
Mignères (45) 64 A6
Mignerette (45) 64 A5
Mignéville (54) 70 B1
Mignières (28) 62 A2
Mignovillard (39) 103 G5
Migny (36) 97 E3
Migré (17) 107 G5
Migron (17) 121 G2
Mijanès (09) 199 H2
Mijoux (01) 118 B3
la Milesse (72) 60 A5
Milhac (46) 138 B6
Milhac-d'Auberoche (24) 137 G3
Milhac-de-Nontron (24) 123 F6
Milhars (81) 153 G6
Milhas (31) 184 B5
Milhaud (30) 174 A3
Milhavet (81) 170 B1
Milizac (29) 30 D4
Millac (86) 109 G5
Millam (59) 2 B3
Millançay (41) 80 D6
Millas (66) 201 E2
Millau (12) 172 A1
Millay (58) 100 B5
Millebosc (76) 6 B5
Millemont (78) 41 H4
Millencourt (80) 8 A5
Millencourt-en-Ponthieu (80) 7 E3
Millery (21) 84 D4
Millery (54) 48 C4
Millery (69) 130 A4
Millevaches (19) 125 G4
Millières (50) 12 D6
Millières (52) 68 B4
Millonfosse (59) 9 F1
Milly (50) 37 G5
Milly-la-Forêt (91) 63 H2
Milly-Lamartine (71) 116 A3
Milly-sur-Bradon (55) 24 D5
Milly-sur-Thérain (60) 20 A4
Milon-la-Chapelle (78) 42 B5
Mimbaste (40) 165 E4
Mimet (13) 192 C3
Mimeure (21) 101 E2
Mimizan (40) 148 A5
Minaucourt-le-Mesnil-
  lès-Hurlus (51) 46 B1
Minerve (34) 187 G2
Mingot (65) 183 F1
Mingoval (62) 8 A2
Miniac-Morvan (35) 35 E5
Miniac-sous-Bécherel (35) 56 D2
Minihy-Tréguier (22) 33 E2
Minorville (54) 48 B4
Minot (21) 85 G4
Minversheim (67) 51 E4
Minzac (24) 136 B4

Minzier (74) 118 B6
Miolles (81) 171 E3
Mionnay (01) 130 B2
Mions (69) 130 B4
Mios (33) 148 C1
Miossens-Lanusse (64) 166 B6
Mirabeau (84) 177 E1
Mirabeau (04) 176 B4
Mirabel (07) 157 H2
Mirabel (82) 152 C6
Mirabel-aux-Baronnies (26) 158 C5
Mirabel-et-Blacons (26) 158 D1
Miradoux (32) 168 A2
Miramas (13) 191 G3
Mirambeau (17) 135 F1
Mirambeau (31) 184 C1
Miramont-
  de-Comminges (31) 184 B4
Miramont-de-Guyenne (47) 150 D2
Miramont-de-Quercy (82) 152 A5
Miramont-Latour (32) 168 A4
Miramont-Sensacq (40) 166 B5
Mirande (32) 167 G6
Mirandol-Bourgnounac (81) 153 H6
Mirannes (32) 167 G5
Miraumont (80) 8 A4
Miraval-Cabardès (11) 187 E2
Mirbel (49) 67 H6
Mire (49) 77 F3
Mirebeau (86) 94 A5
Mirebeau-sur-Bèze (21) 86 B5
Mirebel (39) 103 E6
Mirecourt (88) 69 F3
Mirefleurs (63) 127 F4
Miremont (31) 185 F2
Miremont (63) 126 C2
Mirepeisset (11) 188 A3
Mirepeix (64) 182 C3
Mirepoix (32) 167 H4
Mirepoix (09) 186 B4
Mirepoix-sur-Tarn (31) 169 G3
Mireval (34) 173 F6
Mireval-Lauragais (11) 186 B3
Miribel (01) 130 B2
Miribel (26) 144 C2
Miribel-Lanchâtre (38) 145 F4
Miribel-les-Échelles (38) 131 G6
Mirmande (26) 158 B1
le Miroir (71) 117 E2
Mirvaux (80) 7 G5
Mirville (76) 15 G1
Miscon (26) 159 F2
Miserey (27) 41 E2
Miserey-Salines (25) 87 F6
Misérieux (01) 130 A1
Misery (80) 21 G1
Mison (04) 160 A5
Missé (79) 93 G4
Missècle (81) 170 B4
Missègre (11) 187 E5
Missery (21) 84 D6
Missillac (44) 73 H3
Missiriac (56) 56 A5
Misson (40) 165 E4
Missy (14) 14 A4
Missy-aux-Bois (02) 21 H5
Missy-lès-Pierrepont (02) 22 D2
Missy-sur-Aisne (02) 22 B5
Misy-sur-Yonne (77) 64 D2
Mitry-Mory (77) 43 E3
Mittainville (78) 41 G5
Mittainvilliers (28) 61 H1
Mittelbergheim (67) 71 G1
Mittelbronn (57) 50 B4
Mittelhausbergen (67) 51 E5
Mittelhausen (67) 51 E4
Mittelschaeffolsheim (67) 51 E4
Mittelwihr (68) 71 F4
Mittersheim (67) 49 H3
Mittlach (68) 71 E5
Mittois (14) 39 F2
Mitzach (68) 71 E6
Mizérieux (42) 129 E3
Mizoën (38) 146 B3
Moca-Croce (2A) 207 E1
Modane (73) 147 E2
Modène (84) 175 G1
Moëlan-sur-Mer (29) 54 A4
les Moëres (59) 2 C2
Mœrnach (68) 89 F4
Moëslains (52) 46 C5
Mœurs-Verdey (51) 45 E5
Mœuvres (59) 8 D3
Moëze (17) 120 C1
Moffans-et-Vacheresse (70) 88 A3
Mogeville (55) 25 F6
Mogneneins (01) 116 B5
Mognéville (55) 46 D4
Mogues (08) 25 E2
Mohon (56) 55 H3
Moidieu-Détourbe (38) 130 B5
Moigny-sur-École (91) 63 G2
Moigné (35) 57 E3
Moimay (70) 88 A4
Moings (17) 121 G5
Moinville-la-Jeurie (28) 62 D2
Moirans (38) 145 F1
Moirans-en-Montagne (39) 117 H2
Moirax (47) 151 F5
Moiré (69) 129 H2
Moiremont (51) 46 C1
Moirey-Flabas-Crépion (55) 25 E5
Moiron (39) 102 D6
Moiry (08) 25 E3
Moisdon-la-Rivière (44) 75 E2
Moisenay (77) 64 A1
Moislains (80) 8 C5
Moissac (82) 168 D1
Moissac-
  Vallée-Française (48) 156 C5
Moissannes (87) 124 D2
Moissat (63) 127 G3
Moisselles (95) 42 D2
Moissey (39) 102 C2
Moissieu-sur-Dolon (38) 130 B6
Moissy-Cramayel (77) 43 E6
Moissy-Moulinot (58) 83 H6
Moisville (27) 41 E4
Moisy (41) 79 H1
Moïta (2B) 205 G2
les Moitiers-d'Allonne (50) 12 B3
les Moitiers-en-Bauptois (50) 12 D4
Moitron (21) 85 F4
Moitron-sur-Sarthe (72) 59 H3
Moivre (51) 46 B3
Moivrons (54) 48 D4
Molac (56) 56 A6
Molagnies (76) 19 G3
Molain (02) 9 F4
Molamboz (39) 102 D4
Molandier (11) 185 H3
Molas (31) 184 B2
Molay (39) 102 C3
Molay (70) 86 D3
Môlay (89) 83 H3
le Molay-Littry (14) 13 G5
Molèdes (15) 141 E3
Molène (29) 30 A4
Moléans (28) 61 H4
Molère (65) 183 F4
Molesme (21) 66 C6
Molesmes (89) 83 F4
Molezon (48) 156 B5
Moliens (60) 19 H3
Molières (24) 137 F6
Molières (82) 152 C6
Molières (46) 139 F6
les Molières (91) 42 B5
Molières-Cavaillac (30) 172 D3
Molières-Glandaz (26) 159 E1
Molières-sur-Cèze (30) 157 E5
Moliets-et-Maa (40) 164 C2
Molinchart (02) 22 B3
Molines-en-Queyras (05) 147 G6

Molinet (03) 114 D2
Molineuf (41) 79 H4
Molinges (39) 117 H3
Molinons (89) 65 F4
Molins (16) 121 H6
Mollans (70) 87 H3
Mollans-sur-Ouvèze (26) 158 D5
Mollau (68) 70 D6
Mollégès (13) 175 F3
Molles (03) 114 B6
les Mollettes (73) 132 A5
Molleville (11) 186 A3
Molliens-au-Bois (80) 7 G5
Molliens-Dreuil (80) 7 E6
Mollkirch (67) 50 D6
Molompize (15) 141 F2
Molosmes (89) 84 B1
Moloy (21) 85 G4
Molphey (21) 84 C6
Molpré (39) 103 G5
Molring (57) 49 G3
Molsheim (67) 50 D6
Moltifao (2B) 205 E1
les Molunes (39) 118 A3
Momas (64) 166 A6
Mombrier (33) 135 E3
Momères (65) 183 E3
Momerstroff (57) 27 E5
Mommenheim (67) 51 E4
Momuy (40) 165 G4
Momy (64) 166 C6
Monacia-d'Aullène (2A) 207 E4
Monacia-d'Orezza (2B) 205 G1
Monampteuil (02) 22 C4
Monassut-Audiracq (64) 166 B6
le Monastère (12) 154 C4
le Monastier-
  Pin-Moriès (48) 155 G3
le Monastier-
  sur-Gazeille (43) 142 D5
Monay (39) 102 D5
Monbahus (47) 151 E2
Monbalen (47) 151 F4
Monbardon (32) 184 B1
Monbazillac (24) 136 D6
Monbéqui (82) 168 D2
Monblanc (32) 184 C1
Monbrun (32) 168 C4
Moncale (2B) 204 C2
Moncassin (32) 183 H1
Moncaup (32) 184 B1
Moncaup (64) 183 E1
Moncaut (47) 151 E5
Moncayolle-Larrory-
  Mendibieu (64) 181 G2
Moncé-en-Belin (72) 78 A1
Moncé-en-Saosnois (72) 60 C3
Monceau-le-Neuf-
  et-Faucouzy (02) 22 C1
Monceau-lès-Leups (02) 22 B2
Monceau-Saint-Waast (59) 9 H3
Monceau-sur-Oise (02) 9 G6
les Monceaux (14) 15 E5
Monceaux (60) 20 D5
Monceaux-en-Bessin (14) 13 H5
Monceaux-l'Abbaye (60) 19 H2
Monceaux-le-Comte (58) 83 G6
Monceaux-
  sur-Dordogne (19) 139 F3
Moncel-lès-Lunéville (54) 49 E6
Moncel-sur-Seille (54) 49 E4
Moncel-sur-Vair (88) 68 D2
la Moncelle (08) 24 C2
Moncetz-Longevas (51) 45 H3
Moncey (25) 87 G5
Monchaux-Soreng (76) 6 C5
Monchaux-sur-Écaillon (59) 9 F2
Moncheaux (59) 8 D1
Moncheaux-lès-Frévent (62) 7 G2
Monchecourt (59) 8 D2
Monchel-sur-Canche (62) 7 F2
Moncheux (57) 48 D2
Monchiet (62) 8 A3
Monchy-au-Bois (62) 8 A3
Monchy-Breton (62) 7 H1
Monchy-Cayeux (62) 7 G1
Monchy-Humières (60) 21 E4
Monchy-Lagache (80) 8 C6
Monchy-le-Preux (62) 8 B3
Monchy-Saint-Éloi (60) 20 D6
Monchy-sur-Eu (76) 6 B5
Moncla (64) 166 C5
Monclar (32) 166 C4
Monclar (47) 151 E3
Monclar-de-Quercy (82) 169 G2
Monclar-sur-Losse (32) 167 G6
Moncley (25) 87 F6
Moncontour (22) 33 H6
Moncontour (86) 93 H3
Moncorneil-Grazan (32) 184 A1
Moncourt (57) 49 F4
Moncoutant (79) 92 D6
Moncrabeau (47) 167 F1
Moncy (61) 38 A4
Mondavezan (31) 184 D3
Mondelange (57) 26 B4
Mondement-
  Montgivroux (51) 45 E4
Mondescourt (60) 21 H3
Mondevert (35) 58 A4
Mondeville (91) 63 H1
Mondeville (14) 14 C5
Mondicourt (62) 7 H3
Mondigny (08) 24 A3
Mondilhan (31) 184 B2
Mondion (86) 94 C4
Mondon (25) 87 H5
Mondonville (31) 169 E5
Mondonville-Saint-Jean (28) 62 D3
Mondorff (57) 26 C2
Mondoubleau (41) 61 F6
Mondouzil (31) 169 F5
Mondragon (84) 158 A5
Mondrainville (14) 14 B5
Mondrepuis (02) 10 B6
Mondreville (78) 41 G4
Mondreville (77) 63 H4
Monein (64) 182 A2
Monès (31) 184 D1
Monesple (09) 185 G4
Monestier (03) 114 A5
Monestier (07) 143 G2
Monestier (24) 136 C6
le Monestier (63) 128 A5
Monestier-d'Ambel (38) 145 H6
Monestier-de-Clermont (38) 145 F4
le Monestier-du-Percy (38) 145 G6
Monestier-Merlines (19) 126 B4
Monestier-Port-Dieu (19) 126 B6
Monestiés (81) 170 B1
Monestrol (31) 185 H2
Monétay-sur-Allier (03) 113 H3
Monétay-sur-Loire (03) 114 C2
Monéteau (89) 83 F2
Monêtier-Allemont (05) 160 A4
le Monêtier-les-Bains (05) 146 D4
Monfaucon (24) 136 C5
Monfaucon (65) 183 E1
Monferran-Plavès (32) 167 H6
Monferran-Savès (32) 184 C1
Monflanquin (47) 151 G2
Monfort (32) 168 B3
Monfréville (14) 13 F5
Mongaillard (47) 167 F1
Mongausy (32) 184 A1
Mongauzy (33) 150 B2
Monget (40) 165 H5
Monguilhem (32) 166 C3
Monheurt (47) 150 D4
Monhoudou (72) 60 B3
Monieux (84) 175 H1
Monistrol-d'Allier (43) 142 A4
Monistrol-sur-Loire (43) 143 E1
Monlaur-Bernet (32) 183 H2
Monléon-Magnoac (65) 183 H3
Monlet (43) 142 B2

Monlezun (32) 167 E6
Monlezun-d'Armagnac (32) 166 C3
Monlong (65) 183 H3
Monmadalès (24) 137 E6
Monmarvès (24) 151 F1
Monnai (61) 39 H4
Monnaie (37) 79 E4
Monneren (57) 26 D3
la Monnerie-le-Montel (63) 128 A2
Monnerville (91) 63 E3
Monnes (02) 44 A1
Monnet-la-Ville (39) 103 F5
Monnetay (39) 117 F2
Monnetier-Mornex (74) 118 C5
Monneville (60) 20 A6
Monnières (39) 102 C2
Monnières (44) 75 E6
Monoblet (30) 173 F2
Monpardiac (32) 167 F6
Monpazier (24) 151 H1
Monpezat (64) 166 B6
Monplaisant (24) 137 H6
Monprimblanc (33) 149 H1
Mons (16) 122 A2
Mons (17) 121 G2
Mons (30) 173 H1
Mons (31) 169 G5
Mons (34) 171 H6
Mons (63) 127 H1
Mons (83) 178 A4
Mons-Boubert (80) 6 C3
Mons-en-Baroeul (59) 3 G5
Mons-en-Laonnois (02) 22 C3
Mons-en-Montois (77) 64 D1
Mons-en-Pévèle (59) 3 F6
Monsac (24) 137 F6
Monsaguel (24) 137 E6
Monsec (24) 123 E6
Monségur (64) 166 C6
Monségur (40) 165 H5
Monségur (47) 151 G3
Monségur (33) 150 B2
la Monselie (15) 140 B1
Monsempron-Libos (47) 151 H3
Monsireigne (85) 92 B5
Monsols (69) 115 H5
Monsteroux-Milieu (38) 130 B6
Monsures (80) 20 B2
Monswiller (67) 50 C4
Mont (64) 165 H6
Mont (65) 197 F1
Mont (71) 114 D1
le Mont (88) 70 D1
Mont-Bernanchon (62) 2 D5
Mont-Bertrand (14) 37 G2
Mont-Bonvillers (54) 25 H5
Mont-Cauvaire (76) 17 G5
Mont-d'Astarac (32) 183 H2
Mont-Dauphin (05) 161 F1
Mont-de-Lans (38) 146 B3
Mont-de-Laval (25) 104 C1
Mont-de-Marrast (32) 183 G1
Mont-de-Marsan (40) 166 A2
Mont-de-Vougney (25) 104 C1
Mont-devant-Sassey (55) 24 D4
le Mont-Dieu (08) 24 B3
Mont-Disse (64) 166 C5
Mont-Dol (35) 35 E4
Mont-Dore (83) 126 C4
Mont-d'Origny (02) 9 G6
Mont-et-Marré (58) 99 G3
Mont-Laurent (08) 23 H4
Mont-le-Vernois (70) 87 F3
Mont-le-Vignoble (54) 48 B5
Mont-lès-Lamarche (88) 69 E5
Mont-lès-Neufchâteau (88) 68 C3
Mont-lès-Seurre (71) 102 A4
Mont-l'Étroit (54) 68 D1
Mont-l'Évêque (60) 43 E1
Mont-Louis (66) 200 A4
Mont-Notre-Dame (02) 22 C5
Mont-Ormel (61) 39 F4
Mont-près-Chambord (41) 80 A4
le Mont-Saint-Adrien (60) 20 B4
Mont-Saint-Aignan (76) 17 G6
Mont-Saint-Éloi (62) 8 A2
Mont-Saint-Jean (02) 23 H2
Mont-Saint-Jean (21) 84 D6
Mont-Saint-Jean (72) 59 G3
Mont-Saint-Léger (70) 87 E3
Mont-Saint-Martin (02) 22 C6
Mont-Saint-Martin (38) 145 G1
Mont-Saint-Martin (08) 24 A4
Mont-Saint-Martin (54) 25 H3
le Mont-Saint-Michel (50) 35 F4
Mont-Saint-Père (02) 44 B2
Mont-Saint-Remy (08) 23 H5
Mont-Saint-Sulpice (89) 65 G6
Mont-Saint-Vincent (71) 100 D6
Mont-sous-Vaudrey (39) 102 D3
Mont-sur-Courville (51) 22 C6
Mont-sur-Meurthe (54) 49 E6
Mont-sur-Monnet (39) 103 F6
Montabard (61) 39 E4
Montabon (72) 78 B2
Montabot (50) 37 F2
Montacher-Villegardin (89) 64 C3
Montadet (32) 184 B1
Montady (34) 188 B2
Montagagne (09) 185 G5
Montagna-
  le-Reconduit (39) 117 E2
Montagna-le-Templier (39) 117 F2
Montagnac (30) 173 H2
Montagnac (34) 188 D1
Montagnac-
  d'Auberoche (24) 137 G2
Montagnac-
  la-Crempse (24) 137 E5
Montagnac-Montpezat (04) 177 E3
Montagnac-
  sur-Auvignon (47) 151 E5
Montagnac-sur-Lède (47) 151 G2
Montagnat (01) 117 E5
Montagne (33) 135 H5
Montagne (38) 144 D2
la Montagne (70) 88 B1
la Montagne (44) 74 C5
Montagne-Fayel (80) 7 E6
Montagney (70) 86 D6
Montagney-Servigney (25) 87 H4
Montagnieu (01) 131 E2
Montagnieu (38) 131 E4
Montagnol (12) 171 G3
Montagnole (73) 131 H5
Montagny (73) 133 E4
Montagny (69) 129 H4
Montagny (42) 115 F6
Montagny-en-Vexin (60) 41 H1
Montagny-lès-Beaune (21) 101 G3
Montagny-lès-Buxy (71) 101 F6
Montagny-les-Lanches (74) 132 A2
Montagny-lès-Seurre (21) 102 B3
Montagny-
  près-Louhans (71) 102 B6
Montagny-
  Sainte-Félicité (60) 43 F1
Montagoudin (33) 150 B2
Montagrier (24) 136 D2
Montagudet (82) 152 A5
Montagut (64) 166 A5
Montaignac-
  Saint-Hippolyte (19) 139 F1
Montaigu (39) 102 D6
Montaigu (02) 22 D3
Montaigu (85) 91 H2
Montaigu-de-Quercy (82) 151 H4
Montaigu-la-Brisette (50) 12 D2
Montaigu-le-Blin (03) 114 B4
Montaigu-les-Bois (50) 37 E2
Montaiguët-en-Forez (03) 114 C4
Montaigut (63) 112 D5
Montaigut-le-Blanc (23) 111 F5
Montaigut-le-Blanc (63) 127 F5
Montaigut-sur-Save (31) 168 D4
Montaillé (72) 61 E6

Montailleur (73)........132 C4
Montaillou (09)........199 G1
Montaimont (73)........132 C6
Montain (82)........102 D6
Montaïn (82)........168 D2
Montainville (68)........62 B3
Montainville (78)........42 A3
Montaigu-de-Château (66)........200 D2
Montalembert (79)........108 D5
Montalet-le-Bois (78)........41 H2
Montalieu-Vercieu (38)........131 E2
Montalzat (82)........152 B6
Montamat (32)........168 B6
Montambert (58)........99 H5
Montamel (46)........152 C2
Montamise (86)........109 F1
Montamy (14)........38 A2
Montanay (69)........130 A2
Montancy (25)........88 D5
Montandon (25)........88 C6
Montanel (50)........35 C5
Montaner (64)........183 E2
Montanges (01)........117 H5
Montans (81)........170 A3
Montapas (58)........99 G3
Montarcher (42)........128 D6
Montardit (09)........185 E4
Montardon (64)........182 C1
Montaren-et-
  Saint-Médiers (30)........174 B1
Montargis (45)........64 A6
Montarlot (77)........64 B3
Montarlot-lès-Rioz (70)........87 F5
Montarnaud (34)........173 E5
Montaron (58)........99 H4
Montastruc (47)........151 E4
Montastruc (65)........183 F3
Montastruc (82)........169 E1
Montastruc-de-Salies (31)........184 C5
Montastruc-
  la-Conseillère (31)........169 G4
Montastruc-Savès (31)........184 D2
le Montat (46)........152 C4
Montataire (60)........20 D6
Montauban (82)........169 F2
Montauban-de-Bretagne (35)........56 C2
Montauban-de-Luchon (31)........197 F1
Montauban-
  sur-l'Ouvèze (26)........159 F5
Montaud (34)........173 G4
Montaud (38)........145 F2
Montaudin (53)........58 B2
Montaulieu (26)........159 E4
Montaulin (10)........66 B3
Montaure (27)........18 C6
Montauriol (11)........186 A4
Montauriol (47)........151 F2
Montauriol (66)........201 E3
Montauriol (81)........170 D1
Montauroux (83)........178 A4
Montaut (09)........185 H3
Montaut (24)........137 E6
Montaut (31)........185 E2
Montaut (32)........183 H1
Montaut (40)........165 H4
Montaut (47)........151 F2
Montaut (64)........182 C3
Montaut-les-Créneaux (32)........167 H4
Montautour (35)........58 A3
Montauville (54)........48 B3
Montay (59)........9 F4
Montayral (47)........151 H3
Montazeau (24)........136 B5
Montazels (11)........186 D6
Montbard (21)........84 C3
Montbarla (82)........152 A5
Montbarrey (39)........102 D3
Montbarrois (45)........63 G5
Montbartier (82)........169 F1
Montbavin (02)........22 B3
Montbazens (12)........154 A3
Montbazin (34)........173 E6
Montbazon (37)........78 D6
Montbel (09)........186 B5
Montbel (48)........156 C2
Montbéliard (25)........88 C4
Montbéliardot (25)........104 C1
Montbellet (71)........116 B2
Montbenoît (25)........104 B3
Montberaud (31)........185 E4
Montbernard (31)........184 B2
Montberon (31)........169 F4
Montbert (44)........91 G1
Montberthault (21)........84 B4
Montbeton (82)........169 E2
Montbeugny (03)........114 A2
Montbizot (72)........60 A4
Montblainville (55)........24 C6
Montblanc (34)........188 B1
Montboillon (70)........87 E5
Montboissier (28)........60 D4
Montbolo (66)........200 D4
Montbonnot-
  Saint-Martin (38)........145 G2
Montboucher (23)........124 D1
Montboucher-
  sur-Jabron (26)........158 B2
Montboudif (15)........140 C1
Montbouton (90)........88 D4
Montbouy (45)........82 B4
Montboyer (16)........136 B1
Montbozon (70)........87 G4
Montbras (55)........68 C1
Montbray (50)........37 F3
Montbré (51)........45 F1
Montbrehain (02)........9 E5
Montbrison (42)........128 D4
Montbron (16)........123 E4
Montbronn (57)........28 B6
Montbrun (46)........153 F3
Montbrun (48)........156 B4
Montbrun-Bocage (31)........185 E4
Montbrun-
  des-Corbières (11)........187 G3
Montbrun-Lauragais (31)........185 G1
Montbrun-les-Bains (26)........159 F6
Montcabrier (46)........152 A2
Montcabrier (81)........169 H5
Montcaret (24)........136 B5
Montcarra (38)........131 E4
Montcavrel (62)........1 G6
Montceau-
  et-Écharnant (21)........101 F3
Montceau-les-Mines (71)........100 D6
Montceaux (01)........116 B6
Montceaux-lès-Meaux (77)........43 H3
Montceaux-lès-Provins (77)........44 B5
Montceaux-l'Étoile (71)........115 E4
Montceaux-Ragny (71)........116 B1
Montcel (63)........127 E1
Montcel (73)........131 H3
Montcenis (71)........100 D5
Montcet (01)........116 D4
Montcey (70)........87 G3
Montchaboud (38)........145 G3
Montchal (42)........129 F2
Montchamp (14)........38 A3
Montchamp (15)........141 F4
Montchanin (71)........100 D5
Montcharvot (52)........86 D2
Montchaton (50)........36 D2
Montchaude (16)........121 H5
Montchauvet (14)........38 A2
Montchauvet (78)........41 G3
Montchenu (26)........144 B2
Montcheutin (08)........24 B5
Montchevrel (61)........39 G6
Montchevrier (36)........111 F1
Montclar (04)........160 D3
Montclar (11)........186 D4
Montclar (12)........171 F2

Montcléra (46)........152 B2
Montclus (05)........159 H3
Montclus (30)........157 G5
Montcombroux-
  les-Mines (03)........114 C3
Montcony (71)........102 B6
Montcorbon (45)........64 C6
Montcornet (02)........11 E6
Montcornet (08)........11 E6
Montcourt (70)........69 E6
Montcourt-Fromonville (77)........64 A3
Montcoy (71)........101 H5
Montcresson (45)........82 B1
Montcuit (50)........37 E1
Montcuq (46)........152 B4
Montcusel (39)........117 G3
Montcy-Notre-Dame (08)........24 B1
Montdardier (30)........172 D2
Montdauphin (77)........44 B4
Montdidier (57)........49 G1
Montdidier (80)........20 D2
Montdoré (70)........69 F6
Montdoumerc (46)........152 D5
Montdragon (81)........170 A3
Montdurausse (81)........169 G2
Monte (2B)........203 G6
Monteaux (41)........79 G5
Montebourg (50)........12 D3
Montech (82)........168 D2
Montécheroux (25)........88 C5
Montegrosso (2B)........202 C5
Montégut (32)........167 H5
Montégut (40)........166 A4
Montégut (65)........183 H4
Montégut-Arros (32)........183 F1
Montégut-Bourjac (31)........184 D2
Montégut-
  en-Couserans (09)........184 D5
Montégut-Lauragais (31)........186 B1
Montégut-Plantaurel (09)........185 G4
Montégut-Savès (31)........184 C1
Monteignet-
  sur-l'Andelot (03)........113 H6
le Monteil (03)........140 B2
le Monteil (43)........142 C4
le Monteil-au-Vicomte (23)........125 F1
Monteille (14)........39 E1
Monteils (12)........153 G5
Monteils (30)........173 H1
Monteils (82)........153 E5
Montel-de-Gelat (63)........126 B1
Montéléger (26)........144 B5
Montélier (26)........144 C5
Montélimar (26)........158 A2
le Montellier (01)........130 C1
Montels (09)........185 G5
Montels (34)........188 B2
Montels (81)........170 A2
Montembœuf (16)........123 E3
Montenach (57)........26 C2
Montenay (53)........58 C3
Montendre (17)........135 G1
Montenescourt (62)........8 A2
Monteneuf (56)........56 B5
Montenils (77)........44 C4
Montenois (25)........88 B4
Montenoison (58)........99 F1
Montenoy (54)........48 D4
Montépilloy (60)........21 E6
Monteplain (39)........103 E2
Montépreux (51)........45 G5
Monterblanc (56)........55 G5
Montereau (45)........82 B1
Montereau-Fault-Yonne (77)........64 C2
Montereau-sur-le-Jard (77)........43 F6
Monterfil (35)........56 D3
Montérolier (76)........19 E2
Monterrein (56)........56 A4
Montertelot (56)........56 A4
Montescot (66)........201 F3
Montescourt-Lizerolles (02)........22 A2
Montespan (31)........184 C4
Montesquieu (34)........172 A5
Montesquieu (47)........150 D5
Montesquieu (82)........152 A6
Montesquieu-Avantès (09)........185 E5
Montesquieu-
  des-Albères (66)........201 F4
Montesquieu-Guittaut (31)........184 B2
Montesquieu-Lauragais (31)........185 H1
Montesquieu-Volvestre (31)........185 E3
Montesquiou (32)........167 F5
Montessaux (70)........88 A2
Montesson (78)........42 C3
Montestruc-sur-Gers (32)........167 H3
le Montet (03)........113 F3
Montet-et-Bouxal (46)........153 G1
Monteton (47)........150 C2
Monteux (84)........175 F1
Montévrain (77)........43 F4
Monteynard (38)........145 G4
Montézic (12)........154 C1
Montfa (09)........185 E4
Montfa (81)........170 C4
Montfalcon (38)........144 C2
Montfarville (50)........13 E2
Montfaucon (02)........44 B3
Montfaucon (25)........103 G1
Montfaucon (30)........174 D1
Montfaucon (46)........152 C2
Montfaucon-d'Argonne (55)........24 C6
Montfaucon-en-Velay (43)........143 F2
Montfaucon-Montigné (49)........75 F6
Montfermeil (93)........43 E3
Montfermier (82)........152 C5
Montfermy (63)........126 D2
Montferrand (11)........186 A2
Montferrand-
  du-Périgord (24)........137 G6
Montferrand-la-Fare (26)........159 F4
Montferrand-
  le-Château (25)........103 F1
Montferrat (38)........131 F5
Montferrat (83)........177 H5
Montferrer (66)........200 D4
Montferrier (09)........186 A6
Montferrier-sur-Lez (34)........173 F5
Montfey (10)........65 H5
Montfiquet (14)........13 G6
Montfleur (39)........117 F3
Montflovin (25)........104 A3
Montfort (25)........103 F2
Montfort (04)........160 C5
Montfort (25)........103 F2
Montfort (49)........77 G5
Montfort (64)........181 G1
Montfort-en-Chalosse (40)........165 H4
Montfort-l'Amaury (78)........41 H4
Montfort-le-Gesnois (72)........60 C5
Montfort-sur-Argens (83)........177 F6
Montfort-sur-Boulzane (11)........200 B2
Montfort-sur-Meu (35)........56 D2
Montfort-sur-Risle (27)........18 A5
Montfranc (12)........171 F3
Montfrin (30)........174 C3
Montfroc (26)........159 G6
Montfuron (04)........176 C3
Montgaillard (09)........185 H6
Montgaillard (11)........187 G6
Montgaillard (40)........166 A4
Montgaillard (65)........183 E4
Montgaillard (81)........169 G3
Montgaillard (82)........152 A6
Montgaillard-de-Salies (31)........184 C4
Montgaillard-Lauragais (31)........185 H1
Montgaillard-sur-Save (31)........184 B3
Montgardin (05)........160 C2
Montgardon (50)........36 C1
Montgaroult (61)........38 D4
Montgauch (09)........184 D5
Montgaudry (61)........60 B2
Montgazin (31)........185 F2
Montgé-en-Goële (77)........43 F2
Montgeard (31)........185 H2
Montgellafrey (73)........132 C6
Montgenèvre (05)........147 F4

Montgenost (51)........44 D6
Montgérain (60)........20 D3
Montgermont (35)........57 E2
Montgeron (91)........42 D5
Montgeroult (95)........42 B2
Montgesoye (25)........103 H2
Montgesty (46)........152 B3
Montgey (81)........170 A6
Montgibaud (19)........124 C5
Montgilbert (73)........132 C5
Montgiscard (31)........185 G1
Montgivray (36)........111 G1
Montgobert (02)........21 H5
Montgon (08)........24 A3
Montgradail (11)........186 C4
Montgras (31)........184 D1
Montgreleix (15)........140 D1
Montgru-Saint-Hilaire (02)........44 B1
Montguers (26)........159 F5
Montgueux (10)........66 A3
Montguillon (49)........76 C2
Montguyon (17)........135 H2
les Monthairons (55)........47 F2
Montharville (28)........62 A4
Monthault (35)........37 F6
Monthelie (21)........101 G3
Monthelon (51)........45 E2
Monthelon (71)........100 C4
Monthenault (02)........22 C4
Montherlant (60)........20 A5
Monthermé (08)........11 E6
Monthiers (02)........44 B2
Monthieux (01)........130 B1
Monthion (73)........132 C4
Monthodon (37)........79 E3
Monthoiron (86)........94 D6
Monthois (08)........24 B5
Montholier (39)........102 D4
Monthou-sur-Bièvre (41)........79 H5
Monthou-sur-Cher (41)........79 H6
Monthuchon (50)........37 E1
Monthurel (02)........44 C2
Monthureux-le-Sec (88)........69 F4
Monthureux-sur-Saône (88)........69 E5
Monthyon (77)........43 G2
Monticello (2B)........202 D5
Montier-en-Der (52)........67 F1
Montier-en-l'Isle (10)........67 E3
Montiéramey (10)........66 C4
Montierchaume (36)........96 D5
Montiers (60)........20 D4
Montiers-sur-Saulx (55)........68 A1
Monties (32)........184 B1
Montignac (24)........138 A3
Montignac (33)........149 H1
Montignac (65)........183 F3
Montignac-Charente (16)........122 B3
Montignac-de-Lauzun (47)........151 E2
Montignac-le-Coq (16)........136 C1
Montignac-Toupinerie (47)........150 D2
Montignargues (30)........173 H2
Montigné (16)........122 A2
Montigné (79)........107 H4
Montigné-le-Brillant (53)........58 C5
Montigné-lès-Rairies (49)........77 G3
Montigny (14)........38 B3
Montigny (18)........98 A1
Montigny (45)........63 E5
Montigny (54)........69 G1
Montigny (72)........60 B1
Montigny (76)........18 C4
Montigny-aux-Amognes (58)........99 E3
Montigny-
  devant-Sassey (55)........24 D4
Montigny-en-Arrouaise (02)........9 F5
Montigny-en-Cambrésis (59)........9 F4
Montigny-en-Gohelle (62)........8 C1
Montigny-en-Morvan (58)........100 A2
Montigny-en-Ostrevent (59)........8 D2
Montigny-la-Resle (89)........83 G1
Montigny-l'Allier (02)........43 H2
Montigny-le-Bretonneux (78)........42 B5
Montigny-le-Chartif (28)........61 G3
Montigny-le-Franc (02)........22 D2
Montigny-le-Gannelon (28)........61 H1
Montigny-le-Guesdier (77)........65 E2
Montigny-Lencoup (77)........64 C2
Montigny-Lengrain (02)........21 H5
Montigny-lès-Arsures (39)........103 E4
Montigny-lès-Cherlieu (70)........87 E2
Montigny-lès-Condé (02)........44 C2
Montigny-lès-Cormeilles (95)........42 C3
Montigny-lès-Jongleurs (80)........7 F3
Montigny-lès-Metz (57)........26 B5
Montigny-lès-Monts (10)........66 A5
Montigny-
  lès-Vaucouleurs (55)........47 H6
Montigny-lès-Vesoul (70)........87 F3
le Montigny (03)........113 H3
Montigny-Montfort (21)........84 C3
Montigny-Mornay-Villeneuve-
  sur-Vingeanne (21)........86 B4
Montigny-
  Saint-Barthélemy (21)........84 C5
Montigny-sous-Marle (02)........22 D1
Montigny-sur-Armançon (21)........84 D5
Montigny-sur-Aube (21)........85 G1
Montigny-sur-Avre (28)........40 D5
Montigny-sur-Canne (58)........99 G4
Montigny-sur-Crécy (02)........22 C2
Montigny-sur-l'Ain (39)........103 E6
Montigny-sur-l'Hallue (80)........7 H5
Montigny-sur-Loing (77)........64 A3
Montigny-sur-Meuse (08)........11 E4
Montigny-sur-Vence (08)........24 A2
Montigny-sur-Vesle (51)........22 D5
Montilliers (49)........93 E1
Montillot (89)........83 G4
Montilly (03)........113 H1
Montilly-sur-Noireau (61)........38 B4
Montils (17)........121 F4
les Montils (41)........79 H4
Montipouret (36)........111 G1
Montirat (11)........187 E3
Montirat (81)........153 H6
Montireau (28)........61 E3
Montiron (32)........168 B5
Montivernage (25)........88 A6
Montivilliers (76)........15 F1
Montjardin (11)........186 B5
Montjaux (12)........171 H1
Montjavoult (60)........19 G6
Montjay (05)........159 G4
Montjay (71)........102 B5
Montjean (16)........121 H2
Montjean (53)........58 B5
Montjean-sur-Loire (49)........75 H4
Montjoi (11)........187 F5
Montjoi (82)........151 H5
Montjoie-en-Couserans (09)........185 E5
Montjoie-le-Château (25)........88 D5
Montjoie-Saint-Martin (50)........35 H5
Montjoire (31)........169 G4
Montjoux (26)........158 C3
Montjoyer (26)........158 B3
Montjustin (04)........176 B3
Montjustin-et-Velotte (70)........87 H3
Montlandon (28)........61 F3
Montlaur (11)........187 F4
Montlaur (12)........171 G3
Montlaur (31)........169 G6
Montlaur-en-Diois (26)........159 F2
Montlaux (04)........176 C1
Montlauzun (46)........152 B5
Montlay-en-Auxois (21)........84 C6
Montlebon (25)........104 B3
Montlevicq (36)........111 H1
Montlevon (02)........44 C3
Montliard (45)........63 G6
Montlieu-la-Garde (17)........135 G2
Montlignon (95)........42 C2
Montliot-et-Courcelles (21)........85 E1
Montlivault (41)........80 A3
Montlognon (60)........43 F1
Montloué (02)........23 E2
Montlouis (18)........97 F5
Montlouis-sur-Loire (37)........79 E6
Montluçon (03)........112 D4
Montluel (01)........130 C2
Montmachoux (77)........64 C3
Montmacq (60)........21 F4
Montmagny (95)........42 D3

Montmahoux (25)........103 G3
Montmain (21)........102 A3
Montmain (76)........17 H6
Montmançon (21)........86 B6
Montmarault (03)........113 F4
Montmarlon (39)........103 F4
Montmartin (60)........21 E4
Montmartin-en-Graignes (50)........13 F5
Montmartin-le-Haut (10)........67 E4
Montmartin-sur-Mer (50)........36 D2
Montmaur (05)........160 A2
Montmaur (11)........185 H1
Montmaur-en-Diois (26)........159 E1
Montmaurin (31)........184 A3
Montmédy (55)........25 E3
Montmeillant (08)........23 G2
Montmelard (71)........115 G4
Montmelas-Saint-Sorlin (69)........129 G1
Montmélian (73)........132 A5
Montmerle-sur-Saône (01)........116 B6
Montmerrei (61)........39 E5
Montmeyan (83)........177 F5
Montmeyran (26)........144 B6
Montmirail (51)........44 C4
Montmirail (72)........61 E5
Montmiral (26)........144 C3
Montmirat (30)........173 H3
Montmirey-la-Ville (39)........102 C1
Montmirey-le-Château (39)........102 C1
Montmoreau-
  Saint-Cybard (16)........122 B6
Montmorency (95)........42 D3
Montmorency-Beaufort (10)........42 D2
Montmorillon (86)........109 H3
Montmorin (05)........159 G3
Montmorin (63)........127 G4
Montmorot (39)........102 D6
Montmort (71)........100 B6
Montmort-Lucy (51)........45 E3
Montmotier (88)........69 G6
Montmoyen (21)........85 F2
Montmurat (15)........153 H2
Montner (66)........200 D2
Montoillot (21)........101 F1
Montoir-de-Bretagne (44)........73 H4
Montoire-sur-le-Loir (41)........79 E2
Montois-la-Montagne (57)........26 B4
Montoison (26)........144 B6
Montoldre (03)........114 A4
Montolieu (11)........186 D2
Montolivet (77)........44 B4
Montonvillers (80)........7 G5
Montory (64)........181 G4
Montot (21)........102 A2
Montot (70)........86 D4
Montot-sur-Rognon (52)........68 A3
Montouliers (34)........188 A2
Montoulieu (09)........185 H5
Montoulieu (34)........173 F3
Montoulieu-
  Saint-Bernard (31)........184 C3
Montournais (85)........92 C5
Montours (35)........35 H5
Montourtier (53)........59 E3
Montoussé (65)........183 G4
Montoussin (31)........184 D2
Montoy-Flanville (57)........26 C5
Montpascal (73)........132 C6
Montpellier (34)........173 F5
Montpellier-de-Médillan (17)........121 E4
Montpensier (63)........113 H6
Montperreux (25)........104 A4
Montpeyroux (12)........155 F4
Montpeyroux (24)........136 B5
Montpeyroux (34)........173 E4
Montpeyroux (63)........127 F4
Montpezat (30)........173 H3
Montpezat (32)........168 C6
Montpezat (47)........151 E4
Montpezat-
  sous-Bauzon (07)........157 F1
Montpinchon (50)........37 E2
Montpinier (81)........170 C5
Montpitol (31)........169 G4
Montplonne (55)........47 E5
Montpollin (49)........77 G3
Montpon-Ménestérol (24)........136 B4
Montpont-en-Bresse (71)........116 D1
Montpothier (10)........44 C6
Montpouillan (47)........150 B3
Montrabé (31)........169 F5
Montrabot (50)........37 G2
Montracol (01)........116 D5
Montréal (07)........157 F2
Montréal (11)........186 C3
Montréal (32)........167 E2
Montréal (89)........84 B4
Montréal-la-Cluse (01)........117 G5
Montréal-les-Sources (26)........159 E4
Montrécourt (59)........9 F3
Montredon (46)........153 H2
Montredon-
  des-Corbières (11)........188 A3
Montredon-
  Labessonnié (81)........170 C4
Montregard (43)........143 F3
Montréjeau (31)........184 A4
Montrelais (44)........76 A5
Montrem (24)........137 E3
Montrésor (37)........95 H2
Montret (71)........102 A6
Montreuil (28)........41 E4
Montreuil (62)........6 C1
Montreuil (85)........107 E2
Montreuil (93)........42 D4
Montreuil-au-Houlme (61)........38 D5
Montreuil-aux-Lions (02)........44 A2
Montreuil-Bellay (49)........93 G2
Montreuil-Bonnin (86)........108 D1
Montreuil-des-Landes (35)........58 A3
Montreuil-en-Auge (14)........15 E5
Montreuil-en-Caux (76)........18 D2
Montreuil-en-Touraine (37)........79 F5
Montreuil-Juigné (49)........76 D4
Montreuil-la-Cambe (61)........39 E3
Montreuil-l'Argillé (27)........39 H3
Montreuil-le-Chétif (72)........59 H3
Montreuil-le-Gast (35)........57 E1
Montreuil-le-Henri (72)........78 D1
Montreuil-Poulay (53)........59 E2
Montreuil-sous-Pérouse (35)........57 H2
Montreuil-sur-Barse (10)........66 C4
Montreuil-sur-Blaise (52)........67 G1
Montreuil-sur-Brêche (60)........20 C4
Montreuil-sur-Epte (95)........41 G1
Montreuil-sur-Ille (35)........57 F1
Montreuil-sur-Loir (49)........77 E3
Montreuil-sur-Lozon (50)........13 E6
Montreuil-sur-Maine (49)........76 D3
Montreuil-sur-Thérain (60)........20 B4
Montreuil-
  sur-Thonnance (52)........68 A1
Montreuillon (58)........100 A2
Montreux (54)........70 A1
Montreux-Château (90)........88 D3
Montreux-Jeune (68)........88 D3
Montreux-Vieux (68)........88 D3
Montrevault (49)........75 F5
Montrevel (38)........131 E5
Montrevel (39)........117 F2
Montrevel-en-Bresse (01)........116 D3
Montréverd (85)........91 H2
Montrichard-Albanné (73)........146 C2
Montricoux (82)........169 G1
Montrieux-en-Sologne (41)........80 C4
Montrigaud (26)........144 C2
Montriond (74)........119 F4
Montrodat (48)........155 H3
Montrol-Sénard (87)........110 C5
Montrollet (16)........123 G1
Montromant (69)........129 G3
Montrond (05)........159 H4
Montrond (39)........103 E5
Montrond-le-Château (25)........103 G2
Montrond-les-Bains (42)........129 E4
Montrosier (81)........153 F5
Montrottier (69)........129 G3
Montroty (76)........19 F4

Montrouge (92)........42 D4
Montrouveau (41)........79 E2
Montroy (17)........106 D5
Montrozier (12)........154 D4
Montry (77)........43 G3
Monts (35)........78 D6
Monts (60)........20 A5
Monts-en-Bessin (14)........14 A5
Monts-en-Ternois (62)........7 G2
Monts-sur-Guesnes (86)........94 B4
les Monts-Verts (48)........141 F5
Montsalès (12)........153 G3
Montsalier (04)........176 B1
Montsalvy (15)........154 C1
Montsapey (73)........132 C5
Montsauche-
  les-Settons (58)........100 B1
Montsaugeon (52)........86 B3
Montsaunès (31)........184 C4
Montsec (55)........47 H3
Montsecret (61)........38 A4
Montségur (09)........185 H6
Montségur-sur-Lauzon (26)........158 B4
Montselgues (07)........157 E3
Montséret (11)........187 H4
Montsérié (65)........183 H4
Montseron (09)........185 F5
Montseveroux (38)........130 B6
Montsoreau (49)........93 H2
Montsoué (40)........166 A4
Montsoult (95)........42 D2
Montsûrs (53)........59 E4
Montsurvent (50)........36 D1
Montsuzain (10)........66 B2
Montureux-et-Prantigny (70)........86 D4
Montureux-lès-Baulay (70)........87 F1
Montusclat (43)........142 D4
Montussaint (25)........88 A5
Montussan (33)........135 F5
Montvalen (81)........169 G3
Montvalent (46)........138 D5
Montvalezan (73)........133 F4
Montvendre (26)........144 C5
Montverdun (42)........128 D3
Montvernier (73)........146 C1
Montvert (15)........139 G4
Montvicq (03)........113 E4
Montville (76)........17 G5
Montviette (14)........39 F2
Montville (14)........39 F2
Montviron (50)........35 H3
Montzéville (55)........25 E6
Monviel (47)........151 E2
Monze (11)........187 E4
Moon-sur-Elle (50)........13 F6
Moosch (68)........88 D1
Mooslargue (68)........89 E4
Moragne (17)........106 D6
Moraines (51)........45 E5
Morainville (28)........62 D3
Morainville-Jouveaux (27)........15 G4
Morainvilliers (78)........42 A3
Morancé (69)........129 H2
Morancez (28)........62 B2
Morancourt (52)........67 G2
Morand (37)........79 F4
Morangis (51)........45 E3
Morangis (91)........42 D5
Morangles (60)........42 C1
Morannes (49)........77 E2
Moranville (55)........25 G6
Moras (38)........130 D5
Moras-en-Valloire (26)........144 B1
Morbecque (59)........3 H5
Morbier (39)........118 A1
Morcenx (40)........165 F1
Morchain (80)........21 G1
Morchies (62)........8 C4
Morcourt (02)........22 A1
Morcourt (80)........8 B6
Mordelles (35)........57 E3
Moréac (56)........55 F4
Morée (41)........79 H1
Moreilles (85)........106 D2
Morelmaison (88)........69 E2
Morembert (10)........66 C1
Morestel (38)........131 E4
Moret-sur-Loing (77)........64 B3
Morette (38)........145 E1
Moreuil (80)........20 D1
Morey (71)........101 H5
Morey-Saint-Denis (21)........101 H1
Morez (39)........118 B2
Morfontaine (54)........25 H4
Morganx (40)........165 H5
Morgemoulin (55)........25 G6
Morgny (27)........19 F5
Morgny-en-Thiérache (02)........23 E1
Morgny-la-Pommeraye (76)........17 H5
Morhange (57)........49 F3
Moriani-Plage (2B)........203 G6
Morienne (76)........19 F1
Morienval (60)........21 G5
Morières-lès-Avignon (84)........175 E2
Moriers (28)........61 H4
Morieux (22)........33 H4
Moriez (04)........177 H2
Morigny (50)........37 G3
Morigny-Champigny (91)........63 F2
Morillon (74)........119 F5
Moringhem (62)........3 E4
Morionvilliers (52)........68 B2
Morisel (80)........20 D1
Moriville (88)........69 H2
Moriviller (54)........69 G1
Morizécourt (88)........69 E5
Morizès (33)........150 A2
Morlaàs (64)........182 C1
Morlac (18)........97 G6
Morlaix (29)........32 A3
Morlancourt (80)........7 H6
Morlanne (64)........165 H6
Morlet (71)........101 E4
Morley (55)........47 F6
Morlhon-le-Haut (12)........153 G5
Morlincourt (60)........21 G3
Mormaison (85)........91 G2
Mormant (77)........43 H6
Mormant-sur-Vernisson (45)........64 A6
Mormès (32)........166 C3
Mormoiron (84)........175 G1
Mornac (16)........122 C3
Mornac-sur-Seudre (17)........120 C3
Mornand-en-Forez (42)........128 D4
Mornans (26)........158 C2
Mornant (69)........129 H4
Mornay (71)........115 G2
Mornay-Berry (18)........98 C3
Mornay-sur-Allier (18)........98 D4
Moroges (71)........101 F5
Morogues (18)........97 H1
Morosaglia (2B)........203 F6
Morre (25)........103 G1
Morsain (02)........21 H4
Morsains (51)........44 C4
Morsalines (50)........13 E3
Morsan (27)........15 H4
Morsang-sur-Orge (91)........42 D5
Morsang-sur-Seine (91)........43 E6
Morsbach (57)........27 G5
Morsbronn-les-Bains (67)........51 E3
Morschwiller (67)........50 D3
Morschwiller-le-Bas (68)........89 F2
Morsiglia (2B)........203 F2
Mortagne (88)........70 B2
Mortagne-au-Perche (61)........60 D1
Mortagne-du-Nord (59)........4 A6
Mortagne-sur-Gironde (17)........120 D5
Mortagne-sur-Sèvre (85)........92 B3
Mortain (50)........37 G5
Mortcerf (77)........43 G4
la Morte (38)........145 H4
Morteau (25)........104 B3
Morteaux-Coulibœuf (14)........39 E3
Mortefontaine (02)........21 H6
Mortefontaine (60)........43 E1
Mortefontaine-en-Thelle (60)........20 B6
Mortemart (87)........110 B5
Mortemer (60)........21 E3
Mortemer (76)........19 F2
Mortery (77)........44 A4

Morthomiers (18)........97 G3
Mortiers (02)........22 C2
Mortiers (17)........121 G6
Morton (86)........93 H2
Mortrée (61)........39 E5
Mortroux (23)........111 H3
Mortzwiller (68)........88 D2
Morval (62)........8 C4
Morvillars (90)........88 D4
Morville (50)........12 D3
Morville (88)........68 D3
Morville-en-Beauce (45)........63 F3
Morville-lès-Vic (57)........49 F4
Morville-sur-Andelle (76)........19 E4
Morville-sur-Nied (57)........49 E2
Morville-sur-Seille (54)........48 C3
Morvillers (60)........19 H3
Morvillers-Saint-Saturnin (80)........19 H1
Morvilliers (10)........67 E2
Morvilliers (28)........40 D5
Mory (62)........8 B3
Mory-Montcrux (60)........20 C3
Morzine (74)........119 F4
Mosles (14)........13 H5
Moslins (51)........45 E3
Mosnac (16)........122 A4
Mosnac (17)........121 F5
Mosnay (36)........111 E1
Mosnes (37)........79 G5
Mosset (66)........200 B3
Mosson (21)........85 E1
Mostuéjouls (12)........155 G6
Motey-Besuche (70)........86 D6
Motey-sur-Saône (70)........86 D4
la Mothe-Achard (85)........91 E5
la Mothe-Saint-Héray (79)........108 B3
Mothern (67)........51 G2
la Motte (22)........55 G1
la Motte (83)........177 H6
la Motte-Chalancon (26)........159 E3
la Motte-d'Aigues (84)........176 B4
la Motte-d'Aveillans (38)........145 G4
la Motte-de-Galaure (26)........144 B2
la Motte-du-Caire (04)........160 B4
la Motte-en-Bauges (73)........132 B3
la Motte-
  en-Champsaur (05)........146 B6
la Motte-Fanjas (26)........144 D4
la Motte-Feuilly (36)........111 H1
la Motte-Fouquet (61)........38 D6
la Motte-Saint-Jean (71)........114 D2
la Motte-Saint-Martin (38)........145 G4
la Motte-Servolex (73)........131 H4
la Motte-Ternant (21)........84 C6
la Motte-Tilly (10)........65 F1
Mottereau (28)........61 G3
Motteville (76)........17 F4
Mottier (38)........131 E5
Mouacourt (54)........49 F5
Mouais (44)........74 D1
Mouans-Sartoux (06)........178 C5
Mouaville (54)........25 H6
Mouazé (35)........57 F2
Mouchamps (85)........92 A5
Mouchan (32)........167 F3
Mouchard (39)........103 E3
la Mouche (50)........35 H2
Mouchès (32)........167 G5
Mouchin (59)........4 A6
Mouchy-le-Châtel (60)........20 C5
Moudeyres (43)........142 D5
Mouen (14)........14 B5
Mouettes (27)........41 F3
Mouffy (89)........83 F3
Mouflaines (27)........19 F6
Mouflers (80)........7 F4
Mouflières (80)........6 D5
Mougins (06)........178 C5
Mougon (79)........108 A4
Mouguerre (64)........164 B6
Mouhers (36)........111 F1
Mouhet (36)........110 D3
Mouhous (64)........182 B1
Mouilleron (52)........86 D2
Mouilleron-en-Pareds (85)........92 B6
Mouilleron-le-Captif (85)........91 G4
Mouilly (55)........47 G2
Moulainville (55)........47 G1
Moularès (81)........170 D1
Moulay (53)........59 E3
Moulayrès (81)........170 B4
Moulédous (65)........183 F3
Moulès-et-Baucels (34)........173 F3
Mouleydier (24)........137 E5
Moulézan (30)........173 H2
Moulhard (28)........61 G4
Moulicent (61)........40 C6
Moulidars (16)........122 A4
Mouliets-et-Villemartin (33)........136 A5
Mouliherne (49)........77 G5
Moulin-Mage (81)........171 F4
Moulin-Neuf (09)........186 B4
Moulin-Neuf (24)........136 B4
Moulin-sous-Touvent (60)........21 H4
Moulineaux (76)........18 B5
Moulines (14)........14 B6
Moulines (50)........37 H5
Moulinet (06)........179 F2
Moulinet (47)........151 F2
le Moulinet-sur-Solin (45)........82 B3
Moulins (02)........22 D4
Moulins (35)........57 G4
Moulins (79)........92 D6
Moulins-en-Tonnerrois (89)........84 B2
Moulins-Engilbert (58)........100 A3
Moulins-la-Marche (61)........39 H6
Moulins-le-Carbonnel (72)........59 H2
Moulins-lès-Metz (57)........26 B5
Moulins-Saint-Hubert (55)........24 D3
Moulins-sur-Céphons (36)........96 B3
Moulins-sur-Orne (61)........39 E4
Moulins-sur-Ouanne (89)........83 E3
Moulins-sur-Yèvre (18)........97 H2
Moulis (09)........185 E5
Moulis-en-Médoc (33)........134 D3
Moulismes (86)........109 H3
Moulle (62)........3 F4
Moulon (33)........135 H5
Moulon (45)........63 H6
Moulotte (55)........25 H6
Moult (14)........14 C5
Moumour (64)........181 H3
Mounes-Prohencoux (12)........171 G4
Mourède (32)........167 F3
Mourens (33)........149 H1
Mourenx (64)........182 A2
Mouret (12)........154 C3
Moureuille (63)........126 C1
Mourèze (34)........172 C5
Mouriès (13)........191 F3
Mouriez (62)........7 E2
Mourioux-Vieilleville (23)........111 F6
Mourjou (15)........154 A1
Mourmelon-le-Grand (51)........45 H1
Mourmelon-le-Petit (51)........45 H2
Mournans-Charbonny (39)........103 F5
Mouron (08)........24 B5
Mouron-sur-Yonne (58)........99 H2
Mouroux (77)........43 H4
Mours (95)........42 C2
Mours-Saint-Eusèbe (26)........144 C3
Mourvilles-Basses (31)........185 H1
Mourvilles-Hautes (31)........186 A1
Mouscardès (40)........165 G5
Moussac (30)........173 H2
Moussac (86)........109 G4
Moussages (15)........140 B2
Moussan (11)........188 A3
Moussé (35)........57 H4
les Mousseaux (78)........41 H4
Mousseaux-lès-Bray (77)........64 D2
Mousseaux-Neuville (27)........41 E3
Mousseaux-sur-Seine (78)........41 G2
Moussey (10)........66 B4
Moussey (57)........49 G5

Moussey (88)........70 D1
les Moussières (39)........118 A3
Mousson (54)........48 C3
Moussonvillers (61)........40 B6
Moussoulens (11)........186 D3
Moussy (51)........45 E2
Moussy (58)........99 E2
Moussy (95)........42 A2
Moussy-le-Neuf (77)........43 E2
Moussy-le-Vieux (77)........43 E2
Moussy-Verneuil (02)........22 C4
Mousteru (22)........32 D4
Moustey (40)........149 E4
Moustier (47)........150 D1
Moustier-en-Fagne (59)........10 C4
Moustier-Ventadour (19)........125 G6
Moustiers-
  Sainte-Marie (04)........177 E3
le Moustoir (22)........32 C6
Moustoir-Ac (56)........55 F4
Moustoir-Remungol (56)........55 F3
la Moutade (63)........127 F1
le Moutaret (38)........132 A6
Mouterhouse (67)........50 C2
Mouterre-Silly (86)........93 H3
Mouterre-sur-Blourde (86)........109 G5
Mouthe (25)........103 H6
le Moutherot (25)........103 E1
Mouthier-en-Bresse (71)........102 C4
Mouthier-Haute-Pierre (25)........103 H3
Mouthiers-sur-Boëme (16)........122 B5
Mouthoumet (11)........187 F5
Moutier-d'Ahun (23)........111 H6
Moutier-Malcard (23)........111 G3
Moutier-Rozeille (23)........125 F2
Moutiers (28)........62 C4
Moutiers (35)........58 A5
Moutiers (54)........26 A4
Moutiers-au-Perche (61)........61 E1
les Moutiers-en-Auge (14)........39 E3
les Moutiers-en-Cinglais (14)........14 B6
les Moutiers-en-Puisaye (89)........82 D4
les Moutiers-en-Retz (44)........74 A6
les Moutiers-Hubert (14)........39 G2
Moutiers-les-Mauxfaits (85)........91 G6
Moutiers-Saint-Jean (21)........84 B4
Moutiers-
  sous-Chantemerle (79)........92 D6
Moutiers-sur-le-Lay (85)........106 C1
Moutonne (39)........117 G2
Moutonneau (16)........122 C2
Moutoux (39)........103 F6
Moutrot (54)........48 B6
Mouvaux (59)........4 D4
Moux (11)........187 G3
Moux-en-Morvan (58)........100 C2
Mouxy (73)........131 H3
Mouy (60)........20 C5
Mouy-sur-Seine (77)........64 D2
Mouzay (37)........95 F2
Mouzay (55)........24 D4
Mouzeil (44)........75 E3
Mouzens (24)........137 H5
Mouzens (81)........170 A5
Mouzeuil-Saint-Martin (85)........106 D2
Mouzieys-Panens (81)........170 A1
Mouzieys-Teulet (81)........170 D3
Mouzillon (44)........75 E6
Mouzon (08)........24 D3
Mouzon (16)........123 E2
Moval (90)........88 D3
Moyaux (14)........15 F4
Moydans (05)........159 F4
Moye (74)........131 H2
Moyemont (88)........70 A2
Moyen (54)........70 A1
Moyencourt (80)........21 G2
Moyencourt-lès-Poix (80)........20 A1
Moyenmoutier (88)........70 C2
Moyenneville (60)........21 F3
Moyenneville (62)........8 B3
Moyenneville (80)........6 D4
Moyenvic (57)........49 F4
Moyeuvre-Grande (57)........26 B4
Moyeuvre-Petite (57)........26 B4
Moyon (50)........37 F2
Moyrazès (12)........154 B4
Moyvillers (60)........21 E4
Mozac (63)........127 F2
Mozé-sur-Louet (49)........76 D5
Muchedent (76)........17 H3
Mudaison (34)........173 G5
Muel (35)........56 C2
Muespach (68)........89 G3
Muespach-le-Haut (68)........89 G3
Mugron (40)........165 G3
Muhlbach-sur-Bruche (67)........50 B6
Muhlbach-sur-Munster (68)........70 D5
Muides-sur-Loire (41)........80 B3
Muidorge (60)........20 B3
Muids (27)........18 D6
Muille-Villette (80)........21 G2
Muirancourt (60)........21 G3
Muizon (51)........22 D6
les Mujouls (06)........178 C3
la Mulatière (69)........129 H3
Mulcent (78)........41 H4
Mulcey (57)........49 F4
Mulhausen (67)........50 D3
Mulhouse (68)........89 F2
Mulsanne (72)........60 B6
Mulsans (41)........80 A2
Mun (65)........183 F3
Munchhausen (67)........51 G2
Muncq-Nieurlet (62)........3 E3
Mundolsheim (67)........51 E5
Muneville-le-Bingard (50)........12 D6
Muneville-sur-Mer (50)........36 D1
le Mung (17)........121 E3
Munster (57)........49 H3
Munster (68)........71 E5
Muntzenheim (68)........71 F4
Munwiller (68)........71 F6
Mur-de-Barrez (12)........140 C6
Mûr-de-Bretagne (22)........55 E1
Mur-de-Sologne (41)........80 B5
Murasson (12)........171 E4
Murat (03)........113 F3
Murat (15)........140 D3
Murat-le-Quaire (63)........126 D4
Murat-sur-Vèbre (81)........171 F4
Murato (2B)........203 F5
la Muraz (74)........118 C5
Murbach (68)........71 E6
la Mure (38)........145 G5
la Mure-Argens (04)........177 H2
Mureaumont (60)........19 H3
les Mureaux (78)........42 A2
Mureils (26)........144 B2
Mûres (74)........132 A2
Muret (31)........185 F1
Muret-et-Crouttes (02)........22 B6
Muret-le-Château (12)........154 C3
la Murette (38)........131 F6
Murianette (38)........145 G2
Murinais (38)........144 D2
Murles (34)........173 E5
Murlin (58)........98 D2
Muro (2B)........202 C5
Murol (63)........127 E5
Murols (12)........154 C2
Muron (17)........107 E5
Mûrs-Erigné (49)........76 D5
Murs (36)........95 H4
Murs (84)........175 G2
Murs-et-Gélignieux (01)........131 F3
Murtin-et-Bogny (08)........23 H1
Murvaux (55)........24 D4
Murviel-lès-Béziers (34)........188 B1
Murviel-lès-Montpellier (34)........173 E5
Murville (54)........25 H5
Mus (30)........173 H4
Muscourt (02)........22 D5

Musculdy (64) 181 F3
Musièges (74) 118 A6
Musigny (21) 101 E2
Mussey-sur-Marne (52) 67 H2
Mussidan (24) 136 D4
Mussig (67) 71 G3
Mussy-la-Fosse (21) 84 D4
Mussy-sous-Dun (71) 115 G4
Mussy-sur-Seine (10) 66 D6
Mutigney (39) 86 C6
Mutigny (51) 45 F2
Mutrécy (14) 14 B5
Muttersholtz (67) 71 G3
Mutzenhouse (67) 50 D2
Mutzig (67) 50 C6
le Muy (83) 178 A6
Muzeray (55) 25 G5
Muzillac (56) 73 F2
Muzy (27) 41 E3
Myans (73) 132 A5
Myennes (58) 82 C5
Myon (25) 103 F3

Nabas (64) 181 G1
Nabinaud (16) 136 C1
Nabirat (24) 138 B6
Nabringhen (62) 1 G4
Nachamps (17) 107 G6
Nadaillac (24) 138 B4
Nadaillac-de-Rouge (46) 138 C5
Nades (03) 152 D2
Nadillac (46) 152 D2
Nagel-Séez-Mesnil (27) 40 C3
Nages (81) 171 G5
Nages-et-Solorgues (30) ...199 H4
Nahuja (66) 199 H4
Nailhac (24) 138 A2
Naillat (23) 111 E4
Nailloux (31) 185 H4
Nailly (89) 64 D4
Naintré (86) 94 B2
Nainville-les-Roches (91) ...63 H1
Naisey-les-Granges (25) ...103 H1
Naives-en-Blois (55) 47 G2
Naives-Rosières (55) 47 E4
Naix-aux-Forges (55) 47 F6
Naizin (56) 55 F3
Najac (12) 153 G5
Nalliers (86) 109 H1
Nalliers (85) 107 H1
Nalzen (09) 186 A6
Nambsheim (68) 71 G6
Nampcel (60) 19 E6
Nampcelles-la-Cour (02) 23 E1
Nampont (80) 6 D4
Namps-Maisnil (80) 20 B1
Nampteuil-sous-Muret (02) ..22 B5
Nampty (80) 20 B1
Nan-sous-Thil (21) 84 D6
Nanc-lès-Saint-Amour (39) ..117 E3
Nançay (18) 81 H5
Nance (39) 102 C5
Nances (73) 131 G4
Nanclars (16) 122 C2
Nancray (25) 103 G1
Nancray-sur-Rimarde (45) ...63 G5
Nancuise (39) 117 F2
Nancy (54) 48 D5
Nancy-sur-Cluses (74) 119 E6
Nandax (42) 115 F6
Nandy (77) 43 E6
Nangeville (45) 63 G3
Nangis (77) 63 H1
Nangy (74) 118 D5
Nannay (58) 99 E1
Nans (25) 88 A4
Nans-les-Pins (83) 192 D3
Nans-sous-
   Sainte-Anne (25) 103 F3
Nant (12) 172 B2
Nant-le-Grand (55) 47 E5
Nant-le-Petit (55) 47 E5
Nanteau-sur-Essonne (77) ...63 E3
Nanteau-sur-Lunain (77) 64 B3
Nanterre (92) 42 C3
Nantes (44) 74 D5
Nantes-en-Ratier (38) 145 H4
Nanteuil (79) 108 B3
Nanteuil-Auriac-
   de-Bourzac (24) 122 C6
Nanteuil-en-Vallée (16) ...109 E6
Nanteuil-la-Forêt (51) 45 E1
Nanteuil-la-Fosse (02) 22 B4
Nanteuil-le-Haudouin (60) ..43 F1
Nanteuil-lès-Meaux (77) 43 G3
Nanteuil-Notre-Dame (02) ...22 B6
Nanteuil-sur-Aisne (08) 23 G3
Nanteuil-sur-Marne (77) 44 A3
Nantey (39) 117 F3
Nantheuil (24) 123 G6
Nanthiat (24) 123 H6
Nantiat (87) 124 A1
Nantillé (17) 121 F2
Nantillois (55) 24 D5
Nantilly (70) 86 C5
Nantoin (38) 130 D6
Nantois (55) 47 F6
Nanton (71) 116 B1
Nantouillet (77) 43 F2
Nantoux (21) 101 G3
Nantua (01) 117 G5
Naours (80) 7 G5
Narbéfontaine (57) 27 E5
Narbief (25) 104 C2
Narbonne (11) 188 A3
Narcastet (64) 182 C2
Narcy (52) 67 G1
Narcy (58) 98 D1
Nargis (45) 64 B5
Narnhac (15) 140 D5
Narp (64) 181 G1
Narrosse (40) 164 E4
Nasbinals (48) 155 F2
Nassandres (27) 40 B1
Nassiet (40) 165 G5
Nassigny (03) 112 D2
Nastringues (24) 136 B5
Nattages (01) 131 G3
Natzwiller (67) 71 E1
Naucelle (12) 154 A4
Naucelles (15) 140 A5
Naujac-sur-Mer (33) 134 C1
Naujan-et-Postiac (33) 135 H6
Nauroy (02) 8 C6
Naussac (12) 153 H3
Naussac (48) 156 C1
Naussannes (24) 137 F6
Nauvay (72) 60 C3
Nauviale (12) 154 B3
Navacelles (30) 157 F6
Navailles-Angos (64) 182 C1
Navarrenx (64) 181 G2
Naveil (41) 79 F2
Navenne (70) 87 G3
Naves (03) 113 G5
Naves (19) 139 E1
Naves (59) 9 E3
Naves-Parmelan (74) 132 A1
Navilly (71) 102 A4
le Nayrac (12) 154 D2
Nazelles-Négron (37) 79 F5
Néac (33) 135 H4
Néant-sur-Yvel (56) 56 B3
Neau (53) 59 E3
Neauphe-sous-Essai (61) 39 F6
Neauphe-sur-Dive (61) 15 H6

Neauphle-le-Château (78) ...42 A4
Neauphle-le-Vieux (78) 42 A4
Neauphlette (78) 41 H3
Néaux (42) 129 E1
Nébian (34) 172 C5
Nébias (11) 186 C6
Nébouzat (63) 126 D3
Nécy (61) 39 E4
Nedde (87) 125 E3
Nédon (62) 2 A6
Nédonchel (62) 2 B6
Neewiller-près-
   Lauterbourg (67) 51 G2
Neffes (05) 160 B3
Neffiès (34) 172 C6
Néfiach (66) 200 D2
Neffes (82) 169 F1
Négreville (50) 12 C3
Négrondes (24) 137 G1
Néhou (50) 12 C4
Nelling (57) 49 G2
Nemours (77) 64 A3
Nempont-Saint-Firmin (62) ...6 C3
Nénigan (31) 184 B2
Néons-sur-Creuse (36) 95 F5
Néoules (83) 193 F3
Néoux (23) 125 H2
Nepvant (55) 24 D3
Nérac (47) 150 D6
Nerbis (40) 165 G3
Nercillac (16) 121 H3
Néré (17) 121 H1
Néret (36) 112 A1
Nérigean (33) 135 G5
Nérignac (86) 109 G4
Néris-les-Bains (03) 112 D4
Nernier (74) 118 D3
Néron (28) 41 F6
Néronde (42) 129 E2
Néronde-sur-Dore (63) 127 H3
Nérondes (18) 98 B3
Ners (30) 173 H1
Nersac (16) 122 B4
Nervieux (42) 129 E3
Nerville-la-Forêt (95) 42 C2
Néry (60) 21 F6
Neschers (63) 127 F5
Nescus (09) 185 H5
Nesle (80) 21 F1
Nesle-et-Massoult (21) 84 D2
Nesle-Hodeng (76) 19 F2
Nesle-la-Reposte (51) 44 C6
Nesle-le-Repons (51) 44 D2
Nesle-l'Hôpital (80) 6 C6
Nesle-Normandeuse (76) 6 C6
Nesles (62) 1 F5
Nesles-la-Montagne (02) 44 A3
Nesles-la-Vallée (95) 42 C1
Neslette (80) 6 D5
Nesmy (85) 91 G5
Nesploy (45) 63 G6
Nespouls (19) 138 C4
Nessa (2B) 202 D5
Nestier (65) 183 H4
Nettancourt (55) 46 D3
Neublans-Abergement (39) ..102 B4
Neubois (67) 71 F2
le Neubourg (27) 40 C1
Neuchâtel-Urtière (25) 88 C5
Neuf-Berquin (59) 3 H5
Neuf-Brisach (68) 71 G5
Neuf-Église (63) 113 E6
Neuf-Marché (76) 19 G4
Neuf-Mesnil (59) 10 A2
Neufbosc (76) 19 E3
le Neufbourg (50) 37 G5
Neufchâteau (88) 68 D2
Neufchâtel-en-Bray (76) 19 E2
Neufchâtel-en-Saosnois (72) .60 B2
Neufchâtel-Hardelot (62) 1 F5
Neufchâtel-sur-Aisne (02) ..23 E4
Neufchef (57) 26 B3
Neufchelles (60) 43 H1
Neuffons (33) 150 B1
Neuffontaines (58) 83 H6
Neufgrange (57) 27 H5
Neuflieux (02) 21 H3
Neuflize (08) 23 G4
Neufmaison (08) 23 H1
Neufmaisons (54) 70 C1
Neufmanil (08) 24 B1
Neufmesnil (50) 12 C5
Neufmoulin (80) 7 E4
Neufmoutiers-en-Brie (77) ..43 G5
le Neufour (55) 46 D1
Neufvillage (57) 49 G2
Neufvy-sur-Aronde (60) 21 E4
Neugartheim-Ittlenheim (67) .50 D5
Neuhaeusel (67) 51 G3
Neuil (37) 94 D2
Neuilh (65) 183 E4
Neuillac (17) 121 G5
Neuillay-les-Bois (36) 96 B5
Neuillé (49) 77 H6
Neuillé-le-Lierre (37) 79 F4
Neuillé-Pont-Pierre (37) ...78 C4
Neuilly (27) 41 F3
Neuilly (58) 99 F1
Neuilly (89) 83 F1
Neuilly-en-Donjon (03) 114 D3
Neuilly-en-Dun (18) 98 B5
Neuilly-en-Sancerre (18) ...82 A6
Neuilly-en-Thelle (60) 20 C6
Neuilly-en-Vexin (95) 42 B1
Neuilly-la-Forêt (14) 13 F5
Neuilly-lès-Dijon (21) 102 A1
Neuilly-l'Évêque (52) 68 B6
Neuilly-l'Hôpital (80) 6 D3
Neuilly-Plaisance (93) 43 E4
Neuilly-Saint-Front (02) ...44 A2
Neuilly-sous-Clermont (60) ..20 C5
Neuilly-sur-Eure (61) 61 F1
Neuilly-sur-Marne (93) 43 E4
Neuilly-sur-Seine (92) 42 C3
Neuilly-sur-Suize (52) 67 H5
Neulette (62) 7 F1
Neulise (42) 129 E2
Neulles (17) 121 G5
Neulliac (56) 55 F2
Neung-sur-Beuvron (41) 80 D4
Neunkirch-
   lès-Bouzonville (57) 27 E3
Neure (03) 98 C6
Neurey-en-Vaux (70) 87 G2
Neurey-lès-la-Demie (70) ...87 G3
Neussargues-Moissac (15) ..141 E3
Neuve-Chapelle (62) 3 E5
Neuve-Église (67) 71 F2
la Neuve-Lyre (27) 40 A3
Neuve-Maison (02) 10 D6
Neuvecelle (74) 119 E3
Neuvéglise (15) 141 E4
Neuvelle-lès-Cromary (70) ..87 F5
Neuvelle-lès-la-Charité (70) .87 F4
la Neuvelle-lès-Lure (70) ..88 A2
la Neuvelle-lès-Scey (70) ..87 E2
la Neuvelle-lès-Voisey (52) .86 D1
Neuves-Maisons (54) 48 C6
la Neuveville-
   devant-Lépanges (88) 70 B4
la Neuveville-
   sous-Châtenois (88) 68 D3
la Neuveville-
   sous-Montfort (88) 69 F3
Neuvic (19) 140 A1
Neuvic (24) 136 D4
Neuvic-Entier (87) 124 D3
Neuvicq (17) 135 H2
Neuvicq-le-Château (17) ...121 H2
Neuvillalais (72) 59 H4
Neuville (19) 139 E3
la Neuville (59) 10 A5
la Neuville (59) 3 F4

la Neuville-à-Maire (08) 24 B3
la Neuville-au-Bois (80) 6 D5
la Neuville-au-Plain (50) ...12 D4
la Neuville-au-Pont (51) 46 C1
la Neuville-aux-Bois (45) ...63 E5
la Neuville-aux-Bois (51) ...46 C3
la Neuville-aux-Joûtes (08) .10 C6
la Neuville-aux-Larris (51) .45 E1
la Neuville-Bosc (60) 20 A6
la Neuville-Bosmont (02) 22 D2
la Neuville-Bourjonval (62) ..8 C4
la Neuville-Chant-d'Oisel (76) .18 D5
la Neuville-Coppegueule (80) .20 B2
la Neuville-d'Aumont (60) ...20 B5
la Neuville-Day (08) 24 A4
la Neuville-de-Poitou (86) ..94 B6
la Neuville-du-Bosc (27) 18 B6
la Neuville-en-Avesnois (59) ..9 G3
la Neuville-en-Beaumont (50) .12 C4
la Neuville-en-Beine (02) ...21 H2
la Neuville-en-Ferrain (59) ...3 H3
la Neuville-en-Hez (60) 20 C5
la Neuville-
   en-Tourne-à-Fuy (08) 23 G5
la Neuville-en-Verdunois (55) .47 F3
la Neuville-Ferrières (76) ..19 F2
la Neuville-Garnier (60) 20 A5
la Neuville-Housset (02) 22 D1
la Neuville-lès-Bray (80) 8 B5
la Neuville-lès-Dames (01) .116 C5
la Neuville-lès-Decize (58) ..99 E5
la Neuville-lès-Dorengt (02) ..9 G5
la Neuville-lès-Loeuilly (80) .20 B1
la Neuville-lès-This (08) ...24 A1
la Neuville-lès-Vaucouleurs (55) .47 H6
la Neuville-lès-Wasigny (08) .23 G2
la Neuville-près-Sées (61) ..39 G6
la Neuville-Roy (60) 20 D4
la Neuville-Saint-Amand (02) .22 A1
la Neuville-Saint-Pierre (60) .20 C4
la Neuville-Saint-Vaast (62) ..8 B2
la Neuville-Sire-Bernard (80) .20 D1
la Neuville-sous-Montreuil (62) .1 G6
la Neuville-sur-Aillette (02) .22 C4
la Neuville-sur-Ain (01) ...117 F6
la Neuville-sur-Authou (27) .15 H4
la Neuville-sur-Brenne (37) .79 E3
la Neuville-sur-Escaut (59) ..9 E2
la Neuville-sur-Essonne (45) .63 G4
la Neuville-sur-Margival (02) .22 B4
la Neuville-sur-Oise (95) ...42 B2
la Neuville-sur-Ornain (55) .46 D4
la Neuville-sur-Oudeuil (60) .20 A3
la Neuville-sur-Ressons (60) .21 E3
la Neuville-sur-Saône (69) .130 A2
la Neuville-sur-Sarthe (72) ..60 A5
la Neuville-sur-Seine (10) ..66 D5
la Neuville-sur-Touques (61) .39 G3
la Neuville-sur-Vanne (10) ..65 H3
la Neuville-Vault (60) 20 A4
la Neuville-Vitasse (62) 8 B3
la Neuville-Roche (67) 71 E1
Neuviller-la-Roche (67) 71 E1
Neuviller-lès-Badonviller (54) .49 H6
Neuvillers-sur-Moselle (54) .69 G1
Neuvillette (02) 21 G6
Neuvillette (80) 7 F5
Neuvillette-en-Charnie (72) .59 G5
Neuvilley (39) 102 D4
Neuvilly (59) 9 F4
Neuvilly-en-Argonne (55) ...46 D1
Neuvireuil (62) 8 C3
Neuvizy (08) 23 H2
Neuvy (03) 113 H2
Neuvy (41) 80 B4
Neuvy (51) 44 C5
Neuvy-au-Houlme (61) 38 D4
Neuvy-Bouin (79) 93 E5
Neuvy-Deux-Clochers (18) ...98 B1
Neuvy-en-Beauce (28) 62 D3
Neuvy-en-Champagne (72) 59 H5
Neuvy-en-Dunois (28) 62 B4
Neuvy-en-Sullias (45) 81 F2
Neuvy-Grandchamp (71) 114 D1
Neuvy-le-Barrois (18) 98 B5
Neuvy-le-Roi (37) 78 D3
Neuvy-Pailloux (36) 96 D5
Neuvy-Saint-Sépulchre (36) .111 F1
Neuvy-Sautour (89) 65 G4
Neuvy-sur-Barangeon (18) ...81 F6
Neuvy-sur-Loire (58) 82 C4
Néville (76) 17 E3
Néville-sur-Mer (50) 13 E1
Nevoy (45) 81 H3
Nevy-lès-Dole (39) 102 C3
Nevy-sur-Seille (39) 102 D5
Nexon (87) 124 A4
Ney (39) 103 F5
Neydens (74) 118 B5
les Neyrolles (01) 117 G5
Neyron (01) 130 B2
Nézel (78) 42 A3
Nézignan-l'Évêque (34) 188 D1
Niafles (53) 76 B1
Niaux (09) 199 E1
Nibas (80) 6 C4
Nibelle (45) 63 G6
Nibles (04) 160 B5
Nice (06) 195 F3
Nicey (21) 84 C1
Nicey-sur-Aire (55) 47 F3
Nicole (47) 150 C4
Nicorps (50) 37 E1
Niderhoff (57) 49 H5
Niderviller (57) 50 A4
Niederbronn-les-Bains (67) .28 B6
Niederbruck (68) 88 D1
Niederentzen (68) 71 F5
Niederhaslach (67) 50 C6
Niederhausbergen (67) 51 E5
Niederhergheim (68) 71 F5
Niederlauterbach (67) 51 G2
Niedermodern (67) 50 D3
Niedermorschwihr (68) 71 F4
Niedernai (67) 71 G1
Niederrœdern (67) 51 G2
Niederschaeffolsheim (67) ..51 E4
Niedersoultzbach (67) 50 D3
Niedersteinbach (67) 51 E1
Niederstinzel (57) 49 H4
Niedervisse (57) 27 E5
Nielles-lès-Ardres (62) 2 A3
Nielles-lès-Bléquin (62) 1 H5
Nielles-lès-Calais (62) 1 G2
Nieppe (59) 3 G5
Niergnies (59) 9 E4
Nieudan (15) 139 H5
Nieuil (16) 123 F2
Nieuil-l'Espoir (86) 109 F2
Nieul (87) 124 A1
Nieul-le-Dolent (85) 91 F5
Nieul-le-Virouil (17) 121 F6
Nieul-lès-Saintes (17) 120 D3
Nieul-sur-l'Autise (85) 107 F2
Nieul-sur-Mer (17) 106 C4
Nieulle-sur-Seudre (17) ...120 C3
Nieurlet (59) 2 B3
Niévroz (01) 130 C2
Niffer (68) 89 G2
Niherne (36) 96 B5
Nijon (52) 68 C4
Nilvange (57) 26 B3
Nîmes (30) 174 A3
Ninville (52) 68 B5
Niort (79) 107 H4
Niort-de-Sault (11) 199 H1
Niozelles (04) 177 E2
Nissan-lez-Enserune (34) ..188 B3
Nistos (65) 183 G5
Nitry (89) 83 H3
Nitting (57) 50 A5

Nivelle (59) 9 F1
Nivillac (56) 73 G2
Nivillers (60) 20 B4
Nivolas-Vermelle (38) 130 D5
Nivollet-Montgriffon (01) .117 F6
Nixéville-Blercourt (55) ...47 F1
le Nizan (33) 149 H3
Nizan-Gesse (31) 184 A3
Nizas (32) 184 D1
Nizas (34) 172 C6
Nizerolles (03) 114 B6
Nizy-le-Comte (02) 23 E3
Noailhac (12) 154 B2
Noailhac (19) 138 D4
Noailhac (81) 170 D6
Noaillac (33) 150 B2
Noaillan (33) 149 G3
Noailles (19) 138 C3
Noailles (60) 20 B5
Noailles (81) 170 B2
Noailly (42) 115 E5
Noalhac (48) 141 F6
Noards (27) 15 H4
Nocario (2B) 205 F1
Noce (61) 61 E2
Noceta (2B) 205 F3
Nochize (71) 115 F3
la Nocle-Maulaix (58) 99 H5
Nod-sur-Seine (21) 85 E2
Nods (25) 104 A2
Noé (31) 185 E2
Noé (89) 65 E4
la Noë-Blanche (35) 57 E5
Noë-les-Mallets (10) 67 E5
la Noë-Poulain (27) 15 H4
Noël-Cerneux (27) 104 C2
Noëllet (49) 75 G1
les Noës (42) 114 D6
les Noës-près-Troyes (10) ..66 B3
Nœux-lès-Auxi (62) 7 F3
Nœux-les-Mines (62) 2 D6
Nogaret (31) 170 A6
Nogaro (32) 166 C3
Nogent (52) 68 B5
Nogent-en-Othe (10) 65 H5
Nogent-l'Abbesse (51) 23 F6
Nogent-l'Artaud (02) 44 B3
Nogent-le-Bernard (72) 60 C3
Nogent-le-Phaye (28) 62 B2
Nogent-le-Roi (28) 41 G6
Nogent-le-Rotrou (28) 61 E3
Nogent-le-Sec (27) 41 E3
Nogent-lès-Montbard (21) ...84 D3
Nogent-sur-Aube (10) 66 C1
Nogent-sur-Eure (28) 62 A2
Nogent-sur-Loir (72) 78 B3
Nogent-sur-Marne (94) 43 E4
Nogent-sur-Oise (60) 20 D6
Nogent-sur-Seine (10) 65 F1
Nogent-sur-Vernisson (45) ..82 A2
Nogentel (02) 44 B2
Nogna (39) 117 G1
Noguères (64) 182 A1
Nohanent (63) 127 E3
Nohant-en-Goût (18) 98 A2
Nohant-en-Graçay (18) 96 D3
Nohant-Vic (36) 97 G6
Nohèdes (66) 200 B3
Nohic (82) 169 F3
Noidan (21) 85 E6
Noidans-le-Ferroux (70) 87 F4
Noidans-lès-Vesoul (70) 87 G3
Noidant-Chatenoy (52) 86 B1
Noidant-le-Rocheux (52) 86 A1
Noilhan (32) 168 B4
Nointel (60) 20 D5
Nointel (95) 42 C1
Nointot (76) 15 H1
Noircourt (02) 23 F2
Noirefontaine (25) 88 C5
Noirémont (60) 20 B3
Noirétable (42) 128 B3
Noirlieu (51) 46 C3
Noirmoutier-en-l'Île (85) ..90 B1
Noiron (70) 86 C5
Noiron-sous-Gevrey (21) ...101 H2
Noiron-sur-Bèze (21) 86 B5
Noiron-sur-Seine (21) 66 D6
Noironte (25) 87 E6
Noisiel (77) 43 E4
Noisseville (57) 26 C5
Noisy-le-Grand (93) 43 E4
Noisy-le-Roi (78) 42 B4
Noisy-le-Sec (93) 42 D3
Noisy-Rudignon (77) 64 C3
Noizay (37) 79 F5
Nojals-et-Clotte (24) 137 G6
Nojeon-en-Vexin (27) 19 F5
Nolay (21) 101 F4
Nolay (58) 99 E1
Noléval (76) 19 F4
Nollieux (42) 128 D3
Nomain (59) 9 E1
Nomdieu (47) 167 G1
Nomécourt (52) 67 G3
Nomeny (54) 48 D3
Nomexy (88) 69 G3
Nommay (25) 88 C4
Nompatelize (88) 70 C2
Nonac (16) 122 B6
Nonancourt (27) 41 E4
Nonant (14) 14 A4
Nonant-le-Pin (61) 39 F5
Nonards (19) 139 E4
Nonaville (16) 122 B5
Noncourt-sur-
   le-Rongeant (52) 68 A2
Nonette (63) 127 G5
Nonglard (74) 132 A1
Nonhigny (54) 49 H6
Nonières (07) 143 G5
Nonsard-Lamarche (55) 48 A3
Nontron (24) 123 E5
Nonville (77) 64 B4
Nonville (88) 69 E4
Nonvilliers-Grandhoux (28) .61 F3
Nonza (2B) 203 F3
Nonzeville (88) 70 B3
Noordpeene (59) 2 C3
Nordausques (62) 1 H3
Nordheim (67) 50 D5
Nordhouse (67) 71 H1
Noreuil (62) 8 C4
Norges-la-Ville (21) 85 H5
Normandel (61) 40 B5
Normanville (27) 18 B6
Normanville (76) 16 D4
Normée (51) 45 F5
Norolles (14) 15 H4
Noron-la-Poterie (14) 13 H6
Noron-l'Abbaye (14) 38 D3
Noroy (60) 20 D4
Noroy-le-Bourg (70) 87 H3
Noroy-sur-Ourcq (02) 21 H6
Norrent-Fontes (62) 2 C5
Norrey-en-Auge (14) 39 E3
Norrois (51) 46 B5
Norroy (88) 68 D3
Norroy-le-Sec (54) 25 H5
Norroy-le-Veneur (57) 26 B5
Norroy-lès-Pont-
   à-Mousson (54) 48 B3
Nort-Leulinghem (62) 2 A3
Nort-sur-Erdre (44) 74 D3
Nortkerque (62) 1 H3
Norville (76) 15 H2
la Norville (91) 42 D6
Nossage-et-Bénévent (05) ...159 H4
Nossoncourt (88) 70 B2
Nostang (56) 54 D5
Noth (23) 111 E4
Nothalten (67) 71 F2
Notre-Dame-
   d'Aliermont (76) 17 H2
Notre-Dame-d'Allençon (49) .77 H5
Notre-Dame-
   de-Bellecombe (73) 132 D2

Notre-Dame-
   de-Bliqueteuit (76) 17 E5
Notre-Dame-
   de-Boisset (42) 128 D1
Notre-Dame-
   de-Bondeville (76) 18 C4
Notre-Dame-de-Cenilly (50) .37 F2
Notre-Dame-
   de-Commiers (38) 145 G4
Notre-Dame-
   de-Courson (14) 15 F6
Notre-Dame-
   de-Gravenchon (76) 15 H2
Notre-Dame-
   de-la-Rouvière (30) 173 E1
Notre-Dame-de-l'Isle (27) ..41 F1
Notre-Dame-de-Livaye (14) ..15 E5
Notre-Dame-de-Livoye (50) ..37 F4
Notre-Dame-
   de-Londres (34) 173 F3
Notre-Dame-de-l'Osier (38) .145 E2
Notre-Dame-
   de-Mésage (38) 145 G3
Notre-Dame-de-Monts (85) ...90 D2
Notre-Dame-de-Riez (85) 90 D3
Notre-Dame-
   de-Sanilhac (24) 137 F3
Notre-Dame-de-Vaulx (38) ..145 G4
Notre-Dame-d'Elle (50) 37 G1
Notre-Dame-d'Épine (27) 15 H4
Notre-Dame-des-Landes (44) .74 C3
Notre-Dame-
   des-Millières (73) 132 C4
Notre-Dame-d'Estrées (14) ..15 E5
Notre-Dame-d'Oé (37) 78 D5
Notre-Dame-du-Bec (76) 15 F1
Notre-Dame-du-Cruet (73) ..132 C6
Notre-Dame-du-Hamel (27) ...39 H3
Notre-Dame-du-Parc (76) 18 C1
Notre-Dame-du-Pré (72) 77 F2
Notre-Dame-du-Pré (73) 133 E5
Notre-Dame-du-Rocher (61) ..38 D4
Notre-Dame-du-Touchet (50) .37 G6
Nottonville (28) 62 B5
la Nouaille (23) 125 G2
Nouaillé-Maupertuis (86) ..109 F2
Nouainville (50) 12 C2
Nouan-le-Fuzelier (41) 81 E4
Nouans (72) 60 A3
Nouans-les-Fontaines (37) ..96 A2
Nouart (08) 24 C4
Nouâtre (37) 94 D3
la Nouaye (35) 56 D2
la Noue (51) 44 D5
Nouelles (62) 18 A5
Nougaroulet (32) 168 A4
Nouhant (23) 112 B4
Nouic (87) 110 A6
Nouilhan (65) 183 F2
les Nouillers (17) 121 E1
Nouillonpont (55) 25 F5
Nouilly (57) 26 C5
Noulens (32) 167 E3
Nourard-le-Franc (60) 20 C4
Nourray (41) 79 G2
Nousse (40) 165 G4
Nousseviller-lès-Bitche (57) .50 C1
Nousseviller-
   Saint-Nabor (57) 49 H1
Nousty (64) 182 C2
Nouvelle-Église (62) 1 H2
Nouvion (80) 6 D3
le Nouvion-en-Thiérache (02) .9 H6
Nouvion-et-Catillon (02) ...22 B2
Nouvion-le-Comte (02) 22 B2
Nouvion-le-Vineux (02) 22 C4
Nouvion-sur-Meuse (08) 24 B2
Nouvoitou (35) 57 F3
Nouvron-Vingré (02) 21 H4
Nouzerines (23) 111 H3
Nouzerolles (23) 111 F3
Nouziers (23) 111 G3
Nouzilly (37) 79 E4
Nouzonville (08) 24 B1
Novacelles (63) 128 A5
Novale (2B) 205 G2
Novéant-sur-Moselle (57) ...26 B6
Novel (74) 119 G3
Novella (2B) 203 F5
Noves (13) 175 E3
Noviant-aux-Prés (54) 48 B4
Novillard (90) 88 D3
Novillars (25) 87 G6
Novillers (60) 20 B6
Novion-Porcien (08) 23 G3
Novy-Chevrières (08) 23 H3
Noyal (22) 34 A5

Nuzéjouls (46) 152 C3
Nyer (66) 200 B3
Nyoiseau (49) 75 H1
Nyons (26) 158 D4

Obenheim (67) 71 H2
Oberbronn (67) 50 D2
Oberbruck (68) 88 D1
Oberdorf (68) 89 F3
Oberdorf-Spachbach (67) 51 E2
Oberdorff (57) 27 E4
Oberentzen (68) 71 F5
Obergailbach (57) 28 A5
Oberhaslach (67) 50 C6
Oberhausbergen (67) 51 E5
Oberhergheim (68) 71 F5
Oberhoffen-
   lès-Wissembourg (67) 51 F1
Oberhoffen-sur-Moder (67) ..51 F4
Oberlarg (68) 89 F4
Oberlauterbach (67) 51 G2
Obermodern-Zutzendorf (67) .50 D3
Obermorschwihr (68) 71 F5
Obermorschwiller (68) 89 F3
Obernai (67) 71 G1
Oberrœdern (67) 51 F2
Obersaasheim (68) 71 G5
Oberschaeffolsheim (67) 50 D5
Obersoultzbach (67) 50 D3
Obersteinbach (67) 51 E1
Oberstinzel (57) 50 A4
Obervisse (57) 27 E5
Obies (59) 9 H2
Objat (19) 138 C2
Oblinghem (62) 2 D5
Obrechies (59) 10 A3
Obreck (57) 49 F3
Obsonville (77) 63 H4
Obterre (36) 95 F4
Obtrée (21) 85 E1
Ocana (2A) 204 D5
Occagnes (61) 39 E4
Occey (52) 86 A3
Occhiatana (2B) 202 D5
Occoches (80) 7 F4
Ochancourt (80) 6 C4
Oches (08) 24 C3
Ochey (54) 48 C6
Ochtezeele (59) 2 C3
Ocquerre (77) 43 H2
Ocqueville (76) 17 E3
Octeville-l'Avenel (50) 12 D3
Octeville-sur-Mer (76) 15 F1
Octon (34) 172 C5
Odars (31) 169 G6
Odenas (69) 116 A6
Oderen (68) 88 D1
Odomez (59) 9 F2
Odos (65) 183 E3
Odratzheim (67) 50 D5
Oëlleville (88) 69 F2
Oermingen (67) 27 H6
Œting (57) 27 G5
Œuf-en-Ternois (62) 7 F2
Œuilly (02) 22 C5
Œuilly (51) 45 E2
Oeyregave (40) 165 E5
Oeyreluy (40) 165 E4
Offekerque (62) 1 H2
Offemont (90) 88 C3
Offendorf (67) 51 F4
Offignies (80) 19 H1
Offin (62) 6 D2
l'Orbrie (85) 107 F2
Offlanges (39) 102 D1
Offoy (60) 21 G1
Offoy (80) 21 G1
Offranville (76) 17 G2
Offrethun (62) 1 F4
Offroicourt (88) 69 F3
Offwiller (67) 50 D3
Ogenne-Camptort (64) 181 H2
Oger (51) 45 F3
Ogeu-les-Bains (64) 182 A3
Ogéviller (54) 49 G6
Ogliastro (2B) 203 F3
Ognes (02) 22 A2
Ognes (51) 45 E5
Ognes (60) 43 G1
Ognéville (54) 69 E1
Ognolles (60) 21 G2
Ognon (60) 21 E5
Ogy (57) 26 C5
Ohain (59) 10 B4
Oherville (76) 17 E3
Ohis (02) 10 C6
Ohlungen (67) 51 E3
Ohnenheim (67) 71 G3
l'Oie (85) 92 A4
Oigney (70) 87 E2
Oigny (21) 85 F3
Oigny (41) 61 F5
Oigny-en-Valois (02) 21 H6
Oingt (69) 129 G2
Oinville-Saint-Liphard (28) .62 D4
Oinville-sous-Auneau (28) ..62 C3
Oinville-sur-Montcient (78) .42 A2
Oiron (79) 93 H3
Oiry (51) 45 F2
Oiselay-et-Grachaux (70) ...87 E5
Oisemont (80) 20 B1
Oisilly (21) 86 B5
Oisly (41) 79 H5
Oison (45) 62 D5
Oisseau (53) 58 D2
Oisseau-le-Petit (72) 59 H2
Oissel (76) 18 C5
Oissery (77) 43 F2
Oissy (80) 20 C1
Oisy (02) 9 G6
Oisy (58) 83 E5
Oisy (59) 9 E2
Oisy-le-Verger (62) 8 D3
Oizé (72) 78 A2
le Noyer (05) 160 B1
le Noyer (18) 82 A6
le Noyer (73) 132 A3
le Noyer-en-Ouche (27) 40 B2
Noyers (27) 41 F1
Noyers (45) 81 H2
Noyers (52) 86 B1
Noyers (89) 83 H2
Noyers-Auzécourt (55) 46 D3
Noyers-Bocage (14) 14 A5
Noyers-Pont-Maugis (08) 24 C2
Noyers-Saint-Martin (60) ...20 C3
Noyers-sur-Cher (41) 96 A1
Noyers-sur-Jabron (04) 160 A6
Noyon (60) 21 G3
Nozay (10) 65 H1
Nozay (44) 74 C2
Nozay (91) 42 C6
Nozeroy (39) 103 G5
Nozières (07) 143 G4
Nozières (18) 97 H6
Nuaillé (49) 75 H6
Nuaillé-d'Aunis (17) 107 E4
Nuaillé-sur-Boutonne (17) ..107 H6
Nuars (58) 83 G5
Nubécourt (55) 47 E2
Nucourt (95) 42 A1
Nueil-les-Aubiers (79) 92 D3
Nueil-sous-Faye (86) 94 B4
Nueil-sur-Layon (49) 93 F2
Nuelles (69) 129 G3
Nuillé-le-Jalais (72) 60 C5
Nuillé-sur-Vicoin (53) 58 C6
Nuisement-sur-Coole (51) ...45 G3
Nuits (89) 84 B2
Nuits-Saint-Georges (21) ..101 H1
Nullemont (76) 19 H1
Nully (52) 67 E2
Nuncq-Hautecôte (62) 7 F2
Nurieux-Volognat (01) 117 G5
Nurlu (80) 8 C5
Oborne (73) 131 G5

Oltingue (68) 89 G4
Olwisheim (67) 51 E4
Omblèze (26) 144 C5
Omécourt (60) 19 H3
Omelmont (54) 69 E1
les Omergues (04) 159 G6
Omerville (95) 41 H1
Omessa (2B) 205 E2
Omex (65) 183 E4
Omey (51) 46 A4
Omicourt (08) 24 B2
Omiécourt (80) 21 F1
Ommeray (57) 49 F4
Ommoy (61) 39 E3
Omont (08) 24 B3
Omonville (76) 17 F3
Omonville-la-Petite (50) ...12 A1
Omonville-la-Rogue (50) 12 A1
Omps (15) 139 H5
Oms (66) 201 E3
Onans (25) 88 B4
Onard (40) 165 F3
Onay (70) 86 D5
Oncieu (01) 131 E1
Oncourt (88) 69 H3
Ondefontaine (14) 14 A6
Ondes (31) 169 E4
Ondres (40) 164 B5
Ondreville-sur-Essonne (45) .63 G4
Onesse-et-Laharie (40) 148 B6
Onet-le-Château (12) 154 C4
Oneux (80) 7 E3
Ongles (04) 176 C1
Onglières (39) 103 G5
Onjon (10) 66 B2
Onlay (58) 100 A4
Onnaing (59) 9 G2
Onnion (74) 119 E5
Onoz (39) 117 G2
Ons-en-Bray (60) 19 H4
Ontex (73) 131 G3
Onville (54) 26 A6
Onzain (41) 79 H4
Oô (31) 197 E1
Oost-Cappel (59) 2 C2
Opio (06) 178 C4
Opoul-Périllos (66) 187 H6
Oppède (84) 175 G3
Oppedette (04) 176 B2
Oppenans (70) 87 H3
Oppy (62) 8 C3
Optevoz (38) 130 D3
Oraás (64) 165 G6
Oradour (15) 141 E5
Oradour (16) 122 A1
Oradour-Fanais (16) 109 H5
Oradour-Saint-Genest (87) ..110 B4
Oradour-sur-Glane (87) 123 H1
Oradour-sur-Vayres (87) ...123 G3
Orain (21) 86 B3
Orainville (02) 23 E5
Oraison (04) 176 D2
Orange (84) 158 B6
Orbagna (39) 117 F1
Orbais-l'Abbaye (51) 44 D3
Orban (81) 170 B3
Orbec (14) 15 G6
Orbeil (63) 127 G5
Orbessan (32) 167 H6
Orbey (68) 71 E4
Orbigny (37) 95 G2
Orbigny-au-Mont (52) 86 B1
Orbigny-au-Val (52) 86 B1
Orcay (41) 97 F1
Orcemont (78) 41 H5
Orcenais (18) 97 H6
Orcet (63) 127 F4
Orcevaux (52) 86 A2
Orchaise (41) 79 G4
Orchamps (39) 102 D1
Orchamps-Vennes (25) 104 B2
Orches (86) 94 B4
Orcières (05) 146 B6
Orcier (74) 119 E3
Orcières (05) 146 B6
Orcinas (26) 158 D2
Orcines (63) 127 E3
Orcival (63) 126 D4
Orconte (51) 46 C4
Ordan-Larroque (32) 167 G4
Ordiarp (64) 181 F3
Ordizan (65) 183 F4
Ordonnac (33) 134 D1
Ordonnaz (01) 131 F2
Ore (31) 184 A4
Orègue (64) 181 E1
Oreilla (66) 200 B3
Orelle (73) 146 D2
Oresmaux (80) 20 C1
Organ (65) 183 H2
Orgeans-
   Blanchefontaine (25) 88 B5
Orgedeuil (16) 123 E3
Orgeix (09) 199 G2
Orgelet (39) 117 F2
Orgères (35) 57 F4
Orgères (61) 39 G4
Orgères-en-Beauce (28) 62 C4
Orgerus (78) 41 H4
Orges (52) 67 G5
Orgeux (21) 86 A6
Orgeval (02) 22 C4
Orgeval (78) 42 B3
Orgibet (09) 184 B5
Orglandes (50) 12 D4
Orgnac-l'Aven (07) 157 G5
Orgnac-sur-Vézère (19) 138 C1
Orgon (13) 175 F3
Orgueil (82) 169 F3
Oricourt (70) 87 H4
Orieux (65) 183 G3
Orignac (65) 183 F4
Origne (33) 149 F3
Origné (53) 58 C6
Orignolles (17) 135 H1
Origny (21) 85 E3
Origny-en-Thiérache (02) ...10 A6
Origny-le-Butin (61) 60 C2
Origny-le-Roux (61) 60 C2
Origny-le-Sec (10) 65 G2
Origny-Sainte-Benoite (02) ..9 G6
Orin (64) 182 A3
Orincles (65) 183 E4
Oriocourt (57) 49 F3
Oriol-en-Royans (26) 144 D4
Oriolles (16) 122 A6
Orion (64) 181 G1
Oris-en-Rattier (38) 145 H4
Orival (16) 122 B6
Orival (76) 18 C5
Orléans (45) 80 D1
Orléat (63) 127 H2
Orleix (65) 183 F3
Orliac (24) 152 A1
Orliac-de-Bar (19) 138 D2
Orliaguet (24) 138 B5
Orliénas (69) 129 H4
Orlu (09) 199 G2
Orlu (32) 168 B4
Orly (94) 42 D5
Orly-sur-Morin (77) 44 A3
Ormancey (52) 86 B1
Ormenans (70) 87 G5
Ormersviller (57) 28 B4
Ormes (10) 66 B1
Ormes (27) 40 D2
Ormes (45) 62 D6
Ormes (51) 23 E6
Ormes (71) 116 B1
les Ormes (86) 94 D4
les Ormes (89) 65 F6
les Ormes-sur-Voulzie (77) .64 D2
Ormesson (77) 64 A3
Ormesson-sur-Marne (94) 43 E4

Ormoiche (70).....87 H1
Ormoy (28).....41 F6
Ormoy (70).....87 G4
Ormoy (89).....65 F6
Ormoy (91).....42 D6
Ormoy-la-Rivière (91).....63 G2
Ormoy-le-Davien (60).....43 G1
Ormoy-lès-Sexfontaines (52).....67 H4
Ormoy-Villers (60).....43 G1
Ornacieux (38).....130 D6
Ornaisons (11).....187 H3
Ornans (25).....103 G2
Ornes (55).....25 F6
Ornex (01).....118 B4
Ornézan (32).....167 H6
Orniac (46).....153 E3
Ornolac-Ussat-
les-Bains (09).....199 E1
Ornon (38).....146 A3
Orny (57).....26 C6
Oroër (60).....22 A4
Oroix (65).....183 E2
Oron (57).....49 E3
Oroux (79).....93 G6
Orphin (78).....41 H6
Orpierre (05).....159 H4
Orquevaux (52).....68 A3
les Orres (05).....161 E2
Orret (21).....85 F4
Orriule (64).....181 G1
Orrouer (28).....61 G3
Orrouy (60).....21 H6
Orry-la-Ville (60).....43 E1
Ors (59).....9 G4
Orsan (30).....158 A6
Orsanco (64).....181 E2
Orsans (11).....186 B4
Orsans (25).....103 G2
Orsay (91).....42 C5
Orschwihr (68).....71 F5
Orschwiller (67).....71 F3
Orsennes (36).....111 F2
Orsinval (59).....9 G2
Orsonnette (63).....127 G6
Orsonville (78).....62 D1
Ortaffa (66).....201 F3
Ortale (2B).....205 G2
Orthevielle (40).....164 D5
Orthez (64).....165 G6
Orthoux-
Sérignac-Quilhan (30).....173 G3
Ortillon (10).....66 C1
Ortiporio (2B).....203 F6
Ortoncourt (88).....70 A2
Orus (09).....198 D1
Orval (18).....97 H6
Orval (50).....36 D2
Orvault (44).....74 C4
Orvaux (27).....40 D3
Orve (25).....88 B6
Orveau (91).....63 F2
Orveau-Bellesauve (45).....63 G3
Orville (21).....85 H2
Orville (36).....96 D2
Orville (45).....63 G4
Orville (61).....39 G3
Orville (62).....7 G4
Orvillers-Sorel (60).....21 F3
Orvilliers (78).....41 G4
Orvilliers-Saint-Julien (10).....65 H2
Orx (40).....164 C5
Os-Marsillon (64).....182 A1
Osani (2A).....204 B2
Osches (55).....47 E2
Osenbach (68).....71 E5
Oslon (71).....101 H5
Osly-Courtil (02).....22 A5
Osmanville (14).....13 F5
Osmery (18).....98 A4
Osmets (65).....183 F2
Osmoy (18).....97 G3
Osmoy (78).....41 H4
Osmoy-Saint-Valery (76).....19 E1
Osne-le-Val (52).....68 A1
Osnes (08).....24 D2
Osny (95).....42 B2
Ossages (40).....165 F5
Ossas-Suhare (64).....181 G3
Osse (25).....87 G6
Ossé (35).....57 G3
Osse-en-Aspe (64).....181 H4
Osséja (66).....199 H5
Osselle (25).....103 E2
Ossen (65).....182 D4
Ossenx (64).....181 G2
Osserain-Rivareyte (64).....181 F1
Ossès (64).....180 D2
Ossey-les-Trois-Maisons (10).....65 G2
Ossun (65).....183 E3
Ossun-Ez-Angles (65).....183 E4
Ostabat-Asme (64).....181 E2
Ostel (02).....22 B4
Ostheim (68).....71 F4
Osthoffen (67).....50 D5
Osthouse (67).....71 H1
Ostreville (62).....7 G1
Ostricourt (59).....8 C1
Ostwald (67).....51 E6
Ota (2A).....204 C3
Othe (54).....25 F3
Othis (77).....43 F2
Ottange (57).....26 A2
Ottersthal (67).....50 C4
Otterswiller (67).....50 C4
Ottmarsheim (88).....89 G1
Ottonville (57).....26 D4
Ottrott (67).....71 F1
Ottwiller (67).....50 B3
Ouagne (58).....83 F6
Ouainville (76).....16 D3
Ouanne (89).....83 F3
Ouarville (28).....62 C3
les Oubeaux (14).....13 F5
Ouchamps (41).....79 H5
Ouches (42).....128 C1
Oucques (41).....79 H2
Oudalle (76).....15 F2
Oudan (58).....83 E6
Oudeuil (60).....21 H3
Oudezeele (59).....2 D3
Oudincourt (52).....67 H4
l'Oudon (14).....39 E2
Oudon (44).....75 E4
Oudrenne (57).....26 C3
Oudry (71).....115 F1
Oueilloux (65).....183 F3
Ouerre (28).....41 E5
Ouessant (29).....30 A4
Ouézy (14).....39 E1
Ouffières (14).....14 B6
Ouge (70).....86 D2
Ouges (21).....102 A1
Ougney (39).....102 D1
Ougney-Douvot (25).....87 G6
Ougny (58).....99 H3
Ouhans (25).....103 H4
Ouides (43).....142 B5
Ouillon (64).....182 C2
Ouilly-du-Houley (14).....15 G5
Ouilly-le-Tesson (14).....38 D2
Ouilly-le-Vicomte (14).....15 F5
Ouistreham (14).....14 C4
Oulches (36).....110 D1
Oulches-
la-Vallée-Foulon (02).....22 D4
Oulchy-la-Ville (02).....22 A6
Oulchy-le-Château (02).....22 A6
Oulins (28).....41 F4
Oulles (38).....146 A3
Oullins (69).....130 A3
Oulmes (85).....107 G2
Oulon (58).....99 E1
Ounans (39).....102 D3
Oupia (34).....188 A3
Our (39).....102 D2
Ourches (26).....144 C6
Ourches-sur-Meuse (55).....47 H5
Ourde (65).....183 H5
Ourdis-Cotdoussan (65).....183 E4
Ourdon (65).....183 E4

Ourouër (58).....99 E3
Ourouer-les-Bourdelins (18).....98 B4
Ouroux (69).....116 A4
Ouroux-en-Morvan (58).....100 A2
Ouroux-sous-
le-Bois-Sainte-Marie (71).....115 G3
Ouroux-sur-Saône (71).....101 H6
Oursbelille (65).....183 E2
Oursel-Maison (60).....20 B3
Ourton (62).....7 H1
Ourville-en-Caux (76).....16 D3
Ousse (64).....182 C2
Ousse-Suzan (40).....165 G2
Oussières (39).....102 D4
Ousson-sur-Loire (45).....82 B4
Oussoy-en-Gâtinais (45).....82 A1
Oust (09).....198 C2
Oust-Marest (80).....6 B4
Ousté (65).....183 E4
Outarville (45).....63 E4
Outines (51).....67 E1
Outreau (62).....1 F4
Outrebois (80).....7 G3
Outremécourt (52).....68 D3
Outrepont (51).....46 B4
Outriaz (01).....117 G6
Ouvans (25).....88 A6
Ouve-Wirquin (62).....2 A5
Ouveillan (11).....188 A2
Ouville (50).....37 E2
Ouville-la-Bien-Tournée (14).....39 E2
Ouville-l'Abbaye (76).....17 F2
Ouville-la-Rivière (76).....17 F2
Ouvrouer-les-Champs (45).....81 F2
Ouzilly (86).....94 C4
Ouzouer-des-Champs (45).....82 A1
Ouzouer-le-Doyen (41).....62 A5
Ouzouer-le-Marché (41).....80 B1
Ouzouer-sous-
Bellegarde (45).....63 G6
Ouzouer-sur-Loire (45).....81 H2
Ouzouer-sur-Trézée (45).....82 B3
Ouzous (65).....182 D4
Ovanches (70).....87 F3
Ovillers-la-Boisselle (80).....8 A5
Oxelaëre (59).....2 C3
Oyé (71).....115 F4
Oye-et-Pallet (25).....104 A4
Oye-Plage (62).....1 H2
Oyes (51).....45 E4
Oyeu (38).....131 E6
Oyonnax (01).....117 G4
Oyré (86).....94 D4
Oyrières (70).....86 C3
Oysonville (28).....62 D2
Oytier-Saint-Oblas (38).....130 B5
Oz (38).....146 A3
Ozan (01).....116 C3
Oze (05).....159 H3
Ozenay (71).....116 B2
Ozenx-Montestrucq (64).....165 G6
Ozerailles (54).....25 H6
Ozeville (50).....13 E3
Ozières (52).....68 B4
Ozillac (17).....121 G6
Ozolles (71).....115 G3
Ozon (07).....144 A3
Ozon (65).....183 F3
Ozouer-le-Voulgis (77).....43 F5
Ozourt (40).....165 F4

P

Paars (02).....22 C5
Pabu (22).....33 E3
la Pacaudière (42).....114 D5
Pacé (35).....57 E2
Pacé (61).....60 A1
Pact (38).....144 B1
Pacy-sur-Armançon (89).....84 B2
Pacy-sur-Eure (27).....41 F2
Padern (11).....187 G6
Padiès (81).....170 D1
Padirac (46).....139 E6
Padoux (88).....70 A2
Pageas (87).....123 H4
Pagney (39).....102 D1
Pagney-derrière-Barine (54).....48 A5
Pagnoz (39).....103 E3
Pagny-la-Blanche-Côte (55).....48 A6
Pagny-la-Ville (21).....102 A2
Pagny-le-Château (21).....102 A2
Pagny-lès-Goin (57).....48 D2
Pagny-sur-Meuse (55).....48 A5
Pagny-sur-Moselle (54).....48 B3
les Paroches (55).....47 F3
Pagolle (64).....181 F2
Pailhac (65).....183 G6
Pailhès (09).....185 G4
Pailherols (15).....140 C5
Pailhès (34).....188 B1
Paillart (60).....20 C2
Paillé (17).....107 H6
Paillencourt (59).....9 E3
Paillet (33).....135 F6
Pailloles (47).....151 F3
le Pailly (52).....86 B2
Pailly (89).....65 E3
Paimbœuf (44).....74 A4
Paimpol (22).....33 F2
Paimpont (35).....56 C4
Painblanc (21).....101 F2
Pair-et-Grandrupt (88).....70 D3
Paissy (02).....22 C4
Paisy-Cosdon (10).....65 G4
Paizay-le-Chapt (79).....108 B5
Paizay-le-Sec (86).....109 H1
Paizay-le-Tort (79).....108 B5
Paizay-Naudouin-
Embourie (16).....108 C6
Pajay (38).....144 C1
Paladru (38).....131 F5
Palairac (11).....187 G5
Palaiseau (91).....42 C5
Palaiseul (52).....86 B2
Palaja (11).....187 E3
Palaminy (31).....184 D3
Palante (70).....88 B3
Palantine (25).....103 F2
Palasca (2B).....202 D5
Palau-de-Cerdagne (66).....199 G5
Palau-del-Vidre (66).....201 F3
Palavas-les-Flots (34).....173 G6
Palazinges (19).....138 D3
Paley (77).....64 B4
Palhers (48).....155 H3
Paligny (77).....115 F2
Palis (10).....65 G3
Palise (25).....87 F6
Palisse (19).....125 H6
Palladuc (63).....128 A1
Pallanne (32).....167 F5
Palleau (71).....101 H4
Pallegney (88).....69 H2
le Pallet (44).....75 E6
Palleville (81).....170 B6
la Pallu (53).....59 F1
Palluau (85).....91 E3
Palluau-sur-Indre (36).....96 A4
Palluaud (16).....136 C1
Pallud (73).....132 C3
Palluel (62).....8 C2
Palmas (12).....155 E4
la Palme (11).....188 A5
Palneca (2A).....205 F5
Palogneux (42).....128 C3
la Palud-sur-Verdon (04).....177 G3
Paluel (76).....16 D3
Pamfou (77).....64 B2
Pamiers (09).....185 H4
Pampelonne (81).....154 A6
Pamplie (79).....107 H2
Pampoux (79).....108 C2
Panassac (32).....184 A1

Panazol (87).....124 B2
Pancé (35).....57 F5
Pancey (52).....68 A1
Pancheraccia (2B).....205 G3
Pancy-Courtecon (02).....22 C4
Pandrignes (19).....139 E2
Pange (57).....26 C5
Panilleuse (27).....41 F1
Panissage (38).....131 E5
Panissières (42).....129 F3
Panjas (32).....166 B3
Pannecé (44).....75 F3
Pannecières (45).....63 E3
Pannes (45).....64 A6
Pannes (54).....48 A3
Pannesière (39).....102 D6
Panon (72).....60 B2
Panossas (38).....130 C4
la Panouse (48).....156 B1
Pantin (93).....43 E3
Panzoult (37).....94 C2
Papleux (02).....9 H5
Paradou (13).....191 E2
Parassy (18).....97 H1
Parata (2B).....205 G1
Paray-Douaville (78).....62 D2
Paray-le-Frésil (03).....114 B1
Paray-le-Monial (71).....115 H3
Paray-sous-Briailles (03).....114 A4
Paray-Vieille-Poste (91).....42 D5
Paraza (11).....187 H3
Parbayse (64).....182 A2
Parc-d'Anxtot (76).....15 G1
Parçay-les-Pins (49).....78 A5
Parçay-Meslay (37).....79 E5
Parçay-sur-Vienne (37).....94 C2
Parcé (35).....58 A3
Parcé-sur-Sarthe (72).....77 G1
Parcey (39).....102 C4
Parcieux (01).....130 A2
Parcoul (24).....136 B2
le Parcq (62).....7 F1
Parcy-et-Tigny (02).....22 A6
Pardailhan (34).....187 H1
Pardaillan (47).....150 D1
Pardies (64).....182 A2
Pardies-Piétat (64).....182 C3
Pardines (63).....127 F5
Paréac (65).....183 E4
Pareid (55).....47 H1
Parempuyre (33).....135 E4
Parennes (72).....59 G4
Parent (63).....127 F4
Parentignat (63).....127 G5
Parentis-en-Born (40).....148 B4
Parey-Saint-Césaire (54).....48 C6
Parey-sous-Montfort (88).....69 E3
Parfondeval (02).....23 F1
Parfondeval (61).....60 D1
Parfondru (02).....22 C4
Parfondrupt (55).....47 H1
Pargny (80).....21 G1
Pargny-Filain (02).....22 B4
Pargny-la-Dhuys (02).....44 D3
Pargny-les-Bois (02).....22 C2
Pargny-lès-Reims (51).....45 F1
Pargny-sous-Mureau (88).....68 C2
Pargny-sur-Saulx (51).....46 C4
Pargues (10).....66 C5
Parigné (35).....58 A1
Parigné-l'Évêque (72).....60 B6
Parigné-le-Pôlin (72).....78 A1
Parigny (42).....128 D1
Parigny (50).....37 F5
Parigny-la-Rose (58).....83 F6
Parigny-les-Vaux (58).....98 D3
Paris (75).....42 D4
Paris-l'Hôpital (71).....101 F4
Parisot (81).....169 H1
Parisot (82).....153 F5
Parlan (15).....139 G6
Parleboscq (40).....166 D2
Parly (89).....83 E2
Parmain (95).....42 C1
Parmilieu (38).....130 D2
Parnac (36).....110 C1
Parnac (46).....152 C3
Parnans (26).....144 C3
Parnay (18).....98 A5
Parnay (49).....93 H1
Parné-sur-Roc (53).....58 D5
Parnes (60).....21 G6
Parnoy-en-Bassigny (52).....68 D5
les Paroches (55).....47 F3
Paron (89).....64 D3
Paroy (25).....103 E3
Paroy (77).....64 D1
Paroy-en-Othe (89).....65 F5
Paroy-sur-Saulx (52).....68 B2
Paroy-sur-Tholon (89).....65 E5
Parpeçay (36).....96 C1
Parpeville (02).....22 B2
Parranquet (47).....151 G1
Parroy (54).....49 F5
Pars-lès-Chavanges (10).....66 D1
Pars-lès-Romilly (10).....65 G1
Parsac (23).....112 A5
Parthenay (79).....93 F6
Parthenay-de-Bretagne (35).....57 E2
Partinello (2A).....204 B2
Parux (54).....49 H6
Parves (01).....131 G3
Parville (27).....40 D2
Parvillers-le-Quesnoy (80).....21 E1
Parzac (16).....122 D1
le Pas (53).....59 E1
Pas-de-Jeu (79).....93 H3
Pas-en-Artois (62).....7 H3
le Pas-Saint-l'Homer (61).....61 E2
Pasilly (89).....84 B3
Paslières (63).....128 A2
Pasly (02).....22 A5
Pasques (21).....85 G6
le Pasquier (39).....103 F5
Passa (66).....201 E3
le Passage (38).....131 E5
le Passage (47).....151 E5
Passais (61).....37 H6
Passavant (25).....87 H6
Passavant-en-Argonne (51).....46 D2
Passavant-la-Rochère (70).....69 E6
Passavant-sur-Layon (49).....93 F3
Passel (60).....21 G3
Passenans (39).....102 D5
Passins (38).....131 E4
Passirac (16).....136 A1
Passonfontaine (25).....104 A3
Passy (71).....116 B3
Passy (74).....133 E1
Passy (89).....65 E4
Passy-en-Valois (02).....44 A1
Passy-Grigny (51).....45 E2
Passy-sur-Marne (02).....44 C2
Passy-sur-Seine (77).....65 E2
Patay (45).....62 D5
Patornay (39).....117 G1
Patrimonio (2B).....203 F4
Pau (64).....182 B2
Paucourt (45).....64 B5
Paudy (36).....96 D3
Pauilhac (32).....168 A3
Pauillac (33).....134 D1
Paule (22).....54 C1
Paulhac (15).....141 E3
Paulhac (31).....169 G4
Paulhac (43).....141 H2
Paulhac-en-Margeride (48).....141 G5
Paulhaguet (43).....141 H2
Paulhan (34).....172 C6
Paulhe (12).....155 F6
Paulhenc (15).....140 D5
Paulhiac (47).....151 H2
Pauligne (11).....186 D5
Paulin (24).....138 C5
Paulinet (81).....171 E1

Paulmy (37).....95 F3
Paulnay (36).....95 G5
Paulx (44).....91 E1
Paunat (24).....137 G5
Paussac-et-
Saint-Vivien (24).....137 E1
Pautaines-Augeville (52).....68 A3
Pauvres (08).....23 H4
Pavant (02).....44 B3
Pavezin (42).....129 H6
le Pavillon-Sainte-Julie (10).....66 A2
les Pavillons-sous-Bois (93).....43 E3
Pavilly (76).....17 F5
Payns (10).....66 A2
Payra-sur-l'Hers (11).....186 B3
Payrac (46).....138 C6
Payré (86).....108 D3
Payrignac (46).....138 C6
Payrin-Augmontel (81).....170 D6
Payros-Cazautets (40).....166 B5
Payroux (86).....109 F4
Payssous (31).....184 B5
Payzac (07).....157 E3
Payzac (24).....138 B3
Pazayac (24).....138 D4
Paziols (11).....187 G6
Pazy (58).....99 G1
le Péage-de-Roussillon (38).....144 A1
Péas (51).....45 F5
Peaugres (07).....143 H2
Péault (85).....106 C2
Pébées (32).....168 A6
Pébrac (43).....141 H4
Pech (09).....198 D1
Pech-Luna (11).....186 A3
Péchabou (31).....169 F6
Pécharic-et-le-Py (11).....186 A3
Péchaudier (81).....170 A6
Pechbonnieu (31).....169 F4
Pechbusque (31).....169 F6
le Pêchereau (36).....111 E1
Pécorade (40).....166 B4
le Pecq (78).....42 B3
Pecquencourt (59).....8 D1
Pecqueuse (91).....42 B6
Pécy (77).....43 H6
Pédernec (22).....32 D3
Pégairolles-de-Buèges (34).....172 C4
Pégairolles-
de-l'Escalette (34).....172 C4
Pégomas (06).....178 C5
le Pègue (26).....158 C3
Péguilhan (31).....184 B2
Peigney (52).....86 B1
Peillac (56).....56 B6
Peille (06).....195 G2
Peillon (06).....195 G2
Peillonnex (74).....118 D5
Peintre (39).....102 C1
les Peintures (33).....136 A3
Peipin (04).....160 B6
Peisey-Nancroix (73).....133 F4
Pel-et-Der (10).....66 D2
Pélissanne (13).....191 G3
Pellafol (38).....145 H6
Pelleautier (05).....160 B3
le Pellerin (44).....74 B5
la Pellerine (49).....77 H5
la Pellerine (53).....58 B2
Pellefigue (32).....168 B6
Pellegrue (33).....136 B6
Pelleport (31).....168 C4
Pellevoisin (36).....96 A4
Pellouailles-les-Vignes (49).....77 E4
Pelonne (26).....159 F4
Pelousey (25).....87 E6
Peltre (57).....48 D1
Pélussin (42).....129 H6
Pelves (62).....8 C3
Pelvoux (05).....146 D5
Penchard (77).....43 G3
Pencran (29).....31 F4
Pendé (80).....6 B3
Pénestin (56).....73 F2
Penguily (22).....34 A6
Penin (62).....7 H2
Penly (76).....17 H1
Penmarch (29).....53 E5
Pennautier (11).....187 E3
la Penne (06).....178 C2
Penne (81).....169 H1
Penne-d'Agenais (47).....151 H4
la Penne-sur-Huveaune (13).....192 D4
la Penne-sur-l'Ouvèze (26).....159 E5
Pennedepie (14).....15 E3
Pennes-le-Sec (26).....159 E3
les Pennes-Mirabeau (13).....192 A3
Pennesières (70).....87 F4
Penol (38).....130 C6
Pensol (87).....123 G4
Penta-Acquatella (2B).....205 G2
Penta-di-Casinca (2B).....203 G6
Penvénan (22).....32 D1
Péone (06).....161 H6
Pépieux (11).....187 G2
Pérassay (36).....112 A2
Peray (72).....60 C3
Perceneige (89).....65 E2
Percey (89).....84 A2
Percey-le-Grand (70).....86 B3
le Perchay (95).....42 A1
la Perche (18).....112 C1
Perchède (32).....166 B3
Percy (50).....37 F3
Percy-en-Auge (14).....39 E2
Perdreauville (78).....41 G3
Péré (17).....107 E5
Péré (65).....183 G4
Péreille (09).....186 A5
Perelli (2B).....205 G2
Pérenchies (59).....3 F5
Péret (34).....172 C6
Péret-Bel-Air (19).....125 G4
Péreuil (16).....122 A5
Péreyres (07).....143 E5
Pergain-Taillac (32).....167 H1
Peri (2A).....204 D5
le Périer (38).....146 A4
Périers (50).....12 D6
Périers-en-Auge (14).....14 D4
Périers-sur-le-Dan (14).....14 C4
Pérignac (16).....122 A5
Pérignac (17).....121 F4
Pérignat-lès-Sarliève (63).....127 F3
Pérignat-sur-Allier (63).....127 F4
Périgné (79).....108 A5
Périgneux (42).....129 E6
Périgny (03).....114 B3
Périgny (14).....38 C3
Périgny (17).....106 D5
Périgny (41).....79 G2
Périgny (94).....43 E5
Périgny-la-Rose (10).....65 F1
Périgueux (24).....137 F2
Périssac (33).....135 G4
Perles-et-Castelet (09).....199 F1
Pern (46).....152 C4
Pernand-Vergelesses (21).....101 G2
Pernant (02).....22 A5
Pernay (37).....78 C5
la Pernelle (50).....13 E2
Pernes (62).....7 G1
Pernes-les-Boulogne (62).....1 F4
Pernes-les-Fontaines (84).....175 F2
Pernois (80).....7 F4
Pero-Casevecchie (2B).....203 G6
Pérols (34).....173 G6
Pérols-sur-Vézère (19).....125 F5
Péron (01).....118 A4
Péronnas (01).....116 D5
Péronne (71).....116 B4
Péronne (80).....8 C5
Péronne-en-Mélantois (59).....3 G5
Péronville (28).....62 B5

Pérouges (01).....130 C2
la Pérouille (36).....96 B6
Pérouse (90).....88 D3
Péroy-les-Gombries (60).....43 G1
Perpezac-le-Blanc (19).....138 C2
Perpezac-le-Noir (19).....138 D1
Perpezat (63).....126 D4
Perpignan (66).....201 F2
Perquie (40).....166 B2
les Perques (50).....12 C3
Perrancey-
les-Vieux-Moulins (52).....86 A1
le Perray-en-Yvelines (78).....42 A5
Perrecy-les-Forges (71).....115 F1
le Perréon (69).....116 A6
Perret (22).....55 E1
Perreuil (71).....101 E5
Perreux (42).....115 E6
Perreux (89).....82 D2
le Perreux-sur-Marne (94).....43 E4
Perrex (01).....116 C4
Perrier (63).....127 F5
le Perrier (85).....90 C3
la Perrière (61).....60 C2
la Perrière (73).....133 E5
Perrières (14).....39 E2
Perriers-la-Campagne (27).....40 B1
Perriers-sur-Andelle (27).....19 E4
Perrignier (74).....118 D3
Perrigny (39).....102 D6
Perrigny (89).....83 F2
Perrigny-lès-Dijon (21).....101 H1
Perrigny-sur-Armançon (89).....84 C3
Perrigny-sur-l'Ognon (21).....86 B6
Perrigny-sur-Loire (71).....114 D2
Perrogney-les-Fontaines (52).....86 A2
le Perron (50).....37 H1
Perros-Guirec (22).....32 C1
Perrou (61).....38 B6
Perrouse (70).....87 F5
Perruel (27).....19 E4
Perrusse (52).....68 C5
Perrusson (37).....95 F2
Pers (79).....108 C4
Pers (15).....139 H5
Pers-en-Gâtinais (45).....64 B5
Pers-Jussy (74).....118 C5
Persac (86).....109 G3
Persan (95).....42 C1
Pesmes (70).....86 C5
Pessac (33).....135 E5
Pessac-sur-Dordogne (33).....136 B5
Pessan (32).....167 H5
Pessans (25).....103 F2
Pessat-Villeneuve (63).....127 F2
la Pesse (39).....118 A3
Pessines (17).....121 E3
Pessoulens (32).....168 B3
Petersbach (67).....50 B3
le Petit-Abergement (01).....117 G6
Petit-Auverné (44).....75 E2
Petit-Bersac (24).....136 C1
le Petit-Bornand-
les-Glières (74).....118 D6
le Petit-Celland (50).....37 F5
Petit-Couronne (76).....18 C5
Petit-Croix (90).....88 D3
Petit-Failly (54).....25 E4
Petit-Fayt (59).....9 H4
le Petit-Fougeray (35).....57 F4
Petit-Landau (68).....89 G2
Petit-Mars (44).....74 D3
le Petit-Mercey (39).....103 E1
Petit-Noir (39).....102 C4
le Petit-Palais-
et-Cornemps (33).....136 A4
le Petit-Pressigny (37).....95 F4
le Petit-Quevilly (76).....18 C5
Petit-Réderching (57).....28 A5
Petit-Tenquin (57).....49 G2
Petit-Verly (02).....9 F5
la Petite-Boissière (79).....92 C4
Petite-Chaux (25).....103 H6
la Petite-Fosse (88).....70 D2
la Petite-Marche (03).....112 C5
la Petite-Pierre (67).....50 B3
la Petite-Raon (88).....70 D1
Petite-Rosselle (57).....27 F4
la Petite-Verrière (71).....100 C3
Petitefontaine (90).....88 D2
les Petites-Armoises (08).....24 B4
les Petites-Loges (51).....45 G1
Petitmagny (90).....88 D2
Petitmont (54).....49 H6
Petiville (14).....14 D4
Petiville (76).....15 H2
Petosse (85).....107 E2
Petreto-Bicchisano (2A).....206 D2
Pettoncourt (57).....49 E4
Pettonville (54).....49 G6
Peujard (33).....135 G3
Peumérit (29).....53 E3
Peumerit-Quintin (22).....32 D5
Peuplingues (62).....1 G2
Peuton (53).....58 C6
Peuvillers (55).....25 E5
Peux-et-Couffouleux (12).....171 G4
Pévange (57).....49 F3
Pévy (51).....22 D6
Pexiora (11).....186 C3
Pexonne (54).....49 G6
Pey (40).....164 D4
Peymeinade (06).....178 C4
Peynier (13).....192 C3
Peypin (13).....192 C3
Peypin-d'Aigues (84).....176 C3
Peyrabout (23).....111 F6
le Peyrat (09).....186 A5
Peyrat-de-Bellac (87).....110 B5
Peyrat-la-Nonière (23).....112 A6
Peyrat-le-Château (87).....125 E3
la Peyratte (79).....93 F6
Peyraube (65).....183 F3
Peyraud (07).....144 A1
Peyre (40).....165 H5
Peyrecave (32).....168 B1
Peyrefitte-du-Razès (11).....186 C4
Peyrefitte-sur-l'Hers (11).....186 B3
Peyregoux (81).....170 C5
Peyrehorade (40).....164 D5
Peyreleau (12).....172 A1
Peyrelevade (19).....125 G4
Peyrelongue-Abos (64).....182 D1
Peyremale (30).....157 E5
Peyrens (11).....186 C2
Peyrestortes (66).....201 E2
Peyret-Saint-André (65).....183 H3
Peyriac-de-Mer (11).....188 A4
Peyriac-Minervois (11).....187 F3
Peyriat (01).....117 F5
Peyrieu (01).....131 G4
Peyrignac (24).....138 C3
Peyriguère (65).....183 F3
Peyrilhac (87).....124 A1
Peyrilles (46).....152 C2
Peyrins (26).....144 C3
Peyrissac (19).....124 D6
Peyrissas (31).....184 C2
Peyrole (81).....170 A4
Peyrolles (11).....187 E5
Peyrolles (13).....176 B4
Peyrolles-en-Provence (13).....176 B4
Peyrouse (65).....182 D4
Peyrouzet (31).....184 B3
Peyruis (04).....160 B6
Peyrun (65).....183 F2
Peyrus (26).....144 C5
Peyrusse (15).....141 E2
Peyrusse-Grande (32).....167 E5
Peyrusse-le-Roc (12).....153 H3
Peyrusse-Massas (32).....167 H4
Peyrusse-Vieille (32).....167 E5
Peyssies (31).....185 E2
Peyzac-le-Moustier (24).....137 H4
Peyzieux-sur-Saône (01).....116 B5
Pézarches (77).....43 H5
Pezé-le-Robert (72).....59 H4
Pézenas (34).....188 D1
Pézènes-les-Mines (34).....172 B5
Pezens (11).....186 D3
Pézilla-de-Conflent (66).....200 C2
Pézilla-la-Rivière (66).....201 E2
Pezou (41).....79 G1
Pezuls (24).....137 F5
Pfaffenheim (68).....71 F5
Pfalzweyer (67).....50 B4
Pfastatt (68).....89 F1
Pfetterhouse (68).....89 E4
Pfettisheim (67).....50 D5
Pfulgriesheim (67).....51 E5
Phaffans (90).....88 D3
Phalempin (59).....3 F6
Phalsbourg (57).....50 B4
Philippsbourg (57).....28 C6
Philondenx (40).....166 A5
Phlin (54).....48 D3
Pia (66).....201 F2
Piacé (72).....59 H3
le Pian-Médoc (33).....135 E4
le Pian-sur-Garonne (33).....149 H2
Piana (2A).....204 B3
Pianello (2B).....205 G2
Piano (2B).....205 G1
Pianottoli-Caldarello (2A).....207 E4
les Piards (39).....117 H2
la Piarre (05).....159 G3
Piazzali (2B).....205 G2
Piazzole (2B).....205 G1
Piblange (57).....26 D4
Pibrac (31).....169 E5
Picarreau (39).....103 E5
Picauville (50).....12 D4
Pichanges (21).....85 H5
Picquigny (80).....7 F5
Pie-d'Orezza (2B).....205 G1
Pied-de-Borne (48).....156 D3
Piedicorte-di-Gaggio (2B).....205 G3
Piedicroce (2B).....205 G1
Piedigriggio (2B).....203 F6
Piedipartino (2B).....205 G1
Piégon (26).....158 D4
Piégros-la-Clastre (26).....158 D1
Piégut (04).....160 C3
Piégut-Pluviers (24).....123 F4
Piencourt (27).....15 G5
Piennes (54).....25 H5
Piennes-Onvillers (80).....21 E2
Pierlas (06).....178 D1
la Pierre (38).....145 H1
Pierre-Bénite (69).....130 A3
Pierre-Buffière (87).....124 B4
Pierre-Châtel (38).....145 H4
Pierre-de-Bresse (71).....102 B4
Pierre-la-Treiche (54).....48 B5
Pierre-Levée (77).....43 H3
Pierre-Morains (51).....45 F4
Pierre-Percée (54).....70 C1
Pierre-Perthuis (89).....83 H5
Pierreclos (71).....116 A4
Pierrecourt (70).....86 C3
Pierrecourt (76).....6 C6
Pierrefeu (06).....195 E1
Pierrefeu-du-Var (83).....193 G4
Pierrefiche (12).....155 E3
Pierrefiche (48).....156 C1
Pierrefiques (76).....16 B3
Pierrefitte (19).....124 D5
Pierrefitte (23).....111 H5
Pierrefitte (79).....93 F4
Pierrefitte (88).....69 G3
Pierrefitte-en-Auge (14).....15 F4
Pierrefitte-en-Beauvaisis (60).....20 A4
Pierrefitte-en-Cinglais (14).....38 C2
Pierrefitte-ès-Bois (45).....82 B4
Pierrefitte-Nestalas (65).....182 D6
Pierrefitte-sur-Aire (55).....47 F3
Pierrefitte-sur-Loire (03).....114 C2
Pierrefitte-sur-Sauldre (41).....81 F4
Pierrefitte-sur-Seine (93).....42 D3
Pierrefonds (60).....21 G5
Pierrefontaine-
lès-Blamont (25).....88 C5
Pierrefontaine-
les-Varans (25).....104 B1
Pierrefort (15).....140 D5
Pierregot (80).....7 G5
Pierrelatte (26).....158 A4
Pierrelaye (95).....42 C2
Pierrelongue (26).....159 E5
Pierremande (02).....21 H3
Pierremont (62).....7 G1
Pierremont-sur-Amance (52).....86 D2
Pierrepont (02).....22 D2
Pierrepont (14).....38 C3
Pierrepont (54).....25 G4
Pierrepont-sur-Avre (80).....20 D2
Pierrepont-sur-l'Arentèle (88).....70 B3
Pierrerue (04).....176 D2
Pierrerue (34).....188 A1
Pierres (14).....38 A3
Pierres (28).....41 G6
Pierreval (76).....18 D4
Pierrevert (04).....176 C3
Pierreville (50).....12 B4
Pierreville (54).....48 C6
Pierric (44).....74 C1
Pierry (51).....45 F2
Pietra-di-Verde (2B).....205 G2
Pietracorbara (2B).....203 G2
Pietralba (2B).....203 F5
Pietraserena (2B).....205 G3
Pietricaggio (2B).....205 G2
Pietrosella (2A).....206 C2
Pietroso (2B).....205 F3
Piets-Plasence-
Moustrou (64).....166 A6
Pieusse (11).....186 D4
les Pieux (50).....12 B3
Piève (2B).....203 F5
Piffonds (89).....64 D4
Pigerolles (23).....125 G3
Pigna (2B).....202 D5
Pignan (34).....173 F6
Pignans (83).....193 G3
Pignicourt (02).....23 E4
Pigny (18).....97 H2
Pihem (62).....2 B4
Pihen-lès-Guînes (62).....1 G3
Pila-Canale (2A).....206 D1
Pillac (16).....136 C1
Pillemoine (39).....103 F5
les Pilles (26).....158 D4
Pillon (55).....25 E4
Pimbo (40).....166 A5
Pimelles (89).....84 B2
Pimorin (39).....117 F2
Pimprez (60).....21 G4
le Pin (03).....114 D3
le Pin (14).....15 F5
le Pin (17).....135 G1
le Pin (30).....174 C1
le Pin (32).....166 C3

le Pin (38).....131 E6
le Pin (39).....102 D6
le Pin (44).....75 E2
le Pin (77).....43 F3
le Pin (79).....92 D3
le Pin (82).....168 C2
le Pin-au-Haras (61).....39 F4
Pin-Balma (31).....169 F5
le Pin-en-Mauges (49).....75 H5
le Pin-la-Garenne (61).....60 D2
le Pin-Murelet (31).....184 D2
Pinas (65).....183 H4
Pinay (42).....129 E2
Pincé (72).....77 F2
Pindères (47).....150 C5
Pindray (86).....109 H2
les Pineaux (85).....106 C1
Pinel-Hauterive (47).....151 F3
Pinet (34).....189 E1
Pineuilh (33).....136 C5
Piney (10).....66 C2
Pino (2B).....203 F2
Pinols (43).....141 H4
Pinon (02).....22 B4
Pins-Justaret (31).....169 E6
Pinsac (46).....138 C5
Pinsaguel (31).....169 E6
Pinsot (38).....132 B6
Pintac (65).....183 F2
Pinterville (27).....18 D6
les Pinthières (28).....41 G5
Piobetta (2B).....205 G2
Pioggiola (2B).....202 D5
Piolenc (84).....158 B6
Pionnat (23).....111 H5
Pionsat (63).....112 D6
Pioussay (79).....108 C5
Pipriac (35).....56 D5
Piquecos (82).....169 E1
Pirajoux (01).....117 E3
Piré-sur-Seiche (35).....57 G4
Pirey (25).....87 E6
Piriac-sur-Mer (44).....73 F3
Pirmil (72).....59 G6
Pirou (50).....12 C6
Pis (32).....168 A3
Pisany (17).....120 D3
Piscop (95).....42 D2
Piseux (27).....40 C4
Pisieu (38).....130 C6
Pisseleu (60).....20 A3
Pisseleux (02).....43 H1
la Pisseure (70).....87 G1
Pissos (40).....148 D3
Pissotte (85).....107 F2
Pissy (80).....7 F6
Pissy-Pôville (76).....17 G5
Pisy (89).....84 B4
Pitgam (59).....2 C3
Pithiviers (45).....63 F4
Pithiviers-le-Vieil (45).....63 E4
Pithon (02).....21 H2
Pîtres (27).....18 D5
Pittefaux (62).....1 F4
Pizay (01).....130 C2
Pizieux (72).....60 B3
le Pizou (24).....136 B4
le Pla (09).....199 H2
Plabennec (29).....31 E4
Placé (53).....58 C3
Plachy-Buyon (80).....20 B1
Placy (14).....14 B6
Placy-Montaigu (50).....37 G2
le Plagnal (07).....156 D1
la Plagne (73).....133 F4
Plagnole (31).....184 D2
Plaigne (11).....186 A3
Plailly (60).....43 E2
Plaimbois-du-Miroir (25).....104 C1
Plaimbois-Vennes (25).....104 B1
Plaimpied-Givaudins (18).....97 H3
la Plaine (49).....92 B2
Plaine (67).....71 E1
Plaine-de-Walsch (57).....50 A5
Plaine-Haute (22).....33 G5
la Plaine-sur-Mer (44).....73 G5
Plaines-Saint-Lange (10).....66 D6
Plainfaing (88).....70 D3
Plainoiseau (39).....102 D5
les Plains-et-
Grands-Essarts (25).....88 D3
Plaintel (22).....33 G5
Plainval (60).....20 C3
Plainville (27).....15 G6
Plainville (60).....20 D2
Plaisance (12).....171 F2
Plaisance (24).....137 F6
Plaisance (32).....167 E4
Plaisance (86).....109 H3
Plaisance-du-Touch (31).....169 E5
Plaisia (39).....117 F2
Plaisians (26).....159 E5
Plaisir (78).....42 B4
Plaissan (34).....172 C6
Plaizac (16).....122 A3
le Plan (31).....184 D3
Plan (38).....145 E1
Plan-d'Aups-
Sainte-Baume (83).....192 D3
Plan-de-Baix (26).....144 C6
Plan-de-Cuques (13).....192 B3
le Plan-de-la-Tour (83).....194 B3
Plan-d'Orgon (13).....175 F3
Planay (21).....84 C2
Planay (73).....133 F5
la Planche (44).....91 G1
Plancher-Bas (70).....88 C2
Plancher-les-Mines (70).....88 C1
Plancherine (73).....132 C3
les Planches-
en-Montagne (39).....103 G6
les Planches-
près-Arbois (39).....103 E4
Planchez (58).....100 B2
Plancoët (22).....34 C4
Plancy-l'Abbaye (10).....45 H6
la Planée (25).....103 H4
Planès (66).....200 A4
Planèzes (66).....200 D2
Planfoy (42).....143 F1
Planguenoual (22).....33 H4
le Planois (71).....102 C5
le Planquay (27).....15 G6
Planquery (14).....13 G6
Planques (62).....7 E1
Planrupt (52).....67 E1
les Plans (30).....157 F6
les Plans (34).....172 B4
le Plantay (01).....116 D5
les Plantiers (30).....173 E1
le Plantis (61).....60 B1
Planty (10).....65 G4
Planzolles (07).....157 E3
Plappeville (57).....26 B5
Plasne (39).....102 D5
Plasnes (27).....15 G6
Plassac (17).....121 F5
Plassac (33).....135 E2
Plassac-Rouffiac (16).....122 B5
Plassay (17).....121 E3
Plaudren (56).....55 H5
Plauzat (63).....127 F4
Plavilla (11).....186 B4
Pléboulle (22).....34 B4
Pléchâtel (35).....57 E5
Plédéliac (22).....34 B5
Plédran (22).....33 G5
Pléguien (22).....33 F3

Pléhédel (22)................33 F3
Pleine-Fougères (35).........35 G5
Pleine-Selve (02)............22 B1
Pleine-Selve (33)...........135 E1
Plélan-le-Grand (35).........17 E3
Plélan-le-Petit (22).........34 C5
Plélauff (22)................54 D1
Plélo (22)...................33 F4
Plémet (22)..................55 H2
Plémy (22)...................55 G2
Plénée-Jugon (22)............34 A4
Pléneuf-Val-André (22).......34 A4
Plénise (39)................103 G5
Plénisette (39).............103 G5
Plerguer (35)................35 E5
Plérin (22)..................33 G4
Plerneuf (22)................33 F4
Plescop (56).................34 D5
Plesder (35).................34 D5
Plésidy (22).................33 E5
Pleslin-Trigavou (22)........34 D4
Plesnois (57)................26 C1
Plesnoy (52).................86 C1
Plessala (22)................55 H1
Plessé (44)..................74 B2
le Plessier-Huleu (02).......22 C6
le Plessier-Rozainvilliers (80)..20 D3
le Plessier-sur-Bulles (60)..20 C4
le Plessier-sur-Saint-Just (60)..20 C4
le Plessis-aux-Bois (77).....43 F2
Plessis-Barbuise (10)........44 C1
le Plessis-Belleville (60)...43 F2
le Plessis-Bouchard (95).....42 C2
le Plessis-Brion (60)........21 E4
le Plessis-Dorin (41)........61 F1
le Plessis-Feu-Aussoux (77)..43 H5
le Plessis-Gassot (95).......43 E2
le Plessis-Grammoire (49)....77 E4
le Plessis-Grimoult (14).....14 A6
le Plessis-Hébert (27).......41 F2
le Plessis-Lastelle (50).....12 D5
le Plessis-l'Échelle (41)....80 A2
le Plessis-l'Évêque (77).....43 F2
le Plessis-Luzarches (95)....42 D2
le Plessis-Macé (49).........76 D4
le Plessis-Pâté (91).........42 D6
le Plessis-Patte-d'Oie (60)..21 G2
le Plessis-Placy (77)........43 H2
le Plessis-Robinson (92).....42 C4
Plessis-Saint-Benoist (91)...63 E3
le Plessis-Saint-Jean (89)...65 E3
le Plessis-
   Sainte-Opportune (27)....40 C2
le Plessis-Trévise (94)......43 E4
Plessis-Balisson (22)........34 C4
Plestan (22).................34 A5
Plestin-les-Grèves (22)......32 B3
Pleubian (22)................33 E1
Pleucadeuc (56)..............56 A5
Pleudaniel (22)..............33 E2
Pleudihen-sur-Rance (22).....36 A4
Pleugriffet (56).............55 G3
Pleumartin (86)..............95 E5
Pleumeur-Bodou (22)..........32 C2
Pleumeur-Gautier (22)........33 E1
Pleure (39).................102 C4
Pleurs (51)..................45 E5
Pleurtuit (35)...............34 D4
Pleuvezain (88)..............69 E2
Pleuville (16)..............109 H6
Pléven (22)..................34 B5
Plévenon (22)................34 B3
Plévin (22)..................32 B1
Pleyben (29).................31 G6
Pleyber-Christ (29)..........31 H4
Pliboux (79)...............108 D5
Plichancourt (51)............46 C5
Plieux (32).................168 A2
Plivot (51)..................45 F2
Plobannalec-Lesconil (29)....53 F4
Plobsheim (67)...............71 H1
Ploemel (56).................55 E6
Ploemeur (56)................54 C5
Ploërdut (56)................54 D2
Ploëren (56).................56 A4
Ploeuc-sur-Lié (22)..........33 G6
Ploéven (29).................53 F1
Ploëzal (22).................33 E2
Plogastel-Saint-Germain (29).53 E3
Plogoff (29).................52 C2
Plogonnec (29)...............53 F2
Plomb (50)...................35 H3
Plombières-les-Bains (88)....70 A6
Plombières-lès-Dijon (21)....85 G6
Plomelin (29)................53 F3
Plomeur (29).................53 E4
Plomion (02).................23 E1
Plomodiern (29)..............53 F1
Plonéis (29).................53 F2
Plonéour-Lanvern (29)........53 E3
Plonévez-du-Faou (29)........31 H6
Plonévez-Porzay (29).........53 F1
Plorec-sur-Arguenon (22).....34 B4
Plottes (71)................116 B2
Plou (18)....................97 F3
Plouagat (22)................33 F4
Plouaret (22)................32 C3
Plouarzel (29)...............30 A5
Plouasne (22)................34 D6
Plouay (56)..................54 C4
Ploubalay (22)...............34 C4
Ploubazlanec (22)............33 F2
Ploubezre (22)...............32 C2
Ploudalmézeau (29)...........30 D3
Ploudaniel (29)..............31 F3
Ploudiry (29)................31 F4
Plouëc-du-Trieux (22)........33 E3
Plouédern (29)...............31 F4
Plouégat-Guérand (29)........32 B3
Plouégat-Moysan (29).........32 B3
Plouénan (29)................31 H3
Plouër-sur-Rance (22)........36 A4
Plouescat (29)...............31 G2
Plouézec (22)................33 F2
Plouezoc'h (29)..............32 A3
Ploufragan (22)..............33 G4
Plougar (29).................31 G3
Plougasnou (29)..............32 A3
Plougastel-Daoulas (29)......31 E5
Plougonvelin (29)............30 C5
Plougonven (29)..............32 A4
Plougonver (22)..............32 C4
Plougoulm (29)...............31 G2
Plougoumelen (56)............55 F6
Plougourvest (29)............31 G3
Plougras (22)................32 B4
Plougrescant (22)............33 E1
Plouguenast (22).............55 G1
Plouguerneau (29)............31 E2
Plouguernével (22)...........54 D1
Plouguiel (22)...............32 D1
Plouguin (29)................30 D3
Plouha (22)..................33 F3
Plouharnel (56)..............72 B1
Plouhinec (29)...............52 D2
Plouhinec (56)...............54 D3
Plouider (29)................31 F3
Plouigneau (29)..............32 B3
Plouisy (22).................33 E3
Ploulec'h (22)...............32 C2
Ploumagoar (22)..............33 E3
Ploumilliau (22).............32 C2
Ploumoguer (29).............30 C4
Plounéour-Ménez (29).........31 H4
Plounéour-Trez (29)..........31 F2
Plounérin (22)...............32 B4
Plounéventer (29)............31 F3
Plounévez-Lochrist (29)......31 G3
Plounévez-Moëdec (22)........32 C4
Plounévez-Quintin (22).......32 D6
Plourac'h (22)...............32 B5
Plouray (56).................54 D3

Plourhan (22)................33 G3
Plourin (29).................30 C3
Plourin-lès-Morlaix (29).....32 A4
Plourivo (22)................33 E2
Plouvain (62)................8 C2
Plouvara (22)................33 F4
Plouvien (29)................31 E3
Plouvorn (29)................31 G3
Plouyé (29)..................32 A6
Plouzané (29)................30 C5
Plouzélambre (22)............32 C3
Plouzévédé (29)..............31 G3
Plovan (29)..................53 E3
Ployart-et-Vaurseine (02)....22 D4
le Ployron (60)..............20 D3
Plozévet (29)................52 D2
Pludual (22).................33 F3
Pluduno (22).................34 B4
Plufur (22)..................32 B3
Pluguffan (29)...............53 F3
Pluherlin (56)...............55 A6
Plumaudan (22)...............34 C6
Plumaugat (22)...............34 B1
Plumelec (56)................55 G5
Pluméliau (56)...............55 F3
Plumelin (56)................55 F3
Plumergat (56)...............55 F5
Plumetot (14)................14 C4
Plumieux (22)................55 H2
Plumont (39)................103 E2
Pluneret (56)................55 F6
Plurien (22).................34 B3
Plusquellec (22).............32 C5
Plussulien (22)..............33 E6
Pluvault (21)...............102 B1
Pluvet (21).................102 B1
Pluvigner (56)...............55 E5
Pluzunet (22)................32 D3
Pocancy (51).................45 G3
Pocé-les-Bois (35)...........57 H3
Pocé-sur-Cisse (37)..........79 F5
Podensac (33)...............149 G1
le Poët (05).................160 A5
le Poët-Célard (26)..........58 C2
le Poët-en-Percip (26).......159 F5
le Poët-Laval (26)...........158 C3
le Poët-Sigillat (26)........159 E4
Pœuilly (80).................8 D6
Poey-de-Lescar (64).........182 B1
Poey-d'Oloron (64)...........181 H2
Pœzat (03)..................113 G6
Poggio-di-Nazza (2B)........205 F4
Poggio-di-Venaco (2B).......205 F3
Poggio-d'Oletta (2B)........203 F4
Poggio-Marinaccio (2B)......203 F6
Poggio-Mezzana (2B).........203 G6
Poggiolo (2A)...............204 D3
Pogny (51)...................46 A4
Poids-de-Fiole (39).........117 G1
Poigny (77)..................64 C1
Poigny-la-Forêt (78).........41 H5
Poil (58)...................100 B4
Poilcourt-Sydney (08)........23 F4
Poilhes (34)................188 B2
Poil-sur-Vègre (72)..........59 F6
Poillé (53)..................59 E6
Poilley (35).................35 H5
Poilley (50).................35 H4
Poilly (45)..................82 B2
Poilly (51)..................22 D6
Poilly-lez-Gien (45).........81 H3
Poilly-sur-Serein (89).......84 A2
Poilly-sur-Tholon (89).......83 E1
Poinçon-lès-Larrey (21)......85 E1
le Poinçonnet (36)...........96 C5
Poincy (77)..................43 G3
Poinsenot (52)...............85 G2
Poinson-lès-Fayl (52)........86 C2
Poinson-lès-Grancey (52).....85 G3
Poinson-lès-Nogent (52)......68 B6
Pointel (61).................38 C5
Pointis-de-Rivière (31).....184 A4
Pointis-Inard (31)..........184 C2
Pointre (39).................102 C1
Pointvillers (25)...........103 F2
Poinville (28)...............62 D4
Poiroux (85).................91 F6
Poisat (38).................145 G2
Poiseul (52).................68 C6
Poiseul-la-Grange (21).......85 F4
Poiseul-la-Ville-
   et-Laperrière (21).......85 E4
Poiseul-lès-Saulx (21).......85 H4
Poiseux (58).................99 E2
Poisieux (18)................97 F3
le Poislay (41)..............61 G5
Poisson (71)................115 E3
Poissons (52)................68 A2
Poissy (78)..................42 B3
Poisvilliers (28)............62 B1
Poisy (74)..................132 A1
la Poitevinière (49).........75 H5
Poitiers (86)...............109 E1
Poivres (10).................45 G5
Poix (51)....................45 H3
Poix-de-Picardie (80)........20 A1
Poix-du-Nord (59)............9 G3
Poix-Terron (08).............24 A2
le Poizat (01)..............117 H5

Pompey (54)..................48 C4
Pompiac (32)................168 C6
le Pompidou (48)............156 B6
Pompierre (88)...............68 D3
Pompierre-sur-Doubs (25).....88 A4
Pompiey (47)................150 C5
Pompignac (33)..............135 F5
Pompignan (30)..............173 F3
Pompignan (82)..............169 E3
Pompogne (47)...............150 B5
Pomponne (77)................43 F4
Pomport (24)................136 D6
Pomps (64)..................165 H6
Pomy (11)...................186 D5
Poncé-sur-le-Loir (72).......78 D2
Poncey-lès-Athée (21).......102 C1
Poncey-sur-l'Ignon (21)......85 F4
le Ponchel (62)..............7 E3
Ponches-Estruval (80)........6 D2
Ponchon (60).................20 B5
Poncin (01).................117 F6
Poncins (42)................129 E3
Pondaurat (33)..............150 A2
le Pondy (18)................98 A5
Ponet-et-Saint-Auban (26)...144 D6
Ponlat-Taillebourg (31).....184 A4
Pons (17)...................121 F4
Ponsampère (32).............183 G1
Ponsan-Soubiran (32)........183 H2
Ponsas (26).................144 A2
Ponson-Debat-Pouts (64).....182 D2
Ponson-Dessus (64)..........182 D2
Ponsonnas (38)..............145 G5
Pont (21)...................102 B2
Pont-à-Marcq (59)............8 D1
Pont-à-Mousson (54)..........48 C3
Pont-à-Vendin (62)...........3 E6
Pont-Arcy (02)...............22 C5
Pont-Audemer (27)............15 H3
Pont-Authou (27).............18 A6
Pont-Aven (29)...............54 A4
Pont-Bellanger (14).........37 G2
le Pont-Chrétien-
   Chabenet (36)............110 D1
Pont-Croix (29)..............52 D2
Pont-d'Ain (01).............117 E6
Pont-de-Barret (26).........158 C2
Pont-de-Beauvoisin (38).....131 E2
le Pont-de-Beauvoisin (73)..131 F5
Pont-de-Buis-
   lès-Quimerch (29)........31 G6
Pont-de-Chéruy (38).........130 D2
le Pont-de-Claix (38).......145 G3
le Pont-de-Labeaume (07)....157 F1
Pont-de-l'Arche (27).........18 D5
Pont-de-Larn (81)...........170 D6
Pont-de-l'Isère (26)........144 A4
le Pont-de-Metz (80).........7 F6
le Pont-de-Montvert (48)....156 C5
le Pont-de-Planches (70).....87 E4
Pont-de-Poitte (39).........117 G1
Pont-de-Roide (25)...........88 C5
Pont-de-Ruan (37)............94 D1
Pont-de-Salars (12).........154 D4
Pont-de-Vaux (01)...........116 C3
Pont-de-Veyle (01)..........116 B4
Pont-d'Héry (39)............103 F4
Pont-d'Ouilly (14)...........38 C3
Pont-du-Bois (70)............69 F6
Pont-du-Casse (47)..........151 F5
Pont-du-Château (63)........127 G3
Pont-du-Navoy (39)..........103 E6
Pont-en-Royans (38).........144 D3
Pont-et-Massène (21).........84 D5
Pont-Évêque (38)............130 B5
Pont-Farcy (14)..............37 G2
Pont-Hébert (50).............13 F6
Pont-la-Ville (52)...........67 G5
Pont-l'Abbé (29).............53 F4
Pont-l'Abbé-d'Arnoult (17)..120 D2
Pont-lès-Bonfays (88)........69 F3
Pont-les-Moulins (25)........88 A6
Pont-l'Évêque (14)...........15 F4
Pont-l'Évêque (60)...........21 G3
Pont-Melvez (22).............32 D4
Pont-Noyelles (80)...........7 H5
Pont-Remy (80)...............6 D5
Pont-Saint-Esprit (30)......158 A5
Pont-Saint-Mard (02).........22 A4
Pont-Saint-Martin (44).......74 C6
Pont-Saint-Pierre (27).......18 D5
Pont-Saint-Vincent (54)......48 C6
Pont-Sainte-Marie (10).......66 B3
Pont-Sainte-Maxence (60).....20 D5
Pont-Scorff (56).............54 C4
Pont-sur-l'Ognon (70)........87 H4
Pont-sur-Madon (88)..........69 F2
Pont-sur-Meuse (55)..........47 G4
Pont-sur-Sambre (59).........9 H3
Pont-sur-Seine (10)..........65 F2
Pont-sur-Vanne (89)..........65 F4
Pont-sur-Yonne (89)..........64 D4
Pont-Trambouze (69).........115 G6
Pontacq (64)................182 C3
Pontailler-sur-Saône (21)....86 B6
Pontaix (26)................144 D6

Porchères (33)..............136 A4
la Porcherie (87)...........124 D5
Porcheux (60)................19 H5
Porcheville (78).............41 H3
Porcieu-Amblagnieu (38).....131 E2
Pordic (22)..................33 G4
le Porge (33)...............134 B5
Pornic (44)..................73 H6
Pornichet (44)...............73 G4
Porquéricourt (60)...........21 F3
Porri (2B)..................203 G6
Porspoder (29)...............30 C3
Port (01)...................117 G5
Port-Brillet (53)............58 B4
Port-de-Bouc (13)...........191 G5
Port-de-Lanne (40)..........164 D5
Port-de-Piles (86)...........94 D3
Port-d'Envaux (17)..........121 E2
Port-des-Barques (17)........120 C1
Port-en-Bessin-Huppain (14)..13 H5
la Port-Nouvelle (11).......188 B5
Port-Launay (29).............31 G6
le Port-Marly (78)...........42 B4
Port-Mort (27)...............41 F1
Port-Saint-Louis-
   du-Rhône (13)...........191 E5
Port-Saint-Père (44).........74 B6
Port-Sainte-Foy-
   et-Ponchapt (24)........136 C5
Port-sur-Saône (70)..........87 F3
Port-sur-Seille (54).........48 C3
Port-Vendres (66)...........201 G4
Porta (66)..................199 F4
Portbail (50)................12 B4
Porte-Joie (27)..............18 D5
Porté-Puymorens (66)........199 G3
Portel-des-Corbières (11)...188 A5
Portes (27)..................40 C2
Portes (30).................157 E5
Portes-en-Ré (17)...........106 A4
Portes-lès-Valence (26).....144 B5
Portet (64).................166 A6
Portet-d'Aspet (31).........184 D5
Portet-de-Luchon (31).......197 E1
Portet-sur-Garonne (31).....169 F6
Portets (33)................149 G1
Portieux (88)................69 G2
Portiragnes (34)............187 D2
Porto (2A)..................204 B4
Porto-Vecchio (2A)..........207 G3
Ports (37)...................94 D3
Posanges (21)................85 E5
Poses (27)...................18 D5
Possesse (51)................46 C3
la Possonnière (49)..........76 D5
Postroff (57)................49 H3
Potangis (51)................44 D6
Potelières (30).............157 F5
Potelle (59)................9 G3
la Poterie-au-Perche (61)....40 B6
la Poterie-Cap-d'Antifer (76)..16 B4
la Poterie-Mathieu (27)......15 H4
Pothières (21)...............84 D1
Potigny (14).................38 D2
Pottes (21)..................27 E1
Pouan-les-Vallées (10).......66 B1
Pouançay (86)................93 H2
Pouancé (49).................58 A6
Pouant (86)..................94 B3
Poubeau (31)................197 E1
Poucharramet (31)...........185 E1
Poudenas (47)...............167 E1
Poudenx (40)................165 H5
Poudis (81).................170 B6
Poueyferré (65).............182 D4
la Pouëze (49)...............76 C3
Pouffonds (79)..............108 B4
la Pouge (23)...............125 F1
le Pouget (34)..............172 D5
Pougnadoresse (30)..........174 C1
Pougne-Hérisson (79)........108 A2
Pougny (01).................118 A5
Pougny (58)..................82 C6
Pougues-les-Eaux (58).......98 D3
Pougy (10)...................66 C2
Pouillac (17)...............135 G1
Pouillat (01)...............117 F3
Pouillé (41).................79 H6
Pouillé (85)................107 E2
Pouillé (86)................109 E2
Pouillé-les-Côteaux (44).....75 F3
Pouillenay (21)..............84 D4
Pouilley-Français (25).......103 F1
Pouilley-les-Vignes (25)....103 E1
Pouilloux (71)..............115 G2
Pouilly (57).................26 C6
Pouilly (60).................20 A6
Pouilly-en-Auxois (21)......101 E1
Pouilly-le-Monial (69)......129 H1
Pouilly-lès-Feurs (42)......129 E3
Pouilly-les-Nonains (42)....115 E6
Pouilly-sous-Charlieu (42)..115 E5
Pouilly-sur-Loire (58).......98 C1
Pouilly-sur-Meuse (55).......24 D3
Pouilly-sur-Saône (21)......102 A3
Pouilly-sur-Serre (02).......22 C2
Pouilly-sur-Vingeanne (21)...86 B4
le Poujol-sur-Orb (34)......172 C6
Poujols (34)................172 C4
Poulaines (36)...............96 C2
Poulainville (80)............7 G5
Poulan-Pouzols (81).........170 B3
Poulangy (52)................68 A5
Pouldergat (29)..............53 E2
Pouldouran (22)..............33 E2
Pouldreuzic (29).............53 E2
Poule-les-Écharmeaux (69)...115 G5
Pouliacq (64)...............166 B6
les Poulières (88)...........70 C3
Pouligney-Lusans (25)........87 H6
Pouligny-Notre-Dame (36)....111 H2
Pouligny-Saint-Martin (36)..111 H2
Pouligny-Saint-Pierre (36)...95 G6
Poulx (30)..................174 B2
Poumarous (65)..............183 F3
Poupas (82).................168 B2
Poupry (28)..................62 D5
Pouques-Lormes (58)..........83 H6
Pourcharesses (48).........156 D3
Pourchères (07).............157 G1
Pourcieux (83)..............176 C6
Pourcy (51)..................45 E1
Pourlans (71)...............102 B4
Pournoy-la-Chétive (57)......26 B6
Pournoy-la-Grasse (57).......48 C1
Pourrain (89)................83 F2
Pourrières (83).............176 C6
Poursac (16)................122 C1
Poursay-Garnaud (17)........121 F1
Poursiugues-Boucoue (64)....166 B5
Pouru-aux-Bois (08)..........24 D2
Pouru-Saint-Remy (08).......24 D2
Poussan (34)................173 E6
Poussanges (23).............125 H2
Poussay (88).................69 F2
Pousseaux (58)...............83 G5
Poussignac (47).............150 B4
Pousthomy (12)..............171 F3
le Pout (33)................135 G6
Pouvrai (61).................60 D3
Pouxeux (88).................70 B4
Pouy (65)...................184 A1
Pouy-de-Touges (31).........184 D2
Pouy-Loubrin (32)...........167 H6
Pouy-Roquelaure (32)........167 H1

Pouy-sur-Vannes (10).........65 G3
Pouyastruc (65).............183 F2
Pouydesseaux (40)...........166 B2
Pouydraguin (32)............166 D4
Pouzac (65).................183 F4
Pouzauges (85)...............92 C5
Pouzay (37)..................94 D2
Pouze (31)..................185 G1
Pouzilhac (30)..............174 C1
le Pouzin (07)..............144 A6
Pouzol (63).................113 F6
Pouzolles (34)..............188 C1
Pouzols (34)................173 G5
Pouzols-Minervois (11)......187 H2
Pouzy-Mésangy (03)...........98 C6
Poyanne (40)................165 F3
Poyans (70)..................86 C4
Poyartin (40)...............165 F4
Poyols (26).................159 F2
Pozières (80)................8 B5
le Pradal (34)..............172 C5
les Pradeaux (63)...........127 G5
Pradelle (26)...............159 E2
Pradelles (43)..............142 C6
Pradelles (59)...............3 E4
Pradelles-Cabardès (11).....187 F1
Pradelles-en-Val (11).......187 H2
Pradère-les-Bourquets (31)..168 D5
Prades (07).................157 F1
Prades (09).................199 G1
Prades (43).................142 A4
Prades (66).................200 C3
Prades (81).................170 A5
Prades-d'Aubrac (12)........155 E3
Prades-le-Lez (34)..........173 F4
Prades-Salars (12)..........154 D5
le Pradet (83)..............193 F5
Pradières (09)..............185 H6
Pradiers (15)...............141 E2
Pradinas (12)...............154 B5
Pradines (19)...............124 C6
Pradines (42)...............129 E1
Pradines (46)...............152 C3
Pradons (07)................157 G3
Prads-Haute-Bléone (04).....161 E5
Pragnac (19)................138 D3
Prahecq (79)................108 A4
Prailles (79)...............108 A3
Pralognan-la-Vanoise (73)...133 G5
Prâlon (21)..................85 F6
Pralong (42)................129 E4
Pranles (07)................143 G6
Pranzac (16)................122 D4
Praslay (52).................85 H2
Praslin (10).................66 B5
Prasville (28)...............62 C3
Prat (22)....................32 D3
Prat-Bonrepaux (09).........184 D5
Prato-di-Giovellina (2B)....203 E6
Prats-de-Carlux (24)........138 C5
Prats-de-Mollo-
   la-Preste (66)..........200 C5
Prats-de-Sournia (66).......199 H2
Prats-du-Périgord (24)......152 A1
Pratviel (81)...............170 A5
Pratz (39)..................117 H3
Prauthoy (52)................86 A3
Pray (41)....................79 G3
Prayols (09)................185 H6
Prayssac (46)...............152 B3
Prayssas (47)...............151 E5
Praz-sur-Arly (74)..........133 E2
le Pré-d'Auge (14)...........15 E5
Pré-en-Pail (53).............59 F1
Pré-Saint-Évroult (28).......62 C4
le Pré-Saint-Gervais (93)....42 D3
Pré-Saint-Martin (28).......62 C4
les Préaux (27)..............15 H3
Préaux (36)..................96 B4
Préaux (53)..................59 F6
Préaux (76)..................18 C3
Préaux-Bocage (14)...........14 B6
Préaux-du-Perche (61)........60 D2
Préaux-Saint-Sébastien (14)..15 H6
Prébois (38)................145 G6
Précey (50)..................35 H4
Préchac (32)................167 H3
Préchac (33)................149 G3
Préchac (65)................182 D5
Préchac-sur-Adour (32)......166 D4
Préchacq-Josbaig (64).......181 H2
Préchacq-les-Bains (40).....165 F3
Préchacq-Navarrenx (64).....181 H2
Précieux (42)...............129 E5
Précigné (72)................77 F2
Précilhon (64)..............182 A3
Précorbin (50)...............37 G1
Précy (18)...................98 B2
Précy-le-Sec (89)............83 H4
Précy-Notre-Dame (10)........66 C2
Précy-Saint-Martin (10)......66 C2
Précy-sous-Thil (21)........84 D5
Précy-sur-Marne (77).........43 F3
Précy-sur-Oise (60)..........20 C6
Précy-sur-Vrin (89)..........64 D6
Prédefin (62)................7 F1
Préfailles (44)..............73 F5
Préfontaines (45)............63 H4
Prégilbert (89)..............83 G3
Préguillac (17).............121 E3
Préhy (89)...................83 H2
Preignac (33)...............149 H2
Preignan (32)...............167 H4
Preigney (70)................87 E2
Preixan (11)................186 D4
Prémanon (39)...............118 B1
Premeaux-Prissey (21).......101 H2
Prémery (58).................98 D2
Prémesques (59)..............3 F5
Prémeyzel (01)..............131 F2
Prémian (34)................171 H6
Premières (21)..............102 B1
Prémilhat (03)..............112 B4
Prémillieu (01).............131 F1
Prémont (02).................9 E5
Prémontré (02)...............22 B3
Prendeignes (46)............153 H1
Préneron (32)...............167 F3
la Prénessaye (22)...........55 H2
Prenois (21).................85 G5
Prénouvellon (41)............62 C6
Prénovel (39)...............117 H2
Prény (54)...................48 B3
Préporché (58)..............100 A4
Prépotin (61)................40 A6
les Prés (26)...............159 F3
Présailles (43).............142 D5
Préseau (59).................9 F2
Présentevillers (25)........88 C4
Préserville (31)............169 H6
Présilly (39)...............117 G2
Présilly (74)...............118 A5
Presle (73).................132 B5
Presles (14).................37 H2
Presles (38)................145 E3
Presles (95).................42 C1
Presles-en-Brie (77).........43 G5
Presles-et-Boves (02).......22 C5
Presles-et-Thierny (02)......22 C4
Presly (18)..................81 G6
Presnoy (45).................63 G6
Pressac (86)................109 F5
Pressagny-l'Orgueilleux (27)..41 F1
Pressiat (01)...............117 E3
Pressignac (16).............123 F3
Pressignac-Vicq (24)........137 F5
Pressigny (52)...............86 D2
Pressigny (79)...............93 G5
Pressigny-les-Pins (45)......63 H5
Pressins (38)...............131 E4
Pressy (62)..................7 G1
Pressy-sous-Dondin (71).....115 H2
la Prétière (25).............88 B5
Pretin (39).................103 F4
Prétot-Sainte-Suzanne (50)...12 D5
Prétot-Vicquemare (76).......17 F3

Prétreville (14).............15 F6
Préty (71)..................116 B2
Pretz-en-Argonne (55)........47 E3
Preuilly (18)................97 F2
Preuilly-la-Ville (36).......95 H5
Preuilly-sur-Claise (37).....95 G4
Preures (62).................6 D2
Preuschdorf (67).............51 E2
Preuseville (76).............19 H2
Preutin-Higny (54)...........25 H5
Preux-au-Bois (59)...........9 G3
Preux-au-Sart (59)...........9 G2
Préval (72)..................60 D3
Prévelles (72)...............60 C4
Prévenchères (48)...........156 D3
Préveranges (18)............112 A3
Prévessin-Moëns (01)........118 B4
la Prévière (49).............76 A2
Prévillers (60)..............20 A3
Prévinquières (12)..........154 B4
Prévocourt (57)..............49 E3
Prey (27)....................41 E3
Prey (88)....................70 C3
Preyssac-d'Excideuil (24)...138 A1
Prez (08)....................23 G2
Prez-sous-Lafauche (52)......68 C3
Priaires (79)...............107 G4
Priay (01)..................117 F6
Priez (02)...................44 A1
Prignac (17)................121 G2
Prignac-en-Médoc (33).......120 C6
Prignac-et-Marcamps (33)....135 F4
Prigonrieux (24)............136 D5
Primarette (38).............130 B6
Primelin (29)................52 C2
Primelles (18)...............97 F4
Prin-Deyrançon (79).........107 G4
Prinçay (86).................94 B4
Princé (35)..................58 B3
Pringy (51)..................46 B3
Pringy (74).................132 A1
Pringy (77)..................63 H1
Prinquiau (44)...............74 A3
Prinsuéjols (48)............155 G2
Printzheim (67)..............50 C4
Prisces (02).................23 E1
Prisches (59)................9 H4
Prissac (36)................110 C2
Prissé (71).................116 B4
Prissé-la-Charrière (79)....107 G5
Privas (07).................157 H1
Privezac (12)...............153 H4
Prix-lès-Mézières (08).......24 A1
Priziac (56).................54 C2
Prizy (71)..................115 F3
la Proiselière-et-Langle (70)..88 A1
Proissans (24)...............138 B4
Proisy (02)..................23 F1
Proix (02)...................23 E2
Projan (32).................166 C4
Promilhanes (46)............153 F4
Prompsat (63)...............126 C3
Prondines (63)..............126 C3
Pronleroy (60)...............20 D4
Pronville (62)...............8 C3
Propiac (26)................158 D5
Propières (69)..............115 G5
Propriano (2A)..............206 D3
Prosnes (51).................45 H1
Prouais (28).................41 G5
Prouilly (51)................22 D5
Proupiary (31)..............184 C3
Proussy (14).................38 B3
Prouvais (02)................23 E4
Prouville (80)...............7 F4
Prouvy (59)..................9 F2
Prouzel (80).................20 B1
Provemont (27)...............19 G6
Provenchère (25).............88 B6
Provenchère (70).............87 H2
Provenchères-
   lès-Darney (88).........69 E4
Provenchères-sur-Fave (88)...70 D2
Provenchères-sur-Meuse (52)..86 D1
Provency (89)...............84 A5
Proverville (10).............66 D4
Proveysieux (38)............145 G2
Provin (59)..................3 E6
Provins (77).................64 D1
Proviseux-et-Plesnoy (02)....23 E4
Proyart (80).................8 A6
Prudemanche (28).............41 E5
Prudhomat (46)..............139 E5
Prugnanes (66)..............200 C1
Prugny (10)..................66 A4
Pruillé (49).................76 D3
Pruillé-le-Chétif (72).......60 A6
Pruillé-l'Éguillé (72).......78 C1
Pruines (12)................154 B3
Prunay (51)..................45 H1
Prunay-Belleville (10).......65 H2
Prunay-Cassereau (41)........79 F3
Prunay-en-Yvelines (78)......62 D2
Prunay-le-Gillon (28)........62 C2
Prunay-le-Temple (78)........41 G4
Prunay-sur-Essonne (91)......63 G4
Prunelli-di-Casacconi (2B)..203 F5
Prunelli-di-Fiumorbo (2B)...205 F5
Prunet (07).................157 F2
Prunet (15).................140 B5
Prunet (31).................170 A6
Prunet-et-Belpuig (66)......200 C3
Prunières (05)..............160 D3
Prunières (38)..............145 G6
Prunières (48)..............141 F6
Pruniers (36)................97 E5
Pruniers-en-Sologne (41).....96 D1
Pruno (2B)..................203 G6
Prunoy (89)..................82 D1
Prusly-sur-Ource (21)........85 E1
Pruzilly (71)...............116 A4
Puberg (67)..................50 B3
Publy (39)..................117 G1
Puceul (44)..................74 C2
le Puch (09)................199 H2
Puch-d'Agenais (47).........150 C4
Puchay (27)..................19 F6
Puchevillers (80)............7 G4
le Puech (34)...............172 C5
Puéchabon (34)..............173 E3
Puéchoursi (81).............170 A6
Puechredon (30).............173 H3
Puellemontier (52)...........67 E2
Puessans (25)................87 H5
le Puget (34)...............173 H6
Puget (84)..................175 H4
Puget-Rostang (06)..........179 E2
Puget-sur-Argens (83).......178 B6
Puget-Théniers (06).........178 D2
Puget-Ville (83)............192 D4
Pugey (25)..................103 F1
Pugieu (01).................131 F2
Puginier (11)...............186 B3
Pugnac (33).................135 F3
Pugny (79)..................107 H4
Pugny-Chatenod (73).........132 A3
Puichéric (11)..............187 G3
le Puid (88).................70 D1
Puihardy (79)...............107 H2
Puilacher (34)..............173 E5
Puilaurens (11).............200 B2
Puilboreau (17).............106 D4
Puilly-et-Charbeaux (08).....24 D2
Puimichel (04)..............177 F2
Puimisson (34)..............188 C1
Puimoisson (04).............177 F2
la Puisaye (28)..............40 D6
Puiseaux (45)................63 G4
Puiselet-le-Marais (91)......63 F3
Puisenval (76)...............19 H2
le Puiset (28)...............62 D4
le Puiset-Doré (49)..........75 G5
Puiseux (08).................24 B4
Puiseux (28).................41 F5
Puiseux-en-Bray (60).........19 H4
Puiseux-en-France (95).......43 E2
Puiseux-en-Retz (02).........21 H5
Puiseux-le-Hauberger (60)....20 B6
Puiseux-Pontoise (95).......42 B2
Puisieulx (51)...............45 G1
Puisieux (62)................8 A4
Puisieux (77)................43 G2

Puisieux-et-Clanlieu (02)....9 G6
Puissalicon (34)............188 C1
Puisseguin (33).............136 A4
Puisserguier (34)...........188 B2
Puits (71)...................84 D2
Puits-et-Nuisement (10)......66 D4
Puits-la-Vallée (60).........20 B3
Puivert (11)................186 C6
Pujaudran (32)..............168 D5
Pujaut (30).................174 D2
Pujo (65)...................183 E2
Pujo-le-Plan (40)...........166 B3
les Pujols (09).............185 H4
Pujols (33).................135 H6
Pujols (47).................151 F4
Pujols-sur-Ciron (33).......149 G2
le Puley (71)...............101 E6
Puligny-Montrachet (21).....101 G4
Pullay (27)..................40 C5
Pulligny (54)................48 C6
Pulney (54)..................69 E2
Pulnoy (54)..................48 D5
Pulvérières (63)............126 C2
Pulversheim (68).............89 F1
Punchy (80)..................8 B6
Punerot (88).................68 D2
Puntous (65)................183 H2
Pupillin (39)...............103 E4
Pure (08)....................24 D2
Purgerot (70)................87 F2
Pusey (70)...................87 F3
Pusignan (69)...............130 C3
Pussay (91)..................63 E3
Pussigny (37)................94 D3
Pusy-et-Épenoux (70).........87 F3
Putanges-Pont-Écrepin (61)...38 D4
Puteaux (92).................42 C4
Putot-en-Auge (14)...........14 D4
Putot-en-Bessin (14).........14 A5
Puttelange-aux-Lacs (57).....49 H1
Puttelange-lès-Thionville (57)..26 C2
Puttigny (57)................49 F3
Puxe (54)....................48 A3
Puxieux (54).................48 A3
le Puy (25)..................87 G6
le Puy (33).................150 B1
Puy-d'Arnac (19)............138 D4
Puy-de-Serre (85)...........107 F1
Puy-du-Lac (17).............121 E1
le Puy-en-Velay (43)........142 C4
Puy-Guillaume (63)..........127 H1
Puy-l'Évêque (46)...........152 A3
Puy-Malsignat (23)..........112 A6
le Puy-Notre-Dame (49).......93 G2
Puy-Saint-André (05)........147 E5
Puy-Saint-Eusèbe (05).......160 D3
Puy-Saint-Gulmier (63)......126 C3
Puy-Saint-Martin (26).......158 C2
Puy-Saint-Pierre (05).......147 E5
Puy-Saint-Vincent (05)......146 D5
le Puy-
   Sainte-Réparade (13)....176 A5
Puy-Sanières (05)...........161 E3
Puybarban (33)..............150 A2
Puybegon (81)...............170 A4
Puybrun (46)................139 E5
Puycalvel (81)..............170 B5
Puycasquier (32)............168 A3
Puycelci (81)...............169 H2
Puycornet (82)..............152 C6
Puydaniel (31)..............185 F2
Puydarrieux (65)............183 G2
la Puye (86)................109 H1
Puygaillard-
   de-Lomagne (82).........168 B2
Puygaillard-de-Quercy (82)..169 G1
Puygouzon (81)..............170 C3
Puygros (73)................132 A4
Puyjourdes (46).............153 F4
Puylagarde (82).............153 E5
Puylaroque (82).............152 D5
Puylaurens (81).............170 B6
Puylausic (32)..............168 C6
Puymangou (24)..............136 B3
Puymaurin (31)..............184 B2
Puyméras (84)...............158 D5
Puymiclan (47)..............150 D3
Puymirol (47)...............151 G6
Puymoyen (16)...............122 B4
Puynormand (33).............136 A4
Puyol-Cazalet (40)..........166 A5
Puyoô (64)..................165 F6
Puyravault (17).............107 E5
Puyravault (85).............106 D3
Puyréaux (16)...............122 C2
Puyrenier (24)..............122 D5
Puyrolland (17).............107 F5
Puységur (32)...............167 H4
Puysségur (31)..............168 D3
Puysserampion (47)..........150 D3
Puyvalador (66).............199 H3
Puyvert (84)................175 H4
Puzeaux (80).................8 B6
Puzieux (57).................48 D2
Puzieux (88).................69 F2
Py (66).....................200 B4
la Pyle (27).................18 B6
Pys (80).....................8 B4

Q

Quaëdypre (59)...............2 C2
Quaix-en-Chartreuse (38)....145 G2
Quantilly (18)...............97 H1
Quarante (34)...............188 B2
Quarouble (59)...............9 G1
Quarré-les-Tombes (89)......84 A4
la Quarte (70)...............86 D2
le Quartier (63)............113 E6
Quasquara (2A)..............205 E6
Quatre-Champs (08)...........24 B4
les Quatre-Routes-
   du-Lot (46).............138 D4
Quatremare (27)..............18 D6
Quatzenheim (67).............50 D5
Quéant (62)..................8 C3
Queaux (86).................109 G3
Québriac (35)................35 E6
Quédillac (35)...............56 C1
Queige (73).................132 D3
Quelaines-Saint-Gault (53)...58 C6
Quelmes (62).................2 A4
Quelneuc (56)................56 C5
Quéménéven (29)..............53 F1
Quemigny-Poisot (21)........101 G1
Quemigny-sur-Seine (21)......85 E3
Quemper-Guézennec (22).......33 E3
Quemperven (22)..............32 D3
Quend (80)...................6 B3
Quenne (89)..................83 G2
Quenoche (70)................87 G4
Quenza (2A).................207 F2
Quercamps (62)...............2 A4
Quercitello (2B)............203 F6
Quérénaing (59)..............9 F2
Quérigut (09)...............199 H2
Querqueville (50)...........12 C1
Querré (49)..................76 D2
Querrien (29)................54 B3
Querrieu (80)................7 H5
Quers (70)...................87 H2
Quesmy (60)..................21 F3
le Quesne (80)...............7 E6
le Quesnel (80)..............20 D2
le Quesnel-Aubry (60)........20 C4
le Quesnoy (59)..............9 G3
le Quesnoy-en-Artois (62)....7 E3
Quesnoy-le-Montant (80)......6 D4
Quesnoy-sur-Airaines (80)....7 F5
Quesnoy-sur-Deûle (59).......3 F4
Quesques (62)................2 A5
Quessigny (27)...............41 F3
Quessoy (22).................33 G5
Questembert (56).............56 A6
Questrecques (62)............1 F5

Quet-en-Beaumont (38)......145 H5
Quetigny (21)......85 H6
Quettehou (50)......13 E2
Quettetot (50)......12 C3
Quetteville (14)......15 F3
Quettreville-sur-Sienne (50)......35 G1
Queudes (51)......44 D6
la Queue-en-Brie (94)......43 E4
la Queue-les-Yvelines (78)......41 H4
Queuille (63)......126 D1
Quevauvillers (80)......20 B1
Quéven (56)......54 C5
Quévert (34)......34 C5
Quevillon (76)......17 F6
Quevilloncourt (54)......69 F1
Quévreville-la-Poterie (76)......18 D5
Queyrac (33)......120 C6
Queyrières (43)......142 D3
Queyssac (24)......137 E5
Queyssac-les-Vignes (19)......139 E4
Quézac (15)......185 H1
Quézac (48)......156 A4
Quiberon (56)......72 B2
Quiberville (76)......17 F2
Quibou (50)......37 F1
Quié (09)......199 E1
Quiers (77)......63 G1
Quiers-sur-Bézonde (45)......63 G6
Quiéry-la-Motte (62)......8 C2
Quiéry (02)......21 H3
Quiestède (62)......2 B4
Quiévelon (59)......10 B3
Quièvrechain (59)......9 G1
Quièvrecourt (76)......19 E1
Quiévy (59)......9 F3
Quilen (62)......1 G6
Quillan (11)......186 D6
Quilleboeuf-sur-Seine (27)......15 H2
le Quillio (22)......55 F1
Quilly (08)......24 A4
Quilly (44)......74 A3
Quily (56)......56 A4
Quimper (29)......53 F3
Quimperlé (29)......54 B4
Quincampoix (76)......18 A4
Quincampoix-Fleuzy (60)......19 G1
Quincay (86)......108 D1
Quincerot (21)......84 C3
Quincerot (89)......66 B6
Quincey (21)......101 H2
Quincey (70)......87 G3
Quincié-en-Beaujolais (69)......116 A5
Quincieu (38)......145 E1
Quincieux (69)......130 A2
Quincy (18)......97 E2
Quincy-Basse (02)......22 A4
Quincy-Landzécourt (55)......25 E4
Quincy-le-Vicomte (21)......84 C4
Quincy-sous-le-Mont (02)......22 B5
Quincy-sous-Sénart (91)......43 E5
Quincy-Voisins (77)......43 G3
Quingey (25)......103 F2
Quinquempoix (60)......20 C3
Quins (12)......154 B5
Quinsac (24)......123 F6
Quinsac (33)......135 F6
Quinson (04)......177 E4
Quinssaines (03)......112 C4
Quint-Fonsegrives (31)......169 F5
Quintal (74)......132 A2
la Quinte (72)......59 H5
Quintenas (07)......143 H2
Quintenic (22)......34 A4
Quintigny (39)......102 D5
Quintillan (11)......187 G5
Quintin (22)......33 F5
le Quiou (22)......34 D6
Quirbajou (11)......200 A1
le Quiou-le-Sec (80)......20 C2
Quissac (30)......173 G3
Quissac (46)......153 E2
Quistinic (56)......54 D4
Quittebeuf (27)......40 D1
Quivières (80)......21 G1
Quœux-Haut-Maïnil (62)......7 F2

R

Rabastens (81)......169 H3
Rabastens-de-Bigorre (65)......183 F1
Rabat-les-
Trois-Seigneurs (09)......185 G6
la Rabatelière (85)......91 H3
Rablay-sur-Layon (49)......76 D6
Rabodanges (61)......38 C4
Rabou (05)......160 B2
Rabouillet (66)......200 C2
Racécourt (88)......69 F3
Rachecourt-sur-Marne (52)......67 H1
Rachecourt-Suzémont (52)......67 G2
Râches (59)......8 D1
Racines (10)......65 H5
la Racineuse (71)......102 A5
Racquinghem (62)......2 B4
Racrange (57)......49 F3
Raddon-et-Chapendu (70)......88 A1
Radenac (56)......55 G3
Radepont (27)......19 E5
Radinghem (62)......2 A6
Radinghem-en-Weppes (59)......3 E5
Radon (61)......60 A1
Radonvilliers (10)......66 D3
Raedersdorf (68)......89 F4
Raedersheim (68)......71 F6
Raffetot (76)......15 H1
Rageade (15)......141 G3
Rahart (41)......79 G1
Rahay (72)......78 D1
Rahling (57)......28 A6
Rahon (25)......88 B6
Rahon (39)......102 C3
Rai (61)......40 A4
Raids (50)......12 D6
Raillencourt-Sainte-Olle (59)......8 D3
Railleu (66)......200 A3
Raillicourt (08)......24 A2
Raillimont (08)......23 F2
Raimbeaucourt (59)......8 D1
Rainans (39)......102 C2
Raincheval (80)......7 G4
Raincourt (70)......87 E1
le Raincy (93)......43 E3
Rainfreville (76)......17 F3
Rainneville (80)......7 H5
Rainville (88)......69 E2
Rainvillers (60)......20 A4
les Rairies (49)......77 G3
Raissac (09)......186 A6
Raissac-d'Aude (11)......187 H3
Raissac-sur-Lampy (11)......186 D3
Raival (55)......47 F3
Raix (16)......108 C6
Raizeux (78)......41 G6
Ramasse (01)......117 E5
Ramatuelle (83)......194 B4
Rambaud (05)......160 C2
Rambervillers (88)......70 B2
Rambluzin-
et-Benoîte-Vaux (55)......47 F2
Rambouillet (78)......41 H6
Rambucourt (55)......48 A4
Rambures (80)......6 C5
Ramburelles (80)......6 C5
Ramecourt (62)......7 G2
Ramecourt (88)......69 F3
Ramecourt (02)......9 E5
Ramillies (59)......8 D3
Rammersmatt (68)......89 E1
Ramonchamp (88)......70 B6
Ramonville-Saint-Agne (31)......169 F5
Ramoulu (45)......63 F4
Ramous (64)......165 H5
Ramousies (59)......10 A4
Ramouzens (32)......167 E3

Rampan (50)......13 F6
Rampieux (24)......151 G1
Rampillon (77)......64 C1
Rampoux (46)......152 C2
Rancé (01)......130 A1
Rancenay (25)......103 F1
Rances (08)......11 F4
Ranchal (39)......115 G5
Ranchot (39)......103 E2
Ranchy (14)......13 H5
Rancogne (16)......122 D3
Rancon (87)......110 B5
Ranconnières (68)......68 C6
Rancourt (80)......8 C5
Rancourt (88)......69 F3
Rancourt-sur-Ornain (55)......46 D4
Rancy (71)......116 D1
Randan (63)......127 G1
Randens (73)......132 C5
Randevillers (25)......88 A6
Randonnai (61)......40 A5
Rânes (61)......38 D5
Rang (25)......88 B5
Rang-du-Fliers (62)......6 C1
Rangecourt (52)......68 C5
Rangen (67)......50 C5
Ranguevaux (57)......26 B4
Rannée (35)......57 H4
Rans (39)......103 E2
Ransart (62)......8 A3
Ranspach (68)......70 D6
Ranspach-le-Bas (68)......89 G3
Ranspach-le-Haut (68)......89 G3
Rantechaux (25)......104 A2
Rantigny (60)......20 D5
Ranton (86)......93 H3
Rantzwiller (68)......89 G2
Ranville (14)......14 C4
Ranville-Breuillaud (16)......122 A1
Ranzevelle (70)......69 F6
Ranzières (55)......47 G2
Raon-aux-Bois (88)......70 A5
Raon-lès-Leau (54)......71 G1
Raon-l'Étape (88)......70 C2
Raon-sur-Plaine (88)......50 A6
Rapaggio (2B)......205 G1
Rapale (2B)......203 F5
Rapey (88)......69 G3
Rapilly (14)......38 C3
Rapsécourt (51)......46 C2
Raray (60)......21 E6
Rarécourt (55)......47 E2
Rasiguères (66)......200 D1
Raslay (86)......93 H2
Rasteau (84)......158 C5
Ratenelle (71)......116 C2
Ratières (26)......144 B2
Ratte (71)......117 E1
Rattwiller (67)......50 B2
Raucoules (43)......143 E2
Raucourt (54)......48 D3
Raucourt-au-Bois (59)......9 G3
Raulhac (15)......140 B5
Rauret (43)......142 B6
Rauville-la-Bigot (50)......12 C3
Rauville-la-Place (50)......12 D4
Rauwiller (67)......50 A4
Rauzan (33)......135 H6
Raveau (58)......98 D2
Ravel (63)......127 G3
Ravenel (60)......20 D4
Ravenoville (50)......13 E3
Raves (88)......70 D3
Ravières (89)......84 B2
Ravigny (53)......59 H1
Raville (57)......49 E1
Raville-sur-Sânon (54)......49 E5
Ravilloles (39)......117 H2
la Ravoire (73)......131 H5
Ray-sur-Saône (70)......87 E3
Raye-sur-Authie (62)......7 E2
Rayet (47)......151 G1
Raymond (18)......98 A4
Raynans (25)......88 C4
Rayol-Canadel-sur-Mer (83)......194 A5
Rayssac (81)......170 D3
Razac-de-Saussignac (24)......136 C6
Razac-d'Eymet (24)......151 E1
Razac-sur-l'Isle (24)......137 E2
Raze (70)......87 F3
Razecueillé (31)......184 B5
Razengues (32)......168 C5
Razès (87)......110 C6
Razimet (47)......150 C4
Razines (37)......94 B4
Réal (66)......200 A4
Réalcamp (76)......6 C6
Réallon (05)......160 D2
Réalmont (81)......170 C4
Réalville (82)......169 F1
Réans (32)......166 D3
Réau (77)......43 E6
Réaumont (38)......131 F6
Réaumur (85)......92 C5
Réauville (26)......158 B3
Réaux (17)......121 G5
Rebais (77)......44 A4
Rebecques (62)......2 B5
Rébénacq (64)......182 B3
Rebergues (62)......1 H4
Rebets (76)......19 E3
Rebeuville (88)......68 D2
Rebigue (31)......169 F6
Rebréchien (45)......63 E6
Rebreuve-Ranchicourt (62)......7 H1
Rebreuve-sur-Canche (62)......7 G2
Rebreuviette (62)......7 G2
Recanoz (39)......102 C5
Recey-sur-Ource (21)......85 G2
Réchésy (90)......89 G4
Réchicourt-la-Petite (54)......49 F4
Réchicourt-le-Château (57)......49 G5
Récicourt (55)......47 E1
Réclainville (28)......62 C3
Reclesne (71)......100 C3
Reclinghem (62)......2 A5
Réclonville (54)......49 G6
Recloses (77)......64 A3
Recologne (25)......87 F6
Recologne (70)......86 D4
Recologne-lès-Rioz (70)......87 F4
Recoubeau-Jansac (26)......159 F1
Recoules-d'Aubrac (48)......155 F1
Recoules-de-Fumas (48)......155 G4
Recoules-Prévinquières (12)......155 E4
Récourt (62)......8 C3
Récourt-le-Creux (55)......47 G2
Recouvrance (90)......88 D3
le Recoux (48)......155 F5
Recques-sur-Course (62)......1 G6
Recques-sur-Hem (62)......2 A3
Recquignies (59)......10 A2
le Reculey (14)......37 H3
Reculfoz (25)......103 G6
Recurt (65)......183 H3
Recy (51)......45 H3
Rédange (57)......26 A2
Rédené (29)......54 B4
Redessan (30)......174 C3
Réding (57)......50 A4
Redon (35)......73 H1
la Redorte (11)......187 G3
Redortiers (04)......176 A2
Réez-Fosse-Martin (60)......43 H1
Reffannes (79)......108 B2
Reffroy (55)......47 F6
Reffuveille (50)......37 F5
Régades (31)......184 B3
Régat (09)......186 A4
Regnauville (62)......7 E2
Régnéville-sur-Mer (50)......36 D2
Régnéville-sur-Meuse (55)......25 E6
Regney (88)......69 G3
Régnié-Durette (69)......116 A5

Regnière-Écluse (80)......6 D2
Regniowez (08)......10 D5
Regny (02)......22 B1
Régny (42)......129 E1
la Regrippière (44)......75 F5
Réguiny (56)......55 G3
Réguisheim (68)......71 F6
Régusse (83)......177 F4
Rehaincourt (88)......70 A2
Rehainviller (54)......49 E6
Rehaupal (88)......70 B4
Reherrey (54)......49 H6
Réhon (54)......25 H3
Reichsfeld (67)......71 F2
Reichshoffen (67)......50 D2
Reichstett (67)......51 E5
Reignac (16)......121 H6
Reignac (33)......135 F2
Reignac-sur-Indre (37)......95 F1
Reignat (63)......127 G3
Reignier (63)......118 C5
Reigny (18)......112 B1
Reilhac (15)......140 A4
Reilhac (46)......153 E1
Reilhaguet (46)......138 C6
Reilhanette (26)......159 F6
Reillanne (04)......176 B3
Reillon (54)......49 G6
Reilly (60)......19 H6
Reims (51)......23 H6
Reims-la-Brûlée (51)......46 B5
Reinhardsmunster (67)......50 B5
Reiningue (68)......89 F2
Reipertswiller (67)......50 C2
Reithouse (39)......117 G1
Réjaumont (32)......167 H3
Réjaumont (65)......183 H3
Relanges (88)......69 F4
Relans (39)......102 C5
le Relecq-Kerhuon (29)......31 E4
Relevant (01)......116 C6
Rely (62)......2 B5
Remaisnil (80)......7 F3
Rémalard (61)......61 E2
Remaucourt (02)......9 E6
la Remaudière (44)......75 E5
Remaugies (80)......21 E3
Remauville (77)......64 B4
Rembercourt-
Sommaisne (55)......46 D3
Rembercourt-sur-Mad (54)......48 B2
Rémécourt (60)......20 D5
Rémelfang (57)......26 D4
Rémelfing (57)......27 H5
Rémeling (57)......26 D2
Remennecourt (55)......46 D4
Remenoville (54)......69 H1
Rémérangles (60)......20 C4
Réméréville (54)......49 E5
Rémering (57)......27 E4
Rémering-
lès-Puttelange (57)......49 H2
Remicourt (51)......46 C3
Remicourt (88)......69 F3
Remiencourt (80)......20 D2
Remies (02)......22 B2
Remigny (02)......22 A2
Remigny (71)......101 F4
Remilly (57)......49 E2
Remilly (58)......100 A5
Remilly-Aillicourt (08)......24 C2
Remilly-en-Montagne (21)......85 F6
Remilly-les-Pothées (08)......23 H1
Remilly-sur-Lozon (50)......13 E6
Remilly-sur-Tille (21)......86 A6
Remilly-Wirquin (62)......2 A5
Réminiac (56)......56 B5
Remiremont (88)......70 B5
Remoiville (55)......25 F4
Remollon (05)......160 C3
Remomeix (88)......70 D3
Remoncourt (54)......49 G5
Remoncourt (88)......69 F2
Rémondans-Vaivre (25)......88 C5
Remoray-Boujeons (25)......103 H5
Remouillé (44)......91 G1
Remoulins (30)......174 C2
Removille (88)......69 E2
Rempnat (87)......125 F4
la Remuée (76)......15 G1
Remungol (56)......55 F3
Rémuzat (26)......159 E4
Rémy (60)......21 E4
Rémy (62)......8 C3
Renac (35)......56 D6
Renage (38)......145 E1
Renaison (42)......114 D6
Renansart (02)......22 B2
Renaucourt (70)......86 D3
la Renaudie (63)......128 B3
la Renaudière (49)......75 F6
Renauvoid (88)......69 H4
Renay (41)......79 G1
Renazé (53)......76 A1
Rencurel (38)......145 E3
René (72)......60 B3
Renédale (25)......103 H3
Renescure (59)......2 B4
Renève (21)......86 B5
Réning (57)......49 G3
Rennemoulin (78)......42 B4
Rennepont (52)......67 F4
Rennes (35)......57 F3
Rennes-en-Grenouilles (53)......59 F1
Rennes-le-Château (11)......186 D6
Rennes-les-Bains (11)......187 E6
Rennes-sur-Loure (35)......103 F3
Renneval (02)......23 E2
Renneville (08)......23 E2
Renneville (27)......19 E4
Renneville (31)......186 A2
Renno (2A)......204 C3
Renoued (61)......38 D6
Rentières (63)......127 F6
Renty (62)......1 H5
Renung (40)......166 B4
Renwez (08)......11 E6
la Réole (33)......150 B2
la Réorthe (85)......92 A6
Réotier (05)......161 F1
Repaix (54)......49 G5
la Répara-Auriples (26)......158 C1
Réparsac (16)......121 H3
Repel (88)......69 E2
Repentigny (14)......15 E4
le Reposoir (74)......119 E6
les Repôts (39)......102 C6
Reppe (90)......88 D2
Requeil (72)......78 A2
Réquista (12)......171 E1
Résenlieu (61)......39 G4
la Résie-Saint-Martin (70)......86 D6
Résigny (02)......23 F1
Resson (55)......47 E4
Ressons-l'Abbaye (60)......20 B5
Ressons-le-Long (02)......21 H5
Ressons-sur-Matz (60)......21 E3
les Ressuintes (28)......40 C6
Restigné (37)......78 A6
Restinclières (34)......173 G4
le Retail (79)......107 H1
Reterre (23)......112 C6
Rétaud (17)......121 E3
Rethel (08)......23 G4
Retheuil (02)......21 H6
Rethondes (60)......21 F4
Rethonvillers (80)......21 F1
Retiers (35)......57 G4
Retjons (40)......149 G6
Rétonval (76)......19 F1
Retournac (43)......142 D2
Retschwiller (67)......51 F2
Rettel (57)......26 C2
Rety (62)......1 G4
Retzwiller (68)......89 E3

Reugney (25)......103 H3
Reugny (03)......112 D2
Reugny (37)......79 F5
Reuil (51)......45 E2
Reuil-en-Brie (77)......44 A3
Reuil-sur-Brêche (60)......20 B3
Reuilly (27)......41 E2
Reuilly (36)......97 E3
Reuilly-Sauvigny (02)......44 C2
Reulle-Vergy (21)......101 G2
la Réunion (47)......150 B4
Reutenbourg (67)......50 C4
Reuves (51)......45 E4
Reuville (76)......17 F3
Réveillon (51)......44 C4
Réveillon (61)......60 D1
Revel (31)......186 C1
Revel (38)......145 H2
Revel-Tourdan (38)......130 B6
Revens (30)......172 B1
Reventin-Vaugris (38)......130 A6
Revercourt (28)......40 D5
Revest-des-Brousses (04)......176 B2
Revest-du-Bion (04)......176 B1
le Revest-les-Eaux (83)......193 E5
Revest-les-Roches (06)......195 E1
Revest-Saint-Martin (04)......176 C1
Reviers (14)......14 B3
Revigny (39)......102 D6
Revigny-sur-Ornain (55)......46 D4
Réville (50)......13 E2
Réville-aux-Bois (55)......25 E5
Révillon (02)......22 D5
Revin (08)......11 E5
Revonnas (01)......117 E5
Rexpoède (59)......2 C2
Reyersviller (57)......50 C1
Reygade (19)......139 F4
Reynel (52)......68 B3
Reynès (66)......200 D5
Reyniès (82)......169 F2
Reyrevignes (46)......153 F2
Reyrieux (01)......130 A1
Reyssouze (01)......116 C3
Reyvroz (74)......119 E2
Rezay (18)......97 F6
Rézentières (15)......141 F3
Rezonville (57)......26 A5
Rezza (2A)......204 D4
Rhèges (10)......66 A1
le Rheu (35)......57 E3
Rhinau (67)......71 H2
Rhodes (57)......49 H4
Rhodon (41)......79 H2
Rhuis (60)......21 E5
Ri (61)......38 D4
Ria-Sirach (66)......200 C3
Riaillé (44)......75 F3
le Rialet (81)......171 E6
Rians (18)......98 A2
Rians (83)......192 D1
Riantec (56)......54 C5
Riaucourt (52)......67 H4
Riaville (55)......47 H1
Ribagnac (24)......136 D6
Ribaute (11)......187 G4
Ribaute-les-Tavernes (30)......173 H1
le Ribay (53)......59 F2
Ribeaucourt (55)......68 B1
Ribeaucourt (80)......7 F4
Ribeauville (02)......22 D1
Ribeauvillé (68)......71 F3
Ribécourt-Dreslincourt (60)......21 F4
Ribécourt-la-Tour (59)......8 D4
Ribemont (02)......22 B1
Ribemont-sur-Ancre (80)......7 H5
Ribennes (48)......155 H2
Ribérac (24)......136 D2
Ribes (07)......157 F3
Ribeyret (05)......159 G3
Ribiers (05)......160 A5
Ribouisse (11)......186 B3
Ribute (11)......187 G4
Ricarville (76)......17 E4
Ricarville-du-Val (76)......17 H3
Ricaud (11)......186 B2
Ricaud (65)......183 F3
les Riceys (10)......66 C6
la Richardais (35)......36 A5
Richardménil (54)......48 C6
Richarville (91)......63 E1
la Riche (37)......78 D5
Riché (57)......49 E3
Richebourg (52)......67 H5
Richebourg (62)......2 D5
Richebourg (78)......41 G3
Richecourt (55)......48 A3
Richelieu (37)......94 B3
Richeling (57)......49 H2
Richemont (57)......26 B4
Richemont (76)......19 F2
Richerenches (84)......158 C4
Richeval (57)......49 H5
Richeville (27)......19 F6
Richtolsheim (67)......71 G3
Richwiller (68)......89 F2
Ricourt (32)......167 E5
Ricquebourg (60)......21 E3
Riec-sur-Belon (29)......54 A4
Riedisheim (68)......89 F2
Riedseltz (67)......51 F2
Riedwihr (68)......71 G4
Riel-les-Eaux (21)......67 E6
Riencourt (80)......7 G6
Riencourt-lès-Bapaume (62)......8 B4
Riencourt-lès-Cagnicourt (62)......8 C3
Riervescemont (90)......88 C2
Riespach (68)......89 F3
Rieucazé (31)......184 B4
Rieucros (09)......186 A4
Rieulay (59)......9 E2
Rieumajou (31)......186 A1
Rieumes (31)......184 D1
Rieupeyroux (12)......154 A4
Rieussec (34)......187 G2
Rieutort-de-Randon (48)......156 A2
Rieux-en-Val (11)......187 F4
Rieux-Minervois (11)......187 F3
Riez (04)......177 E3
Rigarda (66)......200 C3
Rigaud (06)......194 C1
Rignac (12)......154 A4
Rignac (46)......138 D6
Rigney (25)......87 G5
Rignieux-le-Franc (01)......130 C1
Rignosot (25)......87 H5
Rignovelle (70)......88 A2
Rigny (70)......86 D5
Rigny-la-Nonneuse (10)......65 G2
Rigny-la-Salle (55)......47 G5
Rigny-le-Ferron (10)......65 G4
Rigny-Saint-Martin (55)......48 A6
Rigny-sur-Arroux (71)......115 E2
Rigny-Ussé (37)......94 B1
Riguepeu (32)......167 F5
Rilhac-Lastours (87)......124 A4
Rilhac-Rancon (87)......124 B2
Rilhac-Treignac (19)......124 D5
Rilhac-Xaintrie (19)......139 H3
Rillans (25)......87 H5
Rillé (37)......78 B5
Rilleux-la-Pape (69)......130 B2
Rilly-la-Montagne (51)......45 F1
Rilly-Sainte-Syre (10)......66 A2
Rilly-sur-Aisne (08)......24 A4
Rilly-sur-Loire (41)......79 G5
Rilly-sur-Vienne (37)......94 D3

Rimaucourt (52)......68 B3
Rimbach-
près-Guebwiller (68)......71 E6
Rimbach-
près-Masevaux (68)......88 D1
Rimbachzell (68)......71 E6
Rimbez-et-Baudiets (40)......167 E1
Rimboval (62)......1 H6
Rimeize (48)......141 G6
Rimling (57)......28 A5
Rimogne (08)......10 D6
Rimon-et-Savel (26)......159 E1
Rimondeix (23)......111 H5
Rimons (33)......150 B1
Rimont (09)......185 F5
Rimou (35)......35 F6
Rimplas (06)......162 C6
Rimsdorf (67)......50 A2
Ringeldorf (67)......50 D3
Ringendorf (67)......50 D3
Rinxent (62)......1 F3
Riocaud (33)......136 C6
Riolas (31)......184 C2
Riols (34)......171 G6
le Riols (81)......153 G6
Riom (63)......127 F2
Riom-ès-Montagnes (15)......140 C2
Rioms (35)......159 F5
Riorges (42)......115 E6
Riotord (43)......143 F2
Rioux (17)......121 E4
Rioux-Martin (16)......136 A2
Rioz (70)......87 F5
Riquewihr (68)......71 F4
Ris (63)......128 A1
Ris (65)......183 G6
Ris-Orangis (91)......42 D6
Riscle (32)......166 D4
Risoul (05)......161 F1
Ristolas (05)......147 G6
Rittershoffen (67)......51 F2
Ritzing (57)......26 D3
Riupeyrous (64)......182 C1
Rivarennes (36)......110 D1
Rivarennes (37)......94 C1
Rive-de-Gier (42)......129 G5
Rivecourt (60)......21 E5
Rivedoux-Plage (17)......106 C4
Rivehaute (64)......181 G1
Rivel (11)......186 B4
Riventosa (2B)......205 E3
Rivèrenert (09)......185 E5
Riverie (69)......129 G4
Rivery (80)......7 H6
les Rives (34)......172 B3
Rives (38)......145 E1
Rives (47)......151 G1
Rivesaltes (66)......201 F1
Rivière (37)......94 B2
la Rivière (33)......135 G4
la Rivière (38)......145 F2
la Rivière-de-Corps (10)......66 A3
la Rivière-Drugeon (25)......103 H4
la Rivière-Enverse (74)......119 F5
les Rivières-Henruel (51)......46 B5
Rivières (16)......122 D2
Rivières-le-Bois (52)......86 C1
la Rivière (76)......16 D3
Rivolet (69)......129 G1
Rix (09)......185 F6
Rix (39)......103 G4
Rixheim (68)......89 G2
la Rixouse (39)......118 A2
Rizaucourt-Buchey (52)......67 F3
Roaillan (33)......149 H3
Roaix (84)......158 C5
Roanne (42)......115 E6
Roannes-Saint-Mary (15)......140 A5
Robécourt (88)......68 C4
Robecq (62)......2 C5
Robersart (59)......9 G3
Robert-Espagne (55)......46 D5
Robert-Magny-
Laneuville-à-Rémy (52)......67 F1
Robertot (76)......17 E3
Roberval (60)......21 E5
Robiac-Rochessadoule (30)......157 E5
la Robine-sur-Galabre (04)......160 C6
Robion (84)......175 H3
le Roc (46)......138 C5
le Roc-Saint-André (56)......56 A4
Rocamadour (46)......138 D6
Rocbaron (83)......193 F3
Rocé (41)......79 G2
Roche (38)......130 C4
Roche (42)......128 D3
la Roche-Bernard (56)......73 G2
la Roche-Blanche (44)......75 F4
la Roche-Blanche (63)......127 F4
la Roche-Canillac (19)......139 F2
la Roche-Chalais (24)......136 A3
Roche-Charles-
la-Mayrand (63)......127 E6
la Roche-Clermault (37)......94 B2
la Roche-d'Agoux (63)......112 D6
la Roche-de-Glun (26)......144 A4
la Roche-de-Rame (05)......147 F6
la Roche-Derrien (22)......32 D2
la Roche-des-Arnauds (05)......160 B2
la Roche-en-Brenil (21)......84 B6
Roche-en-Régnier (43)......142 C2
la Roche-Guyon (95)......41 G2
la Roche-la-Molière (42)......129 F5
la Roche-l'Abeille (87)......124 B4
la Roche-Mabile (61)......59 H2
la Roche-Maurice (29)......31 F4
la Roche-Morey (70)......86 D2
la Roche-Noire (63)......127 F4
la Roche-Posay (86)......95 E5
la Roche-Rigault (86)......94 A3
Roche-Saint-Secret-
Béconne (26)......158 C3
la Roche-sur-Foron (74)......118 D6
la Roche-sur-Grane (26)......158 C1
la Roche-sur-le-Buis (26)......159 E5
Roche-sur-Linotte-et-
Sorans-les-Cordiers (70)......87 G4
la Roche-sur-Yon (85)......91 G4
la Roche-Vanneau (21)......85 E5
la Roche-Vineuse (71)......116 A3
Rochebaudin (26)......158 C2
la Rochebeaucourt-
et-Argentine (24)......123 E5
Rochebrune (05)......160 C3
Rochebrune (26)......159 E4
Rochechinard (26)......144 C3
Rochechouart (87)......123 F3
Rochecolombe (07)......157 G3
Rochecorbon (37)......79 E5
Rochefort (21)......84 C6
Rochefort (73)......131 G4
Rochefort-du-Gard (30)......174 D2
Rochefort-en-Terre (56)......73 G1
Rochefort-en-Valdaine (26)......158 B3
Rochefort-en-Yvelines (78)......42 B6
Rochefort-Montagne (63)......126 D4
Rochefort-Samson (26)......144 C4
Rochefort-sur-Brévon (21)......85 F2
Rochefort-sur-la-Côte (52)......67 H4
Rochefort-sur-Loire (49)......76 D5
Rochefort-sur-Nenon (39)......102 D2
la Rochefoucauld (16)......122 D3
Rochefourchat (26)......159 D2
la Rochegiron (04)......176 B1
Rochegude (30)......157 G5
Rochegude (26)......158 C4
Rochejean (25)......103 H5

Rompon (07)......144 A6
Rônai (61)......38 D4
Roncenay (10)......66 B4
le Roncenay-Authenay (27)......40 D2
Roncey (50)......37 E2
Ronchamp (70)......88 B2
Ronchaux (25)......103 F3
Ronchères (02)......44 C1
Ronchères (89)......82 D4
Roncherolles-en-Bray (76)......19 F3
Roncherolles-
sur-le-Vivier (76)......17 H6
Ronchin (59)......3 F5
Ronchois (76)......19 G2
Roncourt (57)......26 B5
Roncq (59)......3 G3
la Ronde (17)......107 F3
la Ronde-Haye (50)......12 D6
Rondefontaine (25)......103 H5
Ronel (81)......170 B4
Ronfeugerai (61)......38 B4
Rongères (03)......114 A4
Ronnet (03)......112 D5
Ronno (69)......129 F1
Ronquerolles (95)......42 C1
Ronsenac (16)......122 C5
Ronssoy (80)......8 D5
Rontalon (69)......129 H4
Rontignon (64)......182 C2
Ronvaux (55)......47 G1
Roost-Warendin (59)......8 D1
Roppe (90)......88 D2
Roppenheim (67)......51 G3
Roppentzwiller (68)......89 F3
Roppeviller (57)......28 C5
la Roque-Alric (84)......158 D6
la Roque-Baignard (14)......15 E5
la Roque-d'Anthéron (13)......175 H4
la Roque-Esclapon (83)......178 A4
la Roque-Gageac (24)......138 A6
la Roque-
Sainte-Marguerite (12)......172 B1
la Roque-sur-Cèze (30)......157 H5
la Roque-sur-Pernes (84)......175 G2
Roquebillière (06)......163 E6
Roquebrun (34)......172 A6
Roquebrune (32)......167 F4
Roquebrune (33)......150 B1
Roquebrune-
Cap-Martin (06)......195 G2
Roquebrune-
sur-Argens (83)......178 A6
Roquecor (82)......152 B4
Roquecourbe (81)......170 D5
Roquecourbe-
Minervois (11)......187 G3
Roquedur (30)......173 E2
Roquefère (11)......187 F2
Roquefeuil (11)......199 H1
Roquefixade (09)......186 A6
Roquefort (32)......167 F4
Roquefort (40)......166 C1
Roquefort (47)......151 E6
Roquefort-de-Sault (11)......200 A2
Roquefort-
des-Corbières (11)......188 A6
Roquefort-la-Bédoule (13)......192 C4
Roquefort-
les-Cascades (09)......186 A6
Roquefort-les-Pins (06)......195 E3
Roquefort-sur-Garonne (31)......184 C3
Roquefort-sur-Soulzon (12)......171 H2
Roquelaure (32)......167 H4
Roquelaure-
Saint-Aubin (32)......168 C4
Roquemaure (30)......174 D1
Roquemaure (81)......169 F3
Roquepine (32)......167 G2
Roqueredonde (34)......172 B4
Roques (31)......185 E1
Roques (32)......167 F3
Roquesérière (31)......169 G4
Roquessels (34)......172 B6
Roquesteron (06)......178 C6
Roquesteron-Grasse (06)......178 C6
Roquetaillade (11)......186 D5
Roquetoire (62)......2 B4
la Roquette (27)......19 E6
la Roquette-sur-Siagne (06)......178 C4
la Roquette-sur-Var (06)......195 E2
Roquettes (31)......185 E1
Roquevaire (13)......192 C3
Roquevidal (81)......170 A5
Roquiague (64)......181 G3
la Roquille (33)......136 C6
Rorbach-lès-Dieuze (57)......49 G3
Rorschwihr (68)......71 F3
Rosans (05)......159 F3
Rosay (39)......117 F2
Rosay (76)......19 E2
Rosay (78)......41 G3
Rosay-sur-Lieure (27)......19 E4
Rosazia (2A)......204 C4
Rosbruck (57)......27 F5
Roscanvel (29)......30 C6
Roscoff (29)......31 H2
Rosel (14)......14 B4
Rosenau (68)......89 H2
Rosenwiller (67)......71 E1
Roset-Fluans (25)......103 E2
Rosey (70)......87 F4
Rosey (71)......101 F5
Rosheim (67)......71 E1
la Rosière (70)......88 B1
Rosières (07)......157 F3
Rosières (43)......142 D3
Rosières (60)......21 F5
Rosières (81)......170 D1
Rosières-aux-Salines (54)......48 D6
Rosières-en-Haye (54)......48 B4
Rosières-en-Santerre (80)......21 F1
Rosières-près-Troyes (10)......66 B3
Rosières-sur-Barbèche (25)......88 B6
Rosières-sur-Mance (70)......87 E1
Rosiers-de-Juillac (19)......138 B1
Rosiers-d'Égletons (19)......139 F1
les Rosiers-sur-Loire (49)......77 F5
Rosis (34)......171 H5
Rosnay (36)......95 H6
Rosnay (51)......45 E1
Rosnay (85)......107 E1
Rosnay-l'Hôpital (10)......66 D2
Rosnoën (29)......31 F6
Rosny-sous-Bois (93)......43 E3
Rosny-sur-Seine (78)......41 G2
Rosoy (60)......20 D5
Rosoy (89)......65 E4
Rosoy-en-Multien (60)......43 H2
Rospez (22)......32 D2
Rospigliani (2B)......205 F3
Rosporden (29)......53 H3
Rosselange (57)......26 B4
Rossfeld (67)......71 G2
Rossillon (01)......131 F2
Rosteig (67)......50 B2
Rostrenen (22)......54 C1
Rosureux (25)......104 C1
Rotalier (39)......117 F1
Rotangy (60)......20 B3
Rothau (67)......71 E1
Rothbach (67)......50 D3
Rotherens (73)......132 B5
la Rothière (10)......67 E3
Rothois (60)......20 B3
Rothonay (39)......117 F2
les Rotours (61)......38 D4
Rots (14)......14 B4
Rott (67)......51 F1
Rottelsheim (67)......51 E4
Rottier (26)......159 E3
Rou-Marson (49)......93 H1
Rouairoux (81)......171 F6
la Rouaudière (53)......75 H1
Roubaix (59)......3 G4
Roubia (11)......187 H3
Roubion (06)......162 C6
Roucamps (14)......14 A6
Roucourt (59)......8 D2

Roucy (02) 22 D5
Roudouallec (56) 54 A2
Rouécourt (52) 67 H3
Rouède (31) 184 C4
Rouellé (61) 38 A6
Rouelles (52) 85 H2
Rouen (76) 17 G6
Rouessé-Fontaine (72) 60 A3
Rouessé-Vassé (72) 59 G4
Rouet (34) 173 F3
Rouez (72) 59 G4
Rouffach (68) 71 F5
Rouffange (39) 103 E1
Rouffiac (15) 139 G4
Rouffiac (16) 136 B1
Rouffiac (17) 121 F3
Rouffiac (81) 170 B3
Rouffiac-d'Aude (11) 186 D4
Rouffiac-des-Corbières (11) 187 F6
Rouffiac-Tolosan (31) 169 F5
Rouffignac (17) 135 F1
Rouffignac-de-Sigoulès (24) 136 D6
Rouffignac-Saint-Cernin-de-Reilhac (24) 137 H4
Rouffigny (50) 37 E4
Rouffilhac (46) 138 C6
Rouffy (51) 45 F3
Rougé (44) 57 G6
la Rouge (61) 61 E3
Rouge-Perriers (27) 40 C1
Rougefay (62) 7 F2
Rougegoutte (90) 88 C2
Rougemont (21) 84 C3
Rougemont (25) 87 H4
Rougemont-le-Château (90) 88 D2
Rougemontiers (27) 18 A5
Rougemontot (25) 87 G5
Rougeou (41) 80 B6
Rougeries (02) 22 D1
les Rouges-Eaux (88) 70 C3
le Rouget (15) 139 H5
Rougeux (52) 86 C2
Rougiers (83) 193 E3
Rougnac (16) 122 D5
Rougnat (23) 112 C6
Rougon (04) 177 G3
Rouhe (25) 103 F2
Rouhling (57) 27 G5
Rouillac (16) 122 A3
Rouillac (22) 34 B6
Rouillé (86) 108 C2
Rouillon (72) 60 A5
Rouilly (77) 44 B6
Rouilly-Sacey (10) 66 C3
Rouilly-Saint-Loup (10) 66 B3
Roujan (34) 172 C6
Roulans (25) 87 G6
le Roulier (88) 70 B4
Roullée (72) 60 B1
Roullens (11) 186 D4
Roullet-Saint-Estèphe (16) 122 B4
Roullours (14) 37 H3
Roumagne (47) 150 D2
Roumare (76) 17 F5
Roumazières-Loubert (16) 123 E2
Roumégoux (15) 139 H5
Roumégoux (81) 170 C4
Roumengoux (09) 186 B4
Roumens (31) 186 B1
Roumoules (04) 177 E3
Rountzenheim (67) 51 F3
Roupeldange (57) 26 D4
Rouperroux (61) 39 E6
Rouperroux-le-Coquet (72) 60 C3
Roupy (02) 21 H1
la Rouquette (12) 153 G5
Roure (06) 162 C6
le Rouret (06) 178 D4
Rousies (59) 10 A2
Roussac (87) 110 C6
Roussas (26) 158 B3
Roussay (49) 75 G6
Roussayrolles (81) 170 A1
Rousseloy (60) 20 C5
Roussennac (12) 154 A3
Roussent (62) 6 D2
les Rousses (39) 118 B2
Rousses (48) 156 B6
Rousset (05) 160 C3
Rousset (13) 176 B6
le Rousset (71) 115 G1
Rousset-les-Vignes (26) 158 D4
la Roussière (27) 40 A3
Roussieux (26) 159 F4
Roussillon (38) 144 A1
Roussillon (84) 175 H2
Roussillon-en-Morvan (71) 100 C3
Roussines (16) 123 E3
Roussines (36) 110 D2
Rousson (30) 157 E6
Rousson (89) 65 E5
Roussy-le-Village (57) 26 B2
Routelle (25) 103 E2
Routes (76) 17 E3
Routier (11) 186 C4
Routot (27) 18 A5
Rouvenac (11) 186 C6
Rouves (54) 48 C3
la Rouvière (30) 174 A2
Rouvignies (59) 9 F2
Rouville (60) 21 F6
Rouville (76) 15 H1
Rouvillers (60) 21 E4
Rouvray (21) 84 B5
Rouvray (27) 41 E2
Rouvray (89) 83 G1
Rouvray-Catillon (76) 19 F3
Rouvray-Saint-Denis (28) 62 D3
Rouvray-Saint-Florentin (28) 62 B3
Rouvray-Sainte-Croix (45) 62 C5
Rouvrel (80) 20 C1
Rouvres (14) 38 D2
Rouvres (28) 41 F4
Rouvres (77) 43 F2
Rouvres-en-Multien (60) 43 H1
Rouvres-en-Plaine (21) 102 A1
Rouvres-en-Woëvre (55) 25 G6
Rouvres-en-Xaintois (88) 69 F3
Rouvres-la-Chétive (88) 68 D3
Rouvres-les-Bois (36) 96 C3
Rouvres-les-Vignes (10) 67 F3
Rouvres-Saint-Jean (45) 63 F3
Rouvres-sous-Meilly (21) 101 E1
Rouvres-sur-Aube (52) 85 G1
Rouvrois-sur-Meuse (55) 47 G3
Rouvrois-sur-Othain (55) 25 G5
Rouvroy (02) 9 E6
Rouvroy (62) 8 C1
Rouvroy-en-Santerre (80) 21 E1
Rouvroy-les-Merles (60) 20 C2
Rouvroy-Ripont (51) 24 B6
Rouvroy-sur-Audry (08) 23 H1
Rouvroy-sur-Marne (52) 67 H2
Rouvroy-sur-Serre (02) 23 F2
le Roux (07) 157 E1
Rouxeville (50) 37 G1
la Rouxière (44) 75 G3
Rouxmesnil-Bouteilles (76) 17 G2
Rouy (58) 99 G3
Rouy-le-Grand (80) 21 G1
Rouy-le-Petit (80) 21 G1
Rouze (09) 199 H2
Rouzède (16) 123 E3
Rouziers (15) 139 H6
Rouziers-de-Touraine (37) 78 D4
le Rove (13) 192 A3
Roville-aux-Chênes (88) 70 A2
Roville-devant-Bayon (54) 69 G1
Rovon (38) 145 E2
Roy-Boissy (60) 19 H3
Royan (17) 120 C4
Royas (38) 130 C5
Royat (63) 127 E3
Royaucourt (60) 20 D3
Royaucourt-et-Chailvet (02) 22 B3
Royaumeix (54) 48 B4
Roybon (38) 144 D2
Roye (70) 88 A3
Roye (80) 21 F2
Roye-sur-Matz (60) 21 F3
Royer (71) 116 B1
Royère-de-Vassivière (23) 125 F2
Royères (87) 124 C2
Roynac (26) 158 C2
Royon (62) 1 H6
Royville (76) 17 F3
Roz-Landrieux (35) 35 E4
Roz-sur-Couesnon (35) 35 F4
Rozay-en-Brie (77) 43 G5
le Rozel (50) 12 B3
Rozelieures (54) 69 H1
Rozérieulles (57) 26 B5
Rozerotte (88) 69 F3
Rozès (32) 167 G3
Rozet-Saint-Albin (02) 44 B1
le Rozier (48) 155 G6
Rozier-Côtes-d'Aurec (42) 142 D1
Rozier-en-Donzy (42) 129 E3
Rozières-en-Beauce (45) 62 C6
Rozières-sur-Crise (02) 22 A5
Rozières-sur-Mouzon (88) 68 D4
Roziers-Saint-Georges (87) 124 D3
Rozoy-Bellevalle (02) 44 C3
Rozoy-le-Vieil (45) 64 C5
Rozoy-sur-Serre (02) 23 F2
Ruages (58) 83 G6
Ruan (45) 62 D5
Ruan-sur-Egvonne (41) 61 G6
Ruaudin (72) 60 B6
Rubécourt-et-Lamécourt (08) 24 C2
Rubelles (77) 64 A1
Rubempré (80) 7 G5
Rubercy (14) 13 G5
Rubescourt (80) 20 D3
Rubigny (08) 23 F2
Rubrouck (59) 2 B3
Ruca (22) 34 B4
Ruch (33) 136 A6
Rucqueville (14) 14 A4
Rudeau-Ladosse (24) 123 E5
Rudelle (46) 153 F1
Rue (80) 6 C2
la Rue-Saint-Pierre (60) 20 C4
la Rue-Saint-Pierre (76) 17 H5
Ruederbach (68) 89 F3
Rueil-la-Gadelière (28) 40 C5
Rueil-Malmaison (92) 42 C4
Ruelisheim (68) 89 F1
Ruelle-sur-Touvre (16) 122 C3
les Rues-des-Vignes (59) 9 E4
Ruesnes (59) 9 G3
Rueyres (46) 153 F1
Ruffec (16) 108 D6
Ruffec (36) 110 B1
Ruffey-le-Château (25) 87 E6
Ruffey-lès-Beaune (21) 101 G3
Ruffey-lès-Echirey (21) 85 H6
Ruffey-sur-Seille (39) 102 C5
Ruffiac (47) 150 B4
Ruffiac (56) 56 B5
Ruffieu (01) 131 F1
Ruffieux (73) 131 G2
Ruffigné (44) 57 G6
Rugles (27) 40 B4
Rugney (88) 69 G2
Rugny (89) 84 B1
Ruhans (70) 87 G5
Ruillé-en-Champagne (72) 59 H5
Ruillé-Froid-Fonds (53) 58 D6
Ruillé-le-Gravelais (53) 58 B5
Ruillé-sur-Loir (72) 78 D2
Ruisseauville (62) 2 A6
Ruitz (62) 8 A1
Rullac-Saint-Cirq (12) 154 B6
Rully (14) 38 A4
Rully (60) 21 E6
Rully (71) 101 F4
Rumaucourt (62) 8 C3
Rumegies (59) 4 A6
Rumersheim-le-Haut (68) 71 G6
Rumesnil (14) 15 E4
Rumigny (08) 23 G1
Rumigny (80) 20 C1
Rumilly (62) 1 H5
Rumilly (74) 131 H2
Rumilly-en-Cambrésis (59) 8 D4
Rumilly-lès-Vaudes (10) 66 C4
Ruminghem (62) 2 A3
Rumont (55) 47 F4
Rumont (77) 63 H3
Runan (22) 33 E2
Rungis (94) 42 D5
Ruoms (07) 157 G3
Rupéreux (77) 44 B6
Ruppes (88) 68 D1
Rupt (52) 67 H2
Rupt-aux-Nonains (55) 47 E5
Rupt-devant-Saint-Mihiel (55) 47 F3
Rupt-en-Woëvre (55) 47 G2
Rupt-sur-Moselle (88) 70 B6
Rupt-sur-Othain (55) 25 F4
Rupt-sur-Saône (70) 87 E3
Rurange-lès-Thionville (57) 26 C4
Rurey (25) 103 F2
Rusio (2B) 205 F2
Russ (67) 50 B6
Russange (57) 26 A2
le Russey (25) 104 C1
Russy (14) 13 H5
Russy-Bémont (60) 21 G6
Rustenhart (68) 71 G6
Rustiques (11) 187 F3
Rustrel (84) 176 A2
Rustroff (57) 26 D2
Rutali (2B) 203 F5
Ruvigny (10) 66 B3
Ruy (38) 130 D4
Ruyaulcourt (62) 8 C4
Ruynes-en-Margeride (15) 141 F4
Ry (76) 19 E4
Rye (39) 102 C4
Ryes (14) 14 A3

S

Saâcy-sur-Marne (77) 44 A3
Saales (67) 70 D2
Saâne-Saint-Just (76) 17 F3
Saasenheim (67) 71 H3
Sabadel-Latronquière (46) 153 G1
Sabadel-Lauzès (46) 152 D2
Sabaillan (32) 184 B1
Sabalos (65) 183 F2
Sabarat (09) 185 F4
Sabarros (65) 183 H3
Sabazan (32) 166 D4
Sablé-sur-Sarthe (72) 77 F1
les Sables-d'Olonne (85) 91 E6
Sablet (84) 158 C6
Sablières (07) 157 E3
Sablonceaux (17) 120 D3
Sablonnières (77) 44 B4
Sablons (33) 135 H4
Sablons (38) 144 A1
Sabonnères (31) 184 D1
la Sabotterie (08) 24 A3
Sabran (30) 157 H6
Sabres (40) 149 E6
Saccourvielle (31) 197 F1
Sacé (53) 58 D4
Sacey (50) 35 G5
Saché (37) 94 D1
Sachin (62) 2 B6
Sachy (08) 24 D2
Sacierges-Saint-Martin (36) 110 D2
Saclas (91) 63 E2
Saclay (91) 42 C5
Saconin-et-Breuil (02) 21 H5
Sacoué (65) 184 A5
le Sacq (27) 40 D3
Sacquenay (21) 86 B4
Sacquenville (27) 40 D2
Sacy (51) 45 E1
Sacy (89) 83 H3
Sacy-le-Grand (60) 20 D5
Sacy-le-Petit (60) 21 E5
Sadeillan (32) 183 G1
Sadillac (24) 136 D6
Sadirac (33) 135 F6
Sadournin (65) 183 G2
Sadroc (19) 138 D2
Saessolsheim (67) 50 D4
Saffais (54) 48 D6
Saffloz (39) 103 F6
Saffré (44) 74 D2
Saffres (21) 85 E6
Sagelat (24) 137 H6
Sagnat (23) 111 E4
Sagnes-et-Goudoulet (07) 143 E6
Sagonne (18) 98 B5
Sagy (71) 117 E1
Sagy (95) 42 A2
Sahorre (66) 200 B4
Sahune (26) 159 E4
Sahurs (76) 18 B5
Sai (61) 39 E4
Saignes (15) 140 B1
Saignes (46) 139 E6
Saigneville (80) 6 C4
Saignon (84) 176 A3
Saiguède (31) 168 D6
Sail-les-Bains (42) 114 D4
Sail-sous-Couzan (42) 128 C3
Sailhan (65) 196 D1
Saillac (19) 138 D4
Saillac (46) 153 E4
Saillagouse (66) 199 H4
Saillans (26) 158 D1
Saillans (33) 135 G4
Saillant (63) 128 C6
Saillat-sur-Vienne (87) 123 G2
Saillenard (71) 102 C6
Sailly (08) 24 D2
Sailly (52) 68 A2
Sailly (71) 115 H2
Sailly (78) 41 H2
Sailly-Achâtel (57) 48 D3
Sailly-au-Bois (62) 8 A4
Sailly-en-Ostrevent (62) 8 C2
Sailly-Flibeaucourt (80) 6 D3
Sailly-Labourse (62) 2 D6
Sailly-Laurette (80) 8 A6
Sailly-le-Sec (80) 8 A6
Sailly-lez-Cambrai (59) 8 D3
Sailly-lez-Lannoy (59) 3 G5
Sailly-Saillisel (80) 8 C5
Sailly-sur-la-Lys (62) 3 E5
Sain-Bel (69) 129 G3
Saincaize-Meauce (58) 98 D4
Sainghin-en-Mélantois (59) 3 G5
Sainghin-en-Weppes (59) 3 E6
Sainneville (76) 15 F1
Sainpuits (89) 83 E4
Sains (35) 35 F4
Sains-du-Nord (59) 10 A4
Sains-en-Amiénois (80) 20 C1
Sains-en-Gohelle (62) 8 A1
Sains-lès-Fressin (62) 1 H6
Sains-lès-Marquion (62) 8 D3
Sains-lès-Pernes (62) 2 B6
Sains-Morainvillers (60) 20 D3
Sains-Richaumont (02) 22 C1
le Saint (56) 54 B2
Saint-Abit (64) 182 C3
Saint-Abraham (56) 56 A5
Saint-Acheul (80) 7 F3
Saint-Adjutory (16) 123 E3
Saint-Adrien (22) 33 E4
Saint-Affrique (12) 171 G2
Saint-Affrique-les-Montagnes (81) 170 C6
Saint-Agathon (22) 33 E4
Saint-Agil (41) 61 F5
Saint-Agnan (02) 44 C2
Saint-Agnan (58) 84 B6
Saint-Agnan (71) 114 D2
Saint-Agnan (81) 169 H4
Saint-Agnan (89) 64 C3
Saint-Agnan-de-Cernières (27) 39 H3
Saint-Agnan-en-Vercors (26) 145 E5
Saint-Agnan-le-Malherbe (14) 14 A6
Saint-Agnan-sur-Erre (61) 61 E3
Saint-Agnan-sur-Sarthe (61) 39 H6
Saint-Agnant (17) 120 C1
Saint-Agnant-de-Versillat (23) 111 E4
Saint-Agnant-près-Crocq (23) 126 A3
Saint-Agne (24) 137 E5
Saint-Agnet (40) 166 B5
Saint-Agnin-sur-Bion (38) 130 D5
Saint-Agoulin (63) 113 G6
Saint-Agrève (07) 143 F4
Saint-Aignan (08) 24 B2
Saint-Aignan (33) 135 G4
Saint-Aignan (41) 96 A1
Saint-Aignan (56) 55 E1
Saint-Aignan (72) 60 B4
Saint-Aignan (82) 168 C1
Saint-Aignan-de-Couptrain (53) 59 F1
Saint-Aignan-de-Cramesnil (14) 38 D1
Saint-Aignan-des-Gués (45) 81 G1
Saint-Aignan-des-Noyers (18) 98 B5
Saint-Aignan-Grandlieu (44) 74 C6
Saint-Aignan-le-Jaillard (45) 81 G2
Saint-Aignan-sur-Roë (53) 76 A1
Saint-Aignan-sur-Ry (76) 19 E4
Saint-Aigny (36) 110 B1
Saint-Aigulin (17) 136 A2
Saint-Ail (54) 26 A5
Saint-Albain (71) 116 B3
Saint-Alban (01) 117 F6
Saint-Alban (22) 34 A4
Saint-Alban (31) 169 F4
Saint-Alban-Auriolles (07) 157 F4
Saint-Alban-d'Ay (07) 143 H2
Saint-Alban-de-Montbel (73) 131 G5
Saint-Alban-de-Roche (38) 130 D4
Saint-Alban-des-Hurtières (73) 132 C5
Saint-Alban-des-Villards (73) 146 B1
Saint-Alban-du-Rhône (38) 130 A6
Saint-Alban-en-Montagne (07) 156 D1
Saint-Alban-les-Eaux (42) 128 C1
Saint-Alban-Leysse (73) 131 H4
Saint-Alban-sur-Limagnole (48) 141 G6
Saint-Albin-de-Vaulserre (38) 131 G5
Saint-Alexandre (30) 158 A5
Saint-Algis (02) 9 H6
Saint-Allouestre (56) 55 G4
Saint-Alpinien (23) 125 H1
Saint-Alyre-d'Arlanc (63) 142 A1
Saint-Alyre-ès-Montagne (63) 141 E1
Saint-Amadou (09) 185 H4
Saint-Amancet (81) 186 C1
Saint-Amand (23) 125 H1
Saint-Amand (50) 37 G1
Saint-Amand (62) 7 H3
Saint-Amand-de-Belvès (24) 137 H6
Saint-Amand-de-Coly (24) 138 B4
Saint-Amand-de-Vergt (24) 137 F4
Saint-Amand-des-Hautes-Terres (27) 18 B6
Saint-Amand-en-Puisaye (58) 82 C4
Saint-Amand-Jartoudeix (23) 124 D2
Saint-Amand-le-Petit (87) 125 E3
Saint-Amand-les-Eaux (59) 9 F1
Saint-Amand-Longpré (41) 79 F3
Saint-Amand-Magnazeix (87) 110 D5
Saint-Amand-Montrond (18) 97 H6
Saint-Amand-sur-Fion (51) 46 B4
Saint-Amand-sur-Ornain (55) 47 F6
Saint-Amand-sur-Sèvre (79) 92 C4
Saint-Amandin (15) 140 C1
Saint-Amans (09) 185 G4
Saint-Amans (11) 186 B3
Saint-Amans (48) 156 A2
Saint-Amans-de-Pellagal (82) 152 A5
Saint-Amans-des-Cots (12) 154 C1
Saint-Amans-du-Pech (82) 151 G4
Saint-Amans-Soult (81) 187 F1
Saint-Amans-Valtoret (81) 187 F1
Saint-Amant (16) 122 B6
Saint-Amant-de-Boixe (16) 122 B2
Saint-Amant-de-Bonnieure (16) 122 C2
Saint-Amant-de-Nouère (16) 122 B3
Saint-Amant-Roche-Savine (63) 128 A5
Saint-Amant-Tallende (63) 127 F4
Saint-Amarin (68) 70 D6
Saint-Ambreuil (71) 101 G6
Saint-Ambroix (18) 97 F4
Saint-Ambroix (30) 157 F5
Saint-Amé (88) 70 B5
Saint-Amour (39) 117 E2
Saint-Amour-Bellevue (71) 116 B4
Saint-Andelain (58) 82 C6
Saint-Andéol (26) 144 D6
Saint-Andéol (38) 145 F4
Saint-Andéol-de-Berg (07) 157 H3
Saint-Andéol-de-Clerguemort (48) 156 D5
Saint-Andéol-de-Fourchades (07) 143 F5
Saint-Andéol-de-Vals (07) 157 G1
Saint-Andéol-le-Château (69) 129 H5
Saint-Andeux (21) 84 B5
Saint-Andiol (13) 175 E3
Saint-André (31) 184 C2
Saint-André (32) 168 B6
Saint-André (66) 201 F3
Saint-André (73) 147 E2
Saint-André (81) 171 E2
Saint-André-Capcèze (48) 156 D4
Saint-André-d'Allas (24) 138 A5
Saint-André-d'Apchon (42) 114 D6
Saint-André-de-Bâgé (01) 116 C4
Saint-André-de-Boëge (74) 118 D4
Saint-André-de-Bohon (50) 13 E5
Saint-André-de-Briouze (61) 38 C4
Saint-André-de-Buèges (34) 173 E3
Saint-André-de-Chalencon (43) 142 C2
Saint-André-de-Corcy (01) 130 B1
Saint-André-de-Cruzières (07) 157 F5
Saint-André-de-Cubzac (33) 135 F4
Saint-André-de-Double (24) 136 C3
Saint-André-de-la-Marche (49) 75 G6
Saint-André-de-la-Roche (06) 195 F2
Saint-André-de-Lancize (48) 156 C5
Saint-André-de-l'Épine (50) 13 F6
Saint-André-de-l'Eure (27) 41 E3
Saint-André-de-Lidon (17) 120 D4
Saint-André-de-Majencoules (30) 173 E2
Saint-André-de-Messei (61) 38 B5
Saint-André-de-Najac (12) 153 G6
Saint-André-de-Roquelongue (11) 187 H4
Saint-André-de-Roquepertuis (30) 157 G5
Saint-André-de-Rosans (05) 159 F4
Saint-André-de-Sangonis (34) 172 D5
Saint-André-de-Seignanx (40) 164 C5
Saint-André-de-Valborgne (30) 156 B6
Saint-André-de-Vézines (12) 155 G6
Saint-André-d'Embrun (05) 161 E2
Saint-André-des-Eaux (22) 34 D6
Saint-André-des-Eaux (44) 73 G4
Saint-André-d'Hébertot (14) 15 F3
Saint-André-d'Huiriat (01) 116 C5
Saint-André-d'Olérargues (30) 157 H6
Saint-André-du-Bois (33) 149 H2
Saint-André-en-Barrois (55) 47 E2
Saint-André-en-Bresse (71) 102 A6
Saint-André-en-Morvan (58) 83 H5
Saint-André-en-Royans (38) 144 D3
Saint-André-en-Terre-Plaine (89) 84 B5
Saint-André-en-Vivarais (07) 143 F3
Saint-André-et-Appelles (33) 136 C6
Saint-André-Farivillers (60) 20 C3
Saint-André-Goule-d'Oie (85) 92 A4
Saint-André-la-Côte (69) 129 G4
Saint-André-Lachamp (07) 157 E3
Saint-André-le-Bouchoux (01) 116 D5
Saint-André-le-Coq (63) 127 G1
Saint-André-le-Désert (71) 115 H2
Saint-André-le-Gaz (38) 131 F5
Saint-André-le-Puy (42) 129 E4
Saint-André-les-Alpes (04) 177 H2
Saint-André-les-Vergers (10) 66 B3
Saint-André-lez-Lille (59) 3 F5
Saint-André-sur-Cailly (76) 17 H5
Saint-André-sur-Orne (14) 14 B5
Saint-André-sur-Sèvre (79) 92 D5
Saint-André-sur-Vieux-Jonc (01) 116 D5
Saint-André-Treize-Voies (85) 91 G2
Saint-Androny (33) 135 E2
Saint-Ange-et-Torçay (28) 41 E6
Saint-Ange-le-Viel (77) 64 B3
Saint-Angeau (16) 122 C2
Saint-Angel (03) 112 D3
Saint-Angel (19) 125 H5
Saint-Angel (63) 127 E1
Saint-Anthème (63) 128 C5
Saint-Anthot (21) 85 E6
Saint-Antoine (15) 154 A1
Saint-Antoine (25) 104 A5
Saint-Antoine (32) 168 B1
Saint-Antoine (33) 135 F4
Saint-Antoine-Cumond (24) 136 C2
Saint-Antoine-d'Auberoche (24) 137 G3
Saint-Antoine-de-Breuilh (24) 136 B5
Saint-Antoine-de-Ficalba (47) 151 F4
Saint-Antoine-du-Queyret (33) 136 A6
Saint-Antoine-du-Rocher (37) 78 D4
Saint-Antoine-la-Forêt (76) 15 G1
Saint-Antoine-l'Abbaye (38) 144 D2
Saint-Antoine-sur-l'Isle (33) 136 B4
Saint-Antonin (06) 178 C2
Saint-Antonin (32) 168 B4
Saint-Antonin-de-Lacalm (81) 170 D4
Saint-Antonin-de-Sommaire (27) 40 A4
Saint-Antonin-du-Var (83) 193 G1
Saint-Antonin-Noble-Val (82) 153 E6
Saint-Antonin-sur-Bayon (13) 176 B6
Saint-Aoustrille (36) 96 D4
Saint-Août (36) 97 E6
Saint-Apollinaire (05) 160 D2
Saint-Apollinaire (21) 85 H6
Saint-Apollinaire-de-Rias (07) 143 G5
Saint-Appolinaire (69) 129 F1
Saint-Appolinard (38) 144 D2
Saint-Appolinard (42) 143 H1
Saint-Aquilin (24) 136 D2
Saint-Aquilin-de-Corbion (61) 39 H6
Saint-Aquilin-de-Pacy (27) 41 F2
Saint-Araille (31) 184 D2
Saint-Arailles (32) 167 F5
Saint-Arcons-d'Allier (43) 142 A4
Saint-Arcons-de-Barges (43) 142 C6
Saint-Arey (38) 145 G5
Saint-Armel (35) 57 F4
Saint-Armel (56) 72 D1
Saint-Armou (64) 182 C1
Saint-Arnac (66) 200 C1
Saint-Arnoult (14) 15 E3
Saint-Arnoult (41) 79 F3
Saint-Arnoult (60) 19 H2
Saint-Arnoult (76) 17 E5
Saint-Arnoult-des-Bois (28) 61 H1
Saint-Arnoult-en-Yvelines (78) 42 A6
Saint-Arroman (32) 183 H1
Saint-Arroman (65) 183 G4
Saint-Arroumex (82) 168 C2
Saint-Astier (24) 137 E3
Saint-Astier (47) 136 C6
Saint-Auban (06) 178 B3
Saint-Auban-d'Oze (05) 160 A3
Saint-Auban-sur-l'Ouvèze (26) 159 F5
Saint-Aubert (59) 9 F3
Saint-Aubert-sur-Orne (61) 38 C4
Saint-Aubin (02) 21 H4
Saint-Aubin (10) 65 F1
Saint-Aubin (21) 101 F4
Saint-Aubin (36) 97 E5
Saint-Aubin (39) 102 B3
Saint-Aubin (40) 165 G4
Saint-Aubin (47) 151 G3
Saint-Aubin (59) 10 A3
Saint-Aubin (62) 6 C1
Saint-Aubin (91) 42 B5
Saint-Aubin-Celloville (76) 18 D5
Saint-Aubin-Château-Neuf (89) 83 E2
Saint-Aubin-d'Appenai (61) 60 C1
Saint-Aubin-d'Arquenay (14) 14 C4
Saint-Aubin-d'Aubigné (35) 57 F1
Saint-Aubin-de-Blaye (33) 135 F1
Saint-Aubin-de-Bonneval (61) 39 G3
Saint-Aubin-de-Branne (33) 135 H6
Saint-Aubin-de-Cadelech (24) 151 E1
Saint-Aubin-de-Courteraie (61) 39 H6
Saint-Aubin-de-Crétot (76) 18 A3
Saint-Aubin-de-Lanquais (24) 137 E6
Saint-Aubin-de-Locquenay (72) 59 H3
Saint-Aubin-de-Luigné (49) 76 D6
Saint-Aubin-de-Médoc (33) 134 D4
Saint-Aubin-de-Nabirat (24) 152 B1
Saint-Aubin-de-Scellon (27) 15 G5
Saint-Aubin-de-Terregatte (50) 35 H4
Saint-Aubin-d'Écrosville (27) 40 C1
Saint-Aubin-des-Bois (14) 37 F3
Saint-Aubin-des-Bois (28) 62 A1
Saint-Aubin-des-Châteaux (44) 57 G6
Saint-Aubin-des-Chaumes (58) 83 H5
Saint-Aubin-des-Coudrais (72) 60 D4
Saint-Aubin-des-Grois (61) 60 D2
Saint-Aubin-des-Hayes (27) 40 B2
Saint-Aubin-des-Landes (35) 57 H3
Saint-Aubin-des-Ormeaux (85) 92 B3
Saint-Aubin-des-Préaux (50) 35 G2
Saint-Aubin-du-Cormier (35) 57 G1
Saint-Aubin-du-Désert (53) 59 G3
Saint-Aubin-du-Pavail (35) 57 G3
Saint-Aubin-du-Perron (50) 12 D6
Saint-Aubin-du-Plain (79) 93 E4
Saint-Aubin-du-Thenney (27) 15 G6
Saint-Aubin-en-Bray (60) 19 H4
Saint-Aubin-en-Charollais (71) 115 F2
Saint-Aubin-Épinay (76) 17 H6
Saint-Aubin-Fosse-Louvain (53) 58 C1
Saint-Aubin-la-Plaine (85) 106 D1
Saint-Aubin-le-Cauf (76) 17 H2
Saint-Aubin-le-Cloud (79) 93 F6
Saint-Aubin-le-Dépeint (37) 78 C3
Saint-Aubin-le-Guichard (27) 40 B2
Saint-Aubin-le-Monial (03) 113 F2
Saint-Aubin-le-Vertueux (27) 15 H6
Saint-Aubin-lès-Elbeuf (76) 18 C5
Saint-Aubin-les-Forges (58) 99 E2
Saint-Aubin-Montenoy (80) 7 E6
Saint-Aubin-Rivière (80) 6 D6
Saint-Aubin-Routot (76) 15 G2
Saint-Aubin-sous-Erquery (60) 20 D4
Saint-Aubin-sur-Aire (55) 47 G5
Saint-Aubin-sur-Gaillon (27) 41 E1
Saint-Aubin-sur-Loire (71) 114 C1
Saint-Aubin-sur-Mer (14) 14 B3
Saint-Aubin-sur-Mer (76) 17 F2
Saint-Aubin-sur-Quillebeuf (27) 15 H2
Saint-Aubin-sur-Scie (76) 17 G2
Saint-Aubin-sur-Yonne (89) 65 E6
Saint-Augustin (17) 120 B3
Saint-Augustin (19) 125 E6
Saint-Augustin (77) 43 H4
Saint-Augustin-des-Bois (49) 75 H3
Saint-Aulaire (19) 138 B2
Saint-Aulais-la-Chapelle (16) 122 A6
Saint-Aulaye (24) 136 B2
Saint-Aunès (34) 173 G5
Saint-Aunix-Lengros (32) 166 D5
Saint-Aupre (38) 131 F6
Saint-Austremoine (43) 141 G3
Saint-Auvent (87) 123 G2
Saint-Avaugourd-des-Landes (85) 91 F6
Saint-Avé (56) 55 G6
Saint-Aventin (31) 197 F1
Saint-Avertin (37) 79 E6
Saint-Avit (16) 136 B2
Saint-Avit (26) 144 B2
Saint-Avit (40) 166 A2
Saint-Avit (41) 61 F5
Saint-Avit (47) 150 C2
Saint-Avit (63) 126 B2
Saint-Avit (81) 170 B6
Saint-Avit-de-Soulège (33) 136 B6
Saint-Avit-de-Tardes (23) 125 H2
Saint-Avit-de-Vialard (24) 137 G5
Saint-Avit-Frandat (32) 168 A2
Saint-Avit-le-Pauvre (23) 125 G1
Saint-Avit-les-Guespières (28) 61 H3
Saint-Avit-Rivière (24) 137 G6
Saint-Avit-Saint-Nazaire (33) 136 C5
Saint-Avit-Sénieur (24) 137 F6
Saint-Avold (57) 49 F1
Saint-Avre (73) 132 C6
Saint-Ay (45) 80 C1
Saint-Aybert (59) 9 G1
Saint-Babel (63) 127 G5
Saint-Baldoph (73) 131 H5
Saint-Bandry (02) 21 H5
Saint-Baraing (39) 102 C3
Saint-Barbant (87) 109 H5
Saint-Bard (23) 126 A2
Saint-Bardoux (26) 144 B3
Saint-Barnabé (22) 55 G2
Saint-Barthélemy (38) 144 C1
Saint-Barthélemy (40) 164 C5
Saint-Barthélemy (50) 37 G5
Saint-Barthélemy (56) 55 E4
Saint-Barthélemy (70) 88 B2
Saint-Barthélemy (77) 44 B4
Saint-Barthélemy-d'Agenais (47) 150 D3
Saint-Barthélemy-d'Anjou (49) 77 E4
Saint-Barthélemy-de-Bellegarde (24) 136 C3
Saint-Barthélemy-de-Bussière (24) 123 F4
Saint-Barthélemy-de-Séchilienne (38) 145 H3
Saint-Barthélemy-de-Vals (26) 144 A3
Saint-Barthélemy-Grozon (07) 143 H4
Saint-Barthélemy-le-Meil (07) 143 G5
Saint-Barthélemy-le-Plain (07) 144 A4
Saint-Barthélemy-Lestra (42) 129 F3
Saint-Basile (07) 143 G4
Saint-Baslemont (88) 69 F4
Saint-Baudel (18) 97 F5
Saint-Baudelle (53) 58 D3
Saint-Baudille-de-la-Tour (38) 130 D3
Saint-Baudille-et-Pipet (38) 145 G6
Saint-Bauld (37) 95 F2
Saint-Baussant (54) 48 A3
Saint-Bauzeil (09) 185 G4
Saint-Bauzély (30) 173 H2
Saint-Bauzile (07) 158 A1
Saint-Bauzile (48) 156 A3
Saint-Bauzille-de-la-Sylve (34) 172 D5
Saint-Bauzille-de-Montmel (34) 173 G4
Saint-Bauzille-de-Putois (34) 173 E3
Saint-Bazile (87) 123 G3
Saint-Bazile-de-la-Roche (19) 139 F3
Saint-Bazile-de-Meyssac (19) 139 E4
Saint-Béat (31) 184 A6
Saint-Beaulize (12) 172 A3
Saint-Beauzeil (82) 151 H4
Saint-Beauzély (12) 155 E6
Saint-Beauzile (81) 169 H2
Saint-Beauzire (43) 141 G2
Saint-Beauzire (63) 127 F2
Saint-Bénézet (30) 173 H2
Saint-Bénigne (01) 116 C3
Saint-Benin (59) 9 F4
Saint-Benin-d'Azy (58) 99 F3
Saint-Benin-des-Bois (58) 99 F2
Saint-Benoist-sur-Mer (85) 106 B2
Saint-Benoist-sur-Vanne (10) 65 G4
Saint-Benoît (01) 131 F3
Saint-Benoît (04) 178 B2
Saint-Benoît (11) 186 C5
Saint-Benoît (86) 109 E1
Saint-Benoît-de-Carmaux (81) 170 C1
Saint-Benoît-des-Ombres (27) 15 H4
Saint-Benoît-des-Ondes (35) 35 E4
Saint-Benoît-d'Hébertot (14) 15 F3
Saint-Benoît-du-Sault (36) 110 D3
Saint-Benoit-en-Diois (26) 159 E1
Saint-Benoît-la-Chipotte (88) 70 B2
Saint-Benoît-la-Forêt (37) 94 B1
Saint-Benoît-sur-Loire (45) 81 F2
Saint-Benoît-sur-Seine (10) 66 A2
Saint-Bérain (43) 142 A4
Saint-Berain-sous-Sanvignes (71) 100 D6
Saint-Bérain-sur-Dheune (71) 101 F5
Saint-Bernard (01) 129 H1
Saint-Bernard (21) 101 H2
Saint-Bernard (38) 145 H1
Saint-Bernard (68) 89 E2
Saint-Béron (73) 131 G5
Saint-Berthevin (53) 58 C5
Saint-Berthevin-la-Tannière (53) 58 B2
Saint-Bertrand-de-Comminges (31) 184 A5
Saint-Biez-en-Belin (72) 78 B1
Saint-Bihy (22) 33 F5
Saint-Blaise (06) 195 F2
Saint-Blaise (74) 118 B6
Saint-Blaise-du-Buis (38) 131 F6
Saint-Blaise-la-Roche (67) 71 E1
Saint-Blancard (32) 184 A2
Saint-Blimont (80) 6 C4
Saint-Blin (52) 68 B3
Saint-Boès (64) 165 F5
Saint-Bohaire (41) 79 H3
Saint-Boil (71) 101 F6
Saint-Boingt (54) 69 H1
Saint-Bois (01) 131 F3
Saint-Bomer (28) 61 E4
Saint-Bômer-les-Forges (61) 38 A5
Saint-Bon (51) 44 C5
Saint-Bon-Tarentaise (73) 133 E5
Saint-Bonnet (16) 122 A5
Saint-Bonnet-Avalouze (19) 139 E2
Saint-Bonnet-Briance (87) 124 C3
Saint-Bonnet-de-Bellac (87) 110 A5
Saint-Bonnet-de-Chavagne (38) 144 D3
Saint-Bonnet-de-Chirac (48) 155 G3
Saint-Bonnet-de-Condat (15) 140 D2
Saint-Bonnet-de-Cray (71) 115 E5
Saint-Bonnet-de-Four (03) 113 F4
Saint-Bonnet-de-Joux (71) 115 G2
Saint-Bonnet-de-Montauroux (48) 142 B6
Saint-Bonnet-de-Mure (69) 130 B4
Saint-Bonnet-de-Rochefort (03) 113 G5
Saint-Bonnet-de-Salendrinque (30) 173 F1
Saint-Bonnet-de-Salers (15) 140 B3
Saint-Bonnet-de-Valclérieux (26) 144 C2
Saint-Bonnet-de-Vieille-Vigne (71) 115 F2
Saint-Bonnet-des-Bruyères (69) 115 H4
Saint-Bonnet-des-Quarts (42) 114 D5
Saint-Bonnet-du-Gard (30) 174 C2
Saint-Bonnet-Elvert (19) 139 F3
Saint-Bonnet-en-Bresse (71) 102 A4
Saint-Bonnet-en-Champsaur (05) 160 B1
Saint-Bonnet-la-Rivière (19) 138 B1
Saint-Bonnet-le-Bourg (63) 128 A6
Saint-Bonnet-le-Chastel (63) 128 A6
Saint-Bonnet-le-Château (42) 128 D6
Saint-Bonnet-le-Courreau (42) 128 C4
Saint-Bonnet-le-Froid (43) 143 F3
Saint-Bonnet-le-Troncy (69) 115 G6
Saint-Bonnet-l'Enfantier (19) 138 C1
Saint-Bonnet-lès-Allier (63) 127 G3
Saint-Bonnet-les-Oules (42) 129 F5
Saint-Bonnet-les-Tours-de-Merle (19) 139 G4
Saint-Bonnet-près-Bort (19) 126 A5
Saint-Bonnet-près-Orcival (63) 126 D4
Saint-Bonnet-près-Riom (63) 127 F2
Saint-Bonnet-sur-Gironde (17) 121 E6
Saint-Bonnet-Tronçais (03) 112 D1
Saint-Bonnot (58) 99 E1
Saint-Bouize (18) 98 C1
Saint-Brancher (89) 84 A5
Saint-Branchs (37) 95 E1
Saint-Brandan (22) 33 F5
Saint-Brès (30) 157 F5
Saint-Brès (32) 168 A4
Saint-Brès (34) 173 G5
Saint-Bresson (30) 173 E2
Saint-Bresson (70) 88 A1
Saint-Bressou (46) 153 G1
Saint-Brevin-les-Pins (44) 73 H4
Saint-Briac-sur-Mer (35) 34 C4
Saint-Brice (16) 121 G3
Saint-Brice (33) 150 A1
Saint-Brice (50) 35 H3
Saint-Brice (53) 77 E1
Saint-Brice (61) 38 A6
Saint-Brice (77) 65 E1
Saint-Brice-Courcelles (51) 23 E6
Saint-Brice-de-Landelles (50) 37 F6
Saint-Brice-en-Coglès (35) 35 H6
Saint-Brice-sous-Forêt (95) 42 D2
Saint-Brice-sous-Rânes (61) 38 D5
Saint-Brice-sur-Vienne (87) 123 H2
Saint-Brieuc (22) 33 G4
Saint-Brieuc-de-Mauron (56) 56 B3
Saint-Brieuc-des-Iffs (35) 57 E1
Saint-Bris-des-Bois (17) 121 F3
Saint-Bris-le-Vineux (89) 83 G2
Saint-Brisson (58) 100 B1
Saint-Brisson-sur-Loire (45) 82 A3
Saint-Broing (70) 86 D5
Saint-Broing-les-Moines (21) 85 F3
Saint-Broingt-le-Bois (52) 86 B2
Saint-Broingt-les-Fosses (52) 86 A2
Saint-Broladre (35) 35 F4
Saint-Bueil (38) 131 G5
Saint-Calais (72) 61 E6
Saint-Calais-du-Désert (53) 59 G1
Saint-Calez-en-Saosnois (72) 60 B3
Saint-Cannat (13) 175 H5
Saint-Caprais (03) 112 D2
Saint-Caprais (18) 97 G4
Saint-Caprais (32) 168 A5
Saint-Caprais (46) 152 B2
Saint-Caprais-de-Blaye (33) 135 F1
Saint-Caprais-de-Bordeaux (33) 135 F6
Saint-Caprais-de-Lerm (47) 151 F5
Saint-Capraise-de-Lalinde (24) 137 E5
Saint-Capraise-d'Eymet (24) 151 E1
Saint-Caradec (22) 55 F1
Saint-Caradec-Trégomel (56) 54 C3
Saint-Carné (22) 34 D5
Saint-Carreuc (22) 33 G5
Saint-Cassien (24) 151 G1
Saint-Cassien (38) 145 F1
Saint-Cassin (73) 131 H5
Saint-Cast-le-Guildo (22) 34 B3
Saint-Castin (64) 182 C1
Saint-Célerin (72) 60 C4
Saint-Céneré (53) 58 D4
Saint-Céneri-le-Gérei (61) 59 H2
Saint-Céols (18) 98 A1
Saint-Céré (46) 139 F5
Saint-Cergues (74) 118 D4
Saint-Cernin (15) 140 A4
Saint-Cernin (46) 152 D2
Saint-Cernin-de-Labarde (24) 137 E6
Saint-Cernin-de-Larche (19) 138 C3
Saint-Cernin-de-l'Herm (24) 152 A2
Saint-Césaire (17) 121 F3
Saint-Césaire-de-Gauzignan (30) 173 H1
Saint-Cézaire-sur-Siagne (06) 178 B4
Saint-Cézert (31) 168 D4
Saint-Chabrais (23) 112 A5
Saint-Chaffrey (05) 147 E4
Saint-Chamant (15) 140 A3
Saint-Chamant (19) 139 F3
Saint-Chamarand (46) 152 C1
Saint-Chamas (13) 191 G3
Saint-Chamassy (24) 137 G5
Saint-Chamond (42) 129 G6
Saint-Champ (01) 131 G3
Saint-Chaptes (30) 174 A2
Saint-Charles-de-Percy (14) 37 H3
Saint-Charles-la-Forêt (53) 59 E6
Saint-Chartier (36) 111 G1
Saint-Chef (38) 130 D4
Saint-Chels (46) 153 F3
Saint-Chély-d'Apcher (48) 141 G6
Saint-Chély-d'Aubrac (12) 155 E2
Saint-Chéron (51) 46 A6
Saint-Chéron (91) 63 E1
Saint-Chinian (34) 188 A1
Saint-Christ-Briost (80) 8 C6
Saint-Christaud (31) 184 D3
Saint-Christaud (32) 167 F6
Saint-Christo-en-Jarez (42) 129 G5
Saint-Christol (07) 143 F5
Saint-Christol (34) 173 H4
Saint-Christol (84) 176 A1
Saint-Christol-de-Rodières (30) 157 H5
Saint-Christol-lès-Alès (30) 173 H1
Saint-Christoly-de-Blaye (33) 135 F3
Saint-Christoly-Médoc (33) 120 D6
Saint-Christophe (03) 114 B5
Saint-Christophe (16) 123 G1
Saint-Christophe (17) 107 E5
Saint-Christophe (23) 111 G6
Saint-Christophe (28) 62 A5
Saint-Christophe (69) 115 H4
Saint-Christophe (73) 131 G6
Saint-Christophe (81) 153 G6
Saint-Christophe (86) 94 C4
Saint-Christophe-á-Berry (02) 21 H4
Saint-Christophe-d'Allier (43) 142 B5
Saint-Christophe-de-Chaulieu (61) 37 H4
Saint-Christophe-de-Double (33) 136 A3
Saint-Christophe-de-Valains (35) 35 G6
Saint-Christophe-des-Bardes (33) 135 H5
Saint-Christophe-des-Bois (35) 57 H2
Saint-Christophe-Dodinicourt (10) 66 D2
Saint-Christophe-du-Bois (49) 92 B2
Saint-Christophe-du-Foc (50) 12 B2
Saint-Christophe-du-Jambet (72) 59 H3
Saint-Christophe-du-Ligneron (85) 91 E3
Saint-Christophe-du-Luat (53) 59 E4
Saint-Christophe-en-Bazelle (36) 96 C2
Saint-Christophe-en-Boucherie (36) 97 F6
Saint-Christophe-en-Bresse (71) 101 H5
Saint-Christophe-en-Brionnais (71) 115 F4
Saint-Christophe-en-Champagne (72) 59 G6
Saint-Christophe-en-Oisans (38) 146 B4
Saint-Christophe-et-le-Laris (26) 144 C2
Saint-Christophe-la-Couperie (49) 75 F5
Saint-Christophe-le-Chaudry (18) 112 B1
Saint-Christophe-le-Jajolet (61) 39 E5
Saint-Christophe-sur-Avre (27) 40 B5
Saint-Christophe-sur-Condé (27) 15 H4
Saint-Christophe-sur-Dolaison (43) 142 C4

241

Saint-Christophe-sur-Guiers (38) 131 G6
Saint-Christophe-sur-le-Nais (37) 78 C3
Saint-Christophe-sur-Roc (79) 108 A2
Saint-Christophe-Vallon (12) 154 B3
Saint-Cibard (33) 136 A4
Saint-Cierge-la-Serre (07) 143 H6
Saint-Cierge-sous-le-Cheylard (07) 143 G5
Saint-Ciergues (52) 86 A1
Saint-Ciers-Champagne (17) 121 G5
Saint-Ciers-d'Abzac (33) 135 G3
Saint-Ciers-de-Canesse (33) 135 E3
Saint-Ciers-du-Taillon (17) 121 E6
Saint-Ciers-sur-Bonnieure (16) 122 C2
Saint-Ciers-sur-Gironde (33) 135 E1
Saint-Cirgue (81) 170 D2
Saint-Cirgues (43) 141 H3
Saint-Cirgues (46) 153 H1
Saint-Cirgues-de-Jordanne (15) 140 B4
Saint-Cirgues-de-Malbert (15) 140 A4
Saint-Cirgues-de-Prades (07) 157 F2
Saint-Cirgues-en-Montagne (07) 142 D6
Saint-Cirgues-la-Loutre (19) 139 G3
Saint-Cirgues-sur-Couze (63) 127 F5
Saint-Cirice (82) 168 B1
Saint-Cirq (24) 137 G5
Saint-Cirq (82) 152 D6
Saint-Cirq-Lapopie (46) 153 E3
Saint-Cirq-Madelon (46) 138 B6
Saint-Cirq-Souillaguet (46) 152 C1
Saint-Civran (36) 110 D2
Saint-Clair (07) 143 H2
Saint-Clair (46) 152 C1
Saint-Clair (82) 151 H6
Saint-Clair (86) 94 A4
Saint-Clair-d'Arcey (27) 40 A2
Saint-Clair-de-Halouze (61) 38 A5
Saint-Clair-de-la-Tour (38) 131 E4
Saint-Clair-du-Rhône (38) 130 A6
Saint-Clair-sur-Epte (95) 19 G6
Saint-Clair-sur-Galaure (38) 144 C2
Saint-Clair-sur-l'Elle (50) 13 F6
Saint-Clair-sur-les-Monts (76) 17 E4
Saint-Clar (32) 168 A3
Saint-Clar-de-Rivière (31) 185 E1
Saint-Claud (16) 123 E2
Saint-Claude (39) 118 A3
Saint-Claude-de-Diray (41) 80 A3
Saint-Clément (02) 23 E1
Saint-Clément (03) 114 C6
Saint-Clément (07) 143 E5
Saint-Clément (15) 140 C4
Saint-Clément (19) 138 D1
Saint-Clément (30) 173 G3
Saint-Clément (54) 49 F6
Saint-Clément (89) 65 E4
Saint-Clément-á-Arnes (08) 23 H5
Saint-Clément-de-la-Place (49) 76 C4
Saint-Clément-de-Régnat (63) 127 G1
Saint-Clément-de-Rivière (34) 173 F5
Saint-Clément-de-Valorgue (63) 128 C5
Saint-Clément-de-Vers (69) 115 G5
Saint-Clément-des-Baleines (17) 106 A4
Saint-Clément-des-Levées (49) 77 G6
Saint-Clément-les-Places (69) 129 F3
Saint-Clément-Rancoudray (50) 37 H5
Saint-Clément-sur-Durance (05) 161 E1
Saint-Clément-sur-Guye (71) 115 H1
Saint-Clément-sur-Valsonne (69) 129 F2
Saint-Clémentin (79) 93 E3
Saint-Clet (22) 33 E3
Saint-Cloud (92) 42 C4
Saint-Cloud-en-Dunois (28) 62 A5
Saint-Colomb-de-Lauzun (47) 151 E2
Saint-Colomban (44) 91 F1
Saint-Colomban-des-Villards (73) 146 B1
Saint-Côme (33) 149 H3
Saint-Côme-de-Fresné (14) 14 A3
Saint-Côme-d'Olt (12) 154 D3
Saint-Côme-du-Mont (50) 13 E4
Saint-Côme-et-Maruéjols (30) 173 H3
Saint-Congard (56) 56 B5
Saint-Connan (22) 33 E5
Saint-Connec (22) 55 F1
Saint-Constant (15) 154 A1
Saint-Contest (14) 14 B4
Saint-Corneille (72) 60 B5
Saint-Cornier-des-Landes (61) 38 A4
Saint-Cosme (68) 89 E2
Saint-Cosme-en-Vairais (72) 60 C3
Saint-Couat-d'Aude (11) 187 G3
Saint-Couat-du-Razès (11) 186 C5
Saint-Coulitz (29) 53 G1
Saint-Coulomb (35) 35 E3
Saint-Coutant (16) 109 F6
Saint-Coutant (79) 108 C4
Saint-Coutant-le-Grand (17) 121 E1
Saint-Créac (32) 168 B2
Saint-Créac (65) 183 E4
Saint-Crépin (05) 147 E6
Saint-Crépin (17) 107 F6
Saint-Crépin-aux-Bois (60) 21 G4
Saint-Crépin-d'Auberoche (24) 137 G3
Saint-Crépin-de-Richemont (24) 123 E6
Saint-Crépin-et-Carlucet (24) 138 B4
Saint-Crépin-Ibouvillers (60) 20 A6
Saint-Crespin (76) 18 D1
Saint-Crespin-sur-Moine (49) 75 F6
Saint-Cricq (32) 168 C4
Saint-Cricq-Chalosse (40) 165 G4
Saint-Cricq-du-Gave (40) 165 E5
Saint-Cricq-Villeneuve (40) 166 B2
Saint-Cybardeaux (16) 122 A3
Saint-Cybranet (24) 138 A6
Saint-Cyprien (19) 138 B2
Saint-Cyprien (24) 137 H5
Saint-Cyprien (42) 129 E5
Saint-Cyprien (46) 152 B5
Saint-Cyprien (66) 201 G3
Saint-Cyprien-sur-Dourdou (12) 154 B3
Saint-Cyr (07) 143 H2
Saint-Cyr (50) 12 D3
Saint-Cyr (71) 101 G6
Saint-Cyr (86) 94 C6
Saint-Cyr (87) 123 H3
Saint-Cyr-au-Mont-d'Or (69) 130 A2
Saint-Cyr-de-Favières (42) 128 D1
Saint-Cyr-de-Salerne (27) 18 A6
Saint-Cyr-de-Valorges (42) 129 E2
Saint-Cyr-des-Gâts (85) 107 E1
Saint-Cyr-du-Bailleul (50) 37 H6
Saint-Cyr-du-Doret (17) 107 E4
Saint-Cyr-du-Gault (41) 79 F3
Saint-Cyr-du-Ronceray (14) 15 F6
Saint-Cyr-en-Arthies (95) 41 H2
Saint-Cyr-en-Bourg (49) 93 H1
Saint-Cyr-en-Pail (53) 59 G1
Saint-Cyr-en-Talmondais (85) 91 G6
Saint-Cyr-en-Val (45) 80 D2
Saint-Cyr-la-Campagne (27) 18 C6
Saint-Cyr-la-Lande (79) 93 G2
Saint-Cyr-la-Rivière (91) 63 F3
Saint-Cyr-la-Roche (19) 138 B2
Saint-Cyr-la-Rosière (61) 60 D3
Saint-Cyr-le-Chatoux (69) 115 H6
Saint-Cyr-le-Gravelais (53) 58 B5
Saint-Cyr-l'École (78) 42 B4
Saint-Cyr-les-Champagnes (24) 138 B1
Saint-Cyr-les-Colons (89) 83 G2
Saint-Cyr-les-Vignes (42) 129 E4
Saint-Cyr-Montmalin (39) 103 E4
Saint-Cyr-sous-Dourdan (91) 42 B6
Saint-Cyr-sur-le-Rhône (69) 130 A5
Saint-Cyr-sur-Loire (37) 78 D5
Saint-Cyr-sur-Menthon (01) 116 C4
Saint-Cyr-sur-Mer (83) 192 D5
Saint-Cyr-sur-Morin (77) 44 A3
Saint-Cyran-du-Jambot (36) 95 G3
Saint-Dalmas-le-Selvage (06) 161 G4
Saint-Daunès (46) 152 B4
Saint-Denis (11) 186 D2
Saint-Denis (30) 157 F5
Saint-Denis (89) 65 E4
Saint-Denis (93) 42 D3
Saint-Denis-Catus (46) 152 C2
Saint-Denis-Combarnazat (63) 127 G1
Saint-Denis-d'Aclon (76) 17 F2
Saint-Denis-d'Anjou (53) 77 E1
Saint-Denis-d'Augerons (27) 39 H3
Saint-Denis-d'Authou (28) 61 F3
Saint-Denis-de-Cabanne (42) 115 F5
Saint-Denis-de-Gastines (53) 58 C2
Saint-Denis-de-Jouhet (36) 111 G2
Saint-Denis-de-l'Hôtel (45) 81 E1
Saint-Denis-de-Mailloc (14) 15 F5
Saint-Denis-de-Méré (14) 38 B3
Saint-Denis-de-Palin (18) 97 H4
Saint-Denis-de-Pile (33) 135 H4
Saint-Denis-de-Vaux (71) 101 F5
Saint-Denis-de-Villenette (61) 59 E1
Saint-Denis-des-Coudrais (72) 60 C4
Saint-Denis-des-Monts (27) 18 B6
Saint-Denis-des-Murs (87) 124 D3
Saint-Denis-des-Puits (28) 61 G2
Saint-Denis-d'Oléron (17) 106 B6
Saint-Denis-d'Orques (72) 59 F5
Saint-Denis-du-Béhélan (27) 40 C3
Saint-Denis-du-Maine (53) 59 E6
Saint-Denis-du-Payré (85) 106 C2
Saint-Denis-du-Pin (17) 107 G6
Saint-Denis-en-Bugey (01) 130 D1
Saint-Denis-en-Margeride (48) 156 A1
Saint-Denis-en-Val (45) 80 D1
Saint-Denis-la-Chevasse (85) 91 G3
Saint-Denis-le-Ferment (27) 19 G5
Saint-Denis-le-Gast (50) 35 H1
Saint-Denis-le-Thiboult (76) 19 E4
Saint-Denis-le-Vêtu (50) 37 E2
Saint-Denis-lès-Bourg (01) 116 D5
Saint-Denis-lès-Martel (46) 138 D5
Saint-Denis-les-Ponts (28) 61 H5
Saint-Denis-lès-Rebais (77) 44 A4
Saint-Denis-Maisoncelles (14) 37 H2
Saint-Denis-sur-Coise (42) 129 F4
Saint-Denis-sur-Huisne (61) 60 D1
Saint-Denis-sur-Loire (41) 80 A3
Saint-Denis-sur-Ouanne (89) 82 D2
Saint-Denis-sur-Sarthon (61) 59 H1
Saint-Denis-sur-Scie (76) 17 G4
Saint-Deniscourt (60) 19 H3
Saint-Denœux (62) 1 G6
Saint-Denoual (22) 34 B4
Saint-Derrien (29) 31 F3
Saint-Désert (71) 101 F5
Saint-Désir (14) 15 F5
Saint-Désirat (07) 144 A2
Saint-Désiré (03) 112 C2
Saint-Dézéry (30) 174 A2
Saint-Didier (21) 84 C6
Saint-Didier (35) 57 G3
Saint-Didier (39) 102 C6
Saint-Didier (58) 83 G6
Saint-Didier (84) 175 G2
Saint-Didier-au-Mont-d'Or (69) 130 A2
Saint-Didier-d'Allier (43) 142 B4
Saint-Didier-d'Aussiat (01) 116 D4
Saint-Didier-de-Bizonnes (38) 130 D5
Saint-Didier-de-Formans (01) 130 A1
Saint-Didier-de-la-Tour (38) 131 E5
Saint-Didier-des-Bois (27) 18 C6
Saint-Didier-en-Bresse (71) 102 A4
Saint-Didier-en-Brionnais (71) 115 E4
Saint-Didier-en-Donjon (03) 114 D3
Saint-Didier-en-Velay (43) 143 E1
Saint-Didier-la-Forêt (03) 113 H5
Saint-Didier-sous-Aubenas (07) 157 G2
Saint-Didier-sous-Écouves (61) 39 E6
Saint-Didier-sous-Riverie (69) 129 G4
Saint-Didier-sur-Arroux (71) 100 C5
Saint-Didier-sur-Beaujeu (69) 115 H5
Saint-Didier-sur-Chalaronne (01) 116 B5
Saint-Didier-sur-Doulon (43) 142 A1
Saint-Didier-sur-Rochefort (42) 128 C3
Saint-Dié-des-Vosges (88) 70 D3
Saint-Dier-d'Auvergne (63) 127 H4
Saint-Diéry (63) 127 E5
Saint-Dionizy (30) 174 A3
Saint-Disdier (05) 145 H6
Saint-Divy (29) 31 E4
Saint-Dizant-du-Bois (17) 121 F6
Saint-Dizant-du-Gua (17) 121 E5
Saint-Dizier (52) 46 D6
Saint-Dizier-en-Diois (26) 159 F3
Saint-Dizier-la-Tour (23) 112 A5
Saint-Dizier-les-Domaines (23) 111 H4
Saint-Dizier-l'Évêque (90) 88 D4
Saint-Dizier-Leyrenne (23) 111 F6
Saint-Dolay (56) 73 H2
Saint-Domet (23) 112 B6
Saint-Domineuc (35) 35 E6
Saint-Donan (22) 33 F5
Saint-Donat (63) 126 C6
Saint-Donat-sur-l'Herbasse (26) 144 B3
Saint-Dos (64) 165 E6
Saint-Doulchard (18) 97 G2
Saint-Drézéry (34) 173 G4
Saint-Dyé-sur-Loire (41) 80 B3
Saint-Ébremond-de-Bonfossé (50) 37 F1
Saint-Edmond (71) 115 F5
Saint-Égrève (38) 145 G2
Saint-Élier (27) 40 C3
Saint-Éliph (28) 61 G2
Saint-Élix (32) 168 A6
Saint-Élix-le-Château (31) 185 E2
Saint-Élix-Séglan (31) 184 C3
Saint-Élix-Theux (32) 183 H1
Saint-Ellier-du-Maine (53) 58 B2
Saint-Ellier-les-Bois (61) 59 H1
Saint-Éloi (01) 130 C1
Saint-Éloi (23) 111 F6
Saint-Éloi (58) 99 E4
Saint-Éloi-de-Fourques (27) 18 B6
Saint-Eloy (29) 31 G5
Saint-Éloy-d'Allier (03) 112 B2
Saint-Éloy-de-Gy (18) 97 G2
Saint-Éloy-la-Glacière (63) 128 A5
Saint-Éloy-les-Mines (63) 113 E5
Saint-Éloy-les-Tuileries (19) 124 B6
Saint-Éman (28) 61 H3
Saint-Émiland (71) 101 E4
Saint-Émilion (33) 135 H5
Saint-Ennemond (03) 99 F6
Saint-Épain (37) 94 D2
Saint-Epvre (57) 49 E2
Saint-Erblon (35) 57 F3
Saint-Erblon (53) 76 A1
Saint-Erme-Outre-et-Ramecourt (02) 22 D4
Saint-Escobille (91) 63 E2
Saint-Esteben (64) 181 E1
Saint-Estèphe (24) 123 F4
Saint-Estèphe (33) 134 D1
Saint-Estève (66) 201 F2
Saint-Estève-Janson (13) 176 A4
Saint-Étienne (42) 129 F6
Saint-Étienne-á-Arnes (08) 23 H5
Saint-Étienne-au-Mont (62) 1 F4
Saint-Étienne-au-Temple (51) 45 H2
Saint-Étienne-aux-Clos (19) 126 B5
Saint-Étienne-Cantalès (15) 139 H5
Saint-Étienne-d'Albagnan (34) 171 G6
Saint-Étienne-de-Baïgorry (64) 180 D3
Saint-Étienne-de-Boulogne (07) 157 G1
Saint-Étienne-de-Brillouet (85) 106 D1
Saint-Étienne-de-Carlat (15) 140 B5
Saint-Étienne-de-Chigny (37) 78 C5
Saint-Étienne-de-Chomeil (15) 140 B1
Saint-Étienne-de-Crossey (38) 131 F6
Saint-Étienne-de-Cuines (73) 146 C1
Saint-Étienne-de-Fontbellon (07) 157 G2
Saint-Étienne-de-Fougères (47) 151 E3
Saint-Étienne-de-Fursac (23) 111 E5
Saint-Étienne-de-Gourgas (34) 172 C4
Saint-Étienne-de-Lisse (33) 135 H5
Saint-Étienne-de-l'Olm (30) 173 H1
Saint-Étienne-de-Lugdarès (07) 156 D2
Saint-Étienne-de-Maurs (15) 153 H1
Saint-Étienne-de-Mer-Morte (44) 91 E2
Saint-Étienne-de-Montluc (44) 74 B4
Saint-Étienne-de-Puycorbier (24) 136 C3
Saint-Étienne-de-Saint-Geoirs (38) 144 D1
Saint-Étienne-de-Serre (07) 143 G6
Saint-Étienne-de-Tinée (06) 161 H5
Saint-Étienne-de-Tulmont (82) 169 F1
Saint-Étienne-de-Valoux (07) 144 A2
Saint-Étienne-de-Vicq (03) 114 B5
Saint-Étienne-de-Villeréal (47) 151 G2
Saint-Étienne-des-Champs (63) 126 B2
Saint-Étienne-des-Guérets (41) 79 G4
Saint-Étienne-des-Oullières (69) 116 A6
Saint-Étienne-des-Sorts (30) 158 A6
Saint-Étienne-d'Orthe (40) 164 D5
Saint-Étienne-du-Bois (01) 117 E4
Saint-Étienne-du-Bois (85) 91 F3
Saint-Étienne-du-Grès (13) 191 E1
Saint-Étienne-du-Gué-de-l'Isle (22) 55 H2
Saint-Étienne-du-Rouvray (76) 18 C5
Saint-Étienne-du-Valdonnez (48) 156 B3
Saint-Étienne-du-Vauvray (27) 18 D6
Saint-Étienne-du-Vigan (43) 142 C6
Saint-Étienne-en-Bresse (71) 102 A6
Saint-Étienne-en-Coglès (35) 35 H6
Saint-Étienne-en-Dévoluy (05) 160 A1
Saint-Étienne-Estréchoux (34) 172 A5
Saint-Étienne-la-Cigogne (79) 107 G5
Saint-Étienne-la-Geneste (19) 126 A6
Saint-Étienne-la-Thillaye (14) 15 E4
Saint-Étienne-la-Varenne (69) 116 A6
Saint-Étienne-l'Allier (27) 15 H4
Saint-Étienne-Lardeyrol (43) 142 D4
Saint-Étienne-le-Laus (05) 160 C3
Saint-Étienne-le-Molard (42) 128 D3
Saint-Étienne-les-Orgues (04) 176 C1
Saint-Étienne-lès-Remiremont (88) 70 B5
Saint-Étienne-Roilaye (60) 21 G5
Saint-Étienne-sous-Bailleul (27) 41 F1
Saint-Étienne-sous-Barbuise (10) 66 B1
Saint-Étienne-sur-Blesle (43) 141 F1
Saint-Étienne-sur-Chalaronne (01) 116 B5
Saint-Étienne-sur-Reyssouze (01) 116 C3
Saint-Étienne-sur-Suippe (51) 23 F5
Saint-Étienne-sur-Usson (63) 127 H5
Saint-Étienne-Vallée-Française (48) 156 C6
Saint-Eugène (02) 44 C2
Saint-Eugène (17) 121 G5
Saint-Eugène (71) 100 C6
Saint-Eulien (51) 46 C5
Saint-Euphraise-et-Clairizet (51) 22 D6
Saint-Euphrône (21) 84 D5
Saint-Eusèbe (71) 101 E6
Saint-Eusèbe (74) 131 H1
Saint-Eusèbe-en-Champsaur (05) 146 A6
Saint-Eustache (74) 132 B2
Saint-Eustache-la-Forêt (76) 15 G1
Saint-Eutrope (16) 122 B6
Saint-Eutrope-de-Born (47) 151 F2
Saint-Évarzec (29) 53 G3
Saint-Evroult-de-Montfort (61) 39 G4
Saint-Evroult-Notre-Dame-du-Bois (61) 39 H4
Saint-Exupéry (33) 150 A1
Saint-Exupéry-les-Roches (19) 126 A5
Saint-Fargeau (89) 82 C3
Saint-Fargeau-Ponthierry (77) 63 H1
Saint-Fargeol (03) 112 D5
Saint-Faust (64) 182 B2
Saint-Félicien (07) 143 H3
Saint-Féliu-d'Amont (66) 201 E2
Saint-Féliu-d'Avall (66) 201 E2
Saint-Félix (03) 114 A5
Saint-Félix (16) 122 A6
Saint-Félix (17) 107 G5
Saint-Félix (46) 153 H2
Saint-Félix (60) 20 C5
Saint-Félix (74) 131 H2
Saint-Félix-de-Bourdeilles (24) 123 E6
Saint-Félix-de-Foncaude (33) 150 A1
Saint-Félix-de-l'Héras (34) 172 B3
Saint-Félix-de-Lodez (34) 172 D5
Saint-Félix-de-Lunel (12) 154 C2
Saint-Félix-de-Pallières (30) 173 G2
Saint-Félix-de-Reillac-et-Mortemart (24) 137 G4
Saint-Félix-de-Rieutord (09) 185 H5
Saint-Félix-de-Sorgues (12) 171 H3
Saint-Félix-de-Tournegat (09) 186 A4
Saint-Félix-de-Villadeix (24) 137 F5
Saint-Félix-Lauragais (31) 186 B1
Saint-Fergeux (08) 23 F3
Saint-Ferjeux (70) 88 A4
Saint-Ferme (33) 150 B1
Saint-Ferréol (74) 132 C3
Saint-Ferréol-d'Auroure (43) 143 E1
Saint-Ferréol-de-Comminges (31) 184 B2
Saint-Ferréol-des-Côtes (63) 128 B5
Saint-Ferréol-Trente-Pas (26) 159 E3
Saint-Ferriol (11) 186 D6
Saint-Fiacre (22) 33 E5
Saint-Fiacre (77) 43 G3
Saint-Fiacre-sur-Maine (44) 74 D6
Saint-Fiel (23) 111 G5
Saint-Firmin (05) 146 A6
Saint-Firmin (54) 69 F2
Saint-Firmin (58) 99 F3
Saint-Firmin (71) 101 E5
Saint-Firmin-des-Bois (45) 64 B6
Saint-Firmin-des-Prés (41) 79 G1
Saint-Firmin-sur-Loire (45) 82 A3
Saint-Flavy (10) 65 H2
Saint-Florent (2B) 203 F4
Saint-Florent (45) 81 H3
Saint-Florent-des-Bois (85) 91 H5
Saint-Florent-le-Vieil (49) 76 B5
Saint-Florent-sur-Auzonnet (30) 157 E5
Saint-Florent-sur-Cher (18) 97 G3
Saint-Florentin (36) 96 D3
Saint-Florentin (89) 65 G6
Saint-Floret (63) 127 F5
Saint-Floris (62) 2 C5
Saint-Flour (15) 141 F4
Saint-Flour (63) 127 H4
Saint-Flour-de-Mercoire (48) 156 C1
Saint-Flovier (37) 95 G3
Saint-Floxel (50) 12 D3
Saint-Folquin (62) 2 A2
Saint-Fons (69) 130 A3
Saint-Forgeot (71) 100 D3
Saint-Forget (78) 42 B5
Saint-Forgeux (69) 129 G2
Saint-Forgeux-Lespinasse (42) 114 D5
Saint-Fort (53) 76 D1
Saint-Fort-sur-Gironde (17) 121 E5
Saint-Fort-sur-le-Né (16) 121 G4
Saint-Fortunat-sur-Eyrieux (07) 143 H6
Saint-Fraigne (16) 122 B1
Saint-Fraimbault (61) 58 D1
Saint-Fraimbault-de-Prières (53) 59 E2
Saint-Frajou (31) 184 C2
Saint-Franc (73) 131 G5
Saint-Franchy (58) 99 F2
Saint-François-de-Sales (73) 132 A3
Saint-François-Lacroix (57) 26 D3
Saint-François-Longchamp (73) 132 C6
Saint-Frégant (29) 31 E3
Saint-Fréjoux (19) 126 A5
Saint-Frézal-d'Albuges (48) 156 C2
Saint-Frézal-de-Ventalon (48) 156 C5
Saint-Frichoux (11) 187 F3
Saint-Frion (23) 125 H2
Saint-Fromond (50) 13 F6
Saint-Front (16) 122 C2
Saint-Front (43) 143 E4
Saint-Front-d'Alemps (24) 137 F1
Saint-Front-de-Pradoux (24) 136 D3
Saint-Front-la-Rivière (24) 123 F5
Saint-Front-sur-Lémance (47) 151 H2
Saint-Front-sur-Nizonne (24) 123 E5
Saint-Froult (17) 120 C1
Saint-Fulgent (85) 92 A4
Saint-Fulgent-des-Ormes (61) 60 C3
Saint-Fuscien (80) 7 G6
Saint-Gabriel-Brécy (14) 14 A3
Saint-Gal (48) 156 A1
Saint-Gal-sur-Sioule (63) 113 F6
Saint-Galmier (42) 129 F5
Saint-Gand (70) 87 E4
Saint-Ganton (35) 56 D6
Saint-Gatien-des-Bois (14) 15 F3
Saint-Gaudens (31) 184 B4
Saint-Gaudent (86) 109 E5
Saint-Gaudéric (11) 186 B4
Saint-Gaultier (36) 110 D1
Saint-Gauzens (81) 170 A4
Saint-Gein (40) 166 B3
Saint-Gelais (79) 107 H3
Saint-Gelven (22) 55 E1
Saint-Gély-du-Fesc (34) 173 F5
Saint-Génard (79) 108 B5
Saint-Gence (87) 124 A1
Saint-Généroux (79) 93 G4
Saint-Genès-Champanelle (63) 127 E3
Saint-Genès-Champespe (63) 126 C6
Saint-Genès-de-Blaye (33) 135 E2
Saint-Genès-de-Castillon (33) 136 A5
Saint-Genès-de-Fronsac (33) 135 G4
Saint-Genès-de-Lombaud (33) 135 F6
Saint-Genès-du-Retz (63) 113 G6
Saint-Genès-la-Tourette (63) 127 H5
Saint-Genest (03) 112 D4
Saint-Genest (88) 70 A2
Saint-Genest-d'Ambière (86) 94 C5
Saint-Genest-de-Beauzon (07) 157 F3
Saint-Genest-de-Contest (81) 170 C4
Saint-Genest-Lachamp (07) 143 F5
Saint-Genest-Lerpt (42) 129 F6
Saint-Genest-Malifaux (42) 143 F1
Saint-Genest-sur-Roselle (87) 124 C3
Saint-Geneys-près-Saint-Paulien (43) 142 C3
Saint-Gengoulph (02) 44 A1
Saint-Gengoux-de-Scissé (71) 116 B2
Saint-Gengoux-le-National (71) 116 A1
Saint-Geniès (24) 138 B4
Saint-Geniès-Bellevue (31) 169 F5
Saint-Geniès-de-Comolas (30) 174 D1
Saint-Geniès-de-Fontedit (34) 188 C1
Saint-Geniès-de-Malgoirès (30) 174 A2
Saint-Geniès-de-Varensal (34) 171 H5
Saint-Geniès-des-Mourgues (34) 173 G4
Saint-Geniez (04) 160 B5
Saint-Geniez-d'Olt (12) 155 E3
Saint-Geniez-ô-Merle (19) 139 G3
Saint-Genis (05) 159 H4
Saint-Genis-de-Saintonge (17) 121 F5
Saint-Génis-des-Fontaines (66) 201 F3
Saint-Genis-d'Hiersac (16) 122 B3
Saint-Genis-du-Bois (33) 150 A1
Saint-Genis-l'Argentière (69) 129 G3
Saint-Genis-Laval (69) 130 A4
Saint-Genis-les-Ollières (69) 129 H3
Saint-Genis-Pouilly (01) 118 B4
Saint-Genis-sur-Menthon (01) 116 C4
Saint-Genix-sur-Guiers (73) 131 F4
Saint-Genou (36) 96 A4
Saint-Genouph (37) 78 D5
Saint-Geoire-en-Valdaine (38) 131 F6
Saint-Geoirs (38) 145 E1
Saint-Georges (15) 141 F4
Saint-Georges (16) 122 C1
Saint-Georges (32) 168 B4
Saint-Georges (47) 151 H3
Saint-Georges (57) 49 H5
Saint-Georges (62) 7 F2
Saint-Georges (82) 153 E5
Saint-Georges-Antignac (17) 121 F5
Saint-Georges-Armont (25) 88 B5
Saint-Georges-Blancaneix (24) 136 C5
Saint-Georges-Buttavent (53) 58 D2
Saint-Georges-d'Annebecq (61) 38 D5
Saint-Georges-d'Aunay (14) 38 A2
Saint-Georges-d'Aurac (43) 142 A3
Saint-Georges-de-Baroille (42) 128 D2
Saint-Georges-de-Bohon (50) 13 E5
Saint-Georges-de-Chesné (35) 57 H1
Saint-Georges-de-Commiers (38) 145 G4
Saint-Georges-de-Didonne (17) 120 C4
Saint-Georges-de-Gréhaigne (35) 35 G4
Saint-Georges-de-la-Couée (72) 78 D1
Saint-Georges-de-la-Rivière (50) 12 B4
Saint-Georges-de-Lévéjac (48) 155 G5
Saint-Georges-de-Livoye (50) 37 F4
Saint-Georges-de-Longuepierre (17) 107 H6
Saint-Georges-de-Luzençon (12) 171 H1
Saint-Georges-de-Mons (63) 126 D1
Saint-Georges-de-Montaigu (85) 91 H2
Saint-Georges-de-Montclard (24) 137 E5
Saint-Georges-de-Noisné (79) 108 A2
Saint-Georges-de-Pointindoux (85) 91 F4
Saint-Georges-de-Poisieux (18) 97 H6
Saint-Georges-de-Reintembault (35) 37 E6
Saint-Georges-de-Reneins (69) 116 A6
Saint-Georges-de-Rex (79) 107 F4
Saint-Georges-de-Rouelley (50) 37 H5
Saint-Georges-d'Elle (50) 13 G6
Saint-Georges-des-Agoûts (17) 121 E6
Saint-Georges-des-Coteaux (17) 121 E2
Saint-Georges-des-Gardes (49) 92 C1
Saint-Georges-des-Groseillers (61) 38 B4
Saint-Georges-des-Hurtières (73) 132 C5
Saint-Georges-des-Sept-Voies (49) 77 F5
Saint-Georges-d'Espéranche (38) 130 C5
Saint-Georges-d'Oléron (17) 106 B6
Saint-Georges-d'Orques (34) 173 F5
Saint-Georges-du-Bois (17) 107 F5
Saint-Georges-du-Bois (49) 77 F4
Saint-Georges-du-Bois (72) 60 A6
Saint-Georges-du-Mesnil (27) 15 H4
Saint-Georges-du-Rosay (72) 60 C4
Saint-Georges-du-Vièvre (27) 15 H4
Saint-Georges-en-Auge (14) 15 E6
Saint-Georges-en-Couzan (42) 128 C4
Saint-Georges-Haute-Ville (42) 128 D5
Saint-Georges-la-Pouge (23) 125 F1
Saint-Georges-Lagricol (43) 142 C1
Saint-Georges-le-Fléchard (53) 59 E5
Saint-Georges-le-Gaultier (72) 59 G3
Saint-Georges-lès-Baillargeaux (86) 94 C6
Saint-Georges-les-Bains (07) 144 A5
Saint-Georges-les-Landes (87) 110 C3
Saint-Georges-Montcocq (50) 37 G1
Saint-Georges-Motel (27) 41 F4
Saint-Georges-Nigremont (23) 125 H2
Saint-Georges-sur-Allier (63) 127 G4
Saint-Georges-sur-Arnon (36) 97 F3
Saint-Georges-sur-Baulche (89) 83 F2
Saint-Georges-sur-Cher (41) 79 G6
Saint-Georges-sur-Erve (53) 59 F4
Saint-Georges-sur-Eure (28) 62 A2
Saint-Georges-sur-Fontaine (76) 17 H5
Saint-Georges-sur-la-Prée (18) 97 E1
Saint-Georges-sur-l'Aa (59) 2 A2
Saint-Georges-sur-Layon (49) 93 F1
Saint-Georges-sur-Loire (49) 76 C5
Saint-Georges-sur-Moulon (18) 97 H2
Saint-Georges-sur-Renon (01) 116 C6
Saint-Geours-d'Auribat (40) 165 F3
Saint-Geours-de-Maremne (40) 164 D4
Saint-Gérand (56) 55 F2
Saint-Gérand-de-Vaux (03) 114 A3
Saint-Gérand-le-Puy (03) 114 B4
Saint-Géraud (47) 150 C2
Saint-Géraud-de-Corps (24) 136 C4
Saint-Géréon (44) 75 F4
Saint-Germain (07) 157 G2
Saint-Germain (10) 66 A3
Saint-Germain (54) 69 H1
Saint-Germain (70) 88 A2
Saint-Germain (86) 109 H1
Saint-Germain-au-Mont-d'Or (69) 130 A2
Saint-Germain-Beaupré (23) 111 E4
Saint-Germain-Chassenay (58) 99 F5
Saint-Germain-d'Anxure (53) 58 D3
Saint-Germain-d'Arcé (72) 78 B3
Saint-Germain-d'Aunay (61) 39 G3
Saint-Germain-de-Belvès (24) 137 H6
Saint-Germain-de-Calberte (48) 156 C5
Saint-Germain-de-Clairefeuille (61) 39 G5
Saint-Germain-de-Confolens (16) 109 G6
Saint-Germain-de-Coulamer (53) 59 G3
Saint-Germain-de-Fresney (27) 41 E3
Saint-Germain-de-Grave (33) 149 H1
Saint-Germain-de-Joux (01) 117 H5
Saint-Germain-de-la-Coudre (61) 60 D3
Saint-Germain-de-la-Grange (78) 42 A4
Saint-Germain-de-la-Rivière (33) 135 G4
Saint-Germain-de-Livet (14) 15 F6
Saint-Germain-de-Longue-Chaume (79) 93 F5
Saint-Germain-de-Lusignan (17) 121 F5
Saint-Germain-de-Marencennes (17) 107 F5
Saint-Germain-de-Martigny (61) 39 H6
Saint-Germain-de-Modéon (21) 84 B6
Saint-Germain-de-Montbron (16) 122 D4
Saint-Germain-de-Montgommery (14) 39 F3
Saint-Germain-de-Pasquier (27) 18 C6
Saint-Germain-de-Prinçay (85) 92 B5
Saint-Germain-de-Salles (03) 113 G5
Saint-Germain-de-Tallevende-la-Lande-Vaumont (14) 37 H4
Saint-Germain-de-Tournebut (50) 12 D3
Saint-Germain-de-Varreville (50) 13 E4
Saint-Germain-de-Vibrac (17) 121 G6
Saint-Germain-d'Ectot (14) 38 A1
Saint-Germain-d'Elle (50) 37 H1
Saint-Germain-des-Angles (27) 40 D2
Saint-Germain-des-Bois (18) 97 H4
Saint-Germain-des-Bois (58) 83 F6
Saint-Germain-des-Champs (89) 84 A5
Saint-Germain-des-Essourts (76) 19 E3
Saint-Germain-des-Fossés (03) 114 A5
Saint-Germain-des-Grois (61) 61 E2
Saint-Germain-des-Prés (24) 137 H1
Saint-Germain-des-Prés (45) 64 B6
Saint-Germain-des-Prés (49) 75 H3
Saint-Germain-des-Prés (81) 170 B6
Saint-Germain-des-Vaux (50) 12 A1
Saint-Germain-d'Esteuil (33) 134 D1
Saint-Germain-d'Étables (76) 17 H2
Saint-Germain-du-Bel-Air (46) 152 C2
Saint-Germain-du-Bois (71) 102 B5
Saint-Germain-du-Corbéis (61) 60 A2
Saint-Germain-du-Crioult (14) 38 B3
Saint-Germain-du-Pert (14) 13 F5
Saint-Germain-du-Pinel (35) 58 A5
Saint-Germain-du-Plain (71) 101 H6
Saint-Germain-du-Puch (33) 135 G5
Saint-Germain-du-Puy (18) 97 H2
Saint-Germain-du-Salembre (24) 136 D3
Saint-Germain-du-Seudre (17) 121 E5
Saint-Germain-du-Teil (48) 155 G3
Saint-Germain-en-Brionnais (71) 115 F3
Saint-Germain-en-Coglès (35) 35 H6
Saint-Germain-en-Laye (78) 42 B3
Saint-Germain-en-Montagne (39) 103 F5
Saint-Germain-et-Mons (24) 137 E5
Saint-Germain-la-Blanche-Herbe (14) 14 B4
Saint-Germain-la-Campagne (27) 15 G6
Saint-Germain-la-Chambotte (73) 131 H3
Saint-Germain-la-Montagne (42) 115 G5
Saint-Germain-la-Poterie (60) 20 A4
Saint-Germain-la-Ville (51) 46 A3
Saint-Germain-l'Aiguiller (85) 92 C6
Saint-Germain-Langot (14) 38 C3
Saint-Germain-Laprade (43) 142 C4
Saint-Germain-Laval (42) 128 D2
Saint-Germain-Laval (77) 64 C2
Saint-Germain-Lavolps (19) 125 H4
Saint-Germain-Laxis (77) 43 F6
Saint-Germain-le-Châtelet (90) 88 D2
Saint-Germain-le-Fouilloux (53) 58 C4
Saint-Germain-le-Gaillard (28) 61 H2
Saint-Germain-le-Gaillard (50) 12 B3
Saint-Germain-le-Guillaume (53) 58 C3
Saint-Germain-le-Rocheux (21) 85 E2
Saint-Germain-le-Vasson (14) 14 C6
Saint-Germain-le-Vieux (61) 39 G6
Saint-Germain-Lembron (63) 127 G6
Saint-Germain-lès-Arlay (39) 102 D5
Saint-Germain-lès-Arpajon (91) 42 C6
Saint-Germain-les-Belles (87) 124 C4
Saint-Germain-lès-Buxy (71) 101 G6
Saint-Germain-lès-Corbeil (91) 43 E6
Saint-Germain-les-Paroisses (01) 131 F3
Saint-Germain-lès-Senailly (21) 84 C4
Saint-Germain-les-Vergnes (19) 138 D2
Saint-Germain-Lespinasse (42) 114 D6
Saint-Germain-l'Herm (63) 128 A6
Saint-Germain-près-Herment (63) 126 B3
Saint-Germain-sous-Cailly (76) 17 H5
Saint-Germain-sous-Doue (77) 44 A4
Saint-Germain-sur-Avre (27) 41 E4
Saint-Germain-sur-Ay (50) 12 C5
Saint-Germain-sur-Bresle (80) 6 C6
Saint-Germain-sur-Eaulne (76) 19 F1
Saint-Germain-sur-École (77) 63 H1
Saint-Germain-sur-Ille (35) 57 F1
Saint-Germain-sur-l'Arbresle (69) 129 G2
Saint-Germain-sur-Meuse (55) 47 H5
Saint-Germain-sur-Moine (49) 75 F6
Saint-Germain-sur-Morin (77) 43 G4
Saint-Germain-sur-Renon (01) 116 D6
Saint-Germain-sur-Rhône (74) 117 H6
Saint-Germain-sur-Sarthe (72) 60 A3
Saint-Germain-sur-Sèves (50) 12 D5
Saint-Germain-sur-Vienne (37) 94 A1
Saint-Germain-Village (27) 15 H3
Saint-Germainmont (08) 23 F4
Saint-Germé (32) 166 C4
Saint-Germer-de-Fly (60) 19 G4
Saint-Germier (31) 186 A1
Saint-Germier (32) 168 C5
Saint-Germier (79) 108 C2
Saint-Germier (81) 170 C5
Saint-Géron (43) 141 G1
Saint-Gérons (15) 139 H5
Saint-Gervais (30) 157 H6
Saint-Gervais (33) 135 F4
Saint-Gervais (38) 145 E2
Saint-Gervais (85) 90 C2
Saint-Gervais (95) 41 H1
Saint-Gervais-d'Auvergne (63) 126 D1
Saint-Gervais-de-Vic (72) 79 E1
Saint-Gervais-des-Sablons (61) 39 F3
Saint-Gervais-du-Perron (61) 39 F6
Saint-Gervais-en-Belin (72) 78 B1
Saint-Gervais-en-Vallière (71) 101 H4
Saint-Gervais-la-Forêt (41) 80 A4
Saint-Gervais-les-Bains (74) 133 E1
Saint-Gervais-les-Trois-Clochers (86) 94 C4
Saint-Gervais-sous-Meymont (63) 128 A4
Saint-Gervais-sur-Couches (71) 101 E4
Saint-Gervais-sur-Mare (34) 172 A5
Saint-Gervais-sur-Roubion (26) 158 B2
Saint-Gervasy (30) 174 B3
Saint-Gervazy (63) 127 F6
Saint-Géry (24) 136 C4
Saint-Géry (46) 152 D3
Saint-Geyrac (24) 137 G3
Saint-Gibrien (51) 45 H3
Saint-Gildas (22) 33 F5
Saint-Gildas-de-Rhuys (56) 72 D2
Saint-Gildas-des-Bois (44) 74 A2
Saint-Gilles (30) 174 B5
Saint-Gilles (35) 57 E2
Saint-Gilles (36) 110 D2
Saint-Gilles (50) 37 F1
Saint-Gilles (51) 22 C6
Saint-Gilles (71) 101 F4
Saint-Gilles-Croix-de-Vie (85) 90 D4
Saint-Gilles-de-Crétot (76) 18 A3
Saint-Gilles-de-la-Neuville (76) 15 G1
Saint-Gilles-des-Marais (61) 38 A6
Saint-Gilles-du-Mené (22) 55 H1
Saint-Gilles-les-Bois (22) 33 E3
Saint-Gilles-les-Forêts (87) 124 D4
Saint-Gilles-Pligeaux (22) 33 E5
Saint-Gilles-Vieux-Marché (22) 55 F1
Saint-Gineis-en-Coiron (07) 157 H2
Saint-Gingolph (74) 119 G3
Saint-Girod (73) 131 H3
Saint-Girons (09) 185 E5
Saint-Girons-d'Aiguevives (33) 135 F2
Saint-Girons-en-Béarn (64) 165 F5
Saint-Gladie-Arrive-Munein (64) 181 F1
Saint-Glen (22) 34 A6
Saint-Goazec (29) 54 A1
Saint-Gobain (02) 22 A3
Saint-Gobert (02) 22 D1
Saint-Goin (64) 181 H2
Saint-Gondon (45) 81 H3
Saint-Gondran (35) 57 E1
Saint-Gonlay (35) 56 C2
Saint-Gonnery (56) 55 G2
Saint-Gor (40) 166 C1
Saint-Gorgon (56) 73 G1
Saint-Gorgon (88) 70 B2
Saint-Gorgon-Main (25) 104 A3
Saint-Gouéno (22) 55 H1
Saint-Gourgon (41) 79 F3
Saint-Gourson (16) 122 D1
Saint-Goussaud (23) 111 E6
Saint-Gratien (80) 7 G5
Saint-Gratien (95) 42 C3
Saint-Gratien-Savigny (58) 99 H4
Saint-Gravé (56) 56 B6
Saint-Grégoire (35) 57 F2
Saint-Grégoire (81) 170 C2
Saint-Grégoire-d'Ardennes (17) 121 F5
Saint-Grégoire-du-Vièvre (27) 15 H4
Saint-Griède (32) 166 C4
Saint-Groux (16) 122 C2
Saint-Guen (22) 55 F1
Saint-Guilhem-le-Désert (34) 172 D4
Saint-Guillaume (38) 145 F4
Saint-Guinoux (35) 35 E4
Saint-Guiraud (34) 172 C5
Saint-Guyomard (56) 55 H5
Saint-Haon (43) 142 B6
Saint-Haon-le-Châtel (42) 114 D6
Saint-Haon-le-Vieux (42) 114 D6
Saint-Héand (42) 129 F5
Saint-Hélen (22) 36 A6
Saint-Hélier (21) 85 F5
Saint-Hellier (76) 17 H3
Saint-Herblain (44) 74 C5
Saint-Herblon (44) 75 F3
Saint-Hérent (63) 127 F6
Saint-Hernin (29) 54 B1
Saint-Hervé (22) 33 G6
Saint-Hilaire (03) 113 F2
Saint-Hilaire (11) 186 D4
Saint-Hilaire (25) 87 G6
Saint-Hilaire (31) 185 E1
Saint-Hilaire (38) 145 H1
Saint-Hilaire (43) 141 H1
Saint-Hilaire (46) 139 G6
Saint-Hilaire (63) 112 D6
Saint-Hilaire (91) 63 E2
Saint-Hilaire-au-Temple (51) 45 H2
Saint-Hilaire-Bonneval (87) 124 B3
Saint-Hilaire-Cottes (62) 2 C5
Saint-Hilaire-Cusson-la-Valmitte (42) 142 D1
Saint-Hilaire-de-Beauvoir (34) 173 G4
Saint-Hilaire-de-Brens (38) 130 D4
Saint-Hilaire-de-Brethmas (30) 173 H1
Saint-Hilaire-de-Briouze (61) 38 C5
Saint-Hilaire-de-Chaléons (44) 74 B6
Saint-Hilaire-de-Clisson (44) 91 H1
Saint-Hilaire-de-Court (18) 97 E1
Saint-Hilaire-de-Gondilly (18) 98 C3
Saint-Hilaire-de-la-Côte (38) 130 D6
Saint-Hilaire-de-la-Noaille (33) 150 B2
Saint-Hilaire-de-Lavit (48) 156 D5
Saint-Hilaire-de-Loulay (85) 91 H1
Saint-Hilaire-de-Lusignan (47) 151 E5
Saint-Hilaire-de-Riez (85) 90 D4
Saint-Hilaire-de-Villefranche (17) 121 F2
Saint-Hilaire-de-Voust (85) 107 G1
Saint-Hilaire-des-Landes (35) 35 H6
Saint-Hilaire-des-Loges (85) 107 F2

Saint-Hilaire-d’Estissac (24) 137 E4
Saint-Hilaire-d’Ozilhan (30) 174 C2
Saint-Hilaire-du-Bois (17) 121 F6
Saint-Hilaire-du-Bois (33) 150 A1
Saint-Hilaire-du-Harcouët (50) 37 F6
Saint-Hilaire-du-Maine (53) 58 C3
Saint-Hilaire-du-Rosier (38) 144 D3
Saint-Hilaire-en-Lignières (18) 97 F6
Saint-Hilaire-en-Morvan (58) 100 A3
Saint-Hilaire-en-Woëvre (55) 47 H1
Saint-Hilaire-Foissac (19) 139 G1
Saint-Hilaire-Fontaine (58) 99 G5
Saint-Hilaire-la-Croix (63) 113 F6
Saint-Hilaire-la-Forêt (85) 91 F6
Saint-Hilaire-la-Gérard (61) 39 E6
Saint-Hilaire-la-Gravelle (41) 61 H6
Saint-Hilaire-la-Palud (79) 107 F4
Saint-Hilaire-la-Plaine (23) 111 G5
Saint-Hilaire-la-Treille (87) 110 C4
Saint-Hilaire-le-Château (23) 125 F1
Saint-Hilaire-le-Châtel (61) 39 H6
Saint-Hilaire-le-Grand (51) 46 A1
Saint-Hilaire-le-Lierru (72) 60 D5
Saint-Hilaire-le-Petit (51) 23 G6
Saint-Hilaire-le-Vouhis (85) 92 A5
Saint-Hilaire-les-Andrésis (45) 64 C5
Saint-Hilaire-les-Courbes (19) 125 E4
Saint-Hilaire-les-Monges (63) 126 C3
Saint-Hilaire-les-Places (87) 124 A4
Saint-Hilaire-lez-Cambrai (59) 9 F3
Saint-Hilaire-Luc (19) 139 H1
Saint-Hilaire-Petitville (50) 13 E5
Saint-Hilaire-Peyroux (19) 138 D2
Saint-Hilaire-Saint-Mesmin (45) 80 D1
Saint-Hilaire-sous-Charlieu (42) 115 F5
Saint-Hilaire-sous-Romilly (10) 65 G1
Saint-Hilaire-sur-Benaize (36) 110 B1
Saint-Hilaire-sur-Erre (61) 61 E3
Saint-Hilaire-sur-Helpe (59) 10 A4
Saint-Hilaire-sur-Puiseaux (45) 82 A1
Saint-Hilaire-sur-Risle (61) 39 H5
Saint-Hilaire-sur-Yerre (28) 61 H5
Saint-Hilaire-Taurieux (19) 139 E4
Saint-Hilarion (78) 41 H6
Saint-Hilliers (77) 44 A6
Saint-Hippolyte (12) 154 C1
Saint-Hippolyte (15) 140 C2
Saint-Hippolyte (17) 120 D1
Saint-Hippolyte (25) 88 C6
Saint-Hippolyte (33) 135 H5
Saint-Hippolyte (37) 95 G3
Saint-Hippolyte (66) 201 F1
Saint-Hippolyte (68) 71 F3
Saint-Hippolyte-de-Caton (30) 173 H1
Saint-Hippolyte-de-Montaigu (30) 174 C1
Saint-Hippolyte-du-Fort (30) 173 F2
Saint-Hippolyte-le-Graveyron (84) 158 D6
Saint-Honoré (38) 145 H4
Saint-Honoré (76) 17 H3
Saint-Honoré-les-Bains (58) 100 A4
Saint-Hostien (43) 142 D4
Saint-Hubert (57) 26 C4
Saint-Huruge (71) 115 H1
Saint-Hymer (14) 15 F4
Saint-Hymetière (39) 117 G3
Saint-Igeaux (22) 33 E6
Saint-Igest (12) 153 G4
Saint-Ignan (31) 184 B3
Saint-Ignat (63) 127 G2
Saint-Igny-de-Roche (71) 115 F5
Saint-Igny-de-Vers (69) 115 G4
Saint-Illide (15) 139 H4
Saint-Illiers-la-Ville (78) 41 G3
Saint-Illiers-le-Bois (78) 41 F3
Saint-Ilpize (43) 141 G2
Saint-Imoges (51) 45 F1
Saint-Inglevert (62) 1 F3
Saint-Ismier (38) 145 H2
Saint-Izaire (12) 171 F2
Saint-Jacques (04) 177 G2
Saint-Jacques-d’Aliermont (76) 17 H2
Saint-Jacques-d’Ambur (63) 126 D2
Saint-Jacques-d’Atticieux (07) 143 H1
Saint-Jacques-de-la-Lande (35) 57 E3
Saint-Jacques-de-Néhou (50) 12 C4
Saint-Jacques-de-Thouars (79) 93 G3
Saint-Jacques-des-Arrêts (69) 115 H4
Saint-Jacques-des-Blats (15) 140 C4
Saint-Jacques-des-Guérets (41) 79 E2
Saint-Jacques-en-Valgodemard (05) 146 A6
Saint-Jacques-sur-Darnétal (76) 17 H6
Saint-Jacut-de-la-Mer (22) 34 C4
Saint-Jacut-du-Mené (22) 56 A1
Saint-Jacut-les-Pins (56) 56 B6
Saint-Jal (19) 124 D6
Saint-James (50) 35 H5
Saint-Jammes (64) 182 C1
Saint-Jans-Cappel (59) 2 D4
Saint-Jean (31) 169 F5
Saint-Jean-aux-Amognes (58) 99 E3
Saint-Jean-aux-Bois (08) 23 G2
Saint-Jean-aux-Bois (60) 21 F5
Saint-Jean-Bonnefonds (42) 129 F6
Saint-Jean-Brévelay (56) 55 G5
Saint-Jean-Cap-Ferrat (06) 195 F3
Saint-Jean-Chambre (07) 143 G5
Saint-Jean-d’Aigues-Vives (09) 186 B6
Saint-Jean-d’Alcapiès (12) 171 H2
Saint-Jean-d’Angély (17) 121 F1
Saint-Jean-d’Angle (17) 120 C2
Saint-Jean-d’Ardières (69) 116 B5
Saint-Jean-d’Arves (73) 146 C2
Saint-Jean-d’Arvey (73) 132 A4
Saint-Jean-d’Assé (72) 60 A4
Saint-Jean-d’Ataux (24) 136 D3
Saint-Jean-d’Aubrigoux (43) 142 B1
Saint-Jean-d’Aulps (74) 119 F4
Saint-Jean-d’Avelanne (38) 131 F5
Saint-Jean-de-Barrou (11) 187 H5
Saint-Jean-de-Bassel (57) 49 H4
Saint-Jean-de-Beauregard (91) 42 C5
Saint-Jean-de-Belleville (73) 132 D6
Saint-Jean-de-Beugné (85) 106 D1
Saint-Jean-de-Blaignac (33) 135 H6
Saint-Jean-de-Bœuf (21) 101 F1
Saint-Jean-de-Boiseau (44) 74 C5
Saint-Jean-de-Bonneval (10) 66 B4
Saint-Jean-de-Bournay (38) 130 C5
Saint-Jean-de-Braye (45) 80 D1
Saint-Jean-de-Buèges (34) 173 E3
Saint-Jean-de-Ceyrargues (30) 174 A1
Saint-Jean-de-Chevelu (73) 131 G3
Saint-Jean-de-Côle (24) 123 G6
Saint-Jean-de-Cornies (34) 173 G4
Saint-Jean-de-Couz (73) 131 G5
Saint-Jean-de-Crieulon (30) 173 G2
Saint-Jean-de-Cuculles (34) 173 F4
Saint-Jean-de-Daye (50) 13 F5
Saint-Jean-de-Duras (47) 150 D1
Saint-Jean-de-Folleville (76) 15 H2
Saint-Jean-de-Fos (34) 172 D4
Saint-Jean-de-Gonville (01) 118 A4
Saint-Jean-de-la-Blaquière (34) 172 C4
Saint-Jean-de-la-Croix (49) 76 D5
Saint-Jean-de-la-Forêt (61) 60 D2
Saint-Jean-de-la-Haize (50) 35 H3
Saint-Jean-de-la-Léqueraye (27) 15 H4
Saint-Jean-de-la-Motte (72) 77 H2
Saint-Jean-de-la-Neuville (76) 15 G1
Saint-Jean-de-la-Porte (73) 132 B5
Saint-Jean-de-la-Rivière (50) 12 B4
Saint-Jean-de-la-Ruelle (45) 80 D1
Saint-Jean-de-Laur (46) 153 F4
Saint-Jean-de-Lier (40) 165 F3
Saint-Jean-de-Linières (49) 76 D4
Saint-Jean-de-Liversay (17) 107 E4
Saint-Jean-de-Livet (14) 15 F5
Saint-Jean-de-Losne (21) 102 B2
Saint-Jean-de-Luz (64) 180 B1
Saint-Jean-de-Marcel (81) 170 C1
Saint-Jean-de-Marsacq (40) 164 D4
Saint-Jean-de-Maruéjols-et-Avéjan (30) 157 F5
Saint-Jean-de-Maurienne (73) 146 C1
Saint-Jean-de-Minervois (34) 187 H2
Saint-Jean-de-Moirans (38) 145 F1
Saint-Jean-de-Monts (85) 90 C3
Saint-Jean-de-Muzols (07) 144 A3
Saint-Jean-de-Nay (43) 142 B4
Saint-Jean-de-Niost (01) 130 D2
Saint-Jean-de-Paracol (11) 186 C6
Saint-Jean-de-Rebervilliers (28) 41 E6
Saint-Jean-de-Rives (81) 169 H4
Saint-Jean-de-Sauves (86) 94 A4
Saint-Jean-de-Savigny (50) 13 F6
Saint-Jean-de-Serres (30) 173 G2
Saint-Jean-de-Sixt (74) 132 C1
Saint-Jean-de-Soudain (38) 131 E5
Saint-Jean-de-Tholome (74) 118 D5
Saint-Jean-de-Thouars (79) 93 G3
Saint-Jean-de-Thurac (47) 151 F6
Saint-Jean-de-Thurigneux (01) 130 A1
Saint-Jean-de-Touslas (69) 129 H5
Saint-Jean-de-Trézy (71) 101 E5
Saint-Jean-de-Valériscle (30) 157 E5
Saint-Jean-de-Vals (81) 170 C5
Saint-Jean-de-Vaulx (38) 145 G4
Saint-Jean-de-Vaux (71) 101 F5
Saint-Jean-de-Védas (34) 173 F6
Saint-Jean-de-Verges (09) 185 H5
Saint-Jean-Delnous (12) 171 E1
Saint-Jean-des-Baisants (50) 37 G1
Saint-Jean-des-Bois (61) 37 H4
Saint-Jean-des-Champs (50) 35 G2
Saint-Jean-des-Échelles (72) 61 E4
Saint-Jean-des-Essartiers (14) 37 H2
Saint-Jean-des-Mauvrets (49) 77 E5
Saint-Jean-des-Ollières (63) 127 H4
Saint-Jean-des-Vignes (69) 129 H2
Saint-Jean-d’Estissac (24) 137 E4
Saint-Jean-d’Étreux (39) 117 E3
Saint-Jean-devant-Possesse (51) 46 C4
Saint-Jean-d’Eyraud (24) 136 D4
Saint-Jean-d’Hérans (38) 145 G5
Saint-Jean-d’Heurs (63) 127 H3
Saint-Jean-d’Illac (33) 134 D5
Saint-Jean-d’Ormont (88) 70 D2
Saint-Jean-du-Bois (72) 77 H1
Saint-Jean-du-Bouzet (82) 168 B2
Saint-Jean-du-Bruel (12) 172 C2
Saint-Jean-du-Cardonnay (76) 17 G5
Saint-Jean-du-Castillonnais (09) 184 C5
Saint-Jean-du-Corail (50) 37 G5
Saint-Jean-du-Corail-des-Bois (50) 37 F4
Saint-Jean-du-Doigt (29) 32 A2
Saint-Jean-du-Falga (09) 185 H4
Saint-Jean-du-Gard (30) 173 F1
Saint-Jean-du-Pin (30) 173 G1
Saint-Jean-du-Thenney (27) 15 G6
Saint-Jean-en-Royans (26) 144 D4
Saint-Jean-en-Val (63) 127 G5
Saint-Jean-et-Saint-Paul (12) 171 H2
Saint-Jean-Froidmentel (41) 61 H6
Saint-Jean-Kerdaniel (22) 33 F4
Saint-Jean-Kourtzerode (57) 50 B4
Saint-Jean-la-Bussière (69) 129 F1
Saint-Jean-la-Fouillouse (48) 156 B1
Saint-Jean-la-Poterie (56) 73 H1
Saint-Jean-la-Vêtre (42) 128 B3
Saint-Jean-Lachalm (43) 142 B5
Saint-Jean-Lagineste (46) 139 E6
Saint-Jean-Lasseille (66) 201 F3
Saint-Jean-le-Blanc (14) 38 A3
Saint-Jean-le-Blanc (45) 80 D1
Saint-Jean-le-Centenier (07) 157 H2
Saint-Jean-le-Comtal (32) 167 G5
Saint-Jean-le-Thomas (50) 35 G3
Saint-Jean-le-Vieux (01) 117 F6
Saint-Jean-le-Vieux (38) 145 H2
Saint-Jean-le-Vieux (64) 181 E3
Saint-Jean-lès-Buzy (55) 47 H1
Saint-Jean-les-Deux-Jumeaux (77) 43 H3
Saint-Jean-lès-Longuyon (54) 25 F4
Saint-Jean-Lespinasse (46) 139 E5
Saint-Jean-Lherm (31) 169 G4
Saint-Jean-Ligoure (87) 124 B4
Saint-Jean-Mirabel (46) 153 H2
Saint-Jean-Pied-de-Port (64) 180 D3
Saint-Jean-Pierre-Fixte (28) 61 E3
Saint-Jean-Pla-de-Corts (66) 201 E4
Saint-Jean-Poudge (64) 166 C6
Saint-Jean-Poutge (32) 167 G4
Saint-Jean-Rohrbach (57) 49 G2
Saint-Jean-Roure (07) 143 F5
Saint-Jean-Saint-Germain (37) 95 G2
Saint-Jean-Saint-Gervais (63) 127 G6
Saint-Jean-Saint-Maurice-sur-Loire (42) 128 D1
Saint-Jean-Saint-Nicolas (05) 160 C1
Saint-Jean-Saverne (67) 50 C4
Saint-Jean-Soleymieux (42) 128 D5
Saint-Jean-sur-Couesnon (35) 57 H1
Saint-Jean-sur-Erve (53) 59 F5
Saint-Jean-sur-Mayenne (53) 58 D4
Saint-Jean-sur-Moivre (51) 46 B3
Saint-Jean-sur-Reyssouze (01) 116 C3
Saint-Jean-sur-Tourbe (51) 46 B1
Saint-Jean-sur-Veyle (01) 116 C4
Saint-Jean-sur-Vilaine (35) 57 H3
Saint-Jean-Trolimon (29) 53 E4
Saint-Jeannet (04) 177 E2
Saint-Jeannet (06) 195 E2
Saint-Jeanvrin (18) 112 A1
Saint-Jeoire (74) 119 E5
Saint-Jeoire-Prieuré (73) 132 A5
Saint-Jeure-d’Andaure (07) 143 G4
Saint-Jeure-d’Ay (07) 143 H3
Saint-Jeures (43) 143 E3
Saint-Joachim (44) 73 G3
Saint-Jodard (42) 128 D2
Saint-Joire (55) 47 G6
Saint-Jores (50) 12 D5
Saint-Jorioz (74) 132 B2
Saint-Jory (31) 169 E4
Saint-Jory-de-Chalais (24) 123 G5
Saint-Jory-las-Bloux (24) 137 H1
Saint-Joseph (42) 129 G5
Saint-Joseph (50) 12 C3
Saint-Joseph-de-Rivière (38) 131 G6
Saint-Joseph-des-Bancs (07) 157 G1
Saint-Josse (62) 1 F6
Saint-Jouan-de-l’Isle (22) 56 C1
Saint-Jouan-des-Guérets (35) 36 A5
Saint-Jouin (14) 14 D4
Saint-Jouin-Bruneval (76) 16 B4
Saint-Jouin-de-Blavou (61) 60 C1
Saint-Jouin-de-Marnes (79) 93 H4
Saint-Jouin-de-Milly (79) 92 D5
Saint-Jouvent (87) 124 A1
Saint-Juan (25) 87 H6
Saint-Judoce (22) 34 D6
Saint-Juéry (12) 171 F3
Saint-Juéry (48) 141 F6
Saint-Juéry (81) 170 C2
Saint-Juire-Champgillon (85) 106 D1
Saint-Julia (31) 170 A6
Saint-Julia-de-Bec (11) 186 D6
Saint-Julien (21) 86 A5
Saint-Julien (22) 33 G5
Saint-Julien (34) 171 H6
Saint-Julien (39) 117 F3
Saint-Julien (69) 116 A6
Saint-Julien (83) 176 D4
Saint-Julien (88) 69 E5
Saint-Julien-aux-Bois (19) 139 G3
Saint-Julien-Beychevelle (33) 134 D2
Saint-Julien-Boutières (07) 143 F4
Saint-Julien-Chapteuil (43) 142 D4
Saint-Julien-d’Ance (43) 142 C1
Saint-Julien-d’Armagnac (40) 166 C2
Saint-Julien-d’Arpaon (48) 156 B5
Saint-Julien-d’Asse (04) 177 E2
Saint-Julien-de-Bourdeilles (24) 137 E1
Saint-Julien-de-Briola (11) 186 B4
Saint-Julien-de-Cassagnas (30) 157 F6
Saint-Julien-de-Chédon (41) 79 G6
Saint-Julien-de-Civry (71) 115 F3
Saint-Julien-de-Concelles (44) 75 E5
Saint-Julien-de-Coppel (63) 127 G4
Saint-Julien-de-Crempse (24) 137 E4
Saint-Julien-de-Gras-Capou (09) 186 A5
Saint-Julien-de-Jonzy (71) 115 F4
Saint-Julien-de-la-Liègue (27) 41 E1
Saint-Julien-de-la-Nef (30) 173 E2
Saint-Julien-de-Lampon (24) 138 B5
Saint-Julien-de-l’Escap (17) 121 F1
Saint-Julien-de-l’Herms (38) 130 C6
Saint-Julien-de-Mailloc (14) 15 F5
Saint-Julien-de-Peyrolas (30) 157 H5
Saint-Julien-de-Raz (38) 145 F1
Saint-Julien-de-Toursac (15) 139 H6
Saint-Julien-de-Vouvantes (44) 75 F1
Saint-Julien-des-Chazes (43) 142 A4
Saint-Julien-des-Landes (85) 91 E4
Saint-Julien-des-Points (48) 156 D5
Saint-Julien-d’Eymet (24) 151 E1
Saint-Julien-d’Oddes (42) 128 D2
Saint-Julien-du-Gua (07) 143 G6
Saint-Julien-du-Pinet (43) 142 D3
Saint-Julien-du-Puy (81) 170 B4
Saint-Julien-du-Sault (89) 65 E5
Saint-Julien-du-Serre (07) 157 G1
Saint-Julien-du-Terroux (53) 59 F1
Saint-Julien-du-Tournel (48) 156 B3
Saint-Julien-du-Verdon (04) 177 H2
Saint-Julien-en-Beauchêne (05) 159 H2
Saint-Julien-en-Born (40) 148 A6
Saint-Julien-en-Champsaur (05) 160 C1
Saint-Julien-en-Genevois (74) 118 B5
Saint-Julien-en-Quint (26) 144 D5
Saint-Julien-en-Saint-Alban (07) 143 H6
Saint-Julien-en-Vercors (26) 145 E4
Saint-Julien-Gaulène (81) 170 D2
Saint-Julien-la-Geneste (63) 112 D6
Saint-Julien-la-Genête (23) 112 C5
Saint-Julien-la-Vêtre (42) 128 B3
Saint-Julien-Labrousse (07) 143 G5
Saint-Julien-l’Ars (86) 109 F1
Saint-Julien-le-Châtel (23) 112 B6
Saint-Julien-le-Faucon (14) 15 E6
Saint-Julien-le-Pèlerin (19) 139 G4
Saint-Julien-le-Petit (87) 125 E2
Saint-Julien-le-Roux (07) 143 H5
Saint-Julien-le-Vendômois (19) 124 B6
Saint-Julien-lès-Gorze (54) 26 A6
Saint-Julien-lès-Metz (57) 26 C5
Saint-Julien-lès-Montbéliard (25) 88 B4
Saint-Julien-les-Rosiers (30) 157 E6
Saint-Julien-lès-Russey (25) 104 C1
Saint-Julien-les-Villas (10) 66 B3
Saint-Julien-Maumont (19) 138 D4
Saint-Julien-Molhesabate (43) 143 F2
Saint-Julien-Molin-Molette (42) 143 H1
Saint-Julien-Mont-Denis (73) 146 C1
Saint-Julien-près-Bort (19) 126 A6
Saint-Julien-Puy-Lavèze (63) 126 C4
Saint-Julien-sous-les-Côtes (55) 47 H4
Saint-Julien-sur-Bibost (69) 129 G3
Saint-Julien-sur-Calonne (14) 15 F4
Saint-Julien-sur-Cher (41) 96 D1
Saint-Julien-sur-Dheune (71) 101 E5
Saint-Julien-sur-Garonne (31) 185 E3
Saint-Julien-sur-Reyssouze (01) 116 D3
Saint-Julien-sur-Sarthe (61) 60 C1
Saint-Julien-sur-Veyle (01) 116 C5
Saint-Julien-Vocance (07) 143 G3
Saint-Junien (87) 123 G2
Saint-Junien-la-Bregère (23) 125 E2
Saint-Junien-les-Combes (87) 110 B6
Saint-Jure (57) 48 D3
Saint-Jurs (04) 177 F2
Saint-Just (01) 117 E5
Saint-Just (07) 157 H5
Saint-Just (15) 141 F5
Saint-Just (18) 97 H3
Saint-Just (24) 137 E1
Saint-Just (27) 41 F1
Saint-Just (34) 173 H5
Saint-Just (35) 56 D6
Saint-Just (63) 128 B6
Saint-Just-Chaleyssin (38) 130 B4
Saint-Just-d’Avray (69) 129 F1
Saint-Just-de-Claix (38) 144 D3
Saint-Just-en-Bas (42) 128 C3
Saint-Just-en-Brie (77) 43 H6
Saint-Just-en-Chaussée (60) 20 D4
Saint-Just-en-Chevalet (42) 128 C2
Saint-Just-et-le-Bézu (11) 186 D6
Saint-Just-et-Vacquières (30) 174 A1
Saint-Just-Ibarre (64) 181 E3
Saint-Just-la-Pendue (42) 129 E2
Saint-Just-le-Martel (87) 124 C2
Saint-Just-Luzac (17) 120 C2
Saint-Just-Malmont (43) 143 F1
Saint-Just-près-Brioude (43) 141 G2
Saint-Just-Saint-Rambert (42) 129 E5
Saint-Just-Sauvage (51) 65 H1
Saint-Just-sur-Dive (49) 93 H1
Saint-Just-sur-Viaur (12) 154 B6
Saint-Justin (32) 167 E6
Saint-Justin (40) 166 C2
Saint-Juvat (22) 34 D6
Saint-Juvin (08) 24 C5
Saint-Lactencin (36) 96 B4
Saint-Lager (69) 116 A6
Saint-Lager-Bressac (07) 158 A1
Saint-Lamain (39) 102 D5
Saint-Lambert (14) 38 B3
Saint-Lambert (78) 42 B5
Saint-Lambert-du-Lattay (49) 76 D6
Saint-Lambert-et-Mont-de-Jeux (08) 24 A4
Saint-Lambert-la-Potherie (49) 76 D4
Saint-Lambert-sur-Dive (61) 39 F4
Saint-Langis-lès-Mortagne (61) 60 D1
Saint-Lanne (65) 166 D5
Saint-Laon (86) 93 H3
Saint-Lary (09) 184 C6
Saint-Lary (32) 167 G4
Saint-Lary-Boujean (31) 184 B3
Saint-Lary-Soulan (65) 196 D1
Saint-Lattier (38) 144 D3
Saint-Launeuc (22) 56 B1
Saint-Laure (63) 127 G2
Saint-Laurent (08) 24 B1
Saint-Laurent (18) 97 F1
Saint-Laurent (22) 32 D3
Saint-Laurent (23) 111 G5
Saint-Laurent (31) 184 B2
Saint-Laurent (47) 150 D5
Saint-Laurent (74) 118 D6
Saint-Laurent-Blangy (62) 8 B2
Saint-Laurent-Bretagne (64) 182 C1
Saint-Laurent-Chabreuges (43) 141 G2
Saint-Laurent-d’Agny (69) 129 H4
Saint-Laurent-d’Aigouze (30) 173 H5
Saint-Laurent-d’Andenay (71) 101 E6
Saint-Laurent-d’Arce (33) 135 F3
Saint-Laurent-de-Belzagot (16) 122 B6
Saint-Laurent-de-Brèvedent (76) 15 F1
Saint-Laurent-de-Carnols (30) 157 H5
Saint-Laurent-de-Cerdans (66) 200 D5
Saint-Laurent-de-Céris (16) 123 E1
Saint-Laurent-de-Chamousset (69) 129 F3
Saint-Laurent-de-Cognac (16) 121 G3
Saint-Laurent-de-Condel (14) 14 B6
Saint-Laurent-de-Cuves (50) 37 F4
Saint-Laurent-de-Gosse (40) 164 C5
Saint-Laurent-de-Jourdes (86) 109 F3
Saint-Laurent-de-la-Barrière (17) 107 F6
Saint-Laurent-de-la-Cabrerisse (11) 187 G4
Saint-Laurent-de-la-Plaine (49) 75 H4
Saint-Laurent-de-la-Prée (17) 106 D6
Saint-Laurent-de-la-Salanque (66) 201 G1
Saint-Laurent-de-la-Salle (85) 107 E1
Saint-Laurent-de-Lévézou (12) 155 E6
Saint-Laurent-de-Lin (37) 78 B4
Saint-Laurent-de-Mure (69) 130 B4
Saint-Laurent-de-Muret (48) 155 G2
Saint-Laurent-de-Neste (65) 183 H4
Saint-Laurent-de-Terregatte (50) 37 E6
Saint-Laurent-de-Trèves (48) 156 B5
Saint-Laurent-de-Vaux (69) 129 H3
Saint-Laurent-de-Veyrès (48) 141 F6
Saint-Laurent-des-Arbres (30) 174 D1
Saint-Laurent-des-Autels (49) 75 F4
Saint-Laurent-des-Bâtons (24) 137 F4
Saint-Laurent-des-Bois (27) 41 E4
Saint-Laurent-des-Bois (41) 80 A1
Saint-Laurent-des-Combes (16) 136 B1
Saint-Laurent-des-Combes (33) 135 H5
Saint-Laurent-des-Hommes (24) 136 C4
Saint-Laurent-des-Mortiers (53) 77 E2
Saint-Laurent-des-Vignes (24) 136 D6
Saint-Laurent-d’Oingt (69) 129 G1
Saint-Laurent-d’Olt (12) 155 F3
Saint-Laurent-d’Onay (26) 144 C2
Saint-Laurent-du-Bois (33) 150 A1
Saint-Laurent-du-Cros (05) 160 B1
Saint-Laurent-du-Mont (14) 15 E5
Saint-Laurent-du-Mottay (49) 76 B5
Saint-Laurent-du-Pape (07) 144 A6
Saint-Laurent-du-Plan (33) 150 A1
Saint-Laurent-du-Pont (38) 131 G6
Saint-Laurent-du-Tencement (27) 39 H3
Saint-Laurent-du-Var (06) 195 F3
Saint-Laurent-du-Verdon (04) 177 E4
Saint-Laurent-en-Beaumont (38) 145 H5
Saint-Laurent-en-Brionnais (71) 115 F4
Saint-Laurent-en-Caux (76) 17 F3
Saint-Laurent-en-Gâtines (37) 79 E4
Saint-Laurent-en-Grandvaux (39) 118 A1
Saint-Laurent-en-Royans (26) 144 D4
Saint-Laurent-la-Conche (42) 129 E4
Saint-Laurent-la-Gâtine (28) 41 G5
Saint-Laurent-la-Roche (39) 117 F1
Saint-Laurent-la-Vallée (24) 137 H6
Saint-Laurent-la-Vernède (30) 174 B1
Saint-Laurent-l’Abbaye (58) 82 C6
Saint-Laurent-le-Minier (30) 173 E2
Saint-Laurent-les-Bains (07) 156 D2
Saint-Laurent-les-Églises (87) 124 C1
Saint-Laurent-les-Tours (46) 139 F5
Saint-Laurent-Lolmie (46) 152 B5
Saint-Laurent-Médoc (33) 134 D2
Saint-Laurent-Nouan (41) 80 B3
Saint-Laurent-Rochefort (42) 128 C3
Saint-Laurent-sous-Coiron (07) 157 G2
Saint-Laurent-sur-Gorre (87) 123 H3
Saint-Laurent-sur-Manoire (24) 137 F3
Saint-Laurent-sur-Mer (14) 13 G4
Saint-Laurent-sur-Othain (55) 25 F4
Saint-Laurent-sur-Oust (56) 56 B5
Saint-Laurent-sur-Saône (01) 116 B4
Saint-Laurent-sur-Sèvre (85) 92 C3
Saint-Laurs (79) 107 G1
Saint-Léger (06) 178 B1
Saint-Léger (16) 122 B5
Saint-Léger (17) 121 F4
Saint-Léger (47) 150 D5
Saint-Léger (53) 59 E5
Saint-Léger (62) 8 B3
Saint-Léger (73) 132 C6
Saint-Léger (77) 44 A4
Saint-Léger-aux-Bois (60) 21 G4
Saint-Léger-aux-Bois (76) 6 C6
Saint-Léger-Bridereix (23) 111 E4
Saint-Léger-de-Balson (33) 149 F3
Saint-Léger-de-Fougeret (58) 100 A3
Saint-Léger-de-la-Martinière (79) 108 B4
Saint-Léger-de-Montbrillais (86) 93 H2
Saint-Léger-de-Montbrun (79) 93 G3
Saint-Léger-de-Peyre (48) 155 H2
Saint-Léger-de-Rôtes (27) 40 A1
Saint-Léger-des-Aubées (28) 62 C2
Saint-Léger-des-Bois (49) 76 D4
Saint-Léger-des-Prés (35) 35 F6
Saint-Léger-des-Vignes (58) 99 F5
Saint-Léger-du-Bois (71) 101 E3
Saint-Léger-du-Bourg-Denis (76) 18 D4
Saint-Léger-du-Gennetey (27) 18 A5
Saint-Léger-du-Malzieu (48) 141 G5
Saint-Léger-du-Ventoux (84) 159 E5
Saint-Léger-Dubosq (14) 14 D4
Saint-Léger-en-Bray (60) 20 A5
Saint-Léger-en-Yvelines (78) 41 H5
Saint-Léger-la-Montagne (87) 110 D6
Saint-Léger-le-Guérétois (23) 111 F5
Saint-Léger-le-Petit (18) 98 C2
Saint-Léger-lès-Authie (80) 7 H4
Saint-Léger-lès-Domart (80) 7 F4
Saint-Léger-les-Mélèzes (05) 160 C1
Saint-Léger-lès-Paray (71) 115 E2
Saint-Léger-les-Vignes (44) 74 B6
Saint-Léger-Magnazeix (87) 110 C4
Saint-Léger-près-Troyes (10) 66 B4
Saint-Léger-sous-Beuvray (71) 100 B4
Saint-Léger-sous-Brienne (10) 66 D2
Saint-Léger-sous-Cholet (49) 92 C2
Saint-Léger-sous-la-Bussière (71) 115 H4
Saint-Léger-sous-Margerie (10) 66 D1
Saint-Léger-sur-Bresle (80) 6 C6
Saint-Léger-sur-Dheune (71) 101 F5
Saint-Léger-sur-Roanne (42) 115 E6
Saint-Léger-sur-Sarthe (61) 60 C1
Saint-Léger-sur-Vouzance (03) 114 D3
Saint-Léger-Triey (21) 86 B6
Saint-Léger-Vauban (89) 84 B6
Saint-Léomer (86) 110 A3
Saint-Léon (03) 114 C3
Saint-Léon (31) 185 G1
Saint-Léon (33) 135 G6
Saint-Léon (47) 150 C5
Saint-Léon-d’Issigeac (24) 151 F1
Saint-Léon-sur-l’Isle (24) 137 E3
Saint-Léon-sur-Vézère (24) 137 H4
Saint-Léonard (32) 168 A3
Saint-Léonard (51) 23 F6
Saint-Léonard (62) 1 F4
Saint-Léonard (76) 16 C3
Saint-Léonard (88) 70 D3
Saint-Léonard-de-Noblat (87) 124 C2
Saint-Léonard-des-Bois (72) 59 H2
Saint-Léonard-des-Parcs (61) 39 G5
Saint-Léonard-en-Beauce (41) 80 A1
Saint-Léons (12) 155 F6
Saint-Léopardin-d’Augy (03) 98 D6
Saint-Léry (56) 56 B3
Saint-Leu-d’Esserent (60) 20 C6
Saint-Leu-la-Forêt (95) 42 C2
Saint-Lézer (65) 183 E1
Saint-Lézin (49) 76 C6
Saint-Lieux-Lafenasse (81) 170 C4
Saint-Lieux-lès-Lavaur (81) 169 H4
Saint-Lin (79) 108 A1
Saint-Lions (04) 177 G1
Saint-Lizier (09) 184 D5
Saint-Lizier-du-Planté (32) 184 C1
Saint-Lô (50) 37 G1
Saint-Lô-d’Ourville (50) 12 C4
Saint-Lon-les-Mines (40) 164 D5
Saint-Longis (72) 60 C2
Saint-Lormel (22) 34 C4
Saint-Lothain (39) 102 D5
Saint-Loube (32) 184 D1
Saint-Loubert (33) 150 A2
Saint-Loubès (33) 135 F4
Saint-Loubouer (40) 166 A4
Saint-Louet-sur-Seulles (14) 38 A1
Saint-Louet-sur-Vire (50) 37 G2
Saint-Louis (57) 50 B4
Saint-Louis (68) 89 H3
Saint-Louis-de-Montferrand (33) 135 F4
Saint-Louis-en-l’Isle (24) 136 D3
Saint-Louis-et-Parahou (11) 200 B1
Saint-Louis-lès-Bitche (57) 50 C2
Saint-Loup (03) 114 A3
Saint-Loup (17) 107 G6
Saint-Loup (23) 112 B5
Saint-Loup (39) 102 B3
Saint-Loup (41) 96 D1
Saint-Loup (50) 35 H3
Saint-Loup (51) 45 E5
Saint-Loup (58) 82 C5
Saint-Loup (69) 129 G2
Saint-Loup (82) 168 B1
Saint-Loup-Cammas (31) 169 F4
Saint-Loup-de-Buffigny (10) 65 G2
Saint-Loup-de-Fribois (14) 15 E5
Saint-Loup-de-Gonois (45) 64 C5
Saint-Loup-de-Naud (77) 64 D1
Saint-Loup-de-Varennes (71) 101 G6
Saint-Loup-des-Chaumes (18) 97 G5
Saint-Loup-des-Vignes (45) 63 G5
Saint-Loup-d’Ordon (89) 64 D6
Saint-Loup-du-Dorat (53) 59 E6
Saint-Loup-du-Gast (53) 59 E2
Saint-Loup-en-Champagne (08) 23 F4
Saint-Loup-en-Comminges (31) 184 A3
Saint-Loup-Géanges (71) 101 G4
Saint-Loup-Hors (14) 13 H5
Saint-Loup-Lamairé (79) 93 G5
Saint-Loup-Nantouard (70) 86 D5
Saint-Loup-sur-Aujon (52) 85 H1
Saint-Loup-sur-Semouse (70) 87 G1
Saint-Loup-Terrier (08) 24 A3
Saint-Loyer-des-Champs (61) 39 E5
Saint-Lubin-de-Cravant (28) 40 D5
Saint-Lubin-de-la-Haye (28) 41 G4
Saint-Lubin-des-Joncherets (28) 41 E4
Saint-Lubin-en-Vergonnois (41) 79 H3
Saint-Luc (27) 41 E3
Saint-Lucien (28) 41 G6
Saint-Lumier-en-Champagne (51) 46 B4
Saint-Lumier-la-Populeuse (51) 46 C5
Saint-Lumine-de-Clisson (44) 75 E6
Saint-Lumine-de-Coutais (44) 74 B6
Saint-Lunaire (35) 34 C3
Saint-Luperce (28) 61 H2
Saint-Lupicin (39) 117 H3
Saint-Lupien (10) 65 G2
Saint-Lyé (10) 66 A2
Saint-Lyé-la-Forêt (45) 63 E5
Saint-Lyphard (44) 73 G3
Saint-Lys (31) 168 D6
Saint-Macaire (33) 149 H2
Saint-Macaire-du-Bois (49) 93 F2
Saint-Macaire-en-Mauges (49) 75 G6
Saint-Maclou (27) 15 G3
Saint-Maclou-de-Folleville (76) 18 D2
Saint-Maclou-la-Brière (76) 16 C4
Saint-Macoux (86) 108 D5
Saint-Maden (22) 34 C6
Saint-Magne (33) 149 E2
Saint-Magne-de-Castillon (33) 136 A5
Saint-Maigner (63) 112 D6
Saint-Maigrin (17) 121 G6
Saint-Maime (04) 176 C2
Saint-Maime-de-Péreyrol (24) 137 E4
Saint-Maixant (23) 125 H1
Saint-Maixant (33) 149 H2
Saint-Maixent (72) 60 D5
Saint-Maixent-de-Beugné (79) 107 G2
Saint-Maixent-l’École (79) 108 B3
Saint-Maixent-sur-Vie (85) 90 D3
Saint-Maixme-Hauterive (28) 40 D6
Saint-Malo (35) 36 A5
Saint-Malo-de-Beignon (56) 56 C4
Saint-Malo-de-Guersac (44) 73 H4
Saint-Malo-de-la-Lande (50) 36 D1
Saint-Malo-de-Phily (35) 57 E5
Saint-Malo-des-Trois-Fontaines (56) 56 A3
Saint-Malô-du-Bois (85) 92 C3
Saint-Malo-en-Donziois (58) 83 E6
Saint-Malon-sur-Mel (35) 56 C3
Saint-Mamert (69) 115 H4
Saint-Mamert-du-Gard (30) 173 H3
Saint-Mamet (31) 197 F1
Saint-Mamet-la-Salvetat (15) 139 H5
Saint-Mammès (77) 64 B2
Saint-Mandé (94) 42 D4
Saint-Mandé-sur-Brédoire (17) 108 A6
Saint-Mandrier-sur-Mer (83) 193 E5
Saint-Manvieu-Bocage (14) 37 G3
Saint-Manvieu-Norrey (14) 14 B4
Saint-Marc (15) 141 F5
Saint-Marc-á-Frongier (23) 125 G2
Saint-Marc-á-Loubaud (23) 125 F2
Saint-Marc-du-Cor (41) 61 F6
Saint-Marc-Jaumegarde (13) 176 B6
Saint-Marc-la-Lande (79) 107 H2
Saint-Marc-le-Blanc (35) 35 G6
Saint-Marc-sur-Couesnon (35) 57 H1
Saint-Marc-sur-Seine (21) 85 E3
Saint-Marcan (35) 35 F4
Saint-Marceau (08) 24 A2
Saint-Marceau (72) 60 A4
Saint-Marcel (01) 130 B1
Saint-Marcel (08) 23 H1
Saint-Marcel (27) 41 F2
Saint-Marcel (36) 111 E1
Saint-Marcel (54) 26 A5
Saint-Marcel (56) 56 A5
Saint-Marcel (70) 87 E1
Saint-Marcel (71) 101 G5
Saint-Marcel (73) 132 D5
Saint-Marcel-Bel-Accueil (38) 130 D4
Saint-Marcel-Campes (81) 170 B1
Saint-Marcel-d’Ardèche (07) 158 A4
Saint-Marcel-de-Careiret (30) 157 H6
Saint-Marcel-de-Félines (42) 129 E2
Saint-Marcel-du-Périgord (24) 137 F5
Saint-Marcel-d’Urfé (42) 128 C2
Saint-Marcel-en-Marcillat (03) 112 D5
Saint-Marcel-en-Murat (03) 113 F4
Saint-Marcel-l’Éclairé (69) 129 F2
Saint-Marcel-lès-Annonay (07) 143 H2
Saint-Marcel-lès-Sauzet (26) 158 B2
Saint-Marcel-lès-Valence (26) 144 B4
Saint-Marcel-Paulel (31) 169 G5
Saint-Marcel-sur-Aude (11) 188 A3
Saint-Marcelin-de-Cray (71) 115 H2
Saint-Marcellin (38) 144 D3
Saint-Marcellin-en-Forez (42) 129 E5
Saint-Marcellin-lès-Vaison (84) 158 D5
Saint-Marcet (31) 184 B3
Saint-Marcory (24) 151 H1
Saint-Marcouf (14) 13 F5
Saint-Marcouf (50) 13 E3
Saint-Mard (02) 22 C5
Saint-Mard (17) 107 F5
Saint-Mard (54) 69 G1
Saint-Mard (77) 43 F2
Saint-Mard (80) 21 E2
Saint-Mard-de-Réno (61) 60 D1
Saint-Mard-de-Vaux (71) 101 F5
Saint-Mard-lès-Rouffy (51) 45 F3
Saint-Mard-sur-Auve (51) 46 B2
Saint-Mard-sur-le-Mont (51) 46 C3
Saint-Mards (76) 17 G3
Saint-Mards-de-Blacarville (27) 15 H3
Saint-Mards-de-Fresne (27) 15 G6
Saint-Mards-en-Othe (10) 65 H4
Saint-Marien (23) 112 A3
Saint-Mariens (33) 135 F3
Saint-Mars-de-Coutais (44) 74 B6
Saint-Mars-de-Locquenay (72) 60 C6
Saint-Mars-d’Égrenne (61) 38 A6
Saint-Mars-d’Outillé (72) 78 B1
Saint-Mars-du-Désert (44) 75 E4
Saint-Mars-du-Désert (53) 59 G3
Saint-Mars-la-Brière (72) 60 C5
Saint-Mars-la-Jaille (44) 75 F2
Saint-Mars-la-Réorthe (85) 92 B4
Saint-Mars-sous-Ballon (72) 60 B4
Saint-Mars-sur-Colmont (53) 58 D2
Saint-Mars-sur-la-Futaie (53) 58 B1
Saint-Mars-Vieux-Maisons (77) 44 B5
Saint-Marsal (66) 200 D4
Saint-Martial (07) 143 E5
Saint-Martial (15) 141 E5
Saint-Martial (16) 122 B6
Saint-Martial (17) 107 H6
Saint-Martial (30) 173 E1
Saint-Martial (33) 150 A1
Saint-Martial-d’Albarède (24) 137 H1
Saint-Martial-d’Artenset (24) 136 C4
Saint-Martial-de-Gimel (19) 139 F2
Saint-Martial-de-Mirambeau (17) 121 E6
Saint-Martial-de-Nabirat (24) 152 B1
Saint-Martial-de-Valette (24) 123 F5
Saint-Martial-de-Vitaterne (17) 121 F5
Saint-Martial-Entraygues (19) 139 F3
Saint-Martial-le-Mont (23) 111 H6
Saint-Martial-le-Vieux (23) 125 H4
Saint-Martial-sur-Isop (87) 109 H5
Saint-Martial-sur-Né (17) 121 G4
Saint-Martial-Viveyrol (24) 136 D1
Saint-Martin (32) 167 F6
Saint-Martin (54) 49 G6
Saint-Martin (65) 183 E3
Saint-Martin (66) 200 C1
Saint-Martin (67) 71 F2
Saint-Martin (83) 193 E1
Saint-Martin-au-Bosc (76) 6 C6
Saint-Martin-au-Laërt (62) 2 B4
Saint-Martin-aux-Arbres (76) 17 F4
Saint-Martin-aux-Bois (60) 20 D3
Saint-Martin-aux-Buneaux (76) 16 D2
Saint-Martin-aux-Champs (51) 46 A4
Saint-Martin-aux-Chartrains (14) 15 F3
Saint-Martin-Belle-Roche (71) 116 B3
Saint-Martin-Bellevue (74) 132 B1
Saint-Martin-Boulogne (62) 1 F4
Saint-Martin-Cantalès (15) 139 H3
Saint-Martin-Château (23) 125 E2
Saint-Martin-Choquel (62) 1 G4
Saint-Martin-Curton (47) 150 B4
Saint-Martin-d’Abbat (45) 81 F1
Saint-Martin-d’Ablois (51) 45 E2
Saint-Martin-d’Août (26) 144 B2
Saint-Martin-d’Arberoue (64) 181 E1
Saint-Martin-d’Arc (73) 146 D2
Saint-Martin-d’Arcé (49) 77 G4
Saint-Martin-d’Ardèche (07) 157 H5
Saint-Martin-d’Armagnac (32) 166 D4
Saint-Martin-d’Arrossa (64) 180 D2
Saint-Martin-d’Ary (17) 135 H2
Saint-Martin-d’Aubigny (50) 12 D6
Saint-Martin-d’Audouville (50) 12 D3
Saint-Martin-d’Auxigny (18) 97 H1
Saint-Martin-d’Auxy (71) 101 E6
Saint-Martin-de-Bavel (01) 131 F2
Saint-Martin-de-Beauville (47) 151 G5
Saint-Martin-de-Belleville (73) 132 D6
Saint-Martin-de-Bernegoue (79) 107 H4
Saint-Martin-de-Bienfaite-la-Cressonnière (14) 15 G6
Saint-Martin-de-Blagny (14) 13 G5
Saint-Martin-de-Bonfossé (50) 37 F1
Saint-Martin-de-Boscherville (76) 17 F6
Saint-Martin-de-Bossenay (10) 65 G2
Saint-Martin-de-Boubaux (48) 156 D6
Saint-Martin-de-Bréthencourt (78) 62 D1
Saint-Martin-de-Brômes (04) 176 D3
Saint-Martin-de-Caralp (09) 185 G5
Saint-Martin-de-Castillon (84) 176 A3
Saint-Martin-de-Cenilly (50) 37 E2
Saint-Martin-de-Clelles (38) 145 F5
Saint-Martin-de-Commune (71) 101 E4
Saint-Martin-de-Connée (53) 59 G3
Saint-Martin-de-Coux (17) 135 H3
Saint-Martin-de-Crau (13) 191 E2
Saint-Martin-de-Fontenay (14) 14 B5
Saint-Martin-de-Fraigneau (85) 107 F2
Saint-Martin-de-Fressengeas (24) 123 G6
Saint-Martin-de-Fugères (43) 142 C5
Saint-Martin-de-Goyne (32) 167 H2
Saint-Martin-de-Gurson (24) 136 B4
Saint-Martin-de-Hinx (40) 164 C5
Saint-Martin-de-Juillers (17) 121 G1
Saint-Martin-de-Jussac (87) 123 G2
Saint-Martin-de-la-Brasque (84) 176 B4
Saint-Martin-de-la-Cluze (38) 145 G4
Saint-Martin-de-la-Lieue (14) 15 F5
Saint-Martin-de-la-Mer (21) 100 C1
Saint-Martin-de-la-Place (49) 77 G6
Saint-Martin-de-la-Porte (73) 146 D2
Saint-Martin-de-Lamps (36) 96 B3
Saint-Martin-de-Landelles (50) 37 F6
Saint-Martin-de-Lansuscle (48) 156 C6
Saint-Martin-de-l’Arçon (34) 171 H6
Saint-Martin-de-Laye (33) 135 H3
Saint-Martin-de-Lenne (12) 155 E4
Saint-Martin-de-Lerm (33) 150 B1
Saint-Martin-de-Lixy (71) 115 F5
Saint-Martin-de-Londres (34) 173 E4
Saint-Martin-de-Mâcon (79) 93 G3
Saint-Martin-de-Mailloc (14) 15 F5
Saint-Martin-de-Mieux (14) 38 D3
Saint-Martin-de-Nigelles (28) 41 G6
Saint-Martin-de-Queyrières (05) 147 E5
Saint-Martin-de-Ré (17) 106 B4
Saint-Martin-de-Ribérac (24) 136 D2
Saint-Martin-de-Saint-Maixent (79) 108 B3
Saint-Martin-de-Salencey (71) 115 H2
Saint-Martin-de-Sallen (14) 14 A6
Saint-Martin-de-Sanzay (79) 93 G2
Saint-Martin-de-Seignanx (40) 164 C5
Saint-Martin-de-Sescas (33) 150 A2
Saint-Martin-de-Valamas (07) 143 F5
Saint-Martin-de-Valgalgues (30) 157 E6
Saint-Martin-de-Varreville (50) 13 E4
Saint-Martin-de-Vaulserre (38) 131 G5
Saint-Martin-de-Vers (46) 152 D2
Saint-Martin-de-Villeréal (47) 151 G2
Saint-Martin-de-Villereglan (11) 186 D4
Saint-Martin-d’Écublei (61) 40 A4
Saint-Martin-d’Entraunes (06) 161 G6
Saint-Martin-des-Besaces (14) 37 H2
Saint-Martin-des-Bois (41) 79 E2
Saint-Martin-des-Champs (18) 98 C2
Saint-Martin-des-Champs (29) 32 A3
Saint-Martin-des-Champs (50) 35 H3
Saint-Martin-des-Champs (77) 44 B4
Saint-Martin-des-Champs (78) 41 H3
Saint-Martin-des-Champs (89) 82 C3
Saint-Martin-des-Combes (24) 137 E4

Saint-Martin-des-Entrées (14) 14 A4
Saint-Martin-des-Fontaines (85) 107 E1
Saint-Martin-des-Lais (03) 99 G6
Saint-Martin-des-Landes (61) 38 D6
Saint-Martin-des-Monts (72) 60 D4
Saint-Martin-des-Noyers (85) 92 A5
Saint-Martin-des-Olmes (63) 128 B5
Saint-Martin-des-Pézerits (61) 39 H6
Saint-Martin-des-Plains (63) 127 G5
Saint-Martin-des-Prés (22) 33 F6
Saint-Martin-des-Puits (11) 187 F5
Saint-Martin-des-Tilleuls (85) 92 B3
Saint-Martin-d'Estréaux (42) 114 C5
Saint-Martin-d'Hardinghem (62) 2 A5
Saint-Martin-d'Hères (38) 145 G2
Saint-Martin-d'Heuille (58) 99 E3
Saint-Martin-d'Ollières (63) 127 H6
Saint-Martin-Don (14) 37 G3
Saint-Martin-d'Oney (40) 165 H2
Saint-Martin-d'Ordon (89) 64 D6
Saint-Martin-d'Oydes (09) 185 G3
Saint-Martin-du-Bec (76) 15 F1
Saint-Martin-du-Bois (33) 135 G4
Saint-Martin-du-Bois (49) 76 C2
Saint-Martin-du-Boschet (77) 44 B5
Saint-Martin-du-Clocher (16) 108 D6
Saint-Martin-du-Fouilloux (49) 76 D5
Saint-Martin-du-Fouilloux (79) 108 B1
Saint-Martin-du-Frêne (01) 117 G5
Saint-Martin-du-Lac (71) 115 E4
Saint-Martin-du-Limet (53) 76 B1
Saint-Martin-du-Manoir (76) 15 F1
Saint-Martin-du-Mesnil-Oury (14) 15 E6
Saint-Martin-du-Mont (01) 117 E5
Saint-Martin-du-Mont (21) 85 F5
Saint-Martin-du-Mont (71) 117 E1
Saint-Martin-du-Puy (33) 150 B1
Saint-Martin-du-Puy (58) 83 H6
Saint-Martin-du-Tartre (71) 116 A1
Saint-Martin-du-Tertre (89) 65 E4
Saint-Martin-du-Tertre (95) 42 D1
Saint-Martin-du-Tilleul (27) 15 H5
Saint-Martin-du-Var (06) 195 E2
Saint-Martin-du-Vieux-Bellême (61) 60 D2
Saint-Martin-du-Vivier (76) 18 D4
Saint-Martin-d'Uriage (38) 145 H3
Saint-Martin-en-Bière (77) 63 H2
Saint-Martin-en-Bresse (71) 102 A5
Saint-Martin-en-Campagne (76) 17 H1
Saint-Martin-en-Gâtinois (71) 101 H4
Saint-Martin-en-Haut (69) 129 G4
Saint-Martin-en-Vercors (26) 145 E4
Saint-Martin-Gimois (32) 168 B6
Saint-Martin-la-Campagne (27) 40 D2
Saint-Martin-la-Garenne (78) 41 H2
Saint-Martin-la-Méanne (19) 139 F3
Saint-Martin-la-Patrouille (71) 115 H1
Saint-Martin-la-Plaine (42) 129 G5
Saint-Martin-la-Sauveté (42) 128 C2
Saint-Martin-Labouval (46) 153 E3
Saint-Martin-Lacaussade (33) 135 E2
Saint-Martin-Laguépie (81) 153 G6
Saint-Martin-l'Aiguillon (61) 38 D6
Saint-Martin-Lalande (11) 186 C2
Saint-Martin-l'Ars (86) 109 F4
Saint-Martin-Lars-en-Sainte-Hermine (85) 107 E1
Saint-Martin-l'Astier (24) 136 C3
Saint-Martin-le-Beau (37) 79 F6
Saint-Martin-le-Bouillant (50) 37 F4
Saint-Martin-le-Châtel (01) 116 D4
Saint-Martin-le-Colonel (26) 144 D4
Saint-Martin-le-Gaillard (76) 6 A5
Saint-Martin-le-Gréard (50) 12 C2
Saint-Martin-le-Hébert (50) 12 C3
Saint-Martin-le-Mault (87) 110 C3
Saint-Martin-le-Noeud (60) 20 A5
Saint-Martin-le-Pin (24) 123 E5
Saint-Martin-le-Redon (46) 152 A3
Saint-Martin-le-Vieil (11) 186 C2
Saint-Martin-le-Vieux (87) 124 A3
Saint-Martin-le-Vinoux (38) 145 G2
Saint-Martin-les-Eaux (04) 176 C3
Saint-Martin-lès-Langres (52) 86 A1
Saint-Martin-lès-Melle (79) 108 B4
Saint-Martin-lès-Seyne (04) 160 D4
Saint-Martin-Lestra (42) 129 F3
Saint-Martin-l'Heureux (51) 23 G6
Saint-Martin-l'Hortier (76) 19 E1
Saint-Martin-Longueau (60) 21 E5
Saint-Martin-Lys (11) 200 A1
Saint-Martin-Osmonville (76) 17 H4
Saint-Martin-Petit (47) 150 B2
Saint-Martin-Rivière (02) 9 F4
Saint-Martin-Saint-Firmin (27) 15 H4
Saint-Martin-Sainte-Catherine (23) 124 D1
Saint-Martin-Sepert (19) 124 C6
Saint-Martin-sous-Montaigu (71) 101 F5
Saint-Martin-sous-Vigouroux (15) 140 D5
Saint-Martin-sur-Armançon (89) 84 B1
Saint-Martin-sur-Cojeul (62) 8 B3
Saint-Martin-sur-Écaillon (59) 9 F3
Saint-Martin-sur-la-Chambre (73) 132 C6
Saint-Martin-sur-Lavezon (07) 158 A2
Saint-Martin-sur-le-Pré (51) 45 H3
Saint-Martin-sur-Nohain (58) 82 C6
Saint-Martin-sur-Ocre (45) 82 A3
Saint-Martin-sur-Ocre (89) 83 E2
Saint-Martin-sur-Ouanne (89) 82 D1
Saint-Martin-sur-Oust (56) 56 B6
Saint-Martin-Terressus (87) 124 C2
Saint-Martin-Valmeroux (15) 140 A3
Saint-Martin-Vésubie (06) 162 D6
Saint-Martinien (03) 112 C4
Saint-Martory (31) 184 C4
Saint-Mary (16) 122 D2
Saint-Mary-le-Plain (15) 141 F3
Saint-Masmes (51) 23 G5
Saint-Mathieu (87) 123 F3
Saint-Mathieu-de-Tréviers (34) 173 F4
Saint-Mathurin (85) 91 E5
Saint-Mathurin-sur-Loire (49) 77 F5
Saint-Matré (46) 152 A4
Saint-Maudan (22) 55 G2
Saint-Maudez (22) 34 C5
Saint-Maugan (35) 56 C2
Saint-Maulvis (80) 6 D6
Saint-Maur (18) 112 B1
Saint-Maur (32) 167 F6
Saint-Maur (36) 96 C5
Saint-Maur (39) 117 G1
Saint-Maur (60) 19 H3
Saint-Maur-des-Bois (50) 37 F3
Saint-Maur-des-Fossés (94) 43 E4
Saint-Maur-sur-le-Loir (28) 62 A4
Saint-Maurice (52) 86 B1
Saint-Maurice (58) 99 G2
Saint-Maurice (63) 127 F4
Saint-Maurice (67) 71 F2
Saint-Maurice (94) 42 D4
Saint-Maurice-aux-Forges (54) 49 G6
Saint-Maurice-aux-Riches-Hommes (89) 65 F3
Saint-Maurice-Colombier (25) 88 B5
Saint-Maurice-Crillat (39) 117 H1
Saint-Maurice-d'Ardèche (07) 157 G3
Saint-Maurice-de-Beynost (01) 130 B2
Saint-Maurice-de-Cazevieille (30) 174 A1
Saint-Maurice-de-Gourdans (01) 130 C2
Saint-Maurice-de-Lestapel (47) 151 E2
Saint-Maurice-de-Lignon (43) 143 E2
Saint-Maurice-de-Rémens (01) 130 D1
Saint-Maurice-de-Rotherens (73) 131 G4
Saint-Maurice-de-Satonnay (71) 116 B3
Saint-Maurice-de-Tavernole (17) 121 G5
Saint-Maurice-de-Ventalon (48) 156 C5
Saint-Maurice-des-Champs (71) 116 A1
Saint-Maurice-des-Lions (16) 123 F1
Saint-Maurice-des-Noues (85) 107 F1
Saint-Maurice-d'Ételan (76) 15 H2
Saint-Maurice-d'Ibie (07) 157 G3
Saint-Maurice-du-Désert (61) 38 C6
Saint-Maurice-en-Chalencon (07) 143 G5
Saint-Maurice-en-Cotentin (50) 12 B4
Saint-Maurice-en-Gourgois (42) 129 E6
Saint-Maurice-en-Quercy (46) 153 G1
Saint-Maurice-en-Rivière (71) 101 H5
Saint-Maurice-en-Trièves (38) 145 G6
Saint-Maurice-en-Valgodemard (05) 146 B6
Saint-Maurice-la-Clouère (86) 109 E3
Saint-Maurice-la-Fougereuse (79) 93 E3
Saint-Maurice-la-Souterraine (23) 110 D5
Saint-Maurice-le-Girard (85) 92 C6
Saint-Maurice-le-Vieil (89) 83 E2
Saint-Maurice-les-Brousses (87) 124 B3
Saint-Maurice-lès-Charencey (61) 40 B5
Saint-Maurice-lès-Châteauneuf (71) 115 F5
Saint-Maurice-lès-Couches (71) 101 F4
Saint-Maurice-l'Exil (38) 130 A6
Saint-Maurice-Montcouronne (91) 42 B6
Saint-Maurice-Navacelles (34) 172 D3
Saint-Maurice-près-Crocq (23) 126 A2
Saint-Maurice-près-Pionsat (63) 112 D6
Saint-Maurice-Saint-Germain (28) 61 G1
Saint-Maurice-sous-les-Côtes (55) 47 H2
Saint-Maurice-sur-Adour (40) 166 A3
Saint-Maurice-sur-Aveyron (45) 82 C1
Saint-Maurice-sur-Dargoire (69) 129 H5
Saint-Maurice-sur-Eygues (26) 158 C5
Saint-Maurice-sur-Fessard (45) 64 A6
Saint-Maurice-sur-Huisne (61) 61 E2
Saint-Maurice-sur-Mortagne (88) 70 A2
Saint-Maurice-sur-Moselle (88) 88 C1
Saint-Maurice-sur-Vingeanne (21) 86 B4
Saint-Maurice-Thizouaille (89) 83 E2
Saint-Maurin (47) 151 G5
Saint-Max (54) 48 D5
Saint-Maxent (80) 6 C5
Saint-Maximin (30) 174 B2
Saint-Maximin (38) 132 A6
Saint-Maximin (60) 20 D6
Saint-Maximin-la-Sainte-Baume (83) 193 E2
Saint-Maxire (79) 107 H3
Saint-May (26) 159 E3
Saint-Mayeux (22) 55 E1
Saint-Méard (87) 124 D4
Saint-Méard-de-Drône (24) 136 D2
Saint-Méard-de-Gurçon (24) 136 B5
Saint-Médard (16) 121 H5
Saint-Médard (17) 121 G6
Saint-Médard (31) 184 B4
Saint-Médard (32) 167 G6
Saint-Médard (36) 95 H3
Saint-Médard (46) 152 B3
Saint-Médard (57) 49 F4
Saint-Médard (64) 165 H5
Saint-Médard (79) 108 A4
Saint-Médard-d'Aunis (17) 106 D5
Saint-Médard-de-Guizières (33) 136 A4
Saint-Médard-de-Mussidan (24) 136 D4
Saint-Médard-de-Presque (46) 139 E5
Saint-Médard-d'Excideuil (24) 137 H1
Saint-Médard-d'Eyrans (33) 135 F6
Saint-Médard-en-Forez (42) 129 F4
Saint-Médard-en-Jalles (33) 134 D5
Saint-Médard-la-Rochette (23) 112 A6
Saint-Médard-Nicourby (46) 139 F6
Saint-Médard-sur-Ille (35) 57 F1
Saint-Méen (29) 31 F3
Saint-Méen-le-Grand (35) 56 C2
Saint-Melaine-sur-Aubance (49) 77 E5
Saint-Mélany (07) 157 E3
Saint-Méloir-des-Bois (22) 34 B5
Saint-Méloir-des-Ondes (35) 35 E3
Saint-Même-le-Tenu (44) 91 E1
Saint-Même-les-Carrières (16) 121 H4
Saint-Memmie (51) 45 H3
Saint-Menge (88) 69 E3
Saint-Menges (08) 24 C1
Saint-Menoux (03) 113 G1
Saint-Merd-de-Lapleau (19) 139 G2
Saint-Merd-la-Breuille (23) 126 A3
Saint-Merd-les-Oussines (19) 125 G4
Saint-Méry (77) 43 G6
Saint-Meslin-du-Bosc (27) 18 B6
Saint-Mesmes (77) 43 F3
Saint-Mesmin (10) 66 A2
Saint-Mesmin (21) 85 E6
Saint-Mesmin (24) 138 A1
Saint-Mesmin (85) 92 C5
Saint-Mexant (19) 138 D2
Saint-Mézard (32) 167 H1
Saint-M'Hervé (35) 58 A4
Saint-M'Hervon (35) 56 C1
Saint-Micaud (71) 101 E6
Saint-Michel (02) 10 B6
Saint-Michel (09) 185 G4
Saint-Michel (16) 122 B4
Saint-Michel (31) 184 D3
Saint-Michel (32) 183 H1
Saint-Michel (34) 172 C3
Saint-Michel (45) 63 G5
Saint-Michel (64) 180 D3
Saint-Michel (82) 168 C1
Saint-Michel-Chef-Chef (44) 73 H5
Saint-Michel-d'Aurance (07) 143 G5
Saint-Michel-de-Bannières (46) 138 D4
Saint-Michel-de-Boulogne (07) 157 G1
Saint-Michel-de-Castelnau (33) 150 A5
Saint-Michel-de-Chabrillanoux (07) 143 H6
Saint-Michel-de-Chaillol (05) 160 C1
Saint-Michel-de-Chavaignes (72) 60 D5
Saint-Michel-de-Dèze (48) 156 D5
Saint-Michel-de-Double (24) 136 C3
Saint-Michel-de-Feins (53) 76 D2
Saint-Michel-de-Fronsac (33) 135 G4
Saint-Michel-de-la-Pierre (50) 12 D6
Saint-Michel-de-la-Roë (53) 58 A6
Saint-Michel-de-Lanès (11) 186 A2
Saint-Michel-de-Lapujade (33) 150 B2
Saint-Michel-de-Livet (14) 15 E6
Saint-Michel-de-Llotes (66) 200 D3
Saint-Michel-de-Maurienne (73) 146 D2
Saint-Michel-de-Montaigne (24) 136 A5
Saint-Michel-de-Montjoie (50) 37 G4
Saint-Michel-de-Plélan (22) 34 C5
Saint-Michel-de-Rieufret (33) 149 G1
Saint-Michel-de-Saint-Geoirs (38) 145 E1
Saint-Michel-de-Vax (81) 169 H1
Saint-Michel-de-Veisse (23) 125 G1
Saint-Michel-de-Villadeix (24) 137 F4
Saint-Michel-de-Volangis (18) 97 H2
Saint-Michel-des-Andaines (61) 38 C6
Saint-Michel-d'Euzet (30) 157 H6
Saint-Michel-d'Halescourt (76) 19 G3
Saint-Michel-en-Beaumont (38) 145 H5
Saint-Michel-en-Brenne (36) 95 G5
Saint-Michel-en-Grève (22) 32 B2
Saint-Michel-en-l'Herm (85) 106 C3
Saint-Michel-Escalus (40) 164 D2
Saint-Michel-et-Chanveaux (49) 75 F1
Saint-Michel-Labadié (81) 171 E2
Saint-Michel-le-Cloucq (85) 107 F2
Saint-Michel-les-Portes (38) 145 F5
Saint-Michel-l'Observatoire (04) 176 C2
Saint-Michel-Loubéjou (46) 139 E5
Saint-Michel-Mont-Mercure (85) 92 C4
Saint-Michel-sous-Bois (62) 1 G6
Saint-Michel-sur-Loire (37) 78 B6
Saint-Michel-sur-Meurthe (88) 70 C2
Saint-Michel-sur-Orge (91) 42 C6
Saint-Michel-sur-Rhône (42) 129 H6
Saint-Michel-sur-Savasse (26) 144 C3
Saint-Michel-sur-Ternoise (62) 7 G1
Saint-Michel-Tuboeuf (61) 40 B4
Saint-Mihiel (55) 47 G3
Saint-Mitre-les-Remparts (13) 191 G4
Saint-Molf (44) 73 F3
Saint-Momelin (59) 2 B3
Saint-Mont (32) 166 C4
Saint-Montan (07) 158 A3
Saint-Moré (89) 83 H4
Saint-Moreil (23) 124 D2
Saint-Morel (08) 24 A5
Saint-Morillon (33) 149 F1
Saint-Mury-Monteymond (38) 145 H2
Saint-Myon (63) 127 F1
Saint-Nabor (67) 71 F1
Saint-Nabord (88) 70 A5
Saint-Nabord-sur-Aube (10) 66 C1
Saint-Nauphary (82) 169 F2
Saint-Nazaire (30) 158 A6
Saint-Nazaire (44) 73 G4
Saint-Nazaire (66) 201 G2
Saint-Nazaire-d'Aude (11) 187 H3
Saint-Nazaire-de-Ladarez (34) 172 A6
Saint-Nazaire-de-Pézan (34) 173 H5
Saint-Nazaire-de-Valentane (82) 151 H5
Saint-Nazaire-des-Gardies (30) 173 G2
Saint-Nazaire-en-Royans (26) 144 D3
Saint-Nazaire-le-Désert (26) 159 E2
Saint-Nazaire-les-Eymes (38) 145 H2
Saint-Nazaire-sur-Charente (17) 120 C1
Saint-Nectaire (63) 127 E5
Saint-Nexans (24) 137 E6
Saint-Nic (29) 31 F6
Saint-Nicodème (22) 32 D6
Saint-Nicolas (62) 8 B2
Saint-Nicolas-aux-Bois (02) 22 B3
Saint-Nicolas-d'Aliermont (76) 17 H2
Saint-Nicolas-d'Attez (27) 40 C4
Saint-Nicolas-de-Bliquetuit (76) 17 E5
Saint-Nicolas-de-Bourgueil (37) 78 A6
Saint-Nicolas-de-la-Balerme (47) 151 G6
Saint-Nicolas-de-la-Grave (82) 168 C1
Saint-Nicolas-de-la-Haie (76) 15 H1
Saint-Nicolas-de-la-Taille (76) 15 G2
Saint-Nicolas-de-Macherin (38) 131 F6
Saint-Nicolas-de-Pierrepont (50) 12 C4
Saint-Nicolas-de-Port (54) 48 D5
Saint-Nicolas-de-Redon (44) 74 A1
Saint-Nicolas-de-Sommaire (61) 40 A4
Saint-Nicolas-des-Biefs (03) 114 C6
Saint-Nicolas-des-Bois (50) 37 F4
Saint-Nicolas-des-Bois (61) 59 H1
Saint-Nicolas-des-Laitiers (61) 39 H4
Saint-Nicolas-des-Motets (37) 79 F4
Saint-Nicolas-du-Bosc (27) 18 B6
Saint-Nicolas-du-Pélem (22) 33 E6
Saint-Nicolas-du-Tertre (56) 56 B5
Saint-Nicolas-la-Chapelle (10) 65 F1
Saint-Nicolas-la-Chapelle (73) 132 D2
Saint-Nicolas-lès-Cîteaux (21) 101 H2
Saint-Nizier-d'Azergues (69) 115 H6
Saint-Nizier-de-Fornas (42) 128 D6
Saint-Nizier-du-Moucherotte (38) 145 F2
Saint-Nizier-le-Bouchoux (01) 116 D2
Saint-Nizier-le-Désert (01) 116 D6
Saint-Nizier-sous-Charlieu (42) 115 E5
Saint-Nizier-sur-Arroux (71) 100 C5
Saint-Nolff (56) 55 G6
Saint-Nom-la-Bretèche (78) 42 B4
Saint-Offenge-Dessous (73) 132 A3
Saint-Offenge-Dessus (73) 132 A3
Saint-Omer (14) 38 C3
Saint-Omer (62) 2 B4
Saint-Omer-Capelle (62) 2 A2
Saint-Omer-en-Chaussée (60) 20 A3
Saint-Ondras (38) 131 F5
Saint-Onen-la-Chapelle (35) 56 C2
Saint-Oradoux-de-Chirouze (23) 126 A3
Saint-Oradoux-près-Crocq (23) 126 A2
Saint-Orens (32) 168 B4
Saint-Orens-de-Gameville (31) 169 F6
Saint-Orens-Pouy-Petit (32) 167 G2
Saint-Ost (32) 183 H1
Saint-Ouen (17) 121 H2
Saint-Ouen (41) 79 G2
Saint-Ouen (80) 7 F5
Saint-Ouen (93) 42 D3
Saint-Ouen-d'Attez (27) 40 C4
Saint-Ouen-d'Aunis (17) 106 D4
Saint-Ouen-de-la-Cour (61) 60 D2
Saint-Ouen-de-Mimbré (72) 60 A3
Saint-Ouen-de-Pontcheuil (27) 18 C6
Saint-Ouen-de-Sécherouvre (61) 39 H6
Saint-Ouen-de-Thouberville (27) 18 B5
Saint-Ouen-des-Alleux (35) 57 G1
Saint-Ouen-des-Besaces (14) 37 H2
Saint-Ouen-des-Champs (27) 15 H3
Saint-Ouën-des-Toits (53) 58 C4
Saint-Ouën-des-Vallons (53) 59 E4
Saint-Ouen-Domprot (51) 45 H6
Saint-Ouen-du-Breuil (76) 17 G4
Saint-Ouen-du-Mesnil-Oger (14) 39 E1
Saint-Ouen-du-Tilleul (27) 18 B5
Saint-Ouen-en-Belin (72) 78 B1
Saint-Ouen-en-Brie (77) 64 C1
Saint-Ouen-en-Champagne (72) 59 G6
Saint-Ouen-la-Rouërie (35) 35 G5
Saint-Ouen-l'Aumône (95) 42 B2
Saint-Ouen-le-Brisoult (61) 59 F1
Saint-Ouen-le-Houx (14) 39 F2
Saint-Ouen-le-Mauger (76) 17 F3
Saint-Ouen-le-Pin (14) 15 E5
Saint-Ouen-lès-Parey (88) 68 D4
Saint-Ouen-les-Vignes (37) 79 F5
Saint-Ouen-Marchefroy (28) 41 G4
Saint-Ouen-sous-Bailly (76) 6 A6
Saint-Ouen-sur-Gartempe (87) 110 B5
Saint-Ouen-sur-Iton (61) 40 B5
Saint-Ouen-sur-Loire (58) 99 E4
Saint-Ouen-sur-Maire (61) 38 D5
Saint-Ouen-sur-Morin (77) 44 A3
Saint-Oulph (10) 65 H1
Saint-Ours (63) 126 D2
Saint-Ours (73) 132 A3
Saint-Outrille (18) 96 D2
Saint-Ovin (50) 37 E5
Saint-Oyen (73) 132 D5
Saint-Pabu (29) 30 D3
Saint-Paër (76) 17 F5
Saint-Pair (14) 14 C5
Saint-Pair-sur-Mer (50) 35 G2
Saint-Pal-de-Chalencon (43) 142 C1
Saint-Pal-de-Mons (43) 143 E2
Saint-Pal-de-Senouire (43) 142 A2
Saint-Palais (03) 112 B3
Saint-Palais (18) 97 H1
Saint-Palais (33) 135 E1
Saint-Palais (64) 181 F1
Saint-Palais-de-Négrignac (17) 135 H1
Saint-Palais-de-Phiolin (17) 121 E5
Saint-Palais-du-Né (16) 121 G5
Saint-Palais-sur-Mer (17) 120 B3
Saint-Pancrace (24) 123 F6
Saint-Pancrace (73) 146 C1
Saint-Pancrasse (38) 145 H1
Saint-Pancré (54) 25 G3
Saint-Pandelon (40) 165 E4
Saint-Pantaléon (46) 152 B4
Saint-Pantaléon (84) 175 G3
Saint-Pantaléon-de-Lapleau (19) 139 H1
Saint-Pantaléon-de-Larche (19) 138 C3
Saint-Pantaléon-les-Vignes (26) 158 C4
Saint-Pantaly-d'Ans (24) 137 H2
Saint-Pantaly-d'Excideuil (24) 137 H1
Saint-Papoul (11) 186 C2
Saint-Pardon-de-Conques (33) 149 H2
Saint-Pardoult (17) 107 H6
Saint-Pardoux (63) 113 F6
Saint-Pardoux (79) 108 A1
Saint-Pardoux (87) 110 C6
Saint-Pardoux-Corbier (19) 124 C6
Saint-Pardoux-d'Arnet (23) 126 A2
Saint-Pardoux-de-Drône (24) 136 D2
Saint-Pardoux-du-Breuil (47) 150 C3
Saint-Pardoux-et-Vielvic (24) 137 H6
Saint-Pardoux-Isaac (47) 150 D2
Saint-Pardoux-la-Croisille (19) 139 F2
Saint-Pardoux-la-Rivière (24) 123 F5
Saint-Pardoux-le-Neuf (19) 126 A4
Saint-Pardoux-le-Neuf (23) 125 H2
Saint-Pardoux-le-Vieux (19) 125 H4
Saint-Pardoux-les-Cards (23) 111 H6
Saint-Pardoux-l'Ortigier (19) 138 D1
Saint-Pardoux-Morterolles (23) 125 E2
Saint-Pargoire (34) 172 D6
Saint-Parize-en-Viry (58) 99 F6
Saint-Parize-le-Châtel (58) 99 E5
Saint-Parres-aux-Tertres (10) 66 B3
Saint-Parres-lès-Vaudes (10) 66 C4
Saint-Parthem (12) 154 A2
Saint-Pastour (47) 151 F3
Saint-Pastous (65) 182 D5
Saint-Paterne (72) 60 A2
Saint-Paterne-Racan (37) 78 C3
Saint-Pathus (77) 43 F2
Saint-Patrice (37) 78 B6
Saint-Patrice-de-Claids (50) 12 D5
Saint-Patrice-du-Désert (61) 38 C6
Saint-Paul (06) 195 E3
Saint-Paul (19) 139 F2
Saint-Paul (33) 135 E2
Saint-Paul (60) 20 A4
Saint-Paul (61) 38 A4
Saint-Paul (65) 183 H4
Saint-Paul (73) 131 G4
Saint-Paul (87) 124 C3
Saint-Paul (88) 69 E2
Saint-Paul-aux-Bois (02) 21 H3
Saint-Paul-Cap-de-Joux (81) 170 B5
Saint-Paul-de-Baïse (32) 167 G4
Saint-Paul-de-Fenouillet (66) 200 C1
Saint-Paul-de-Fourques (27) 18 B6
Saint-Paul-de-Jarrat (09) 185 H6
Saint-Paul-de-Loubressac (46) 152 C5
Saint-Paul-de-Salers (15) 140 B3
Saint-Paul-de-Serre (24) 137 E3
Saint-Paul-de-Tartas (43) 142 C6
Saint-Paul-de-Varax (01) 116 D6
Saint-Paul-de-Varces (38) 145 F3
Saint-Paul-de-Vern (46) 139 F6
Saint-Paul-de-Vézelin (42) 128 D2
Saint-Paul-des-Landes (15) 139 H5
Saint-Paul-d'Espis (82) 151 H6
Saint-Paul-d'Izeaux (38) 145 E1
Saint-Paul-d'Oueil (31) 197 F1
Saint-Paul-du-Bois (49) 93 E2
Saint-Paul-du-Vernay (14) 13 H6
Saint-Paul-d'Uzore (42) 128 D4
Saint-Paul-en-Born (40) 148 B5
Saint-Paul-en-Chablais (74) 119 F3
Saint-Paul-en-Cornillon (42) 129 E6
Saint-Paul-en-Forêt (83) 178 B5
Saint-Paul-en-Gâtine (79) 92 D6
Saint-Paul-en-Jarez (42) 129 G5
Saint-Paul-en-Pareds (85) 92 B4
Saint-Paul-et-Valmalle (34) 173 E5
Saint-Paul-la-Coste (30) 156 D6
Saint-Paul-la-Roche (24) 123 H5
Saint-Paul-le-Froid (48) 142 A6
Saint-Paul-le-Gaultier (72) 59 G3
Saint-Paul-le-Jeune (07) 157 E4
Saint-Paul-lès-Dax (40) 165 E4
Saint-Paul-lès-Durance (13) 176 C4
Saint-Paul-les-Fonts (30) 174 C1
Saint-Paul-lès-Monestier (38) 145 F5
Saint-Paul-lès-Romans (26) 144 C3
Saint-Paul-Lizonne (24) 136 C1
Saint-Paul-Mont-Penit (85) 91 E3
Saint-Paul-sur-Isère (73) 132 D4
Saint-Paul-sur-Save (31) 168 D4
Saint-Paul-sur-Ubaye (04) 161 G2
Saint-Paul-Trois-Châteaux (26) 158 B4
Saint-Paulet (11) 186 B1
Saint-Paulet-de-Caisson (30) 157 H5
Saint-Paulien (43) 142 B3
Saint-Pavace (72) 60 A5
Saint-Pé-d'Ardet (31) 184 A5
Saint-Pé-de-Bigorre (65) 182 D4
Saint-Pé-de-Léren (64) 165 E6
Saint-Pé-Delbosc (31) 184 B2
Saint-Pé-Saint-Simon (47) 167 E1
Saint-Pée-sur-Nivelle (64) 180 B1
Saint-Pellerin (28) 61 G5
Saint-Pellerin (50) 13 E5
Saint-Péran (35) 56 C3
Saint-Péravy-la-Colombe (45) 62 C6
Saint-Péray (07) 144 A5
Saint-Perdon (40) 165 H2
Saint-Perdoux (24) 137 E6
Saint-Perdoux (46) 153 G1
Saint-Père (35) 36 A5
Saint-Père (58) 82 C5
Saint-Père (89) 83 H5
Saint-Père-en-Retz (44) 73 H5
Saint-Père-sur-Loire (45) 81 G2
Saint-Péreuse (58) 99 H3
Saint-Pern (35) 56 D1
Saint-Perreux (56) 73 H1
Saint-Péver (22) 33 E4
Saint-Pey-d'Armens (33) 135 H5
Saint-Pey-de-Castets (33) 136 A6
Saint-Phal (10) 66 A5
Saint-Philbert-de-Bouaine (85) 91 F1
Saint-Philbert-de-Grand-Lieu (44) 91 F1
Saint-Philbert-des-Champs (14) 15 F4
Saint-Philbert-du-Peuple (49) 77 H5
Saint-Philbert-en-Mauges (49) 75 G6
Saint-Philbert-sur-Boissey (27) 18 B6
Saint-Philbert-sur-Orne (61) 38 C3
Saint-Philbert-sur-Risle (27) 18 A5
Saint-Philibert (21) 101 H1
Saint-Philibert (56) 72 C1
Saint-Philippe-d'Aiguille (33) 136 A5
Saint-Philippe-du-Seignal (33) 136 C5
Saint-Piat (28) 62 B1
Saint-Pierre (04) 178 C2
Saint-Pierre (15) 140 A1
Saint-Pierre (31) 169 G5
Saint-Pierre (39) 118 A1
Saint-Pierre (51) 45 G3
Saint-Pierre (67) 71 G2
Saint-Pierre-á-Arnes (08) 23 H5
Saint-Pierre-Aigle (02) 21 H5
Saint-Pierre-Avez (05) 159 H5
Saint-Pierre-Azif (14) 15 E3
Saint-Pierre-Bellevue (23) 125 F2
Saint-Pierre-Bénouville (76) 17 F3
Saint-Pierre-Bois (67) 71 F2
Saint-Pierre-Brouck (59) 2 A2
Saint-Pierre-Canivet (14) 38 D3
Saint-Pierre-Chérignat (23) 124 D1
Saint-Pierre-Colamine (63) 127 E5
Saint-Pierre-d'Albigny (73) 132 B4
Saint-Pierre-d'Allevard (38) 132 A6
Saint-Pierre-d'Alvey (73) 131 G4
Saint-Pierre-d'Amilly (17) 107 F5
Saint-Pierre-d'Argençon (05) 159 H3
Saint-Pierre-d'Arthéglise (50) 12 B4
Saint-Pierre-d'Aubézies (32) 167 E5
Saint-Pierre-d'Aurillac (33) 149 H2
Saint-Pierre-d'Autils (27) 41 F1
Saint-Pierre-de-Bailleul (27) 41 F1
Saint-Pierre-de-Bat (33) 149 H1
Saint-Pierre-de-Belleville (73) 132 C5
Saint-Pierre-de-Bœuf (42) 130 A6
Saint-Pierre-de-Bressieux (38) 144 D1
Saint-Pierre-de-Buzet (47) 150 C5
Saint-Pierre-de-Cernières (27) 39 H3
Saint-Pierre-de-Chandieu (69) 130 B4
Saint-Pierre-de-Chartreuse (38) 145 G1
Saint-Pierre-de-Chérennes (38) 145 E3
Saint-Pierre-de-Chevillé (72) 78 C3
Saint-Pierre-de-Chignac (24) 137 G3
Saint-Pierre-de-Clairac (47) 151 G6
Saint-Pierre-de-Côle (24) 137 F1
Saint-Pierre-de-Colombier (07) 157 F1
Saint-Pierre-de-Cormeilles (27) 15 G4
Saint-Pierre-de-Coutances (50) 36 D1
Saint-Pierre-de-Curtille (73) 131 G3
Saint-Pierre-de-Frugie (24) 123 H5
Saint-Pierre-de-Fursac (23) 111 E5
Saint-Pierre-de-Genebroz (73) 131 G6
Saint-Pierre-de-Jards (36) 97 E2
Saint-Pierre-de-Juillers (17) 121 G1
Saint-Pierre-de-la-Fage (34) 172 C4
Saint-Pierre-de-Lages (31) 169 G6
Saint-Pierre-de-Lamps (36) 96 B4
Saint-Pierre-de-l'Île (17) 107 H6
Saint-Pierre-de-Maillé (86) 95 E6
Saint-Pierre-de-Mailloc (14) 15 F6
Saint-Pierre-de-Manneville (76) 18 B4
Saint-Pierre-de-Méaroz (38) 145 H5
Saint-Pierre-de-Mésage (38) 145 G3
Saint-Pierre-de-Mézoargues (13) 174 D3
Saint-Pierre-de-Mons (33) 149 H2
Saint-Pierre-de-Nogaret (48) 155 G3
Saint-Pierre-de-Plesguen (35) 34 D5
Saint-Pierre-de-Rivière (09) 185 G5
Saint-Pierre-de-Salerne (27) 18 A6
Saint-Pierre-de-Semilly (50) 37 G1
Saint-Pierre-de-Soucy (73) 132 B5
Saint-Pierre-de-Trivisy (81) 171 E4
Saint-Pierre-de-Varengeville (76) 17 F5
Saint-Pierre-de-Varennes (71) 101 E5
Saint-Pierre-de-Vassols (84) 175 G1
Saint-Pierre-dels-Forcats (66) 200 A4
Saint-Pierre-d'Entremont (38) 131 H6
Saint-Pierre-d'Entremont (61) 38 A4
Saint-Pierre-d'Entremont (73) 131 H6
Saint-Pierre-des-Bois (72) 59 G6
Saint-Pierre-des-Champs (11) 187 F5
Saint-Pierre-des-Corps (37) 79 E5
Saint-Pierre-des-Échaubrognes (79) 92 D3
Saint-Pierre-des-Fleurs (27) 18 C6
Saint-Pierre-des-Ifs (14) 15 E5
Saint-Pierre-des-Ifs (27) 15 H4
Saint-Pierre-des-Jonquières (76) 6 B6
Saint-Pierre-des-Landes (53) 58 B3
Saint-Pierre-des-Loges (61) 39 H4
Saint-Pierre-des-Nids (53) 59 H2
Saint-Pierre-des-Ormes (72) 60 C3
Saint-Pierre-des-Tripiers (48) 155 G5
Saint-Pierre-d'Exideuil (86) 108 D5
Saint-Pierre-d'Eyraud (24) 136 C5
Saint-Pierre-d'Irube (64) 164 B6
Saint-Pierre-d'Oléron (17) 120 A1
Saint-Pierre-du-Bosguérard (27) 18 B6
Saint-Pierre-du-Bû (14) 38 D3
Saint-Pierre-du-Champ (43) 142 C2
Saint-Pierre-du-Chemin (85) 92 D6
Saint-Pierre-du-Fresne (14) 38 A2
Saint-Pierre-du-Jonquet (14) 14 D5
Saint-Pierre-du-Lorouër (72) 78 C2
Saint-Pierre-du-Mesnil (27) 40 A3
Saint-Pierre-du-Mont (14) 13 G4
Saint-Pierre-du-Mont (40) 166 A2
Saint-Pierre-du-Mont (58) 83 F6
Saint-Pierre-du-Palais (17) 135 H2
Saint-Pierre-du-Perray (91) 43 E6
Saint-Pierre-du-Regard (61) 38 B3
Saint-Pierre-du-Val (27) 16 C6
Saint-Pierre-du-Vauvray (27) 18 D6
Saint-Pierre-Église (50) 12 D1
Saint-Pierre-en-Faucigny (74) 118 D6
Saint-Pierre-en-Port (76) 16 D3
Saint-Pierre-en-Val (76) 6 B5
Saint-Pierre-en-Vaux (21) 101 E3
Saint-Pierre-es-Champs (60) 19 G4
Saint-Pierre-Eynac (43) 142 D4
Saint-Pierre-la-Bourlhonne (63) 128 B4
Saint-Pierre-la-Bruyère (61) 61 E2
Saint-Pierre-la-Cour (53) 58 B4
Saint-Pierre-la-Garenne (27) 41 F1
Saint-Pierre-la-Noaille (42) 115 E5
Saint-Pierre-la-Palud (69) 129 G3
Saint-Pierre-la-Rivière (61) 39 F4
Saint-Pierre-la-Roche (07) 158 A2
Saint-Pierre-la-Vieille (14) 38 B3
Saint-Pierre-Lafeuille (46) 152 C3
Saint-Pierre-Langers (50) 35 G2
Saint-Pierre-Laval (03) 114 C5
Saint-Pierre-Lavis (76) 18 A2
Saint-Pierre-le-Bost (23) 112 A3
Saint-Pierre-le-Chastel (63) 126 D3
Saint-Pierre-le-Moûtier (58) 98 D5
Saint-Pierre-le-Vieux (48) 141 G6
Saint-Pierre-le-Vieux (71) 115 H4
Saint-Pierre-le-Vieux (76) 17 F2
Saint-Pierre-le-Vieux (85) 107 F3
Saint-Pierre-le-Viger (76) 17 F3
Saint-Pierre-lès-Bitry (60) 21 G4
Saint-Pierre-les-Bois (18) 97 G6
Saint-Pierre-lès-Elbeuf (76) 18 C6
Saint-Pierre-les-Étieux (18) 98 A6
Saint-Pierre-lès-Franqueville (02) 22 D1
Saint-Pierre-lès-Nemours (77) 64 A3
Saint-Pierre-Montlimart (49) 75 G5
Saint-Pierre-Quiberon (56) 72 B2
Saint-Pierre-Roche (63) 126 D3
Saint-Pierre-Saint-Jean (07) 157 E3
Saint-Pierre-sur-Dives (14) 39 E2
Saint-Pierre-sur-Doux (07) 143 G3
Saint-Pierre-sur-Dropt (47) 150 C1
Saint-Pierre-sur-Erve (53) 59 F5
Saint-Pierre-sur-Orthe (53) 59 G3
Saint-Pierre-sur-Vence (08) 24 A2
Saint-Pierre-Tarentaine (14) 37 H2
Saint-Pierre-Toirac (46) 153 G3
Saint-Pierremont (02) 22 D2
Saint-Pierremont (08) 24 C4
Saint-Pierremont (88) 70 A1
Saint-Pierreville (07) 143 G6
Saint-Pierrevillers (55) 25 G4
Saint-Plaisir (03) 113 F1
Saint-Plancard (31) 184 A3
Saint-Planchers (50) 35 G2
Saint-Plantaire (36) 111 F2
Saint-Point (71) 116 A3
Saint-Point-Lac (25) 103 H5
Saint-Pois (50) 37 G4
Saint-Poix (53) 58 B5
Saint-Pol-de-Léon (29) 31 H2
Saint-Pol-sur-Mer (59) 2 B1
Saint-Pol-sur-Ternoise (62) 7 G1
Saint-Polgues (42) 128 C2
Saint-Polycarpe (11) 186 D5
Saint-Pompain (79) 107 G2
Saint-Pompont (24) 152 A1
Saint-Poncy (15) 141 F3
Saint-Pons (04) 161 F3
Saint-Pons (07) 157 H2
Saint-Pons-de-Mauchiens (34) 172 D6
Saint-Pons-de-Thomières (34) 187 G1
Saint-Pons-la-Calm (30) 174 C1
Saint-Pont (03) 113 H5
Saint-Porchaire (17) 120 D2
Saint-Porquier (82) 168 D2
Saint-Pôtan (22) 34 B4
Saint-Pouange (10) 66 B4
Saint-Pourçain-sur-Besbre (03) 114 B2
Saint-Pourçain-sur-Sioule (03) 113 H4
Saint-Prancher (88) 69 E2
Saint-Préjet-Armandon (43) 142 A2
Saint-Préjet-d'Allier (43) 142 A5
Saint-Prest (28) 62 B1
Saint-Preuil (16) 121 H4
Saint-Priest (07) 157 H1
Saint-Priest (23) 112 B6
Saint-Priest (69) 130 B3
Saint-Priest-Bramefant (63) 127 H1
Saint-Priest-d'Andelot (03) 113 G6
Saint-Priest-de-Gimel (19) 139 F1
Saint-Priest-des-Champs (63) 126 D1
Saint-Priest-en-Jarez (42) 129 F6
Saint-Priest-en-Murat (03) 113 F3
Saint-Priest-la-Feuille (23) 111 E5
Saint-Priest-la-Marche (18) 112 A3
Saint-Priest-la-Plaine (23) 111 E5
Saint-Priest-la-Prugne (42) 128 B1
Saint-Priest-la-Roche (42) 128 D2
Saint-Priest-la-Vêtre (42) 128 B3
Saint-Priest-les-Fougères (24) 123 H5
Saint-Priest-Ligoure (87) 124 B4
Saint-Priest-Palus (23) 124 D2
Saint-Priest-sous-Aixe (87) 124 A2
Saint-Priest-Taurion (87) 124 C2
Saint-Prim (38) 130 A6
Saint-Privat (07) 157 G2
Saint-Privat (19) 139 G3
Saint-Privat (34) 172 C4
Saint-Privat-d'Allier (43) 142 B4
Saint-Privat-de-Champclos (30) 157 G5
Saint-Privat-de-Vallongue (48) 156 C5
Saint-Privat-des-Prés (24) 136 C2
Saint-Privat-des-Vieux (30) 157 E6
Saint-Privat-du-Dragon (43) 141 H2
Saint-Privat-du-Fau (48) 141 G5
Saint-Privat-la-Montagne (57) 26 B5
Saint-Privé (71) 101 E6
Saint-Privé (89) 82 C3
Saint-Prix (03) 114 B5
Saint-Prix (07) 143 G5
Saint-Prix (71) 100 B4
Saint-Prix (95) 42 C2
Saint-Prix-lès-Arnay (21) 101 E2
Saint-Projet (46) 152 D1
Saint-Projet (82) 153 F5
Saint-Projet-de-Salers (15) 140 B3
Saint-Projet-Saint-Constant (16) 122 D3
Saint-Prouant (85) 92 B5
Saint-Pryvé-Saint-Mesmin (45) 80 D1
Saint-Puy (32) 167 G3
Saint-Python (59) 9 F3
Saint-Quantin-de-Rançanne (17) 121 E5
Saint-Quay-Perros (22) 32 C1
Saint-Quay-Portrieux (22) 33 G3
Saint-Quentin (02) 9 E6
Saint-Quentin-au-Bosc (76) 6 A5
Saint-Quentin-de-Baron (33) 135 G5
Saint-Quentin-de-Blavou (61) 60 C1
Saint-Quentin-de-Caplong (33) 136 B6
Saint-Quentin-de-Chalais (16) 136 B2
Saint-Quentin-des-Isles (27) 15 H6
Saint-Quentin-des-Prés (60) 19 G3
Saint-Quentin-du-Dropt (47) 151 F1
Saint-Quentin-en-Mauges (49) 75 H4
Saint-Quentin-en-Tourmont (80) 6 C2
Saint-Quentin-Fallavier (38) 130 C4
Saint-Quentin-la-Chabanne (23) 125 G2
Saint-Quentin-la-Motte-Croix-au-Bailly (80) 6 B4
Saint-Quentin-la-Poterie (30) 174 B1
Saint-Quentin-la-Tour (09) 186 B5
Saint-Quentin-le-Petit (08) 23 E3
Saint-Quentin-le-Verger (51) 44 D6
Saint-Quentin-les-Anges (53) 76 C2
Saint-Quentin-lès-Beaurepaire (49) 77 G3
Saint-Quentin-les-Chardonnets (61) 38 A4
Saint-Quentin-les-Marais (51) 46 B4
Saint-Quentin-sur-Charente (16) 123 F2
Saint-Quentin-sur-Coole (51) 45 H4
Saint-Quentin-sur-Indrois (37) 95 G1
Saint-Quentin-sur-Isère (38) 145 F1
Saint-Quentin-sur-le-Homme (50) 35 H4
Saint-Quentin-sur-Nohain (58) 82 C6
Saint-Quentin-sur-Sauxillanges (63) 127 G5
Saint-Quintin-sur-Sioule (63) 113 G6
Saint-Quirc (09) 185 G2
Saint-Quirin (57) 50 A5
Saint-Rabier (24) 138 A3
Saint-Racho (71) 115 G4
Saint-Rambert-d'Albon (26) 144 A1
Saint-Rambert-en-Bugey (01) 131 E1
Saint-Raphaël (24) 137 H1
Saint-Raphaël (83) 194 C2
Saint-Régis-du-Coin (42) 143 F2
Saint-Règle (37) 79 G5
Saint-Remèze (07) 157 H4
Saint-Remimont (54) 69 G1
Saint-Remimont (88) 69 E3
Saint-Rémy (01) 116 D5
Saint-Rémy (12) 153 G4
Saint-Rémy (14) 38 B3
Saint-Rémy (19) 125 H4
Saint-Rémy (21) 84 C3
Saint-Rémy (24) 136 B4
Saint-Remy (70) 87 F1
Saint-Rémy (71) 101 G5
Saint-Rémy (79) 107 G3
Saint-Remy (88) 70 C2
Saint-Rémy-au-Bois (62) 6 D2
Saint-Rémy-aux-Bois (54) 69 H2
Saint-Rémy-Blanzy (02) 22 A6
Saint-Rémy-Boscrocourt (76) 6 B5
Saint-Rémy-Chaussée (59) 9 H3
Saint-Rémy-de-Blot (63) 113 F6
Saint-Rémy-de-Chargnat (63) 127 G5
Saint-Rémy-de-Chaudes-Aigues (15) 141 E6
Saint-Rémy-de-Maurienne (73) 132 C6
Saint-Rémy-de-Provence (13) 191 F1
Saint-Rémy-de-Sillé (72) 59 H4
Saint-Rémy-des-Landes (50) 12 C5
Saint-Rémy-des-Monts (72) 60 C3
Saint-Remy-du-Nord (59) 10 A3
Saint-Rémy-du-Plain (35) 35 F6
Saint-Rémy-du-Val (72) 60 B2
Saint-Remy-en-Bouzemont-Saint-Genest-et-Isson (51) 46 B6
Saint-Remy-en-l'Eau (60) 20 D4
Saint-Rémy-en-Mauges (49) 75 G5
Saint-Rémy-en-Rollat (03) 114 A5
Saint-Remy-la-Calonne (55) 47 H2
Saint-Rémy-la-Vanne (77) 44 A4
Saint-Rémy-la-Varenne (49) 77 F5
Saint-Remy-le-Petit (08) 23 F4
Saint-Rémy-lès-Chevreuse (78) 42 B5
Saint-Rémy-l'Honoré (78) 42 A5
Saint-Remy-sous-Barbuise (10) 66 B1
Saint-Remy-sous-Broyes (51) 44 D5
Saint-Rémy-sur-Avre (28) 41 E4
Saint-Remy-sur-Bussy (51) 46 B2
Saint-Rémy-sur-Creuse (86) 95 E4
Saint-Rémy-sur-Durolle (63) 128 A2
Saint-Renan (29) 30 D4
Saint-Restitut (26) 158 B4
Saint-Révérend (85) 90 D4
Saint-Révérien (58) 99 F1
Saint-Rieul (22) 34 A5
Saint-Rigomer-des-Bois (72) 60 A2
Saint-Rimay (41) 79 F2
Saint-Riquier (80) 7 E4
Saint-Riquier-en-Rivière (76) 6 B6
Saint-Riquier-ès-Plains (76) 17 E2
Saint-Rirand (42) 114 D6
Saint-Rivoal (29) 31 G5
Saint-Robert (19) 138 B2
Saint-Robert (47) 151 G5
Saint-Roch (37) 78 D5
Saint-Roch-sur-Égrenne (61) 38 A6
Saint-Rogatien (17) 106 D5
Saint-Romain (16) 136 B1
Saint-Romain (21) 101 F3
Saint-Romain (63) 128 C5
Saint-Romain (86) 109 E4
Saint-Romain-au-Mont-d'Or (69) 130 A2
Saint-Romain-d'Ay (07) 143 H3

Saint-Romain-de-Benet (17) 120 D3
Saint-Romain-de-Colbosc (76) 15 G1
Saint-Romain-de-Jalionas (38) 130 D3
Saint-Romain-de-Lerps (07) 144 A4
Saint-Romain-de-Monpazier (24) 151 G1
Saint-Romain-de-Popey (69) 129 G2
Saint-Romain-de-Surieu (38) 130 B6
Saint-Romain-d'Urfé (42) 128 B2
Saint-Romain-en-Gal (69) 130 A5
Saint-Romain-en-Gier (69) 129 H5
Saint-Romain-en-Jarez (42) 129 G5
Saint-Romain-en-Viennois (84) 158 D5
Saint-Romain-et-Saint-Clément (24) 123 G6
Saint-Romain-la-Motte (42) 115 E6
Saint-Romain-la-Virvée (33) 135 F4
Saint-Romain-Lachalm (43) 143 F2
Saint-Romain-le-Noble (47) 151 G6
Saint-Romain-le-Preux (89) 64 D6
Saint-Romain-le-Puy (42) 128 D5
Saint-Romain-les-Atheux (42) 143 F1
Saint-Romain-sous-Gourdon (71) 115 G1
Saint-Romain-sous-Versigny (71) 115 F1
Saint-Romain-sur-Cher (41) 80 A6
Saint-Romain-sur-Gironde (17) 120 D5
Saint-Roman (26) 159 F1
Saint-Roman-de-Codières (30) 173 F2
Saint-Roman-de-Malegarde (84) 158 C5
Saint-Romans (38) 144 D3
Saint-Romans-des-Champs (79) 107 H4
Saint-Romans-lès-Melle (79) 108 B4
Saint-Rome (31) 185 H1
Saint-Rome-de-Cernon (12) 171 H2
Saint-Rome-de-Dolan (48) 155 G5
Saint-Rome-de-Tarn (12) 171 H1
Saint-Romphaire (50) 37 F1
Saint-Rustice (31) 169 E3
Saint-Saëns (76) 17 H4
Saint-Saire (76) 19 F2
Saint-Salvadou (12) 153 H5
Saint-Salvadour (19) 125 E6
Saint-Salvi-de-Carcavès (81) 171 F4
Saint-Salvy (47) 151 E5
Saint-Salvy-de-la-Balme (81) 170 D5
Saint-Samson (14) 14 D4
Saint-Samson (53) 59 G1
Saint-Samson-de-Bonfossé (50) 37 F1
Saint-Samson-de-la-Roque (27) 15 G2
Saint-Samson-la-Poterie (60) 19 G3
Saint-Samson-sur-Rance (22) 36 A6
Saint-Sandoux (63) 127 F4
Saint-Santin (12) 153 H2
Saint-Santin-Cantalès (15) 139 H4
Saint-Santin-de-Maurs (15) 153 H2
Saint-Sardos (47) 151 E4
Saint-Sardos (82) 168 D3
Saint-Satur (18) 82 B6
Saint-Saturnin (15) 140 D2
Saint-Saturnin (16) 122 B4
Saint-Saturnin (18) 112 A2
Saint-Saturnin (48) 155 G4
Saint-Saturnin (51) 45 E6
Saint-Saturnin (63) 127 F4
Saint-Saturnin (72) 60 A5
Saint-Saturnin-de-Lenne (12) 155 F4
Saint-Saturnin-de-Lucian (34) 172 D5
Saint-Saturnin-du-Bois (17) 107 F5
Saint-Saturnin-du-Limet (53) 76 A1
Saint-Saturnin-lès-Apt (84) 175 H2
Saint-Saturnin-lès-Avignon (84) 175 E2
Saint-Saturnin-sur-Loire (49) 77 E5
Saint-Saud-Lacoussière (24) 123 G5
Saint-Sauflieu (80) 20 C1
Saint-Saulge (58) 99 G2
Saint-Saulve (59) 9 F2
Saint-Saury (15) 139 G5
Saint-Sauvant (17) 121 F3
Saint-Sauvant (86) 108 C3
Saint-Sauves-d'Auvergne (63) 126 C4
Saint-Sauveur (05) 161 E2
Saint-Sauveur (21) 86 B6
Saint-Sauveur (24) 137 E5
Saint-Sauveur (29) 31 G4
Saint-Sauveur (31) 169 F4
Saint-Sauveur (33) 134 D2
Saint-Sauveur (38) 144 D3
Saint-Sauveur (54) 49 H6
Saint-Sauveur (60) 21 F5
Saint-Sauveur (70) 87 H1
Saint-Sauveur (80) 7 F5
Saint-Sauveur (86) 94 D5
Saint-Sauveur-Camprieu (30) 172 D1
Saint-Sauveur-d'Aunis (17) 107 E4
Saint-Sauveur-de-Carrouges (61) 38 D6
Saint-Sauveur-de-Cruzières (07) 157 F5
Saint-Sauveur-de-Flée (49) 76 C2
Saint-Sauveur-de-Ginestoux (48) 156 B1
Saint-Sauveur-de-Landemont (49) 75 E4
Saint-Sauveur-de-Meilhan (47) 150 B3
Saint-Sauveur-de-Montagut (07) 143 G6
Saint-Sauveur-de-Peyre (48) 155 G2
Saint-Sauveur-de-Pierrepont (50) 12 C4
Saint-Sauveur-de-Puynormand (33) 136 A4
Saint-Sauveur-d'Émalleville (76) 15 F1
Saint-Sauveur-des-Landes (35) 35 H6
Saint-Sauveur-en-Diois (26) 158 D1
Saint-Sauveur-en-Puisaye (89) 82 D3
Saint-Sauveur-en-Rue (42) 143 G2
Saint-Sauveur-Gouvernet (26) 159 E4
Saint-Sauveur-la-Pommeraye (50) 35 G2
Saint-Sauveur-la-Sagne (63) 128 B6
Saint-Sauveur-la-Vallée (46) 152 D2
Saint-Sauveur-Lalande (24) 136 C4
Saint-Sauveur-le-Vicomte (50) 12 C4
Saint-Sauveur-Lendelin (50) 12 D6
Saint-Sauveur-lès-Bray (77) 64 D2
Saint-Sauveur-Marville (28) 41 E6
Saint-Sauveur-sur-École (77) 63 H1
Saint-Sauveur-sur-Tinée (06) 162 C6
Saint-Sauvier (03) 112 B3
Saint-Sauvy (32) 168 B4
Saint-Savin (33) 135 F2
Saint-Savin (38) 130 D4
Saint-Savin (65) 182 D5
Saint-Savin (86) 109 H1
Saint-Savinien (17) 121 E1
Saint-Saviol (86) 108 D5
Saint-Savournin (13) 192 B3
Saint-Sébastien (23) 111 E3
Saint-Sébastien (38) 145 G5
Saint-Sébastien-d'Aigrefeuille (30) 173 G1
Saint-Sébastien-de-Morsent (27) 40 D2
Saint-Sébastien-de-Raids (50) 12 D6
Saint-Sébastien-sur-Loire (44) 74 D5
Saint-Secondin (86) 109 F3
Saint-Ségal (29) 31 G6
Saint-Séglin (35) 56 D5
Saint-Seine (58) 100 A6
Saint-Seine-en-Bâche (21) 102 C2
Saint-Seine-l'Abbaye (21) 85 F5
Saint-Seine-sur-Vingeanne (21) 86 B4
Saint-Selve (33) 149 F1
Saint-Senier-de-Beuvron (50) 35 H4
Saint-Senier-sous-Avranches (50) 35 H3
Saint-Senoch (37) 95 F3
Saint-Senoux (35) 57 E4
Saint-Sériès (34) 173 H4
Saint-Sernin (07) 157 G2
Saint-Sernin (11) 186 A3
Saint-Sernin (47) 150 C1
Saint-Sernin-du-Bois (71) 101 E5
Saint-Sernin-du-Plain (71) 101 F4
Saint-Sernin-lès-Lavaur (81) 170 B6
Saint-Sernin-sur-Rance (12) 171 F3
Saint-Sérotin (89) 64 D4
Saint-Servais (22) 32 C5
Saint-Servais (29) 31 G4
Saint-Servant (56) 55 H4
Saint-Setiers (19) 125 G4
Saint-Seurin-de-Bourg (33) 135 E3
Saint-Seurin-de-Cadourne (33) 134 D1
Saint-Seurin-de-Cursac (33) 135 E2
Saint-Seurin-de-Palenne (17) 121 F4
Saint-Seurin-de-Prats (24) 136 B5
Saint-Seurin-sur-l'Isle (33) 136 A4
Saint-Sève (33) 150 B2
Saint-Sever (40) 165 H3
Saint-Sever-Calvados (14) 37 G3
Saint-Sever-de-Rustan (65) 183 F2
Saint-Sever-de-Saintonge (17) 121 F3
Saint-Sever-du-Moustier (12) 171 F4
Saint-Séverin (16) 136 C1
Saint-Séverin-d'Estissac (24) 136 D3
Saint-Séverin-sur-Boutonne (17) 107 H5
Saint-Siffret (30) 174 B2
Saint-Sigismond (45) 62 C6
Saint-Sigismond (49) 76 B4
Saint-Sigismond (74) 119 F5
Saint-Sigismond (85) 107 F3
Saint-Sigismond-de-Clermont (17) 121 F5
Saint-Silvain-Bas-le-Roc (23) 112 A4
Saint-Silvain-Bellegarde (23) 125 H1
Saint-Silvain-Montaigut (23) 111 F5
Saint-Silvain-sous-Toulx (23) 112 A4
Saint-Siméon (27) 15 H4
Saint-Siméon (61) 58 D1
Saint-Siméon (77) 44 A4
Saint-Siméon-de-Bressieux (38) 144 D1
Saint-Simeux (16) 122 A4
Saint-Simon (02) 21 H1
Saint-Simon (15) 140 B5
Saint-Simon (16) 122 A4
Saint-Simon (46) 153 F1
Saint-Simon-de-Bordes (17) 121 F6
Saint-Simon-de-Pellouaille (17) 121 E4
Saint-Sixt (74) 118 D6
Saint-Sixte (42) 128 C3
Saint-Sixte (47) 151 G6
Saint-Solve (19) 138 C1
Saint-Sorlin (69) 129 H4
Saint-Sorlin-d'Arves (73) 146 B2
Saint-Sorlin-de-Conac (17) 121 E6
Saint-Sorlin-de-Morestel (38) 131 E4
Saint-Sorlin-de-Vienne (38) 130 B6
Saint-Sorlin-en-Bugey (01) 130 D2
Saint-Sorlin-en-Valloire (26) 144 B1
Saint-Sornin (03) 113 F3
Saint-Sornin (16) 122 D3
Saint-Sornin (17) 120 C2
Saint-Sornin-la-Marche (87) 110 A5
Saint-Sornin-Lavolps (19) 138 B1
Saint-Sornin-Leulac (87) 110 C5
Saint-Soulan (32) 168 B6
Saint-Souplet (59) 9 F4
Saint-Souplet-sur-Py (51) 23 H6
Saint-Soupplets (77) 43 F2
Saint-Sozy (46) 138 D5
Saint-Stail (88) 70 D2
Saint-Suliac (35) 36 A5
Saint-Sulpice (01) 116 C4
Saint-Sulpice (46) 153 F2
Saint-Sulpice (49) 77 E5
Saint-Sulpice (53) 58 D6
Saint-Sulpice (58) 99 F3
Saint-Sulpice (60) 20 B5
Saint-Sulpice (63) 126 C4
Saint-Sulpice (70) 88 A3
Saint-Sulpice (73) 131 H4
Saint-Sulpice (81) 169 G4
Saint-Sulpice-d'Arnoult (17) 120 D2
Saint-Sulpice-de-Cognac (16) 121 G3
Saint-Sulpice-de-Faleyrens (33) 135 H5
Saint-Sulpice-de-Favières (91) 63 F1
Saint-Sulpice-de-Grimbouville (27) 15 G3
Saint-Sulpice-de-Guilleragues (33) 150 B1
Saint-Sulpice-de-Mareuil (24) 123 E5
Saint-Sulpice-de-Pommeray (41) 79 H3
Saint-Sulpice-de-Pommiers (33) 150 A1
Saint-Sulpice-de-Roumagnac (24) 136 D2
Saint-Sulpice-de-Royan (17) 120 C3
Saint-Sulpice-de-Ruffec (16) 122 D1
Saint-Sulpice-des-Landes (35) 57 F6
Saint-Sulpice-des-Landes (44) 75 F2
Saint-Sulpice-des-Rivoires (38) 131 F5
Saint-Sulpice-d'Excideuil (24) 123 H6
Saint-Sulpice-en-Pareds (85) 92 C6
Saint-Sulpice-et-Cameyrac (33) 135 F5
Saint-Sulpice-la-Forêt (35) 57 F2
Saint-Sulpice-Laurière (87) 110 D6
Saint-Sulpice-le-Dunois (23) 111 F4
Saint-Sulpice-le-Guérétois (23) 111 F5
Saint-Sulpice-le-Verdon (85) 91 G2
Saint-Sulpice-les-Bois (19) 125 G4
Saint-Sulpice-les-Champs (23) 125 G1
Saint-Sulpice-les-Feuilles (87) 110 D4
Saint-Sulpice-sur-Lèze (31) 185 F2
Saint-Sulpice-sur-Risle (61) 40 A4
Saint-Supplet (54) 25 H4
Saint-Sylvain (14) 38 D2
Saint-Sylvain (19) 139 F3
Saint-Sylvain (76) 17 E2
Saint-Sylvain-d'Anjou (49) 77 E4
Saint-Sylvestre (07) 144 A4
Saint-Sylvestre (74) 132 A2
Saint-Sylvestre (87) 124 C1
Saint-Sylvestre-Cappel (59) 2 C4
Saint-Sylvestre-de-Cormeilles (27) 15 G4
Saint-Sylvestre-Pragoulin (63) 114 A6
Saint-Sylvestre-sur-Lot (47) 151 G4
Saint-Symphorien (18) 97 G5
Saint-Symphorien (27) 15 G3
Saint-Symphorien (33) 149 F3
Saint-Symphorien (35) 57 E1
Saint-Symphorien (48) 142 A6
Saint-Symphorien (72) 59 G5
Saint-Symphorien (79) 107 G4
Saint-Symphorien-d'Ancelles (71) 116 B5
Saint-Symphorien-de-Lay (42) 129 E1
Saint-Symphorien-de-Mahun (07) 143 G3
Saint-Symphorien-de-Marmagne (71) 100 D5
Saint-Symphorien-de-Thénières (12) 154 D1
Saint-Symphorien-des-Bois (71) 115 F4
Saint-Symphorien-des-Bruyères (61) 40 A4
Saint-Symphorien-des-Monts (50) 37 G6
Saint-Symphorien-d'Ozon (69) 130 A4
Saint-Symphorien-le-Château (28) 62 C1
Saint-Symphorien-le-Valois (50) 12 C5
Saint-Symphorien-sous-Chomérac (07) 158 A1
Saint-Symphorien-sur-Coise (69) 129 F4
Saint-Symphorien-sur-Couze (87) 110 C6
Saint-Symphorien-sur-Saône (21) 102 B2
Saint-Thégonnec (29) 31 H4
Saint-Thélo (22) 55 F1
Saint-Théodorit (30) 173 H2
Saint-Théoffrey (38) 145 G4
Saint-Thibaud-de-Couz (73) 131 H5
Saint-Thibault (10) 66 B4
Saint-Thibault (21) 84 D6
Saint-Thibault (60) 19 H2
Saint-Thibault-des-Vignes (77) 43 F4
Saint-Thibaut (02) 22 C5
Saint-Thibéry (34) 188 D1
Saint-Thiébaud (39) 103 F3
Saint-Thiébault (52) 68 C4
Saint-Thierry (51) 23 E5
Saint-Thois (29) 53 H1
Saint-Thomas (02) 22 D4
Saint-Thomas (31) 168 C6
Saint-Thomas-de-Conac (17) 121 E6
Saint-Thomas-de-Courceriers (53) 59 G3
Saint-Thomas-en-Argonne (51) 46 C1
Saint-Thomas-en-Royans (26) 144 D4
Saint-Thomas-la-Garde (42) 128 D5
Saint-Thomé (07) 158 A3
Saint-Thonan (29) 31 E4
Saint-Thual (35) 34 D6
Saint-Thurial (35) 56 D3
Saint-Thuriau (56) 55 F3
Saint-Thurien (27) 16 D6
Saint-Thurien (29) 54 B3
Saint-Thurin (42) 128 C3
Saint-Tricat (62) 1 G2
Saint-Trimoël (22) 33 H5
Saint-Trinit (84) 159 F6
Saint-Trivier-de-Courtes (01) 116 D2
Saint-Trivier-sur-Moignans (01) 116 C6
Saint-Trojan (33) 135 E3
Saint-Trojan-les-Bains (17) 120 B2
Saint-Tropez (83) 194 B4
Saint-Tugdual (56) 54 C2
Saint-Ulphace (72) 61 E4
Saint-Ulrich (68) 89 E3
Saint-Uniac (35) 56 D2
Saint-Urbain (29) 31 F5
Saint-Urbain (85) 90 C2
Saint-Urbain-Maconcourt (52) 68 A2
Saint-Urcisse (47) 151 G6
Saint-Urcisse (81) 169 G2
Saint-Urcize (15) 155 F1
Saint-Usage (10) 67 E5
Saint-Usage (21) 102 B2
Saint-Usuge (71) 102 B6
Saint-Utin (51) 66 D1
Saint-Uze (26) 144 A2
Saint-Vaast-de-Longmont (60) 21 E5
Saint-Vaast-d'Équiqueville (76) 17 H3
Saint-Vaast-Dieppedalle (76) 17 E3
Saint-Vaast-du-Val (76) 17 G4
Saint-Vaast-en-Auge (14) 15 E4
Saint-Vaast-en-Cambrésis (59) 9 F3
Saint-Vaast-en-Chaussée (80) 7 F5
Saint-Vaast-la-Hougue (50) 13 E2
Saint-Vaast-lès-Mello (60) 20 C6
Saint-Vaast-sur-Seulles (14) 14 A5
Saint-Vaize (17) 121 E2
Saint-Valbert (70) 87 H1
Saint-Valentin (36) 96 D4
Saint-Valérien (85) 107 E1
Saint-Valérien (89) 64 D4
Saint-Valery (60) 19 G2
Saint-Valery-en-Caux (76) 17 E2
Saint-Valery-sur-Somme (80) 6 C3
Saint-Vallerin (71) 101 F6
Saint-Vallier (16) 136 A1
Saint-Vallier (26) 144 A2
Saint-Vallier (71) 115 G1
Saint-Vallier (88) 69 G3
Saint-Vallier-de-Thiey (06) 178 C4
Saint-Vallier-sur-Marne (52) 86 B1
Saint-Varent (79) 93 G4
Saint-Vaury (23) 111 F5
Saint-Venant (62) 2 C5
Saint-Vénérand (43) 142 B5
Saint-Vérain (58) 82 C5
Saint-Véran (05) 147 G6
Saint-Vérand (38) 144 D2
Saint-Vérand (69) 129 G2
Saint-Vérand (71) 116 A4
Saint-Vert (43) 142 A1
Saint-Viance (19) 138 C2
Saint-Viâtre (41) 80 D4
Saint-Viaud (44) 74 A4
Saint-Victeur (72) 60 A3
Saint-Victor (03) 112 D3
Saint-Victor (07) 143 H3
Saint-Victor (15) 139 H4
Saint-Victor (24) 136 D2
Saint-Victor-de-Buthon (28) 61 F2
Saint-Victor-de-Cessieu (38) 131 E5
Saint-Victor-de-Chrétienville (27) 15 H6
Saint-Victor-de-Malcap (30) 157 F5
Saint-Victor-de-Morestel (38) 131 E3
Saint-Victor-de-Réno (61) 61 E1
Saint-Victor-d'Épine (27) 15 H4
Saint-Victor-des-Oules (30) 174 B1
Saint-Victor-en-Marche (23) 111 F5
Saint-Victor-et-Melvieu (12) 171 G1
Saint-Victor-la-Coste (30) 174 C1
Saint-Victor-la-Rivière (63) 127 E5
Saint-Victor-l'Abbaye (76) 18 D2
Saint-Victor-Malescours (43) 143 F2
Saint-Victor-Montvianeix (63) 128 A1
Saint-Victor-Rouzaud (09) 185 G4
Saint-Victor-sur-Arlanc (43) 142 B1
Saint-Victor-sur-Avre (27) 40 C5
Saint-Victor-sur-Ouche (21) 101 F1
Saint-Victor-sur-Rhins (42) 129 E1
Saint-Victoret (13) 191 H4
Saint-Victour (19) 126 A6
Saint-Victurnien (87) 123 H2
Saint-Vidal (43) 142 B3
Saint-Vigor (27) 41 E2
Saint-Vigor-des-Mézerets (14) 38 A3
Saint-Vigor-des-Monts (50) 37 F3
Saint-Vigor-d'Ymonville (76) 15 G2
Saint-Vigor-le-Grand (14) 13 H5
Saint-Vincent (31) 186 A1
Saint-Vincent (43) 142 C3
Saint-Vincent (63) 127 F5
Saint-Vincent (64) 182 D3
Saint-Vincent (82) 152 C6
Saint-Vincent-Bragny (71) 115 E2
Saint-Vincent-Cramesnil (76) 15 G2
Saint-Vincent-de-Barbeyrargues (34) 173 F4
Saint-Vincent-de-Barrès (07) 158 A1
Saint-Vincent-de-Boisset (42) 128 D1
Saint-Vincent-de-Connezac (24) 136 D2
Saint-Vincent-de-Cosse (24) 138 A5
Saint-Vincent-de-Durfort (07) 143 H6
Saint-Vincent-de-Lamontjoie (47) 167 H1
Saint-Vincent-de-Mercuze (38) 131 H6
Saint-Vincent-de-Paul (33) 135 F4
Saint-Vincent-de-Paul (40) 165 E3
Saint-Vincent-de-Pertignas (33) 135 H6
Saint-Vincent-de-Reins (69) 115 G6
Saint-Vincent-de-Salers (15) 140 B2
Saint-Vincent-de-Tyrosse (40) 164 C4
Saint-Vincent-des-Bois (27) 41 F2
Saint-Vincent-des-Landes (44) 74 D1
Saint-Vincent-des-Prés (71) 115 H2
Saint-Vincent-des-Prés (72) 60 C3
Saint-Vincent-d'Olargues (34) 171 G6
Saint-Vincent-du-Boulay (27) 15 G5
Saint-Vincent-du-Lorouër (72) 78 C1
Saint-Vincent-du-Pendit (46) 139 F6
Saint-Vincent-en-Bresse (71) 102 A6
Saint-Vincent-Jalmoutiers (24) 136 C2
Saint-Vincent-la-Châtre (79) 108 C4
Saint-Vincent-la-Commanderie (26) 144 C5
Saint-Vincent-le-Paluel (24) 138 B5
Saint-Vincent-les-Forts (04) 160 D3
Saint-Vincent-Lespinasse (82) 151 H6
Saint-Vincent-Rive-d'Olt (46) 152 B3
Saint-Vincent-Sterlanges (85) 92 A5
Saint-Vincent-sur-Graon (85) 91 G6
Saint-Vincent-sur-Jabron (04) 159 H6
Saint-Vincent-sur-Jard (85) 106 A2
Saint-Vincent-sur-l'Isle (24) 137 G2
Saint-Vincent-sur-Oust (56) 56 C6
Saint-Vit (25) 103 E1
Saint-Vital (73) 132 C4
Saint-Vite (47) 151 H3
Saint-Vitte (18) 112 C2
Saint-Vitte-sur-Briance (87) 124 D4
Saint-Vivien (17) 106 D5
Saint-Vivien (24) 136 B5
Saint-Vivien-de-Blaye (33) 135 F3
Saint-Vivien-de-Médoc (33) 120 C5
Saint-Vivien-de-Monségur (33) 150 B2
Saint-Voir (03) 114 B3
Saint-Vougay (29) 31 G3
Saint-Vrain (51) 46 C5
Saint-Vrain (91) 63 G1
Saint-Vran (22) 56 A1
Saint-Vulbas (01) 130 D2
Saint-Waast (59) 9 G2
Saint-Wandrille-Rançon (76) 17 E5
Saint-Witz (95) 43 E2
Saint-Xandre (17) 106 D4
Saint-Yaguen (40) 165 G2
Saint-Yan (71) 115 E3
Saint-Ybard (19) 124 C6
Saint-Ybars (09) 185 F3
Saint-Yon (91) 63 F1
Saint-Yorre (03) 114 A6
Saint-Yrieix-la-Montagne (23) 125 G2
Saint-Yrieix-la-Perche (87) 124 A5
Saint-Yrieix-le-Déjalat (19) 125 F6
Saint-Yrieix-les-Bois (23) 111 G6
Saint-Yrieix-sous-Aixe (87) 123 H2
Saint-Yrieix-sur-Charente (16) 122 B3
Saint-Ythaire (71) 116 A1
Saint-Yvi (29) 53 G3
Saint-Yvoine (63) 127 G5
Saint-Yzan-de-Soudiac (33) 135 F2
Saint-Yzans-de-Médoc (33) 134 D1
Saint-Zacharie (83) 192 D3
Sainte-Adresse (76) 15 E2
Sainte-Agathe (63) 128 A3
Sainte-Agathe-d'Aliermont (76) 6 A6
Sainte-Agathe-en-Donzy (42) 129 E2
Sainte-Agathe-la-Bouteresse (42) 128 D3
Sainte-Agnès (06) 195 G2
Sainte-Agnès (38) 145 H2
Sainte-Agnès (39) 117 F1
Sainte-Alauzie (46) 152 B5
Sainte-Alvère (24) 137 F4
Sainte-Anastasie (15) 141 E3
Sainte-Anastasie (30) 174 A2
Sainte-Anastasie-sur-Issole (83) 193 F3
Sainte-Anne (25) 103 F3
Sainte-Anne (32) 168 C4
Sainte-Anne (41) 79 G2
Sainte-Anne-d'Auray (56) 55 E6
Sainte-Anne-Saint-Priest (87) 124 D3
Sainte-Anne-sur-Brivet (44) 74 A3
Sainte-Anne-sur-Gervonde (38) 130 D5
Sainte-Anne-sur-Vilaine (35) 57 E6
Sainte-Aulde (77) 44 A3
Sainte-Aurence-Cazaux (32) 183 H1
Sainte-Austreberthe (62) 7 E2
Sainte-Austreberthe (76) 17 F5
Sainte-Barbe (57) 26 C5
Sainte-Barbe (88) 70 B2
Sainte-Barbe-sur-Gaillon (27) 41 E1
Sainte-Bazeille (47) 150 B2
Sainte-Beuve-en-Rivière (76) 19 F1
Sainte-Blandine (38) 131 E5
Sainte-Blandine (79) 108 A4
Sainte-Brigitte (56) 55 E2
Sainte-Camelle (11) 186 A3
Sainte-Catherine (62) 8 B2
Sainte-Catherine (63) 127 H6
Sainte-Catherine (69) 129 G4
Sainte-Catherine-de-Fierbois (37) 94 D2
Sainte-Cécile (36) 96 C2
Sainte-Cécile (50) 37 F3
Sainte-Cécile (71) 116 A3
Sainte-Cécile (85) 92 A5
Sainte-Cécile-d'Andorge (30) 156 D5
Sainte-Cécile-du-Cayrou (81) 169 H2
Sainte-Cécile-les-Vignes (84) 158 B5
Sainte-Céronne-lès-Mortagne (61) 39 H6
Sainte-Cérotte (72) 78 D1
Sainte-Christie (32) 167 H4
Sainte-Christie-d'Armagnac (32) 166 D3
Sainte-Christine (49) 75 H5
Sainte-Christine (63) 113 E6
Sainte-Colombe (05) 159 G5
Sainte-Colombe (16) 122 D2
Sainte-Colombe (17) 135 G1
Sainte-Colombe (21) 84 D5
Sainte-Colombe (25) 103 H4
Sainte-Colombe (33) 136 A5
Sainte-Colombe (35) 57 G5
Sainte-Colombe (40) 165 H4
Sainte-Colombe (46) 153 G1
Sainte-Colombe (50) 12 C4
Sainte-Colombe (69) 130 A5
Sainte-Colombe (76) 17 E3
Sainte-Colombe (77) 65 E1
Sainte-Colombe (89) 84 A4
Sainte-Colombe-de-Duras (47) 150 C1
Sainte-Colombe-de-la-Commanderie (66) 201 E3
Sainte-Colombe-de-Peyre (48) 155 G1
Sainte-Colombe-de-Villeneuve (47) 151 F4
Sainte-Colombe-des-Bois (58) 82 D6
Sainte-Colombe-en-Bruilhois (47) 151 E6
Sainte-Colombe-la-Commanderie (27) 40 C1
Sainte-Colombe-près-Vernon (27) 41 E1
Sainte-Colombe-sur-Gand (42) 129 E2
Sainte-Colombe-sur-Guette (11) 200 B2
Sainte-Colombe-sur-l'Hers (11) 186 B5
Sainte-Colombe-sur-Loing (89) 82 D4
Sainte-Colombe-sur-Seine (21) 85 E1
Sainte-Colome (64) 182 B4
Sainte-Consorce (69) 129 H3
Sainte-Croix (01) 130 B2
Sainte-Croix (02) 22 D4
Sainte-Croix (12) 153 G4
Sainte-Croix (24) 137 G6
Sainte-Croix (26) 144 D6
Sainte-Croix (46) 152 B4
Sainte-Croix (71) 117 E1
Sainte-Croix (81) 170 B2
Sainte-Croix-á-Lauze (04) 176 B2
Sainte-Croix-aux-Mines (68) 71 E3
Sainte-Croix-de-Caderle (30) 173 F1
Sainte-Croix-de-Mareuil (24) 122 D5
Sainte-Croix-de-Quintillargues (34) 173 F4
Sainte-Croix-du-Mont (33) 149 H2
Sainte-Croix-du-Verdon (04) 177 F4
Sainte-Croix-en-Jarez (42) 129 H5
Sainte-Croix-en-Plaine (68) 71 F5
Sainte-Croix-Grand-Tonne (14) 14 A4
Sainte-Croix-Hague (50) 12 B2
Sainte-Croix-sur-Aizier (27) 16 D6
Sainte-Croix-sur-Buchy (76) 19 E3
Sainte-Croix-sur-Mer (14) 14 B3
Sainte-Croix-sur-Orne (61) 38 C4
Sainte-Croix-Vallée-Française (48) 156 C6
Sainte-Croix-Volvestre (09) 185 E4
Sainte-Dode (32) 183 G1
Sainte-Eanne (79) 108 B3
Sainte-Engrâce (64) 181 G4
Sainte-Enimie (48) 155 H4
Sainte-Eugénie-de-Villeneuve (43) 142 A3
Sainte-Eulalie (07) 143 E6
Sainte-Eulalie (11) 186 D3
Sainte-Eulalie (15) 140 A3
Sainte-Eulalie (33) 135 F5
Sainte-Eulalie (48) 141 H6
Sainte-Eulalie-d'Ans (24) 137 H2
Sainte-Eulalie-de-Cernon (12) 172 A2
Sainte-Eulalie-d'Eymet (24) 150 D1
Sainte-Eulalie-d'Olt (12) 155 E3
Sainte-Eulalie-en-Born (40) 148 B4
Sainte-Eulalie-en-Royans (26) 144 D4
Sainte-Euphémie (01) 130 A1
Sainte-Euphémie-sur-Ouvèze (26) 159 F5
Sainte-Eusoye (60) 20 B3
Sainte-Fauste (36) 96 D5
Sainte-Féréole (19) 138 D2
Sainte-Feyre (23) 111 G5
Sainte-Feyre-la-Montagne (23) 125 H2
Sainte-Flaive-des-Loups (85) 91 F5
Sainte-Florence (33) 135 H5
Sainte-Florence (85) 92 A4
Sainte-Florine (43) 127 G6
Sainte-Foi (09) 186 B4
Sainte-Fortunade (19) 139 E2
Sainte-Foy (40) 166 B2
Sainte-Foy (71) 115 E4
Sainte-Foy (76) 18 D1
Sainte-Foy (85) 91 E5
Sainte-Foy-d'Aigrefeuille (31) 169 G6
Sainte-Foy-de-Belvès (24) 152 A1
Sainte-Foy-de-Longas (24) 137 F5
Sainte-Foy-de-Montgommery (14) 39 F3
Sainte-Foy-de-Peyrolières (31) 168 D6
Sainte-Foy-la-Grande (33) 136 C5
Sainte-Foy-la-Longue (33) 150 A2
Sainte-Foy-l'Argentière (69) 129 G3
Sainte-Foy-lès-Lyon (69) 130 A3
Sainte-Foy-Saint-Sulpice (42) 128 D3
Sainte-Foy-Tarentaise (73) 133 F4
Sainte-Gauburge-Sainte-Colombe (61) 39 H5
Sainte-Gemme (17) 120 D2
Sainte-Gemme (32) 168 B4
Sainte-Gemme (33) 150 B2
Sainte-Gemme (36) 96 A5
Sainte-Gemme (51) 44 D1
Sainte-Gemme (79) 93 F4
Sainte-Gemme (81) 170 C1
Sainte-Gemme-en-Sancerrois (18) 82 B5
Sainte-Gemme-la-Plaine (85) 106 D2
Sainte-Gemme-Martaillac (47) 150 C4
Sainte-Gemme-Moronval (28) 41 F5
Sainte-Gemmes (41) 79 H2
Sainte-Gemmes-d'Andigné (49) 75 H1
Sainte-Gemmes-le-Robert (53) 59 F4
Sainte-Gemmes-sur-Loire (49) 76 D5
Sainte-Geneviève (02) 23 E2
Sainte-Geneviève (50) 13 E2
Sainte-Geneviève (54) 48 C3
Sainte-Geneviève (60) 20 B6
Sainte-Geneviève (76) 19 E2
Sainte-Geneviève-des-Bois (45) 82 B2
Sainte-Geneviève-des-Bois (91) 42 D6
Sainte-Geneviève-lès-Gasny (27) 41 G2
Sainte-Geneviève-sur-Argence (12) 140 C6
Sainte-Hélène (33) 134 C4
Sainte-Hélène (48) 156 B3
Sainte-Hélène (56) 54 D5
Sainte-Hélène (71) 101 F5
Sainte-Hélène (88) 70 B3
Sainte-Hélène-Bondeville (76) 16 C3
Sainte-Hélène-du-Lac (73) 132 A5
Sainte-Hélène-sur-Isère (73) 132 C4
Sainte-Hermine (85) 106 D1
Sainte-Honorine-de-Ducy (14) 13 H6
Sainte-Honorine-des-Pertes (14) 13 H5
Sainte-Honorine-du-Fay (14) 14 B5
Sainte-Honorine-la-Chardonne (61) 38 B4
Sainte-Honorine-la-Guillaume (61) 38 C4
Sainte-Innocence (24) 150 D1
Sainte-Jalle (26) 159 E4
Sainte-Jamme-sur-Sarthe (72) 60 A4
Sainte-Julie (01) 130 D2
Sainte-Juliette (82) 152 B5
Sainte-Juliette-sur-Viaur (12) 154 C6
Sainte-Léocadie (66) 199 H4
Sainte-Lheurine (17) 121 G5
Sainte-Livrade (31) 168 D5
Sainte-Livrade-sur-Lot (47) 151 E4
Sainte-Lizaigne (36) 97 E3
Sainte-Luce (38) 145 H5
Sainte-Luce-sur-Loire (44) 74 D5
Sainte-Lucie-de-Tallano (2A) 207 E2
Sainte-Lunaise (18) 97 G4
Sainte-Magnance (89) 84 B5
Sainte-Marguerite (43) 142 A2
Sainte-Marguerite (88) 70 D3
Sainte-Marguerite-de-Carrouges (61) 38 D6
Sainte-Marguerite-de-l'Autel (27) 40 C3
Sainte-Marguerite-de-Viette (14) 15 E6
Sainte-Marguerite-d'Elle (14) 13 F6
Sainte-Marguerite-des-Loges (14) 15 F6
Sainte-Marguerite-en-Ouche (27) 40 A2
Sainte-Marguerite-Lafigère (07) 156 D3
Sainte-Marguerite-sur-Duclair (76) 17 F5
Sainte-Marguerite-sur-Fauville (76) 16 D4
Sainte-Marguerite-sur-Mer (76) 17 F2
Sainte-Marie (05) 159 F3
Sainte-Marie (08) 24 A5
Sainte-Marie (15) 140 D5
Sainte-Marie (25) 88 B4
Sainte-Marie (32) 168 B5
Sainte-Marie (35) 56 C6
Sainte-Marie (58) 99 F2
Sainte-Marie (65) 184 A5
Sainte-Marie (66) 201 G2
Sainte-Marie-á-Py (51) 23 H6
Sainte-Marie-au-Bosc (76) 16 B4
Sainte-Marie-aux-Chênes (57) 26 A5
Sainte-Marie-aux-Mines (68) 71 E3
Sainte-Marie-Cappel (59) 2 C3
Sainte-Marie-d'Alloix (38) 132 A6
Sainte-Marie-d'Alvey (73) 131 G4
Sainte-Marie-de-Chignac (24) 137 G3
Sainte-Marie-de-Cuines (73) 146 C1
Sainte-Marie-de-Gosse (40) 164 D5
Sainte-Marie-de-Ré (17) 106 B5
Sainte-Marie-de-Vatimesnil (27) 19 F6
Sainte-Marie-de-Vaux (87) 123 H2
Sainte-Marie-des-Champs (76) 17 E4
Sainte-Marie-du-Bois (50) 37 G6
Sainte-Marie-du-Bois (53) 59 E1
Sainte-Marie-du-Lac-Nuisement (51) 46 C6
Sainte-Marie-du-Mont (38) 131 H6
Sainte-Marie-du-Mont (50) 13 E4
Sainte-Marie-en-Chanois (70) 88 A1
Sainte-Marie-en-Chaux (70) 87 H2
Sainte-Marie-Kerque (62) 2 A2
Sainte-Marie-la-Blanche (21) 101 G3
Sainte-Marie-la-Robert (61) 38 D5
Sainte-Marie-Lapanouze (19) 126 A6
Sainte-Marie-Laumont (14) 37 H3
Sainte-Marie-Outre-l'Eau (14) 37 G2
Sainte-Marie-sur-Ouche (21) 85 F6
Sainte-Marthe (27) 40 C3
Sainte-Marthe (47) 150 C3
Sainte-Maure (10) 66 B3
Sainte-Maure-de-Peyriac (47) 167 E1
Sainte-Maure-de-Touraine (37) 94 D2
Sainte-Maxime (83) 194 B3
Sainte-Même (17) 121 F2
Sainte-Menehould (51) 46 C2
Sainte-Mère (32) 168 A2
Sainte-Mère-Église (50) 13 E4
Sainte-Mesme (78) 62 D1
Sainte-Mondane (24) 138 B5
Sainte-Montaine (18) 81 G5
Sainte-Nathalène (24) 138 B5
Sainte-Néomaye (79) 108 A3
Sainte-Olive (01) 116 C6
Sainte-Opportune (61) 38 C4
Sainte-Opportune-du-Bosc (27) 40 C1
Sainte-Opportune-la-Mare (27) 15 H2
Sainte-Orse (24) 137 H2
Sainte-Osmane (72) 78 D1
Sainte-Ouenne (79) 107 H2
Sainte-Pallaye (89) 83 G3
Sainte-Paule (69) 129 G1
Sainte-Pazanne (44) 74 B6
Sainte-Pexine (85) 106 D1
Sainte-Pience (50) 35 H3
Sainte-Pôle (54) 49 G6
Sainte-Preuve (02) 22 D3
Sainte-Radegonde (12) 154 C4
Sainte-Radegonde (17) 120 D2
Sainte-Radegonde (24) 151 F1
Sainte-Radegonde (32) 167 H3
Sainte-Radegonde (33) 136 A6
Sainte-Radegonde (71) 100 B6
Sainte-Radegonde (79) 93 G3
Sainte-Radégonde (86) 109 G1
Sainte-Radégonde-des-Noyers (85) 106 D3
Sainte-Ramée (17) 121 E6
Sainte-Reine (70) 87 E4
Sainte-Reine (73) 132 B4
Sainte-Reine-de-Bretagne (44) 73 H3
Sainte-Ruffine (57) 26 B5
Sainte-Sabine (21) 101 F2
Sainte-Sabine-Born (24) 151 G1
Sainte-Sabine-sur-Longève (72) 60 A4
Sainte-Savine (10) 66 B3
Sainte-Scolasse-sur-Sarthe (61) 39 G6
Sainte-Segrée (80) 19 H1
Sainte-Sève (29) 31 H3
Sainte-Sévère (16) 121 H3
Sainte-Sévère-sur-Indre (36) 111 H2
Sainte-Sigolène (43) 143 E2
Sainte-Solange (18) 97 H2
Sainte-Soline (79) 108 C4
Sainte-Souline (16) 122 A6
Sainte-Soulle (17) 106 D4
Sainte-Suzanne (09) 185 F3
Sainte-Suzanne (25) 88 C4
Sainte-Suzanne (53) 59 F4
Sainte-Suzanne-sur-Vire (50) 37 G1
Sainte-Terre (33) 135 H5
Sainte-Thérence (03) 112 C4
Sainte-Thorette (18) 97 F3
Sainte-Tréphine (22) 33 E6
Sainte-Trie (24) 138 A1
Sainte-Tulle (04) 176 C3
Sainte-Valière (11) 187 H3
Sainte-Vaubourg (08) 24 A4
Sainte-Verge (79) 93 G3
Sainte-Vertu (89) 84 A2
Sainteny (50) 13 E5
Saintes (17) 121 E3
Saintes-Maries-de-la-Mer (13) 190 C4
Saintines (60) 21 E5
Saintry-sur-Seine (91) 43 E6
Saints (77) 43 H5
Saints (89) 83 E3
Saints-Geosmes (52) 86 B1
Sainville (28) 62 D2
Saires (86) 94 B4
Saires-la-Verrerie (61) 38 B5
Saissac (11) 186 D2
Saisseval (80) 7 F6
Saisy (71) 101 E4
Saivres (79) 108 A2
le Saix (05) 160 A3
Saïx (81) 170 C6
Saix (86) 93 H2
Saizenay (39) 103 F3
Saizerais (54) 48 C4
Saizy (58) 83 G6
Sajas (31) 184 D2
Salagnac (24) 138 A1
Salagnon (38) 130 D4
Salaise-sur-Sanne (38) 144 A1
Salans (39) 103 E2
Salasc (34) 172 C5
Salaunes (33) 134 D4
Salavas (07) 157 G4
Salavre (01) 117 E3
Salazac (30) 157 H5
Salbris (41) 81 E5
les Salces (48) 155 G3
Saléchan (65) 184 A5
Saleich (31) 184 C5
Saleignes (17) 108 B6
Saleilles (66) 201 F2
les Salelles (07) 157 E4
les Salelles (48) 155 G3
Salency (60) 21 G3
Salenthal (67) 50 C5
Saléon (05) 159 H4
Salérans (05) 159 H5
Salerm (31) 184 B2
Salernes (83) 193 G1
Salers (15) 140 B3
Sales (74) 131 H2
Salesches (59) 9 G3
la Salette-Fallavaux (38) 146 A5
Salettes (26) 158 C2
Salettes (43) 142 C5
Saleux (80) 7 F6
Salice (2A) 204 D4
Saliceto (2B) 205 F1
Saliès (81) 170 C3
Salies-de-Béarn (64) 165 F6
Salies-du-Salat (31) 184 C4
Salignac (04) 160 B6
Salignac (33) 135 G4
Salignac-de-Mirambeau (17) 121 F6
Salignac-Eyvigues (24) 138 B4
Salignac-sur-Charente (17) 121 G3
Saligney (39) 102 D1
Saligny (85) 91 G3
Saligny (89) 65 E4
Saligny-le-Vif (18) 98 B3
Saligny-sur-Roudon (03) 114 C2
Saligos (65) 182 D6
Salindres (30) 157 E6
Salinelles (30) 173 G3
Salins (15) 140 A2
Salins (77) 64 C2
Salins-les-Bains (39) 103 F4
Salins-les-Thermes (73) 132 D5
Salives (21) 85 G3
Sallagriffon (06) 178 C2
Sallanches (74) 133 E1
Sallaumines (62) 8 B1
la Salle (71) 116 B3
la Salle (88) 70 C2
la Salle-de-Vihiers (49) 92 D1
la Salle-en-Beaumont (38) 145 H5
la Salle-et-Chapelle-Aubry (49) 76 B6
la Salle-les-Alpes (05) 147 E4
la Salle-Prunet (48) 156 B5
Salleboeuf (33) 135 F5
Sallèdes (63) 127 G4
Sallèles-Cabardès (11) 187 E2
Sallèles-d'Aude (11) 188 A3
Sallen (14) 37 H1
Sallenelles (14) 14 C4
Sallenôves (74) 118 B6
Sallertaine (85) 90 D2
Salles (33) 148 D2
les Salles (42) 128 B2
Salles (47) 151 G2
Salles (65) 182 D4
Salles (79) 108 B3
Salles (81) 170 B1
Salles-Adour (65) 183 E3
Salles-Arbuissonnas-en-Beaujolais (69) 116 A6
Salles-Courbatiès (12) 153 G3
Salles-Curan (12) 154 D6
Salles-d'Angles (16) 121 G4
Salles-d'Armagnac (32) 166 D3
Salles-d'Aude (11) 188 B3
Salles-de-Barbezieux (16) 121 H5
Salles-de-Belvès (24) 151 H1
les Salles-de-Castillon (33) 136 A5
Salles-de-Villefagnan (16) 122 C1
les Salles-du-Gardon (30) 157 E6
Salles-et-Pratviel (31) 197 F1
Salles-la-Source (12) 154 C4
Salles-Lavalette (16) 122 C6
les Salles-Lavauguyon (87) 123 F3
Salles-Mongiscard (64) 165 F6
Salles-sous-Bois (26) 158 C3
Salles-sur-Garonne (31) 185 E2
Salles-sur-l'Hers (11) 186 A2
Salles-sur-Mer (17) 106 D5
les Salles-sur-Verdon (83) 177 F3
Sallespisse (64) 165 G5
Salmagne (55) 47 F4
Salmaise (21) 85 E5
Salmbach (67) 51 G2
Salmiech (12) 154 C6
Salomé (59) 3 E6
Salon (10) 45 F6
Salon (24) 137 F4
Salon-de-Provence (13) 191 G2
Salon-la-Tour (19) 124 C5
Salonnes (57) 49 E4
Salornay-sur-Guye (71) 115 H2
Salouël (80) 7 F6
Salperwick (62) 2 B4
Salsein (09) 184 D6
Salses-le-Château (66) 201 F1
Salsigne (11) 187 E2
Salt-en-Donzy (42) 129 E3
Salvagnac (81) 169 G3
Salvagnac-Cajarc (12) 153 F3
la Salvetat-Belmontet (82) 169 F2
la Salvetat-Lauragais (31) 169 H6
la Salvetat-Peyralès (12) 153 H5

la Salvetat-Saint-Gilles (31) 169 E5
la Salvetat-sur-Agout (34) 171 F4
Salvezines (11) 200 B1
Salviac (46) 152 B1
Salvizinet (42) 129 E3
Salza (11) 187 F5
Salzuit (43) 141 H2
Samadet (40) 166 A3
Saman (31) 184 A3
Samaran (32) 183 H1
Samatan (32) 168 B4
Samazan (47) 150 B3
Sambin (41) 79 H5
Sambourg (89) 84 A2
Saméon (59) 4 A6
Samer (62) 1 F5
Samerey (21) 102 B2
Sames (64) 164 D6
Sammarçolles (86) 94 A3
Samoëns (74) 119 F5
Samognat (01) 117 G4
Samogneux (55) 25 E6
Samois-sur-Seine (77) 64 B2
Samonac (33) 135 E3
Samoreau (77) 64 B2
Samouillan (31) 184 C3
Samoussy (02) 22 C3
Sampans (39) 102 C2
Sampigny (55) 47 G4
Sampigny-
lès-Maranges (71) 101 E4
Sampolo (2A) 205 E6
Sampzon (07) 157 G4
Samson (25) 103 F3
Samsons-Lion (64) 182 D1
Samuran (31) 184 A5
San-Damiano (2B) 203 G6
San-Gavino-
d'Ampugnani (2B) 203 G6
San-Gavino-di-Carbini (2A) 207 F2
San-Gavino-di-
Fiumorbo (2B) 205 F5
San-Gavino-di-Tenda (2B) 203 F5
San-Giorgio (2B) 203 G6
San-Giuliano (2B) 205 G2
San-Lorenzo (2B) 205 F1
San-Martino-di-Lota (2B) 203 G4
San-Nicolao (2B) 205 G1
Sana (31) 184 D3
Sanary-sur-Mer (83) 192 D5
Sancé (71) 116 B4
Sancergues (18) 98 C2
Sancerre (18) 82 B6
Sancey-le-Grand (25) 88 B6
Sancey-le-Long (25) 88 B6
Sancheville (28) 62 B4
Sanchey (88) 69 H4
Sancoins (18) 98 C5
Sancourt (27) 19 G5
Sancourt (59) 8 D5
Sancourt (80) 21 G1
Sancy (54) 26 A3
Sancy (77) 43 G3
Sancy-les-Cheminots (02) 22 B4
Sancy-lès-Provins (77) 44 B5
Sand (67) 71 G2
Sandarville (28) 62 A3
Sandaucourt (88) 69 E3
Sandillon (45) 81 E1
Sandouville (76) 15 F2
Sandrans (01) 116 C6
Sangatte (62) 1 G2
Sanghen (62) 1 G4
Sanguinet (40) 148 C2
Sanilhac (07) 157 F3
Sanilhac-Sagriès (30) 174 B2
Sannat (23) 112 B6
Sannerville (14) 14 D4
Sannes (84) 176 A4
Sannois (95) 42 C3
Sanous (65) 183 E1
Sanry-lès-Vigy (57) 26 C5
Sanry-sur-Nied (57) 26 D5
Sans-Vallois (88) 69 F4
Sansa (66) 200 A3
Sansac-de-Marmiesse (15) 140 A5
Sansac-Veinazès (15) 154 B1
Sansais (79) 107 G4
Sansan (32) 167 H6
Sanssac-l'Église (43) 142 B4
Sanssat (03) 114 A4
Santa-Lucia-
di-Mercurio (2B) 205 F2
Santa-Lucia-di-Moriani (2B) 205 H1
Santa-Maria-di-Lota (2B) 203 G3
Santa-Maria-Figaniella (2A) 207 E2
Santa-Maria-Poggio (2B) 205 G2
Santa-Maria-Siché (2A) 204 D6
Santa-Reparata-
di-Balagna (2B) 202 D5
Santa-Reparata-
di-Moriani (2B) 205 G2
Sant'Andréa-di-Bozio (2B) 205 F2
Sant'Andréa-di-Cotone (2B) 205 G2
Sant'Andréa-d'Orcino (2A) 204 C5
Santans (39) 102 D3
Sant'Antonino (2B) 202 C5
Santeau (45) 63 F5
Santec (29) 31 G2
Santenay (21) 101 F4
Santenay (41) 79 G4
Santeny (94) 43 E5
Santes (59) 3 F5
Santeuil (28) 62 C2
Santeuil (95) 42 A1
Santigny (89) 84 B4
Santilly (28) 62 D4
Santilly (71) 116 A1
Santo-Pietro-
di-Tenda (2B) 203 F5
Santo-Pietro-
di-Venaco (2B) 205 E3
Santoche (25) 88 A5
Santosse (21) 101 F3
Santranges (18) 82 B5
Sanvensa (12) 153 G5
Sanvignes-les-Mines (71) 100 D6
Sanxay (86) 108 D2
Sanzey (54) 48 A4
Saon (14) 13 G5
Saône (25) 103 G1
Saonnet (14) 13 G5
Saorge (06) 179 G1
Saosnes (72) 60 B3
Saou (26) 158 C2
le Sap (61) 39 G3
le Sap-André (61) 39 G3
Sapignicourt (51) 46 C5
Sapignies (62) 8 B4
Sapogne-et-Feuchères (08) 24 B2
Sapogne-sur-Marche (08) 25 E3
Sapois (39) 103 F5
Sapois (88) 70 B5
Saponay (02) 22 B6
Saponcourt (70) 87 F1
le Sappey (74) 118 C6
le Sappey-
en-Chartreuse (38) 145 G2
Saramon (32) 168 A6
Saran (45) 62 D6
Saraz (25) 103 F3
Sarbazan (40) 166 B1
Sarcé (72) 78 B2
Sarceaux (61) 39 E4
Sarcelles (95) 42 D3
Sarcenas (38) 145 G1
Sarcey (52) 67 H5
Sarcey (69) 129 G2
Sarcos (32) 184 B1
Sarcus (60) 19 H2
Sarcy (51) 22 D6
Sardan (30) 173 H3
Sardent (23) 111 G6
Sardieu (38) 144 D1
Sardon (63) 127 F1
Sardy-lès-Épiry (58) 99 H2
Sare (64) 180 B1
Sargé-lès-le-Mans (72) 60 B5
Sargé-sur-Braye (41) 61 F6
Sari-d'Orcino (2A) 204 C5

Sari-Solenzara (2A) 205 G6
Sariac-Magnoac (65) 183 H2
Sarlabous (65) 183 G4
Sarlande (24) 124 A6
Sarlat-la-Canéda (24) 138 A5
Sarliac-sur-l'Isle (24) 137 G2
Sarniguet (65) 183 E2
Sarnois (60) 19 H2
Saron-sur-Aube (51) 44 D6
Sarp (65) 184 A5
Sarpourenx (64) 165 G6
Sarragachies (32) 166 D4
Sarragachies (47) 150 B3
Sarraguzan (32) 183 G2
Sarralbe (57) 49 H2
Sarraltroff (57) 50 A4
Sarran (19) 125 F6
Sarrance (64) 182 A4
Sarrancolin (65) 183 G5
Sarrant (32) 168 B4
Sarraziet (40) 166 A3
Sarrazac (24) 123 H6
Sarrazac (46) 138 D4
Sarraziet (40) 166 A4
Sarre-Union (67) 50 A2
Sarrebourg (57) 50 A4
Sarrecave (31) 184 A2
Sarreguemines (57) 27 H5
Sarreinsming (57) 27 H5
Sarremezan (31) 184 A3
Sarrewerden (67) 50 A3
Sarrey (52) 68 B5
Sarriac-Bigorre (65) 183 F1
Sarrians (84) 175 F1
Sarrigny (39) 117 G2
Sarrola-Carcopino (2A) 204 C5
Sarron (40) 166 B5
Sarrouilles (65) 183 F3
Sarroux (19) 126 A6
Sarry (51) 45 H3
Sarry (71) 115 E4
Sarry (89) 84 B3
le Sars (62) 8 B4
Sars-et-Rosières (59) 9 E1
Sars-le-Bois (62) 7 H2
Sars-Poteries (59) 10 A3
Sartène (2A) 206 D3
Sartes (88) 68 D3
Sartilly (50) 35 G3
Sarton (62) 7 H4
Sartrouville (78) 42 C3
Sarzay (36) 111 G1
Sarzeau (56) 72 D2
Sasnières (41) 79 F2
Sassangy (71) 101 F6
Sassay (41) 80 A5
Sassegnies (59) 9 H3
Sassenage (38) 145 G2
Sassenay (71) 101 H5
Sassetot-le-Malgardé (76) 17 F3
Sassetot-le-Mauconduit (76) 16 D3
Sasseville (76) 17 E3
Sassey (27) 41 E2
Sassey-sur-Meuse (55) 24 D4
Sassis (65) 182 D6
Sassy (14) 14 D6
Sathonay-Camp (69) 130 A2
Sathonay-Village (69) 130 A2
Satillieu (07) 143 H3
Satolas-et-Bonce (38) 130 C3
Saturargues (34) 173 H4
Saubens (31) 169 E6
Saubion (40) 164 C4
Saubole (64) 182 D2
Saubrigues (40) 164 C5
Saubusse (40) 164 C4
Saucats (33) 149 F1
Saucède (64) 181 H2
la Saucelle (28) 40 D6
Sauchay (76) 17 H2
Sauchy-Cauchy (62) 8 C3
Sauchy-Lestrée (62) 8 C3
Saudemont (62) 8 C3
Saudoy (51) 44 D5
Saudron (52) 68 B1
Saudrupt (55) 46 D5
Saugeot (39) 117 H1
Saugnac-et-Cambran (40) 165 E4
Saugnacq-et-Muret (40) 148 D3
Saugon (33) 135 E2
Saugues (43) 142 A5
Saugues-Saint-Étienne (64) 181 G3
Saugy (18) 97 F4
Saujac (12) 153 F3
Saujon (17) 120 D3
la Saulce (05) 160 B3
Saulce-sur-Rhône (26) 158 B1
Saulces-Champenoises (08) 23 H4
Saulces-Monclin (08) 23 H3
Saulcet (03) 113 H4
le Saulchoy (60) 20 B2
Saulchoy (62) 6 D2
Saulchoy-sous-Poix (80) 20 A1
Saulcy (10) 67 E3
le Saulcy (88) 70 D1
Saulcy-sur-Meurthe (88) 70 D3
Saules (25) 103 G1
Saules (71) 101 F6
Saulgé (86) 109 H4
Saulgé-l'Hôpital (49) 77 F5
Saulges (53) 59 F5
Saulgond (16) 123 F1
Sauliac-sur-Célé (46) 153 E3
Saulieu (21) 100 C1
Saulmory-et-Villefranche (55) 24 D4
Saulnay (36) 95 H4
Saulnes (54) 25 H3
Saulnières (28) 41 F5
Saulnières (35) 57 F4
Saulnot (70) 88 B3
Saulny (57) 26 B5
Saulon-la-Chapelle (21) 102 A1
Saulon-la-Rue (21) 101 H1
Sault (84) 176 A1
Sault-Brénaz (01) 131 E2
Sault-de-Navailles (64) 165 G5
Sault-lès-Rethel (08) 23 G4
Sault-Saint-Remy (08) 23 F4
Saultain (59) 9 F2
Saulty (62) 7 H3
Saulvaux (55) 47 G5
Saulx (70) 87 G2
Saulx-le-Duc (21) 85 H4
Saulx-lès-Champlon (55) 47 H2
Saulx-les-Chartreux (91) 42 C5
Saulx-Marchais (78) 41 H4
Saulxerotte (54) 69 E1
Saulxures (52) 68 D6
Saulxures (67) 71 E2
Saulxures-
lès-Bulgnéville (88) 68 D4
Saulxures-lès-Nancy (54) 48 D5
Saulxures-lès-Vannes (54) 68 D1
Saulxures-sur-Moselotte (88) 70 C6
Saulzais-le-Potier (18) 112 C1
Saulzet (03) 113 H5
Saulzet-le-Froid (63) 126 D4
Saulzoir (59) 9 F3
Saumane (04) 176 C1
Saumane (30) 173 F1
Saumane-de-Vaucluse (84) 175 F2
Sauméjan (47) 150 B5
Saumeray (28) 61 H3
Saumont (47) 151 E5
Saumont-la-Poterie (76) 19 F3
Saumos (33) 134 C4
Saumur (49) 77 H6
Saunay (37) 79 F3
Sauneville (76) 16 D3
Saunières (71) 102 A4
Sauqueville (76) 17 G2
Saurais (79) 108 A1
Sauret-Besserve (63) 126 D1
Saurier (63) 127 E5

Sausheim (68) 89 F1
Saussan (34) 173 F6
Saussay (28) 41 F4
Saussay (76) 17 E4
Saussay-la-Campagne (27) 19 F5
la Saussaye (27) 18 C6
Saussemesnil (50) 12 D2
Saussenac (81) 170 D2
Saussens (31) 169 H5
Sausses (04) 178 B1
Sausset-les-Pins (13) 191 H5
Saussey (21) 101 F3
Saussey (50) 36 D2
Saussignac (24) 136 C6
Saussines (34) 173 G4
Saussy (21) 85 G5
Sautel (09) 186 A5
Sauternes (33) 149 G2
Sauteyrargues (34) 173 G3
Sauto (66) 200 A4
Sautron (44) 74 C4
Sauvagnac (16) 123 F3
Sauvagnas (47) 151 F5
Sauvagnat (63) 126 C3
Sauvagnat-
Sainte-Marthe (63) 127 F5
Sauvagney (25) 87 E6
Sauvagnon (64) 182 B1
Sauvagny (03) 113 E3
Sauvain (42) 128 C4
Sauvat (15) 140 A1
la Sauve (33) 135 G6
la Sauve (30) 135 G6
Sauvelade (64) 181 H1
Sauverny (01) 118 B3
la Sauvetat (32) 167 H3
la Sauvetat (63) 127 F4
la Sauvetat-de-Savères (47) 151 G5
la Sauvetat-du-Dropt (47) 150 D1
la Sauvetat-sur-Lède (47) 151 F4
Sauveterre-
Sainte-Marthe (63) 127 F5
Sauveterre (30) 174 D1
Sauveterre (32) 168 B6
Sauveterre (65) 183 G2
Sauveterre (81) 187 F1
Sauveterre (82) 152 B6
Sauveterre-
de-Comminges (31) 184 A5
Sauveterre-
de-Guyenne (33) 150 A1
Sauveterre-
de-Rouergue (12) 154 A5
Sauveterre-la-Lémance (47) 151 H2
Sauveterre-Saint-Denis (47) 151 F6
Sauviac (32) 183 H1
Sauviac (33) 149 H3
Sauvian (34) 188 C2
Sauviat (63) 128 A3
Sauviat-sur-Vige (87) 124 D2
Sauvignac (16) 135 H1
Sauvigney-lès-Gray (70) 86 D5
Sauvigney-lès-Pesmes (70) 86 C5
Sauvigny (55) 68 D1
Sauvigny-le-Beuréal (89) 84 B4
Sauvigny-le-Bois (89) 84 A4
Sauvigny-les-Bois (58) 99 E4
Sauville (08) 24 B4
Sauville (88) 68 D3
Sauvillers-Mongival (80) 20 D2
Sauvimont (32) 184 C1
Sauvoy (55) 47 H5
Saux (46) 152 A4
Saux-et-Pomarède (31) 184 B3
Sauxillanges (63) 127 G5
Sauze (06) 161 G5
le Sauze-du-Lac (05) 160 D3
Sauzé-Vaussais (79) 108 C5
Sauzelles (36) 95 F6
Sauzet (26) 158 B2
Sauzet (30) 174 A2
Sauzet (46) 152 B4
la Sauzière-Saint-Jean (81) 169 G2
Sauzon (56) 72 A3
Savarthès (31) 184 B4
Savas (07) 143 H1
Savas-Mépin (38) 130 C5
Savasse (26) 158 B2
Savenay (44) 74 A4
Savenès (82) 168 D3
Savennes (23) 111 G6
Savennes (63) 126 B3
Savennières (49) 76 D5
Saverdun (09) 185 G3
Savères (31) 184 D2
Saverne (67) 50 C4
Saveuse (80) 7 F6
Savianges (71) 101 F6
Savières (10) 66 A2
Savigna (39) 117 G2
Savignac (12) 153 G4
Savignac (33) 150 A2
Savignac-de-Duras (47) 150 C1
Savignac-de-l'Isle (33) 135 G4
Savignac-de-Miremont (24) 137 G4
Savignac-de-Nontron (24) 123 F5
Savignac-Lédrier (24) 138 A1
Savignac-les-Églises (24) 137 G2
Savignac-les-Ormeaux (09) 199 F2
Savignac-Mona (32) 168 C6
Savignac-sur-Leyze (47) 151 G3
Savigné (86) 109 E5
Savigné-l'Évêque (72) 60 B5
Savigné-sous-le-Lude (72) 77 H3
Savigné-sur-Lathan (37) 78 B5
Savigneux (01) 116 C6
Savigneux (42) 128 D4
Savignies (60) 20 A4
Savigny (50) 37 E1
Savigny (52) 86 D1
Savigny (69) 129 G2
Savigny (74) 131 H1
Savigny (88) 69 G3
Savigny-en-Revermont (71) 117 F1
Savigny-en-Sancerre (18) 82 B5
Savigny-en-Septaine (18) 98 A3
Savigny-en-Terre-Plaine (89) 84 B4
Savigny-en-Véron (37) 94 A1
Savigny-le-Sec (21) 85 H5
Savigny-le-Temple (77) 43 E6
Savigny-le-Vieux (50) 37 G6
Savigny-lès-Beaune (21) 101 G3
Savigny-Lévescault (86) 109 F2
Savigny-Poil-Fol (58) 100 A5
Savigny-sous-Faye (86) 94 B4
Savigny-sous-Mâlain (21) 85 F6
Savigny-sur-Aisne (08) 24 B5
Savigny-sur-Ardres (51) 22 D6
Savigny-sur-Braye (41) 79 E1
Savigny-sur-Clairis (89) 64 D4
Savigny-sur-Grosne (71) 116 A1
Savigny-sur-Orge (91) 42 D5
Savigny-sur-Seille (71) 116 C1
Savilly (21) 100 D2
Savines-le-Lac (05) 160 D3
Savins (77) 64 D1
Savoillan (84) 159 F5
Savoisy (21) 84 D2
Savolles (21) 86 A5
Savonnières (37) 78 C6
Savonnières-devant-Bar (55) 47 E4
Savonnières-en-Perthois (55) 47 E6
Savouges (21) 101 H2
Savournon (05) 159 H3
Savoyeux (70) 86 D4
Savy (02) 21 H1
Savy-Berlette (62) 8 A2
Saxel (74) 118 D4
Saxi-Bourdon (58) 99 G3
Saxon-Sion (54) 69 F2
Sayat (63) 127 E2
Saze (30) 174 D2
Sazeray (36) 111 H3
Sazeret (03) 113 F3
Sazos (65) 182 D6

Scaër (29) 54 A2
Scata (2B) 203 G6
Sceau-Saint-Angel (24) 123 F5
Sceaux (89) 84 B4
Sceaux (92) 42 C4
Sceaux-d'Anjou (49) 76 D3
Sceaux-du-Gâtinais (45) 63 H5
Sceaux-sur-Huisne (72) 60 D5
Scey-Maisières (25) 103 F2
Scey-sur-Saône-
et-Saint-Albin (70) 87 F3
Schaeferhof (67) 71 H1
Schaffhouse-près-Seltz (67) 51 G2
Schaffhouse-sur-Zorn (67) 50 D4
Schalbach (57) 50 B3
Schalkendorf (67) 50 D3
Scharrachbergheim-
Irmstett (67) 50 D5
Scheibenhard (67) 51 G2
Scherlenheim (67) 50 D4
Scherwiller (67) 71 F2
Schillersdorf (67) 50 D3
Schiltigheim (67) 51 E5
Schirmeck (67) 71 E1
Schirrhein (67) 51 F3
Schirrhoffen (67) 51 F3
Schleithal (67) 51 G2
Schlierbach (68) 89 G2
Schmittviller (57) 28 A6
Schnersheim (67) 50 D5
Schnebusch (57) 50 D5
Schœnau (67) 71 H3
Schœnbourg (67) 50 C3
Schœneck (57) 27 G4
Schœnenbourg (67) 51 F2
Schopperten (67) 50 A2
Schorbach (57) 50 C1
Schweighouse-
sur-Moder (67) 51 E3
Schweighouse-Thann (68) 89 E2
Schwenheim (67) 50 C4
Schweyen (57) 28 A5
Schwindratzheim (67) 50 D4
Schwoben (68) 89 F3
Schwobsheim (67) 71 G3
Sciecq (79) 107 H3
Scientrier (74) 118 D5
Scieurac-et-Flourès (32) 167 E5
Sciez (74) 118 D3
Scillé (79) 107 G1
Scionzier (74) 119 E6
Scolca (2B) 203 F6
Scorbé-Clairvaux (86) 94 C5
Scrignac (29) 32 B5
Scrupt (51) 46 C5
Scy-Chazelles (57) 26 B5
Scye (70) 87 F3
Séailles (32) 167 E4
Sébazac-Concourès (12) 154 C4
Sébécourt (27) 40 B3
Sébéville (50) 13 E4
Seboncourt (02) 9 F6
Sebourg (59) 9 G2
Sébrazac (12) 154 C3
Séby (64) 182 A2
Secenans (70) 88 B4
Séchault (08) 24 B6
Sécheras (07) 144 A3
Sécheval (08) 11 E6
Séchilienne (38) 145 H3
Séchin (25) 87 H6
Seclin (59) 3 F5
Secondigné-sur-Belle (79) 108 A5
Secondigny (79) 107 H1
Secourt (57) 48 D3
Secqueville-en-Bessin (14) 14 B4
Sedan (08) 24 B2
Sédeilhac (31) 184 A3
Séderon (26) 159 G5
Sedze-Maubecq (64) 182 D2
Sedzère (64) 182 D2
Seebach (67) 51 F2
Sées (61) 39 F6
Séez (73) 133 F4
Ségalas (47) 151 E2
Ségalas (65) 183 F1
la Ségalassière (15) 139 H5
Séglien (56) 54 D2
Ségny (01) 118 B3
Segonzac (16) 121 H4
Segonzac (19) 138 B2
Segonzac (24) 136 D2
Ségos (32) 166 B5
Ségoufielle (32) 168 D5
Segré (49) 75 H1
Ségreville (31) 169 H6
Ségrie (72) 59 H4
Ségrie-Fontaine (61) 38 C4
Segrois (21) 101 G2
Ségry (36) 97 E4
la Séguinière (49) 92 B2
Ségur (12) 155 E5
le Ségur (81) 170 B1
Ségur-le-Château (19) 124 B6
Ségur-les-Villas (15) 140 D2
Ségura (09) 185 H5
Séguret (84) 158 D5
Ségus (65) 182 D4
Seich (65) 183 H5
Seichamps (54) 48 D4
Seichebrières (45) 63 F6
Seicheprey (54) 48 A3
Seichebrières (45) 63 F6
Seignalens (11) 186 B4
Seigné (17) 121 H1
Seigneulles (55) 47 E4
Seignosse (40) 164 B4
Seigny (21) 84 D4
Seigy (41) 96 A1
Seilh (31) 169 E4
Seilhac (19) 139 E1
Seilhan (31) 184 A4
Seillac (41) 79 G4
Seillans (83) 178 A4
Seillonnaz (01) 131 E2
Seillons-Source-
d'Argens (83) 176 D6
Seine-Port (77) 63 H1
Seingbouse (57) 27 G5
Seissan (32) 167 H6
Seix (09) 185 E6
le Sel-de-Bretagne (35) 57 F5
Selaincourt (54) 69 E1
Selens (02) 21 H4
Sélestat (67) 71 G3
Séligné (79) 108 A5
Séligney (39) 102 D4
la Selle-Craonnaise (53) 76 A1
la Selle-en-Coglès (35) 35 H6
la Selle-en-Hermoy (45) 64 B6
la Selle-en-Luitré (35) 58 A2
la Selle-Guerchaise (35) 58 A6
la Selle-la-Forge (61) 38 C4
la Selle-sur-le-Bied (45) 64 B5
Selles (27) 16 A4
Selles (51) 23 G5
Selles (62) 1 G4
Selles (70) 69 F6
Selles-Saint-Denis (41) 80 D6
Selles-sur-Cher (41) 96 B1
Selles-sur-Nahon (36) 96 B3
Sellières (39) 102 C5
Selommes (41) 79 G2
Seloncourt (25) 88 C4
Selongey (21) 86 A4
Selonnet (04) 160 D4
Seltz (67) 51 G3
Sélune (61) 38 C5
la Selve (02) 23 E3
la Selve (12) 171 E1
Sem (09) 198 D1
Sémalens (81) 170 B6
Semallé (61) 60 A1
Sembadel (43) 142 B2
Sembas (47) 151 F4
Semblançay (37) 78 C4

Semboués (32) 167 E6
Séméac (65) 183 E3
Séméacq-Blachon (64) 166 C6
Sémécourt (57) 26 B5
Sémelay (58) 100 A5
Semens (33) 149 H2
Sementron (89) 83 E3
Séméries (59) 10 A4
Semerville (41) 61 H5
Semezanges (21) 101 G1
Sémézies-Cachan (32) 168 A6
Semide (08) 24 A5
Semillac (17) 121 F6
Semilly (52) 68 B3
Semmadon (70) 87 E2
Semoine (10) 45 F5
Semond (21) 85 E2
Semondans (25) 88 B4
Semousies (59) 10 A4
Semoussac (17) 121 E6
Semoutiers-Montsaon (52) 67 H5
Semousies (59) 10 A4
Semoutiers-Montsaon (52) 67 H5
Semussac (17) 120 C5
Semuy (08) 24 A4
Sénac (65) 183 F2
Senaide (88) 69 E6
Sénaillac-Latronquière (46) 139 G6
Sénaillac-Lauzès (46) 153 E2
Senailly (21) 84 C4
Senan (89) 83 E1
Senantes (28) 41 G5
Senantes (60) 19 H4
Senarens (31) 184 C2
Sénargent-Mignafans (70) 88 A3
Senarpont (80) 6 D6
Sénas (13) 175 G4
Senaud (39) 117 E3
Senaux (81) 171 F4
Sencenac-Puy-
de-Fourches (24) 137 F1
Senconac (09) 199 F1
Sendets (33) 150 A3
Sendets (64) 182 C2
Séné (56) 73 E1
Sénéchas (30) 157 E5
Sénac (65) 183 F2
Sénaide (88) 69 E6
Sénézergues (15) 154 A1
Séngouagnet (31) 184 B5
Séniergues (46) 152 D1
Senillé (86) 94 D4
Seninghem (62) 1 H4
Senlecques (62) 1 G5
Senlis (60) 20 D6
Senlis (62) 1 H5
Senlis-le-Sec (80) 7 H5
Senlisse (78) 42 B5
Sennecé-lès-Mâcon (71) 42 A2
Sennecey-le-Grand (71) 116 B1
Sennecey-lès-Dijon (21) 85 H6
Sennely (45) 81 F3
Sennevières (37) 95 F2
Senneville-sur-Fécamp (76) 16 C3
Sennevoy-le-Bas (89) 84 C2
Sennevoy-le-Haut (89) 84 C2
Senon (55) 25 G5
Senonches (28) 40 D6
Senoncourt (70) 87 F2
Senoncourt-les-Maujouy (55) 47 F2
Senones (88) 70 D2
Senonges (88) 69 E4
Senonnes (53) 76 A1
Senots (60) 20 A5
Senouillac (81) 170 A2
Sénoville (50) 12 B3
Senozan (71) 116 B3
Sens (89) 65 E4
Sens-Beaujeu (18) 82 A5
Sens-de-Bretagne (35) 57 F1
Sens-sur-Seille (71) 102 B5
Sentein (09) 184 C6
Sentelie (80) 20 A2
Sentenac-de-Sérou (09) 185 F6
Sentenac-d'Oust (09) 185 E6
Sentheim (68) 89 E2
Sentilly (61) 38 D4
la Sentinelle (59) 9 F2
Sentous (65) 183 G2
Senven-Léhart (22) 33 E5
Sépeaux (89) 64 D6
Sepmeries (59) 9 F2
Sepmes (37) 95 E3
Seppois-le-Bas (68) 89 E4
Seppois-le-Haut (68) 89 F4
Sept-Forges (61) 59 E1
Sept-Frères (14) 37 G3
Sept-Meules (76) 6 A5
Sept-Saulx (51) 45 G1
Sept-Sorts (77) 43 H3
Sept-Vents (14) 37 H1
Septème (38) 130 B5
Septèmes-les-Vallons (13) 192 A3
Septeuil (78) 41 G3
Septfonds (82) 152 D6
Septfontaines (25) 103 H3
Septmoncel (39) 118 A2
Septmonts (02) 22 A5
Septsarges (55) 24 D5
Septvaux (02) 22 A3
Sepvigny (55) 68 D1
Sepvret (79) 108 B4
Sept-Vents (14) 37 H1
Sepx (31) 184 C3
Sequedin (59) 3 F5
Sequehart (02) 9 E6
le Sequestre (81) 170 B2
Serain (02) 9 E5
Seraincourt (08) 23 F4
Seraincourt (95) 42 A2
Sérandon (19) 140 A1
Séranon (06) 178 B3
Serans (60) 19 H6
Serans (61) 38 D5
Seraucourt-le-Grand (02) 21 H1
Seraumont (88) 68 C2
Serazereux (28) 41 F6
Serbannes (03) 113 H6
Serbonnes (89) 64 D3
Serches (02) 22 B5
Sercœur (88) 70 A3
Sercus (59) 2 C4
Sercy (71) 116 A1
Serdinya (66) 200 A3
Sère (32) 184 A1
Sère-en-Lavedan (65) 182 D4
Sère-Lanso (65) 183 E4
Sère-Rustaing (65) 183 G2
Serécourt (88) 69 E5
Séreilhac (87) 123 H3
Serémange-Erzange (57) 26 B3
Sérempuy (32) 168 B4
Sérénac (81) 170 D2
Sérent (56) 55 H5
Sérévillers (60) 20 C2
Serez (27) 41 F3
Sérézin-de-la-Tour (38) 130 D5
Sérézin-du-Rhône (69) 130 A4
Sergeac (24) 137 H4
Sergenaux (39) 102 C4
Sergenon (39) 102 C3
Sergines (89) 65 E3
Sergy (01) 118 B4
Sergy (02) 22 C6
Séricourt (62) 7 F2
Sériers (15) 141 E4
Sérifontaine (60) 19 G5
Sérignac (46) 152 A3
Sérignac (82) 168 B2
Sérignac-Péboudou (47) 151 E2

Sérignac-sur-Garonne (47) 151 E5
Sérignan (34) 188 C3
Sérignan-du-Comtat (84) 158 B6
Sérigné (85) 107 E2
Sérigny (61) 60 D2
Sérigny (86) 94 B4
Sérilhac (19) 139 E3
Seringes-et-Nesles (02) 22 C6
Séris (41) 80 B3
Serley (71) 102 B5
Sermages (58) 100 A3
Sermaise (49) 77 G4
Sermaise (91) 63 E1
Sermaises (45) 63 F3
Sermaize (60) 21 G3
Sermaize-les-Bains (51) 46 D4
Sermamagny (90) 88 C2
Sermange (39) 102 D1
Sermano (2B) 205 F2
Sermentizon (63) 127 H3
Sermérieu (38) 131 E4
Sermersheim (67) 71 G2
Sermesse (71) 102 A4
Sermiers (51) 45 F1
Sermizelles (89) 83 H4
Sermoise (02) 22 B5
Sermoise-sur-Loire (58) 99 E4
Sermoyer (01) 116 C2
Sermur (23) 126 A1
Sernhac (30) 174 C2
Serocourt (88) 69 E5
Séron (65) 182 D2
Serpaize (38) 130 B5
la Serpent (11) 186 C6
Serques (62) 2 A3
Serqueux (52) 68 D6
Serqueux (76) 19 F3
Serquigny (27) 40 B1
Serra-di-Ferro (2A) 206 C2
Serra-di-Fiumorbo (2B) 205 G5
Serra-di-Scopamène (2A) 207 E2
Serralongue (66) 200 D5
Serraval (74) 132 C2
la Serre (12) 171 F3
la Serre-Bussière-Vieille (23) 112 B6
Serre-les-Moulières (39) 102 D1
Serre-les-Sapins (25) 103 F1
Serre-Nerpol (38) 145 E2
Serres (11) 186 D5
Serres (54) 49 E5
Serres (11) 187 E6
Serres-Castet (64) 182 B1
Serres-et-Montguyard (24) 151 E1
Serres-Gaston (40) 166 A4
Serres-Morlaàs (64) 182 C2
Serres-Sainte-Marie (64) 182 A1
Serres-sur-Arget (09) 185 G6
Serreslous-et-Arribans (40) 165 H4
Serriera (2A) 204 B2
Serrières (71) 116 A4
Serrières-de-Briord (01) 131 E2
Serrières-
en-Chautagne (73) 131 G2
Serrières-sur-Ain (01) 117 F5
Serrigny (89) 83 H2
Serrigny-en-Bresse (71) 102 A5
Serrouville (54) 26 A3
Serruelles (18) 97 H4
Sers (16) 122 D4
Sers (65) 183 E6
Servais (02) 22 A3
Servance (70) 88 B1
Servanches (24) 136 B3
Servant (63) 113 F5
Servas (01) 117 E5
Servas (30) 157 F6
Servaville-Salmonville (76) 18 D4
Serventes (48) 156 B2
Serves-sur-Rhône (26) 144 A3
Servian (34) 188 C2
Servières (48) 155 H3
Servières-le-Château (19) 139 G3
Serviers-et-Labaume (30) 174 B1
Serviès (81) 170 B5
Serviès-en-Val (11) 187 F4
Servignat (01) 116 D2
Servigney (70) 87 H2
Servigny (50) 37 E1
Servigny-lès-Raville (57) 49 E1
Servigny-lès-
Sainte-Barbe (57) 26 C5
Servilly (03) 114 B3
Servin (25) 88 A6
Servins (62) 8 A1
Servon (50) 35 G4
Servon (77) 43 E5
Servon-Melzicourt (51) 24 B6
Servon-sur-Vilaine (35) 57 F3
Servoz (74) 133 E1
Sery (08) 23 G3
Séry (89) 83 G3
Séry-lès-Mézières (02) 22 B1
Séry-Magneval (60) 21 F6
Serzy-et-Prin (51) 22 D6
Sessenheim (67) 51 G3
Sète (34) 189 F1
Setques (62) 2 A4
Seugy (95) 42 D2
Seuil (08) 23 H4
Seuil-d'Argonne (55) 46 D2
Seuillet (03) 114 A5
Seuilly (37) 94 A2
le Seure (17) 121 G2
Seur (41) 79 H4
Seurre (21) 102 A3
Seux (80) 7 F6
Seuzey (55) 47 H2
Sevelinges (42) 115 F6
Sévenans (90) 88 C3
Séverac (44) 74 A2
Séverac-le-Château (12) 155 F5
Séverac-l'Église (12) 155 E4
Seveux (70) 86 D4
Sévignacq (64) 182 C1
Sévignacq-Meyracq (64) 182 B4
Sévigny (61) 39 E4
Sévigny-la-Forêt (08) 10 D6
Sévigny-Waleppe (08) 23 F3
Sévis (76) 17 H4
Sevrai (61) 39 E5
Sevran (93) 43 E3
Sèvres (92) 42 C4
Sèvres-Anxaumont (86) 109 F1
Sevrey (71) 101 G6
Sévrier (74) 132 B2
Sévry (18) 98 B2
Sewen (68) 88 D1
Sexcles (19) 139 F4
Sexey-aux-Forges (54) 48 C5
Sexey-les-Bois (54) 48 B5
Sexfontaines (52) 67 H4
Seychalles (63) 127 G3
Seyches (47) 150 D3
Seyne (04) 160 D4
la Seyne-sur-Mer (83) 193 E5
Seynes (30) 174 A1
Seynod (74) 132 A2
Seyre (31) 185 H2
Seyresse (40) 165 E4
Seyssel (01) 131 G1
Seyssel (74) 131 G1
Seysses (31) 169 E6
Seysses-Savès (32) 168 C6
Seyssinet-Pariset (38) 145 G2
Seyssins (38) 145 G3
Seyssuel (38) 130 A5
Seythenex (74) 132 C3
Seytroux (74) 119 F4
Sézanne (51) 44 D4
Siarrouy (65) 183 E2
Siaugues-Sainte-Marie (43) 142 A3
Sibiril (29) 31 G2
Sibiville (62) 7 G2
Siccieu-Saint-Julien-
et-Carisieu (38) 130 D3
Sichamps (58) 99 E2

Sickert (68) 88 D1
Sideville (50) 12 C2
Sidiailles (18) 112 B2
Siecq (17) 121 H2
Siegen (67) 51 G2
les Sièges (89) 65 F4
Sierck-les-Bains (57) 26 C2
Sierentz (68) 89 G2
Siersthal (57) 50 B1
Sierville (76) 17 G5
Siest (40) 164 D4
Sieurac (81) 170 B3
Sieuras (09) 185 F3
Siévoz (38) 145 H5
Siewiller (67) 50 B3
Sigale (06) 178 C2
Sigalens (33) 150 A3
Sigean (11) 188 A5
Sigloy (45) 81 F2
Signac (31) 184 A6
Signes (83) 192 D4
Signéville (52) 68 A3
Signy-l'Abbaye (08) 23 G2
Signy-le-Petit (08) 10 C6
Signy-Montlibert (08) 25 E3
Signy-Signets (77) 43 H3
Sigogne (16) 121 H3
Sigoisheim (68) 71 F4
Sigonce (04) 176 D1
Sigottier (05) 159 H3
Sigoulès (24) 136 D6
Sigournais (85) 92 B5
Sigoyer (04) 160 B3
Sigoyer (05) 199 E1
Siguer (09) 198 D1
Sigy (77) 64 D1
Sigy-en-Bray (76) 19 F3
Sigy-le-Châtel (71) 115 H2
Silfiac (56) 55 E2
Silhac (07) 143 H5
Sillans (38) 145 E1
Sillans-la-Cascade (83) 193 G1
Sillars (86) 109 H3
Sillas (33) 150 A3
Sillé-le-Guillaume (72) 59 G4
Sillé-le-Philippe (72) 60 B5
Sillery (51) 23 F6
Silley-Amancey (25) 103 G3
Silley-Bléfond (25) 87 H6
Sillingy (74) 132 A1
Silly-en-Gouffern (61) 39 F4
Silly-en-Saulnois (57) 48 D2
Silly-la-Poterie (02) 44 A1
Silly-le-Long (60) 43 F2
Silly-sur-Nied (57) 26 D5
Silly-Tillard (60) 20 B5
Silmont (55) 47 F5
Siltzheim (67) 27 H5
Silvareccio (2B) 203 G6
Silvarouvres (52) 67 F5
Simandre (71) 116 B1
Simandre-sur-Suran (01) 117 F4
Simandres (69) 130 A4
Simard (71) 102 A5
Simencourt (62) 8 A3
Simeyrols (24) 138 B5
Simiane-Collongue (13) 192 B3
Simiane-la-Rotonde (04) 176 B2
Simorre (32) 184 B1
Simplé (53) 58 C6
Sin-le-Noble (59) 8 D2
Sinard (38) 145 G4
Sinceny (02) 21 H3
Sindères (40) 164 D2
Singles (63) 126 B5
Singleyrac (24) 136 D6
Singly (08) 24 A2
Singrist (67) 50 C5
Sinsat (09) 199 E1
Sinzos (65) 183 F3
Sion (32) 166 D4
Sion-les-Mines (44) 57 F6
Sioniac (19) 139 E4
Sionne (88) 68 C2
Sionviller (54) 49 E5
Siorac-de-Ribérac (24) 136 D2
Siorac-en-Périgord (24) 137 H6
Siouville-Hague (50) 12 B2
Sirac (32) 168 C4
Siracourt (62) 7 G2
Siradan (65) 184 A6
Siran (15) 139 G5
Siran (34) 187 G2
Sireix (65) 182 D5
Sireuil (16) 122 B4
Sirod (39) 103 F5
Siros (64) 182 B1
Sisco (2B) 203 G3
Sissonne (02) 23 E3
Sissy (02) 22 B1
Sistels (82) 168 B1
Sisteron (04) 160 B5
Sivergues (84) 176 A3
Sivignon (71) 115 H3
Sivry-Ante (51) 46 C2
Sivry-Courtry (77) 64 B1
Sivry-la-Perche (55) 47 E1
Sivry-sur-Meuse (55) 25 E5
Six-Fours-les-Plages (83) 193 E5
Sixt-Fer-à-Cheval (74) 119 G5
Sixt-sur-Aff (35) 56 C5
Sizun (29) 31 G5
Smarves (86) 109 E2
Smermesnil (76) 6 B5
Soccia (2A) 204 D4
Sochaux (25) 88 C4
Socx (59) 2 C2
Sode (31) 197 F1
Sœurdres (49) 77 E2
Sognolles-en-Montois (77) 64 D1
Sogny-aux-Moulins (51) 45 G3
Sogny-en-l'Angle (51) 46 C4
Soignolles (14) 38 D2
Soignolles-en-Brie (77) 43 F6
Soindres (78) 41 G3
Soing-Cubry-
Charentenay (70) 87 E3
Soings-en-Sologne (41) 80 B5
Soirans (21) 102 B1
Soissons (02) 22 A5
Soissons-sur-Nacey (21) 102 C1
Soisy-Bouy (77) 65 E1
Soisy-sous-
Montmorency (95) 42 C3
Soisy-sur-École (91) 63 H1
Soisy-sur-Seine (91) 42 D6
Soize (02) 23 E2
Soizé (28) 61 F4
Soizy-aux-Bois (51) 44 D4
Solaize (69) 130 A4
Solante (21) 205 G6
Solbach (67) 71 E1
Soleilhas (04) 178 A3
Solemont (25) 88 C5
Solente (60) 21 F2
Solenzara (2A) 205 G6
le Soler (66) 201 E2
Solérieux (26) 158 B4
Solers (77) 43 F6
Solesmes (59) 9 F3
Solesmes (72) 77 G1
Soleymieu (38) 130 D3
Soleymieux (42) 128 D6
Solférino (40) 148 C6
Solgne (57) 48 D2
Soliers (14) 14 C5
Solignac (87) 124 B3
Solignac-sous-Roche (43) 142 D2
Solignac-sur-Loire (43) 142 C4
Soligny-la-Trappe (61) 39 H6
Soligny-les-Étangs (10) 65 F2
Sollacaro (2A) 206 D2
Solliès-Pont (83) 193 F4
Solliès-Toucas (83) 193 F4
Solliès-Ville (83) 193 F4

Sologny (71)....116 A3
Solomiac (32)....168 B3
Solre-le-Château (59)....10 B3
Solrinnes (59)....10 B3
Solterre (45)....82 A1
Solutré-Pouilly (71)....116 A4
Somain (59)....9 E2
Sombacour (25)....103 H3
Somberon (21)....85 F6
Sombrin (62)....7 H3
Sombrun (65)....166 D6
Somloire (49)....92 D3
Sommaing (59)....9 F2
Sommancourt (52)....67 G1
Sommauthe (08)....24 C4
Somme-Bionne (51)....46 B2
Somme-Suippe (51)....46 B1
Somme-Tourbe (51)....46 B1
Somme-Vesle (51)....46 B3
Somme-Yèvre (51)....46 C3
Sommecaise (89)....82 D1
Sommedieue (55)....47 G1
Sommeilles (55)....46 D3
Sommelans (02)....44 B1
Sommepy-Tahure (51)....23 H6
Sommerance (08)....24 C5
Sommercourt (52)....68 D3
Sommereux (60)....20 A2
Sommeron (02)....11 H6
Sommervieu (14)....14 A3
Sommerviller (54)....49 E5
Sommery (76)....19 E2
Sommesnil (76)....17 E4
Sommesous (51)....45 G5
la Sommette (25)....104 B1
Sommette-Eaucourt (02)....22 A1
Sommeval (10)....66 A4
Sommevoire (52)....67 F2
Sommières (30)....173 H4
Sommières-du-Clain (86)....108 D5
Sompt (79)....108 B5
Sompuis (51)....45 H5
Somsois (51)....46 A4
Son (08)....23 G3
Sonac (46)....153 F1
Sonchamp (78)....42 A6
Soncourt (88)....69 E2
Soncourt-sur-Marne (52)....67 F2
Sondernach (68)....70 D5
Sondersdorf (68)....89 F4
la Sône (38)....144 D3
Songeons (60)....19 H3
Songeson (39)....103 E6
Songieu (01)....131 G1
Songy (51)....46 A4
Sonnac (12)....153 H3
Sonnac (17)....121 H2
Sonnac-sur-l'Hers (11)....186 B5
Sonnay (38)....144 B1
Sonnaz (73)....131 H4
Sonneville (16)....122 A3
Sons-et-Ronchères (02)....22 C1
Sonthonnax-la-Montagne (01)....117 F4
Sonzay (37)....78 C4
Soorts-Hossegor (40)....164 B4
Soppe-le-Bas (68)....89 E2
Soppe-le-Haut (68)....88 D2
Sop (09)....184 D6
Sorans-lès-Breurey (70)....87 F5
Sorbais (02)....10 A6
Sorbets (32)....166 C4
Sorbets (40)....166 A4
Sorbey (55)....25 G4
Sorbey (57)....26 C6
Sorbier (03)....114 B3
Sorbiers (05)....159 G4
Sorbiers (42)....203 G6
Sorbo-Ocagnano (2B)....203 G6
Sorbollano (2A)....207 E2
Sorbon (08)....23 G3
Sorbs (34)....172 C3
Sorcy-Bauthémont (08)....23 H3
Sorcy-Saint-Martin (55)....47 H5
Sorde-l'Abbaye (40)....165 E5
Sore (40)....149 F4
Soréac (65)....183 F2
Sorède (66)....201 F4
Sorel (80)....8 C5
Sorel-en-Vimeu (80)....7 E5
Sorel-Moussel (28)....41 F4
Sorèze (81)....186 C1
Sorgeat (09)....199 G2
Sorges (24)....137 G1
Sorgues (84)....175 E3
Sorigny (37)....95 E1
les Sorinières (44)....74 D6
Sorio (2B)....203 F5
Sormery (89)....65 H5
Sormonne (08)....23 H1
Sornac (19)....125 H4
Sornay (70)....86 D6
Sornay (71)....116 D1
Sornéville (54)....49 E4
Sorquainville (76)....16 D4
Sorrus (62)....6 C1
Sort-en-Chalosse (40)....165 F4
Sortosville (50)....12 D3
Sortosville-en-Beaumont (50)....12 B4
Sos (47)....167 E1
Sospel (06)....195 G1
Sossais (86)....94 C4
Sost (65)....183 H5
Sotta (2A)....207 F4
Sottevast (50)....12 C4
Sotteville (50)....12 B4
Sotteville-lès-Rouen (76)....17 G6
Sotteville-sous-le-Val (76)....18 B5
Sotteville-sur-Mer (76)....17 E2
Soturac (46)....151 H3
Sotzeling (57)....49 F3

Sougy-sur-Loire (58)....99 F5
les Souhesmes-Rampont (55)....47 G2
Souhey (21)....84 D5
le Souich (62)....7 G3
Souilhanels (11)....186 B2
Souilhe (11)....186 B2
Souillac (46)....138 C5
Souillé (72)....60 A4
Souilly (55)....47 F2
Soula (09)....185 H6
Soulac-sur-Mer (33)....120 B5
Soulages (15)....141 G3
Soulages-Bonneval (12)....154 D1
Soulaines-Dhuys (10)....67 F2
Soulaines-sur-Aubance (49)....77 E5
Soulaire-et-Bourg (49)....77 E3
Soulan (09)....185 E6
Soulanges (51)....46 A4
Soulangis (18)....97 H2
Soulangy (14)....38 D3
Soulatgé (11)....187 F6
Soulaucourt-sur-Mouzon (52)....68 D4
Soulaures (24)....151 H1
Soulce-Cernay (25)....88 C6
Soulgé-sur-Ouette (53)....59 E5
le Soulié (34)....171 F6
Soulières (51)....45 E3
Soulignac (33)....149 H1
Souligné-Flacé (72)....59 H6
Souligné-sous-Ballon (72)....60 B4
Soulignonne (17)....120 D2
Souligny (10)....66 A4
Soulitré (72)....60 C5
Soullans (85)....90 D3
Soulom (65)....182 D5
Soulomès (46)....152 D2
Soulosse-sous-Saint-Élophe (88)....68 D2
Soultz-Haut-Rhin (68)....71 E6
Soultz-les-Bains (67)....50 D6
Soultz-sous-Forêts (67)....51 F2
Soultzbach-les-Bains (68)....71 E5
Soultzeren (68)....71 E5
Soultzmatt (68)....71 E5
Soulvache (44)....57 G5
Soumaintrain (89)....65 H6
Soumans (23)....112 B4
Soumensac (47)....150 D1
Souméras (47)....135 F1
Soumont (34)....172 C4
Soumont-Saint-Quentin (14)....38 D2
Soumoulou (64)....182 C2
Soupex (11)....186 B2
Soupir (02)....22 C4
Souppes-sur-Loing (77)....64 A4
Souprosse (40)....165 G3
Souraïde (64)....180 C1
Sourans (25)....88 B5
Sourcieux-les-Mines (69)....129 H3
le Sourd (02)....22 C1
Sourdeval (50)....37 G4
Sourdeval-les-Bois (50)....37 E3
Sourdon (80)....20 C2
le Sourn (56)....55 E3
Sournia (66)....200 C2
Sourniac (15)....140 A2
Sourribes (04)....160 B6
Sours (28)....62 B2
Soursac (19)....139 H3
sous-Parsat (23)....111 G6
Sousceyrac (46)....139 G5
Sousmoulins (17)....135 G1
Souspierre (26)....158 C2
Soussac (33)....150 A1
Soussans (33)....135 E3
Soussey-sur-Brionne (21)....85 E6
Soustelle (30)....156 D6
Soustons (40)....164 B4
Sousville (38)....145 H5
Souternon (42)....128 C2
la Souterraine (23)....110 D4
Soutiers (79)....108 A1
Souvans (39)....102 D3
Souvignargues (30)....173 H3
Souvigné (16)....122 A1
Souvigné (37)....78 C4
Souvigné (79)....108 B2
Souvigné-sur-Même (72)....60 D4
Souvigné-sur-Sarthe (72)....77 F1
Souvigny (03)....113 G2
Souvigny-de-Touraine (37)....79 G5
Souvigny-en-Sologne (41)....81 F3
Souyeaux (65)....183 F3
Souzay-Champigny (49)....93 H1
Souzy (69)....129 G3
Souzy-la-Briche (91)....63 F1
Soveria (2B)....205 E2
Soyans (26)....158 C2
Soyaux (16)....122 C4
Soye (25)....88 A5
Soye-en-Septaine (18)....97 H3
Soyécourt (80)....8 B6
Soyers (52)....86 D1
Soyons (07)....144 A5
Sparsbach (67)....50 C3
Spay (72)....60 A6
Spechbach-le-Bas (68)....89 E2
Spechbach-le-Haut (68)....89 E2
Speloncato (2B)....202 D5
Spéracèdes (06)....178 C4
Spézet (29)....54 A1
Spicheren (57)....27 G4
Spincourt (55)....25 G5
Sponville (54)....48 A2
Spoy (10)....67 E4
Spoy (21)....86 A5
Spycker (59)....2 B2
Squiffiec (22)....33 E3
Staffelfelden (68)....89 F1
Stains (93)....42 D3
Stainville (55)....47 E5
Stattmatten (67)....51 F3
Stazzona (2B)....205 G1
Steenbecque (59)....2 C4
Steene (59)....2 C2
Steenvoorde (59)....2 D3
Steenwerck (59)....3 E4
Steige (67)....71 E2
Steinbach (68)....89 E1
Steinbourg (67)....50 C4
Steinbrunn-le-Bas (68)....89 E2
Steinbrunn-le-Haut (68)....89 F2
Steinseltz (67)....51 F1
Steinsoultz (68)....89 F3
Stenay (55)....24 D4
Sternenberg (68)....89 E2
Stetten (68)....89 G3
Still (67)....50 D6
Stigny (89)....84 B2
Stirling-Wendel (57)....27 G4
Stonne (08)....24 C3
Storckensohn (68)....70 D6
Stosswihr (68)....71 E5
Stotzheim (67)....71 G2
Strasbourg (67)....51 F5
Strazeele (59)....2 D4
Strenquels (46)....138 D4
Strueth (68)....89 E3
Struth (67)....50 B3
Stuckange (57)....26 C3
Stundwiller (67)....51 F2
Stutzheim-Offenheim (67)....50 D5

Sucé-sur-Erdre (44)....74 D4
Sucy-en-Brie (94)....43 E5
Suèvres (41)....80 A3
Sugères (63)....127 H4
Sugny (08)....24 A3
Suhescun (64)....181 E2
Suilly-la-Tour (58)....82 C6
Suin (71)....115 H3
Suippes (51)....46 A1
Suisse (57)....49 G2
Suizy-le-Franc (51)....44 D4
Sulignat (01)....116 C5
Sully (14)....13 H5
Sully (60)....19 G3
Sully (71)....101 E5
Sully-la-Chapelle (45)....63 F6
Sully-sur-Loire (45)....81 G2
Sulniac (56)....55 H6
Sumène (30)....173 E2
Sundhoffen (68)....71 F5
Sundhouse (67)....71 G3
Supt (39)....103 F4
Surat (63)....127 G1
Surba (09)....185 G6
Surbourg (67)....51 E2
Surcamps (80)....7 F4
Surdoux (87)....124 D4
Suré (61)....60 C2
Suresnes (92)....42 C4
Surfonds (72)....60 C6
Surfontaine (02)....22 B1
Surgères (17)....107 F5
Surgy (58)....83 F4
Suriauville (88)....69 E4
Surin (79)....107 H2
Surin (86)....109 E6
Suris (16)....123 E2
Surjoux (01)....117 H6
Surmont (25)....88 B6
Surques (62)....1 G5
Surrain (14)....13 G5
Surtainville (50)....12 B3
Surtauville (27)....18 C6
Survie (61)....39 F4
Surville (14)....15 F3
Surville (27)....18 C6
Survilliers (95)....43 E2
Sury (08)....24 A1
Sury-aux-Bois (45)....63 G6
Sury-en-Vaux (18)....82 B5
Sury-ès-Bois (18)....82 A5
Sury-le-Comtal (42)....129 E5
Sury-près-Léré (18)....82 B5
Surzur (56)....73 E1
Sus (64)....181 G2
Sus-Saint-Léger (62)....7 H3
Susmiou (64)....181 G2
Sussac (87)....124 D4
Sussargues (34)....173 G4
Sussat (03)....113 F5
Sussey (21)....100 D1
Susville (38)....145 G5
Suzan (09)....185 F5
Suzanne (08)....24 A3
Suzanne (80)....8 B5
Suzannecourt (52)....67 H2
Suze (26)....144 C6
Suze-la-Rousse (26)....158 B5
la Suze-sur-Sarthe (72)....77 H1
Suzette (84)....158 D6
Suzoy (60)....21 G3
Suzy (02)....22 B3
Sy (08)....24 B3
Syam (39)....103 F5
Sylvains-les-Moulins (27)....40 D3
Sylvanès (12)....171 H3
le Syndicat (88)....70 B5

T

Tabaille-Usquain (64)....181 G1
Tabanac (33)....135 F6
la Table (73)....132 B5
le Tablier (85)....91 H5
Tabre (09)....186 B5
Tachoires (32)....167 H6
Tacoignières (78)....41 G4
Taconnay (58)....83 F6
Taden (22)....34 C5
Tadousse-Ussau (64)....166 C5
Taglio-Isolaccio (2B)....203 G6
la Tagnière (71)....100 C5
Tagnon (08)....23 G4
Tagolsheim (68)....89 F2
Tagsdorf (68)....89 F3
Tailhac (43)....141 H4
Taillades (84)....175 F3
le Taillan-Médoc (33)....135 E5
Taillancourt (55)....68 D1
Taillant (17)....121 E1
Taillebois (61)....38 C4
Taillebourg (17)....121 E2
Taillebourg (47)....150 D3
Taillecavat (33)....150 C1
Taillecourt (25)....88 C4
la Taillée (85)....107 E3
Taillefontaine (02)....21 G5
Taillepied (50)....12 C4
Taillet (66)....200 D4
Taillette (08)....11 E4
Tailly (08)....24 C4
Tailly (21)....101 G3
Tailly (80)....7 E5
Tain-l'Hermitage (26)....144 A3
Taingy (89)....83 E3
Taintrux (88)....70 C3
Taisnières-en-Thiérache (59)....9 H4
Taisnières-sur-Hon (59)....9 H2
Taissy (51)....23 F6
Taix (81)....170 C2
Taizé (71)....116 A3
Taizé (79)....93 G4
Taizé-Aizie (16)....108 D6
Taizy (08)....23 G3
Tajan (65)....183 H3
Talairan (11)....187 G5
Talais (33)....120 B5
Talange (57)....26 B4
Talant (21)....85 H6
Talasani (2B)....203 G6
la Talaudière (42)....129 F5
Talazac (65)....183 E2
Talcy (18)....82 B5
Talcy (41)....80 B3
Talence (33)....135 E6
Talencieux (07)....144 A2
Talensac (35)....56 D3
Talissieu (01)....131 G2
Talizat (15)....141 E3
Tallans (25)....87 H5
Tallard (05)....160 B3
Tallenay (25)....87 F6
Tallende (63)....127 F4
Taller (40)....165 E2
Talloires (74)....132 B2
Tallone (2B)....205 G3
le Talud-Sainte-Gemme (85)....92 C6
Talmas (80)....7 G5
Talmay (21)....86 C6
Talmont-Saint-Hilaire (85)....91 F6
Talmont-sur-Gironde (17)....120 C4
Talmontiers (60)....19 G5
Talon (58)....83 F6
Talus-Saint-Prix (51)....44 D4
Taluyers (69)....129 H4
Tamerville (50)....12 D3
Tamnay-en-Bazois (58)....99 H3
Tamniès (24)....138 A4
Tanavelle (15)....141 E4
Tanay (21)....86 A5
Tancoigné (49)....93 F1

Tancon (71)....115 F5
Tanconville (54)....49 H5
Tancrou (77)....43 H2
Tangry (62)....7 G1
Taninges (74)....119 E5
Tanis (50)....35 G3
Tanlay (89)....84 B1
Tannay (08)....24 B3
Tannay (58)....83 G6
Tanneron (83)....178 C4
Tannerre-en-Puisaye (89)....82 D2
Tannières (02)....22 B6
Tannois (55)....47 F5
Tanques (61)....39 E5
le Tanu (50)....35 H2
Tanus (81)....170 D1
Tanville (61)....39 E6
Tanzac (17)....121 E4
Taponas (69)....116 B5
Taponnat-Fleurignac (16)....122 D3
Tarabel (31)....169 G6
Taradeau (83)....177 H6
Tarare (69)....129 F2
Tarascon (13)....174 D3
Tarascon-sur-Ariège (09)....199 E1
Tarasteix (65)....183 E2
Tarbes (65)....183 E3
Tarcenay (25)....103 G2
Tardes (23)....112 B5
Tardets-Sorholus (64)....181 G3
la Tardière (85)....92 C6
Tardinghen (62)....1 F3
Tarentaise (42)....143 G1
Tarerach (66)....200 C3
Targassonne (66)....199 H4
Target (03)....113 F4
Targon (33)....135 G6
Tarnac (19)....125 F4
Tarnès (33)....135 G4
Tarnos (40)....164 B5
Taron-Sadirac-Viellenave (64)....166 B6
Tarquimpol (57)....49 G4
Tarrano (2B)....205 G2
Tarsac (32)....166 C4
Tarsacq (64)....182 A1
Tarsul (21)....85 G4
Tart-l'Abbaye (21)....102 B1
Tart-le-Bas (21)....102 B1
Tart-le-Haut (21)....102 A1
Tartaras (42)....129 H5
Tartas (40)....165 G3
Tartécourt (70)....87 F1
Tartiers (02)....21 H4
Tartigny (60)....20 C2
Tartonne (04)....177 G1
le Tartre (71)....102 C5
le Tartre-Gaudran (78)....41 G5
Tarzy (08)....10 C6
Tasque (32)....166 D5
Tassé (72)....77 G1
Tassenières (39)....102 C4
Tassillé (72)....59 G5
Tassin-la-Demi-Lune (69)....130 A3
Tasso (2A)....205 F5
Tatinghem (62)....2 A4
le Tâtre (17)....121 H6
Taugon (17)....107 E3
Taulé (29)....31 H3
Taulignan (26)....158 C3
Taulis (66)....200 C4
Taupont (56)....56 A4
Tauriac (33)....135 F3
Tauriac (46)....139 E5
Tauriac (81)....169 G3
Tauriac-de-Camarès (12)....171 H4
Tauriac-de-Naucelle (12)....154 A6
Tauriers (07)....157 F2
Taurignan-Castet (09)....184 D5
Taurignan-Vieux (09)....184 D5
Taurinya (66)....200 C3
Taurize (11)....187 F4
Taussac (12)....140 C6
Taussac-la-Billière (34)....172 A5
Tautavel (66)....201 E1
Tauves (63)....126 C5
Tauxières-Mutry (51)....45 F2
Tauxigny (37)....95 F1
Tavaco (2A)....204 C5
Tavant (37)....94 C2
Tavaux (39)....102 C3
Tavaux-et-Pontséricourt (02)....22 D2
Tavel (30)....174 D2
Tavera (2A)....204 D4
Tavernay (71)....100 C3
Tavernes (83)....193 F1
Taverny (95)....42 C2
Tavers (45)....80 B2
Tavey (70)....88 C3
Taxat-Senat (03)....113 G5
Taxenne (39)....102 D2
Tayac (33)....136 A4
Taybosc (32)....168 A4
Tayrac (12)....154 A6
Tayrac (47)....151 G5
Tazilly (58)....100 A5
le Tech (66)....200 D5
Têche (38)....145 E2
Técou (81)....170 A3
le Teich (33)....148 C1
Teigny (58)....83 G6
Teilhède (63)....127 E1
Teilhet (09)....186 A4
Teilhet (63)....113 E6
Teillay (35)....57 F5
Teillé (44)....75 E3
Teillé (72)....60 B4
Teillet (81)....170 D2
Teillet-Argenty (03)....112 C4
le Teilleul (50)....37 H6
Teillots (24)....138 A2
Teissières-de-Cornet (15)....140 A4
Teissières-lès-Bouliès (15)....140 B6
Telgruc-sur-Mer (29)....31 E6
Tellancourt (54)....25 G3
Tellecey (21)....86 B6
Tellières-le-Plessis (61)....39 H6
Teloché (72)....78 B1
le Temple (33)....134 C5
le Temple (41)....61 F6
le Temple-de-Bretagne (44)....74 B4
Temple-Laguyon (24)....138 A2
le Temple-sur-Lot (47)....151 E4
Templemars (59)....3 F5
Templeuve (59)....3 G5
Templeux-la-Fosse (80)....8 C5
Templeux-le-Guérard (80)....8 D5
Tenay (01)....131 F1
Tence (43)....143 E3
Tencin (38)....145 H1
Tende (06)....163 H6
Tendon (88)....70 B4
Tendron (18)....98 B4
Tendu (36)....111 F1
Teneur (62)....7 F1
Tennie (72)....59 H4
Tenteling (57)....49 H1
Tercé (86)....109 F2
Tercillat (23)....111 H3
Tercis-les-Bains (40)....165 E4
Terdeghem (59)....2 C3
Terdonne (58)....22 A3
Térjat (03)....112 C5
Termes (08)....24 B5
Termes (11)....187 F5
Termes (48)....141 G6
Termes-d'Armagnac (32)....166 D4
Terminiers (28)....62 C5
Ternand (69)....129 G1
Ternant (17)....121 F1
Ternant (21)....101 H1
Ternant (58)....100 A4
Ternant-les-Eaux (63)....127 F6
Ternas (62)....7 G2
Ternat (52)....85 H2
Ternay (41)....79 F2
Ternay (69)....130 A4
Ternay (86)....93 H3

les Ternes (15)....141 E4
Ternuay-Melay-et-Saint-Hilaire (70)....88 B1
Terny-Sorny (02)....22 A4
Terramesnil (80)....7 G4
la Terrasse (38)....145 H1
la Terrasse-sur-Dorlay (42)....129 G6
Terrasson-Lavilledieu (24)....138 B3
Terrats (66)....201 E3
Terraube (32)....167 H2
Terre-Clapier (81)....170 D3
Terre-Natale (52)....86 C1
Terrebasse (31)....184 C3
Terrehault (72)....60 C4
Terrefondrée (21)....85 G2
Terron-sur-Aisne (08)....24 A4
Terrou (46)....139 F6
Tersanne (26)....144 B2
Tersannes (87)....110 B4
Terssac (81)....170 B2
le Tertre-Saint-Denis (78)....41 G3
Tertry (80)....8 D6
Terville (57)....26 B3
Tessancourt-sur-Aubette (78)....42 A2
Tessé-Froulay (61)....38 D6
Tessel (14)....14 A5
Tesson (17)....121 E4
Tessonnière (79)....93 G5
la Tessoualle (49)....92 C3
Tessy-sur-Vire (50)....37 F2
la Teste-de-Buch (33)....148 B1
Tétaigne (08)....24 D3
Téteghem (59)....2 C1
Téterchen (57)....27 E4
Teting-sur-Nied (57)....49 F1
Teuillac (33)....135 F3
Teulat (81)....169 G5
Teurthéville-Bocage (50)....12 D2
Teurthéville-Hague (50)....12 B2
Teyjat (24)....123 E4
Teyran (34)....173 G5
Teyssières (26)....158 D3
Teyssieu (46)....139 F5
Teyssode (81)....170 A5
Thaas (51)....45 E6
Thaims (17)....120 D4
Thairé (17)....106 D5
Thal-Drulingen (67)....50 B4
Thal-Marmoutier (67)....50 C4
Thalamy (19)....126 B4
Thann (68)....89 E1
Thannenkirch (68)....71 F2
Thanvillé (67)....71 F2
Thaon (14)....14 B4
Thaon-les-Vosges (88)....69 H3
Tharaux (30)....157 F5
Tharoiseau (89)....83 H5
Tharot (89)....84 A4
Thaumiers (18)....98 A5
Thauron (23)....125 E1
Thauvenay (18)....82 B6
Thèbe (65)....184 A5
Théding (57)....49 G1
Thédirac (46)....152 C2
Thégra (46)....139 E6
Théhillac (56)....73 H2
le Theil (03)....113 G3
le Theil (50)....12 D2
le Theil-Bocage (14)....38 A3
le Theil-de-Bretagne (35)....57 G4
le Theil-en-Auge (14)....15 F3
le Theil-Nolent (27)....15 H5
Theil-Rabier (16)....108 C6
le Theil-sur-Vanne (89)....65 F4
Theillay (41)....81 E4
Theillement (27)....18 B5
Theix (56)....73 E1
Theizé (69)....129 G2
Thel (69)....115 G6
Théligny (72)....61 E4
Thélis-la-Combe (42)....143 F3
Thélod (54)....48 C6
Thélonne (08)....24 C2
Thélus (62)....8 B2
Théméricourt (95)....42 A2
Thémines (46)....153 F1
Théminettes (46)....153 F1
Thénac (17)....121 E4
Thénac (24)....136 C6
Thenailles (02)....22 D1
Thenay (36)....111 E1
Thenay (41)....79 H5
Thenelles (02)....22 B1
Thénésol (73)....132 C3
Theneuil (37)....94 C2
Theneuille (03)....113 E1
Thénezay (79)....93 G5
Thénioux (18)....97 E1
Thenissey (21)....85 E4
Thénisy (77)....64 C2
Thennelières (10)....66 B3
Thennes (80)....20 D1
Thénorgues (08)....24 C4
Théoule-sur-Mer (06)....178 C6
Therdonne (60)....20 B4
Thérines (60)....19 H3
Thermes-Magnoac (65)....184 A3
Thérondels (12)....140 D6
Thérouanne (62)....2 B5
Thérouldeville (76)....16 D3
Thervay (39)....102 D1
Thésée (41)....79 H6
Thésy (39)....103 F4
Theuley (70)....87 E2
Théus (05)....160 C3
Theuville (28)....62 B3
Theuville (95)....42 B1
Theuville-aux-Maillots (76)....16 D3
Thevet-Saint-Julien (36)....111 H1
Théville (50)....12 D2
They-sous-Montfort (88)....69 F3
They-sous-Vaudemont (54)....69 F2
Theys (38)....145 H1
Théza (66)....201 F3
Thézac (17)....120 D3
Thézac (47)....151 H4
Thézan-des-Corbières (11)....187 H4
Thézan-lès-Béziers (34)....188 B1
Thèze (04)....160 A4
Thèze (64)....166 B6
Thézey-Saint-Martin (54)....48 D3
Théziers (30)....174 D3
Thézillieu (01)....131 F1
Thézy-Glimont (80)....20 D1
Thiais (94)....42 D5
Thiancourt (90)....88 D3
Thianges (58)....99 G4
Thiant (59)....9 F2
Thiat (87)....110 A4
Thiaucourt-Regniéville (54)....48 B3
Thiaville-sur-Meurthe (54)....70 C2
Thiberville (27)....15 G5
Thibie (51)....45 H3
Thibivillers (60)....19 H5
Thibouville (27)....40 B1
Thicourt (57)....49 F2
Thiébauménil (54)....49 F6
Thiéblemont-Farémont (51)....46 B5
Thiébouhans (25)....88 C6
Thieffrain (10)....66 D3
Thieffrans (70)....87 H4
Thiéfosse (88)....70 B5
Thiel-sur-Acolin (03)....114 B2
Thiembronne (62)....1 H5
Thiénans (70)....87 H4
Thiennes (59)....2 C4
Thiepval (80)....8 A4
Thiergeville (76)....16 D3
Thiernu (02)....22 D1
Thiers (63)....128 A2
Thiers-sur-Thève (60)....43 E1
Thierville (27)....18 B5
Thierville-sur-Meuse (55)....47 F1

Thiéry (06)....178 D1
Thiescourt (60)....21 F3
Thiétreville (76)....16 D3
le Thieulin (28)....61 G2
Thieulloy-la-Ville (80)....19 H1
Thieulloy-l'Abbaye (80)....20 A1
Thieuloye-Saint-Antoine (60)....20 A2
la Thieuloye (62)....7 H1
Thieux (60)....20 C3
Thieux (77)....43 F2
Thiéville (14)....39 E2
Thièvres (62)....7 H4
Thièvres (80)....7 H4
Thiézac (15)....140 C4
Thignonville (45)....63 F3
Thil (01)....130 B2
Thil (10)....67 E3
Thil (27)....18 D4
Thil (31)....168 D4
Thil (51)....23 E5
Thil-Manneville (76)....17 G2
le Thil-Riberpré (76)....19 F2
Thil-sur-Arroux (71)....100 B5
Thilay (08)....11 F5
Thilleux (52)....67 F2
les Thilliers-en-Vexin (27)....19 E6
Thillois (51)....23 E6
Thillombois (55)....47 F3
le Thillot (88)....70 C6
Thilouze (37)....94 D1
Thimert-Gâtelles (28)....61 E2
Thimonville (57)....49 E2
Thimory (45)....81 H1
Thin-le-Moutier (08)....23 H2
Thiolières (63)....128 B4
Thionne (03)....114 B3
Thionville (57)....26 B3
Thiouville (76)....16 D4
Thiraucourt (88)....69 F3
Thiré (85)....106 D1
Thiron-Gardais (28)....61 F3
Thise (25)....87 F6
Thivars (28)....62 A2
Thivencelle (59)....9 G1
Thiverny (60)....20 D6
Thiverval-Grignon (78)....42 A3
Thivet (52)....68 A6
Thiviers (24)....123 G6
Thiville (28)....62 A4
Thizay (36)....96 C4
Thizay (37)....94 B2
Thizy (69)....115 G6
Thizy (89)....84 B3
Thoard (04)....160 C6
Thodure (38)....144 C1
Thoigné (72)....60 B3
Thoiras (30)....173 G1
Thoiré-sous-Contensor (72)....60 B3
Thoiré-sur-Dinan (72)....78 C2
Thoires (21)....85 E1
Thoirette (39)....117 G3
Thoiria (39)....117 H1
Thoiry (01)....118 B4
Thoiry (73)....132 A4
Thoiry (78)....41 H4
Thoissey (01)....116 B5
Thoissia (39)....117 F3
Thoisy-la-Berchère (21)....100 D1
Thoisy-le-Désert (21)....101 E1
Thol-lès-Millières (52)....68 B4
Thollet (86)....110 B3
Thollon-les-Mémises (74)....119 F3
le Tholonet (13)....176 B6
le Tholy (88)....70 B4
Thomer-la-Sôgne (27)....40 D3
Thomery (77)....64 B2
Thomirey (21)....101 E3
Thonac (24)....138 A4
Thônes (74)....132 C2
Thonnance-lès-Joinville (52)....67 H1
Thonnance-les-Moulins (52)....67 H2
Thonne-la-Long (55)....25 E3
Thonne-le-Thil (55)....25 E3
Thonne-les-Près (55)....25 E3
Thonnelle (55)....25 E3
Thonon-les-Bains (74)....119 E3
les Thons (88)....69 E6
Thonville (57)....49 F2
le Thor (84)....175 E3
Thorailles (45)....64 B6
Thoraise (25)....103 F1
Thorame-Basse (04)....161 E6
Thorame-Haute (04)....161 E5
Thoras (43)....142 A5
Thoré-la-Rochette (41)....79 F2
Thorens-Glières (74)....118 C6
Thorenc (06)....178 B3
Thorey (21)....84 D4
Thorey-en-Plaine (21)....102 A1
Thorey-Lyautey (54)....69 F1
Thorey-sous-Charny (21)....84 D6
Thorey-sur-Ouche (21)....101 F2
Thorigné (79)....108 A4
Thorigné-d'Anjou (49)....76 D3
Thorigné-en-Charnie (53)....59 F5
Thorigné-Fouillard (35)....57 F2
Thorigné-sur-Dué (72)....60 D5
Thorigny (85)....91 H5
Thorigny-sur-le-Mignon (79)....107 G5
Thorigny-sur-Marne (77)....43 F3
Thorigny-sur-Oreuse (89)....65 E3
le Thoronet (83)....193 G2
Thorrenc (07)....144 A2
Thors (10)....67 E4
Thors (17)....121 G2
Thory (80)....20 C2
Thory (89)....83 H5
Thoste (21)....84 C5
le Thou (17)....107 E5
Thou (18)....82 A4
Thou (45)....82 C3
Thouarcé (49)....77 E6
Thouaré-sur-Loire (44)....74 D5
Thouars (79)....93 G3
Thouars-sur-Arize (09)....185 F4
Thouars-sur-Garonne (47)....150 D5
Thouarsais-Bouildroux (85)....92 B6
le Thoult-Trosnay (51)....44 D3
le Thour (08)....23 F4
le Thoureil (49)....77 F5
Thourie (35)....57 G5
Thouron (87)....124 B1
Thourotte (60)....21 F4
Thoury (41)....80 C4
Thoury-Férottes (77)....64 C3
Thoux (32)....168 C4
Thubœuf (53)....59 E1
le Thuel (02)....23 E2
Thuès-entre-Valls (66)....200 A4
Thueyts (07)....157 F1
Thugny-Trugny (08)....23 H4
la Thuile (73)....132 A5
les Thuiles (04)....161 F3
Thuilley-aux-Groseilles (54)....48 C6
Thuillières (88)....69 F4
le Thuit (27)....18 D6
le Thuit-Anger (27)....18 C5
le Thuit-Signol (27)....18 C5
le Thuit-Simer (27)....18 C5
Thulay (25)....88 C5
Thumeries (59)....3 F6
Thun-l'Évêque (59)....9 E3
Thun-Saint-Amand (59)....9 F1
Thun-Saint-Martin (59)....9 E3
Thurageau (86)....94 A5
Thuré (86)....94 C5
Thuret (63)....127 G1
Thurey (71)....102 A6
Thurey-le-Mont (25)....87 F5
Thurins (69)....129 H4
Thury (21)....101 E2
Thury (89)....83 E4
Thury-en-Valois (60)....43 H1

Thury-Harcourt (14)....14 B6
Thury-sous-Clermont (60)....20 C5
Thusy (74)....131 H1
Thuy (65)....183 F2
Tibiran-Jaunac (65)....183 H4
Ticheville (61)....39 G3
Tichey (21)....102 B3
Tieffenbach (67)....50 B3
Tiercé (49)....77 E3
Tiercelet (54)....26 A2
le Tiercent (35)....35 G4
Tieste-Uragnoux (32)....166 D5
la Tieule (48)....155 G4
Tiffauges (85)....92 A3
Tigeaux (77)....43 G4
Tigery (91)....43 E6
Tignac (09)....199 F2
Tigné (49)....93 F1
Tignécourt (88)....69 E5
Tignes (73)....133 G5
le Tignet (06)....178 C4
Tignieu-Jameyzieu (38)....130 D3
Tigny-Noyelle (62)....6 C2
Til-Châtel (21)....86 A4
Tilh (40)....165 F5
Tilhouse (65)....183 G4
Tillac (32)....167 E5
Tillay-le-Péneux (28)....62 C4
Tillé (60)....20 B4
Tillenay (21)....102 C2
Tilleul-Dame-Agnès (27)....40 C2
le Tilleul (76)....16 B4
le Tilleul-Lambert (27)....40 C2
le Tilleul-Othon (27)....40 B1
Tilleux (88)....68 D3
Tillières (49)....75 F6
Tillières-sur-Avre (27)....40 D4
Tilloloy (80)....21 E2
Tilloy-et-Bellay (51)....46 B2
Tilloy-Floriville (80)....6 C5
Tilloy-lès-Conty (80)....20 B1
Tilloy-lès-Hermaville (62)....7 H2
Tilloy-lès-Mofflaines (62)....8 B2
Tilloy-lez-Cambrai (59)....8 D3
Tilloy-lez-Marchiennes (59)....9 E1
Tilly (27)....41 G1
Tilly (36)....110 C3
Tilly (78)....41 G4
Tilly-Capelle (62)....7 F1
Tilly-la-Campagne (14)....14 C5
Tilly-sur-Meuse (55)....47 F2
Tilly-sur-Seulles (14)....14 A4
Tilques (62)....2 A4
Tincey-et-Pontrebeau (70)....87 E3
Tinchebray (61)....38 A4
Tincourt-Boucly (80)....8 C5
Tincques (62)....7 H2
Tincry (57)....49 E3
Tingry (62)....1 F5
Tinqueux (51)....23 E6
Tinténiac (35)....35 E5
Tintry (71)....101 E4
Tintury (58)....99 G3
Tiranges (43)....142 D1
Tirent-Pontéjac (32)....168 B6
Tirepied (50)....37 E4
Tissey (89)....84 A1
le Titre (80)....6 D3
Tivernon (45)....62 D4
Tiviers (15)....141 F4
Tizac-de-Curton (33)....135 G5
Tizac-de-Lapouyade (33)....135 G3
Tocane-Saint-Apre (24)....137 E2
Tocqueville (27)....18 D5
Tocqueville (50)....12 D2
Tocqueville-en-Caux (76)....17 F3
Tocqueville-les-Murs (76)....16 D4
Tocqueville-sur-Eu (76)....17 H1
Toeufles (80)....6 D4
Toges (08)....24 B4
Togny-aux-Bœufs (51)....46 A4
Tolla (2A)....204 D5
Tollaincourt (88)....68 D4
Tollent (62)....7 E2
Tollevast (50)....12 C2
Tombebœuf (47)....151 E2
Tomblaine (54)....48 D5
Tomino (2B)....203 G2
les Tonils (26)....158 C2
Tonnac (81)....170 A1
Tonnay-Boutonne (17)....121 E1
Tonnay-Charente (17)....120 D1
Tonneins (47)....150 D4
Tonnerre (89)....84 A1
Tonneville (50)....12 B2
Tonnoy (54)....48 D6
Tonquédec (22)....32 C3
Torcé (35)....57 H3
Torcé-en-Vallée (72)....60 C4
Torcé-Viviers-en-Charnie (53)....59 F4
Torchamp (61)....38 B6
Torchefelon (38)....131 E5
Torcieu (01)....131 E1
Torcy (62)....7 F1
Torcy (71)....101 E5
Torcy (77)....43 F4
Torcy-en-Valois (02)....44 B2
Torcy-et-Pouligny (21)....84 C5
Torcy-le-Grand (10)....66 B2
Torcy-le-Grand (76)....17 H3
Torcy-le-Petit (10)....66 B2
Torcy-le-Petit (76)....17 H3
Tordères (66)....201 E3
Tordouet (14)....15 F6
Torfou (49)....92 A2
Torfou (91)....63 F1
Torigni-sur-Vire (50)....37 G2
Tornac (30)....173 G2
Tornay (52)....86 C2
le Torp-Mesnil (76)....17 F4
Torpes (25)....103 F1
Torpes (71)....102 B5
le Torpt (27)....15 G3
le Torquesne (14)....15 F4
Torreilles (66)....201 G2
Torsac (16)....122 C5
Torsiac (43)....141 G1
Tortebesse (63)....126 C3
Tortefontaine (62)....7 E2
Tortequesne (62)....8 C3
Torteron (18)....98 C3
Torteval-Quesnay (14)....13 H6
Tortezais (03)....113 E2
Torvilliers (10)....66 A3
Torxé (17)....121 E1
Tosny (27)....19 E6
Tossiat (01)....117 E5
Tostat (65)....183 E3
Tostes (27)....18 C6
Totainville (88)....69 F2
Tôtes (76)....17 G4
Touchay (18)....97 F6
la Touche (26)....158 B3
les Touches (44)....74 D3
les Touches-de-Périgny (17)....121 G2
Toucy (89)....83 E2
Toudon (06)....195 E1
Touët-de-l'Escarène (06)....195 G1
Touët-sur-Var (06)....178 C1
Touffailles (82)....152 A5
Touffréville (14)....14 C4
Touffreville (27)....19 F5
Touffreville-la-Cable (76)....17 E5
Touffreville-la-Corbeline (76)....17 E5
Touffreville-sur-Eu (76)....6 A5
Touget (32)....168 B4
Touille (31)....184 C4
Touillon (21)....84 D3
Touillon-et-Loutelet (25)....104 A5
Toul (54)....48 B5

Toulaud (07).............144 A5
Toulenne (33)............149 H2
Touligny (08).............24 A2
Toulis-et-Attencourt (02)..24 C2
Toulon (83)..............193 E5
Toulon-sur-Allier (03)....113 H2
Toulonjac (12)...........153 G4
Toulouges (66)...........201 E2
Toulouse (31)............169 H5
Toulouse-le-Château (39)..102 D5
Toulouzette (40).........165 G3
Toulx-Sainte-Croix (23)...15 E3
Touques (14)..............15 E3
le Touquet-Paris-Plage (62).1 E6
Touquettes (61)...........39 H4
la Tour (06)...............43 H5
la Tour (74).............118 D5
la Tour-Blanche (24).....122 D6
la Tour-d'Aigues (84)....176 B4
la Tour-d'Auvergne (63)..146 C6
Tour-de-Faure (46).......153 E3
la Tour-de-Salvagny (69).129 H2
la Tour-du-Crieu (09)....185 H4
la Tour-du-Meix (39).....117 G2
la Tour-du-Pin (38)......131 E5
Tour-en-Bessin (14)......13 H5
la Tour-en-Jarez (42)....129 F5
Tour-en-Vimeu (80).......80 B4
la Tour-Saint-Gelin (37)..94 C3
la Tour-sur-Orb (34).....172 B5
Tourailles (41)...........79 G3
les Tourailles (61)......38 C4
Tourbes (34).............188 D1
Tourcelles-Chaumont (08)..24 A4
Tourch (29)...............53 H2
Tourcoing (59)............4 D4
Tourdun (32).............167 E5
la Tourette (42).........128 D6
la Tourette-Cabardès (11).187 E2
Tourette-du-Château (06)..195 E1
Tourgéville (14)..........15 E1
la Tourlandry (49).........9 D2
Tourlaville (50)..........12 C2
Tourliac (47)............151 G1
Tourly (60)...............20 A6
Tourmignies (59)..........5 E2
Tourmont (39)............103 E4
Tournai-sur-Dive (61)....39 E4
Tournan (32).............184 B1
Tournan-en-Brie (77).....43 F5
Tournans (25)............87 H5
Tournavaux (08)...........11 F6
Tournay (65).............183 F3
Tournay-sur-Odon (14).....14 A5
le Tourne (33)...........135 H2
Tournebu (14)............38 B6
Tournecoupe (32).........168 B3
Tournedos-Bois-Hubert (27)..40 C2
Tournedos-sur-Seine (27)..18 D6
Tourneuille (31).........169 E5
Tournefort (06)..........178 D2
Tournehem-sur-la-Hem (62)..1 H3
Tournemire (12)..........172 A2
Tournemire (15)..........140 B4
Tournes (08)..............24 A1
le Tourneur (14)..........37 H2
Tourneville (27).........40 D1
Tournières (14)..........13 G6
Tournissan (11)..........187 G4
Tournoisis (45)...........62 B6
Tournon (73).............132 D4
Tournon-d'Agenais (47)...151 H4
Tournon-Saint-Martin (36)..95 F6
Tournon-Saint-Pierre (37)..95 F6
Tournon-sur-Rhône (07)...144 A3
Tournous-darré (65)......183 G2
Tournous-devant (65).....183 G3
Tournus (71)..............71 H4
Tourny (27)...............41 G1
Tourouvre (61)............40 A6
Tourouzelle (11).........187 G3
Tourreilles (11).........186 B5
les Tourreilles (31).....183 H4
Tourrenquets (32)........168 A4
Tourrette-Levens (06)....195 F2
les Tourrettes (26)......158 B1
Tourrettes (83)..........178 B5
Tourrettes-sur-Loup (06).195 E3
Tourriers (16)...........122 C2
Tours (37)................78 D1
Tours-en-Savoie (73).....132 C4
Tours-en-Vimeu (80).......6 D4
Tours-sur-Marne (51)......45 F2
Tours-sur-Meymont (63)...128 A4
Tourteron (08)............24 A3
Tourtoirac (24)..........137 H2
Tourtour (83)............193 G1
Tourtouse (09)...........184 D4
Tourtrès (47)............151 E3
Tourtrol (09)............186 A3
Tourves (83).............193 E2
Tourville-en-Auge (14)....15 E1
Tourville-la-Campagne (27)..18 B6
Tourville-la-Chapelle (76)..17 H2
Tourville-la-Rivière (76)..18 B5
Tourville-les-Ifs (76)....16 C3
Tourville-sur-Arques (76)..17 G2
Tourville-sur-Odon (14)...14 B5
Tourville-
Pont-Audemer (27)....15 H3
Tourville-sur-Sienne (50).36 D1
Toury (28)................62 D4
Toury-Lurcy (58).........100 A6
Toury-sur-Jour (58).......99 E6
Tourzel-Ronzières (63)...127 F5
Toussaint (76)...........16 C3
Toussieu (69)............130 B4
Toussieux (01)...........130 A1
Tousson (77)..............63 G3
Toussus-le-Noble (78)....42 B5
Toutainville (27).........15 G3
Toutencourt (80)..........7 H5
Toutens (31).............186 A1
Toutlemonde (49)..........92 C2
Toury (21)................84 B4
Touvérac (16)............121 H6
le Touvet (38)...........131 H6
Touville (27).............18 A5
Touvois (44)..............91 E2
Touvre (16)..............122 C3
Touzac (16)..............121 H5
Touzac (46)..............152 A3
Tox (2B).................205 G2
Toy-Viam (19)............125 H6
la Tranche-sur-Mer (85)..106 D3
le Tranger (36)..........116 C1
Trancrainville (28)......62 D4

Trangé (72)...............60 A5
le Tranger (36)...........95 H4
Trannes (10)..............67 E3
Tranqueville-Graux (88)...69 E2
Trans (53)................59 F3
Trans-en-Provence (83)...177 H6
Trans-la-Forêt (35).......35 F5
Trans-sur-Erdre (44)......75 E3
le Translay (76)...........6 C5
le Transloy (62)...........8 C4
Tranzault (36)...........111 G1
Trappes (78)..............42 B4
Trassanel (87)...........187 E2
Traubach-le-Bas (68)......89 E3
Traubach-le-Haut (68).....89 E2
Trausse (11).............187 F2
Travaillan (84)..........158 C6
Travecy (02)..............22 A2
Traversères (32).........167 H6
Traves (70)...............87 F3
Trawsfynydd (50)..........56 B5
Trayas (81)...............93 E6
Tréauville (50)...........12 B3
Trébabu (29)............113 G3
Treban (03)..............113 G3
Trébas (81)..............170 D1
Tréban (81)..............171 E2
Trébédan (22)............34 D5
Trèbes (11)..............187 E3
Trébeurden (22)...........32 C2
Trébons (65).............183 E4
Trébons-de-Luchon (31)...197 F1
Trébons-sur-la-Grasse (31).186 A1
Tréboul (22)..............33 H6
Trébry (22)..............102 B1
Trécon (51)...............45 F4
Trédaniel (22)............33 H6
Trédarzec (22)............33 E2
Trédias (22)..............34 B6
Trédion (56)..............55 H5
Trédrez-Locquémeau (22)...32 B2
Tréduder (22).............32 B3
Trefcon (02)...............8 D6
Treffendel (35)...........56 D3
Treffiagat (29)...........53 E4
Treffieux (44)............74 D1
Treffléan (56)............55 H5
Treffort (38)............145 G5
Treffort-Cuisiat (01)....117 E4
Treffrin (22).............32 B6
Tréflaouénan (29)........31 G3
Tréflévénez (29)..........31 F3
Tréflez (29)..............31 F3
Tréfols (51)..............44 C4
Tréfumel (22).............34 D6
Trégarantec (29)..........31 F3
Trégarvan (29)............53 H1
Trégastel (22)............32 C1
Tréglamus (22)............32 D4
Tréglonou (29)............30 D3
Trégomeur (22)............33 H4
Trégon (22)...............34 C4
Trégonneau (22)...........33 E3
Trégourez (29)............53 H2
Trégrom (22)..............32 D3
Tréguennec (29)...........53 E3
Trégueux (22)............33 H4
Tréguidel (22)............33 F3
Tréguier (22).............33 E2
Trégunc (29)..............53 H3
Tréhet (41)...............78 D2
Tréhorenteuc (56).........56 B3
le Tréhou (29)............31 G5
Treignac (19)............125 E5
Treignat (03)............112 B3
Treigny (89)..............83 E4
Treilles (11)............188 A6
Treilles-en-Gâtinais (45)..64 A5
Treillières (44)..........74 C4
Treix (52)................67 F4
Treize-Septiers (85)......91 H1
Treize-Vents (85).........92 C3
Tréjouls (82)............152 B5
Trélans (48).............154 B3
Trélazé (49)..............77 E5
Trélévern (22)............32 D2
Trelins (42).............128 D3
Trélissac (24)...........137 F2
Trélivan (22).............34 C5
Trelly (50)...............35 H1
Trélon (59)...............10 B4
Trélou-sur-Marne (02).....44 C2
Trémaouézan (29).........31 H4
Trémargat (22)............32 D6
Trémauville (76)..........16 D4
la Tremblade (17)........120 B2
Tremblay (35).............35 G6
le Tremblay (49)..........76 B3
Tremblay-en-France (93)...43 E3
Tremblay-les-Villages (28)..41 F6
le Tremblay-Omonville (27)..40 B1
le Tremblay-sur-Mauldre (78)..42 A4
Tremblecourt (54).........48 C4
le Tremblois (70).........86 C5
Tremblois-lès-Carignan (08)..25 E2
Tremblois-lès-Rocroi (08)..10 D6
Trémeheuc (35)............35 F5
Trémel (22)...............32 C3
Tréméloir (22)............33 G4
Trémentines (49)..........75 H6
Tréméoc (29)..............53 F3
Tréméreuc (22)............34 C4
Trémery (57).............26 C3
Trémeur (22)..............34 B6
Tréméven (22).............33 F3
Tréméven (29).............54 B3
Trémilly (52)............67 E2
Tréminis (38)............145 G6
Trémoins (70).............88 B3
Trémolat (24)............137 G5
Trémons (47).............151 H4
Trémont (49)..............93 E1
Trémont (61)..............39 G6
Trémont-sur-Saulx (55)....46 D5
Trémonzey (88)............69 G6
Trémorel (22)............56 B1
Trémouille (15)..........140 C1
Trémouille-Saint-Loup (63)..126 B5
Trémoulès (12)...........171 E1
Trémouilles (09).........185 H4
Trémuson (22).............33 G4
Trenal (39)..............102 C6
Trensacq (40)............149 E5
Trentels (47)............151 G3
Tréogan (22)..............54 A1
Tréogat (29)..............53 E3
Tréon (28)................41 E5
Tréouergat (29)..........30 D3
Trépail (51)..............45 F1
le Tréport (76)...........6 A3
Trépot (25)..............103 G1
Tréprel (14)..............38 C3
Trept (38)...............130 D4
Trésauvaux (55)...........47 H2
Tresbœuf (35).............57 F5
Trescault (62)............8 C4
Treschenu-Creyers (26)...145 F6
Trescléoux (05)..........159 G4
Trésilley (70)............87 F5
Treslon (51)..............22 D6
Tresnay (58)..............99 E6
Trespoux-Rassiels (46)...152 C4
Tresques (30)............158 A6
Tressan (34).............172 C6
Tressandans (25)..........87 H4
Tressange (57)...........26 A3
Tressé (35)...............35 E5
Tresserre (66)...........201 E3
Tresserve (73)...........131 H4
Tressignaux (22).........33 F3
Tressin (59)..............5 E1
Tresson (72)..............78 D1
Treteau (03).............114 A3
la Trétoire (77).........44 B3
Trets (13)...............192 D1
Treux (80)................7 H6
Treuzy-Levelay (77).......64 B3
Trévé (22)................55 G1

Trévenans (90)............88 C3
Tréveneuc (22)............33 G3
Tréveray (55).............47 F6
Tréverec (22).............33 F3
Tréverien (35)............34 D6
Trèves (30)..............172 C1
Trèves (69)..............129 H5
Trévien (81).............170 C1
Trévières (14)............13 G5
Trévignin (73)...........131 H3
Trévillach (66)..........200 C2
Tréville (11)............186 B2
Trévillers (25)...........88 D6
Trévilly (89).............84 B4
Trévol (03)..............113 H1
Trévou-Tréguignec (22)....32 D1
Trévoux (01).............130 A1
le Trévoux (29)...........54 A4
Trévron (22)..............34 D6
Trézelles (03)...........114 B4
Trézény (22)..............32 D2
Tréziers (11)............186 B5
Trézilidé (29)............31 G3
Trézioux (63)............128 A3
le Triadou (34)..........173 E5
Triaize (85).............106 C2
Tribehou (50).............13 E6
Trichey (89)..............66 B6
Tricot (60)...............20 D5
Trie-Château (60).........19 H6
Trie-la-Ville (60)........19 H6
Trie-sur-Baïse (65)......183 G2
Triel-sur-Seine (78)......42 B3
Triembach-au-Val (67).....71 F2
Trieux (54)...............26 A3
Trigance (83)............177 H3
Trignac (44)..............73 G4
Trigny (51)...............22 D5
Trilbardou (77)...........43 F3
Trilla (66)..............200 C2
Trilport (77).............43 G3
Trimbach (67).............51 G2
Trimer (35)...............34 D6
la Trimouille (86).......110 B2
Trinay (45)...............62 D5
la Trinité (06)..........195 E1
la Trinité (27)...........40 C2
la Trinité (50)...........37 E4
la Trinité (73)..........132 B5
la Trinité-de-Réville (27)..39 H3
la Trinité-de-Thouberville (27)..18 B5
la Trinité-des-Laitiers (61)..39 G4
la Trinité-du-Mont (76)....15 H1
la Trinité-Porhoët (56)...55 H2
la Trinité-sur-Mer (56)....72 C1
la Trinité-Surzur (56)....73 E1
Triors (26)..............144 C3
le Trioulou (15).........153 H1
Triplevaults (41).........62 B6
Triqueville (76)..........15 H3
Trizac (15)..............140 C1
Trith-Saint-Léger (59).....9 F3
Tritteling-Redlach (57)...49 F1
Trivy (71)...............115 H2
Trizay (17)..............120 D2
Trizay-Coutretot-
Saint-Serge (28).....61 F3
Trizay-lès-Bonneval (28)..61 H2
Troarn (14)...............14 C5
Troche (19)..............124 C6
Trochères (21)............86 B6
Trocy-en-Multien (77).....43 G2
Troësnes (02).............43 H2
Troguéry (22).............33 E2
Trogues (37)..............94 C2
Trois-Domaines (55).......47 F3
Trois-Fonds (23).........112 A4
Trois-Fontaines-l'Abbaye (51)..46 D5
Trois-Monts (14).........14 B6
les Trois-Moutiers (86)...93 H2
Trois-Palis (16).........122 B4
les Trois-Pierres (76)....15 H1
Trois-Puits (51)..........23 E6
Trois-Vèvres (58).........99 F4
Trois-Villes (64)........181 G1
Troisfontaines (57).......50 A5
Troisfontaines-la-Ville (52)..67 E1
Troisgots (50)............37 G2
Troissereux (60)..........20 A4
Troissy (51)..............44 D2
Troisvaux (62)............7 G1
Troisvilles (59)..........9 F4
Tromarey (70).............86 D6
Tromborn (57).............27 E4
Troncens (32)............167 E6
la Tronche (38)..........145 G2
le Tronchet (35)..........35 E5
le Tronchet (72)..........60 A4
Tronchoy (89).............84 A1
Tronchy (71).............102 A6
le Troncq (27)............18 B6
Trondes (54)..............48 A5
Tronget (03).............113 G3
le Tronquay (14)..........13 G6
le Tronquay (27)..........19 F4
Tronsanges (58)...........98 D2
Tronville (54)............48 B3
Tronville-en-Barrois (55)..47 F5
Troo (41).................79 E2
Trosly-Breuil (60)........21 F4
Trosly-Loire (02).........22 H4
Trouans (10)..............66 A3
Troubat (65).............184 A5
Trouhans (21).............86 B6
Trouhaut (21).............85 F5
Trouillas (66)...........201 E3
Trouley-Labarthe (65)....183 F2
Troussencourt (60)........20 B5
Troussey (55).............47 H4
Troussures (60)...........20 A5
Trouvans (25).............87 H4
Trouville (76)............15 H1
la Trouville-la-Haule (27)..15 H3
Trouville-sur-Mer (14)....15 E3
Trouy (18)................97 G3
Troye-d'Ariège (09)......186 B6
Troyes (10)...............66 B3
Troyon (55)...............47 G2
la Truchère (71).........116 C2
Truchtersheim (67)........51 D5
Trucy (02)................22 D4
Trucy-l'Orgueilleuse (58)..83 F5
Trucy-sur-Yonne (89)......83 G3
le Truel (12)............171 G1
Trugny (21)..............102 A2
Truinas (26).............158 D2
Trumilly (60).............21 F6
Trun (61).................39 E4
Trungy (14)...............13 H6
Truttemer-le-Grand (14)..37 H4
Truttemer-le-Petit (14)..37 H4
Truyes (37)...............95 F1
Tubersent (62)............6 C2
Tuchan (11)..............187 G6
Tucquegnieux (54).........26 A4
Tudeils (19).............139 E4
Tudelle (32).............167 F4
Tuffé (72)................60 D5
Tugéras-Saint-Maurice (17)..121 G6
Tugny-et-Pont (02)........21 H1
Tulette (26).............158 C5
Tulle (19)...............139 E2
Tullins (38).............145 E1
Tully (80)................6 C4
Tupigny (02)..............9 G6
Turbigt-Semons (69)......130 A5
la Turballe (44)..........72 D4
la Turbie (06)...........195 G2
Turcey (21)...............85 F5
Turckheim (68)............71 F4
Turenne (19).............138 D4
Turgon (16)..............122 D2
Turgy (10)................66 B5
Turny (89)................65 H5
Turquant (49).............93 H1
Turqueville (50)..........13 E4
Turquestein-Blancrupt (57)..50 A6

Turquville (50)...........13 E4
Turretot (76).............15 F1
Turriers (04)............160 A3
Tursac (24)..............137 H4
Tusson (16)..............122 B1
Tuzaguet (65)............183 H4
le Tuzan (33)............149 F3
Tuzie (16)...............122 C1

U

Uberach (67)..............50 D3
Ubexy (88)................69 G2
Ubraye (04)..............178 A2
Ucciani (2A).............204 D5
Ucel (07).................157 H2
Uchacq-et-Parentis (40)..165 H2
Uchaud (30)..............174 A4
Uchaux (84)..............158 B5
Uchentein (09)...........184 D6
Uchizy (71)..............116 B2
Uchon (71)...............100 C5
Uckange (57)..............26 C3
Ueberstrass (68)..........89 E3
Uffheim (68)..............89 G2
Uffholtz (68).............89 E1
Ugine (73)...............132 C3
Uglas (65)...............183 H4
Ugnouas (65)..............183 E2
Ugny (51).................25 G4
Ugny-le-Gay (02)..........21 H2
Ugny-l'Équipée (80).......21 G1
Ugny-sur-Meuse (55).......47 H5
Uhart-Cize (64)..........180 C3
Uhart-Mixe (64)..........181 F2
Uhlwiller (67)............51 E3
Uhrwiller (67)............50 D3
Ulcot (79)................93 G3
Ully-Saint-Georges (60)...20 C6
les Ulmes (49)............93 G1
Umpeau (28)...............62 C1
Unac (09)................199 F1
Uncey-le-Franc (21).......85 E6
Unchair (51)..............22 D6
Ungersheim (68)...........71 F6
Unias (42)...............129 E5
Unienville (10)...........67 E3
Unieux (42)..............129 E6
l'Union (31).............169 H5
Unverre (28)..............61 F3
Unzent (09)..............185 G3
Upaix (05)...............160 A4
Upie (26)................144 B6
Ur (66)..................199 G4
Urau (31)................184 C5
Urbalacone (2A)..........204 D6
Urbanya (66).............200 B3
Urbeis (67)...............71 E2
Urbès (68)................89 E1
Urbise (42)..............114 D2
Urçay (03)...............112 D1
Urcel (02)................22 C4
Urcerey (90)..............88 C3
Urciers (36).............112 A1
Urcuit (64)..............164 C6
Urcy (21)................85 G6
Urdens (32)..............168 A3
Urdès (64)...............165 H6
Urdos (64)...............180 C6
Urepel (64)..............180 C4
Urgons (40)..............166 A4
Urgosse (32).............166 D4
Uriménil (88)............69 H4
Urmatt (67)...............50 D6
Urost (64)...............182 D2
Urou-et-Crennes (61)......39 E4
Urrugne (64).............164 A6
Urs (09).................199 F1
Urschenheim (68)..........71 G4
Urt (64).................164 C6
Urtaca (2B)..............203 E5
Urtière (25)..............88 D6
Uruffe (54)...............48 B6
Urval (24)...............137 G6
Urville (10)..............67 E4
Urville (14)..............14 C6
Urville (50)..............12 D3
Urville (88)..............68 D5
Urville-Nacqueville (50)..12 B1
Urvillers (02)............21 A1
Ury (77)..................63 H4
Urzy (58).................99 E3
Us (95)...................42 A2
Usclas-d'Hérault (34)....172 D6
Usclas-du-Bosc (34)......172 C4
Usinens (74).............117 H6
Ussac (19)...............138 C2
Ussat (09)...............199 E1
Usseau (79)..............107 G5
Usseau (86)...............94 B4
Ussel (15)...............141 E3
Ussel (19)...............125 H5
Ussel (46)...............152 D2
Ussel-d'Allier (03)......113 G2
Usson (63)...............127 G5
Usson-du-Poitou (86).....109 F4
Usson-en-Forez (42)......142 C1
Ussy (14).................38 D3
Ussy-sur-Marne (77).......43 H3
Ustaritz (64)............180 C1
Ustou (09)...............197 F1
Utelle (06)..............195 F1
Uttenheim (67)...........71 F1
Uttenhoffen (67)..........50 D3
Uttwiller (67)............50 D3
Uvernet-Fours (04).......161 F4
Uxeau (71)...............100 B6
Uxegney (88)..............69 G3
Uxelles (39).............117 H1
Uxem (59).................2 C1
Uz (65)..................182 D5
Uza (40).................148 C5
Uzan (64)................166 A6
Uzay-le-Venon (18)........97 H5
Uzech (46)...............152 C2
Uzein (64)...............182 B1
Uzel (22)................55 H1
Uzelle (25)...............88 A4
Uzemain (88).............69 G4
Uzer (07)................157 F3
Uzer (11)................187 E6
Uzerche (19).............124 D6
Uzès (30)................174 B2
Uzeste (33)..............149 G3
Uzos (64)................182 B2

V

Vaas (72).................78 B3
Vabre (81)...............170 D1
Vabre-Tizac (12).........153 H5
Vabres (15)..............141 F4
Vabres (30)..............173 G1
Vabres-l'Abbaye (12).....171 G2
Vacheresse (55)...........25 E6
Vachères (04)............176 C2
Vachères-en-Quint (26)...144 D6
Vacheresse (74)..........119 F3
la Vacheresse-et-
la-Rouillie (88).....68 D4
la Vacherie (27)..........40 D1
Vacognes-Neuilly (14).....14 A5
la Vacquerie (14).........37 G1
la Vacquerie-et-Saint-Martin-
de-Castries (34).....172 D4
Vacquerie-le-Boucq (62)....7 F2
Vacqueriette-Erquières (62)..7 F1
Vacqueville (54)..........70 B1
Vacqueyras (84)..........158 C6
Vacquières (34)..........173 E4
Vacquiers (31)...........169 G4

Vadelaincourt (55)........47 F2
Vadenay (51)..............45 H2
Vadencourt (02)...........9 F6
Vadencourt (80)...........7 H5
Vadonville (55)...........47 G4
Vagnas (07)..............157 G4
Vagney (88)...............70 B5
Vahl-Ebersing (57)........49 F1
Vahl-lès-Bénestroff (57)..49 G3
Vahl-lès-Faulquemont (57)..49 E2
Vaiges (53)...............59 E5
Vailhan (34).............172 C6
Vailhauquès (34).........173 E5
Vailhourles (12).........153 F5
Vaillac (46).............152 D1
Vaillant (52).............85 H2
Vailly (10)...............66 D3
Vailly (74)..............118 D3
Vailly-sur-Aisne (02).....22 B4
Vailly-sur-Sauldre (18)...82 A5
Vains (50)................35 H3
Vaire-Arcier (25).........87 G6
Vaire-sous-Corbie (80)....7 H6
Vaire-le-Petit (25).......87 G6
Vaires-sur-Marne (77).....43 E3
Vaison-la-Romaine (84)...158 D5
Vaïssac (82).............169 G1
Vaïvre (70)...............86 D3
la Vaivre (70)............69 H6
Vaivre-et-Montoille (70)..87 G3
le Val (83)..............193 F2
le Val-d'Ajol (88)........70 B6
Val-d'Auzon (10)..........66 C2
le Val-David (27).........41 E2
le Val-de-Bride (57)......49 F4
Val-de-Chalvagne (04)....178 B2
le Val-de-Fier (74)......131 H1
le Val-de-Gouhenans (70)..87 G5
le Val-de-Guéblange (57)..49 H2
Val-de-la-Haye (76).......18 C5
Val-de-Mercy (89)........83 G3
Val-de-Meuse (52).........68 D3
le Val-de-Reuil (27)......18 D6
Val-de-Roulans (25).......87 H5
le Val-de-Saâne (76)......17 E3
Val-de-Vesle (51).........45 G1
Val-de-Vière (51).........46 B3
Val-d'Épy (39)...........117 F3
Val-des-Marais (51).......45 E4
Val-des-Prés (05)........147 E4
le Val-d'Esnoms (52)......86 A3
le Val-d'Isère (73)......133 G5
le Val-d'Izé (35).........57 H2
le Val-d'Ornain (55)......46 D4
le Val-Maravel (26)......159 G2
le Val-Saint-Éloi (70)....87 G2
le Val-Saint-Germain (91)..42 B6
le Val-Saint-Père (50)....35 H3
Val-Suzon (21)............85 G5
Valady (12)..............154 B3
Valailles (27)............15 H5
Valaire (41)..............79 H4
Valanjou (49).............93 E1
Valaurie (26)............158 B3
Valavoire (04)...........160 B4
Valay (70)................86 C6
Valbeleix (63)...........127 E6
Valbelle (04)............160 A4
Valbois (55)..............47 H3
Valbonnais (38)..........145 H5
Valbonne (06)............178 C5
Valcabrère (31)..........184 A4
Valcanville (50)..........13 E2
Valcebollère (66)........199 H4
Valchevrière (38).........87 H2
Valcourt (52).............46 C5
Valdahon (25)............104 A2
Valdampierre (60).........20 A6
Valdeblore (06)..........162 C6
Valderiès (81)...........170 C2
Valderoure (06)..........178 B3
Valdieu-Lutran (68).......89 E3
Valdivienne (86).........109 G2
Valdoie (90)..............88 C2
Valdrôme (26)............159 G3
Valdurenque (81).........170 D6
Valeille (42)............129 E4
Valeilles (82)...........151 H5
Valeins (01).............116 B5
Valempoulières (39)......103 F4
Valençay (36).............96 B2
Valence (16).............122 D2
Valence (26).............144 B4
Valence (82).............151 H6
Valence-d'Albigeois (81)..170 D2
Valence-en-Brie (77)......64 B2
Valence-sur-Baïse (32)...167 G3
Valenciennes (59).........9 F2
Valencin (38)............130 B4
Valencogne (38)..........131 F5
Valennes (72).............61 E6
Valensole (04)...........177 E3
Valentigney (25)..........88 C4
Valentine (31)...........184 A4
Valenton (94).............43 E5
Valergues (34)...........173 H5
Valernes (04)............160 A4
Valescourt (60)...........20 D5
la Valette (38)..........145 H4
la Valette (42)..........142 C1
la Valette-du-Var (83)...193 E5
Valeuil (24).............137 F1
Valeyrac (33)............120 C6
Valezan (73).............133 E4
Valff (67)................71 F1
Valfin-sur-Valouse (39)..117 F3
Valflaunès (34)..........173 F4
Valfleury (42)...........129 F5
Valframbert (61)..........60 A1
Valgorge (07)............157 E3
Valhey (54)...............49 E5
Valhuon (62)...............7 G1
Valiergues (19)..........126 A5
Valignat (03)............113 F4
Valigny (03)..............98 B6
Valines (80)..............6 C4
Valjouffrey (38).........145 H5
Valjouze (15)............141 E2
la Valla-en-Gier (42)....129 G5
la Valla-sur-Rochefort (42)..128 C3
Vallabrègues (30)........174 C3
Vallabrix (30)...........174 B1
Vallan (89)...............83 F2
Vallangoujard (95)........42 C2
Vallant-Saint-Georges (10)..66 A2
Vallauris (06)...........195 E5
Valle-d'Alesani (2B).....205 G2
Valle-di-Campoloro (2B)..205 G2
Valle-di-Mezzana (2A)....204 C5
Valle-di-Rostino (2B)....203 F6
Valle-d'Orezza (2B)......205 G1
la Vallée (17)...........120 D1
la Vallée-au-Blé (02).....9 H6
la Vallée-Mulâtre (02)....9 F5
Valleiry (74)............118 A5
Vallenay (18).............97 G5
Vallentigny (10)..........67 E2
Vallerange (57)...........49 F2
Vallérargues (30)........157 H6
Valleraugue (30).........173 E2
Vallères (37).............78 C6
Valleret (52)............67 E1
Vallereuil (24)..........137 E2
Vallerois-le-Bois (70)....87 G3
Vallerois-Lorioz (70).....87 G3
Valleroy (25).............87 G5
Valleroy (52)............87 E2
Valleroy (54).............48 A3
Valleroy-aux-Saules (88)..69 F3
Valleroy-le-Sec (88)......69 F3
Vallery (89)..............64 C4
Vallesvilles (31)........169 H6
Vallet (44)...............75 E6
Valletot (27).............15 H3
Valliaules (55)..........25 F2

Vallica (2B).............202 D6
Vallières (23)...........125 G2
Vallières (10)............66 B6
Vallières-les-Grandes (41)..79 G5
Valliguières (30)........174 C2
Valliquerville (76)......17 E2
Valloire (73)............146 D2
Vallois (54)..............70 A1
les Vallois (88)..........69 F4
Vallon-en-Sully (03).....112 D2
Vallon-Pont-d'Arc (07)...157 G4
Vallon-sur-Gée (72)......59 H6
Vallon-sur-Gée (72)......59 H6
Vallorcine (74)..........119 H6
Vallouise (05)...........146 D5
Valmanya (66)............200 C4
Valmascle (34)...........172 B5
Valmeinier (73)..........146 D2
Valmestroff (57)..........26 C3
Valmigère (11)...........187 E5
Valmondois (95)...........42 C1
Valmont (57)..............49 F1
Valmont (76)..............16 D3
Valmy (51)................46 C2
Valognes (50)............12 D2
Valojoulx (24)...........138 A4
Valonne (25)..............88 B5
Valoreille (25)...........88 C6
Valouse (26).............158 D3
Valprivas (43)...........142 D1
Valpuiseaux (91)..........63 G3
Valras-Plage (34)........188 C3
Valréas (84).............158 C4
Valros (34)..............188 D1
Valroufié (46)...........152 D3
Vals (09)................186 A3
les Vals-les-Tilles (52)..85 H3
Vals-le-Chastel (43).....141 H2
Vals-les-Bains (07)......157 H2
Vals-près-le-Puy (43)....142 C4
Valsemé (14)..............15 E4
Valserres (05)...........160 B2
Valsonne (69)............129 F1
le Valtin (88)............70 D4
Valuéjols (15)...........141 E4
Valvignères (07).........157 H3
Valz-sous-Châteauneuf (63)..127 H5
Valzergues (12)..........153 H3
Vanault-le-Châtel (51)....46 B3
Vanault-les-Dames (51)....46 C4
Vançais (79).............108 C4
Vancé (72)................78 C1
la Vancelle (67)..........71 F2
Vandelainville (54).......48 B3
Vandeléville (54).........69 E2
Vandélicourt (60).........21 F4
Vandenesse (58)..........100 A4
Vandenesse-en-Auxois (21)..101 F1
Vandeuil (51).............22 D5
Vandières (51)............44 D1
Vandières (54)............48 C3
Vandoncourt (25)..........88 D4
Vandré (17)..............107 F6
Vandrimare (27)...........19 E5
Vandy (08)................24 A4
Vanlay (10)...............66 A5
Vannaire (21).............85 E1
Vannecourt (57)...........49 F3
Vannecrocq (27)..........15 G4
Vannes (56)...............55 G6
Vannes-le-Châtel (54).....48 B6
Vannes-sur-Cosson (45)....81 F3
Vannoz (39)..............103 F5
Vanosc (07)..............143 G2
les Vans (07)............157 E4
Vantoux (57)..............26 C5
Vantoux-et-Longevelle (70)..87 F5
Vanves (92)...............42 C4
Vanvey (21)...............85 F1
Vanville (77).............64 C2
Vany (57).................26 C5
Vanxains (24)...........136 C2
Vanzac (17)..............121 G6
Vanzay (79)..............108 D4
Vanzy (74)...............118 A6
Vaour (81)...............169 H1
Varacieux (38)...........144 D2
Varades (44)..............76 A5
Varages (83).............176 D4
Varaignes (24)...........123 F4
Varaire (46).............153 E4
Varaize (17).............121 F1
Varambon (01)............116 D5
Varanges (21)............102 A1
Varangéville (54).........48 D5
Varaville (14)............14 D4
Varces-Allières-
et-Risset (38).......145 G3
Vareilles (23)...........110 D3
Vareilles (71)...........115 F4
Vareilles (89)............65 F4
Varen (82)...............153 F6
Varengeville-sur-Mer (76)..17 G2
Varenguebec (50)..........12 C4
la Varenne (49)...........75 F5
Varennes (24)............137 H6
Varennes (31)............186 A1
Varennes (37).............94 D2
Varennes (80)............23 E1
Varennes (82)...........169 F2
Varennes (86)............109 E1
Varennes-Changy (45)......82 A1
Varennes-en-Argonne (55)..24 C6
Varennes-Jarcy (91).......43 E5
Varennes-le-Grand (71)...101 G6
Varennes-lès-Mâcon (71)..116 B4
Varennes-lès-Narcy (58)...82 C6
Varennes-Saint-Honorat (43)..142 A3
Varennes-
Saint-Sauveur (71)..117 E2
Varennes-sous-Dun (71)...115 G4
Varennes-sur-Allier (03)..114 A4
Varennes-sur-Fouzon (36)..96 C1
Varennes-sur-Loire (49)...94 A1
Varennes-sur-Morge (63)..127 F1
Varennes-sur-Seine (77)...64 B3
Varennes-sur-Tèche (03)..114 B4
Varennes-sur-Usson (63)..127 G5
Varennes-Vauzelles (58)...98 D3
Varès (47)...............150 D3
Varesnes (60).............21 G3
Varessia (39)............117 F1
Varetz (19)..............138 C2
Varilhes (09)............185 H4
Varinfroy (60)............43 H1
Variscourt (02)...........23 F4
Varize (28)...............61 H4
Varize (57)...............26 D5
Varmonzey (88)............69 G2
Varnéville (55)...........47 H3
Varneville-Bretteville (76)..17 F4
Varogne (70)..............87 G3
Varois-et-Chaignot (21)...86 A6
Varouville (50)...........13 E1
Varrains (49).............93 G1
Varreddes (77)............43 G2
Vars (05)................161 F2
Vars (16)................122 B3
Vars (70).................86 C4
Vars-sur-Roseix (19).....138 B2
Varsberg (57).............27 F5
Varzay (17)..............120 D3
Varzy (58)................83 E5
Vascœuil (27).............19 E4
Vasles (79)..............108 C2
Vasouy (14)...............15 E3
Vasperviller (57).........50 A6
Vassel (63)..............127 G3

Vassens (02)..............21 H4
Vasseny (02)..............22 B5
Vasselay (18).............97 G2
Vasselin (38)............131 E4
Vassens (02)..............21 H4
Vasseur-en-Vercors (26)..145 E5
Vassimont-
et-Chapelaine (51)..45 G5
Vassincourt (55).........47 E4
Vassogne (02).............22 D4
Vassonville (76).........17 F3
Vassy (14)................38 A3
Vassy (89)................84 B3
Vastenville (25)..........19 F6
le Vast (50)..............13 E1
les Vastres (43).........143 E4
Vatan (36)................96 D3
Vathiménil (54)...........70 B1
Vatierville (76)..........19 F1
Vatilieu (38)............145 E2
Vatimont (57).............49 E2
Vatry (51)................45 G4
Vattetot-sous-Beaumont (76)..16 C4
Vattetot-sur-Mer (76).....16 B3
Vatteville (27)...........19 E6
Vatteville-la-Rue (76)....17 E6
Vaubadon (14).............13 G6
Vauban (71)..............115 F4
Vaubecourt (55)..........47 E4
Vaubexy (88)..............69 G3
Vaucelles (14)............13 H5
Vaucelles-et-Beffecourt (02)..22 B3
Vauchamps (25)............87 G6
Vauchamps (51)............44 D4
Vauchassis (10)...........66 A4
Vauchelles (60)...........21 G3
Vauchelles-lès-Authie (80)..7 H4
Vauchelles-lès-Domart (80)..7 G4
Vauchelles-lès-Quesnoy (80)..6 D5
Vauchignon (21)..........101 F3
Vauchonvilliers (10)......66 D3
Vauchoux (70).............87 F3
Vauciennes (51)...........44 D1
Vauciennes (60)...........21 G6
Vauclaix (58)............100 A1
Vauclerc (51).............46 C4
Vaucluse (25).............88 C6
Vauclusotte (25)..........88 C6
Vaucogne (10).............66 C1
Vauconcourt-Nervezain (70)..87 E3
Vaucouleurs (55)..........48 A5
Vaucourtois (77)..........43 G3
Vaucresson (92)...........42 C4
Vaudancourt (60)..........19 H6
Vaudebarrier (71)........115 F3
Vaudelnay (49)............93 F2
Vaudeloges (14)...........39 E3
Vaudemange (51)...........45 F1
Vaudémont (54)............69 E2
Vaudes (10)...............66 B4
Vaudesincourt (51)........23 G6
Vaudesson (02)...........22 B4
Vaudevant (07)...........143 H3
Vaudeville (54)...........69 G1
Vaudeville (88)...........70 A3
Vaudéville-le-Haut (55)...68 B1
Vaudherland (95)..........43 E3
Vaudigny (54).............69 F1
le Vaudioux (39).........103 F5
Vaudoncourt (55)..........25 G5
Vaudoncourt (88)..........68 D2
Vaudreching (57)..........27 E4
Vaudrecourt (52)..........68 C3
Vaudémont (52)............67 G4
le Vaudreuil (27).........18 D6
Vaudreuille (31).........186 C1
Vaudreville (50)..........12 D3
Vaudrey (39).............102 D4
Vaudricourt (62)..........7 H1
Vaudricourt (80)..........6 C4
Vaudrimesnil (50).........12 D6
Vaudringhem (62)...........1 H5
Vaudrivillers (25)........88 A6
Vaudry (14)...............37 H3
Vaugines (84)............176 B4
Vaugneray (69)...........129 H3
Vaugrigneuse (91).........42 C6
Vauhallan (91)............42 D5
Vaujany (38).............146 A2
Vaujours (93).............43 E3
Vaulandry (49)............77 H3
le Vaulmier (15).........140 C2
Vaulnaveys-le-Bas (38)...145 G3
Vaulnaveys-le-Haut (38)..145 G3
Vaulry (87)..............110 D6
Vault-de-Lugny (89).......83 H5
Vaulx (62)................7 E3
Vaulx (74)...............132 A1
Vaulx-en-Velin (69)......130 B3
Vaulx-Milieu (38)........130 C4
Vaulx-Vraucourt (62)......8 B4
le Vaumain (60)...........19 H5
Vaumas (03)..............114 B3
Vaumeilh (04)............160 B5
Vaumoise (60).............21 G6
Vaumort (89)..............65 E4
Vaunac (24)..............137 F1
Vaunaveys-la-Rochette (26)..144 C6
Vaunoise (61).............60 C2
la Vaupalière (76)........17 G6
Vauquois (55)............47 F1
Vauréal (95)..............42 B2
Vaureilles (12)..........153 H3
Vauroux (60).............126 A3
le Vauroux (60)...........19 H5
Vausseroux (79)..........108 B2
Vautebis (79)............108 B2
Vauthiermont (90).........88 D2
Vautorte (53).............58 C3
Vauvenargues (13)........176 B6
Vauvert (30).............174 A4
Vauville (14).............15 E3
Vauville (50).............12 A2
Vauvillers (70)..........69 F6
Vauvillers (80)...........8 A6
Vaux (03)................112 D3
Vaux (31)................186 A1
Vaux (57)................26 B5
Vaux (86)................108 D3
Vaux-Andigny (02).........9 F5
Vaux-Champagne (08).......23 H4
Vaux-devant-Damloup (55)..25 F6
Vaux-en-Amiénois (80).....7 F5
Vaux-en-Beaujolais (69)..115 H6
Vaux-en-Bugey (01).......130 D2
Vaux-en-Dieulet (08).....24 C4
Vaux-en-Pré (71).........115 H1
Vaux-en-Vermandois (02)...21 H1
Vaux-et-Chantegrue (25)..103 H5
Vaux-Lavalette (16)......122 C6
Vaux-le-Moncelot (70).....87 F4
Vaux-le-Pénil (77)........64 A1
Vaux-lès-Mouron (08)......24 B5
Vaux-lès-Mouzon (08)......25 E3
Vaux-lès-Palameix (55)....47 H2
Vaux-lès-Prés (25)........87 E6
Vaux-lès-Rubigny (08).....23 G2
Vaux-lès-Saint-Claude (39)..117 H3
Vaux-Marquenneville (80)...6 D5
Vaux-Montreuil (08).......24 B3
Vaux-Rouillac (16).......122 A3
Vaux-Saules (21)..........85 G5
Vaux-sous-Aubigny (52)....86 A2
Vaux-sur-Aure (14)........13 H5
Vaux-sur-Blaise (52)......67 E1
Vaux-sur-Eure (27)........41 E2
Vaux-sur-Mer (17).........120 B3
Vaux-sur-Poligny (39)....103 E5
Vaux-sur-Saint-Urbain (52)..67 F2
Vaux-sur-Seine (78).......42 B3
Vaux-sur-Seulles (14).....14 A5
Vaux-sur-Somme (80).......7 H6
Vaux-sur-Vienne (86)......94 D4
Vaux-Villaine (08)........24 A1
Vauxaillon (02)..........22 B3
Vauxbons (52)............85 H1